S0-BNE-149

BY ANDREW HUSSIE

BOOK 4

PART 2

ACT 5 ACT 1

Act 5 Act 1

"MOB1US DOUBL3 R34CH4ROUND"

`import universe U1;`

ACT 5 ACT 1
MOB1US DOUBL3 R34CH4ROUND

Ema
001942
Sign

earch: All Platforms go

Home | What's New | Contribute | Features | Boards | My Games | Answers | Help

Platforms: DS | GBA | GameCube | PC | PS2 | PS3 | PSP | Wii | Xbox | Xbox 360 | All Systems

PC >> Miscellaneous >> Immersive Simulation

Sburb Beta

```
================================================================================
[ZZZZ] Rose: Egress.
================================================================================
```

This is my final entry.

My co-players and I have made every earnest attempt, with occasional relapse, to play this game the right way. I have been meticulous in documenting the process to help our peers and successors through the trials should we fail. In my hubris I believed the classes were relegated to the Earth-bound, but even in this quaint supposition I was in error. Our otherworldly antagonists have assured us of our inevitable failure repeatedly, while the gods whisper corroboration in my sleep. I believe them now.

I just blew up my first gate. I'm not sure why I did it, really.

I am not playing by the rules anymore. I will fly around this candy-coated rock and comb the white sand until I find answers. No one can tell me our fate can't be repaired. We've come too far. I jumped out of the way of a burning fucking tree, for God's sake.

We are about to enthusiastically trudge through almost 500 printed pages of Hivebent. But there's a bit of transitional stuff to take a look at first, like this. Post-**Descend** felt like a good time to retire this particular conceit. The idea originally was, I think, to check back on this walkthrough document as Rose updated it, and learn more about the game as she learns. But clearly the game is way off the rails now, so there's not much point in such a linear transcription effort. Also, she's getting moodier, edgier, and tiptoeing ever closer to full-blown grimdarkness. I think 1 Corinthians 13 put it best: "When I was a child, I spoke as a child, I understood as a child, I thought as a child; but when I became a woman, I put away childish things, such as my prolix, ridiculously overblown GameFAQs walkthrough project."

I have used a spell to rip this walkthrough from Earth's decaying network, and sealed it in one of the servers floating in the Furthest Ring. The gods may disperse the signal throughout the cosmos as they wish. Perhaps it will be of use to past or future species who like us have been ensnared by Skaia's malevolent tendrils.

In case it wasn't clear, magic is real.

Pardon my egress. You're on your own now.

We probably all agree that etching your initials with extravagant lettering into the digital canvas of your walkthrough file using *DARK MAGIC* is a pretty Teen-Dramatic thing to do. But you at least have to admit that this signature is pretty cool regardless of the context.

This walkthrough page was actually just one really tall GIF image. We've been scrolling down gradually to reveal just how edgy Rose has become. Bear with us folks, we're making a book here. Bringing you content made for twenty-first-century technology DIRECTLY into a fifteenth-century format.

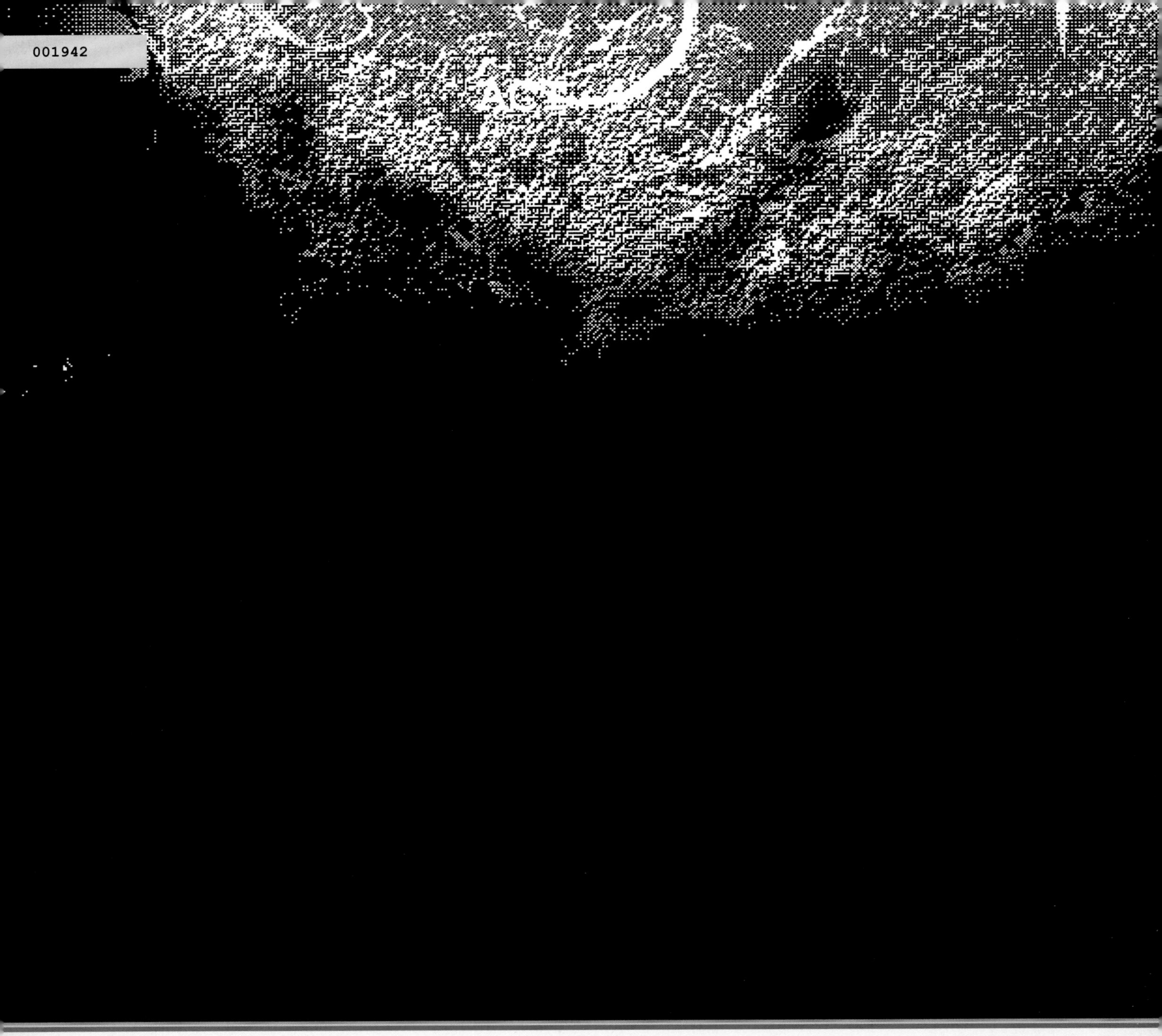

001942

We’re still scrolling. Here are some space monsters.

> Hours in the future...

This is the end of the tall GIF. I believe this is the first time I establish the idea that there are a lot of stray server-like objects floating out in the Furthest Ring. This actually does a pretty admirable job of explaining why trans-universal internet connections are able to be relayed just about anywhere, such as between the human universe and troll universe, and between a session and a home planet. The relay servers are stationed in a continuum that supersedes all these locations. Some of them are special though, like this one. There's another special one we see later that has a flickering pool ball on it.

The warweary calls another broken planet home, another cloth his garb. Land and rags fit for the wayward.

A villein becomes a vagabond.

> the recent past is recalled...

An ACCURSED MASCOT is located among fallen brethren. Its visage, reviled.

These swiftly narrated inter-Act panels get us caught up on some things and connect a few remaining dots. Such as, where'd the exiles get their postapocalyptic clothes?? Burning questions like that.

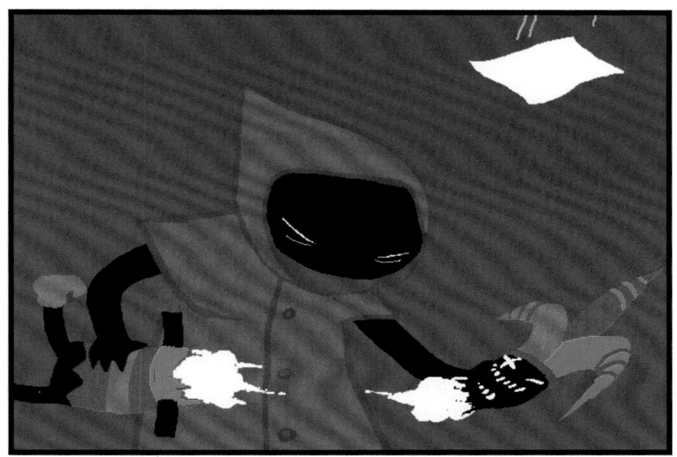

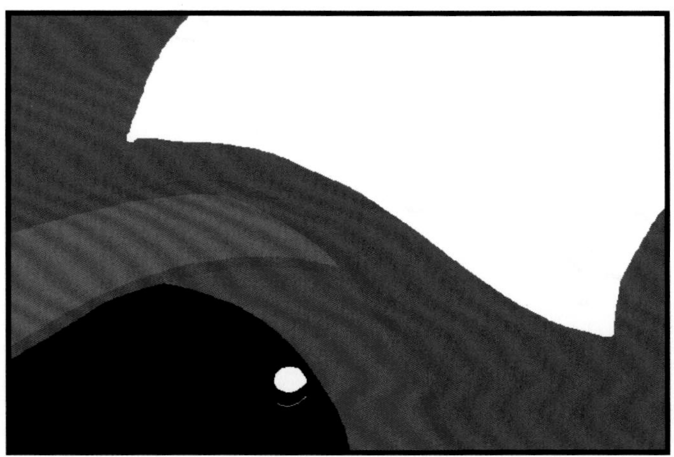

A RAG OF SOULS drifts from the heavens. Its owner, a mystery.

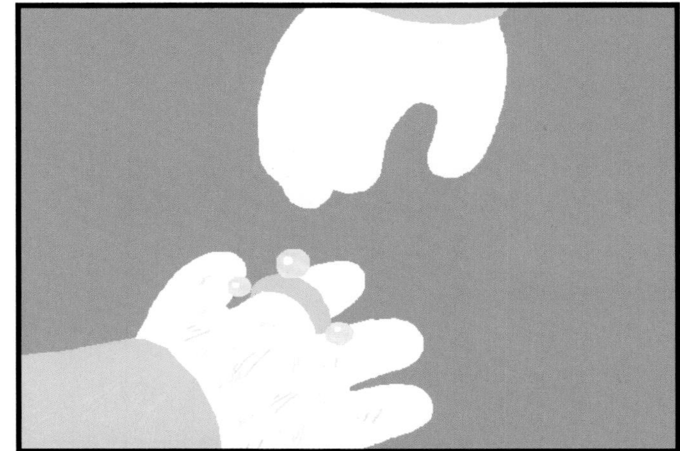

A boy finds a dead friend. Her ring, recovered.

There's a little splotch of oil back there behind John. Mysterious stuff! He doesn't notice though, because he's too busy looting treasure from his dream sister's corpse.

The boy sees himself in a cloud. His destination, revealed.

> Hours in the future...

A mistress becomes a mendicant.

> the recent past is recalled...

This is where PM crash-lands on Earth. She clearly recognizes the need to change clothes. Not just because her Parcel Mistress ensemble is filthy and bloodstained, but she surely recognizes the need to enrobe herself in a hardier cloth shroud more suitable for postapocalyptic life. I'm assuming exiles have certain instincts that kick in after they're exiled. They must know on some level they were designed for the eventual possibility that they will have to survive for hundreds of years in a barren wasteland.

A communication device is borrowed. A rendezvous, arranged.

The slayer is summoned. The collateral, presented.

This mini-arc connects a lot of things but still doesn't actually explain why or how PM got to Earth. But is that really important? Hmm, let's say...NOPE. What's probably more important is showing that she's completing the bargain with Jack to get her package back. She is dogged and determined, particularly when it comes to the mail. Unfortunately for Jack, much later on he will be reminded of her dogged determination when she chases him through outer space for three solid years.

The droll is beckoned. The bargain, honored.

The boy finds the castle. His courier's path, crossed.

CD is always ready and excitable when it comes to performing a menial task for the boss. Since he was near enough for Jack to beckon... I guess this means he was just tailing PM? He must have been. He was following her, ready to present her with this package at any moment, on Jack's orders. He probably couldn't wait.

The mail is delivered. An obligation, satisfied.

The package is opened. Letters, read.

> John!

This little green box has brought her nothing but misery. She's a consummate professional, but that doesn't mean she has to pretend to enjoy this bullshit. Come to think of it, she looked pretty pissed when she finally took Jack down, too.

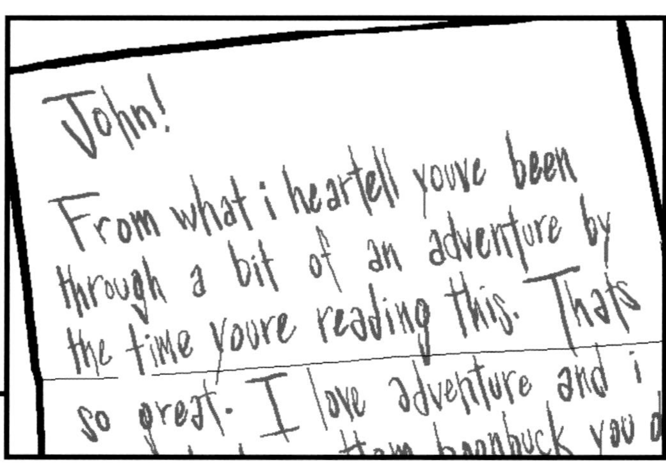

John!

From what i heartell youve been through a bit of an adventure by the time youre reading this. Thats so great. I love adventure and i would bet my bottom boonbuck you do too. I think we are birds of a feather john. I am pretty eager to meet you. Oh yeah i should have mentioned we are going to meet some day. I hear you like movies is that right john? I love movies too. Have you ever seen weekend at bernies? So friggin hilarious. Its hard to talk to jade about movies because she doesnt really know about movies but im sure you know that. Boooring. Ha ha just kidding jade you know i love you and i think youre a blast.

Okay speaking of jade we spent quite a long time working on this present for you. It was a big team effort. Okay i had to do quite a lot of arm twisting to get her to go along with helping me make such an oddball present for you and so well in advance. But i had my arm sort of twisted myself to get this going in the first place. But then she came around to the idea because she can see the future! Pretty amazing if you ask me. Itll all be clear later. Gadzooks with all this arm twisting ive been getting a good workout. We should wrestle when we meet john. I love to wrestle but i dont get a chance to wrestle with anyone that much. Do you like to get into fisticuffs john? Scrums and what not? Me too.

Anyway you should listen to jade from here on out john because she sure seems to know whats best for you. Whatever your adventure throws at you im sure shell tell you you can handle it. She believes in you.

There is another page to this letter...

Jake, get the fuck out of this part of the story. After spending most of Act 6 getting to know you, in hindsight the presence of your voice at this moment feels a bit weird and off-putting.

Oh kicking christ in a dirty diaper
i almost forgot to mention whats in this
box. Sorry this shits so small. I mean
obviously its small. Contents:
Royal Deringer
Quills of Eshidna

There is another letter from a different author...

> dear john,

Sorry I used the entire previous author note to tell Jake to fuck off, in the process gliding over so much pertinent trivia. (It was worth it.) Basically this is a box full of very small weapons (plus a wielder of those weapons, who will appear in a few pages). He lists the weapon names here because why not? It's cool info. There's a lot we don't yet know about Jake (such as the fact his name is Jake), but we surmise he's from the future, in a manner of speaking, and that he's related to Jade or John due to similarities in demeanor and tastes. If we're REALLY on the ball, we're probably also wondering, "Isn't this just young Grandpa Harley?" The answer is yes, of course. The question then is, what does that mean? From what timeline? Why is he helping? Who's twisting his arm? (It's Calliope.) And what, ultimately, is the point of shoving all this deadly stuff in this box and mailing it through time and space anyway? Is the purpose to let Jack use it to kill the queen, fulfilling a dire but critical event in this grand cosmic theater? Or is it something more? The assistance these weapons and this ally would provide later? The answer is never just one thing. In *Homestuck*, something turning out to be "essential" is always justification enough for someone, somewhere, to try to make that thing happen in the first place.

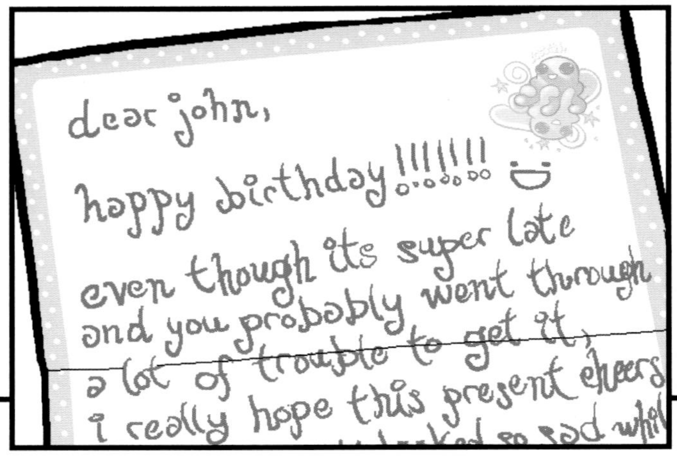

dear john,

happy birthday!!!!!!! :D

even though its super late and you probably went through a lot of trouble to get it, i really hope this present cheers you up! you looked so sad while you were reading my letter. um... which is to say, the one you are reading now. i can explain!!!

you see, when i go to sleep, in my dreams i wake up on the moon of a planet called prospit. by now you must know about this place! i have lived there in my dreams most of my life and i made so many friends there over the years. and you were there too! but you were asleep. the fact that you are awake now i think means all my friends are in trouble. you are awake because it is your job to help them. we will both help them!

but ummm..... i know these things because while i was on the moon, whenever it passed through skaia i could see lots of things in the clouds. the past, the future, stuff about our friends, and stuff about you! now that you are awake, and apparently at the center of skaia (??? WOW!!!) you should be able to see stuff in the clouds too. maybe you already have!

Jade includes a nice note too, to help get the taste of Jake out of our mouths. Very considerate of her. She has no idea John will be reading this over her dead body. This is some choice sadstuck here, guys. Perhaps the first true helping of sadstuck ever? A nice appetizer before Hivebent, which is an arc that does more than anything before it to bust open the floodgates on the tragic teenfeels phase of *Homestuck*'s history. It never quite looks back after that.

about this present! my penpal helped me work on it. he included a letter too! hes really funny and silly, i like him a lot and i think you would too. it took a long time between the two of us. and sure the present looks like a fun and completely ridiculous thing to get, but it is also really important! you are getting it exactly when you need it most. maybe thats hard to believe but its true! i saw it happen already. i dont see everything john, and i definitely dont know everything thats going to happen. but when i do know something, i always try to do my best to help people in the future! when im supposed to that is. youll get the hang of it.

john i am REALLY looking forward to seeing you when you wake up!!!!! its been nice playing with my prospitian friends and all, but also kind of lonely knowing you were in the other tower sleeping and having lousy dreams. :(im not sure where i am when you are reading this but im sure ill make it down to where you are soon! (jeez how did you get down there??? oh well ill find out) i cant wait to fly around the moon with you and show you all my favorite places. itll be so much fun!!!!!!!!! :D

<3
jade

Here's the secret to sadstuck: lay it on thick with the dramatic irony about how she's REALLY excited to do all this fun stuff when they finally meet, when she will be DEFINITELY ALIVE enough to do those things. Also make the kid cry. Come to think of it, since Jade clearly saw John opening this package and reading the letter in a cloud vision, I wonder what she thought he was crying about? Probably tears of happiness due to all the FUN they were both about to have! :D

A boy's grief is interrupted. His ring, sought.

The toy has taken a new master. The tactician, a misstep.

At last, the true contents of the box, revealed. You might have been able to guess another bunny was inside, due to bunnies being inside John's other two packages. You probably wouldn't have anticipated such a garish spectacle, though. It's hard to know what to focus on here. What the hell is going on with that hammer? Actually, let's not talk about the Zillyhoo hammer yet. Jade was right that John would get this unstoppable bunny warrior exactly when he needs it, just in time to defend against an unwelcome, highly premature Jack-murder. And Jack knows he shouldn't mess with this thing, no matter how powerful he currently feels, because this was the exact instrument he used to kill the queen and steal the very powers he has now. He knows he is no match...yet. What Jade doesn't mention (or know) is that this timely assist she helped provide is the very reason for Jack's rise, and therefore John's need for assistance in the first place. Idiots. They're all idiots.

Check.

> Hours in the future...

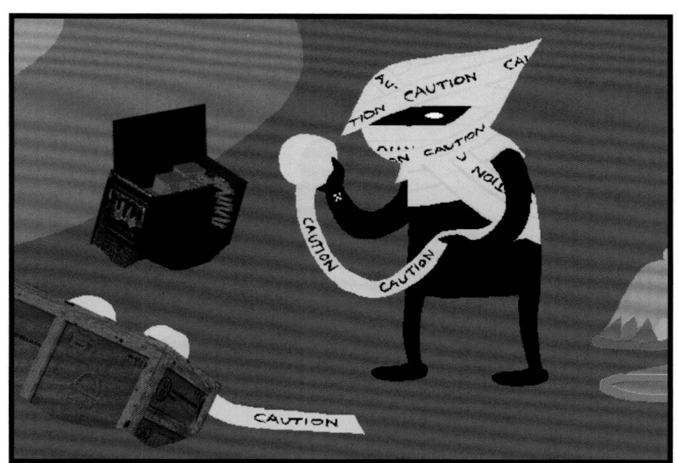

A regulator becomes a renegade.

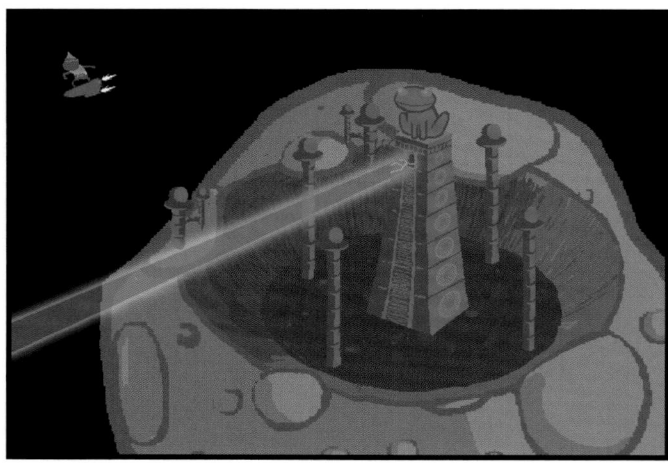

A temple is fled. And soon, revisited.

> the recent past is recalled...

Another exile has landed. There was nothing even wrong with AR's regulator ensemble. It wasn't bloody or ragged or anything. This lends more credence to my theory that exiles quickly change to the nearest possible outfit when they crash in the desert, on pure instinct. Like a hermit crab changing its shell.

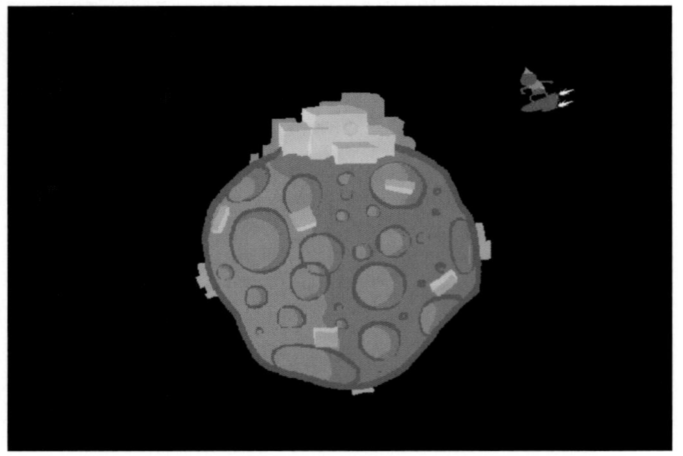

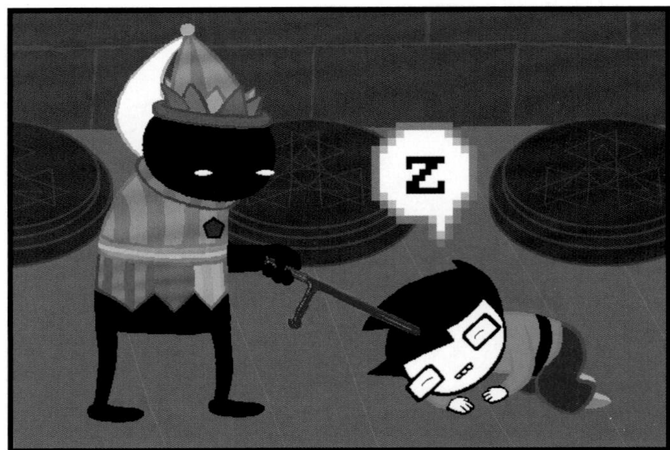

A nearby laboratory is also revisited. Its satellites, dispatched.

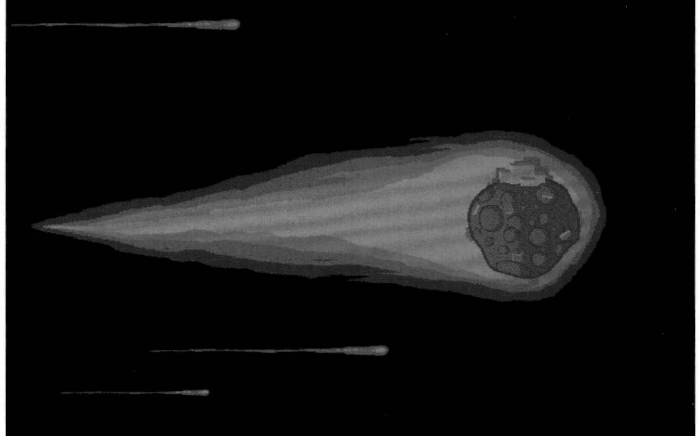

A sleeping boy is found. Rumbling, ominous.

I doubt AR would be so gentle with his baton if he knew this was the thoughtless rapscallion responsible for that DESPICABLE parking violation he ticketed earlier.

The lab is in flight. Its exits, inoperative.

Another public servant makes a sacrifice. A citizen's safety, secured.

A tyrant is retreating. A battleship, landing.

I'm gonna say this was probably another instinctive action made by an exile. They clearly are programmed to understand on a primal level what's important from a gameplay perspective. This kid shouldn't be getting exiled back to Earth with AR. That would be a huge misfire in terms of the flow of the game's strategy and narrative. Dersites are technically the "enemy" and function as a threat to the heroes, but lower-level ones like this will probably make sacrifices to ensure the heroes don't actually leave the boundaries of the game itself.

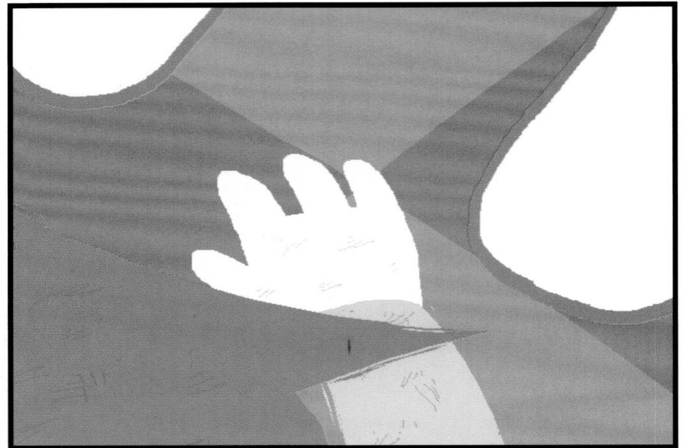

It seems likely Grandpa already knew his dream daughter was dead down here on the Battlefield, due to his comprehensively exploring and studying this session like the intrepid adventure man he is. He's seen cloud visions too, surely. And he's got this big damn battleship somehow, which never has been and never will be explained. Possibly he bartered for it with some chess guys? Who knows. But anyway, if he knew Jade was dead, that means he specifically made the trip to Skaia for the purpose of retrieving her corpse so that he may stuff and mount her in memoriam. He also kindly drops off Dad and Mom so they can begin their honeymoon getaway. Which he probably also knows to be doomed. It's unlikely he told them though.

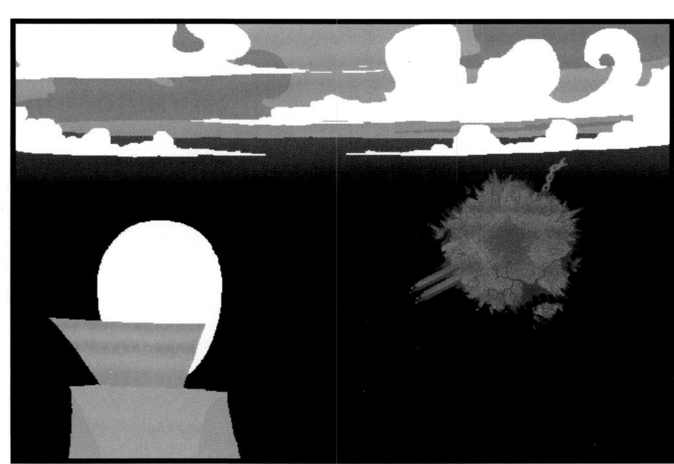

A grandfather mourns.
A family tradition, honored.

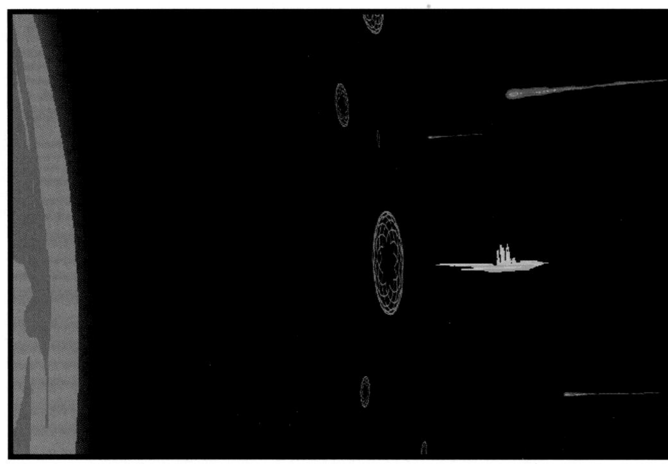

A queen mourns. A kingdom, bid farewell.

Her journey through the windswept must be walked alone. Her entourage, bid farewell.

A queen becomes a questant.

> Hours in the future...

> and then years...

Maybe it doesn't seem that honorable that the queen is abandoning her kingdom and whatever survivors remain. But as a game construct, she's encoded with certain instincts and objectives too. One of her chief priorities is the survival of her people, which in many cases can only be assured through exile, repopulation, and the rebuilding of civilization from scratch. Saying farewell to Prospit may be a common occurrence across all *Sburb* sessions. There are many ways for the game to play out, but it's not unreasonable to imagine the majority of sessions involve Prospit being ravaged in some way.

A key is employed.

The ruined skyscrapers we recognize from Dave's city help us zero in on the location of this station crash site. It's a big broken egg, because the station shape is related to the entry object of the player who lived there—in this case, Dave, who had to wait for an egg to hatch to enter the session. Notice how the egg station is broken in half. Remember how Bro had to chop the meteor in half to buy Dave some time? That's why. Splitting the meteor also split the station it contained. Now WQ has discovered it and must repair it to make it functional.

A command station, repaired.

Fixing a big broken egg I guess is appropriately symbolic for a woman whose job is now to repair and restore life and civilization on this planet. Maybe that's why she landed her gold ship nearby and sought the station out? It's also possible she sought it out because it is indisputably the most baller exile station available. Thing can just hover and teleport anywhere she wants.

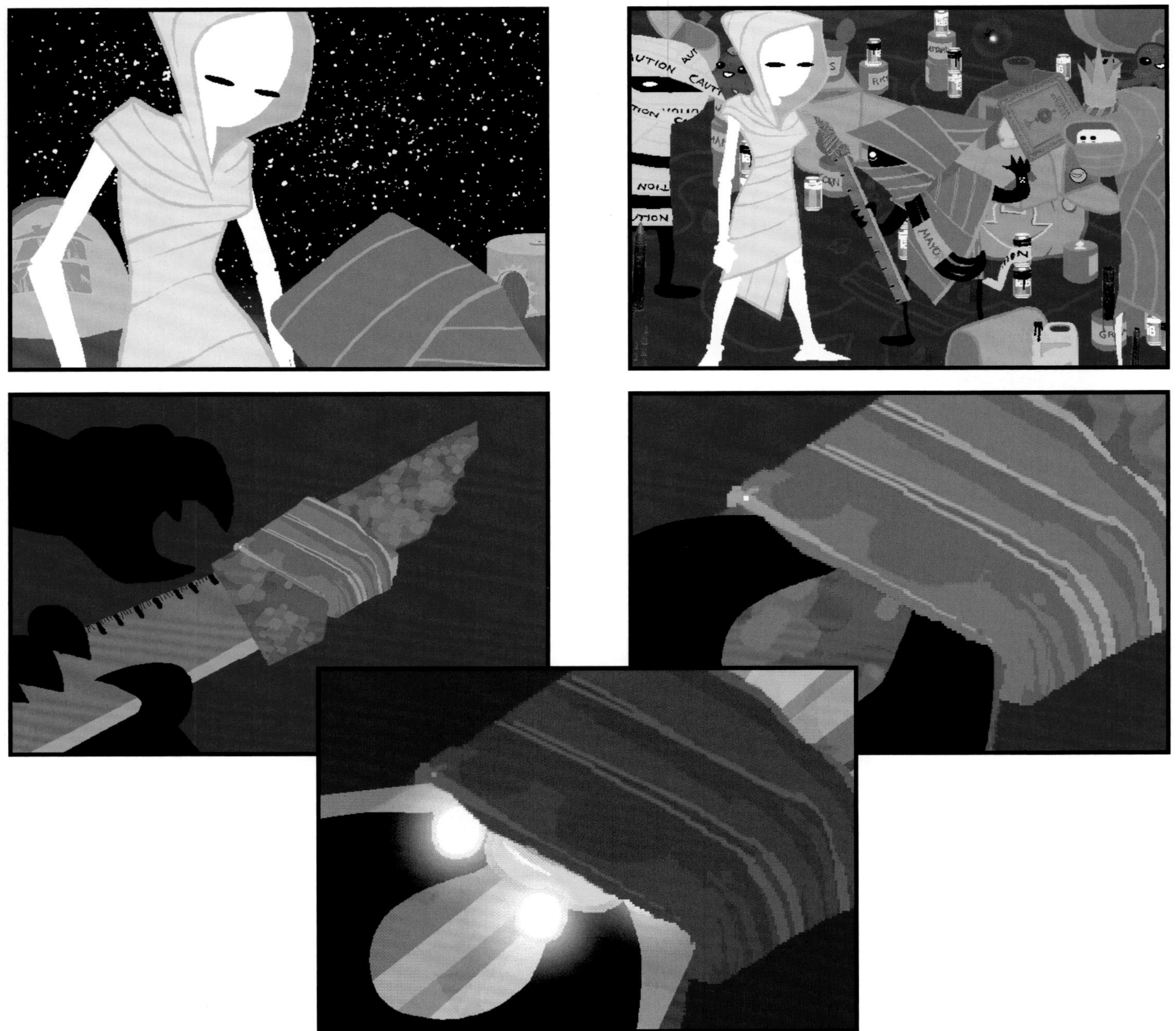

WV is really, really proud of this cool spear he made and he wants to show it off to the queen...wait—okay no, that's not what he's doing at all. But it easily could have been.

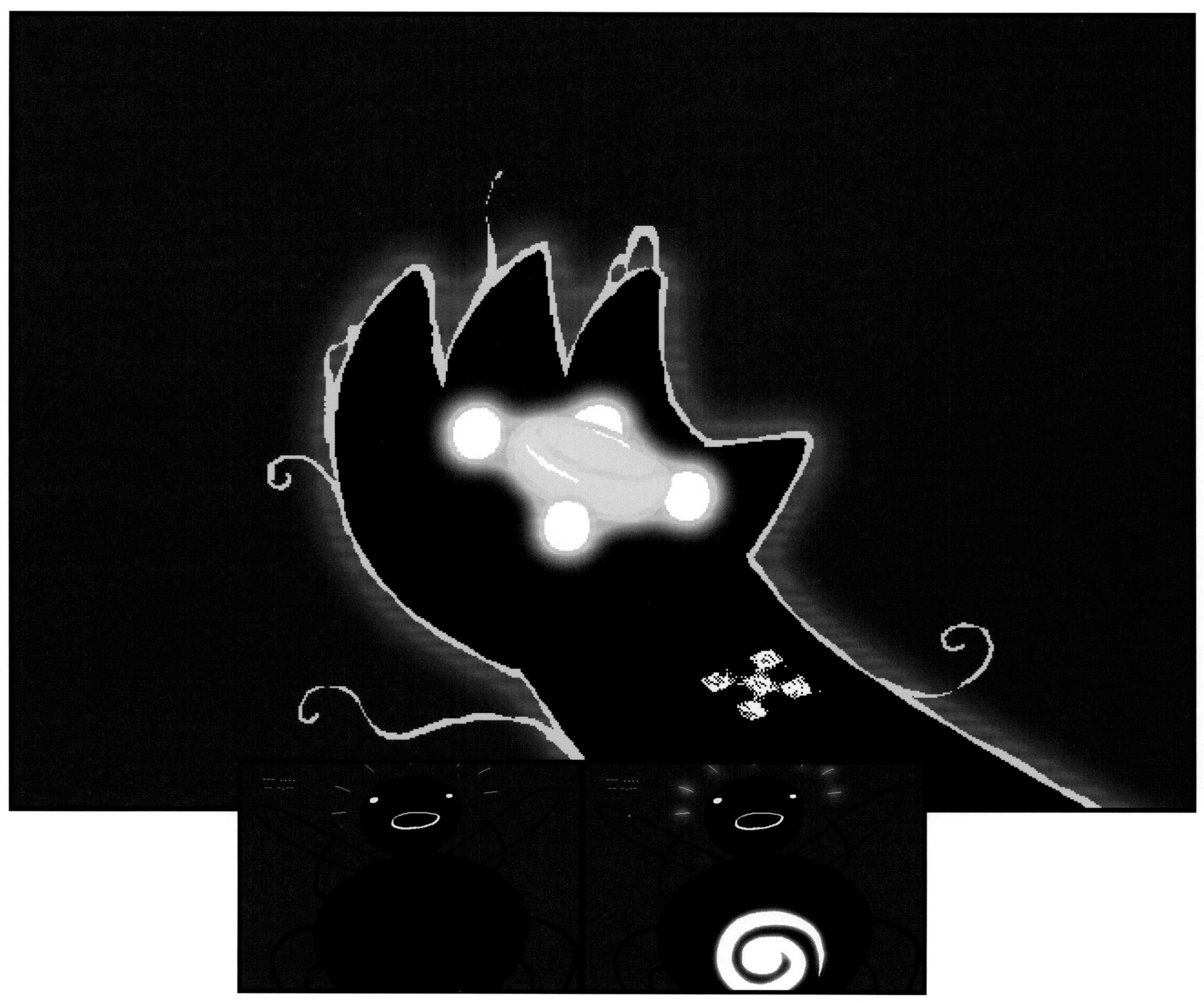

Another tidbit of information revealed to wow us all. (Or at least wow Serenity. She can't even deal.) WV had the ring all along. But we last saw John with it, prying it from Jade's cold, dead finger. So really this reveal just sets up another question for us to keep track of in the ensuing Act: how does the ring make its way from John to WV?

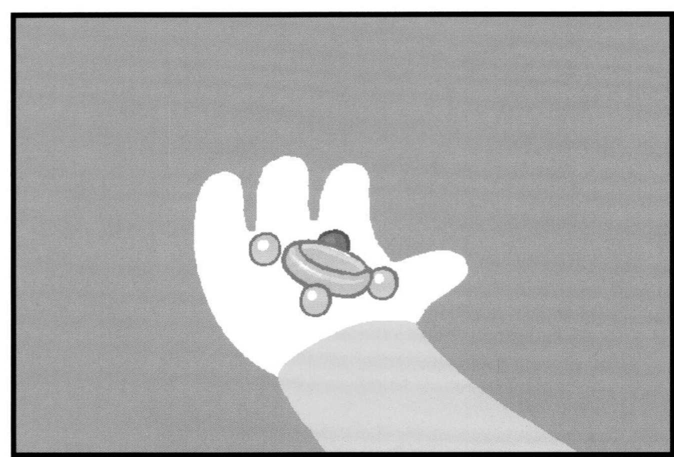

There's another cloud.

I'm glad the bunny put all those other weapons back in a tidy pile inside the box. Not because he looked ridiculous with them, but because they made it a lot harder to draw him.

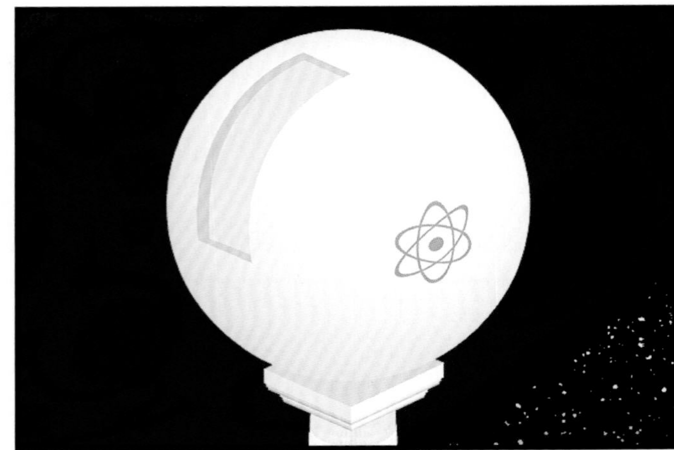

And inside, a dark laboratory, unused for years.

And inside, a FOURTH WALL, pilfered from a bureaucrat's office and absconded with years ago.

It isn't turned on.

But if it was, this is almost certainly what we would see.

> Recap 2.

Now we discover that Grandpa stole the Fourth Wall of Jack's cubicle. He stashed it in here along with his taxidermied loved ones. This Fourth Wall becomes a very important object later, as does the stuffed Jade. Just seeing that they exist in this lab in this one frame is important information to stash in your back pocket. We're still collecting plot tokens to cash in down the road. Do we ever stop? Nope. Don't worry though, at least the dead dog remains safely useless from now on.

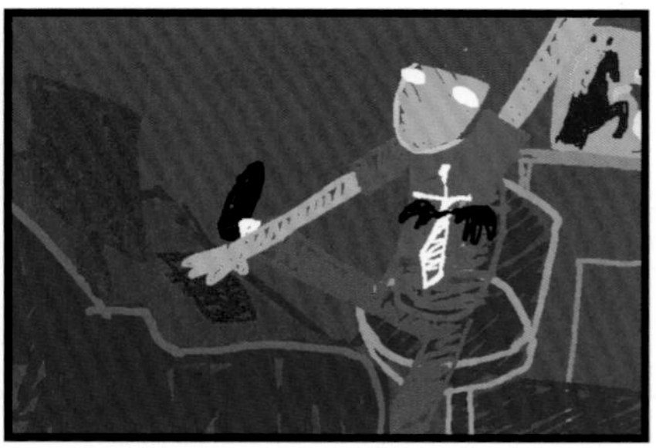

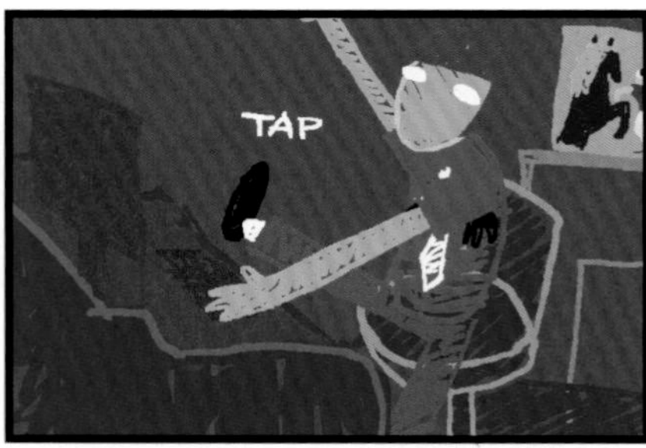

Picking up from where we left off...

I typed a really long recap. Then some other stuff happened.

GC (gallowsCalibrator) helped John fly to the second gate, which took him to Rose's world, LOLAR. He crashed into Rose's room, where he found her asleep. He snooped through her room, and Dave tricked him into giving him the code to duplicate Rose's writing journals. John opened the package Rose made for his birthday. It contained the bunny from Con Air, the same one John got from Dave, but older and dirtier, and modified with Rose's knitting. She'd had the bunny since she was very young.

John leaves Casey the salamander (Bubbles Viceroy Von Salamancer) in the room. He briefly speaks with GA (grimAuxiliatrix) from Rose's computer, and pretends to be Rose. She believes he is, triggering a convoluted series of conversations between her and the real Rose in both the past and future, in no particular order. GA gets help with her computer from TA (twinArmageddons) in time to see Rose at her computer, having woken up.

Before she woke up, Dream Rose was awake on Derse's moon. She now had memories from her future self's doomed alternate reality. She flew to Dream Dave's tower, and got his attention with a ball of yarn, causing real Dave to fall asleep. They had a dream dance party. Dream Rose threw Dream Cal out the window. Bro's rocket board caught Dream Cal. AR? followed the board and Cal to a transportalizer on Derse, which lead to a meteor lab in the veil.

Meanwhile on LOLAR, Rose's mom defeated a huge monster. The pony, Maplehoof, followed her and collected the grist windfall. Both mom and the pony then transported to the meteor lab. John's dad found a clean hat John had deposited into a parcel pyxis. Dad followed Jade's grandpa, who was carrying John's Sassacre book, into some ruins. They both transported to the meteor lab too. Meanwhile, John used the grist collected by the pony to make a normal sized version of a giant hammer, Fear No Anvil, which Davesprite gave him the code for. Dream Rose saw John on Dream Dave's computer, and woke up. She went out to see him, but he had already blasted off. He took the mutant kitten, Vodka Mutini (Doctor Meowgon Spengler), with him.

John found the ruins that mom and the pony went into. He went in and killed some powerful monsters with his new hammer. He transported to the meteor lab as well.

In the lab he found no one, except the pony. Some other stray items were on the floor. Dad's dirty hat, the Sassacre book, Dream Cal. He found some apparatus used to genetically engineer footsoldiers and agents for the white and black armies from chess piece DNA. He also found a junior ectobiologist's lab suit, and a series of terminals much like those the exiles would find in the far future. He would use this apparatus to create paradox clones of himself, his friends, and their guardians. Meanwhile AR? surfed bro's rocket board to a different meteor containing the frog temple that would later root itself near Jade's island. Inside he found the same time capsule she would find later. He also found some more lab equipment used for ectobiology. This equipment would soon be used to create Becquerel, a mutated combination of the genes from an ordinary dog in the early 20th century, and the DNA code in one of Rose's journals. AR? hides in the lab when he hears one of Jack's henchmen, the Draconian Dignitary. DD is carrying Rose's duplicated journals which he stole from Dave, and Dave's beta which was used as a bookmark. He discards the beta into the time capsule. Millions of years later (from the capsule's perspective) Jade would retrieve that beta and use it to connect with Dave, allowing him to enter the medium. Dave created the journal duplicates after an extensive alchemy binge. Rose too had a similar alchemy session, and both kids upgraded their weapons and gear. Rose made a pair of needlewands, crossed with her grimoire, and took up the art of dark magic. She used this magic to burn her journal, thus destroying the genetic code. She was advised to do so by the gods of the Furthest Ring, whom she was now able to communicate with in her dreams. The gods live far beyond the veil, and advise the children of the moon of Derse, and serve as the counterpart to the role Skaia plays for the children of Prospit's moon. They deemed the code which would inevitably be used to create Becquerel to be dangerous. Dave decided to destroy his copy too. But when he went back to his room, he discovered they were stolen. He also found his own dead body, which apparently was him from the very near future attempting to go back in time and stop the thief, DD. Dave decided not to attempt any more time travel, and disposed of the body. GC (gallowsCalibrator) discussed the matter with him, and pledged to help him by telling him his future along the way, so that he would not have to face the death of more future selves, or suffer the sort of embarrassment he went through while entering the medium. Previously unseen, the way Dave entered the medium was as follows. As the large meteor was bearing down on his city, Dave climbed the radio tower on top of his building with his broken sword in hand to reach the nest built by the Crowsprite. The sprite guarded the egg, which unknown to Dave, simply needed time to hatch before he could enter. The sprite pecked his head and he fell. He was saved by bro's rocket board. Meanwhile, bro was on top of the meteor, riding it as it descended. He used his sword to chop it in half, splitting it into two pieces, diverting the initial impact from their building to two separate impact sites. He thus bought a little more time for the egg to hatch, which it did, just before their location was consumed by the blasts. On Prospit's moon, PM? prepared to depart for the Battlefield at the center of Skaia, to seek the king's counsel on what to do with the queen's ring. She was tailed by another of Noir's lackeys, the Courtyard Droll. CD picked her pocket and stole the ring. PM? departed via shuttle to Skaia. Dream Jade then clobbered CD, and recovered the ring. She tried it on, but its power has no effect on humans. Later, CD would travel to the Battlefield and continue tailing PM?. The Battlefield is a planet at the center of Skaia. It undergoes a transformation with each player that enters the medium, and each new prototyped kernel introduced. It starts as a simple 3x3 chessboard with two kings in perpetual stalemate, and expands to a larger board and more exotic collection of pieces with the first player entering. Then it become a much larger cube with the second player. And then an even larger sphere, with oceans, trees, mountains and pastures with the third. It presumably will transform again with the fourth. The armies of the black and white kingdoms duel there. Soldiers are airlifted from meteor facilities in the veil to supply the manpower. Enormous mutant chess-like monsters stalk the landscape. The two kings command their armies from the field. They each have a scepter that serves a similar purpose to the queens' rings. When activated, a scepter causes a king to be a giant, and bear the properties of all the prototypings. A king is able to deactivate a scepter, to hand it off to another so that they will not be affected in that way. When the black king captures the white king's scepter, the Reckoning begins. The Reckoning sends all the meteors in the veil toward Skaia, in stages. First the small ones, then gradually, the bigger ones, over a 24 hour period. There was a Warweary Villein on the Battlefield who was a simple farmer and was tired of the conflict. WV? united a band of soldiers from both armies to lead a rebellion against the black king. Before they could attack the king, Jack Noir, now empowered by the black queen's ring, intercepted the coup. He destroyed the king's scepter, and killed the king. Jack then killed the entire rebellion army, sparing only WV?. Perhaps to leave a survivor to tell the story, or perhaps out of respect for a fellow mutineer. Only he knows. Meanwhile, PM? met with the white king. He disabled his scepter, and gave it to her along with his crown. PM? now had the crowns of the white king and queen, and the white scepter, but discovered she had misplaced the white queen's ring. Jack's muscle, the Hegemonic Brute, had been tailing the white king. HB then followed PM?, and attacked her. She dropped the scepter off a cliff: She would regroup and chop off HB's head with the regisword Jack gave her to kill the white monarchs. CD, who had been tailing both of them, recovered the white scepter, and delivered it to Jack. Jack used it to initiate the Reckoning, and would proceed to go on a more extensive rampage, devastating the Battlefield and Prospit.Back in the meteor lab, John began the ectobiology session which appeared to have been prepared for him in advance by the guardians who had just been there. The four monitors were all locked onto the kids' guardians at certain points in time, each on the day of one of the kid's "birth". On Jade's birthday, nanna was locked onto in John's neighborhood, by the Betty Crocker factory. The meteor carrying baby Jade crashed into the factory and destroyed it. Her grandpa, the owner of that factory, would adopt her. John's dad witnessed, and would spend years investigating. On Dave's birthday, grandpa was locked onto while he was on his yacht, pioneering the island for the first time. He was sailing with baby Jade. Overhead, there was the meteor carrying baby Dave, which would crash into bro's favorite record shop. On Rose's birthday, bro was locked onto as he stood over the crater where he would find baby Dave. He would give him a tiny pair of pointy shades. Overhead, there was a meteor carrying baby Rose, which would land in a lake and destroy it. Rose's mom would retrieve and adopt her. Months later, on John's birthday, mom would bring Rose to John's neighborhood to investigate the destruction of grandpa's factory, and related stellar phenomena. The target was locked on her. Dad came out of the family joke shop to greet her, leaving nanna inside. The meteor carrying baby John destroyed the shop, killing nanna. Dad would adopt John, and Rose's mom disappeared. Dad retrieved her scarf, and filed the clue away for his ongoing investigation. John attempted (unwittingly) to appearify all four guardians. But since removing them from those moments would have caused a paradox, he instead paradoxified their ghost slime imprints. This slime was collected into two pairs of containers. One pair collected nanna and granpa's slime. The other pair collected mom and bro's. The device then created baby paradox clones of the four guardians. These babies would then later be sent back in time to become those guardians themselves. Once those four clones were created, another sequence activated. The two pairs of slime tubes emptied into vats below. The nanna/grandpa slime mixed together, and separately, the mom/bro slime mixed together as well. An additional four paradox clones were created from those two slime concoctions. Baby John and Jade were created from the nanna/grandpa slime. Baby Rose and Dave were created from the mom/bro slime. These four babies would also go back in time to become the four kids, via meteors, in the sequence and on the dates listed above. All eight babies would each ride their own meteors, launched from the veil after Jack started the Reckoning, and into the defense portals deployed by Skaia to protect itself. The defense portals each lead to Earth, as Skaia defends itself, in a way, by sacrificing Earth. While most meteors are sent to the time period when the kids begin the game, many lead to a number of different time periods. Some thirteen years prior to the game (used by the kids), some nearly a century prior (used by nanna and grandpa), some millions of years ago (used, eventually, by the frog temple meteor), and some to the far future (used by the exiles). And all eight of them would travel with an object or animal. John with his Sassacre book, which would become the much older-looking family heirloom stored in dad's safe, with Nannasprite's inscription to John on it. Rose with the dirty bunny Dave gave John for his birthday. Dave with the pony, Maplehoof. Jade with the knit-repaired bunny Rose got John for his birthday, which Rose cherished since "birth". Nanna with dad's dirty hat. Mom with Mutini (Meowgon). Grandpa with two flintlock pistols which older Grandpa left behind for him in the lab (which would eventually both wind up in Jade's room). And bro with Dream Cal, which would later be fitted with a new personalized shirt, and would become real Cal, the same doll that would haunt Dave's waking life, and consequently, his dreams. All of these babies and their items would automatically be transported to their own meteors at the onset of the Reckoning. John made absolutely sure to give baby Rose and Jade their bunnies when he saw an opportunity to reenact a scene from one of his favorite movies, much to the dismay of a watching CG (carcinoGeneticist). While AR? was in the frog temple lab, he would see more of young nanna and grandpa's story. On 4/13, 1910, exactly 99 years prior to John's "birth", baby nanna's meteor destroyed a bakery owned by Betty Crocker. Nanna was adopted by Crocker's husband, Colonel Sassacre, and taken to live in his mansion. 8 days later, grandpa's meteor destroyed the dog house belonging to Sassacre's dog, Halley. Halley was elsewhere, and was unharmed. When Sassacre and nanna went to investigate the crater, Sassacre was shot and killed accidentally with one of grandpa's pistols. Halley then showed up (who young grandpa would tend to pronounce "Harley" due to his speech impediment), and would largely serve as their guardian for the next 13 years, with presumably some parental influence from the wicked Crocker. On his 13th birthday, grandpa would run off with Harley to find adventure. Nanna would stay behind, contend with the batterwitch, and master the art of baking as well as take up her deceased grandfather's tradition of pranksterism. Harley was locked onto by the frog temple's equipment. DD activated the device, and produced a paradox clone of Harley combined with the controversial MEOW code to create puppy Bec. The spectacle terrified AR?, leaving a major impression on him. He would recognize Bec's silhouette carved on WV's pumpkin years later. The pumpkin commanded his fear, and caused him to surrender. Meanwhile, the grown-up versions of mom and dad were on board a flying battleship belonging to grandpa, who piloted it toward Skaia. Dad gave mom her long discarded scarf, from the day he lost his mother and found his son. The two guardians traded gestures of affection. Jade remained asleep through it all, trying to stay on the moon as long as she could until she figured out how to wake John up. She talked about this with AT (adiosToreador), who revealed he preferred his dream life on Prospit more than any aspect of the game, and regretted all the trolls' dream selves were now dead. Jade expressed surprise at the notion of dream self mortality. After Jack used the full power of the ring to devastate the battlefield and the two armies, he turned his attention on Prospit, inflicting severe damage the same way. He then cut the chain connecting the moon to Prospit, sending the moon plummeting through the atmosphere of Skaia, and breaking up in the process. Dream John, still asleep, fell out of his tower and drifted down ahead of the falling moon. Dream Jade flew to intercept him, and spent a moment attempting to wake him before the moon's collision was imminent. At the last minute she flung Dream John out of the blast radius, but was not able to clear the blast herself. She died. The blast left a massive crater on the Battlefield. This was the first thing Dream John saw when he woke up. The death of Dream Jade caused her dreambot to malfunction and explode, destroying her room. Still asleep, Jade fell from her tower as Bec watched from a distance, and an enormous meteor loomed overhead. Elsewhere, on Dave's world LOHAC, bro dueled with Jack briefly. It was a stalemate, until bro plunged his sword into the large floating record platform they were fighting on. This released a mysterious energy from the cracks. Bro escaped. Rose completed her final GameFAQS walkthrough entry, and used magic to seal it in a server in the Furthest Ring, to be accessed by players in worlds beyond their own. She had destroyed her first gate on a whim, and resolved to search for answers to remedy the hopelessness of their doomed session. Meanwhile, Dave entered his first gate, riding into it with his awesome skateboard, Unreal Air. The four exiles arrived on Earth years after its apocalypse, but years before they found their respective command stations. WV wrapped himself in John's dream blanket, which became dirty and unrecognizable over time. He found it along with a Jack-like doll on the Battlefield, which formerly sat in Dream John's bedroom, haunting his dreams. WV? ripped it apart. PM wrapped herself in a Prospit banner, which too faded in time. AR wrapped himself in caution tape, using his own supply, as well as some fresh rolls he was lucky enough to discover near the ruined frog temple in one of grandpa's old crates. This was after he escaped that same temple in the medium, and found

This is a pretty good way to handle this recap page. Is that text even legible? It matters not. Depicted above: that's me banging out these author notes, with sterling fidelity to my posture, attire, and complexion. Some things never change.

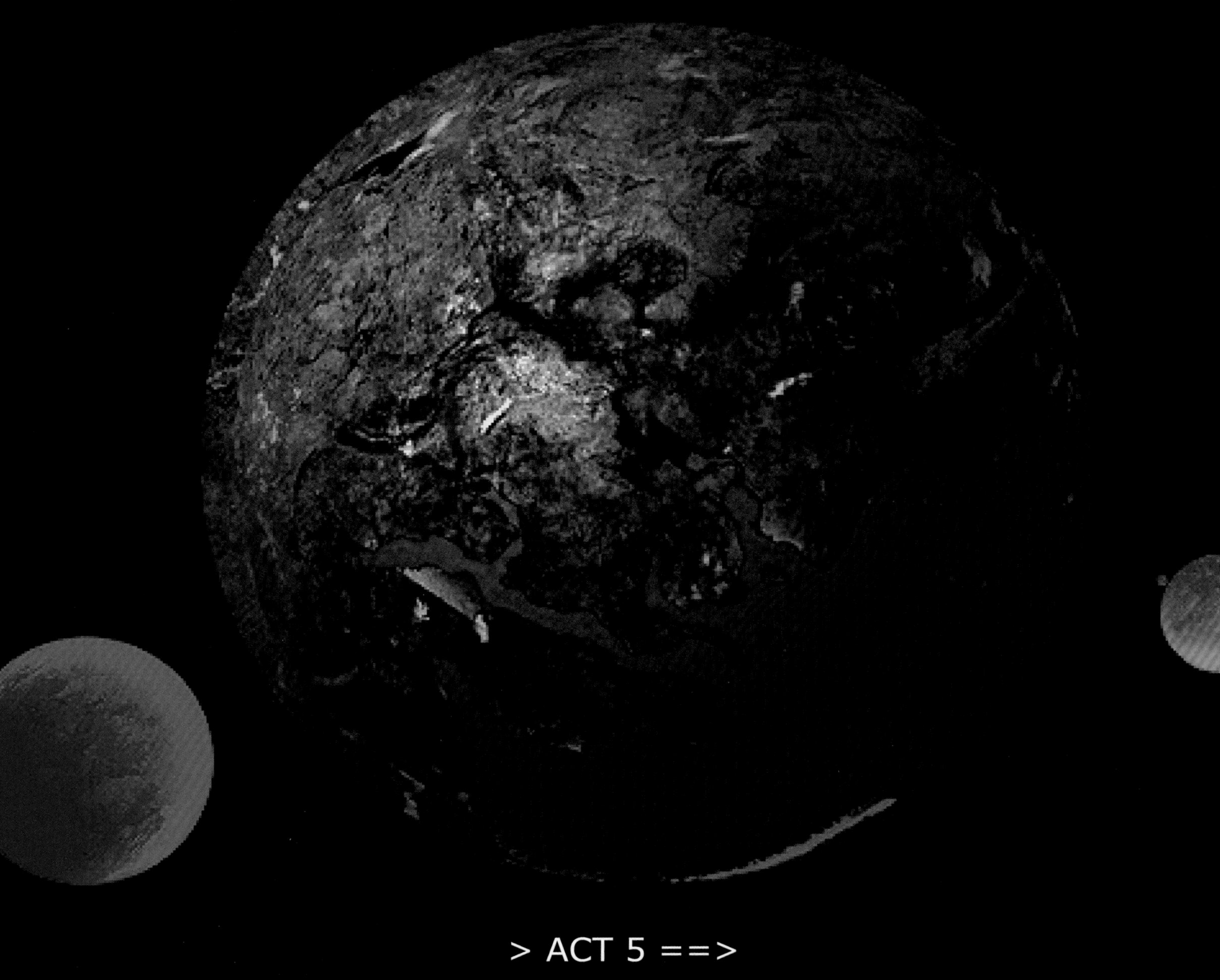

Plowing right ahead with Act 5. This was posted on 6/12/2010. (612 of course instantly became another special *Homestuck* number.) This was barely a week after I posted **[S] Descend**, with all those inter-Act pages coming in the days between. Should I have...stopped for a bit? Planned this big troll arc out? Nah. Onward and upward. Planning is for suckers. About to spend an entire summer building an alien world from scratch, introducing twelve new characters, devising their backstories, tangled web of relationships, and personal arcs, amounting to a rollercoaster ride of teen betrayal and bloodshed? Just fucking do it. We aren't getting any younger.

Elsewhere in paradox space, we examine another planet, forgotten by time.

But we will strive to remember. What was this planet's name?

> Enter name.

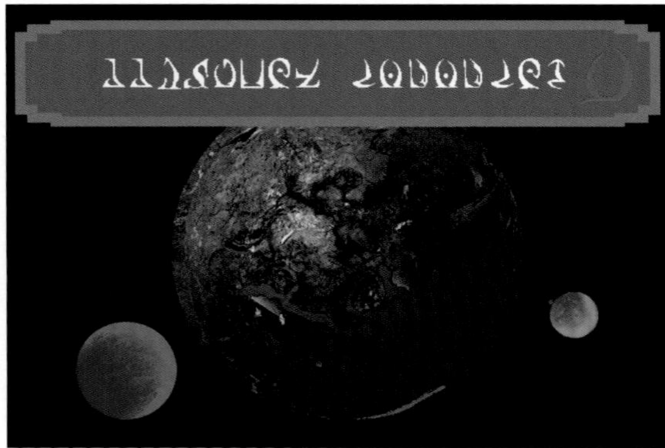

Oh, ha ha! Nice one, smartypants. Really hilarious.

But let's get real here. No more clowning around.

> Try again.

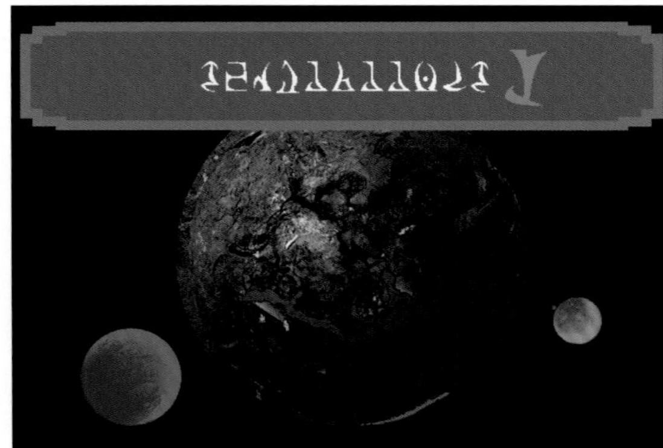

That is much better. In fact, as it happens, your guess is precisely correct. What are the odds??

We examine the planet ALTERNIA. Somewhere on this planet, there is a young troll.

> Hivebent

The original troll font was me performing the creative masterstroke of taking the *Elder Scrolls* font and flipping it upside down. Probably some people wonder why I did this. I guess it was a joke? I couldn't fully explain why it's a joke, or why it's funny. It may not even be funny, in any conventional sense. Suffice it to say that sometimes I perceive humor in that which is so blatantly lazy and stupid, one can barely escape concluding that the intent was to offend the intellect. Okay, so I guess I fucking explained it? Consider it explained. Also the first "failed" planet name was TURDODOR FUCKBALL, I believe. The planetary equivalent of ZOOSMELL POOPLORD. The "real" name was gathered from reader suggestions, like all twelve trolls in this arc. Actually, Toby Fox was the one who suggested Alternia. So let's give him credit for that too, in addition to about a thousand cool songs.

This young troll stands in his respiteblock. It just so happens that today, the 12th bilunar perigee of the 6th dark season's equinox, is the day of this young troll's larval awakening, also known as his wriggling day. Though it was six solar sweeps ago he was given life, it is only today he will be given a name!

Six Alternian solar sweeps, for convenient reference, is equivalent to thirteen Earth years.

Earth, also for convenient reference, is a planet that does not yet exist.

What will the name of this young troll be?

> Enter name.

Homestuck's overarching nature is to be iteratively repetitive. To establish long-term patterns, reach critical moments, "reset" itself in some way or another, then start over and replay the entire pattern with some iterative transformations, evolutions, or deconstructions of those patterns. Launching into Hivebent is the first (of arguably only two) major plot resets that boot up again in this familiar introductory way: the protagonist standing in his or her bedroom, briefly described in this way, awaiting a command from the "player." Because we immediately recognize this introduction template as echoing the first page where John is introduced, that makes a strong basis for almost instantly laying it on thick with the alien worldbuilding bullshit. Respiteblock? That's a silly word for a bedroom. Wriggling day? Guess that's a birthday. Six solar sweeps? That must be what they call years. Oh also, Earth doesn't exist yet? What? That's new information of some interest. Let's put that in our back pocket, along with stuffed Jade and the Fourth Wall, and then make a mental note to buy pants with bigger pockets.

You enter something predictably derogatory and this guy gets fed up by your shenanigans in record time.

This guy has a lot of troll pals and their adventures are going to be quite extensive and convoluted, to an even greater degree than one perhaps may be accustomed. He thinks that if you think that we have time to drag out every little gag and expected pattern along the way, you've got another thing coming. He thinks you should cram that sobering understanding in your chitinous windhole, and tamp it down hard with your ugly stupid looking cartilage nub.

> Try again.

Karkat's fake name which he sliced in half said BULGEREEK NOOKSTAIN. Which I didn't remember, and couldn't actually read in that panel, so I had to go look it up in the *Homestuck* wiki. There's a lot of shit on the wiki. Maybe I should just be pasting huge batches of the wiki directly into these margins and save myself some time. Nah, people would probably get "mad."

Your name is KARKAT VANTAS.

As was previously mentioned, it is your WRIGGLING DAY, which is barely even worth mentioning. It is an anniversary, if anything, to lament the faults of your existence, of which there are assuredly plenty.

Equally plenty, and somewhat related to that topic, are your INTERESTS. You have a passion for RIDICULOUSLY TERRIBLE ROMANTIC MOVIES AND ROMCOMS. You should really be EMBARRASSED for liking this DREADFUL CINEMA, but for some reason you are not. You like to program computers, but you are NOTORIOUSLY PRETTY AWFUL AT IT. Your programs invariably damage the machines on which they are executed, which is just as well, since you like to believe you specialize in COMPUTER VIRUSES. When you mature, you aspire to join the ranks of the most lethal members of your society, the THRESHECUTIONERS. You like to practice with your REALLY COOL SICKLE, but just wind up looking like KIND OF A DOOFUS BY YOURSELF IN YOUR ROOM.

You like to chat with some of your other troll pals, most of which drive you BATSHIT UP THE FUCKING BELFRY. You have been trying out a new chat client beta called TROLLIAN, and you are NOT REALLY SURE WHAT YOU THINK ABOUT IT YET. Your trolltag is carcinoGeneticist and you speak in a manner that is ALMOST EXCLUSIVELY ORNERY, ALL THE TIME.

Later, you will play a game with 5 other friends, and go on a big adventure with them. This game, for convenient reference, is a game that DOES NOT YET EXIST.

But it will soon.

What will you do?

> Karkat: Examine slimy purple pod.

A good joke would be to follow up the note on the previous page by posting a huge block of text from the Karkat section of the wiki right here, and continue on like that for another dozen pages or so. Alas, nope. I'm going to remain disciplined. I'm a FUCKING professional, guys. Anyway that's already a lot of information about Karkat up there, which you can feel free to read and enjoy. Personally, I'm a big fan of the rom-com posters in his room. The fact that he loves romantic comedies is probably the best character trait I gave him, IMO, and maybe one of the best overall character traits of anyone in the story. Troll Will Smith agrees with me. Just look at him there, so smug and confident. You know it's true.

It is your RECUPERACOON full of nourishing SOPOR SLIME. Every young troll enjoys the cozy embrace of such a vessel each night, and the relaxing ooze helps assuage the terrible visions of blood and carnage that plague the dark subconscious of your species.

It is so inviting... a few minutes couldn't hurt.

> Karkat: Get in.

Ok, this sure is cozy and all, but you can't be napping all day like a chump. Dammit, you're a busy guy. You are sort of a big deal.

Goddamn slime. Now you have to change your clothes too. What were you thinking?

Luckily all your clothes are the same. Trolls think fashion is stupid.

> Karkat: Examine movie posters.

Ok, it's time to get serious here. Sweet Troll Jegus. Let's get real and get down to some major business.

You space out and get caught up reading the titles of the films for about five minutes. Wow these movies are great. You don't care what anyone says. Pure magic.

Is that...

Is that John Cusack?

The thing that most people don't realize is that John Cusack is a universal constant.

Sleeping in a huge cocoon full of slime isn't the weirdest possible thing a teen alien could do. But it would be pretty weird if they did so fully clothed. Thankfully, it's implied here that Karkat's aggravated he got his clothes all slimy, which would suggest that it's not customary to jump in fully clothed. On the other hand, I don't know if there's any evidence after this which suggests that trolls take their clothes off before going to sleep? There's one instance I can recall where Terezi is sleeping in her slime while fully clothed. Maybe Terezi is just weird? She didn't have a lusus to teach her how to go to bed properly, after all.

This movie...

Ok, this one even you have a hard time defending. But still, it's so good.

The best thing about it is how Troll Sandler doesn't make you want to punch anything.

Like, nothing at all, really hard or anything.

> Karkat: Captchalogue sickle.

You grab your trusty SICKLE with your ENCRYPTION MODUS. To retrieve it, you'll need to hack the code to open the CARD VAULT left behind.

This will obviously prove to be a completely ridiculous and untenable way of managing an inventory, and lead to a great many follies. Later on, you would swap your modus with your hacker friend, a guy who unlike you happens to be competent with programming. It would only make sense.

But for the time being it makes your life kind of a nightmare. There are so many stupid things that happen because of this modus. So many, you just have no idea.

> Karkat: Take card vault.

A basic, serviceable sickle is readily available for Karkat to wield in lieu of the simple, workmanlike hammer that was available to John. Is there any meaning to draw from the fact that the hammer and sickle combine to form a widely recognized symbol for communism? Doubtful. Except to provide the shippers with a quality name for the Johnkat ship.

GOD.

DAMMIT.

You hear some unhappy grumbling through the hole below. This was not the coolest thing you could have done just now.

> Karkat: Examine large black book.

You make quite sure NOT to captchalogue it, and simply pick it up and read it.

In terms of iterating all the preexisting patterns after this plot reboot, sylladex shenanigans are definitely one of the sillier rodeos we've already been to, ad nauseam, so the only remotely defensible thing to do with it now is to mercilessly mock the entire idea of a sylladex by running with outlandishly unusable versions right off the bat. Consequential slapstick is immediate.

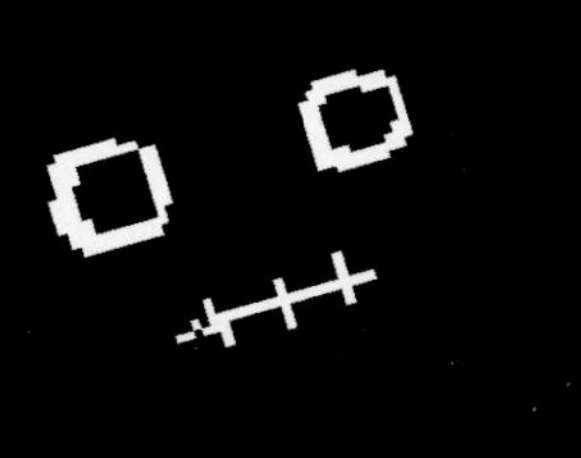

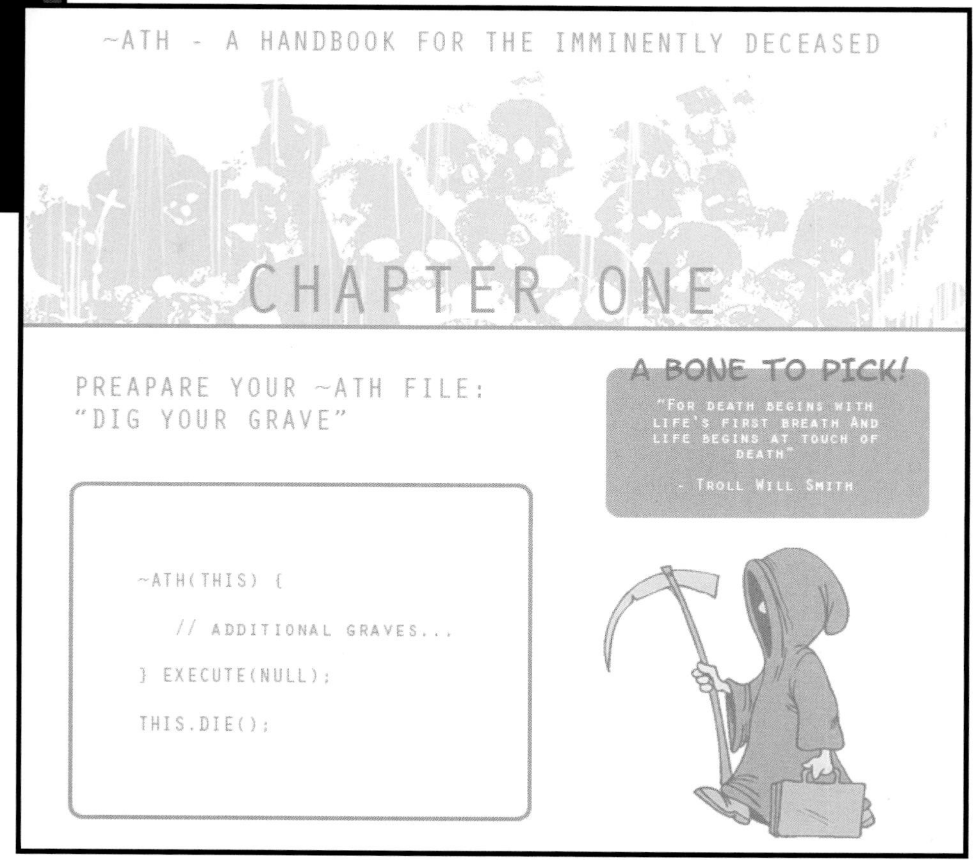

~ATH - A HANDBOOK FOR THE IMMINENTLY DECEASED
CHAPTER ONE
PREAPARE YOUR ~ATH FILE:
"DIG YOUR GRAVE"
A BONE TO PICK!
"For death begins with life's first breath And life begins at touch of death"
- Troll Will Smith
~ATH(THIS) {
// ADDITIONAL GRAVES...
} EXECUTE(NULL);
THIS.DIE();

It is a thick programming manual called "~ATH - A HANDBOOK FOR THE IMMINENTLY DECEASED."

~ATH is an insufferable language to work with. Its logic is composed of nothing but infinite loops, or at best, loops of effectively interminable construction.

The above page in the intro section documents the simplest possible ~ATH code structure. Any code deviating from this basic structure will not compile.

You have a whole bunch of code samples you've been messing around with on your computer. It's been frustrating at best, and debilitating to your machine at worst.

> Karkat: Leave your room.

As far as satirical programming languages go (which is a genre I invented, as far as I'm concerned), ~ATH is a pretty good one. It's pronounced "til death"; that's tilde + ath, for those keeping score at home. It's also not a bad "mascot programming language" for *Homestuck* itself, if you'd like to view it that way. A framework for labyrinthine logic based solely on interminable cyclical patterns, whose exits are predicated on the mortality of certain individuals, or even of the universe itself. Yep, that checks out. The fact that the supreme embodiment of all evil behind everything that ever happens is set to be summoned upon the execution of a ~ATH script supports this idea as well.

You step outside your respiteblock, onto one of your hive's numerous extraterraneal landing slats. You were allowed to design this hive when you were young, after you emerged victorious from your trials deep in the brooding caverns. You have lived here with your CUSTODIAN ever since.

It's almost as if your people have placed great cultural importance on teaching children to become architecturally adept while very young. It has been this way since ancient times. No one seems to know why that is.

Getting to build your own hive at a young age using whatever meandering design you chose likely has left you jaded to the notion of customizing your abode. You certainly wouldn't get all that worked up about a game that happened to allow you to do such a thing.

At least not for that reason.

> Karkat: Examine neighborhood.

Hivebent comes at you fast. It throws so much at you in such compressed narrative spaces. There are a few reasons for this. First, we're plot-rebooting, as I've already pointed out a couple times, so we necessarily have to move through some pedestrian beats very swiftly. Much more so than we did in Act 1, or else it would turn the pacing syrup we're already somewhat mucking with here into pacing cement. Second, we're getting an absolute MEGADOSE of alien worldbuilding so we can familiarize ourselves with the terms and culture of this planet, in order to better understand an actual story that originates there. The one we're about to read. So all this stuff comes in pretty hot for a couple hundred pages. In this instance we learn that the kids get to build their own houses. That's neat! Also that troll babies come out of caves, guardians are custodians, whatever that means, and the planet's customs appear to be oriented around knowledge of *Sburb*. Keeping up???

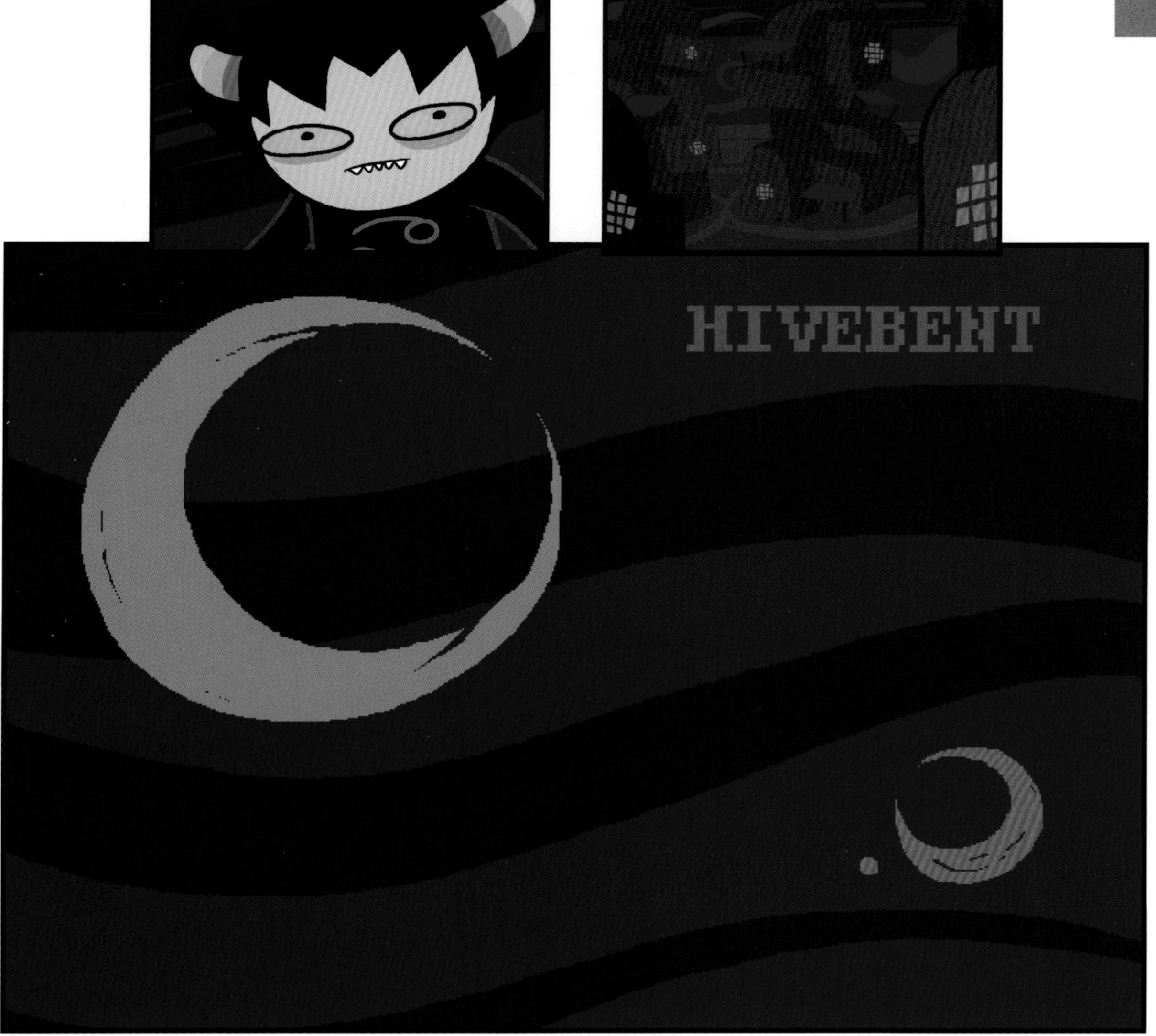

The lawnrings are empty. Blood skims the voids in your porous cranial plates, as if grazing the hollow of a threshed stem, or say, an abandoned cocoon. A sour note is produced. It's the one Agitation plays to make its audience squirm.

It is your sixth wriggling day, and as with all five preceding it blah blah blah blah blah blah blah blah blah blah blah blah blah blah.

Look.

On the subject of Pacing Concerns, and how we're reprising previously established narrative patterns, the subversions of those patterns can often be used to clip certain kinds of action, or certain expectations, in order to achieve the desired brevity outcomes. Here is the expected reprisal of John's navel-gazing moment by his mailbox, listening to the wind. We clip that and move along more quickly, not just because it leads to better pacing, but because it also ties into Karkat's unfolding character portrait. He's IMPATIENT. He's AMBITIOUS. And he is not about to put up with MY. BULLSHIT. In fact, he's already proven he won't, by slicing his fake name in half.

You don't have time for fancy poetry. It's almost as useless as those arm-swing flappy things on mailboxes, assuming you even knew what those were, which you don't. Trolls don't have mail. Mail is almost as useless as poetry to them. Poetry is the swing arm flappy dealy of words, and mail is the red tilty lever doodad of giving people shit.

Frankly you don't know about things skimming voids or grazing hollows or whatever. You've got AMBITION. You were meant to be a bigshot. To be in charge of something huge and really important, and to be totally ruthless about it. You just haven't found the dominion in which you're destined for greatness yet. Or even a vague concept of it. You haven't found your purpose. But you will tonight.

You stew in your own impotent aggravation in the cool dusk breeze. During the dark seasons, it remains dusk for most of the day. It can stay dark for many bilunar perigees at a time. But even if it didn't, you would still have this feeling...

You have a feeling it's going to be a long night.

> Karkat: Go back inside.

It's not just that Karkat's impatient in life, per se, itching to move on to bigger and better things for himself, or to prove his salt as a leader and a warrior—the cues here seem to indicate he's impatient with *Homestuck* itself. The pattern playing itself out again, the familiar points of thematic importance during the Act 1 buildup pertaining to mailboxes, that red flappy lever dealy, the long day (now night): these are the signals that blink at us when rerunning through *Homestuck* as a sort of narrative template, with different Hivebent-specific starting conditions such as protagonist, race, and planet. *Homestuck*, as I will probably keep saying, isn't just a story, it's the confining reality for these kids. The "*Homestuck* = Life" model of interpretation is often clarifying. The story itself is indistinguishable from the alienating, hostile realm the kids are attempting to grow up in. It fully embodies the conditions of adversity, along with all its backdrops and stage props, including the various prescribed challenges and regimented metrics of growth such as quests to fulfill and gods to conquer. CONTINUED -->

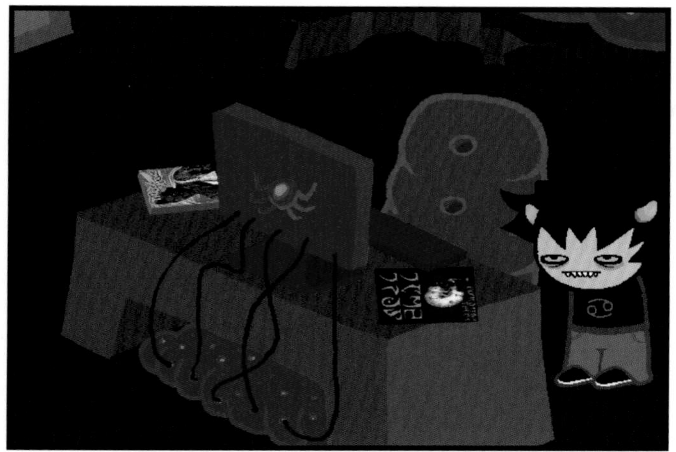

You head back into your block and hit up your computer station. No word from any of your loudmouth pals. No news is good news. Sweet music to your auricular sponge clots.

> Karkat: Check out magazine.

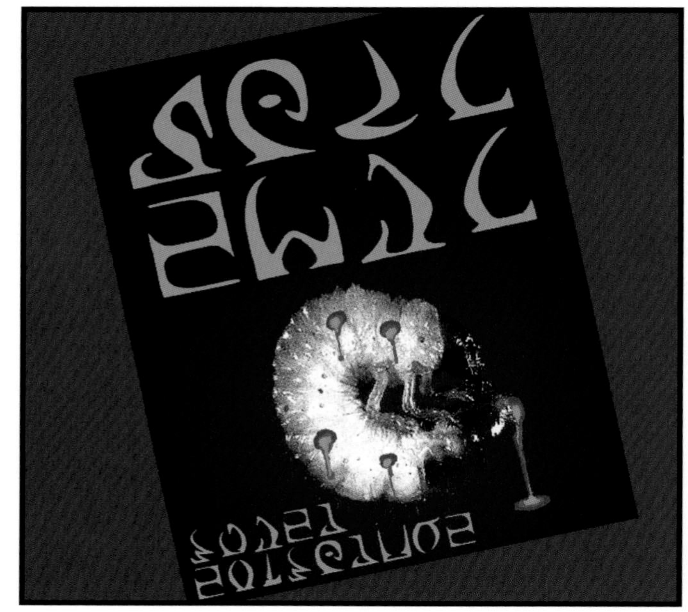

It's the latest issue of GAME GRUB.

This one appears to boast about "exclusive leaks". They all boast about that. You're not even really sure what it means.

> Karkat: Check out DVD.

--> So when Karkat is impatient with and aggravated by these storytelling patterns—the various linguistic tics, beats, and refrains we now recognize as idiomatic to *Homestuck*—he's actually being impatient with life itself, as defined in this metatextual way. Resisting and subverting the various traditions and orthodoxies that *Homestuck* has established as integral to its own telling is the same as resisting and subverting the organic flow of one's own journey through life and personal growth. This idea gets hit pretty hard in Act 6, unavoidably, since the conceit of Act 6 is an even more explicit and unequivocal rebooting of the narrative for a more thoroughly deconstructive reprisal of *Homestuck*. Wait, was this way too much fucking meta to drop under this funny Karkat monologue? Maybe it was. I'M KEEPING IT THOUGH.

It is a DVD of one of your favorite series, THE THRESH PRINCE OF BEL-AIR.

It's about a green threshecutioner cadet who sasses up the bluebloods in his flaysquad pretty good. Their blood is literally blue. Lousy snobs. But Troll Will Smith shows them all how to loosen up. He is pretty much your hero.

Troll TV shows have shorter titles than troll movies because TV is a much newer form of media in their society. Which is a good thing because it would be pretty hard to make this funny joke otherwise.

> Karkat: Get down to business on computer.

Ok enough messing around time to get some work done maybe a little programming or oh god.

It figures that installing this new beta chat client would open the floodgates. All your moron friends are going to be hounding you relentlessly. Not that they needed an excuse before.

You wonder what this chump wants.

> Karkat: Answer troll.

The fact that there are troll versions of our celebrities, starring in troll versions of our shows and movies, MIGHT seem like some really next-level degree of laziness and stupidity in the field of off-the-cuff worldbuilding. But maybe it bears further reflection? Are these figures really troll versions of our celebrities? Since Alternia existed before Earth did, maybe our celebrities are just human versions of them? Maybe the Will Smith we know is better described as Human Troll Will Smith? Something for us all to meditate upon for many years to come.

terminallyCapricious [TC] began trolling carcinoGeneticist [CG]

TC: wHaT iS uUuUuP mY iNvErTeBrOtHeR?
CG: WHAT IN THE SWEET ALMIGHTY TAINTCHAFING FUCK DO YOU WANT.
TC: NoT a MoThErFuCkInG tHiNg BrO.
TC: oThEr ThAn I bE cHeCkIn OuT hOw My BeSt MoThErFuCkIn FrIeNd Is At Yo.
CG: I REALLY CAN'T STAND YOU AND I HATE HOW YOU TYPE, IT JUST BOTHERS ME SO MUCH, HAVE I MENTIONED THAT?
TC: YoU SaY iT pReTtY mUcH eVeRy TiMe We TaLk YeAh.
TC: but uh, i don't have to...
TC: uhhh see?
TC: but i mean man this feels so motherfuckin unnatural and shit.
TC: YoU jUsT gOt To Be GoInG wItH wHaT fEeLs RiGhT aT wHeRe YoUr HeArT's Up In, YoU kNoW?
TC: bEsT fRiEnD.
CG: I WONDER WHAT KIND OF SHITTY THING I DID TO DESERVE SUCH AN AWFUL BEST FRIEND.
CG: OR MAYBE WHAT TERRIBLE THING I'M GOING TO DO AND GET PUNISHED FOR IN ADVANCE.
CG: MAYBE I'M JUST LIKE PREEMPTIVELY THE WORST FUCKING PIECE OF TRASH WHO EVER LIVED AND DON'T EVEN KNOW IT YET, BUT HEY LOOK, YOUR FRIENDSHIP IS EXHIBIT A I GUESS.
TC: It'S sUcH a BeAuTiFuL tHiNg.
TC: ThIs TrOlL dIsEaSe CaLlEd FrIeNdShIp.
CG: FRIENDSHIP ISN'T A DISEASE SHITSPONGE.
CG: IT'S LIKE...
CG: A MISTAKE.
CG: A BIG JOKE OF NATURE.
TC: iT's A mIrAcLe.
CG: OH NO, DON'T.
CG: DON'T START WITH THE MIRACLES AGAIN.
TC: MaN eVeRyWhErE i LoOk...
TC: aLlS i SeE iS mOtHeRfUcKiN mIrAcLeS.
TC: It'S sO sPiRiTuAl, AlL tHeSe mIrAcLeS aNd ShIt.
TC: oK lIkE jUsT bE tAkIn tHiS fUcKiN tItS bOtTlE oF fUcKiN fAyGo I jUsT cRaCkEd Up OpEn.
TC: AnD hOw It'S bEiNg AlL lIkE hIsSiNg AnD sHiT.
TC: mOtHeRfUcKiN hIsSiNg MaN, wHo WeNt AlL aNd ToLd It To Do ThAt?
TC: HoW wOuLd It EvEn Do ThAt, It'S cRaZy.
TC: iT's A mIrAcLe.
CG: IT'S CARBONATION YOU IGNORANT DOUCHE.

This is a huge moment in *Homestuck* history that doesn't really feel like one when you first encounter it. Gamzee is such a sleeper-disaster for the story, a clown horn thrown into the gears, which had been operating in reasonably efficient, mechanically sound fashion up to this point. And well after this too, since it takes quite a while for that horn to grind through the gears and make its way to the heart of the machine, where it can begin doing its real damage. The train wreck has only just left the station. But for now, it feels very innocent. We're just getting to know Karkat's infuriating stoner buddy. What could go wrong?

CG: TRY GETTING SCHOOLFED SOME TIME INSTEAD OF SLURPING DOWN THAT WEIRD SWILL ALL DAY AND FONDLING YOUR STUPID HORNS.
TC: No No BrO, i DoN't WaNnA kNoW, dOn'T eVeN tElL mE.
TC: kNoWiNg ShIt JuSt StEaLs Up AlL tHe FuCkIn MaGiC fRoM mY mIrAcLeS lIkE a MoThErFuCkIn ThIeF.
TC: AnD tHaT aIn'T cOoL.
CG: THE ONLY MIRACLE IS THAT YOU LIKE THAT DISGUSTING SLUDGE, WHERE DO YOU EVEN GET THAT STUFF.
CG: IT'S ALSO A MIRACLE HOW YOU DRESS LIKE AN IMBECILE AND ARE BASICALLY THE STUPIDEST ASSHOLE I'VE EVER KNOWN.
CG: ACTUALLY YOU'RE RIGHT, THERE ARE MIRACLES EVERYWHERE, I'VE BEEN A FOOL.
TC: sEe MaN, i Am StRaIgHt Up TeLlInG yOu.
TC: MiRaClEs.
TC: iT's LiKe, AlRiGhT, cOmPuTeRs, RiGhT?
TC: WhAt ThE fUcK?
TC: mIrAcLeS iS wHaT.
CG: FUCK YOU.
CG: FUCK YOU FOR ME JUST READING THAT.
TC: AnYwAy WhAt'S uP wItH yOuR bAd SeLf, FoR sErIoUs HeRe.
TC: iSn'T sOmEtHiNg BiG aLl GoInG dOwN?
CG: WHAT?
TC: i HeArD sOmEtHiNg bIg WaS gOiNg AlL dOwN.
TC: JuSt AlL bE tElLiNg Me AlL wHaT mOtHeRfUcKiN iT's Up AnD aLl AbOuT.
CG: STOP SAYING ALL. ARE YOU TALKING ABOUT TA'S THING?
TC: yEaH!! fUcK yEaH mAn, So MyStErIoUs.
TC: I'm NeVeR bEiNg GeTtInG cEaSeD tO bE aMaZeD bY aLl ThEsE fUcKiN mYsTeRiEs LiFe'S gOt FoR uS.
CG: UUUUUUGH.
CG: ANYWAY, I DON'T KNOW WHAT'S UP WITH THAT.
CG: MAYBE I'LL TALK TO HIM TONIGHT ABOUT IT. MAYBE I WON'T.
CG: IT'S PROBABLY JUST ANOTHER ONE OF HIS PROJECTS THAT WINDS UP BEING COMPLETELY USELESS AND A HUGE WASTE OF MY TIME.
TC: yEaH mAyBe BuT hE's YoUr BeSt FrIeNd ThOuGh So It'S aLl CoOl.
TC: AnYwAy I tHoUgHt ThIs SoUnDeD lIkE a PrEtTy BiG mOtHeRfUcKiN dEaL mY mAn.
TC: aAaUuUhHh...
CG: WHAT.
TC: Aw BrO nEvErMiNd, I jUsT fUcKiN dId LiKe To ScArE tHe ShIt OuTtA mYsElF hErE.
TC: tHeSe DaMn HoRnS.
CG: YOU'VE GOT TO GET RID OF THOSE THINGS.

Readers who were on the ball immediately recognized this asshole for what he was, which is: the Juggalo Troll. There were groans, there was the rolling of eyes, the gnashing of teeth, each gesture of discontent ABSOLUTELY justified. And that's exactly why I felt it was very important to introduce Gamzee as the first new troll we meet in Hivebent. It really helps set the tone and calibrate reader expectations for this group. It says a lot, right up front. It says, first and foremost, this is going to be an absolute litany of insufferable idiots, so don't get your hopes up too high. It says that many of these characters are going to be defined by common internet-dweller profiles, and more importantly, subculture profiles. It says there is no barrel too shameful or embarrassing to scrape the bottom of for raw material to form into bad characters. Everything going on here is a HUGE shot off the reader's bow regarding what to expect from Hivebent, and even more generally and insidiously, what to expect from the rest of *Homestuck*.

CG: THEY MAKE IT MORE EMBARRASSING TO KNOW YOU.
CG: WHICH IS A FRIGGIN MIRACLE THAT THAT'S EVEN POSSIBLE.
CG: LIKE, WOW, GOD SURE COOKED UP A DOOZY THERE.
CG: TWINKLY EYED SON OF A BITCH JUST KEEPS YOU GUESSING, DOESN'T HE.
TC: MaN yOu KnOw YoU wAnNa GiVe My HoRnS a GoOd SqUeEzE. :o)
CG: ACTUALLY YOU KNOW WHAT WILL BE THE MIRACLE TO END ALL MIRACLES?
CG: IT'LL BE IF I EVER MEET A KID I DESPISE MORE THAN YOU.
CG: THAT WILL MAKE ME A MOTHERFUCKIN CONVERT.
CG: I'LL SEE LIGHT SO BRIGHT I'LL NEED GC TO WALK ME AROUND SO I DON'T BUMP INTO SHIT.
CG: SIGN ME UP FOR YOUR IDIOTIC CLOWN RELIGION OK.
TC: hAhAhAhA yOu fUcKiN gOt It BrOtHeR!

Whoa what the motherfuck, who's this motherfuckin' motherfucker?

It's cool, life is like that sometimes. It's full of mysteries. You'll be doing one thing then something else hits you just like that and you roll with it. That's what you do when life hands you lemons. You sure as fuck don't make lemonade because who the fuck knows where that fuckin' shit comes from?

It's squeezed out of miracles is where.

So what's this motherfucker's name?

> Enter name.

With all that talk of Gamzee in the previous note, there was no space to give a shout-out to how he kept talking about his horns earlier on in the story. Asking Karkat to give them a squeeze, how he scared himself with them... Before seeing him, we had no idea he was referring to literal clown horns. So that was a pretty good quick-setup-and-deliver gag. Just saying! If I don't honk my own fucking horn, who will? Also, the end of this conversation establishes that his whole juggalo shtick is a religious thing, which is a very important detail. He's not a juggalo just because I thought it would be funny (which is still a major factor, to be fair). He promulgates this nonsense as an expression of a certain profoundly idiotic piety to the Mirthful Messiahs, whose specific identities morph over the course of the story depending on context, and on whichever particular interpretation happens to be most convenient at any given moment, either to him, or me.

Your name is GAMZEE MAKARA.

You get pretty excited by CLOWNS OF A GRIM PERSUASION WHICH MAY NOT BE IN FULL POSSESSION OF THEIR MENTAL FACULTIES. You belong to a RATHER OBSCURE CULT, which foretells of a BAND OF ROWDY AND CAPRICIOUS MINSTRELS which will rise one day on a MYTHICAL PARADISE PLANET that does not exist yet. The beliefs of this cult are SOMEWHAT FROWNED UPON by those dwelling in more common lawnrings. But you don't care, you got to be going with what feels right at where your heart's up in, you know? You like to practice on your ONE WHEEL DEVICE, which you are GOD AWFUL AT because your FEET DO NOT REACH THE PEDALS. You enjoy a FINE BEVERAGE, and like to do A LITTLE BAKING SOMETIMES. You've got ALL THESE HORNS all over the place, and sometimes you step on them and SCARE THE SHIT OUT OF YOURSELF.

You like to chat a lot with your pal Karkat, who is usually pretty cranky, but he is your BEST FRIEND. You have a lot of OTHER GREAT FRIENDS who you also like a lot. Your trolltag is terminallyCapricious and you speak in a manner that is JuSt A lItTlE bIt WhImSiCaL.

What will you do?

> Gamzee: Captchalogue bottle of Faygo.

By saying he belongs to a "rather obscure cult," I guess the text seems to be implying that among purple bloods it's rare to dress and act in this clownish way? But this turns out to be untrue. Pretty much the entire blood class is populated by a bunch of shitty clowns. What this really means is that Gamzee's specific religious beliefs are what's obscure and unusual about him, not the clowniness. No, sadly, brutal, nasty clowns are a dime a dozen in his highblood echelon.

You snag a bottle of FAYGO. To consume the beverage is what your fellow devotees refer to as KICKIN' THE WICKED ELIXIR.

It is captchalogued through your MIRACLE MODUS. You have absolutely no idea how this thing works.

And you don't want to know.

> Gamzee: Captchalogue computer.

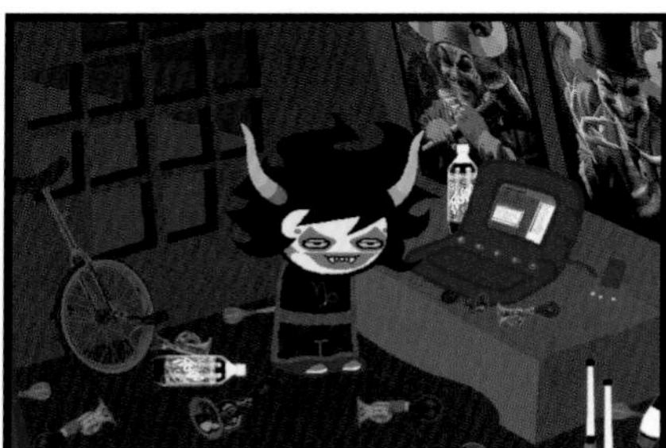

You take your HUSKTOP.

Sometimes you just like to pick stuff up and watch the colors. It's so beautiful. Life is beautiful.

> Gamzee: Ride one wheel device.

The miracle modus, and Gamzee's frequent references to miracles in general, relate to the Insane Clown Posse song "Miracles." I almost feel like I am insulting the intelligence of the reader by pointing this out? On the other hand, this was many years ago. I don't know what the kids today actually consider common knowledge. It would be a damn shame if today's youth was receiving an inadequate education on our clown rap traditions and ancestry.

You decide to give this diabolical contraption another shot. Maybe one of these days you will get one more suited to your proportions. For now this is all you have to work with.

You just have to figure out how to stay on the thing without flying off the handle.

You do some sort of acrobatic fucking pirouette off the handle and into a big pile of horns.

> Gamzee: Sample delicious pie cooling on the counter.

That this very tall unicycle does not match his proportions suggests that his proportions in sprite form are fairly close to actual. So wait a minute. Is Gamzee tall, or is he short?? Some panels in the future suggest he may be taller than usual for trolls. What is going ON here? Consider this page exhibit A in the endless debate on tall vs. short Gamzee, which definitely rages on to this day.

It is still piping hot but you can't help yourself. You sneak a taste of the SOPOR SLIME PIE.

You aren't supposed to eat that slime. It does funny things to a troll's head.

But you were never taught that on account of a lousy upbringing. Your custodian was always out to sea.

That is where he is now. Maybe you will go outside and see if you can spot him.

> Gamzee: Take a juggling club.

The sopor slime is just drugs. Like his weed. Not much else to say about it. Motherfucker fancies his DANK. Moving on.

You grab a JUGGLING CLUB. You'll need it if you are going to go out. It is dangerous to leave unarmed.

> Gamzee: Go outside.

You leave your hive and head out to the beach. There is no sign of your custodian.

You should not stay out here very long. The SEA DWELLERS are quite hostile.

It's probably not actually that dangerous to leave unarmed. This was probably something his goat dad told him a long time ago. But only to scare him, and make sure he stayed inside so no one would ever see him, because he was so embarrassed by him. Goatdad is probably one of the most sympathetic characters in the story. If Gamzee was your son, wouldn't you abandon him too?

Someone is bugging you. This is exciting. You're always down for shooting the wicked shit with anyone that who'll put up with you.

Now if only you could figure out how to get your HUSKTOP out of this stupid thing. It'll be a miracle if you can manage.

> Gamzee: Retrieve husktop.

You say a short prayer to your beloved MIRTHFUL MESSIAHS, and splash a pinch of SPECIAL STARDUST in your face.

He's probably had this modus for years, and he still doesn't know what he's doing. He tries some religious baloney to see if that works, which of course it doesn't. Just like real people who go to church. Please subscribe to my atheism vlog. SMASH that like button if you agree that believing in stuff is DUMB!

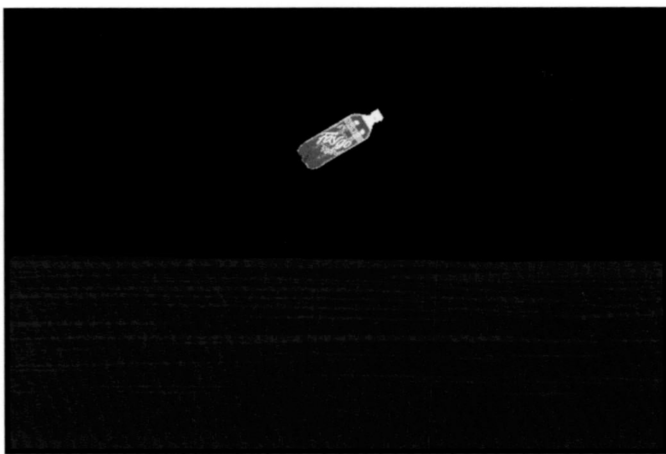

Your sylladex launches your beverage far, far into the ocean.

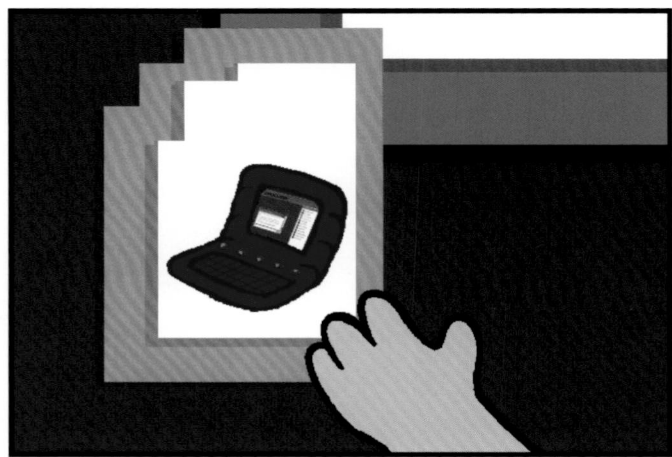

You wonder if you can just...

Just sort of reach over...

And...

> Gamzee: Answer troll.

There goes Chekhov's Faygo, sailing over the sea in search of Eridan's feet. Let's remember to remember this happened, when we see it again. Also, I'm going to speculate that just sort of reaching over...and...taking an object out of a card is probably something you can do with any shitty modus when you feel like you've exhausted all other options. It's just that no one ever actually thinks to try it. They're never stoned enough.

gallowsCalibrator [GC] **began trolling terminallyCapricious [TC]**

GC: H3Y G4MZ33Z YOU W4NT TO PL4Y G4M3Z3Z W1TH M3??
TC: hEy YeAh ThAt SoUnDs LiKe ThE mOtHeRfUcKiN sHiT's BiTcHtItS!
GC: >8\
GC: 1T SUR3 1S H4RD TO 1GNOR3 TH3 W31RD TH1NGS YOU S4Y SOM3T1M3S!
GC: BUT 1M GONN4
GC: TH3 ONLY R34SON 1M 4SK1NG YOU 1S B3C4US3 YOUR N4M3 1S L1K3 G4M3
GC: 4ND NO OTH3R R34SON
GC: G3T 1T??? >:]
TC: HaHa WeLl I hEaRd Of WoRsE fUcKiN rEaSoNs To Be GeTtIn AlL aBoUt To Do SoMeThInG.
TC: :o) hOnK
GC: NO TH4T SHOULD BOTH3R YOU, TH4T R34SON
GC: WHY DONT TH1NGS L1K3 TH4T BOTH3R YOU??
GC: NO WOND3R V4NT4S C4NT ST4ND YOU
GC: BUT WHO C4R3S 4BOUT H1M, W3R3 GO1NG TO H4V3 SOM3 MOTH3RFUCK1NG SH1TTY B1TCH3S PL4Y1NG TOG3TH3R!
GC: OR WH4T3V3R YOU S41D
TC: sO iS tHiS tHe GaMe I'vE hEaRd AbOuT?
TC: ThE bIg MyStErY?
GC: Y34H
TC: wHoA oK uHhH...
TC: ThIs Is GoInG tO bE fUcKiN iNsAnE.
TC: bUt CaN wE pLaY a LiTtLe LaTeR?
TC: I'm OuTsIdE kEePiNg An EyE oUt HeRe FoR tHe OlD gOaT.
TC: yOu KnOw HoW iT iS wItH fAmIlY.
GC: NO, NOT R34LLY!
GC: 4DURRRR DURR DURP
TC: Oh YeAh...
GC: DURRRRRRRRRRRRR
GC: W4Y TO GO, HOW DO3S TH4T STUP1D BOTTL3D SYRUP OF YOURS T4ST3 W1TH YOUR HOOF SO F4R UP YOUR MOUTH???
GC: >:]
TC: sOoOoOoOrY.
TC: AnYwAy I'lL gO iNsIdE iN a WhIlE, wHy DoN't YoU gEt KaRkAt To FiRe Up ThAt MoThErFuCkEr WiTh YoU?
TC: hE lIkEs GaMeS.

Here's another Gamzee conversation that seems very innocent at first but then feels very loaded upon revisiting it once you know the full breadth of *Homestuck*'s Dark Future. These two are in for a hell of a ride. That aside, there's some subtext to sniff out here. Gamzee blunders thoughtlessly into the implication that Terezi is an orphan, which is a tidbit we hadn't gathered yet. He also has no problem with casual use of sexually harassing language, and he displays an utter disinclination to react negatively toward attempts to slight him, which Terezi appears to try with him frequently. These either could be evidence of his latent sociopathy or they're merely symptoms of his drug abuse, and in truth he's just a really nice guy (wrong).

GC: OH NOOOOO.
GC: GOD C4N YOU 1M4G1N3 4LL TH3 B1TCH1NG 4ND MO4N1NG?
GC: 1 US3D TO TRY TO PL4Y STUFF W1TH H1M BUT WOW D1D 1 L34RN MY L3SSON.
TC: AlRiGhT, wElL i'Ll TrY tO gEt In AnD gEt Up On My ChIlL rEaL sOoN aNd We CaN pLaY.
TC: jUsT gIvE mE a MiNuTe!
GC: BULLSH1T!
GC: YOU KNOW YOUR3 JUST GO1NG TO S1T TH3R3 ON TH3 B34CH 4ND SP4C3 OUT 4ND LOS3 TR4CK OF T1M3.
GC: H3LLO?
GC: G4MZ?????
TC: WhAt?
TC: oH mAn SoRrY.
TC: I sPaCeD oUt, DiD yOu KnOw HoW bEaTuFuL tHe SoUnD oF tHe OcEaN iS?
TC: hAvE yOu EvEr EvEn SeEn ThE oCeAn?
TC: oR i MeAn SmElLeD iT...
TC: SoRrY.
GC: >:[

> Karkat: Get some programming done.

It's also pretty telling that when Terezi attempts to start rounding up players for the game, she starts with Gamzee before trying anyone else, even Karkat. It speaks to whatever sort of fraught, mutually unrequited relationship she and Karkat have going on, even this early in their quest. But it also speaks to some deeply misguided fascination she's always had with this shitty clown boy, against her freely admitted better judgment.

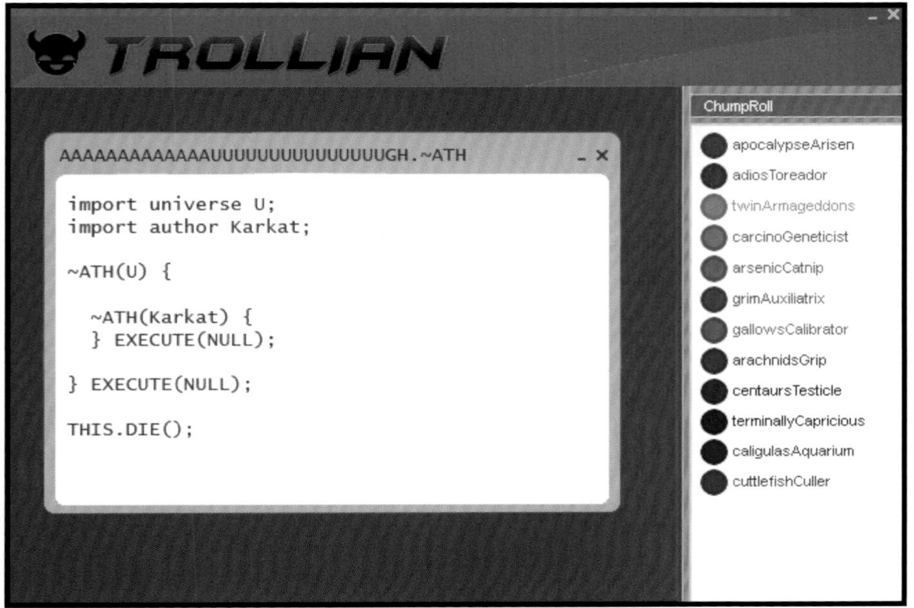

Finally some peace and quiet. Now you can bear down on your coding. This will surely last all evening, without interruption.

You reopen one of your ~ATH projects you started recently. You are still horsing around with the conditions for terminating the loops.

What many ~ATH coders do is import finite constructs and bind the loops to their lifespan. For instance the main loop here will terminate on the death of the universe, labeled U. That way you only have to wait billions of years for it to end instead of forever.

You have bound a subloop to the lifespan of the code's author, which is you. Any routine at the end will execute when you die. You figure this might be handy for coding something to release a final will and testament. Or maybe some doomsday virus. You spend a lot of time thinking of ways to make the perfect doomsday virus.

Conveniently absent from ~ATH's extensive import library are entities with short lifespans. Like a rapidly decaying particle that only lasts a millisecond sure would be handy. Or even a fruit fly or something. But no, coding with this language is all about finding ways to trick it into doing what you want.

Your hacker buddy is obnoxiously good at it. He's sent you some files which you still don't understand, but you're not going to admit that. He is even better at making viruses than you, which really gets stuck in your nook.

> Karkat: Check out one of his files.

The idea of binding a loop to the life span of a universe, so you only have to wait billions of years for it to end instead of forever, sounds like a humorous remark. But really it's some foreshadowing of the exact mechanism by which Lord English is summoned. We see this code get executed when the time is right. It'll be a while, so don't hold your breath. Unless an important ~ATH loop you wrote depends on your death. In which case, go ahead.

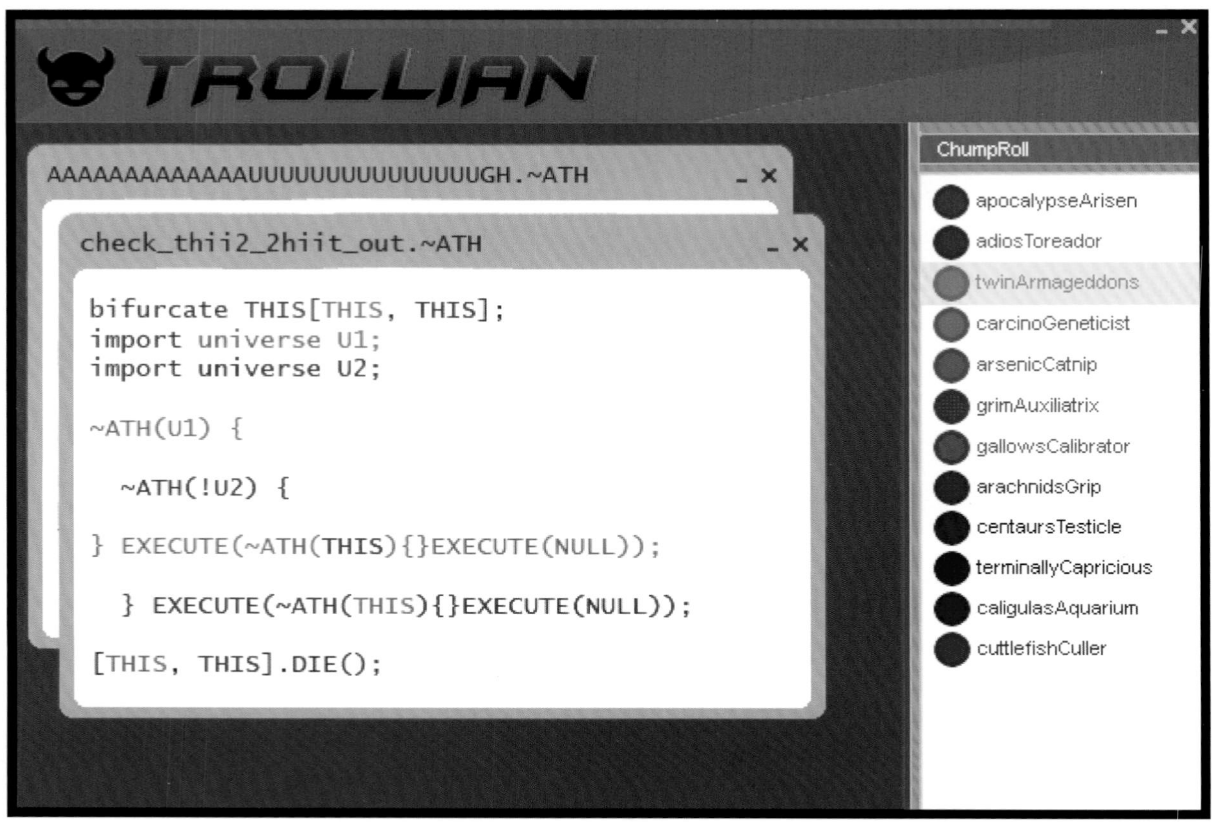

This code, when executed, immediately causes the user's computer to explode, and places a curse on the user forever, along with everyone he knows, and everyone he'll ever meet.

Not surprisingly, later on you would run this code in a fit of stupidity.

You don't know how he does stuff like this. What does this even mean? It's nonsense. Is it even syntactically viable?? Are you allowed to color text like that??? ARGH. Maybe you should ask him about it some time.

Oh speak of the devil. Here he is bugging you about something. Time to put on your game face and pretend you don't think very highly of his abilities.

> Karkat: Answer troll.

This completely bonkers virus Sollux wrote is actually more sophisticated than the syntax for the Lord English–summoning code I just mentioned, which is contingent on the death of only one universe. This one appears to be contingent on the death two universes. And not so much contingent on them, as placing two infinite loops inside each other in a paradoxically interwoven way, making it virtually impossible to execute without causing great harm to whatever machine attempts to do so.

twinArmageddons [TA] **began trolling** carcinoGeneticist [CG]

TA: KK dont fliip your 2hiit about thii2 but iim 2ettiing you up two play a game wiith 2ome people.
CG: WHY WOULD I FLIP MY SHIT ABOUT THAT.
TA: becau2e you fliip your 2hiit about everythiing.
CG: WELL WILL YOU LOOK AT THIS.
CG: HERE IS MY SHIT, AND YET IT REMAINS UNFLIPPED.
CG: JUST SITTING THERE ON THE SKILLET, GETTING BURNED ON ONE SIDE.
CG: IT'S A MIRACLE.
TA: oh no are you iinto miiracle2 now two becau2e iif you are youre fiired preemptiively from the game.
CG: FUCK NO.
TA: ok niice.
CG: MIRACLES ARE LIKE POOP STAINS ON GOD'S UNDERWEAR.
TA: eheheh makiing fun of people2 reliigiion2 i2 the be2t thiing two do.
CG: THAT'S WHY HE HIDES THEM, THEY'RE FUCKING EMBARRASSING.
CG: GOD LAUNDERS IN MYSTERIOUS WAYS.
TA: eheheheheh riight on but let2 2hut our mouth2 a 2econd and talk about thii2 game.
TA: iitll only be a 2econd really you dont have two do two much.
CG: OK, GOOD, BECAUSE I'M PRETTY BUSY TONIGHT.
CG: WHAT IS THIS THING ANYWAY, WHY ALL THE SECRECY.
TA: well the 2hort 2tory ii2 that iit2 an iimmer2iive 2iimulatiion that you play wiith a group.
TA: the long 2tory ii2 that the fate of our ciiviiliizatiion depend2 on u2 playiing iit.
TA: heh ii gue22 the long one wa2 2horter than the 2hort one FUCK.
CG: THAT SOUNDS LIKE MELODRAMATIC BULLSHIT BUT COMING FROM YOU COLOR ME UNSURPRISED.
TA: 2crew you vanta2 thii2 2hiit2 more real than kraft grub2auce.
CG: RIGHT OK.
CG: SO YOU MADE THIS GAME?
TA: no no.
TA: more liike ii adapted iit.
CG: FROM WHAT.
TA: 2ome crazy technology AA dug out of 2ome ruiin2.
TA: havent you talked two her about iit?
CG: MAN, NO.
CG: I CAN'T TALK TO HER, SHE'S SO SPOOKY.
CG: I DON'T KNOW WHY MOST OF OUR FRIENDS ARE SUCH PSYCHOS.
TA: probably iit2 becau2e mo2t troll2 are.

When getting to know the human kids, we never got anything resembling the backstory of how *Sburb* came to be, except for a few vague clues we could piece together. Like, it was developed by Skaianet, which had a lab behind Rose's house, which her mom worked in, and Mom was presumably in touch with Jade's grandpa, who habitually explored ruins, one of which may have contained *Sburb*'s code. We have to make a lot of those leaps ourselves, though. In Hivebent, the narrative is pretty up-front about what happened: Aradia salvaged the code from the frog ruins, and Sollux adapted that code to run as an executable game. They're unambiguously responsible for bringing this upon their friends and their planet. Which makes a certain amount of sense, as they're the two characters who commune with the dead of the future and the past.

TA: iif you heard what ii heard every niight ii mean WOW FUCK.
CG: NO LET'S NOT TALK ABOUT YOUR WEIRD MUTANT BRAIN.
CG: AND DON'T SCAN MINE OR WHATEVER, IT'S OFF LIMITS YOU DOUCHE.
TA: ii told you liike a biilliion tiime2 ii cant do that you nub2lurping fuckpod.
CG: WHY ARE YOU TWO UP TO THIS SECRET STUFF.
CG: WHY HAVEN'T YOU TOLD ME ANYTHING ABOUT THIS?
TA: KK iim 2orry but really iit2 kiind of a priivate matter between me and her and iid appreciiate iit iif that wa2 re2pected.
CG: OH GOD.
CG: STOP BEING SO SENSITIVE.
CG: IT'S A REPUGNANT QUALITY.
TA: ok how about you take your own adviice you are 2uch a blubberiing hypocriite.
TA: youre lucky iim 2o fuckiing magnaniimou2 and chariitable cau2e otherwii2e there2 no chance iid wa2te my tiime on you.
CG: WHAT A LOAD OF SHIT, THIS ACT THAT YOU ACTUALLY THINK YOU'RE A HOTSHOT, YOU KNOW YOU HATE YOURSELF.
TA: nobody hate2 hiim2elf more than you iidiiot.
CG: YEAH WELL I HATE YOU WAY MORE THAN I HATE MYSELF, AND THAT'S FUCKING SAYING SOMETHING.
CG: IN FACT I HATE YOU MORE THAN I HATE MYSELF AND YOU HATE YOURSELF AND YOU HATE ME COMBINED.
TA: oh fuck that noii2e iin every leakiing oriifiice iit2 got you know ii hate the combiined product of you and my2elf more than you could ever begiin two hate me and my2elf and you and your2elf on your wor2t day 2o FUCKIING DEAL WIITH IIT.
CG: OK, TIME OUT FOR THE IDIOT.
CG: THE IDIOT GETS A TIME OUT AND SHUTS UP FOR A SECOND.
CG: THAT'S YOU.
CG: JUST TELL ME WHAT TO DO ABOUT THIS GAME.
TA: ok well iill 2end you a download 2oon.
TA: iim 2ett1ng up two team2.
TA: liike two 2eparate competiing team2 2o that there2 a better chance of at lea2t one group wiinniing.
TA: and al2o ii gue22 two 2ee which one can wiin fa2ter.
CG: OK LET ME GUESS.
CG: THERE'S A RED TEAM AND BLUE TEAM, RIGHT?
TA: yeah.
TA: youre on the red team.
TA: ii wiiill be the leader of the blue.
CG: OK, THEN I GUESS I CAN PICK MY TEAMMATES THEN?
TA: uh...
TA: bro youre not the red team leader.
TA: ii piicked GC for that.
CG: WHAT????????????????????
TA: dude ii diid NOT thiink youd be iintere2ted iin thii2 dont act all offended.

When Sollux says he's setting up two competing teams to improve the chances of one team winning, it's quite possible he's just lying to appease Karkat's curiosity. Either that, or Aradia is lying to Sollux about why there needs to be two teams. It's not to maximize chances of success, since the game doesn't even recognize "teams" anyway. There was always just one big team. They only needed to think there were two, for the purpose of setting up the initial conditions of the session the way they did. My money is on Aradia feeding Sollux this lie. I can hear you ask, why won't I just come out and fucking tell you what's canon, without playing these GAMES? Because it simply is not how I roll.

CG: OH WOW NOW I SEE.
CG: REALLY FUCKING CLEVER, PICKING THE BLIND GIRL TO LEAD THE TEAM YOUR COMPETING WITH.
CG: I KNEW YOU WERE CHEATER LOWLIFE FUCKING SCUMBAG WITH NO SCRUPLES OR SELF ESTEEM AND WERE BASICALLY WORTHLESS ON EVERY LEVEL, BUT SOMEHOW I'M STILL DISAPPOINTED IN YOU.
TA: yeah ii am 2uch an iidiiot for not rewardiing your bubbly per2onaliity and iimpeccable people 2kiill2 wiith a leader2hiip giig.
TA: what an iincon2iiderate knuckle2ponged a22hole ii have been.
CG: I AM A HATCHED LEADER AND YOU KNOW IT.
TA: ii know your fiilthy 2eedflap ii2 flutteriing iin the profane breeze that2 2hootiing out your 2tiinkiing meal tunnel.
TA: ii do know that much.
CG: HOW DO YOU GET OUT OF YOUR COCOON IN THE MORNING KNOWING YOU'RE THE WORST THING A UNIVERSE WAS EVER RESPONSIBLE FOR?
CG: ALSO IT MUST BE HARD WITH YOUR HANDS TO PERSISTENTLY BOTHERING EVERY MUTATED SET OF GENITALS PEPPERING THAT GHASTLY HUSK YOU PAWN OFF AS A BODY.
CG: HAS A FEMALE EVER LOOKED AT YOU WITHOUT AT ONCE TURNING SKYWARD AND ERUPTING LIKE A VOMIT VOLCANO, ANSWER ME THAT.
TA: thii2 ii2 2o iimmature, iim ba2iically ju2t laughiing here at how iimmature you are.
TA: liike ii really giive a fuck who the red leader ii2.
TA: you want two be the leader fiine talk two GC about iit.
CG: I GUESS THESE CONVERSATIONS WE HAVE DO GET KIND OF EMBARRASSING IN RETROSPECT.
CG: ARE WE NOT FRIENDS ANYMORE BECAUSE OF STUFF I SAID.
TA: eheheheh you LIITERALLY a2k me that every tiime are you jokiing.
TA: ii cant even tell anymore.
CG: IT'S A JOKE MORON.
CG: HONESTLY I'M JUST GLAD NOBODY ELSE IS PRIVVY TO OUR CONVERSATIONS.
CG: ACTUALLY WHY DON'T WE MAKE A PACT TO DELETE THIS ONE FROM OUR LOGS, I'M JUST SHUDDERING HERE SCROLLING UP AND READING THIS.
TA: yeah ok.

Sounds like someone downstairs is getting pretty crabby. This is not an encounter you are looking forward to. You'll probably put it off as long as you can manage.

Too late, Karkat. You can't delete your conversation logs, because we already screencapped every single one, and read them over and over, and laughed at you every time. We've got the receipts, all of them, forever. Actually it's worse than that. Your receipts have been published and distributed worldwide. This embarrassing conversation is probably sitting in hundreds of bookstores, RIGHT NOW.

Why, who's this young lady?

> Enter name.

I would posit that, as fun as it is to meet new trolls we've never heard of, like the bad clown one or the sweaty one, it's even more rewarding when we finally get to see the ones we already knew about. Like this blind miscreant right here. Dropping in exciting new characters and rolling out their wild personalities but only tantalizing the reader with little details about them while they troll the heroes from a distance...that's pretty scintillating stuff. So when we start doing the whole tour like this, promising a deep dive on all twelve trolls, you're more likely to look forward to the ones who got teased than the ones who didn't. Now you've finally hit one, and it's exciting. Her room's a HOT MESS. It's colorful, it's fun, it's kind of ridiculous. Is she...in a tree? Is she a damned LAWYER? She could have been anything, but she turned out to be this. I declare such morsels of discovery to be considered amongst the Good Shit™ of *Homestuck*'s wild ride.

Your name is TEREZI PYROPE.

You are pretty enthusiastic about dragons. But you have a PARTICULAR AFFECTION for their COLORFUL SCALES, which you gather and use to decorate your hive. Though you live alone, deep in the woods, you surround yourself with a variety of plushie pals known as SCALEMATES. You often spend your days with them in rounds of LIVE ACTION ROLE PLAYING. You used to engage in various forms of MORE EXTREME ROLEPLAYING with some of your other friends before you had an accident.

You take an interest in justice, holding particular fascination for ORCHESTRATING THE DEMISE OF THE WICKED. You have taken up study of BRUTAL ALTERNIAN LAW, and surround yourself with legal books. You have no need for copies printed in TROLLBRAILLE, because you can SMELL AND TASTE THE WORDS. You hope one day to join the honorable ranks of the LEGISLACERATORS. Your trolltag is gallowsCalibrator and you SP34K W1TH TH3 NUM3R4LS TH3 BL1ND PROPH3TS ONC3 US3D.

You are presently the leader of the RED TEAM, poised to begin a mysterious game with 5 other friends, in direct competition with another 6 of your friends, comprising the BLUE TEAM.

What will you do?

> Terezi: Cut to the chase and begin LARPing immediately.

Terezi's typing quirk is basically leet-speak lite, where the only letter swaps are AIE -> 413. We've observed this already, since we've seen her babble often enough. So we already knew she gets the special distinction of being associated with *Homestuck*'s flagship number, 413. We didn't know why, but here it explains they're numbers the blind prophets once used. Who are the prophets? Come to think of it, this is one of the minor questions which is never expanded on much later. Were they teal bloods, like her? Prophets suggest psychic abilities. Were they rust and yellow bloods, like Aradia and Sollux? Sollux goes blind at some point. Maybe the prophets were yellow bloods who who went blind the way Sollux did, and spoke with Terezi's quirk? Are we getting warmer? Sure, why not. Also, as long as we're piling on the trivia here: 4+1+3 = 7. Teal (Libra) is the seventh blood class, or zodiac sign. Scorpio is the eighth.

It's pretty hard to live action role play when there is no one who is alive nearby. But all of your Scalemates are alive to you.

At least you pretend to believe that to annoy people.

You prepare a new campaign for one of your favorite scenarios, COURTBLOCK DRAMA. His HONORABLE TYRANNY presides. On trial is an especially detestable fellow, SENATOR LEMONSNOUT. You have sparred with this scumbag before. Tonight he faces justice.

You will play the role of the prosecuting attorney. On Alternia, there is no such thing as a defense attorney, or a defense. In a courtblock, the word defense itself is offensive.

> Terezi: Interrogate.

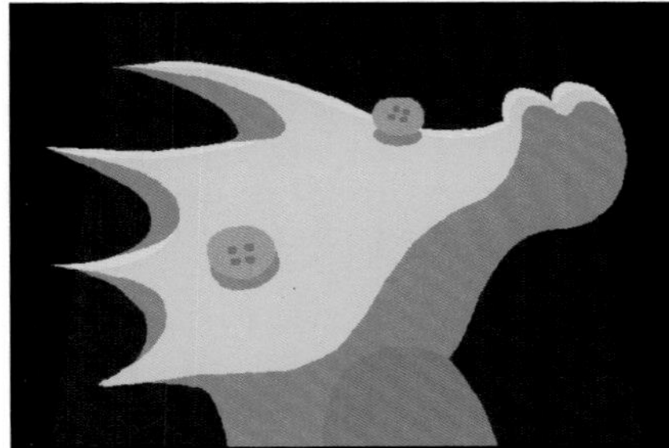

Most of the interrogation is in the intimidating silence.

> Terezi: Slap him around a bit.

Aside from the fact that what this amounts to is Terezi taking delight in torturing, possibly framing, and executing a defendant in a kangaroo court, this whole sequence is pretty cute.

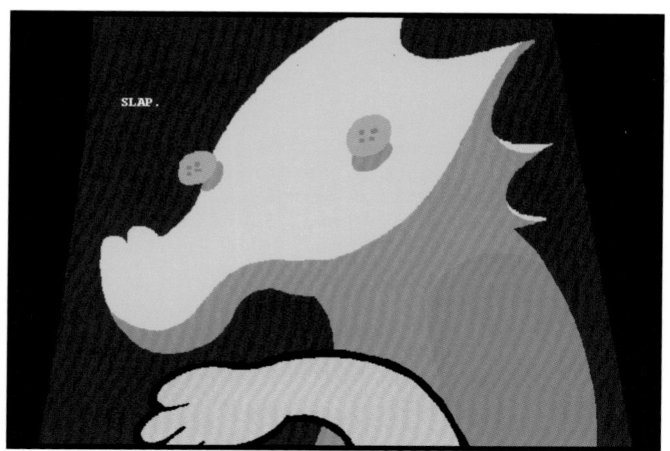

You don't want to slap too hard. Enough to sting, but not to bruise. It must be methodical, business-like. And persistent. You only stop when you smell tears.

Mr. Senator, you smell very nice. Your luscious yellow scales are like the sweetest gumdrops to the prosecution's nose.

But your deceit *STINKS*.

Did you honestly think you could dip your corpulent snout into the imperial beetle coffers like that and get away with it?? Did you think your revolting abuse of the public trust would go unnoticed??? *THINK AGAIN, GOOD SENATOR. WHILE THE PROSECUTION MAY BE BLIND, REST ASSURED THE LEAGUE OF LEGISLACERATORS SEES ALL.*

> Terezi: Call a witness.

Being a good legislacerator when it comes to prosecuting cases in the courtblock probably solely entails putting on a good performance of cruelty for His Honorable Tyranny, who, it cannot be stated enough, is really just a huge, fairly stupid monster who barely understands or cares about anything that's going on around him, let alone the facts of the case.

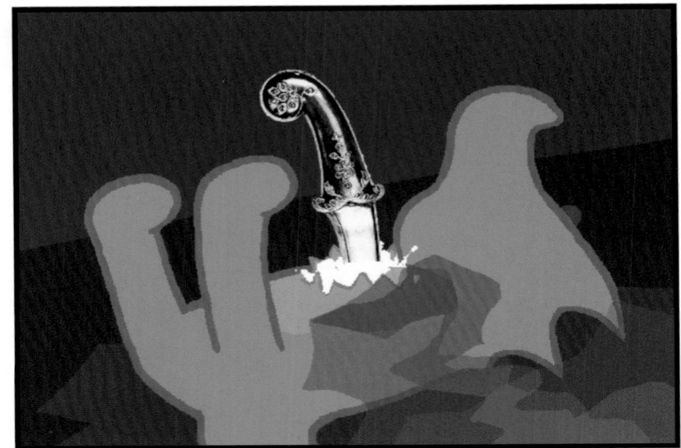

Oh, well played, Lemonsnout. Well played. The prosecution's key witness, murdered. How convenient! The courtblock has little choice but to acknowledge your cunning. You have earned just a teensy sliver of your respect back. For now.

But wait...

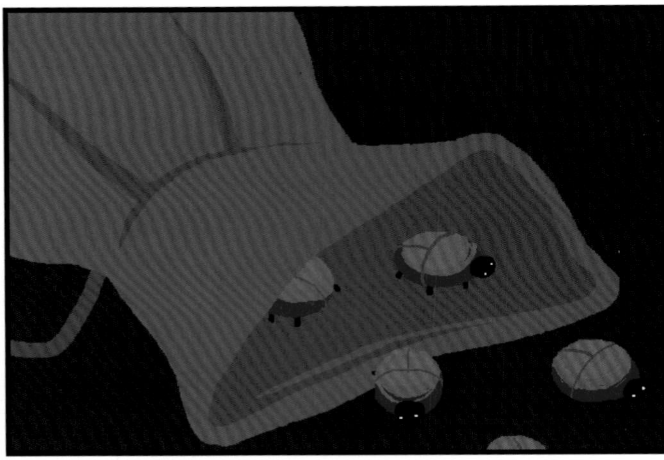

Oh my!

What have we here???

It also seems probable that in a real courtblock, the only thing defendants can do to improve their chances of escaping execution is not presenting a good defense (which the legislacerator only finds irritating), but dazzling the court with various acts of cunning and treachery, such as having witnesses murdered. Lemonsnout knows the game, and he plays it well.

The prosecution begs your pardon, dear senator, but you appear to have dropped something. A personal satchel, perhaps? *CHOCK FULL OF ILLICIT, EMBEZZLED BEETLES, WITH WHICH YOU HAVE THE UNMITIGATED CHEEK TO WALTZ BEFORE HIS TYRANNY, CONCEALED BENEATH YOUR ILL-GOTTEN FINERY??????*

The prosecution requests a short recess from His Honorable Tyranny so that all law abiding and Mother Grub fearing citizens may go outside and puke.

> Terezi: Sentence the criminal.

At the same time, it's just as likely for legislacerators to respond to this gamesmanship with dirty tricks of their own, like planting evidence. Terezi knows that any legislacerator who doesn't at least TRY the "drop a suspicious bag of beetles near the defendant and cry foul" trick should probably be disbarred.

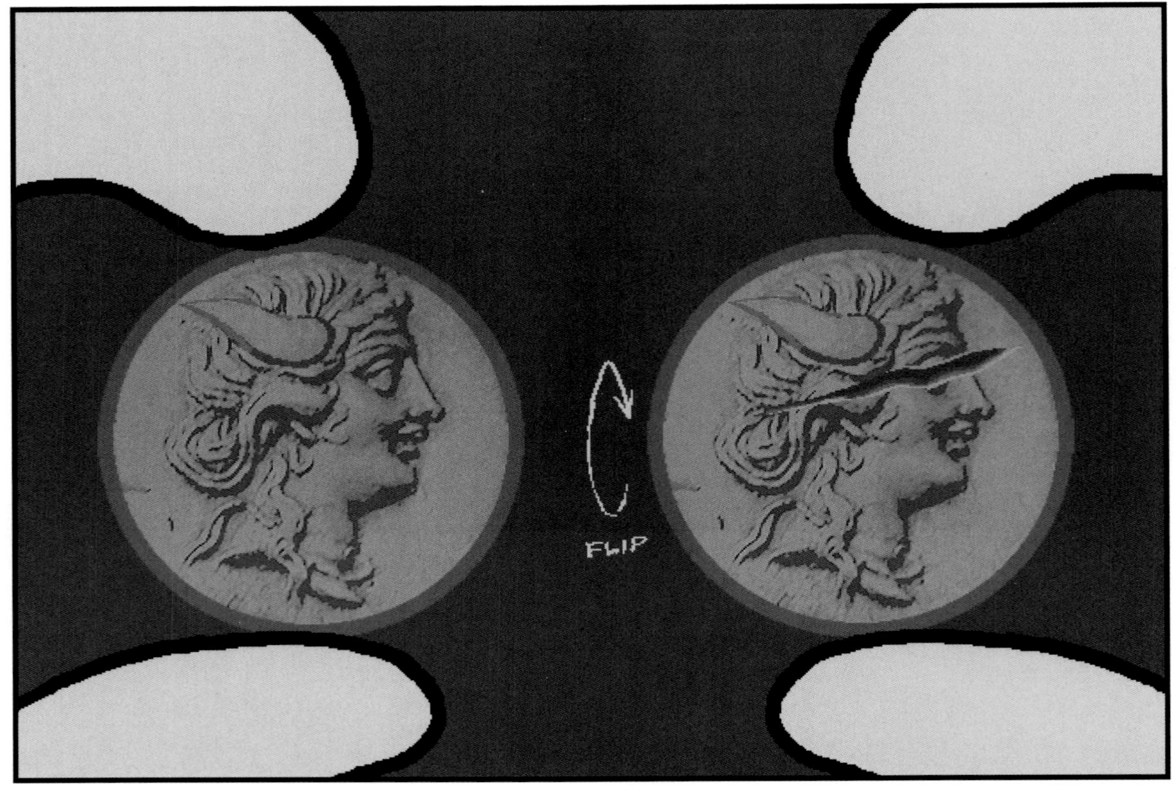

As the prosecutor, it is your job to reach a final verdict and sentence the reprehensible felon, while His Tyranny watches in silence and submits grim approval.

But you take pity on this miserable bureaucrat. You are feeling merciful. You will give him a fighting chance.

You will flip a DOUBLE-HEADED TROLL CAEGAR to decide his fate. You do this quite often when making important decisions. Kind of like Batman's nemesis, Two-Face. Or that guy from No Country for Old Men. It turns out there are lots of badasses out there flipping coins. But those are Earth things and you've never heard of them. It's safe to say you borrowed this gimmick from one of the many, many troll things out there that's got hard boiled dudes flipping coins for major stakes. You base the habit on whichever one smells the most badass.

> Terezi: Flip.

Most court proceedings are designed around the awkward fact nobody really wants to admit, which is that the judge is basically incapable of performing any formal judicial action, except for eating people. So prosecutors have to sentence criminals too. Here's Terezi's special coin. It decides much more significant things later on, aside from the fate of her stuffed dragons. It has Caesar's face on both sides, one blinded with a scratch. Troll Caesar is spelled Troll Caegar, in the same way Troll Jesus is spelled Troll Jegus. And Jegus was only spelled that way due to the SBaHJification of the word Jesus, in a conversation between Dave and Terezi. These explanations are getting pretty esoteric, and frankly, I doubt anyone has benefitted from this explanation at all. We'll be pretty hard pressed to discover information about *Homestuck* that is less useful than this. But don't worry, I will stay vigilant and let you know if I see anything.

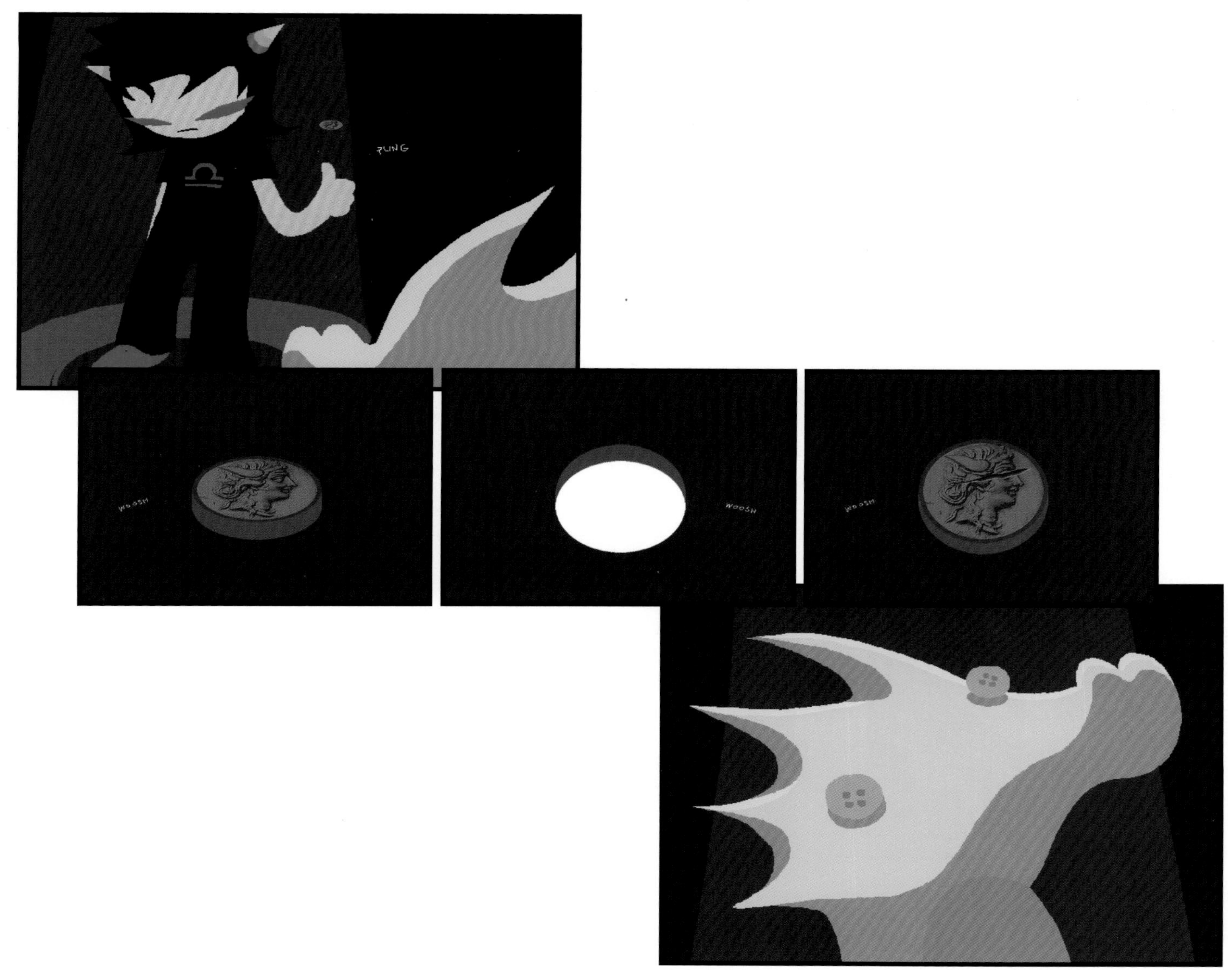

The coin tumbles through the air. Lemonsnout is sweating bullets!!!

You can't tell here, but Lemonsnout is shaking vigorously in fearful anticipation. Terezi is surely the one shaking him. She spares no detail in her roleplay.

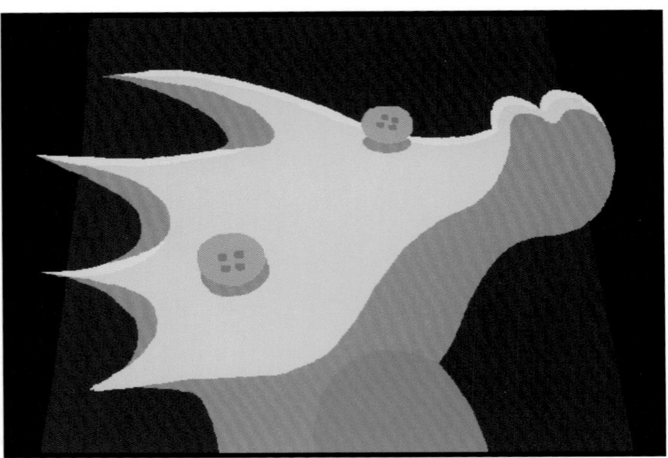

A favorable flip. The senator exhales in relief.

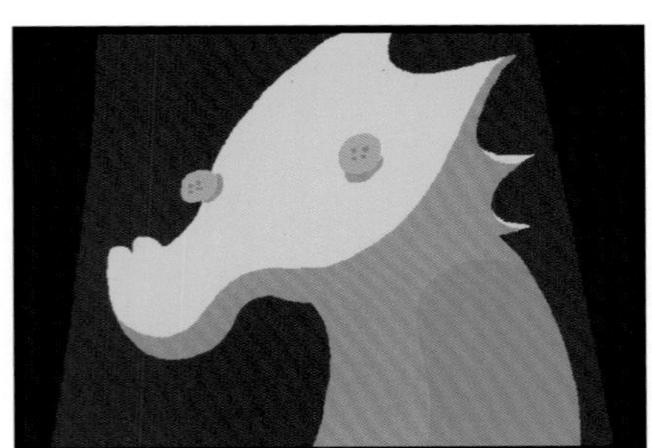

But, what are you so happy about, Mr. Lemonsnout?

He looks a bit confused. He quivers his lowly proboscis at the coin.

See? The coin has exonerated him.

This is some cold-blooded grandstanding, which Terezi is quite proud of. She probably spent hours refining this act, over the course of many plush dragon executions.

Coin? What coin?

Surely you jest, Mr. Senator.
The prosecution sees no coin.

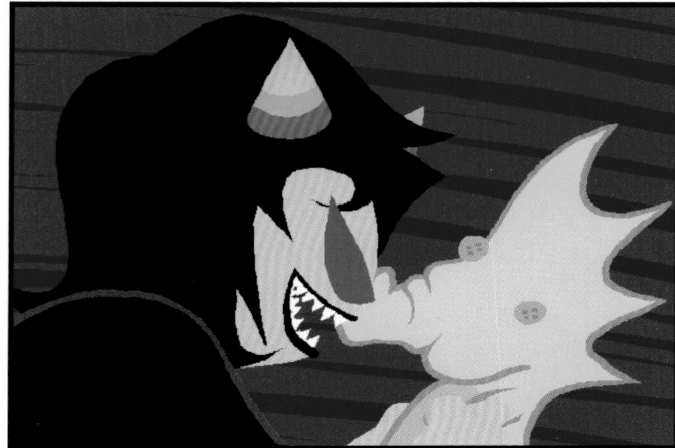

SHE'S BLIND, REMEMBER?

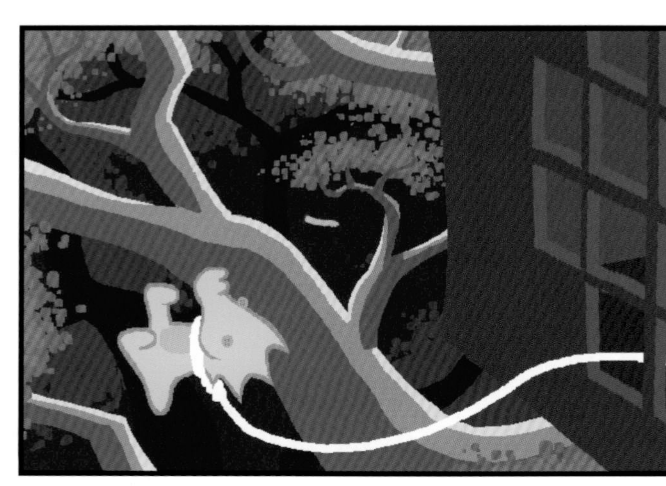

First: another floating arm sighting. Do you see it?? On the coin flip: this is both the first instance of flipping this coin to determine someone's fate, as well as the first time that the result of the coin flip didn't actually matter that much. In this case, a favorable result for the victim, resulting in his death regardless. In the case much later, basically the opposite (followed by a do-over fueled by Seer of Mind powers). There's a theme being established here. Not gonna launch into it too hard, but it concerns the subject of luck, either its irrelevance or subversion in situations where Terezi is concerned, and later, how that specifically ties into her relationship with a certain Scourge Sister who I won't bother mentioning for now.

> Terezi: Adjourn.

Terezi's treehouse hive probably gets the Best Hive Award. It also gets the prize for Hive Most Likely Inspired by an Ewok Village. Well, troll Ewoks I guess. Honorable mention to the cool elevator she rigged, which uses a net full of criminal scalemates as its counterweight. This undoubtedly is the penance they are serving for their vile treasons.

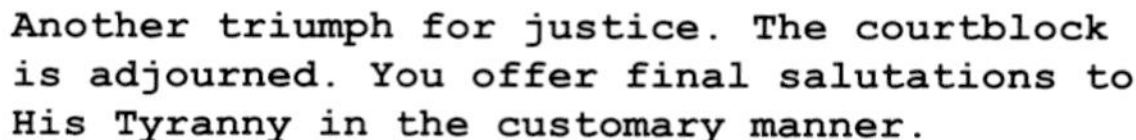

Another triumph for justice. The courtblock is adjourned. You offer final salutations to His Tyranny in the customary manner.

Ok, that's not customary at all. You're just kind of weird.

It's just that your red chalk is THE MOST DELICIOUS CHALK. You cannot get enough of it. Anyone who says there is a more delicious chalk out there simply reeks of deceit.

You sure had to go to a lot of trouble to do that.

> Terezi: Go get cane.

You take your WALKING CANE, which you use as a weapon kind of like Earth Daredevil who you've never heard of. You will use it to wallop enemies when you enter the Medium.

Terezi loves the taste and smell of red the best. Everybody knows this. Especially Karkat.

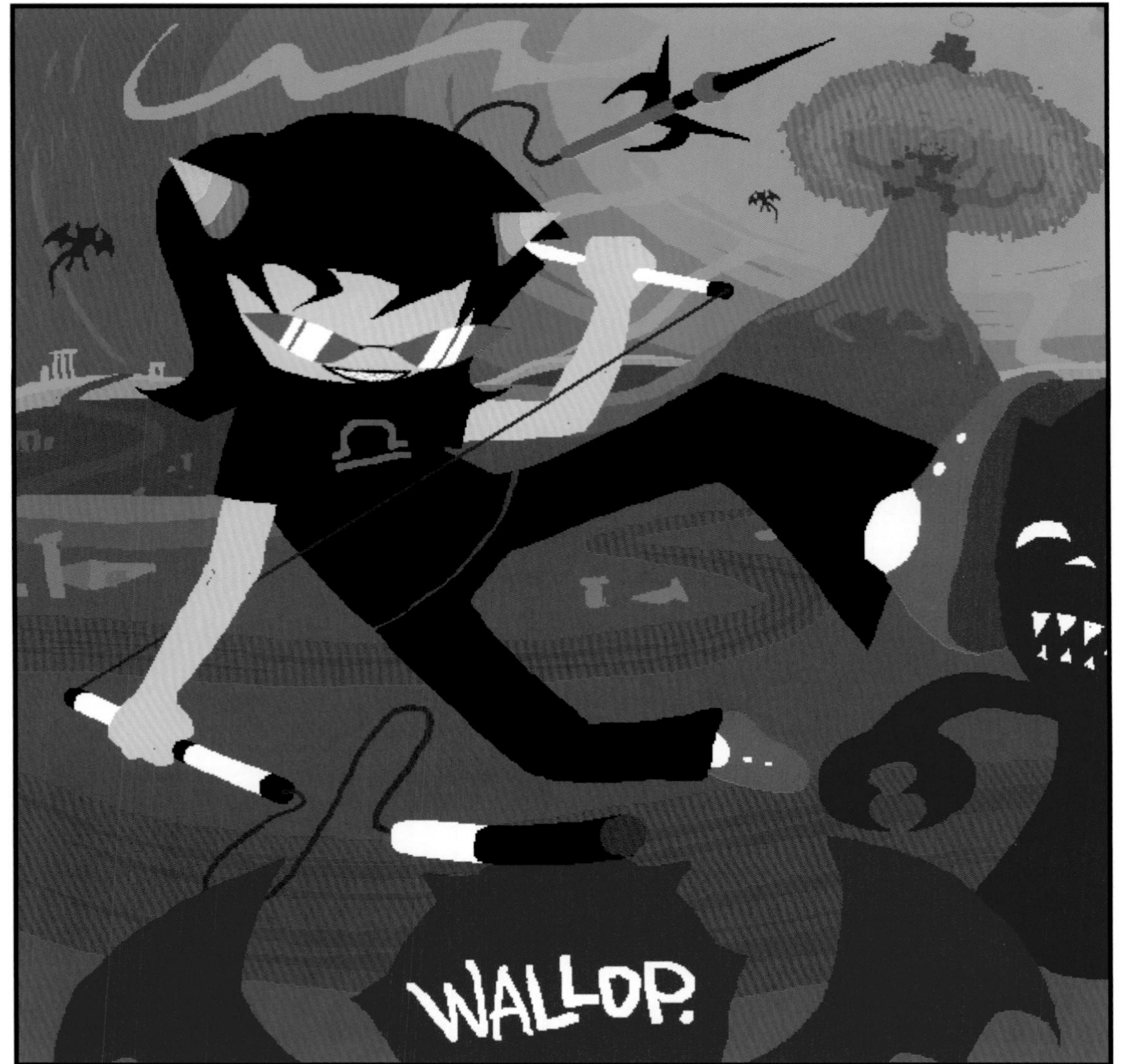

Like this.

> Terezi: Begin recruiting red team members.

Another thing that Hivebent does, in terms of its various fast-and-loose narrative arrangement and pacing methods, is freely hop back and forth through time, utilizing the entire troll adventure, from start to finish, as a sort of Event Palette to draw from. It can use any moment from the full span of their adventure at will, to make any point it needs to or reveal any fact that it deems the audience to be ready for. In this case, we jump way ahead to get a look at Terezi's land, with no fanfare at all, and without any sense that this carries a cost, or risks blowing an important reveal in the wrong way. Because really, it's not an important reveal. It's just an interesting piece of information, and the goal of this arc is to get everybody up to speed on everything about the trolls in a way that feels interesting, and with as much swiftness as possible, given the great extent of what needs to be conveyed.

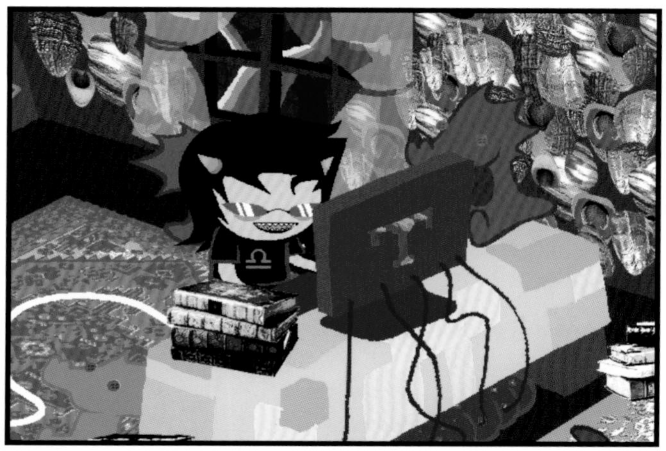

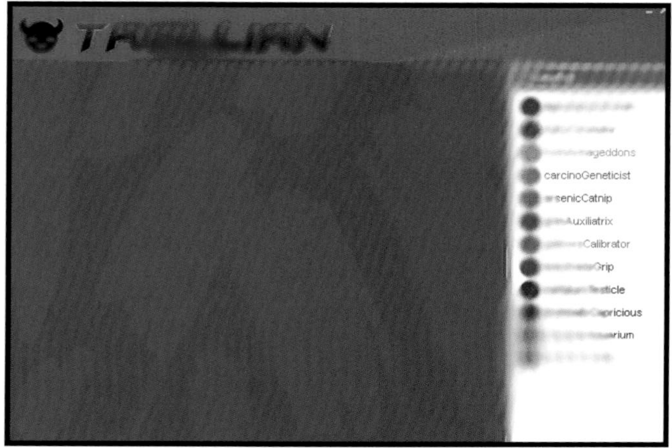

Your nose begins scouring your chumproll through the saliva smears on your monitor for potential teammates so you can start playing. Hmm, no not her. Nope, not her either. DEFINITELY not that guy.

Ok how about this girl. You like to roleplay with her sometimes via chat. You pretend you are a member of the mysterious and noble DRAGONYY'YD RACE, while she does her own goofy thing.

You don't have it in your heart to tell her that your chat RPing is meant f4c3t1ously I mean facetiously.

gallowsCalibrator [GC] **began trolling** arsenicCatnip [AC]

GC: *GC L4NDS ON YOUR WH3LP1NG STOOP 4ND R4PS ON YOUR C4V3 W1TH H3R NOBL3 4ND 3L3G4NT T4LON*
GC: *4ND ONC3 W1TH H3R M1GHTY SNOUT FOR GOOD M34SUR3*
AC: :33 < *ac saunters from her dark cave a little bit sl33py from the recent kill*

There is an implication here with this silly RP session that Terezi and Nepeta at one point were pretty good friends and spent a fair amount of time like this goofing off. It's kind of a cute and fun idea to imagine that this was true. But let's get real. This relationship never went fucking anywhere.

AC: :33 < *ac uses one of her mouths to lick the fresh blood off her paws*
AC: :33 < *and the other one to blow you a kiss!*
GC: >8O
GC: *GC W1TH 4 M1GHTY WH1SK OF H3R M1GHTY T41L PLUCKS TH3 K1SS OUT OF TH3 41R M1GHT1LY*
GC: *GC POCK3TS TH3 K1SS 1N H3R 3NCH4NT3D RUCKS4CK FOR L4T3R, TO DO SOM3TH1NG M4G1C4L, L1K3 M4K3 GOBL1N W1SH3S COM3 TRU3*
AC: :33 < *yes! ac finds that to be a most admirable use of a kiss!*
AC: :33 < *she thinks that goblin wishes n33d to come true too just like any other kind of purrsons wishes*
AC: :33 < *ac begs your pardon while she rips apart this tasty beast to prepare a meal for her cubs*
GC: *GC 3Y3S THE B34ST HUNGR1LY 4ND M1GHT1LY*
AC: :33 < uh oh!
GC: *GC 3Y3S THE CUBS HUNGR1LY!*
GC: *4ND M1GHT1LY*
GC: *3SP3C14LLY M1GHT1LY*
AC: :33 < dont you dare!
AC: :33 < i mean
AC: :33 < *ac shouts dont you dare!*
AC: :33 < *indignantly*
GC: *BUT 1T 1S TOO L4T3! GC SCOOPS UP 4 PLUMP CUB W1TH H3R GL1ST3N1NG M4J3ST1C T41L 4ND FL13S OFF M4G1C4LLY*
GC: *TH3 1NNOC3NT CUB 1S CRY1NG 4ND CRY1NG 4ND CRY1NG*
AC: :33 < *ac says noooooooo and looks a bit crestfallen*
AC: :33 < *ac gets a clever idea to slake the majestic dragons mighty hunger*
AC: :33 < *she prepares the lions share of the slain armored cholerbear for gc*
GC: >:? *GCS M4GN1F1C3NT CUR1OS1TY H4S B33N P3RK3D*
GC: 1S 1T 4 BULL CHOL3RB34R??
GC: OOPS *SH3 4SK3D TH4T*
AC: :33 < *ac pawses a moment and nods knowingly with a couple of smug grins on her face*
AC: :33 < *she confirms it is ind33d the bulliest of bears!*
GC: *GC 1NST4NTLY LOS3S 1NT3R3ST 1N TH3 PUNY CUB 4ND DROPS 1T TO TH3 GROUND F4R B3LOW!*
AC: :33 < *but as it happens the really cute cub lands in a bush safe and sound, whew!*
GC: *GC'S 4L4RM1NG 4ND SPL3ND1F3ROUS G1RTH S3TTL3S OV3R THE SUCCUL3NT CHOL3RB34R ST34K*
GC: *WH3N SH3 F1N1SH3S TH3 S4VORY R3D M34T SH3 L1FTS H3R PROUD W1S3 H34D 4ND OP3NS H3R GR34T B1G MOUTH 4ND SP34KS TH3 4NC13NT TONGU3 OF 4 THOUS4ND W1SDOMS*
GC: *SH3 S4YS:*
GC: H3Y DO YOU W4NT TO PL4Y 4 G4M3 W1TH M3?
AC: :33 < *ac crinkles up her nose and prepares for a really unprecedented marathon of baffling feline obstinacy*

AC stands for arsenicCatnip, as you know. Catnip's active ingredient is nepetalactone. Or, let's say Nepeta for short. She's named after cat weed. She probably likes to toke up in her cave but keeps that on the down low. Just like her ancestor, who also was known to blaze it on occasion if I recall, with her bad clown friend. Okay, this is way off topic now. Nepeta's quirk involves a double cat smile, :33, making use of the number 33, which is the atomic number for arsenic. This is the exact sort of fact that could blow a stoned catgirl's mind.

AC: :33 < *her dragonyyydy suitor will make neither rhyme nor reason of her purrplexing behavior for even an instant!*
GC: NO NO TH4T W4S 4 R34L QU3ST1ON
GC: W4NT TO PL4Y 4 G4M3??
AC: :33 < oh! h33h33
AC: :33 < ok if you mean a computer game then yes that sounds like fun
GC: OK YOU C4N B3 ON MY T34M
AC: :33 < team?
AC: :33 < who else is playing?
GC: 1 H4V3NT D3C1D3D Y3T
GC: 4 WHOL3 BUNCH OF US 1N TWO T34MS
AC: :33 < oh
AC: :33 < well it does sound like it will be a lot of fun but i think i should get purrmission first
GC: BL4R!!!!!
GC: TH4TS SO STUP1D
GC: H3S NOT TH3 BOSS OF YOU
AC: :33 < i know!
AC: :33 < but still im kind of scared of him and i think purrhaps its best to just run it by him first so there isnt a kerfuffle about it or anything
GC: TH1S 1S STUP1D 1N SUCH 4 T3RR1BL3 MYR14D OF DUMB W4YS
GC: YOU SHOULDNT B3 4FR41D OF 4NYON3
GC: YOU K1LL B1G 4N1M4LS W1TH YOUR B4R3 H4NDS!
GC: 4ND 1N 4NY C4S3 H3 L1V3S NOWH3R3 N34R YOU SO TH3 WHOL3 TH1NG 1S 3XTR4 STUP1D
AC: :33 < i knooow
AC: :33 < but i dont think itll be a big deal
AC: :33 < ill just mention it casually and itll be fine im sure and then we can play in just a little bit!
GC: >XO
GC: F11111N3
GC: 1N TH3 M34NT1M3 1 W1LL GO ROUND UP SOME MOR3 P3OPL3 TO PL4Y
AC: :33 < k!

> Terezi: Troll TC.

She's alluding to Equius here, but we don't know that yet. We can only guess which of the unintroduced trolls she's referring to at this point. He also sounds ominous. Possibly abusive? Before we get to know him, there are many clues that Equius is an unspeakably horrid troll. These clues turn out to be pretty misleading. He's actually sort of a powderpuff. A sweaty, creepy, unbelievably racist powderpuff.

gallowsCalibrator [GC] began trolling terminallyCapricious [TC]

GC: H3Y G4MZ33Z YOU W4NT TO PL4Y G4M3Z3Z W1TH M3??
TC: hEy YeAh ThAt SoUnDs LiKe ThE mOtHeRfUcKiN sHiT's BiTcHtItS!
GC: >8\
GC: 1T SUR3 1S H4RD TO 1GNOR3 TH3 W31RD TH1NGS YOU S4Y SOM3T1M3S!

You then proceed to have the rest of this conversation we already read. No luck in getting this guy to play with you right now either.

You guess that leaves...

Oh no. Not Karkat. You were only going to ask him as a last resort. You wonder what he wants? You will try to avoid mentioning the game. Hopefully he hasn't caught wind of it yet.

> Terezi: Deal with Karkat.

Remember how earlier I said that Terezi contacted Gamzee first, of all people? Okay, I was wrong about that. She tried Nepeta first, then the clown. Can you blame her? Maybe Terezi x Nepeta truly did have vast untapped potential. And yet it slipped through our fingers. Gamzee almost certainly derailed this possibility, just like he ruined everything else that was once pure and wholesome about *Homestuck*. Getting in between Neprezi though, and proving to be its poison pill: perhaps this was his most unspeakable crime of all?

carcinoGeneticist [CG] **began trolling** gallowsCalibrator [GC]

CG: HEY GUESS WHAT, BIG NEWS.
CG: LIKE HOLY SHIT STOP THE PRESSES THIS IS A HUMONGOUS DEAL SORT OF NEWS.
GC: BL44444RRRRR WH4T 1S 1T
CG: YOU'RE NOT THE RED TEAM LEADER.
CG: THAT'S ME.
CG: I'M THE LEADER.
CG: IT'S BEEN DECIDED.
CG: ON AN OFFICIAL BASIS.
GC: OK SO 1 GU3SS 1M SUPPOS3D TO M4K3 4 B1G ST1NK 4BOUT TH1S 4ND S4Y W4H W4H 1 W4NT TO B3 TH3 L34D3R >:[>:[>:[
CG: WHAT, NO.
CG: I MEAN YOU CAN BUT IT WON'T DO ANY GOOD BECAUSE I'M THE LEADER AND THAT'S ALL THERE IS TO EVACUATE THROUGH YOUR PROTEIN CHUTE ON THE MATTER.
GC: W3LL 1T M4Y SURPR1S3 YOU TO KNOW TH4T 1 DONT G1V3 4 CR4P WHO G3TS TO B3 L34D3R B3C4US3 UNL1K3 YOU 1 4CTU4LLY H4V3 4 FUCK1NG SM1DG3N OF M4TUR1TY 4ND S3LF R3SP3CT
CG: THAT'S A LIE, YOU'RE MORE OF A MELODRAMA SPAZ QUEEN THAN ME AND YOU KNOW IT AND THIS STUFF YOUR SAYING IS A PRETEND STUNT.
CG: YOU'RE LIKE A ROCKET PROPELLED SPAZ MAGGOT SPRINGLOADED UP THE ASS OF A PSYCHEDELIC FUCKING FREAKOUT WEASEL ON IDIOT DRUGS SO LETS NOT PLAY MAKEBELIEVE GAMES HERE.
CG: LEADER.
CG: ME.
GC: UUUUUUUUHNG
GC: K4RK4T 1 DONT C444R3
GC: YOU C4N B3 TH3 STUP1D L34D3R 1 JUST W4NT TO PL4Y TH1S G4M3
CG: OK, GREAT.
CG: IF IT'S ANY CONSOLATION I HAVE SELECTED YOU TO BE MY SECOND IN COMMAND.
GC: R333334444LLY????
GC: SWOOOOOOOOOOOOOOOOOOOOOOOON >;] <3 <3 <3
CG: FUCK YOU OFFER RESCINDED.
GC: OK BUT S3R1OUSLY
GC: 1 WOULD H4V3 SUGG3ST3D YOU B3 TH3 L34D3R BUT HON3STLY 1T COM3S W1TH S3R1OUS R3SPONS1B1L1T13S 4ND 1 W4SNT SUR3 1F YOU W3R3 UP TO 1T
CG: HOW COULD YOU THINK THAT.
CG: I'M AN INCREDIBLE LEADER WITH ALL KINDS OF PRIORITIZATION AND COMMAND SKILLS.
CG: I'M GOING TO ROCK THE COCK OFF THIS WEATHERVANE AND THE BLUE TEAM WILL WISH THEY NEVER SLITHERED OUT OF THE MOTHER GRUB'S HEINOUS UNDULATING ASSHOLE.

Calling someone a rocket propelled spaz maggot springloaded up the ass of a psychedelic fucking freakout weasel on idiot drugs is definitely something you would call a person if you yourself were not a rocket propelled spaz maggot springloaded up the ass of a psychedelic fucking freakout weasel on idiot drugs.

CG: SO JUST GIVE ME THE FULL BRIEFING, WHAT DO YOU KNOW.
GC: OK TH3 TH1NG YOU N33D TO KNOW 1S TH3 L34D3R ST4RTS OUT BY RUNN1NG THE CL13NT 4PPL1C4T1ON
GC: WH1L3 1 TH3 LOWLY S3COND OFF1C3R CONN3CTS TO YOU W1TH TH3 S3RV3R WH1L3 1 R3M41N G3N3R4LLY 1N 4W3 OF YOUR M4NLY GR4ND3UR
GC: 4ND 1 S1T 4T MY COMPUT3R DO1NG M3N14L CHOR3S 1N SUPPORT OF YOUR H3RO1C 3SC4P4D3S WH1CH HON3STLY 1 DONT TH1NK YOUR3 R34DY FOR BUT WH4T3V3R
CG: SEE THIS IS WHAT I'M TALKING ABOUT.
CG: THIS IS WHAT I WAS MADE FOR.
CG: BEING IN CHARGE OF ADVENTURE, RUNNING AROUND AND STUFF, AND FUCKING SHIT UP LIKE A GODDAMN HERO WITH A RIPPERWASP IN HIS JOCK.
CG: LET'S GET CRACKING HERE.
CG: LAUNCH YOUR SERVER OR WHATEVER, I'LL INSTALL THE HERO PROGRAM.
GC: TH3 CL13NT
CG: YEAH.
GC: OK 1F YOU 1NS1ST
GC: F4R B3 1T FROM M3 TO STOP YOU FROM B31NG SO D4SH1NG 4ND COUR4G3OUS
GC: 4ND TO B3 P3RF3CTLY HON3ST 4 L1TTL3 B1T H4NDSOM3 >:]
CG: YES, EXACTLY.
CG: NOW YOU ARE MAKING SENSE.
CG: THIS IS THE KIND OF THING THAT SANE PEOPLE SAY.
CG: KEEP AT IT, THERE'S HOPE FOR YOU YET.
GC: OK 1LL TRY
GC: 4NYTH1NG TO G3T YOU TO STOP B31NG SUCH 4 B4BY
CG: WHAT'S A BABY.
GC: OH
GC: 1TS L1K3 4 MYTH1C4L L1TTL3 P1NK MONK3Y
GC: SOM3TH1NG MY LUSUS DR34MS 4BOUT
CG: I THOUGHT YOU DIDN'T HAVE ONE.
GC: 1 DONT
GC: Y3T
GC: 1M NOT 4LLOW3D TO
CG: WHY NOT?
CG: WHY HAVE YOU NEVER MENTIONED THIS ANYWAY?
CG: HONESTLY TEREZI IT SOUNDS LIKE MORE FROTHING LOONEYBLOCK NONSENSE.
GC: 1F 1 3V3R D1D H4V3 ON3 1T WOULD M34N TH3 WORLD W4S COM1NG TO 4N 3ND
CG: OH THANK GOD YOU JUST SAID SOMETHING NORMAL, I WAS STARTING TO WORRY THERE.
CG: WHEW BACK IN SANE LAND.
GC: 1TS TRU3! >:P
GC: 1 DONT COMPL3T3LY UND3RST4ND 1T BUT TH4TS WH4T 1T TOLD M3
CG: WE NEED TO GET YOU OUT OF THAT FUCKING TREE AND INTO A PROPER GODDAMN LAWNRING.

Karkat in all his internally conflicted glory can never really decide if he likes Terezi's flirtation or not. One minute he sarcastically rescinds his offer to make her second in command when she throws a bunch of hearts at him. The next, he's saying THIS IS THE KIND OF THING THAT SANE PEOPLE SAY when she calls him handsome. This ship was a fan favorite for a long time, but we should just call it what is, which is: bad. That's what Terezi ended up doing, and in the process ended up literally rewriting huge chunks of the narrative in order to do so.

CG: YOU'VE BEEN STUNTED LIVING UP THERE, BY THE WHISPERS OF FUCKING BARK GNOMES OR SOMETHING.
CG: I THINK ONE OF MY NEIGHBORS WAS JUST CULLED RECENTLY, MAYBE YOU COULD LIVE THERE.
GC: NO W4Y SCR3W L4WNR1NGS!!!
GC: MOR3 L1K3 Y4WNR1NGS
GC: 1 LOV3 MY TR33!
GC: BUT YOUR3 W3LCOM3 TO V1S1T SOM3 T1M3
GC: 1TS 3SP3C14LLY N1C3 1N TH3 TH1RD 4UTUMN
CG: OK WELL
CG: SPEAKING OF THAT
CG: I SHOULD GO DOWNSTAIRS AND DEAL WITH THIS GRUMPY CUSTOMER.
CG: IT'S GOING TO FONDLE MAJOR SEEDFLAP, BUT HOPEFULLY IT'LL BE QUICK.
CG: YOU CAN ESTABLISH YOUR CONNECTION AND DO YOUR TRIVIAL SIDEKICK STUFF I GUESS IN THE MEANTIME.
GC: OK! >:D

> A little later...

And then he's asking her to come live next door, in a dead kid's hive. Talk about mixed signals.

After the KNIGHT OF BLOOD'S heroic arrival to the LAND OF PULSE AND HAZE...

Zapping ahead to the future again, like it's no big deal. Which it isn't. Terezi is an atrocious architect. I guess she's also making use of the implied, but not seen, wall-painting feature in *Sburb/Sgrub*. Which she is also willfully misusing, to Karkat's great irritation, presumably. You get the sense that Terezi uses her blindness as an excuse to troll people all the time. She wildly exaggerates her inability to produce coherent forms using practically any visual media at her disposal. Getting another good excuse to fuck with people was probably the biggest perk of going blind.

You quickly crafted a new weapon, HOMES SMELL YA LATER. Plus some other cool stuff.

> Karkat: Deal with Terezi.

carcinoGeneticist [CG] **began trolling** gallowsCalibrator [GC]

CG: YOU CAN SEE ME RIGHT.
CG: TELL ME WHAT IS WRONG WITH THIS PICTURE.
GC: NO 1 C4NT S33 YOU DUMB4SS
CG: OH YEAH.
CG: ANYWAY, PRESS YOUR NOSE AGAINST YOUR SLOBBERY SCREEN AND TELL ME WHAT IS WRONG WITH THIS PICTURE.
GC: SM3LLS PR3TTY T3RR1BL3!
CG: THAT'S BECAUSE YOU JUST TOOK A HARD DRAG OF MY LOAD GAPER WHICH FOR SOME REASON I HAVE DISCOVERED OUTSIDE ON THIS LITTLE ISLAND.
GC: YOU M34N YOUR TO1L3T?
CG: WELL OOH LA LA.
CG: EXCUSE MY DISDAIN FOR YOUR BLUE BLOODED VERNACULAR.
GC: WH4T COLORS YOUR BLOOD?
CG: WHOA NONE OF YOUR BUSINESS!
CG: SERIOUSLY WAS THAT A SERIOUS QUESTION?
CG: UNBELIEVABLE.
GC: 1 W1LL F1ND OUT SOM3 D4Y
CG: WHAT IS WITH YOUR OBSESSION WITH COLORS.
CG: IT'S BAD ENOUGH YOU WASTE ALL MY HARD EARNED GRIST RAMBLING MY HIVE AROUND LIKE THAT NOT EVEN IN THE DIRECTION OF THE FUCKING GATE.

Yet another instance of a girl server player mistreating the bathroom fixtures of a boy server player. John said the exact same thing when he was sitting in his own bathtub, which Rose placed in his hallway, as you probably remember. Jade also messed with Dave's toilet. This time however, there's no doubt at all that Terezi put Karkat's toilet way down on this tiny island to mess with him. In fact, judging from these two pages, there's virtually no indication that Terezi has been making even the slightest effort to help Karkat play this game properly at all. What a pal.

002061

CG: BUT THEN YOU GO AND SPEND IT ON AN UGLY PAINT JOB.
CG: I KILLED A LOT OF IMPS FOR THAT GRIST.
GC: K4RK4T, PL34S3
GC: DONT PR3T3ND YOU D1DNT 3NJOY GO1NG 4ROUND K1LL1NG TH1NGS
GC: 4ND TH4T YOU WOULDNT 3NJOY K1LL1NG 4 WHOL3 LOT MOR3
GC: PR4NC1NG 4ROUND W1TH YOUR L1TTL3 S1CKL3 B31NG 4LL 4DOR4BL3
CG: YEAH RIGHT.
CG: MORE LIKE...
CG: ADORABLOODTHIRSTY.
CG: I'M PRANCING AROUND BEING THAT, OK?
GC: >:]
CG: ANYWAY THIS IS AWFUL, THIS IS NO WAY FOR A LEADER TO BE TREATED.
GC: SORRY TH1S 1S WH4T YOU W4NT3D
GC: TH3 L34D3R 1S TH3 F1RST ON3 1N
GC: TH1S 1S WH4T TH3 L34D3R 1S SUPPOS3D TO DO
CG: NO, THIS IS NOT ANYTHING EXCEPT FOR WHAT BULLSHIT IS.
CG: A LEADER SHOULDN'T BE AT THE MERCY OF THE HIVE RENOVATION WHIMSY OF A PSYCHOTIC BLIND GIRL.
CG: WHEN DO I GET THE CHANCE TO FUCK UP SOMEONE'S HIVE.
CG: I SHOULD BE THE NEXT ONE TO CONNECT TO A CLIENT.
GC: NO YOU C4NT!
GC: YOU H4V3 TO B3 TH3 L4ST ON3 TO CONNECT TO COMPL3T3 TH3 CH41N
CG: MORE LIES.
GC: TH1NK OF 1T TH1S W4Y
GC: 1M YOUR S3RV3R PL4Y3R SO PR1OR1TY H4S TO B3 ON M3 G3TT1NG 1N TH3 G4M3
GC: B3FOR3 1 G3T K1LL3D BY M3T3ORS
GC: 1N WH1CH C4S3 YOUD B3 SCR3W3D 1N TH3R3
GC: TH3N TH3 N3XT GUY COM3S 1N, TH3N TH3 N3XT
GC: 4ND YOU BR1NG TH3 L4ST ON3 1N
CG: WHOA WAIT, WHAT?
CG: METEORS?
CG: WHAT THE FUCK ARE YOU TALKING ABOUT.
CG: WHAT DOES THIS HAVE TO DO WITH METEORS.
GC: OH BOY YOU N33D TO G3T W1TH TH3 PROGR4M K4RK4T
GC: H4V3 YOU T4LK3D TO 44
CG: 44 WHAT?
GC: 4POC4LYPS34R1S3N SORRY
CG: NO, OF COURSE NOT.
GC: OR T4
GC: OR 4G 1 GU3SS
GC: OR C4
GC: R34LLY TH3R3S L1K3 TH1S WHOL3 CONSP1R4CY 4BOUT TH1S

They keep using screen-name initials for unintroduced characters instead of their real names, just like the kids did. It feels pretty unnatural in hindsight, since after the character intros happen, they never resort to using initials again. Still, I insist this is an important thing for them to do, because *Homestuck* characters don't get to have names until they are formally introduced, PERIOD!!! It's a rule. As for this conversation between them... These exchanges are really dense and packed with interesting tidbits. It's hard to comment on them all in this sad little margin down here all the time. One of the gists here is that Karkat, despite being chuffed to be a big hero in this game, knows virtually nothing about it. He's got a bit of the "last to know" syndrome that John has going on most of the time too. One of the things he is "last to know" about is a substantial clique of his more sinister friends have essentially formed a little doomsday cult around the plans to dredge this game out of the ruins and play it.

GC: 4S 1M F1ND1NG OUT
CG: WELL WHY DON'T YOU JUST TELL ME SO I DON'T HAVE TO TALK TO ANY OF THOSE DOUBLETALKING ASSHOLES.
GC: 1 C4NT!
GC: 1 GOTT4 ST3P OUT OF TH3 TR33 FOR 4 MOM3NT
GC: WH3N 1 COM3 B4CK 1 W1LL 3NT3R TH3 G4M3
GC: CY4!

> A little while ago...

Speaking of the doomsday cult, here's its leader. And in a way, sort of the shadow leader of the troll session. She doesn't really act like a leader or see herself as one, though. She just floats around emotionlessly, setting stuff up, and lets predestination do the rest. Who the hell is she, anyway? We don't know yet, because this isn't even her intro. Just a snapshot tease, as Hivebent continues Hivebending. Is she some sort of...ghost? (Yes.) Guess we'll just (yes) have to wait and see! (She's a ghost.)

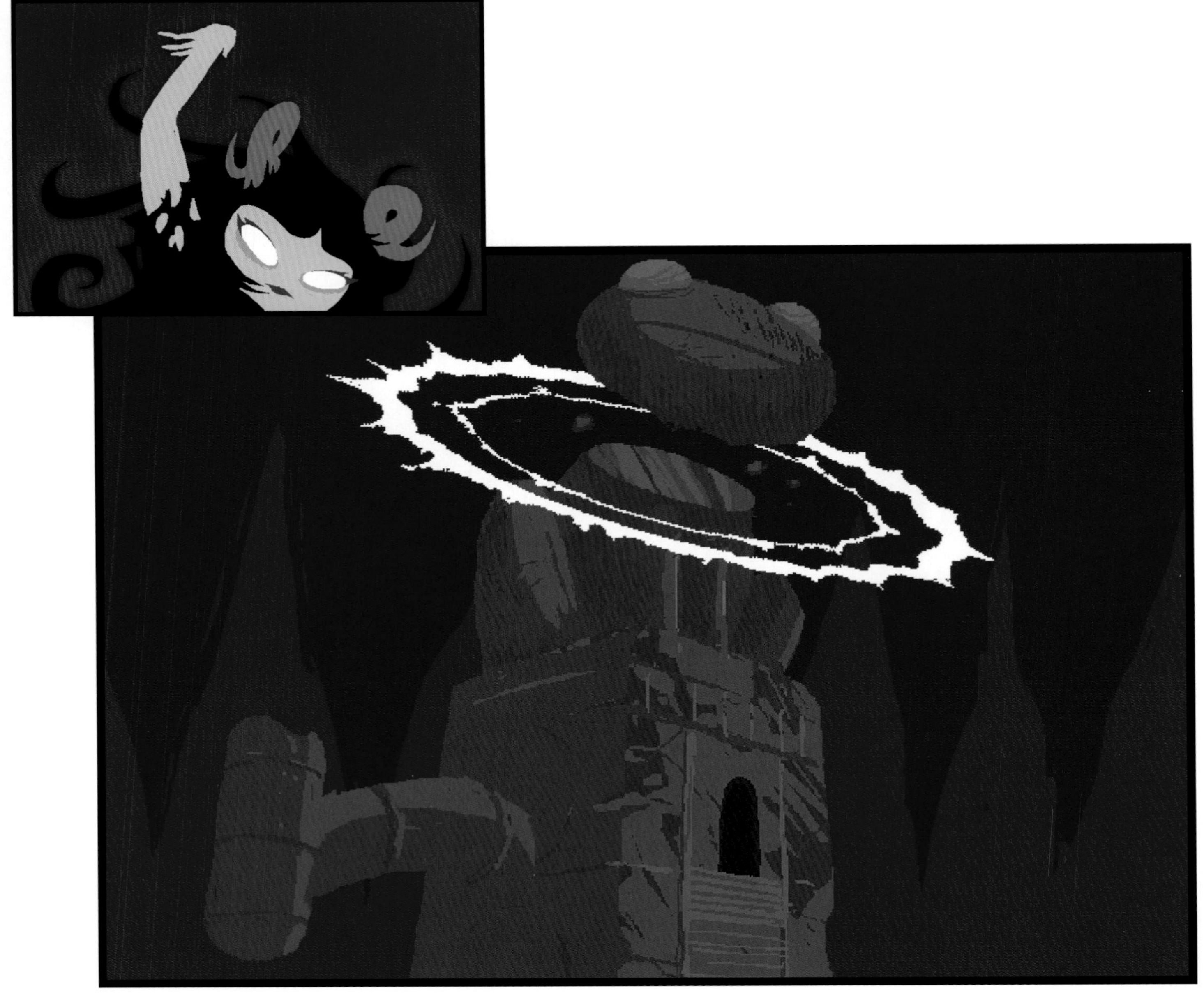

Why exactly IS she doing this? Turns out enjoying random acts of destruction is a character trait. But we've also been sowing the foreshadowing seeds pertaining to frog death, for reasons as yet unknown. The reasons will become less unknown as we approach the end of Act 5. Also like most of these quick drive-by reveals in Hivebent, a huge amount of information is being conveyed without much explanation. We see the trolls have their own set of (blue) frog ruins, with only six planets in orbit. The ruins are underground, presumably in the same subterranean layer as the brooding caverns. Astute folks know this is apocalypseArisen, because of the Aries sign. We see she has telekinesis, and seems to have no problem with acts of desecration. This is a lot to take in, and then without warning, we're looking at Eridan's silly shoes.

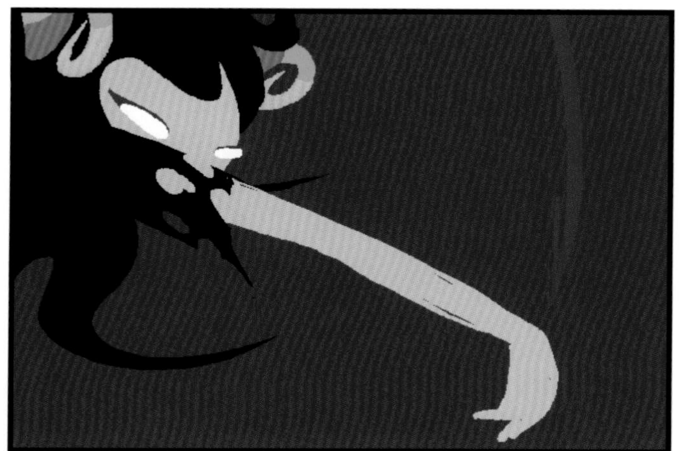

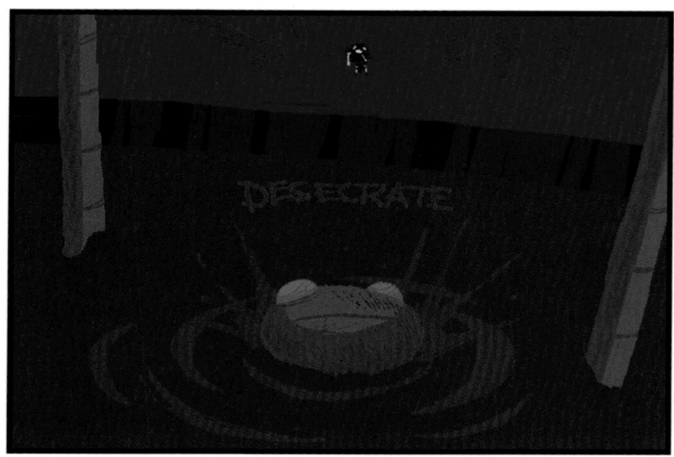

You're not sure why you did that, really.

There'll probably turn out to be a reason. There's a reason for everything. Understanding this lets you be reckless.

Whoever you are.

> A little later...

Somewhere else entirely...

There's the Faygo that Gamzee launched into the sea earlier. For some reason the red liquid in the bottle isn't leveling out in accordance with the pull of gravity. The reason, I would hazard, is that my webcomic consists entirely of one shockingly half-assed piece of garbage after another.

Rubbish from the LAND DWELLERS. Makes you sick.

Whoever you are.

> And later still...

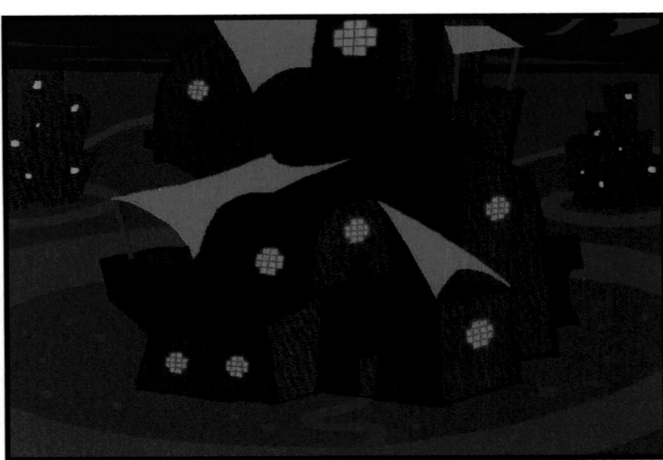

We return to the Land of Pulse and Haze, so that we can rewind a bit. Before all that paint got slopped on your hive and before that mysterious hole was made.

Man how'd that hole get made??

(It was when Karkat ran TA's cursed ~ATH program and his computer blew up. That's what happened. We'll see this happen later. It will be startling and unexpected.)

> Karkat: Deal with crabby customer.

The Aquarius ring signals to readers that these ridiculous hipster accoutrements belong to caligulasAquarium. Just another tease. I probably put a couple character teasers like this in a row because in the previous conversation, Terezi rattled off a bunch of abbreviations, like AA, CA, AG... It seemed like a good idea to start dropping some more concrete visual cues associated with some of these unrevealed characters, to keep them in our minds and help us track who's left to reveal. Twelve characters is quite a lot to introduce in rapid succession. There's an art to doing it in a way that is interesting and makes them all feel distinct from each other, and important in their own ways. Hivebent, for all the things maybe it isn't, totally NAILS being a fun character-rollout arc, IN MY VIEW. Anyway, back to the past, because we weren't done with it yet.

You go downstairs and confront your custodian, which is another term for a frightening beast known as a LUSUS NATURAE.

Your lusus has looked after you since you were very young in lieu of any biological parents, whom you have never known. No young troll ever knows his or her blood parents, nor could such lineage ever be accurately traced. Adult trolls supply their genetic material to the FILIAL PAILS carried by imperial drones and offered to the monstrous MOTHER GRUB deep underground in the brooding caverns. She then combines all the genetic material into one diabolical incestuous slurry, and lays hundreds of thousands of eggs at once.

The eggs hatch into young larval trolls which wriggle about to locate a cozy stalactite from which to spin their cocoons. After they pupate, the young troll with his or her newfound limbs undergoes a series of dangerous trials. If they survive, they are chosen by a member of the diverse and terrifying subterranean monster population native to Alternia. This creature becomes the troll's lusus, and together they surface and choose a location to build a hive. The building process is facilitated by CARPENTER DROIDS left on the planet to cater to the young. But only for building. They're on their own otherwise.

The vast majority of adult trolls are off-planet, serving some role in the forces of ongoing imperial conquest, besieging other star systems in the name of Alternian glory. The culture and civilization on the homeworld is maintained almost entirely by the young.

Trolls sure are weird!

> [S???] ======>

The fact that Karkat's "strife" battle is being shown only now is a good window into the pacing logic of Hivebent, as an expression of "what information and lore to reveal when" as opposed to "what specific events happen, in what order." It also helps indicate that a linear procession through Karkat's early-game events just isn't how we're doing this, and the duel with his guardian (custodian) therefore doesn't have the same narrative weight or meaning that John's clash with his dad had. But aside from pointing that out, this is quite a load of worldbuilding here. The fact that these kids are "raised" by alien beasts is just the right combo of dumb, funny, and genuinely intriguing from a worldbuilding standpoint.

You leap into the domestic fray in an attempt to mollify your nannying aggressor. After a lot of kicking and fussing and gnashing of teeth and carapace, you just pull out a few CHILLED ROE CUBES from the fridge to settle the beast down.

Trolls and their custodians have a peculiar arrangement of codependence. The lusus behaves as a lifelong bodyguard, caretaker, and visceral sort of mentor, while the young troll must learn to function as a sort of zookeeper.

We decide to agree this conflict is not a big enough deal to warrant a detailed examination of the action, or an embedded musical accompaniment. We also agree that while that would have been pretty sweet, we are also in kind of a hurry here. But if it were to be accompanied by something audible, it would probably sound something like this. We decide to listen to that track, close our eyes, and imagine what might have been.

Wow that sure was awesome.

Anyway, moving on.

In fact, we are in such a hurry, you could almost say we need to get moving...

This was also my way of saying "Yeah, I'm not going to bother making a Flash animation for this battle." Flashes, even though I made them pretty fast generally, were brutal to make, even the strife sequences. This would have meant two or three days of no content just to put up a meaningless fray with a crab monster. So I made a joke about it, and linked to a song you could imagine playing during the battle (obviously the song is not available to play in this book). Sometimes by making an obvious demonstration of what I'm NOT doing (while joking about it) is a way of signalling what I consider to be most important to focus on at this moment of the story. And in this case it's: speed. Getting through this wild alien arc as fast as we can, cutting whichever corners I say don't matter.

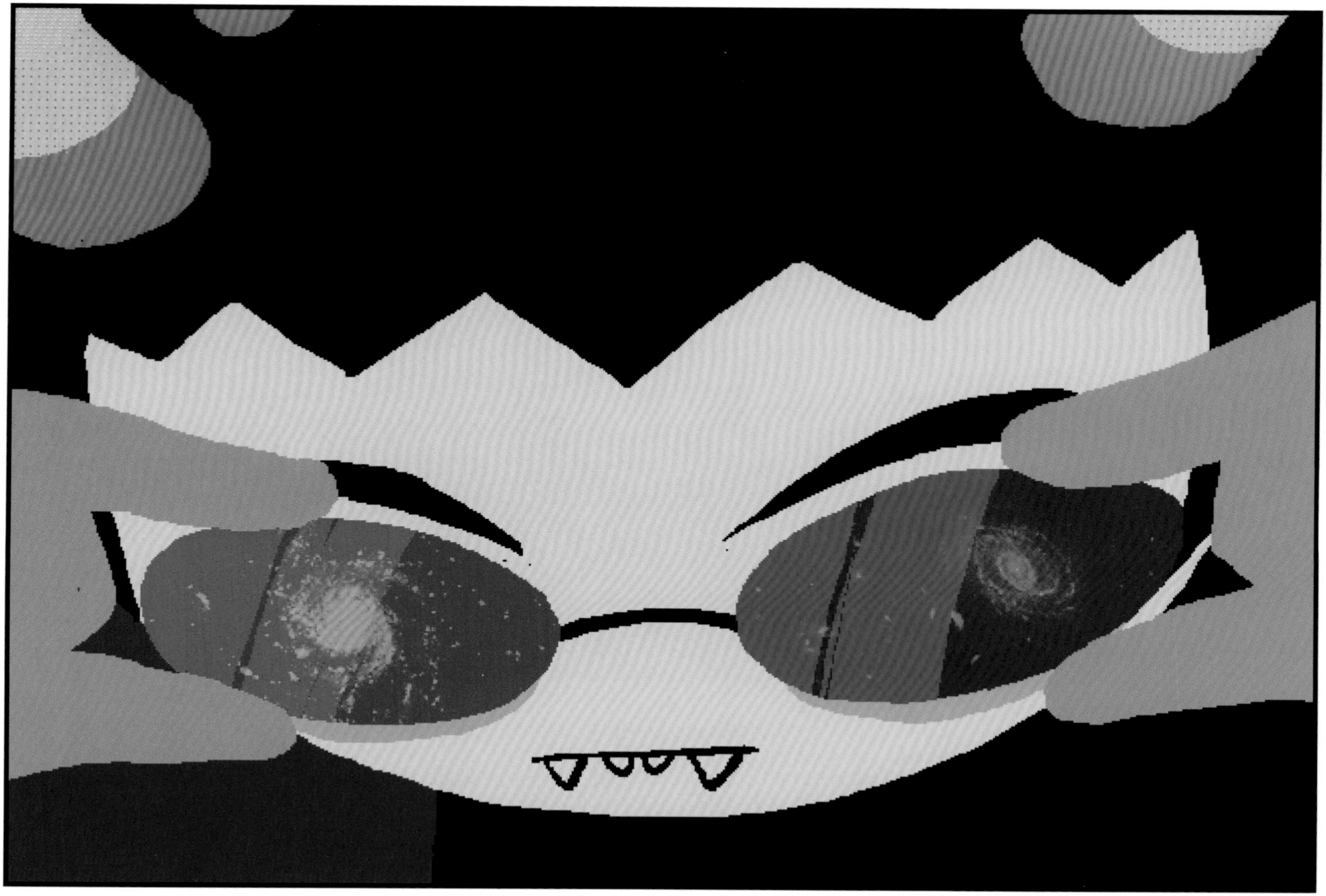

ON THE DOUBLE

> Yeah.

Sollux is doing that meme where the guy puts on the sunglasses and the song by The Who plays where the guy goes YEEEEAAAAAAAAHHHHHHHHH. But that's an old meme and nobody gives a shit about that anymore or thinks it's funny. Pardon me while I get out of my rocking chair to explain certain memes to you sometimes.

There's this pretty cool dude, ok? Some people seem to think he's cool. Sometimes. He guesses they're right. I mean, maybe. If they say so. Actually, you know what? They're right. This guy's dynamite lit in a box of hot shit. Screw the haters. Anyway, he's standing around being all chill, like cool dudes are known to do sometimes, when they're not moping around or nursing migraines or whatever. A cool dude like this probably has a real cool name. Or at least a name that doesn't completely fucking suck. Like at least not the kind of name that belongs to someone you'd want to just perpetually wail on. Maybe just a name that makes you cringe a little, but you guess you can deal with it if you've got to. It's just a guy's name, it's not like it really matters. Who cares? But he probably wouldn't just tell you what it was if you asked. He'd be way too moody for that. In fact, this guy probably thinks you've got some attitude and probably doesn't want a damn thing to do with you.

You could always try to guess his name. But instead of that, here's a better idea. Why don't you just fuck off and go to hell?

Here, name this kooky broad instead.

Sollux is a complete mess. An internal roller coaster careening up and down between self-loathing and bravado. As such, so is his introduction. He's so conflicted, his introduction can't even stay put and follow through with itself. We have to cut away to Nepeta.

Ok, what's her name?

Wait...

You've got to be kidding me.

Looks like we're going back to the other guy again. Alright, hang on...

But we can't actually stay on her for more than a panel, can we? Because she's sort of a joke character. I mean, not REALLY? But she starts out that way, at least in concept. Designing a twelve-troll ensemble before I knew anything about a lot of them meant that a bunch of the designs were sort of these humorous, superficial GESTURES. Ideas that captured internet archetypes that were a bit absurd or cringey. The juggalo troll, the weird horse porn freak troll, the furry girl troll... They all start out as kind of shitty ideas that then receive elaboration and actual character development, which makes them more than the sum of their gimmicks. But the story kind of latches on to her as the poster child for this idea of the "underdeveloped joke character" which some fans would demand additional development well beyond reasonable expectation for the station she holds in the story. So some running gags emerge that focus on dragging poor Nepeta back down to irrelevance, or unfairly target her for tragic outcomes. Hence some "dead Nepeta" jokes that crop up here and there, which maybe seem cruel, but everything has its reason and fits into a greater order. In a way, Nepeta's arc could be seen as the struggle to ultimately free herself from the cycle of narrative marginalization and abuse. If you know where she ends up, do you believe she succeeds at this? I allow YOU to decide.

It appears this cool and moody dude had a change of heart. He feels pretty bad about flying off the handle like that, as if shit wanted nothing to do with the handle. Shit would like to reconcile with the handle, and perhaps seek marital counseling.

So what's his name gonna be?

> Enter name.

The previous page's note contained way too much fucking Nepeta meta. Let's get to some actual Good Shit. Let's talk about Sollux. (Dear God, the Nepeta abuse continues. It never ends.) Sollux, like Nepeta, is another pretty marginal character, and also like her, his metatextual profile seems to acknowledge his marginality, and incorporates it into his personality in a thematically relevant way. He always seems to be falling into the margins of the story as a second-string player, gets used as a pawn a lot, gets led around by others (going blind at one point), and generally just can't catch a damn break. As a psychic, he's aware of things on a lot of levels, such as future visions of doom and gloom, but he also seems intuitively aware of his place in the narrative as just a marginal cast member in a story containing people much more important than he is. His "woe is me," "why don't I just roll over and fucking die already" attitude seems like it's connected to this basic awareness. In other words, his resigned sense of fatalism is inseparable from his narrative impotence, and the basic truth about him is that he was built to be little more than a serviceable part of a big machine. Just like his ancestor.

Your name is SOLLUX CAPTOR.

You are apeshit bananas at computers, and you know ALL THE CODES. All of them. You are the unchallenged authority on APICULTURE NETWORKING. And though all your friends recognize your unparalleled achievements as a TOTALLY SICK HACKER, you feel like you could be better. It's one of a number of things you SORT OF BEAT YOURSELF UP ABOUT for NO VERY GOOD REASON during sporadic and debilitating BIPOLAR MOOD SWINGS. You have a penchant for BIFURCATION, in logic and in life. Your mutant mind is hounded by the psychic screams of the IMMINENTLY DECEASED. Your visions foretell of the planet's looming annihilation, and yet unlike the typical sightless prophet of doom, you are gifted with VISION TWOFOLD.

For now.

You have developed a new game, adapted via CODE PARSED FROM THE RUNES AND GLYPHS IN AN ANCIENT UNDERGROUND TEMPLE. You believe this game to be THE SALVATION OF YOUR RACE, though you are not sure how yet. To ensure success, you will distribute the game to two teams of friends, a RED TEAM and a BLUE TEAM. You will lead the latter group. Your trolltag is twinArmageddons and you tend two 2peak wiith a biit of a lii2p.

What will you do?

> Sollux: Equip throwing stars to strife specibus.

Okay, the previous page's note also contained way too much fucking meta. Let's tone it down, all right? Here's some frivolous shit. The troll names, as you probably know, were drawn from the reader suggestion box, which was only reopened during a troll intro like this. Usually I'd mix and match suggestions, like one person suggests Karkat, another suggests Vantas, and I decide to grab both and stick them together. In this case I think someone just suggested Pollux Castor, which is just the name of the Gemini star system. Which I thought was WAY too on the nose, but otherwise felt promising. So all I did was rearrange the letters a bit. Here's yet more frivolity. Some speculated that Sollux is secretly a reference to every Nic Cage movie ever made. Note the bees (see: *Wicker Man*, when Cage humorously gets his head swarmed with bees), and the code on walls circled with red and blue (see: Cage in *Knowing*), and Sollux's ability to foresee doom in the future (see: Cage in *Next*), NOT TO MENTION Castor and Pollux were the names of Cage and his younger brother in *Face/Off*... The list probably goes on.

Why would you do that?

A high level psionic has no use for any particular specibus allocation.

> Sollux: Fling stars specibus-ward.

You make short work of the specibus and...

Oh God, one of your BEEHOUSE MAINFRAMES. The silicomb was sliced clean through by your foolish maneuver. What were you thinking???

The workers pair up and dance angry messages to you in beenary code.

> Sollux: Taste honey.

Sollux is a special snowflake who does not need a specibus. The amount of times that guys slice game constructs like this in half in order to express defiance... is a thing I have no formal accounting of, sorry. Karkat did it in this very arc. Dave and Bro also do it. I'm sure it happens plenty more than that. Also, let's enjoy this preposterous bee-based computing system I came up with. It's charmingly reminiscent of *Problem Sleuth* lore. Remember the comb raves, the jocose honey, and all that nonsense? It's doubtful you do, tbh.

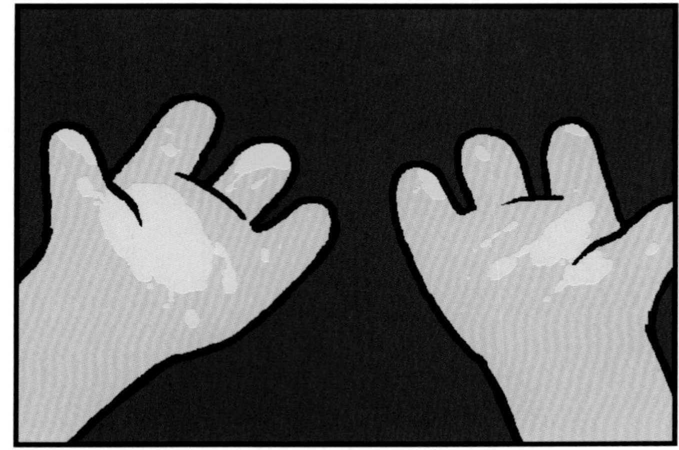

No!!!!!!!!!

You do not under any circumstance eat the MIND HONEY. The consequences are highly unpleasant.

You cultivate this honey for your lusus. It helps him not be such a complete idiot all the time. Merely most of the time instead.

> Sollux: Calm those bees down.

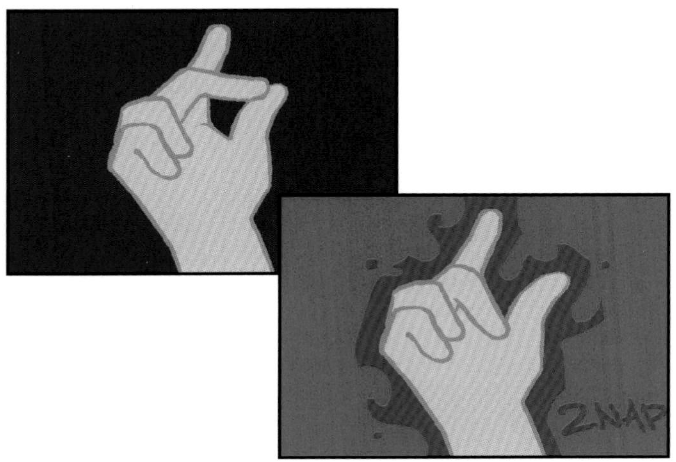

Nap time.

> Sollux: Get to work at computer.

The very common psychic power of being able to put things to sleep is established here. Pretty much any psychic can do this: Sollux, Aradia, Vriska... It happens a lot, often with significant consequences. Note also the exact visual callback to when Dave was staring at the blood on his hands. Same panel, just recolored. For reasons that are never made especially clear, Sollux has certain things in common with Dave. Certain speech patterns, verbal echoes, coolguy with shades look, similar apartment building setup, and callbacks like this where he stares at honey (or blood) on his hands in a way that triggers rumination on certain traumas. But Sollux's traumas are less related to a troubling guardian relationship, and more about the struggle with his own troubled brain. Particularly his bipolar issues, as well as the extreme and volatile mutant abilities he has, the most explosive of which are triggered by this honey.

You are always up to your nook in the newest and hottest games. It is hard to walk around the place without squishing them. Whenever that happens you are screwed, and you have to grow a new one from scratch. Or just pirate it you guess.

But tonight is no night for games.

Well, ok, it is.

But just one game in particular, and this game is no joking matter. It is delirious bugnasty.

> Sollux: Recruit team leader.

twinArmageddons [TA] **began trolling** gallowsCalibrator [GC]

TA: TZ you want two be the leader of one of the team2?
GC: YOU M34N FOR YOUR G4M3 TO S4V3 TH3 WORLD?
TA: yeah.
GC: OK 1 P1CK TH3 R3D T34M!!! >8D
TA: ok ii diidnt 2ay anythiing about a red team, or even that there were two team2, but fiine.
GC: OBV1OUSLY YOU W3R3 GO1NG TO S3T UP R3D 4ND BLU3 T34MS COM3 ON

Maybe I'll come back to the issue of why Sollux is reminiscent of Dave later. I feel like there's more to say there. It touches on a broader issue of personality construction in *Homestuck* overall, which utilizes certain traits as almost elemental, platonic psychological and behavioral forms to build more extensive and widely varied profile composites. It's an approach that resonates with the rest of *Homestuck*'s governing principles involving simple platonic concepts giving rise to greater complexity and chaos. The Alpha Kid personalities in Act 6 are a much clearer demonstration of this principle as applied to character personas. This really is a whole can of worms, though. Let's open a can of grubs instead. Why are video games contained within living grubs, which you must puncture with wires to play? Because everything about troll culture is a bit gross, weird, and stupid. That's why.

TA: you dont know what iim goiing two do, 2top beiing a2 though you can read my miind.

TA: iit2 not a power you have, your 2trength2 are beiing bliind and triickiing people about 2tuff.

TA: and ii gue22 beiing generally 2avvy and pretty decent at other 2tuff, but that2 why iim piickiing you and not 2ome other fuckiing 2chlub from retardatiion row.

GC: SOLLUX, PL34S3

GC: YOU 4R3 MR 4PPL3B3RRY BL4ST 4ND 3V3RYON3 KNOWS THOS3 4R3 YOUR F4VOR1T3 FL4VORS

GC: 3V3N THOUGH YOU TYP3 1N YUCKY MUST4RD

GC: WH1CH 1S W31RD >:

TA: maybe there ii2 more two me than you thiink.

TA: maybe ii am not the two triick hoofbea2t you want two make me out a2.

TA: maybe ii ju2t want two giive the red and blue thiing a re2t for a change and not make iit 2o iit2 liike, oh look iit2 that prediictable fuck wiith tho2e two 2tupiid color2, iit2 amaziing how much everyone fuckiing hate2 hiim.

TA: maybe red and blue arent that great and ii hate them 2uddenly, have you thought of that.

TA: maybe iim more of an aubergiine guy plu2 whatever that putriid color is you type wiith, what ii2 that, turqoii2e?

TA: maybe iit2 makiing me turquea2y.

TA: maybe the new name for that color ii2 2ummer 2hiithead mii2t, have you con2iidered that?

TA: but iim 2tiickiing wiith red and blue 2o maybe you 2hould 2uck on iit.

GC: M4YB3 M4YB3 M4YB3

GC: M4YB3 M4YB3 1S 4 STUP1D WORD

GC: M4YB3 TH4TS TH3 B1G M4YB3 W3 SHOULD 4LL POND3R TON1GHT

GC: OV3R SOM3 HOT SHUT TH3 H3LL UP T34

GC: SO YOU TH1NK 1M S4VVY?? >:]

TA: yeah ii thiink 2o.

TA: piick out whoever you want for the red team and iill lead the blue team.

TA: iill 2end you the download 2oon, talk two you later.

GC: W41T!

GC: M4YB3 YOU SHOULD T3LL M3 MOR3 4BOUT TH3 G4M3 F1RST?

GC: HOW 3X4CTLY 4R3 W3 S4V1NG TH3 WORLD?

TA: ii dont know yet.

TA: ii ju2t know what iive 2een iin my vii2iion2.

TA: that the world wiill end and our whole race diie2 and thii2 ii2 how we 2ave iit.

TA: and aa can back me up on thii2 2o dont be all doubtiing me about iit.

GC: 1 4M NOT DOUBT1NG YOU

GC: 1 TH1NK YOU 4R3 R1GHT!

GC: MOSTLY

TA: mo2tly, what doe2 that mean?

GC: W3LL WH3N YOU T4LK 4BOUT HOW YOUR3 GO1NG TO D13 TOO

TA: ii am goiing two diie.

Terezi says it's weird that Sollux types in yucky mustard, even though his "favorite colors" are red and blue. It's really not weird at all, considering literally everyone in his blood class types in that color. But this idea may not have been fully locked in yet as an ironclad canon fact. While Hivebent continuously provides the scoop on what the facts of this culture are, it is simultaneously exploring certain nebulous ideas before fully committing to them. This is a very good strategy when it comes to improvisational worldbuilding. Also, can I just take a moment to acknowledge the fact that Sollux's typing quirk is a fucking disaster? Definitely one of the more challenging to parse, I think. But unlike other trolls, his quirk evolves to become more readable as he suffers physical ailments.

TA: ii mean we all are.
TA: but e2peciially me.
TA: ii am goiing two get my a22 2erved two me twofold.
TA: double the 2erviice.
TA: liike two dude2 on doublebutler ii2land.
TA: gettiing worked over by a 2iiame2e twiin ma22eu2e.
TA: but before ii diie, iim goiing two go bliind liike you.
TA: iit ha2 two happen liike that.
TA: iim not 2ure why, but ii thiink iit2 liike...
TA: fulfiilliing 2ome requiirement for a true prophet of doom.
TA: iin order for the vii2iion2 two be riight, that ha2 two happen, and the uniiver2e wiill make 2ure iit wiill.
TA: iit2 kiind of liike how a prophet earn2 hii2 2triipe2, by beiing bliind, liike how an angel earn2 iit2 wiing2.
GC: WH4TS 4N 4NG3L
TA: 2ome terriible mythiical demon.
TA: wiith the2e awful feathery wiing2.
GC: Y1K3S
TA: paradox 2pace u2e2 them two u2her iin the end.
GC: HOW DO3S 1T KNOW WH4T 4NG3L TO US3... ....
TA: huh??
GC: >:?
TA: 2o yeah.
TA: we wiill all diie but mo2t e2peciially me, end of 2tory.
GC: BUT
GC: DONT T4K3 TH1S TH3 WRONG W4Y BUT HOW C4N YOU B3 TOT4LLY SUR3 4BOUT 4LL TH4T?
GC: HOW DO YOU KNOW SOM3 OF TH3 R34L V1S1ONS YOUR3 H4V1NG 4R3NT G3TT1NG K1ND OF T4NGL3D UP W1TH UHHH
GC: SORT OF TH3 W4Y YOU 4R3 4BOUT YOURS3LF
TA: what do you mean.
GC: HOW YOU G3T MOP3Y 4ND YOUR3 4LW4YS TH3 V1CT1M OF SOM3TH1NG 4ND HOW SOM3T1M3S YOU TH1NK YOU SUCK WH3N YOU R34LLY DONT
GC: M4YB3 TH4T 1S CLOUD1NG YOUR V1S1ON?
TA: ok that2 ju2t 2ome per2onal priivate emotiional ii22ue2 and iim dealiing wiith that, and hone2tly iid appreciiate you not alway2 throwiing that iin my face every goddamn opportuniity you get.
TA: liike thii2 ii2 a biig ciircu2 act two you, and that ii2 your 2peciial clown piie.
GC: S33, GOD
GC: SO S3NS1T1V3
TA: 2eriiou2ly talk two aa 2he wiill corroborate everythiing.
TA: you and 2he are pretty tiight arent you?

There's an awful lot going on up here too. Many points of lore and prophecy to earmark for later validation by the story. All of it does come to pass, in some way or another. The blindness, the dying twice stuff... Angels turn out to just be flying white monster things that either emerge from, or are composed of, the fearsome force of hope. That sounds kind of meaningless, and maybe it is, but that's what they are. Also, Terezi asking "how does it know which angel to use..." is a pretty confusing line without context. It's just a reference to a *Sweet Bro* comic, where he wonders what angle to use. I'm not sure a lot of these *Sweet Bro and Hella Jeff* funny quote shout-outs really hold up. The whole work seems much more detached from the *Sweet Bro* canon than it used to be. And littering this story with such quotes has simply resulted in the future burden of me having to explain them down here in the gutter when they happen, so y'all aren't too confused. Do you actually appreciate this??? I have my doubts.

GC: NOT R34LLY 4NYMOR3
GC: SH3 US3D TO B3 4 LOT OF FUN
GC: BUT NOW T4LK1NG TO H3R, 1 DONT KNOW
GC: 1T JUST SOM3HOW 4LW4YS M4K3S M3 S4D >:[
TA: ok well toniight2 not about fun, thii2 ii2 2eriiou2.
TA: deliiriiou2ly 2o.
TA: we are iin 2meariiou2 2hiit2taiin ciity.
GC: SCR3W YOU 4ND YOUR SH1TST41NS
GC: 1 W1LL H4V3 4 FUCK1NG BL4ST 4ND YOU C4NT STOP M3
GC: BLU3 T34M 2222222CUM >:]
TA: oh 2h11t 11t2 onnnnnn 2uck4.

What Terezi probably means to say is, it makes her sad to talk to Aradia ever since Vriska mind-controlled Sollux into murdering Aradia with his eye beams and turned her into a depressed ghost. That's probably a pretty awkward fact to bring up, though. Come to think of it, as of this moment, I don't actually remember who is currently aware that Aradia is a ghost? Equius is, because he's building a robot body for her. Vriska PROBABLY is, because she killed her. But I believe everyone else is under the impression that she just...showed up again online after her "accident," and therefore survived somehow. INCLUDING Sollux, who was the triggerman, and Terezi, who maimed Vriska in revenge for this act. This is going to remain my recollection of the facts until the story corrects me on any of this.

That...

Ok that was completely meaningless. What was the point?

Whoever you are.

> Sollux: Deal with apocalypseArisen.

apocalypseArisen [AA] began trolling twinArmageddons [TA]

AA: did y0u set up the teams
TA: 2tiill workiing on iit but yeah more or le22.
TA: we 2hould all be playiing 2oon.
TA: and ii gue22 leaviing thii2 diimen2iion.
TA: that ii2 what happen2, riight??
AA: yes
TA: 2o ii gue22 you 2hould be pretty happy when we fiinally get out of here?

It wasn't meaningless at all. She cleared off the frog torso so she can have a nice, flat surface to stand on when I eventually introduce her. Since becoming a ghost, she has vacated her hive, so she doesn't have the traditional bedroom environment for an intro like everyone else. The desecrated temple must suffice.

AA: i d0nt kn0w ab0ut that
TA: oh.
TA: wiill you at lea2t be able two leave the voiice2 behiind?
AA: i d0nt kn0w ab0ut that either
TA: ii2nt that kiind of depre22iing?
TA: the thought that they miight 2tay wiith you tiil you diie?
AA: n0t really
AA: im 0k with it
AA: im 0k with a l0t 0f things
AA: even 0ur inevitable failure
AA: th0ugh it will briefly masquerade as vict0ry
TA: wow FUCK.
TA: that wa2 2o much more depre22iing than the thiing ii ju2t 2aiid.
TA: terezii wa2 riight, you are 2uch a drag two talk two the2e day2.
AA: she was right ab0ut a l0t 0f things
TA: wow what a my2teriiou2 thiing two 2ay, ii am 2o iintriigued.
TA: do me a favor and 2pare me your 2pooky conundrum2 twoniight, youre kiind of pii22iing me off.
AA: but y0u like t0 talk t0 me
AA: this a fact n0t a questi0n
AA: they t0ld me
TA: oh your 2ource2 have 2poken!
TA: relay a me22age for me, tell them two go haunt my huge creakiing bone bulge.
AA: why d0 y0u like t0 talk t0 me
TA: oh ii dont know, maybe becau2e we are 2uppo2ed two 2ave the world twogether???
TA: ii al2o talk two you becau2e iin ca2e you havent notiiced ii de2pii2e my2elf and perpetually 2eek two dupliicate through emotiional paiin the cacophony of phy2iical paiin my hiideou2 mutant braiin cau2e2 me every day.
TA: oh my god ii ju2t had a breakthrough!!!
TA: thank you 2o much for thii2, iit wa2 great.
TA: that wa2 a joke, here type "ha".
AA: ha
TA: now type iit agaiin.
AA: ha
TA: there you go, you are now offiiciially the liife of the party.
TA: eheheh ii ju2t took an embarra22iing viideo of you cuttiing loo2e there, boy ii 2ure hope thii2 juiicy nugget doe2nt wiind up on the iinternet!
AA: 0_0
AA: s0llux i actually w0uld like it if you were happy
TA: ok. thank you for 2ayiing 2o.

This broad is a stone-cold bummer, folks. She knows many things in advance of the session, making her sort of the wet blanket Jade of the party (until Kanaya, the troll with jade blood, turns out to be an even Jadier Jade of the party). But instead of getting her visions from clouds, Aradia gets them from ghosts, who she can commune with. Also her foreknowledge of the session appears to be nearly exhaustive, including knowledge of their ultimate failure. Maybe if Jade knew her session was doomed from the start, she wouldn't be quite so chipper?? Aradia even understands their failure will "briefly masquerade as victory," which is absolutely right. This was an easy thing to foreshadow though, because I knew two big facts in advance. First, the trolls must "win," because the kids' universe exists, and the trolls created it. Second, something must have gone wrong, because the trolls ended up getting trapped in some vague purgatory state, from which Karkat decided it would be a good idea to uselessly harass the human kids. Unraveling how all this happened and why is what Hivebent is about. But at this moment in the story, we don't even know the first point above. Really, it's kind of wild how little we actually know about this story while we're all caught in the ongoing process of being confused by it.

AA: y0u seem sad and angry all the time
AA: what d0es anger feel like
AA: i f0rg0t
TA: have you ever been angry?
TA: ii dont remember you gettiing angry about anythiing.
AA: maybe i never was
AA: i feel like i was th0ugh
AA: 0nce
TA: why dont you a2k karkat, he2 way angriier than me.
TA: for that matter why dont you get on HII2 ca2e about iit iin2tead of MIINE.
AA: i think his anger serves a greater purp0se
AA: its part 0f his destiny and thus 0urs
AA: it will help him t0 sab0tage his 0wn designs
AA: which are very much in 0pp0siti0n t0 the br0ader purp0se
AA: and will s0w the seeds 0f 0ur failure
AA: a failure which will ir0nically pr0ve t0 be missi0n critical
TA: iif you thiink we are goiing two faiil why wouldnt you get mad about that?
TA: at the voiice2 2endiing you down thii2 bliind alley the whole tiime?
AA: they never lied th0ugh
AA: this is h0w it had t0 be
AA: i have t0 be t0tally h0nest
AA: th0ugh at n0 p0int did i ever lie
AA: but thr0ugh 0missi0n
AA: this game will n0t save the w0rld
TA: the fuck??
AA: and th0ugh it is still very imp0rtant even in 0ur defeat
AA: unf0rtantely it is much cl0ser t0 serving as the instrument 0f 0ur pe0ples demise than that 0f their salvati0n
AA: and we twelve will behave simultane0usly as the pawns and the 0rchestrat0rs of the great und0ing
TA: ii dont want two play anymore then.
AA: y0u will th0ugh
TA: fuck that ju2t watch, thii2 2hiit ii2 du2ted.
TA: check me out, all du2tiing iit liike a 2aucy fuckiin maiid.
AA: it cann0t be st0pped
AA: mete0rs are en r0ute
AA: y0u kn0w this s0llux
TA: who care2, iim yankiing the grubtube on thii2 overpunctured biitch.
TA: iim telliing red team leader two forget the whole thiing.
TA: iim quiittiing a2 blue team leader.
TA: iif you want two 2hamble through thii2 macabre fanta2y of your2 2olo be my gue2t.

Aradia did get mad once. At Vriska, for bullying Tavros. The rest was history. There are other key allusions here, because...there just always are. Like the Great Undoing, referenced now and then throughout Act 5. (That's just when a big old frog dies in **Cascade**.) Aradia talks about lies of omission, which is very much a Doc Scratch thing, his key method of manipulation. It's hard to overstate just how much of everything that happens traces back to his direct orchestration. Recall that he (creepily) raised Aradia's ancestor since she was a grub, and trained her to do his dirty work as the Handmaid. Aradia unwittingly follows in her footsteps with stunts like this.

AA: y0u were never g0ing t0 be the team leader th0ugh
AA: which is t0 say
AA: the first t0 enter
TA: are you me22iing wiith me??
TA: you do realiize iim p2ychiic two.
TA: ii could pull 2o much triippy 2hiit out of my 2piinal creviice, iit would make your head 2piin liike dervii2h iin a fuckiing blender.
TA: 2o GET OFF YOUR HIIGH HOOFBEA2T.
AA: im c0ming up
TA: huh???
TA: up where.
TA: hello??????????????

> Sollux: Abort.

twinArmageddons [TA] began trolling gallowsCalibrator [GC]

TA: hey change of plan, we arent playiing thii2 game anymore.
TA: you dont have two bother recruiitiing, 2orry two wa2te your tiime.
GC: 1M NOT TH3 L34D3R 4NYMOR3
GC: K4RK4T 1S
TA: he ii2?
GC: H3 THR3W 4 T4NTRUM 4BOUT 1T SO 1 L3T H1M B3 TH3 R3D L34D3R

Aradia just means she's gonna stop sulking in her frog hole, come up from the caverns, and put Sollux to sleep so he can't cause trouble. He has fully served his purpose, having programmed the game and gotten the two teams rolling. She now recognizes he will be completely useless until they have entered the session, so he might as well take a long nap. This pathetic situation is a microcosm of Sollux's entire role in the story.

TA: ok that wa2 faiirly prediictable but that2 fiine.
TA: iill talk two hiim about iit.
GC: WH4TS GO1NG ON?
TA: nothiing, thii2 game 2uck2 and aa ii2 full of crap.
TA: 2orry about all thii2.
GC: >:?

twinArmageddons [TA] **began trolling** carcinoGeneticist [CG]

TA: hey change of plan, we arent playiing thii2 game anymore.
CG: HEY.
CG: GUESS WHO THE RED LEADER IS?
CG: I'M THE LEADER. IT'S ME.
CG: YOUR PLAN TO CRIPPLE YOUR RIVAL TEAM HAS FAILED.
TA: ii know, 2he told me, ii dont care.
TA: the game ii2 bad new2, iit wiill cau2e the end of the world, not 2top iit.
TA: 2o forget iit, ju2t go back two whatever you were doiing.
TA: wriitiing your 2hiitty code or whatever.
CG: HAHAHA! SO PATHETIC.
CG: THIS IS YET ANOTHER FEEBLE ATTEMPT TO WEAKEN YOUR OPPOSITION.
CG: TEREZI AND I HAVE ALREADY ESTABLISHED A CONNECTION AND WE ARE MAKING GREAT PROGRESS HERE.
CG: WE ARE A GREAT TEAM, AND I AM A FANTASTIC LEADER.
CG: WE WILL BEAT THIS GAME IN NO TIME, WHILE YOUR TEAM IS CLEARLY STILL ASLEEP AT THE THORAX.
TA: oh god.
TA: no you iidiiot, ii dont care about the game anymore.
TA: ii ju2t quiit, iim not playiing, you 2hould two.
CG: AMAZING.
CG: YOU'RE EITHER BEING REALLY PERSISTENT WITH THIS TRANSPARENT RUSE, OR YOU REALLY ARE JUST THAT SAD AND INCOMPETENT.
CG: NEITHER CASE DESERVES MY RESPECT OR MY FRIENDSHIP.
CG: IN FACT, YOU KNOW WHAT, FRIENDSHIP CANCELED.
CG: THERE IT'S OFFICIAL, BYE BYE FRIENDSHIP!
TA: oh liike you havent 2aiid that liike a biilliion tiime2.
TA: you arent iin any po2iitiion two que2tiion my competence.

"TEREZI AND I HAVE ALREADY ESTABLISHED A CONNECTION AND WE ARE MAKING GREAT PROGRESS HERE" is really an incredibly funny line, consdering we've already observed their "progress." It's unlikely that Karkat will ever mention the toilet incident to anyone. Another thing to note here is that, in a ridiculous way, this conversation actually demonstrates what good friends Karkat and Sollux really are BECAUSE of how often they apparently friend-dump each other, not in spite of it. That's how you know they're solid best bros, instead of kind of shitty, shallow, fake best bros like Karkat and Gamzee are. But that's much more of a Gamzee problem than a Karkat problem, isn't it.

TA: youre the wor2t programmer iive ever 2een, you dont know anythiing about computer2, why do you bother.
TA: the only thiing youre good at ii2 yelliing and makiing huge mii2take2.
TA: and beiing UGLY AND HORRIIBLE IN EVERY WAY, AND HAVIING 2TUPIID LIITTLE NUBBY HORN2.
CG: TO BE HONEST I DON'T SEE WHAT'S SO GREAT ABOUT YOUR PROGRAMMING OR HACKING.
CG: WHAT IS A HACKER EVEN? JUST SOME SMUG ASSHOLE IN MOVIES DOING FAKE THINGS AND MAKING UP WORDS.
CG: IT'S NOT EVEN A REAL THING TO BE, IT'S JUST SOME BULLSHIT TITLE YOU GAVE YOURSELF SO YOU CAN FEEL JUST A TINY BIT LESS LOATHESOME.
TA: oh no, more chiildii2h burn2, ii dont have two prove anythiing two you, iim a great hacker, periiod.
CG: NO IT'S ALL SO CLEAR NOW, YOU WERE A FRAUD ALL ALONG.
CG: WHAT DOES ALL THIS NONSENSICAL CODE YOU WROTE EVEN DO?
CG: IT'S ALL NONSENSE.
CG: LIKE A BLUFF. YOU JUST SAY, OH KARKAT WILL NEVER UNDERSTAND WHAT I WROTE IS BULLSHIT BECAUSE HE'S TOO DUMB TO FIGURE IT OUT.
CG: WELL YOU'RE BUSTED, THESE VIRUSES HERE I BET DO NOTHING AT ALL.
TA: waiit, KK...
CG: I BET IF I RAN THEM NOTHING BAD WOULD HAPPEN.
CG: MIGHT EVEN IMPROVE MY COMPUTER'S PERFORMANCE!
TA: no don't.
CG: HOW ABOUT THIS IDIOTIC PROGRAM WITH THE RED AND BLUE CODE, WHICH IS A MEANINGLESS THING TO DO WITH CODE ANYWAY.
CG: WHAT DOES THAT EVEN MEAN? IT'S ANOTHER ONE OF YOUR SCAMS.
CG: WHY NOT SNEAK SOME BAD CLIP ART INTO THE FILES TOO, AND PRETEND THAT'S CODE???
TA: oh god, no dont run that, iim 2eriiou2.
CG: WHAT WOULD HAPPEN?
TA: iim not 2ure, but iit would be really, really bad iif you ran iit, ju2t dont.
CG: AH HA. JUST AS I THOUGHT, YOU CAN'T EVEN COME UP WITH A GOOD LIE WHEN I PRESS YOU ON IT.
CG: YOUR BLUFF HAS BEEN CALLED.
CG: COMPILING AS WE SPEAK, IT WILL AUTORUN WHEN IT FINISHES.
CG: AND NOW I HAVE TO GO ATTEND TO SOMETHING OUTSIDE, BECAUSE TEREZI IS DOING SOMETHING JUST UNSPEAKABLY STUPID RIGHT NOW.
CG: WHOOPS, FORGET I SAID THAT. IT WAS PRIVILEGED INFORMATION.
TA: you are the dumbe2t grubfucker on the planet, ii 2wear.
CG: LATER DOUCHE BAG.
TA: KK DO NOT RUN THAT CODE.
TA: hello?????????????

carcinoGeneticist's [CG'S] **computer exploded.**

TA: oh my god.

Trollian is impressively versatile software. For example, it can tell you if your buddy's computer exploded. If you want to know how it actually does this, I'm sorry, but I don't think I have an explanation. Gonna drop a truth bomb on your lap, heads up: it makes no sense and strains credulity. Oh, also Trollian can let you talk to people in the future too? That feature is KIND of cool. I GUESS.

You are highly startled by the totally unexpected explosion.

Karkat and his friends and everyone they would ever meet thereafter would experience great misfortune on account of the curse unwittingly implemented through Sollux's esoteric MOBIUS DOUBLE REACHAROUND VIRUS.

Every troll's lusus would soon die. All but one of their kernelsprites would be prototyped with a dead lusus, each prior to entering the Medium. Upon entry, they would each have a bittersweet reunion with the creature after the kernel hatched, triggering the sprite's metamorphosis. For the first time, the trolls would be able to have verbal conversations with their custodians, and would be guided by them along their journeys.

Unfortunately, the underlings and warring royalty would gain the benefits of the monstrous prototypings as well. Each sprite, except for one, would only be prototyped once. The players would learn quickly that while one pre-entry prototyping per player was absolutely necessary for ultimate success, additional pre-entry prototypings merely empowered their enemies unnecessarily.

The notion that this virus cursed them all is pretty questionable. Being experts in the ways of Paradox Space as we all are, we know these tough-luck children are screwed no matter what. The fact that a cursed virus was run at the onset of their journey is probably more of an inauspicious coincidence. Which maybe in a very practical sense is the definition of bad luck?

The game has no explicit rule that demands something dead for prototyping. But in practice, the kernelsprite has particular attraction to the deceased or the doomed. Across every session ever played, exceptions to this pattern are extremely rare.

> Sollux: Lament.

Why did you send Karkat that code? It was such a bad idea. You suppose it was a boastful gesture to get a friend to think more highly of you. But why would flaunting your superior skills accomplish this? It was foolish.

You ought to wipe all these clever viruses you wrote off your computer. They can only bring more trouble.

> Sollux: Delete.

All the trolls' custodians die and become their sprites. This was a swift way of learning a lot about how their session went. Much can be derived from this, including the fact that by the time all the trolls are in the session, the combined prototypings must result in a monstrous combination of features, and the black king they'd ultimately have to defeat would be an insane freakshow of an end boss. It also suggests a lot of probably quite entertaining and heartfelt scenes we never get to see. Such as trolls reuniting with their dead lusii, and getting to speak to the mute parental monsters for the first time ever. Karkat + Crabdad was a tearjerker, no doubt. Same with Terezi and her dragon, who she never met at all as the dragon egg remained unhatched during her lifetime. Tavros and Tinkerbull? Absolute waterworks, trust me. The only one that sucked was Gamzee's reunion with Goatdad. It was complete garbage.

```
$ rm -rf viiru22e2
$ rm -rf moreviiru22e2
$ rm -rf reallybadviiru22e2
$ rm -rf omgholy2hiitneverevercompiilethe2e
$ rm -rf weak2auceviiru22e2
$ vii unhackable.~ath

import universe U;
~
~
~ATH(U) {
~
} EXECUTE(   );
~
THIS.DIE();
~
~
~
```

While deleting your virus folders, you pause on one oddball file you have lying around.

You did not write this virus. You copied it from an obscure server, far beyond your planet's global network. This application is running on that server perpetually.

It is an extremely simple ~ATH program. Its main loop is tied to the lifespan of the universe. When the universe dies, a mysterious subprogram will be executed. You have no way of knowing what that subprogram does. It runs on a protected part of the server. It is completely unhackable.

You delete the file, but it won't do much good. The program is already running elsewhere. Luckily, whatever harm it will do will not be done for many billions of years. And even then, what harm could a virus do after the expiration of the universe? This file always struck you as quite odd.

But Sollux, even with his vision twofold, does not have the perceptional luxuries of our vision omnipresent.

When executed, the subprogram will summon an indestructible demon into the recently voided universe. This monstrous being with the power to travel through time is inconvenienced very little by his arrival upon THE GREAT UNDOING. He has the entire cadaver of the expired universe to pick apart at his whim. From its birth through its swelling maturity and tapering decay. In a reality he is known to have marked for predation, he will go about assembling followers through various epochs, even going as far as personally establishing the parameters for his future summoning.

Sollux couldn't know that the virus is essentially a formality.

The demon is already here.

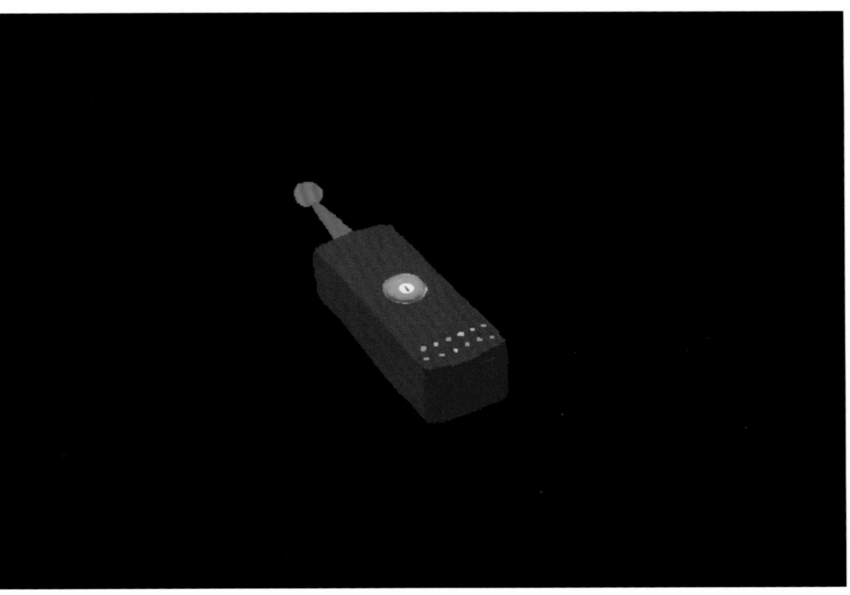

Is this the first use of the "already here" refrain for Lord English? I don't remember if it came up in the Intermission. Anyway, here it is again, if so. Maybe the CATCHPHRASE ITSELF was already here? Maybe it's always been here. The very concept of already being here was already here, and always will be already here. That baloney notwithstanding: the text above refers to English as a demon, but we're not stupid. We recognize the pool ball motif from the Intermission, so we immediately perceive this as being in reference to the summoning of Lord English. Just dragging more bits of lore from the Intermission into the main narrative, thus making it incrementally less irrelevant than we once foolishly assumed.

Sounds like your lusus is agitated about something up there. You already gave him his serving of honey today. If he thinks he can get more, well that's just greedy.

You wonder what could be bothering him?

You keep your enormous BICYCLOPS chained to the roof of your COMMUNAL HIVE STEM. It is the only place there is room for him. Dueling with him on the roof during feeding time is a daily ordeal.

> Be the other girl.

The communal hive stem was an Alternian concept I came up with as an analogue to highrise architecture on Earth. The way it works is, some authority (probably a bunch of drones or something) zones an area for these stems and builds a lot of them. They're completely blank edifices at first, but as lusii bring young trolls they've recently united with from the caverns, they climb the stems and build new apartment-like hives clinging to the sides... Hey, Aradia's here. But there's no time to see what she's up to, because we need to whiplash to another scene change so we can be Kanaya.

You are now one of the five other girls.

Technically we're now Kanaya. But she's not been introduced yet, so we don't know that's her name. So let's pretend we still don't. This scene is more about reminding folks she exists. We'd made it this far with nary a mention of her, so it was about time to say, hey remember this character? It's another instance where we can glean a lot just by visuals alone. She's got a rad chainsaw. All we had to go on before was a lot of snippy dialogue with Rose, which barely told us anything about her. We didn't know she had a sick chainsaw, but now we do, so that's cool.

She also (wow, this is a lot of info...) lives in a desert and has a floating grub lusus. (That's gotta be a mother grub, right? Yes, it is.) She likes putting colorful crap on things. Unlike the other trolls, she goes out during the day. She lives in a carbon copy of Jade's house. This implies that Jade's house is a universally available model to be salvaged from *Sburb* ruins and constructed, which is what Grandpa must have done. And (per the panel on next page) she has her own set of frog ruins, buried in the sand next to her Jade-like house, along with what appears to be the top of a volcano, also buried deep in sand, and also echoing Jade's setup. The sight of red ruins clues us into the fact that this planet has two distinct set of ruins, with six orbiting planets each. This makes sense to us now that we're well versed in the red/blue team logic of this arc, each team with six players. In fact, the presence of blue ruins with six planets made it possible to guess that similar red ruins existed somewhere else for this reason (and I'm sure this was correctly predicted by some people). Also, the sand has the same crazy color scheme as the desert we saw SS in during the Intermission, making it EXTRA obvious this is taking place on the same planet (though the green and pink moons orbiting Alternia already made that obvious).

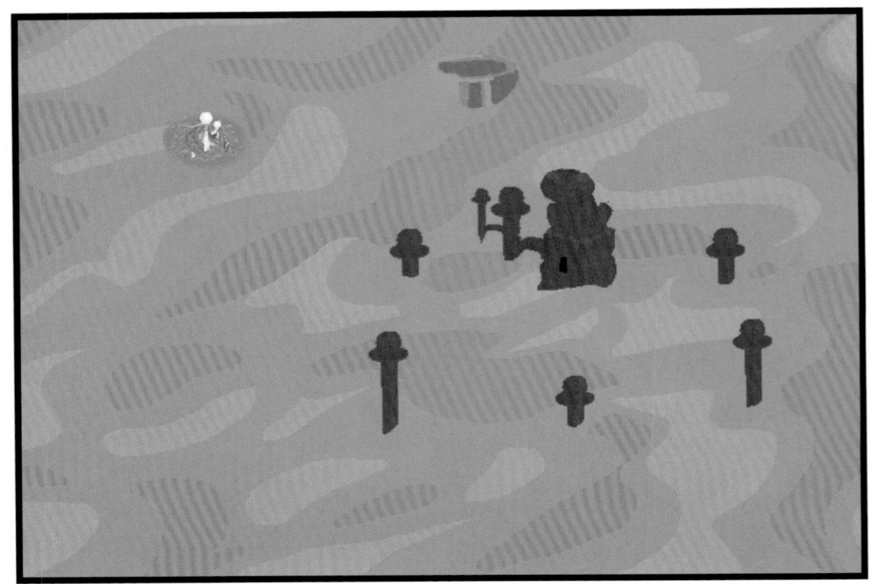

> Stop being the other girl.

You are now no longer the other girl, or any of the other five for that matter.

What's the name of this dude sitting in his FOUR WHEEL DEVICE?

> Enter name.

And just like that, we stop being Kanaya and start being another troll we already met in Act 4 (we were wondering when we'd get around to him), except this time there will actually be an introduction. Also, it should be noted that we aren't *that* excited about this intro, because the dude kinda sucks. Okay, just pulling your chain, Tavros has his fans. You know who you are out there. I mean, he's fine. You can't make a lot of good characters unless you have a few bad ones to provide foils for the good ones, to show by contrast how good they are compared to the lame ones. On the subject of bad characters designed to be shitty foils for good ones, be sure to pay special attention to all the fairy troll posters and wallpaper he's got around. This should wet our whistles for the best character of all, who should be coming up soon. So be strong, be brave, as you soldier through the Tavros Badlands. Things will get better soon, I promise.

Your name is TAVROS NITRAM.

You are known to be heavily arrested by FAIRY TALES AND FANTASY STORIES. You have an acute ability to COMMUNE WITH THE MANY CREATURES OF ALTERNIA, a skill you have utilized to CAPTURE AND TRAIN a great many. They are all your friends, as well as your warriors, which you pit in battle through a variety of related CARD AND ROLE PLAYING GAMES. You used to engage in various forms of MORE EXTREME ROLEPLAYING with some of your other friends before you had an accident.

You like to engage in the noble practice of ALTERNIAN SLAM POETRY, possibly the oldest, most revered, and certainly freshest artform in your planet's rich history. You have a profound fascination with the concept of FLIGHT, and all lore surrounding the topic. You believe in FAIRIES, even though they AREN'T REAL.

Your trolltag is adiosToreador and you uHH, sPEAK IN A SORT OF, uHH, fALTERING MANNER,

What will you do?

> Tavros: Cut to the chase and play card games immediately.

First, this is critical confirmation of something that fandom WILLED into the story, which is that Tavros is in a wheelchair. And the way he got into the wheelchair fueled some important and dramatic backstory, which helped shape the best character's development. So if may I say: good job, fans, for crippling this kid and thereby allowing Vriska to realize her true potential. It would be pretty great if I spent Tavros's entire intro talking up how great Vriska is. In fact, I'd almost consider it authorial malpractice not to.

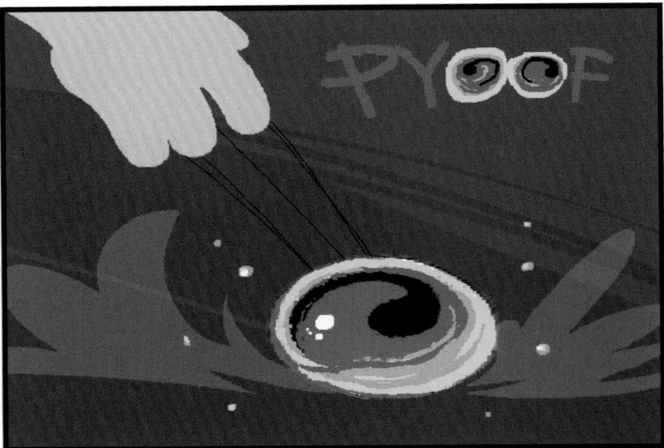

You kickstart a rousing match of FIDUSPAWN, with the only friend you've got to play with in person, your loyal lusus TINKERBULL.

You take a look at the favorable hand you dealt yourself and crack a mischievous smile. With a HOST PLUSH at the ready, you quickly lob an OOGONIBOMB and catch your adversary off guard!!!

Tavros is basically a goofy nerd kid who just likes goofy nerd kid games. Like this fucked-up alien version of *Pokémon*. It's a little more complicated and biologically rigorous than *Pokémon* though, and therefore summoning your creature friend/warrior is a slower process. You have to factor gestation time into your battle strategy. It's doubtful Vriska would mess around with a soft kiddie game like this. She only deals in the hard stuff, like Flarp, and almost certainly bullied Tavros into doing the same. Before his accident, of course.

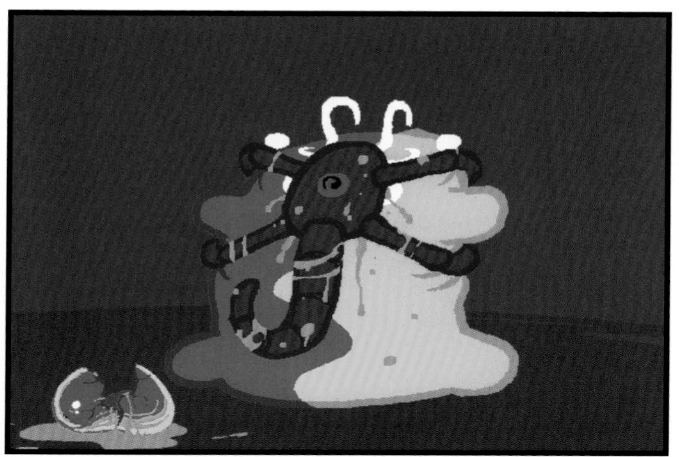

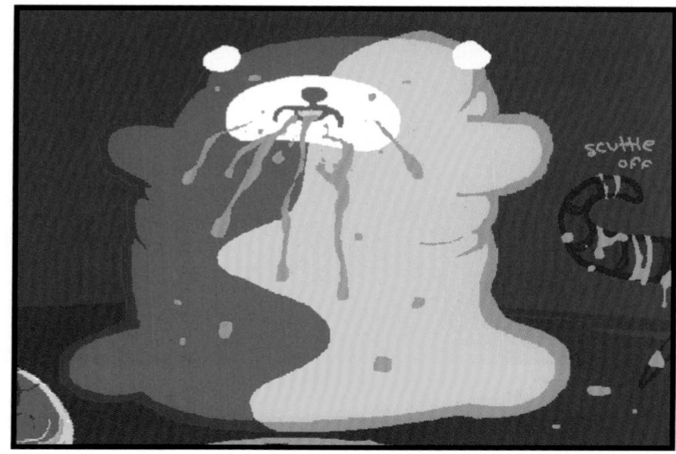

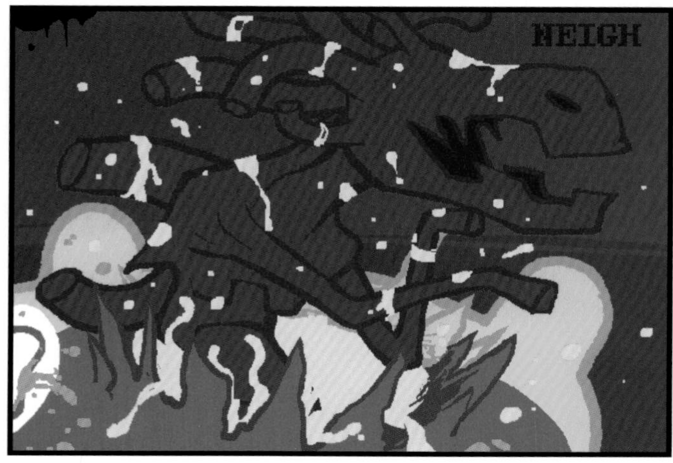

HORSARONI, I CHOOSE YOU!!!!!!

> Tavros: Command faithful steed.

Do I have to say that this references the *Alien* film franchise? Chalk this up as one more reference that I once believed to be so universally recognizable it could go without saying but now am wondering if it actually *does* go without saying, because I just don't know what the touchstones are anymore with the kids today. Anyway, that is what the referance (sic) here. Horsaroni is a respectable choice. Vriska would choose a beast that would turn this sucker into horse meat.

With a brooding whinny, Horsaroni shuffles his mighty hooves and makes short work of the fidusucker, boosting his vitals!

Horsaroni is now primed and raring for battle. Look out Tinkerbull!!!

> Tavros: Horsaroni: Spawntech -> Slumberbuddies.

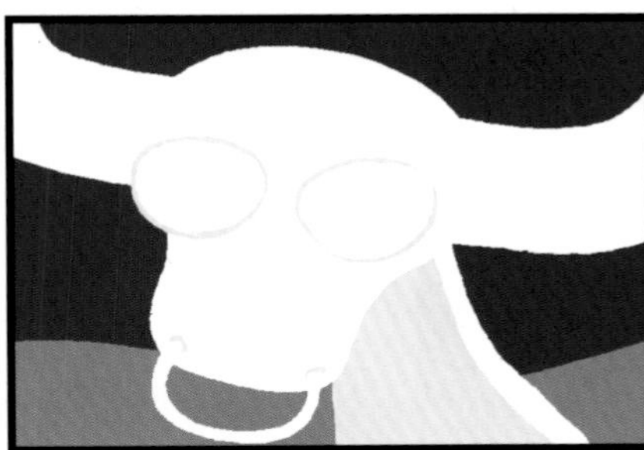

You use your awesome bestial communion abilities and bend the ferocious stallion to your whim. Tinkerbull can't stand the suspense!

This, frankly, is a bit gross. How about we just kick off Tavros's intro with a ton of graphically unpleasant gooey alien shit? Why not. It also establishes his animal communion power, which, to be fair, is a pretty good justification for playing *Fiduspawn*, no matter how lame Vriska thinks it is. Could it be the game of choice for many brown bloods, who also happen to have this ability? No wonder she prefers to pull Tavros into a game that grants her powers a major advantage, rather than his. Wow, she is so smart.

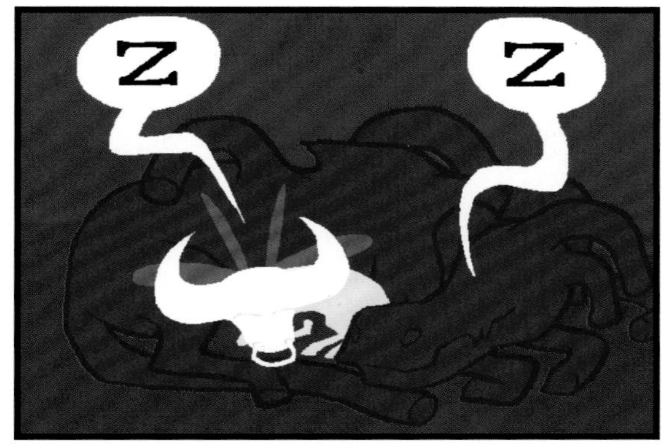

Nap time!

Everybody wins. Horsaroni gains a bunch of levels. In no time he will be ready to breed and you can put him out to stud.

Good game everybody. That was a lot of fun. Time to do some other stuff you guess.

> Tavros: Roll up your ramp.

This is how you get up to your recuperacoon when it's time to rest. It's kind of a production getting in and out.

> Tavros: Hop in.

Another instance of a psychic putting things to sleep. It keeps happening. The ramp up to his cocoon is a nice feature. Not exactly sure how that got installed. My guess? At some point, when Tavros was figuring out how to adjust to his new lifestyle, Vriska came over to sort of patch things up with him, and in a gesture of goodwill, built it for him. You know, after the accident. He's very lucky to have a friend like her.

You can't fit all the way in because of your huge horns. It makes it hard to get any solid shuteye.

Oh great, now you're covered in slime. Why did you do this? You're going to have to change your clothes. There goes another solid hour down the tubes.

Aw damn and there goes your four wheel device down the ramp. That happens a lot.

> Tavros: Take lance.

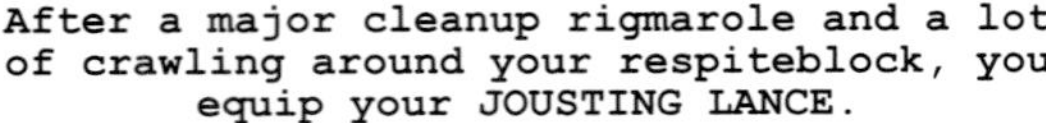
After a major cleanup rigmarole and a lot of crawling around your respiteblock, you equip your JOUSTING LANCE.

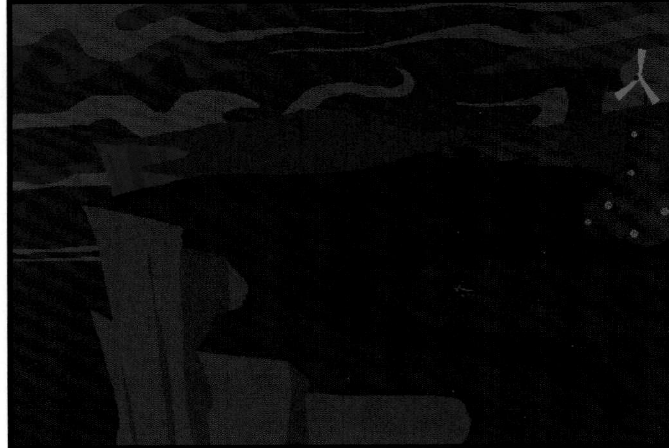

Here's some more incredible food for thought. Do you think Tavros wears a diaper? It's probably more convenient than rolling all the way upstairs to the load gaper. Wait, okay, I'm going to stop talking about this. But...who changes it? Tinkerbull? Tinkerbull might be too small and weak to manage. Oh, I know. I bet Vriska comes over to change it personally every month, because of what a good friend she is, and it's really the least she can do, after the accident. All right, NOW I will stop talking about this, before things start getting unseemly.

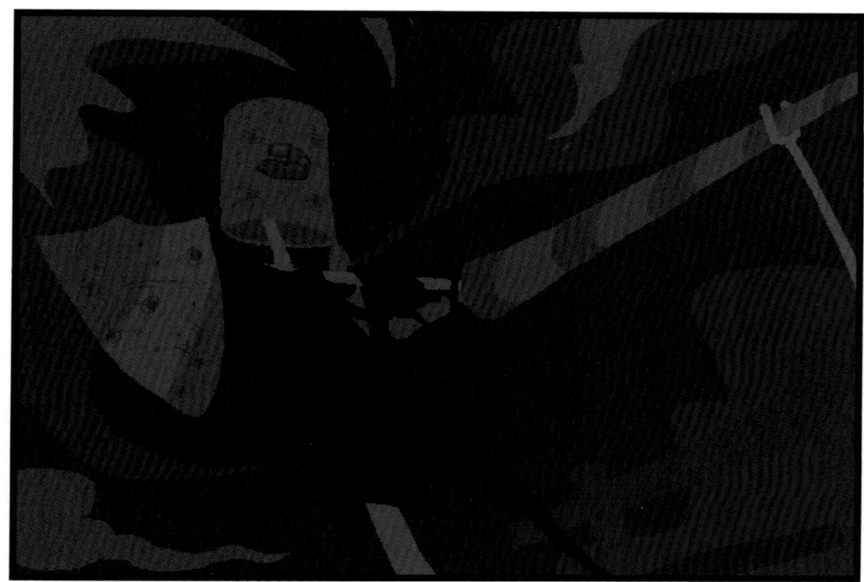

You like to practice your jousting outside. One day you hope to prove yourself worthy of recruitment into the halls of the dreaded imperial CAVALREAPERS. Assuming you are not slated for culling first on account of your disability. Or really any other arbitrary reason.

> Tavros: Admire posters.

You wheel over to your favorite poster featuring PUPA PAN, which is your favorite thing. You have always fantasized that one day intrepid young Pupa would come and take you away, and together you would fly to a beautiful paradise planet of legend, that has all sorts of fanciful stuff like pirates, treasure, a cruel villain with a missing arm and a missing eye, and these weird aliens called "indians". You have left your window open since you were very young, just in case Pupa stopped by one night and decided to splash a pinch of SPECIAL STARDUST in your face.

You have had this interest far prior to your accident. Being paralyzed isn't what made you want to be able to fly. That would be dumb and would make no sense.

Being paralyzed does sort of make you want to be able to walk, though.

> Way in the future...

The jousting dummy is just the same scarecrow WV had on the battlefield, flipped, recolored, and given a lance. Pff, you think I'm gonna DRAW A NEW THING? Dream on, fool. Also the fact that Tavros leaves his window open (i.e. permanently smashed open) on the off chance that a cute fairy girl will fly into his room one night is just about the saddest thing I've ever seen. I bet Vriska would think so too. It's also so unrealistic, from Vriska's point of view. Everyone knows a spider wouldn't venture out to the den of her prey. She'll wait in her own territory, spin a web, set a trap, and let him come to her.

Over the course of your long journey, at one point you were fitted with a cool pair of robolegs. The guy who likes to build robots built them for you.

But then, he does like to break them more than he likes to build them. It's usually why he builds them in the first place.

Occasionally though, he will allow philanthropy to override misanthrobopy.

You were lucky enough to have a friend who didn't mind getting her hands dirty on account of your best interest.

A friend with a chainsaw.

It's a good thing we had a brief snapshot intro to Kanaya a few pages ago, to show her with a chainsaw, so we could then reference it being used in this grisly albeit helpful way. In hindsight though, one wonders how much of this gesture was altruism and how much was just a convenient excuse to have access to a huge surge of fresh brown blood. If there's anyone who'd have a moral objection to this, it wouldn't be Equius, who's too creepy, and it wouldn't be Tavros, who's too stupid. Also, he'd probably be too busy screaming to even notice, having just had his legs chopped off.

The guy who likes to build robots just stood there and watched. It would always make everyone uncomfortable whenever he would just stand there.

And watch.

> And way back again...

But before that you had to scoot around in your wheel device throughout the various worlds of the Medium, and endure all sorts of follies related to your disability, which on account of their great plurality and marginal relevance we will not get to see. Just as well.

Wow, look what happens when you space out and contemplate the future like that. The messages start piling up.

> Tavros: Deal with AG.

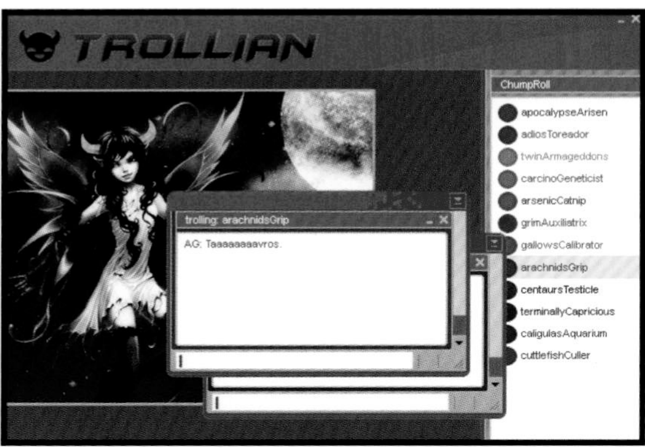

arachnidsGrip [AG] began trolling adiosToreador [AT]

AG: Taaaaaaaavros.
AT: hEY,
AG: Red team is going to 8ite the dust!
AG: And I know you are on the red team.
AT: wHOA, rEALLY,

Oh, here's Vriska. Thank God. We can finally stop tuning out everything Tavros is doing and start paying attention again, because someone important is talking. Wait, oh no. Gamzee is talking to him too. Christ. Okay, we'll have to put up with that bullshit soon as well, I guess. But let's enjoy these precious few nectarean drops of Serket-speak while we're crushingly sandwiched between two heavyweight buffoons.

AG: Yeah, you totally are.
AG: My team's got no use for a 8oy that can't make no use of his legs!
AG: You were f8ed for a team of losers, full of 8lind girls and lame 8oys and cranky iiiiiiim8eciles.
AG: ::::)
AT: oK, yOU'RE PROBABLY RIGHT ABOUT THAT,
AT: bUT i SHOULDN'T BE TALKING TO YOU,
AG: Oh????????
AT: i PROMISED I WOULDN'T TALK TO YOU ANYMORE,
AG: Whaaaaaaaat. Promised who?
AT: rUFIO,
AG: Omg, who's that????????
AG: I h8 this guy already!
AT: hE'S, uHH,
AT: oKAY,
AT: sOMEONE SAID i SHOULD GIVE MY SELF ESTEEM A NAME,
AT: aND TO BE CAREFUL ABOUT WHAT i SAY, tO MAKE SURE i DON'T HURT HIS FEELINGS,
AG: Haha! So he's imaginary! A fake.
AG: Like a made up friend, the way fairies are.
AG: Made up make believe fakey fake fakes.
AG: Who told you to do something so fraudulent?
AT: gA,
AT: bUT i DON'T KNOW IF SHE WAS JOKING ABOUT IT,
AT: iT MIGHT BE A JOKE, uHH, i DON'T KNOW, bUT i DID IT ANYWAY,
AG: Oh maaaaaaaan, what a meddler.
AG: I h8 her meddling! Why is she always meddling?
AG: I don't know if it was a joke, 8ut man.
AT: uH,
AG: I don't think it was a joke. It was more like........
AG: Ok, complete this analogy.
AG: Laughing is to a joke as meddling is to ....?
AT: uUHHH,
AG: Exactly! That's what she just did to you.
AG: It is worse than a joke. It is worse than anything you can do.
AG: Next time tell her to can it! That's what I do.
AG: But she keeps 8ugging me. 8ugging and fussing and meddling. What's her deal!
AG: I guess it's flattering that she wants to talk to me so much though. I guess I don't mind. It's cool.
AG: Anyway Tavros, you've been amazingly 8oring as usual, so I'm going to go.
AT: oKAY,
AG: This show needs to get on the freaking road.

Early Vriska kinda laid the Vriska on a little bit thick, didn't she. Can't say I blame her. Girl's gotta make an entrance, leave her mark. Tavros mentions here his fakey fake made up bullshit friend, Rufio, who he made up due to being some sort of loser, as Vriska wisely points out here. Rufio is the cool, older mohawked kid in the crappy '90s Peter Pan reboot, *Hook*. Although at this point I just know him as my buddy, the actor who played him, Dante Basco, who I only met because I decided to put him in the story as an imaginary friend. This fact is so preposterous, it's best not to think about it too much.

AG: 8elieve it or not, the 8lue team doesn't have a single player in the session yet!
AG: While you guys have like two or three or such!
AG: Un8elievable, I wonder what the holdup is. Oh well, let's face it! You guys need the head start.
AT: uHH,
AG: Ok, anyway, good luck to you. It will be just like old tiiiiiiiimes.
AG: ::::;)
AG: Adios, Toreasnore!!!!!!!!

arachnidsGrip [AG] ceased trolling adiosToreador [AT]

AT: bYE,

> Tavros: Rap with TC.

terminallyCapricious [TC] began trolling adiosToreador [AT]

TC: mOtHeRfUcK mY bRoThEr, Im So SoRrY i KiNd Of ZoNeD oUt ThErE.
AT: hI, tHAT'S OK.
AT: i WASN'T EXPECTING YOU TO NOT BE ZONED OUT FOR ANY REASON.
AT: sO i GUESS, i DON'T UNDERSTAND YOUR APOLOGY.
TC: AlRiGhT, fUcK yEaH, iT's AlL gOoD aNyWaY.

This is about as bad as it gets. Tavros talking to Gamzee, or if you will, the peanut butter and jelly duo. PB&J was a peak woobie ship, very popular among people who go in for that sort of thing, and probably was mostly fueled by this one pointless conversation they had. There are also credible indications that Gamzee has some sort of legitimate red feelings toward Tavros. They are innocent enough in contexts such as this. But later he expresses those feelings inappropriately, by passionately kissing Tavros's severed head.

TC: i JuSt ZoNeD oUt WhEn I wAs SuPpOsEd To Be AlL aBoUt BeInG tO tElL yOu YoU'rE aLl On My TeAm.
AT: uH, yEAH, tHE RED TEAM YOU MEAN,
TC: ShIt MoThErFuCkIn YeAh My WiCkEd MoThErFuCkEr!
TC: :o) hOnK hOnK hOnK
AT: oK, tHAT'S GREAT, i JUST HEARD ABOUT THIS,
AT: fROM SOMEONE i DON'T WANT TO TALK ABOUT,
AT: bUT IT STILL BASICALLY QUALIFIES AS GOOD NEWS,
TC: :o) HoNkHoNkHoNkHoNkHoNk
AT: }:o), hEH,
TC: hAhAh FuUuUuCk, YoU sToLe My FuCkIn NoSe BrO!
TC: WhAt GoT yOu EvEn Up ThE gUmPtIoN tO aLl FuCkIn Do ThE sHiT lIkE tHaT?
AT: eRR, i DON'T KNOW, iT'S JUST,
AT: kIND OF THE OBVIOUS THING TO DO,
AT: sTICK THE CIRCLE IN FRONT OF THE DOTS, aND, bEHIND THE BENDY ONE,
AT: pLUS, oH YEAH, mY HORNS,
TC: hAhAhAhA.
AT: mAYBE WE CAN SLAM ABOUT IT,
TC: YeAh, I cOuLd KiCk ThE sHiT oUt Of SoMe RhYmEs BrO.
TC: aLl StIr Up SoMe FuCkIn HeLl MiRtH aNd RiP oPeN a FuCkIn BaG oF hArShWhImSy.
AT: yEAHHH, yOU CAN TALK ABOUT THE CLOWN THINGS, wHICH,
AT: i DON'T REALLY UNDERSTAND EVER, bUT THAT'S OKAY,
AT: bECAUSE IT'S KIND OF FUNNY,
AT: wHEREAS, i'LL ADDRESS SOME TOPICS PERTAINING TO MY INTERESTS,
AT: aND i GUESS, pERSONAL MOTIFS,
TC: YeAh! FuCk YeAh, ThAt Be HoW sHiT's AlL uSuAlLy Up AnD fUcKiN lOcKeD bRo.
TC: bUt FiRsT hErE's ThE tHiNg WiTh ThE gAmE.
AT: oH YEAH, i ALMOST FORGOT, aBOUT,
AT: tHE RED TEAM GAME,
TC: YeAh Ok If I rEmEmBeR rIgHt ThIs Is HoW wE'rE jUgGlInG tHiS sHiT.
TC: lOt'S oF fUcKiN bAlLs In ThE aIr, HaHaHa.
TC: TeReZi CoNnEcTeD tO kArKaT, sO hE's FuCkIn ChIlL.
TC: tHeN i'M sUpPoSeD tO cOnNeCt To HeR sOoN tO gEt HeR aLl ChIlL tOo.
TC: BuT sHe'S iN tHe WoOdS dOiNg SoMeThInG.
TC: wHeN sHe CoMeS bAcK sHe StArTs PlAyInG.
TC: So In ThE mEaN mOtHeRfUcKiN tImE i'M sUpPoSeD tO gEt YoU tO cOnNeCt To Me.
TC: bUt I fUcKiN sPaCeD oUt AnD fOrGoT.
TC: BeCaUsE i GuEsS i WaS wAy ToO mOtHeRfUcKiN cHiLl AlL uP iN tHiS sHiT, hAhAhAhAhA!
AT: yEAH, i UNDERSTAND,
TC: sO jUsT dOwNlOaD tHiS mOtHeRfUcKeR i'M sEnDiNg YoU sO wE cAn KiCk ThIs BiTcH dOwN tHe StAiRs.

Gamzee's quirk was absolutely the worst one to apply to raw text. There's no basic shortcut like there are with others, involving search/replace functions on certain symbols. You have to brute force it, with alternate caps by hand. So maybe you'll take some solace in the fact that it was just as painful for me to type as it is for you to read. (Although later on, I started using a fan-made quirk conversion script, for Gamzee's lines specifically. Kanaya's too, which have a similarly unhackable quirk.)

AT: oKAY, i'LL DO THAT, aND,
AT: iN THE MEANTIME, sHALL i,
AT: cUE UP THE,
AT: sTRICT BEATS????? }:D
TC: AwWwWw BrOtHeR nOw YoU aLl FuCk AnD uP aNd DoNe It.
TC: yOu ArE fUcKiN wHeEl DeEp In A bIg SlOpPy MaSsAcRe PiE tOpPeD wItH mOtHeRfUcKiN wHiPpEd RhYmE.
TC: HoW sTrIcT aRe ThOsE bEaTs At, MoThErFuCkEr?
AT: wELL, i,
AT: tURNED UP THOSE BITCHES TO PRETTY STERN,
AT: sET BEATS TO LECTURE, aND, i'M KIND OF GOING HOG WILD ON THE CURMUDGEON KNOB,
AT: wHICH, i HAD RECENTLY INSTALLED,
TC: gOd DaMn!!!
TC: TeLl Me MoRe WhIlE i GeT mY rEaCh On FoR tHiS fRoStY bReW.
AT: oKAY,
AT: iMAGINE AN ARRAY OF BEATS THAT SET LIMITS,
AT: tHEY GOT A RULEBOOK, iT DOESN'T PAY TO SKIM IT,
AT: bECAUSE, tHERE'S NOT A LOT OF LATITUDE,
AT: tHEY WON'T STAND FOR AN ATTITUDE,
AT: aND, cROSSING THEM'S A HABIT YOU'D,
AT: (nOT REALLY WANT TO GET INTO BECAUSE, uHH),
AT: tHEY'D GET PRETTY MAD AT YOU,
TC: fUuUuCk, So FuCkIn FrEsH.
TC: YoU nEeD tO bE sLaPpEd FuCkIn SiLlY wItH a MoUtH lIkE tHaT! hAhA.
AT: aND, iF YOU GOT A PROBLEM WITH IT,
AT: tHEN i SUGGEST YOU GO AND RAP IT DUDE,
TC: oK i WiLl.
TC: JuSt LeT mE sNeAk Up On ThIs BoTtLe Of FaYgO aNd SnAp ItS nEcK lIkE iM a FuCkIn LaUgHsSaSsIn.
TC: oK.
TC: ArE tHoSe BeAtS sTiLl ChIlL?
AT: yEAH,
TC: aRe ThEy MoThErFuCkIn StRiCt???
AT: yEAHHHHH,
TC: AiGhT.
TC: cRaCk......
TC: HiSsSsSsSsSsSs.
TC: mOtHeRfUcKiN kIcK iT!!!!!!!!!!!!!!!!!!

You both then proceed to have one of the worst rap-offs in the history of paradox space.

Almost every troll class has a special badass-sounding adult troll profession. Among those mentioned are: threshecutioners, cavalreapers, legislacerators, gamblignants, and probably a bunch of others that go unnamed by the story. Laughsassin is apparently one such career path for purple-blooded clownfolk. I don't know what laughsassins actually do. Probably kill lots of people? I just know that laughsassin is a very good word, and is just one more exhibition of impeccable worldbuilding on my part.

You make your way through the burning woods to meet the lusus you never had.

It's time for her to hatch. It's now or never.

Hero Mode Terezi's forest is on fire. She's Karkat's server player. John's server player was Rose. Rose's forest was also on fire when she had to skedaddle out of there and into the session. Are there more parallels? Yes. Let's look at the next page.

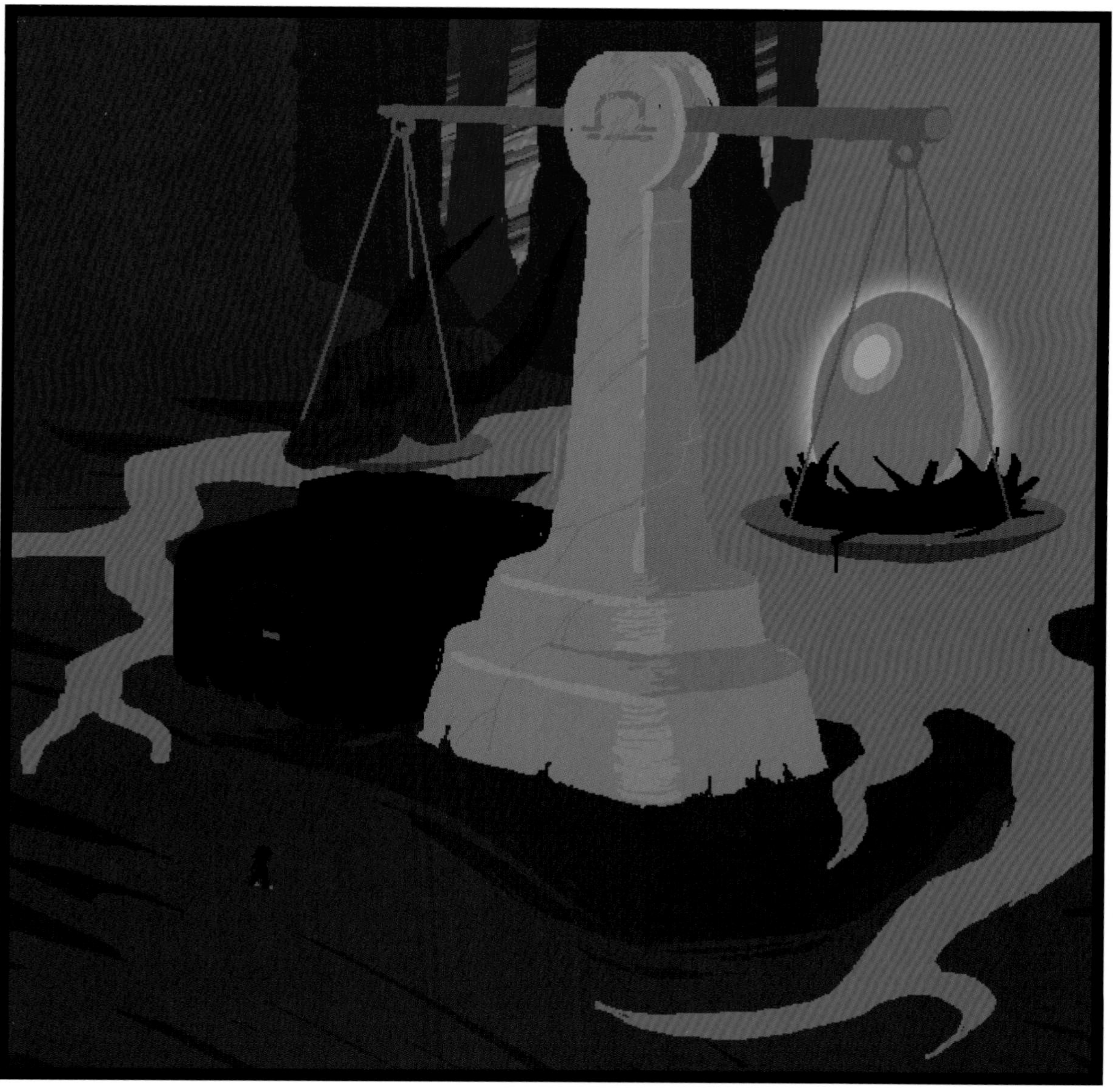

Since the world is about to end anyway, you suppose it no longer matters if the DOOMSDAY SCALE is tipped.

Re: more parallels, that egg there is the same graphic asset as the egg Dave needed to hatch to enter his session. It's a test of patience and resolve, involving the imposition of the need for the character to wait for their surroundings to become warm enough for the egg to hatch. In Dave's case, this entails meteors burning down his city. In this case, meteors burning down this forest. But for Terezi this is not a test of patience so much as a diabolical, fatalistic construction which acknowledges eons in advance that this egg will only hatch under the grimmest of circumstances. When the egg hatches, the baby dragon flies away, and the mother grub skull falls and pushes the doomsday button. Terezi always knew that getting to meet her lusus would coincide with the end of the world. She just didn't know why.

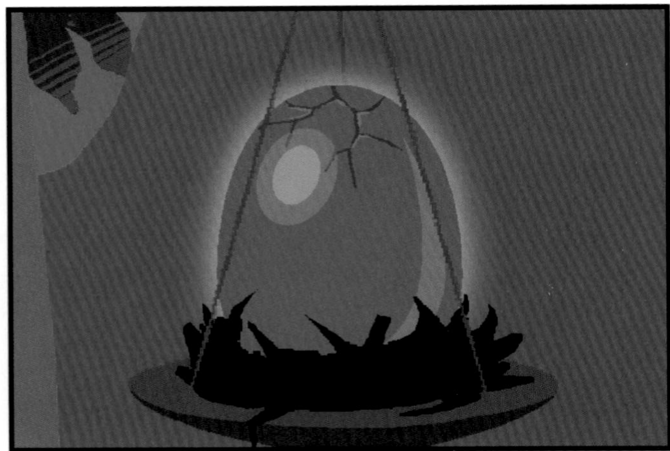

The counterweight is the skull of an ancient mother grub, slain thousands of solar sweeps ago.

The egg contains a rare species of dragon which remains blind until maturity, using its other senses to survive. It has balanced the skull here for millennia, waiting for the warmth of a meteor-sparked forest fire before hatching.

In case it wasn't clear, dragons are real.

While she slept in her egg, she would communicate with you in your sleep.

After your accident, she would use your dreams to teach you to detect the world around you without vision.

Here's some more mixed worldbuilding signals I'm sending. Do trolls sleep in the slime with their clothes on or not?? It's very possible Terezi is just weird and doesn't really care about sliming up her clothes. And here's something worth considering about this dragon egg: given that it's been sitting here for millennia...maybe it's her ancestor's dragon's egg? It's not the craziest point of speculation.

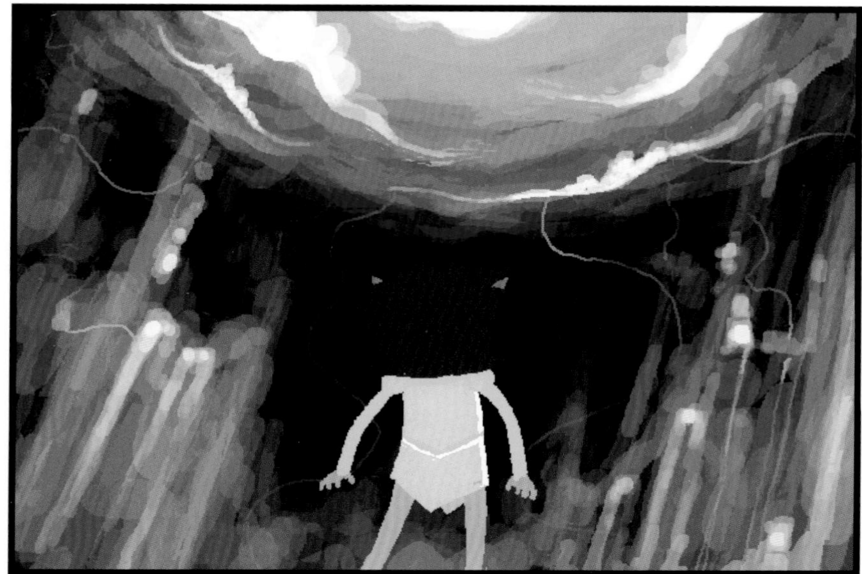

As you learned, your dreams became more vivid. Where before there was darkness, odors and flavors painted a striking picture. You found yourself surrounded by bright honey walls, and in the sky was a huge tasty ball of cotton candy, which is this sweet troll delicacy we wouldn't know anything about.

The first time you caught a glimpse of this world in your dreams, there was no turning back.

The young lusus would take to the sky and promptly get herself killed. This would be much more shocking and maybe a little bit more sad if we didn't already know it was going to happen.

We already knew this. But of course, you didn't.

Terezi's nose-vision needed a certain blurry style. I just used some reduced-opacity brushes to render it, and the same style shows up every now and then. Prospit and Derse are meant to provide good environments for players' various "awakening experiences," which are specific to their circumstances. So it makes some sense that Terezi starts exploring her new sensory abilities in conjunction with her dream self starting to become aware.

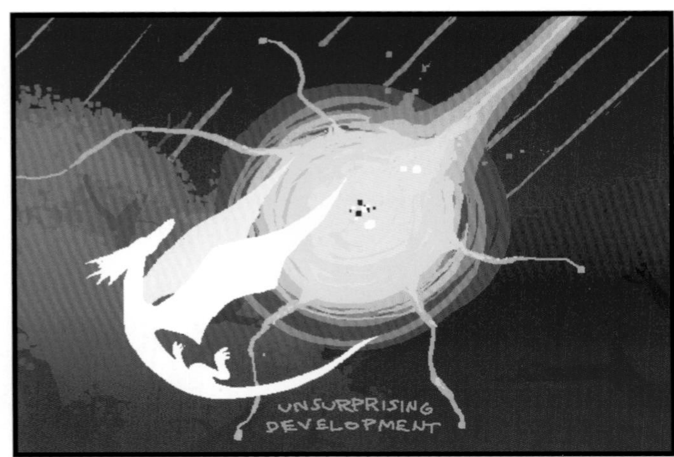

The dragon never smelled it coming.

She would fall to your treehive. On your return, she would be scooped up by a sympathetic ally and deposited into the kernelsprite.

Then you and she could talk! There would be plenty to discuss.

More great and very imaginative sound effects. "GENUINE" seems like maybe it's an unnecessary qualifier, until you consider that Terezi is so full of shit, many things she does could be considered ungenuine. So it pays to point out when she is sad for real, like when her newborn baby mom dies.

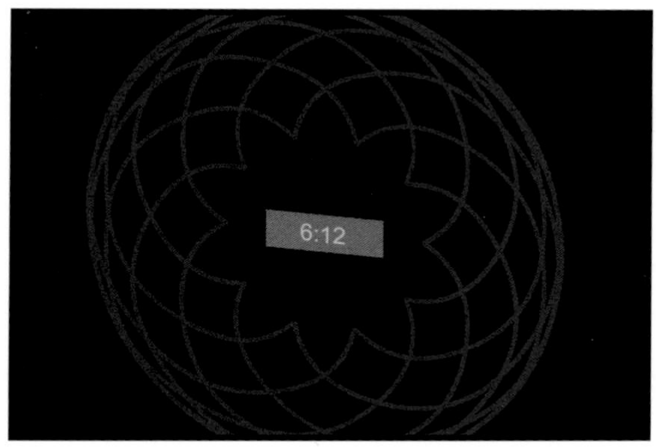

The doomsday device would display the amount of time you had to get back to your hive and enter the Medium before the forest was destroyed.

At the time, it wouldn't occur to you to wonder whether the device was directly responsible for the apocalypse, or merely served as its precisely calibrated harbinger. And it certainly wouldn't occur to you to cast doubt on any perceived difference between those two things.

It wouldn't until later, when you better understood the game you were about to play.

> Be the other other girl.

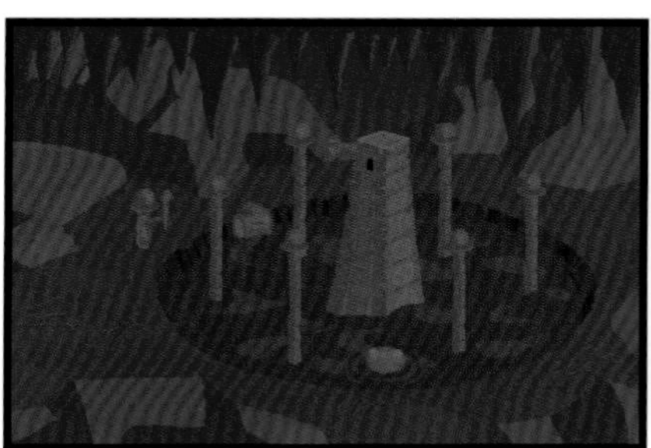

You are now the other other girl.

> Render the girl in a more symbolic manner.

That's better. We can now be properly introduced.

Who's this spooky lady?

> Enter name.

What the fuck is going on with her horns?

Your name is ARADIA MEGIDO.

You once had a number of INTERESTS, which in time you have LOST INTEREST IN. You seem to recollect once having a fondness for ARCHEOLOGY, though now have trouble recalling this passion. It nonetheless has led you to find your PRESENT CALLING, which came through the discovery of these MYSTIC RUINS on which you presently stand, and which you recently DESECRATED OUT OF BOREDOM.

Guiding you to this calling were the VOICES OF THE DEAD, which you have been able to hear since you were young. The voices have become louder as THE GREAT UNDOING approaches. This trend in escalation began after an ACCIDENT involving a CERTAIN KIND OF ROLE PLAYING, which might have been another of your interests once upon a time. It doesn't matter much anymore.

The accident resulted in the DEATH OF YOUR LUSUS, which prompted you to leave your home and take up these ruins as residence. On the instruction of your ANCESTORS, you have recovered MYSTERIOUS TECHNOLOGY from the ruins, and convinced a friend to adapt it into a GAME THAT WILL BRING ABOUT THE DESTRUCTION OF YOUR CIVILIZATION. And by convinced, you suppose you mean tricked.

He has tentatively named the game SGRUB, which is a word that is NOT TERRIBLY ELEGANT. If it were marketed by a legitimate game company instead of rapidly patched together by a young hacker, it would ostensibly be given a better title. He is presently mobilizing twelve friends to play it, including him and yourself. He believes he will lead the blue team. But he is wrong.

Your trolltag is apocalypseArisen and there is typically a pr0n0unced h0ll0wness t0 y0ur w0rds.

What will you do?

> Aradia: Retrieve computer.

The text mentions "ancestors" here pretty casually. This is before ancestors became more of a thing in troll lore. So for now the term appears to be used in the more generic sense, referring to a potentially very large group of nameless, faceless forebears whose ghosts Aradia is communing with. (It's still entirely possible that's what's going on here.) But with the context provided later on, it seems "ancestors" here is actually referencing twelve very specific individuals who are figures of legend in troll history. It's even more likely it's referencing one ancestor in particular: Aradia's, the Handmaid. The Handmaid was groomed by Doc Scratch to serve Lord English by traveling around time causing all kinds of trouble throughout history, specifically to bring about these events. So unlike the other ancestors, the Handmaid is the only one whose job was actually to make all this stuff happen, thus making her the most logical target of this reference. This being the case, it raises the question of how Aradia was receiving "instruction" from the Handmaid. She can commune with the dead, but...the Handmaid isn't dead. She was cursed with immortality for as long as she serves English, and can hop around through time. So does this mean she met with Aradia in person at some point to dispense orders? It's entirely possible. If it happened after Aradia's death, it would also mean Aradia wasn't communing with a dead ancestor to receive instructions. It means a living ancestor was communing with a dead Aradia to give instructions.

It's not up to you to decide what you retrieve from your sylladex. It's up to the spirits.

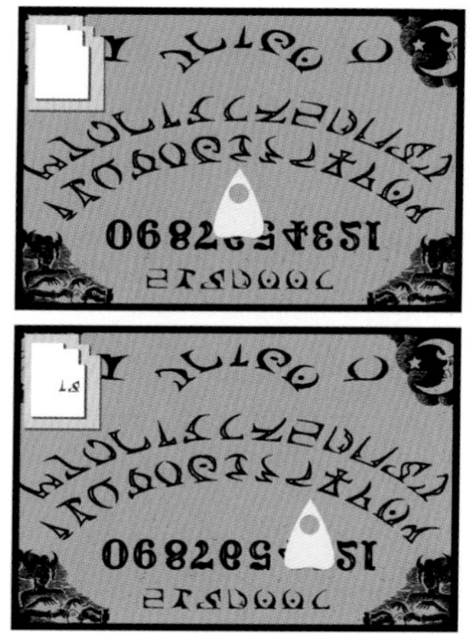

Looks like the spirits are being cooperative today, if a bit cryptic, as usual.

Since Aradia has telekinetic powers, I guess we'll just have to take her word for it that spirits are the ones moving the thing around, not her.

Who's this douchebag?

You found this baffling artifact some time ago on one of your digs. The creature on its facade is completely mystifying. You have taken to using it as your primary computing device on account of its bizarre novelty, as well as convenient portability.

Oh, look who's bothering you again.

She's always bugging you. Bugging and fussing and meddling. What's her deal! You guess it's flattering that she wants to talk to you so much though.

You're ok with it. You're ok with a lot of things.

> Aradia: Humor GA.

We've seen this ridiculously stupid laptop before. Spades Slick found it in the Felt mansion, which we later discovered was on postapocalypse Alternia. And now we see it here, which gives us a small piece of the puzzle to help figure out exactly how the hell this thing ended up here. Aradia found it on an archeological dig. Meaning it was brought here by a meteor, probably. Meaning it was in the troll session at one point. Now we need to look forward to an explanation of how it got to the troll session. Spoiler: it has something to do with the biggest and most unfathomable time loop in the story, the Amazing Adventures of Lil Cal.

grimAuxiliatrix [GA] **began trolling** apocalypseArisen [AA]

GA: Hi Again Aradia
AA: 0h n0000000
GA: So I Guess Tonight Is The Night You Blow Everything Up
AA: 0_0
GA: Is There Nothing I Can Do To Change Your Mind
AA: n0
AA: 0r yes
AA: yes theres n0thing
AA: and n0 y0u cant
AA: but y0u sh0uldnt pretend as if y0u believe this has anything t0 d0 with the state 0f my mind
AA: 0r the decisi0ns it will make 0r has already made
GA: Yeah I Guess Not
GA: I Thought Id Be Friendly Though
GA: And Remind You That You Do In Fact Have A Hand In All The Terrible Things That Are About To Happen
GA: Because Thats What Friends Are For
GA: And The Fact That What Ensues Will Be Terrible
GA: Is An Immutable Fact I Am Stating For The Record
GA: And The Fact That We Will Not Be On The Same Team Is Similarly Immutable
GA: It Does Not Mean That Teamwork Is What Isnt Taking Place Here
AA: s0rry i didnt f0ll0w that
GA: Ill Be Here To Help
GA: If You Need Me
AA: 0k
AA: thanks

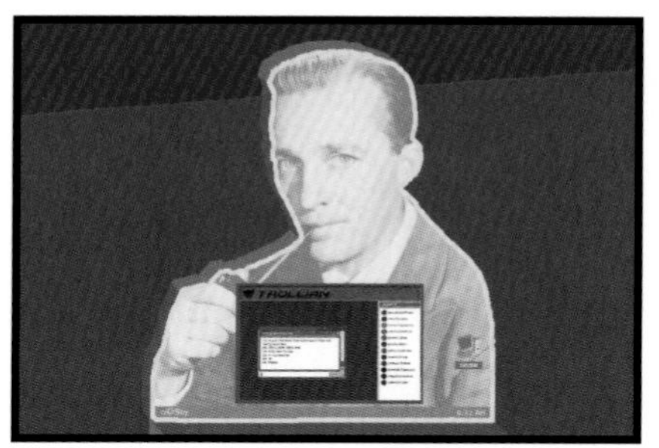

A rare Kanaya/Aradia interaction. Pardon me as I point out the crack pairing convos every single time. Kanaya apparently knows some things about the future too. Why does she know them? Something to look out for. But what's probably more interesting, given that Kanaya is not known to be particularly underhanded or scheming, is that it doesn't seem she's told many people about the dire things that are about to happen. We can wonder why this is, but I don't know if we have to look too much further than one of her known character traits: she tends to consider herself something of a confidante when it comes to her friendships with dangerous girls, and their dark secrets and proclivities (see: Vriska, then later, Rose). That's a flattering way of putting it. Another way would be: she's an enabler.

Tick tock tick tock tick tock.

Waiting for the apocalypse is so boooooring.

You guess you'll check on Sollux to see how he's coming along with those teams.

> Aradia: Check on Sollux.

You then had a conversation we already read, which began like this:

AA: did y0u set up the teams

And ended like this:

AA: im c0ming up

And then you went up.

> Aradia: Go up.

Wildly nonlinear stories like this need these kind of connector moments to help us know when certain things are happening in the context of a lot of stuff we've already seen happen. Performing this kind of transition could use its own verb. For now I'm just gonna say we're tarantinoing on to the next scene, until I can think of something better.

Hmm, you wonder what she wants.

What's with all these girls bugging you? Bugging and fussing and meddling.

> Aradia: Get bugged by AG.

Aradia flew up from her underground lair to incapacitate Sollux so he couldn't cause trouble, but...she's apparently still in no real hurry. She has time to levitate his bicyclops and have a chat with Vriska. She really is so emo-casual, she can barely get her head into keeping her own diabolical schemes on track.

arachnidsGrip [AG] began trolling apocalypseArisen [AA]

AG: Araaaaaaaadiiiiiiia!
AA: 0h b0y thats way t00 many of the same letter in a r0w twice
AG: I know!
AG: So we're a8out to get started right?
AG: Have you tricked Sollux yet?
AG: Do you have Mr. Two Eyes all 8efuddled and flustered in your we8 of lies?
AG: Or Mr. Four Eyes?
AG: Hmmmmmmmmmm.
AG: I don't know. Which nickname do you think would 8e suita8ly derogatory in this case Aradia?
AA: h0w ab0ut
AA: eight eyes
AA: minus seven
AG: ::::P
AA: i didnt trick him
AA: its n0t like that
AG: Ok, whatever. The point is.
AG: Once you have pulled the finely woven silken mesh over his dum8 different colored eyes, you and I will start playing the game and 8e the 8lue team leaders.
AG: That's how this will work right????????
AG: Wait do you mind if we are co-leaders? I forgot to ask! I just assumed it was ok with you.
AA: i d0nt care
AG: Great. That's the spirit!
AG: And when I 8ring you into the game, whatever the hell that means, then we can send each other stuff right? That is how this works right?
AA: yes
AG: Awesome!
AG: 8ecause I have a present for you. It's a surprise, and it's going to 8e great. From me to you.
AG: Just from me. From me alone and no8ody else.
AG: I can't wait to see the look on your face when you see.
AA: 0k well im sure it will be very th0ughtful
AG: Hey speaking of which, what will the name of our team 8e?
AA: uh
AA: the blue team
AG: No no no no no. I know that.

Aradia and Vriska have a pretty interesting thing going on with each other, which is easy to forget since they don't have much to do with each other after Hivebent. Which is understandable, since they mostly work out their issues at the end of the arc. (I.e. Vriska gets beaten senseless. Let that be a lesson to anyone at a loss for how to handle their Serket problems.) The way Vriska behaves toward Aradia says a lot about Vriska. These earlier interactions between them do a lot to establish the finer points of who she is beyond simply being the Huge Bitch of the group. She's fairly obsequious toward Aradia. She looks for approval, she makes appeals to be her equal despite their class disparity, to be "co-leaders," to bond over sticking it to Sollux... Basically to FORCE friendship. Why is she acting like this? Not surprisingly there are a bunch of layers to her psychology. Hey, let's keep talking about this over here. -->

AG: I mean the name of OUR team. You and me. Just uuuuuuuus.
AG: ::::)
AA: i havent given it any th0ught
AA: n0r did i think such a thing was up f0r c0nsiderati0n
AA: but if y0u want t0 pretend we b0th have a separate team t0gether
AA: and name that team
AA: then kn0ck y0urself 0ut
AG: I just thought it would 8e really fitting.
AG: Kind of like a fresh start, you know?
AG: I don't know, what are our shared interests? I guess I never really thought a8out this! I guess I'm used to thinking of you as the enemy. There must 8e some overlap in profiles.
AG: Come oooooooon, let's 8rainstorm!
AA: 0_0
AG: Man, it'll 8e great. We'll 8e unstoppa8le. Surely you must admit it will 8e nice to re8ound from the Team Charge de8acle!
AA: i never think ab0ut that anym0re
AG: Oh maaaaaaaan, I'm so dum8! Here I am running my mouth and opening up old wounds, while at the very same time trying to make amends! What an idiot.
AA: its 0k
AG: Hey speaking of which, that loser isn't going to 8e on the 8lue team is he?
AA: which l0ser
AG: Your old team 8uddy!
AA: n0
AG: Oh thank fucking goodness! Talk a8out dead weight. You made the right choice, leader! I mean co-leader.
AA: i didnt exclude him f0r that reas0n
AA: 0r at all
AA: y0ure just n0t getting it
AA: y0u never listen
AG: Man, now I've got this huge 8eefgrub lodged in my nook just thinking a8out him.
AG: I'm going to go give him a hard time.
AG: Let me know when you're live! Later.

arachnidsGrip [AG] **ceased trolling** apocalypseArisen [AA]

AA: d0nt d0 that its really childish
AA: uh w0w

> Be the mysterious spider girl.

--> Vriska references the Team Charge De8acle, which we later learn resulted in Aradia's death. It's pretty evident that it's mostly Vriska's guilt driving this conversation. Guilt, plus an overbearing need to make things square and thus fully "erase" the misdeeds of the past. She talks about a gift she has in store, only from her, no one else. (She "commissions" Equius to make Aradia a robot body, wants all the credit for the favor, and has no concern for the fact that he may have his own agenda for doing this. Of her many irons in the fire, some tend to be outsourced like this. In her self-obsession, she demands full credit nonetheless and expects to maximize the return on the investment she didn't even make, which is full amnesty for her past crimes.) Everything about what's happening here is wildly overcompensatory, meant to repair damage she's done without really having to face what it is she actually did. Aradia's extremely passive nature as a ghost makes her an easy target for this kind of overbearing attention. Because what Vriska seems to want most is acknowledgement, and more importantly, to foster strong reactions. Good or bad, love or hatred, this seems to be what she demands from everyone. -->

You try to be the mysterious spider girl and fail.

She's way too mysterious for you to be her yet! Seriously, what's up with those glasses? What's up with that robo-arm? What's her deal!

She guesses it's flattering that you want to be her though. She guesses she doesn't mind. It's cool.

We'll learn all about her a little later.

> Sollux: Get back to Aradia.

twinArmageddons [TA] **began trolling apocalypseArisen [AA]**

TA: aradiia ii would liike two apologiize, ii flew off the handle there.
TA: iit wa2 liike the handle wa2 a bald guy goiing really fa2t, and ii wa2 hii2 twoupee.
TA: 2o iim 2orry, iit wa2 my fault.
AA: its Ok
TA: ii hope we are 2tiill friiend2.
AA: yes we are

--> So for that reason, Aradia's impassivity seems to add fuel to Vriska's sycophantic need to make amends. Not caring much one way or another about what Vriska does is guaranteed to drive Vriska crazy. Neutrality is insufferable to her because it makes her feel irrelevant. Being irrelevant is her biggest fear and ultimate enemy. She struggles to keep herself in the spotlight, and when the narrative is finally done with her and tosses her into the gutter, she fights her way back into relevance. Fighting against the forces of narrative marginalization completely define her entire batshit arc, from her introduction here all the way to the end of *Homestuck*. So Aradia's listless attitude is the perfect foil for revealing this about her. It drives her nuts, and later she has a meltdown about it. She won't be done with Aradia until there is a catharsis between them that's up to her standards. In that sense, by finally beating Vriska to a pulp, Aradia is actually sort of doing her a favor.

TA: 2o anyway, ii thiink even though ii quiit a2 leader iim 2tiill goiing two play the game now.
TA: becau2e iit2 eiither that or get totally creamed by all the2e fuckiing 2pace boulder2.
TA: hey maybe we can make the be2t of the game anyway, even though ii guess we are goiing two lo2e.
AA: n0 im s0rry
AA: y0u cant s0llux
AA: n0t yet
TA: oh my god!!!
TA: youre goiing two giive me 2hiit agaiin???
TA: after ii crawled on my belly liike that all groveliing at you.
TA: liike 2ome low cla22 guy wiith... whatever color blood ii2 lower on the hiierarchy than miine.
TA: what2 wor2e than yellow?
TA: fuck thii2 confu2iing ca2te 2y2tem.
TA: anyway 2crew you, iim playiing thii2 game riight now.
AA: n0 y0ure n0t
AA: trust me
TA: waiit what2 thii2...
TA: are you heariing that 2pooky me22age from the grave?
TA: iit ii2 from my abiiliity two giive a 2hiit.
TA: whiich ju2t diied.
TA: thii2 ii2 where you laugh agaiin!
AA: c0me t0 the wind0w
TA: why.
AA: because im 0utside
TA: b2.
AA: take a l00k
TA: ii dont 2ee anythiing out there.
AA: c0me cl0ser y0ull see me
AA: i pr0mise
TA: god ii am ju2t bulge deep iin the fecal matter of a wiildly iincontiinent hoofbea2t but ok, iill iindulge you.
TA: here ii go!

> Sollux: Look out window.

I am going to call bullshit on Sollux being confused by the caste system. There are only two colors lower than his, brown and burgundy, belonging to Tavros and Aradia. Since class is so important in troll culture, if you're in a friend group, you're probably acutely aware at all times of which ones are lower than you, and which ones are higher. I think what he means here (or, rather, what I mean) about the caste system being confusing is that the *reader* is the one who doesn't know much about it yet. We're still in the process of learning that there even *is* a caste system. By asking this fairly disingenuous question "what2 wor2e than yellow?" Sollux is actually informing the reader in a very concrete way that 1) there is definitely a caste system based on blood color, and 2) some colors are worse than yellow and some better. A perceptive reader will probably have already surmised that the castes simply follow the rainbow order that we've seen them arranged by in the Trollian user list already.

Ok, looking out this lousy stupid goddamn window.

Lousy stupid goddamn psychics.

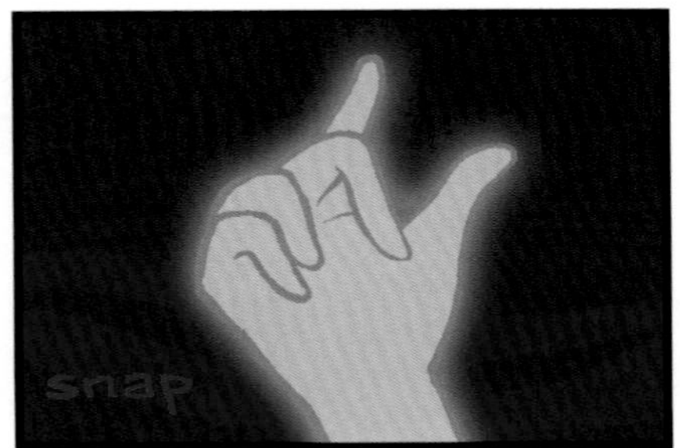

Nap time.

> Much later...

Sleeping with the very bees he put to sleep earlier. Textbook irony. Okay, it's not. I know that. All right then, smart guy, what is it? Oh, it's nothing? It's just a stupid thing that happened? Yeah, I guess you're right.

When you would finally wake up, you'd discover all of your teammates had connected to each other and entered the Medium. You would be the last to enter. Your long nap would facilitate a series of important dreams that would prove essential in support of your teammates.

But here and now, the destruction of your hive would be imminent unless you could quickly establish a connection to the first player of the group and complete the chain.

> Sollux: Wake up.

The mind honey.

Thppppthhhhhh.

Some of it got in your mouth.

YOU DO NOT UNDER ANY CIRCUMSTANCE EAT THE MIND HONEY

Note how Aradia put his lusus to sleep offscreen. Which means she's indirectly responsible for his death on the next page. Just like Sollux was indirectly responsible for hers. Is *this* irony? It still isn't, you say? Very well then.

Since that moody kid is busy flipping his bifurcated lid, we might as well take a moment to get to know this silly cat girl.

Gosh who is she??

> Enter name.

Sollux has eye lasers, like Cyclops from the *X-Men*. Nepeta has Wolverine claws. There are a lot of comic book hero things going on with the troll powers. I think this is obvious enough that it barely warrants mention, but here I am mentioning it, because someone bought ink by the barrel and gave the barrels to me to splash around with for 500 pages. Speaking of Nepeta, the narrative has decided we've endured enough hardship that we should be steeled sufficiently to withstand the secondhand embarrassment of getting to know this cute furry character. So let's get to know her, all right?

Your name is NEPETA LEIJON.

You live in a CAVE that is also a HIVE, but still mostly just a CAVE. You like to engage in FRIENDLY ROLE PLAYING, but not the DANGEROUS KIND. Never the DANGEROUS KIND. It's TOO DANGEROUS! Too many of your good friends have gotten hurt that way.

Your daily routine is dangerous enough as it is. You prowl the wilderness for GREAT BEASTS, and stalk them and take them down with nothing but your SHARP CLAWS AND TEETH! You take them back to your cave and EAT THEM, and from time to time, WEAR THEIR PELTS FOR FUN. You like to paint WALL COMICS using blood and soot and ash, depicting EXCITING TALES FROM THE HUNT! And other goofy stories about you and your numerous pals. Your best pal of all is A LITTLE BOSSY, and people wonder why you even bother with him. But someone has to keep him pacified. If not you, then who? Everyone has an important job to do.

Your trolltag is arsenicCatnip and :33 < *your sp33ch precedes itself with the face of your lusus who is pawssibly the cutest and purrhaps the bestest kitty you have ever s33n!*

What will you do?

> Nepeta: Retrieve claws from arms.

I used the word "embarrassment" in association with Nepeta, staying true to form when it comes to *Homestuck*'s tradition of dumping on this hapless second-string character, who really has not done much to deserve it. The only thing embarrassing is how much there actually is to say about her relative to her importance, when you start digging into it. The troll personas are related to internet culture archetypes, and hers is the first one that correlates pretty closely with fandom itself, at least as the cultural concept was taking shape at that time. Her obsession with shipping is closely connected to the focus on romance that Hivebent injected into *Homestuck*'s bloodstream, forever contaminating it for better or worse. Parsing her as the enthusiastic proto-fandom avatar in this respect reveals her as the Calliope of the story before Calliope shows up in Act 6. However, Nepeta's claim to that ambassadorship was responded to by the narrative with arguably ill-spirited rebuke and mistreatment, which I think was something that evolved before I had the chance to sharpen and clarify any meaningful statement the story intended to make about such an avatar. That refinement happens later with Calliope's character, an enthusiastic fandom avatar who is in explicit danger from such forces, but who is otherwise elevated and designated for protection, revivification, and ultimately, amnesty from the story's various narrative retributions.

You are always wearing your CLAW GLOVES. You never know when you might encounter some unsuspecting prey. Or when some prey might encounter an unsuspecting you!

On Alternia, everything is considered unsuspecting prey by everything else.

> Nepeta: Scratch lusus behind ears.

She sure enjoys a good scratch! POUNCE DE LEON is the best kitty cat. You and she go on adventures together in search of the FOUNTAIN OF CUTE. You ride your sure-pawed mount into the rugged frontier. And sometimes she rides you when she gets tired, which is frequently.

It sure will be sad when she dies. But who knows when or how that will happen.
We might not even really have the time to find out!

The saddest thing about the line "It sure will be sad when she dies" is that it applies just as much to Nepeta herself as it does to Pounce. Speaking of Pounce, if you ask me what's up with her double mouth, the answer obviously is I don't have the slightest idea. The typing quirk came before the lusus design. And the quirk tied to the number 33, arsenic's atomic number. And 3 is a good shape for making a cat face. And there are two of them. So I guess the number always implied a creature with a double cat mouth, and the thing just kind of designed itself? Sometimes that's just how things work. Maybe each mouth connects to a distinct digestive tract, for different types of prey? Maybe for things that are poisonous and things that aren't? I dunno, I've given you enough here to brainstorm with. Get out your workbooks and go worldbuild this stuff yourselves.

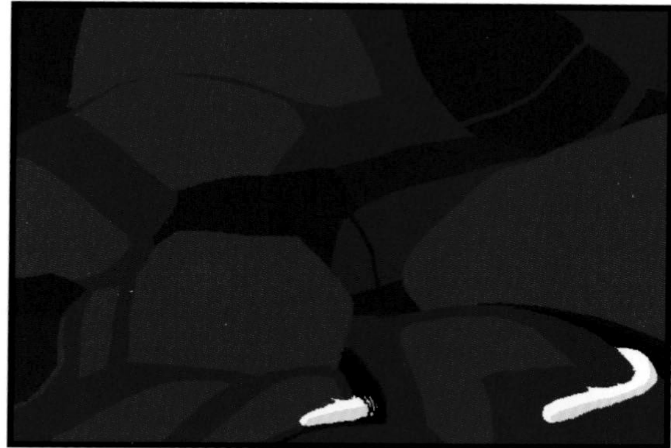

Later there was a cave-in.

> Nepeta: Examine computer.

You saunter over to your DRAWING TABLET COMPUTER. You use this to draw... on a computer!!! It would be cool if this could somehow be adapted to serve as a fetch modus as well. That would be so much more fun than the frustrating one you're using now.

You wonder what this grumpy fellow wants? Probably something to do with that game. That seems to be all ANYBODY'S talking about lately!

> Nepeta: Answer Karkat.

R.I.P. Pounce. Very good smash-cut way of handling that, if I say so myself. Nepeta's also got Jade's tablet modus, except really it's just her computer. In the same way that Nepeta is a proto-Calliope, she's also kind of a neo-Jade. Remember how I was talking about all these characters essentially being reconfigurations of various more fundamental, platonic personality profiles, and that *Homestuck* demonstrates its persona alchemy especially as the roster expands? Nepeta seems to build on Jade as a core persona, adding other dimensions in the process and thereby creating a new fundamental personality index we can reference thereafter as "Nepeta." And the Nepeta index can undergo further permutations to result in a more focused, substantive avatar called "Calliope." Or a less focused (but still substantive) absolute mess of an avatar called "Davepeta."

002161

carcinoGeneticist [CG] **began trolling** arsenicCatnip [AC]

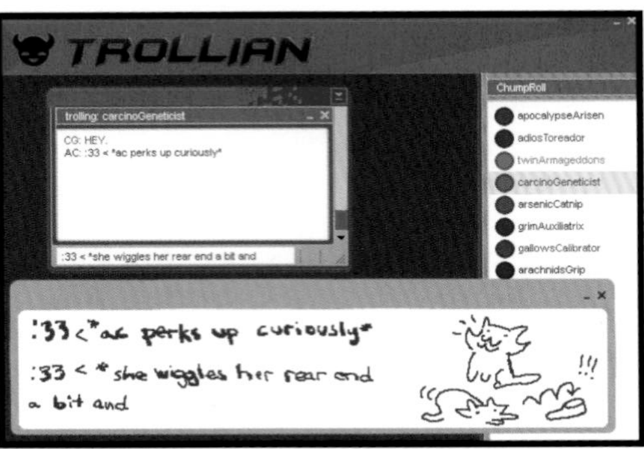

CG: HEY.
AC: :33 < *ac perks up curiously*
AC: :33 < *she wiggles her rear end a bit and then chases something she s33s bounce into one of karkats shoes*
CG: KARKAT CAN'T BELIEVE HE HAS TO SINK THIS LOW.
CG: KARKAT CAN'T BELIEVE HE'S ASKING AN AUTISTIC GIRL IN A CAVE TO JOIN HIS TEAM.
CG: KARKAT MYSTIFIES IN INFINITE BEFUDDLEMENT OVER THE FACT THAT YOU ARE PRESENTLY THE BEST REMAINING CANDIDATE FOR THE RED TEAM.
AC: :33 < i am???
AC: :33 < i mean *ac says i am??? wondrously*
CG: YES AND KARKAT CAN'T FUCKING BELIEVE THAT.
CG: KARKAT THINKS ABOUT THAT A BIT AND HIS JAW DROPS OPEN AND BREAKS A HUGE COLUMN OF BRICKS LIKE A FUCKING KUNG FU MASTER.
AC: :33 < *ac gathers up all the brick pieces and builds a cute little house and invites karkat inside*
CG: OK GOOD, IT'S GOOD THAT YOU'RE TALKING ABOUT BUILDING.
CG: EVEN IF IT'S IN THE MOST INANE POSSIBLE CONTEXT.
CG: YOU'RE GOING TO BE DOING A LOT OF IT.
AC: :33 < yesss that sounds fun
AC: :33 < ok what do i do?
CG: OK, BRIEFING:
CG: ME, TEREZI, GAMZEE AND TAVROS ARE ALL PLAYING NOW.
CG: THE CONNECTION ORDER IS AT -> TC -> GC -> CG.
CG: WE NEED SOMEONE TO CONNECT TO TOREADOR AND GET HIM IN THE GAME.
CG: I HAVE GA LINED UP FOR THE RED TEAM BECAUSE SHE IS ONE OF THE FEW REMAINING SANE ONES LEFT TO PLAY.
CG: OK, THE ONLY SANE ONE.
CG: BUT SHE DOESN'T WANT TO CONNECT YET BECAUSE OF SOME MYSTERIOUS BULLSHIT, SO I WAS LIKE WHATEVER, WHAT ELSE IS NEW.
CG: SO I GUESS THAT LEAVES YOU.
CG: TEREZI SAID SHE HAD YOU LINED UP TO PLAY BACK WHEN SHE WAS THE FAKE LEADER, SO I SAID FINE.
CG: SO JUST CONNECT TO TAVROS AND LATER WE'LL WORRY ABOUT GETTING YOU IN.
AC: :33 < alright! i will talk to him about that
AC: :33 < oh
AC: :33 < *ac pawses and looks up with a little bit of chagrin*
AC: :33 < i forgot i have to talk to someone else about this

Karkat APPEARS to be using ableist rhetoric here. But I'd point out that it is HIGHLY possible, if not probable, that Nepeta is somewhere on the autism spectrum. And no, that's not just me covering my ass retroactively by almost a decade, all right, wise guy?? He's not that tactful in how he mentions it, but you should give him the benefit of the doubt because the full span of the story reveals him to be somewhat Woker Than You Thought. This is all probably an act anyway, this attitude he's exhibiting. He'd probably be happy to have Nepeta on his team, considering the alternatives. And she'd be even happier, since her unrequited Karkat crush is the stuff of legend. It is not to be though. :((

AC: :33 < i have b33n purrcrastinating :((
CG: OH GOD.
CG: ARE YOU REALLY SERIOUS.
AC: :33 < its not that big of a deal!
CG: THIS BOGGLES MY MIND.
CG: HOW CAN YOU BE BEST FRIENDS WITH THE ONLY GUY ON THE PLANET WHO'S A BIGGER ASSHOLE THAN ME.
AC: :33 < hes not so bad!
CG: HE'S SCUM.
CG: BUT DO WHATEVER YOU'VE GOT TO DO I GUESS.
CG: TAVROS IS WAITING.

> Nepeta: Consult with friend on the matter.

arsenicCatnip [AC] **began trolling centaursTesticle [CT]**

AC: :33 < *ac twitches her friendly whiskers at ct*
CT: D --> Hi
AC: :33 < *ct purrplexes over where he put that important wrench that he n33ded for building a fancy robot or something*
AC: :33 < *he says, now where did that silly old wrench go??*
CT: D --> 100k
CT: D --> What are you e%pecting to accomplish with this
AC: :33 < *but oh look! ct p33ks around the corner to find that a very playful kitty has stolen the robot wrench and is now kicking it vigorously with her hind legs!*
CT: D --> This is f001ishness upon one hundred thousand prior, equally unsolicited f001ishnesses
CT: D --> You'll stop now
AC: XOO < rawwrrrrr
AC: :33 < youre so lame!
CT: D --> I'm not
CT: D --> I'm fine
AC: :33 < no! lame
CT: D --> No I'm not
AC: :33 < lame
CT: D --> No
AC: :33 < youve never played a fun purrtend game with me ever even once!

Nepeta x Equius is a good character relationship. I don't mean just that it's entertaining, which it is. It stands out for other reasons. For one thing, it's a strong example of moirallegiance by troll standards. This is a minor point, though. For reasons that are hard to explain, this relationship is of cosmic significance in the grand scheme of the narrative. Arquius x Davepeta, as the terminal for their combined trajectory, illustrates its significance by seemingly placing it on near-equivalent terms with Dave and Dirk's relationship. Why the hell should this be true? Perhaps it's premature to say. I'll save that for the Act 6 book babbling. More generally, key relationship pairs bring a lot out of certain characters, even minor ones. For instance, you could write dozens of paragraphs of meta on Vriska alone. But the moment you stop writing about Vriska in a vacuum, and start writing about Vriska x Terezi, the avenues of analysis seem endless. It's a circuitous, psychologically tortured mutual arc of competitive codependency, which on closer inspection serves as the axis around which virtually the entire plot revolves. Equius and Nepeta bring things out of each other's arcs in a similar way, relative to their lesser roles in the story. They could have ended up being merely two fairly shallow extras swallowed up by a huge ensemble, but the interactions they have make it much harder to write off either of them individually.

AC: :33 < even karkat does it sometimes, even if he does mean it in a grumpy and insincere way
AC: :33 < but at least its still fun!
CT: D --> Yuck
CT: D --> Don't pol100t my incoming data stream with his name, or any sort of e%cremental language you pick up from his ilk
AC: :33 < i s33 right through your stupid act, who are you trying to kid!
AC: :33 < look how you go out of your way to use words that have x's in them so that you can use your silly purrcent signs
AC: :33 < or use these absurd words that you can shoehorn a '100' into, even if its not strictly replacing 'loo'!!!
AC: :33 < you are so transpurrent
AC: :33 < i can tell you like to play games, d33p down you are a guy who likes to play games!
AC: :33 < i can smell a guy who likes to play games from so fur away with this nose, you have no idea X33
CT: D --> If you're 100king for a 100phole through which you may e%tract concessions from me, you'll have to 100k elsewhere
AC: :33 < s33! what the hell???
CT: D --> Nepeta, what did I say about that awful language
CT: D --> I won't stand for it, and you'll stop
AC: :33 < oops
AC: :33 < sorry :((
CT: D --> Your fraternization with the base classes have 100sened your morals, can't you see this
AC: :33 < no! i dont care, they are fun
AC: :33 < and i dont know anything about classes or bases or blood color, it doesn't matter!
AC: :33 < what does gr33n blood even mean! it doesnt mean anything to me and it shouldnt mean anything to anyone else!
CT: D --> Well, green b100d is ok, but it's not great
CT: D --> But that's why you're lucky to have me to 100k out for you
CT: D --> Because you don't know better, and you can't fight the role the mother had in store for you
AC: :33 < rawrgh, you are such a hypurrcrite!
AC: :33 < you pretend to be so high and mighty but i know you're not and i know you like games
AC: :33 < look at that silly little bow and arrow you always type!
AC: :33 < its always there, you never furget
AC: :33 < why would you do that if it wasnt a playful fun thing, i am so on to you!
CT: D --> My bow and arrow are highly dignified symbols
AC: :33 < lol! bs!!!
CT: D --> Archery is among the highest and most e%ceptional crafts, held in tremendous

We don't know much about Equius yet, but we get an awful lot of info about him with this excerpt. He's racist, a huge snob, doesn't like swearing, is stern and controlling, has a patronizing fondness for Nepeta, and thinks archery is cool because of its association with nobility. Combine this with the snapshot of his room we'll see soon, and suddenly we have an extensive character portrait. This was all important to establish quickly, because it helps us understand in record time that Equius is in fact one of the greatest characters ever created.

regard by the most a100f classes for centuries
AC: :33 < you suck at archery
CT: D --> No
AC: :33 < yes
CT: D --> No
AC: :33 < yes
CT: D --> No I don't
AC: :33 < yessssss yes yes yes
AC: :33 < have you ever even successfully fired an arrow?
AC: :33 < like actually got one to leave the bow??
CT: D --> I think
CT: D --> We need to stop talking about archery
AC: :33 < nuh uh
CT: D --> Yes
AC: :33 < no
CT: D --> We will stop talking about archery
CT: D --> The topic is making me
CT: D --> Sweat
AC: :33 < eww
AC: :33 < youre so gross
CT: D --> No, you're the one who e%ercises distasteful practices
AC: :33 < nooo, thats you
AC: :33 < everyone knows youre a weirdo and a cr33p!
AC: :33 < thats why youre lucky to have me to k33p an eye on you
AC: :33 < no one else can stand you!
CT: D --> You e%terminate beautiful, innocent creatures by the hundreds
CT: D --> I can't condone such wretched behavior
CT: D --> Beasts are meant to be 100ked upon with adoration
AC: :33 < but
AC: :33 < i eat them!
AC: :33 < i dont kill anything i dont eat, that would be mean
CT: D --> I guess that's basically acceptable in principle, but I still find it a bit unsavory
AC: :33 < well i think YOUR habits are unsavory!
CT: D --> No they're not
AC: :33 < yuh HUH
CT: D --> You're wrong about me, Nepeta
CT: D --> I do like to play games
CT: D --> But they must be e%tremely important games with very high stakes
CT: D --> Not the kind played by trans100cent green wigglers who let 100se an e%cremental surge hard in their wiggler-bottom diaperstubs
CT: D --> As it happens I have arranged to play just such a game tonight

But wait, there's more. He also sweats a lot, he can't actually wield a bow and arrow because he's too strong and just breaks them, and he detests cruelty to animals, which he adores, especially humongous, nude, anthropomorphic beasts, which is something we don't need to get into now. There's plenty to say about Nepeta too, but when they're talking, it seems Equius starts to bury her in the contest of absurd, eyebrow-raising character traits. In this sense, she's sort of the straight man of the duo's relationship. But then, that's not a bad way to describe what a moirail really is. It's playing the stable, calming straight man to a more erratic or extreme personality, to help keep them grounded.

CT: D --> Aradia and I have a private engagement to be co-leaders of the b100 team
AC: :33 < oh yeah??
AC: :33 < *well just by purrchance it happens that ac has a private and sneaky engagement to play this game as well!*
AC: :33 < *and by a purrsnickety twist of fate, she will be on the R33D TEAM, with her other great friends who like to play their childish diaperpoop games!!!!*
AC: :33 < :PP
CT: D --> Absolutely not
AC: :33 < absolutely :PP
CT: D --> I forbid this
CT: D --> You will take your position on the b100 team with me
AC: :33 < yeah right! i will take my purrsition into this funny pounce ball and tackle you!
CT: D --> That's nonsense, you're nowhere even remotely within my pro%imity that would be necessary to e%ecute such a maneuver
AC: :33 < *ac rolls her eyes almost as hard as she is rolling around in this really interesting smell*
CT: D --> The thought of you fraternizing with and abetting those stink-b100ded h001igans strikes me as scandal beyond measure
CT: D --> I'm afraid you're too delicate to withstand that sort of corruption
CT: D --> It's forbidden
AC: :33 < nuh uuuuuuuuuuuuhhhhhhhhhh
CT: D --> Yes
CT: D --> You won't
AC: :33 < no
AC: :33 < i will
CT: D --> You won't
AC: :33 < you cant stop me!
CT: D --> I am telling you not to
CT: D --> And you will be on my team
CT: D --> That's final
AC: XPO < bllllraaaaaawwwwwlllllrrrrghgghghgh
CT: D --> Quiet
AC: :33 < why do you do this, why are you so confurdent about your stupid commands?
AC: :33 < dont you know you cant ACTUALLY tell me what to do??
AC: :33 < its not like you even have any special mind pawers or telepurrthy or anything!
CT: D --> No
CT: D --> I do not
CT: D --> And yet
CT: D --> You will do as I say

Much of Hivebent involves observing the characters we're in the process of getting to know find out how they're either not on the team they thought they'd be on or won't enter the session in the order they believed. Sometimes people get tricked, sometimes they get sabotaged, and sometimes they get ordered by an abusive friend who has no real power over them, except the power of sheer insistence they have grown accustomed to successfully asserting over the years. Also, there's no such thing as an abusive relationship for trolls, just lots of arrangements that are "normal" due to their terrible culture. There you go, that's my red-hot take of the day for you.

AC: :33 < yes well we will just s33 about that!
CT: D --> Yes we will
CT: D --> You will join me on my team shortly
CT: D --> Stand by for further instru%ion
AC: :33 < hisssssssss!
CT: D --> You're angry, and I appreciate that
CT: D --> But it doesn't matter
CT: D --> Di%ussion over
AC: :33 < :((

> Nepeta: Give Tavros the bad news.

Equius says he appreciates that Nepeta's angry. I guess meaning that he respects an angry disposition, like his own. Especially early on in his characterization, it's suggested he has anger issues (like him taking his rage out on robot dummy combatants). But I'm not sure this trait holds up. Over time, he seems to show a lot more passion about his weird stuff, his passion for archery and muscular horse men, his submissive obsessions, his deference toward those higher on the hemospectrum and fetish-like indulgence in depraved attraction toward those lower. Ultimately he comes off more as a ridiculous nerd, with a soft spot for a lot of silly and creepy shit. My view on this is, it's not that the text lost track of the fact that he was supposed to be angry. It's more that this was his initial state of mind early on, and the more he started blowing off steam with his various indulgences (Aradiabot, etc.) the less he had to be mad about. We just meet him at a really high-strung point in his life. I think it's more accurate to say his "anger" is a form of hyperintense focus on being stern, aloof, proper, and averse to nonsense, which is a facade serving to cover up his inner personality, which is barely in control at all. Like Nepeta suggests, deep down he wants to play the kinds of silly games she plays. He wants to let go completely, and indulge every ludicrous and depraved whim he has. His arc tends to be more about caving to these indulgences, and all the mixed consequences that follow, than resisting them.

arsenicCatnip [AC] began trolling adiosToreador [AT]

AC: :33 < *ac curls up in tavroses lap*
AT: oKAY, *i,
AT: fOR THE TIME BEING, aND,
AT: fOR THE SAKE OF THIS FANTASY SCENARIO, i PRETEND,
AT: tHAT MY CAT ALLERGIES AREN'T THAT BAD,*
AC: :33 < *ac takes a long nap*
AC: :33 < *and then wakes up and frowns because she has bad news*
AT: *oH NO,*
AT: iS,
AT: wHAT i SAY,
AT: aBOUT THE BAD NEWS, nOT THE NAP,
AC: :33 < tavros im sorry i cant be on your team :((
AC: :33 < im not allowed
AT: oH,
AT: tHAT'S OKAY,
AT: tHEN i GUESS HE SAID NO, tHEN,
AC: :33 < yes unfurtunately
AC: :33 < rarg im so mad!
AT: iT'S PROBABLY FOR THE BEST,
AT: tHAT YOU LISTEN TO HIM,
AC: :33 < i dont know
AC: :33 < you think so?
AT: wELL,
AT: iF YOU DIDN'T LISTEN TO HIM BEFORE,
AT: yOU MIGHT HAVE PLAYED GAMES WITH US BEFORE,
AT: aND SOMETHING BAD MIGHT HAVE HAPPENED TO YOU,
AC: :33 < hmm purrhaps
AC: :33 < but i still f33l bad
AT: i'LL FIND ANOTHER PLAYER, iT'S NOT A BIG DEAL,
AT: gOOD LUCK, bEING,
AT: oN THE BLUE TEAM,
AC: :33 < ok thanks :((

Tavros's cat allergies are a throwaway joke here, but actually, it's the second time in the story that a casual, humorous reference to an allergy turns out to be very long-term foreshadowing. John's peanut allergy comes back to haunt Jake when he's assassinated via peanut force-feeding. And much later than that, Tavros fuses with an omnipotent cat and becomes allergic to himself. It's fine though, it's only for the rest of his life. Which has been prolonged eternally through prototyping.

You fondly recall your days of far more intensive role playing. It seems like so long ago now. Aside from a few unfortunate moments, it was a lot of fun. If you had to do it all over again, you suppose you would select better company. Maybe this game you are playing tonight will rekindle some of that excitement.

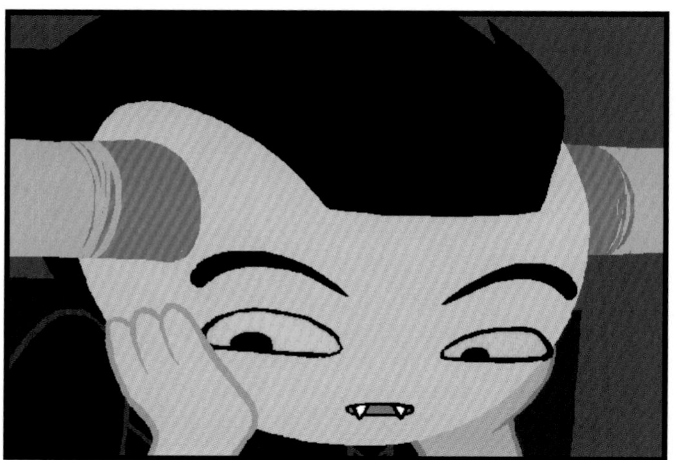

Tinkerbull?

> Some time ago...

Oh, let's not fail to notice the fact that he accidentally slaughtered Tinkerbull with his own wheelchair on the previous page. Good grief, what a fuckup. To tell you the truth, I'm actually a little ashamed I created him.

You stand in your room on a healthy pair of legs and in a plucky little outfit. You are a low level BOY-SKYLARK, and you wield an inexpensive DAGGERLANCE, which is the closest thing to a jousting lance you can wield that is still compatible with your favorite class.

You are about to play a popular game called FLARP, which unlike most games published by major developers, was given a graceful and aesthetically pleasing name. It's a title under the EXTREME ROLE PLAYING genre, and playing it without caution can have serious real world consequences! But that's what makes it fun.

When you activate Flarp's grub, the campaign programmed for tonight will begin. TEAM CHARGE will duel TEAM SCOURGE as usual. This is going to be great.

> Tavros: Contact fellow Team Charge member.

Here we finally dive into the Grim Backstory that Hivebent has been concealing—and ominously alluding to—up to this point. It's a series of events critical enough to almost qualify as the entire point of Hivebent unto itself, that kick off the revenge cycle around which most of the *Homestuck* narrative inadvertently revolves, and continues to revolve around in some ways to the very end. This has a lot more to do with Vriska and Terezi rather than Tavros, lest we get carried away and foolishly assume that Tavros plays any cosmically significant role in this story whatsoever.

adiosToreador [AT] **began trolling** apocalypseArisen [AA]

AT: aRADIA,
AT: mY GRUB IS LAYING NOW, sO
AT: i'LL BE READY SOON,
AA: c00l!
AA: mine t00
AA: i d0nt kn0w where terezi is th0ugh
AA: shes running late
AT: oH, uHH
AT: sHOULD WE WAIT,
AA: n0
AA: ill be here cl0uding her campaign f0r her regardless
AA: with 0r with0ut her!
AA: her l0ss if she d0esnt make it
AA: itll give y0u a chance t0 gain s0me gr0und
AT: oKAY,
AA: y0u picked a t0ugh class tavr0s!
AA: n0ne 0f the really useful c0mbat abilities c0me int0 play until y0u reach a very high level
AA: but i supp0se it will be rewarding when y0u get there
AT: yEAH, i THINK YOU'RE RIGHT, bUT,
AT: iT'S THE CLASS i THINK IS MOST FUN, aND, bATTLE SKILL IS NOT ALL THERE IS,
AT: tO BEING A GREAT ADVENTURER,
AA: i c0uldnt agree m0re
AA: y0u might be the 0nly flarper in the w0rld wh0 really understands the true spirit 0f the game
AA: every0ne else is s0 aggressive and treasure hungry!
AA: but thats what makes beating them all the m0re satisfying
AT: yEAH, i GUESS,
AA: remember y0ur cl0uder isnt g0ing t0 pull any punches t0night
AA: d0nt fall f0r her mind games
AA: ill be here t0 assist 0f c0urse
AA: if y0ure in tr0uble d0nt hesitate t0 ask f0r help
AT: yEAH, i WON'T,
AT: tHANKS, aRADIA,
AA: n0 pr0blem!

> Tavros: Hatch campaign.

Team Charge consists of two kids associated with charging animals, a ram and a bull. Team Scourge consists of...two kids who are just a couple of ruthless bitches, I guess. We can tell here that some things were very different in the old days. Tavros can walk, and Aradia's personality is noticeably different. She seems to be capable of emotion and shows some enthusiasm for certain things. Aradia's personality has a lot of different gears, depending on whether she's alive, dead, or a robot. Also, she references Tavros's Flarp class, which sounds awfully similar to his *Sburb* class. Pages are known to be slow-burning, high-reward players.

Your campaign's GAMING FLAPSTRACTIONS hatch out of their eggs. These comprise all the data and procedures you will need for your adventure tonight.

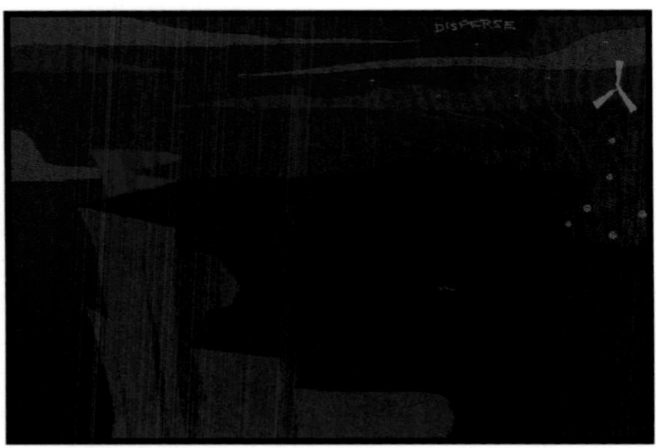

They disperse throughout the terrain surrounding your hive. They follow both preprogrammed and live instructions by your CLOUDER, a member of Team Scourge, whose role is to provide you with a challenging scenario, while your teammate does the same for Scourge's other player.

> Tavros: Go outside and begin adventure.

You take your starting position in the field. The game is afoot, and anything can happen now. It's up to you to consult your maps and work with your teammate to discover the objective of the quest, find treasure, and slay monsters.

Your STAT BAT has bonded with you. This keeps track of every attribute for your character, including vitals. While these attributes in principle remain abstractions, due to the fact that this is EXTREME role playing, they will always relate in some way to your real life attributes as well. You've got to be careful out here!

> A little later...

Flarp is just another gross troll game involving weird creatures laying eggs and such. Flarp, you may be smart enough to deduce, is a portmanteau of LARP (live action roleplay) and, get this, the word "flap," which is a thing that bats do with their wings. I know, how do I come up with this amazing shit? The game has some augmented reality-like features, which makes it feel a bit prescient for something created back in 2010. The "flapstractions" (another incredible portmanteau) are virtual entities that fly around the real world and project certain images, like monsters, to make it feel like the game is taking place around you. Makes me wonder if the makers of *Fiduspawn* ever used this technology to make *Fiduspawn GO*.

arachnidsGrip [AG] **began trolling** adiosToreador [AT]

AG: Wellllllll?
AT: uHH,
AG: Hey 8oy-Skytard, are you going to just stand there all night?
AG: Make your move, make your move, make your move!
AT: i JUST THINK,
AT: tHESE MONSTERS ARE TOO STRONG,
AT: sORRY, bUT, tHEY DON'T SEEM APPROPRIATE FOR THIS CAMPAIGN,
AG: Weak! Weaky weaky weak.
AT: uHH,
AT: wEAKY, iS THAT A REAL,
AT: tHING TO SAY,
AG: Yes. Your 8l8tant excuse making is the weakiest lame that ever shit the coward 8ed.
AG: Roll your dice. Make your move.
AG: Advance or a8scond!
AT: i CAN'T ABSCOND,
AT: tHERE'S NO,
AT: uHH, aBSCONDING PLACE,
AG: 8ut a8sconding is what you do 8est!
AG: I 8n't managed to cloud a scenario yet you couldn't squawk out of in a 8lazing trail of cluck8east feathers.
AG: You cannot hope to 8eat Tavros Nitram in an a8scond-off.
AG: He is simply the 8est there is!
AT: uHH, tHAT SOUNDS FLATTERING, tHEORETICALLY,
AT: bUT, i DON'T THINK,
AG: Hey pipe down!
AG: Make your move!
AG: Advance or a8scond, advance or a8scond!
AG: Roll, Tavros! Roll!!!!!!!!
AT: oKAY,
AT: hOLD ON, fOR ONE MOMENT,

adiosToreador [AT] **began trolling** apocalypseArisen [AA]

AT: aRADIA,
AT: hEY,
AT: aRE YOU THERE,
AT: uHHH,
AT: hMM,

I think we can all agree that Vriska is a harsh DM but a fair one. Something about her quirk to point out: she obviously replaces "ate" sounds in words with "8." But sometimes I made judgment calls on how literal to be about this. Like "blatant" should technically be spelled "8l8ant." But omitting the middle "t" feels like it hurts readability a little too much. "8l8tant" helps the eye pick up what word it's supposed to be more easily. I didn't do this with every word though, just the ones that bugged me.

adiosToreador [AT] **began trolling** gallowsCalibrator [GC]

AT: hEY,
AT: tEREZI,
AT: i HAVE A PROBLEM,
AT: uHHHHHHH,

arachnidsGrip [AG] **began trolling** adiosToreador [AT]

AG: No one can help you, Taaaaaaaavros!
AG: ::::)
AT: oKAY,
AG: Time to decide!
AT: wHERE IS EVERYBODY,
AG: What does that have to do with your present cowardice?
AT: i DON'T KNOW,
AT: pROBABLY NOTHING,
AG: Are you going to roll?
AT: hMM,
AT: nO, i CAN'T,
AG: Why not?
AT: bECAUSE, i WAS THINKING ABOUT THE NUMBERS, aND,
AT: iT'S IMPOSSIBLE FOR THERE TO BE A FAVORABLE OUTCOME,
AT: nO MATTER WHAT THE DICE DO,
AG: So, you give up?
AT: yEAH, mAYBE,
AG: Why not roll and make it official?
AG: Why would you want to cheapsk8 me out of 8onuses like that? It's so thoughtless.
AT: uHH,
AG: Am I going to have to take matters into my own hands?
AG: To make your move for you?
AT: i THOUGHT,
AT: yOU COULDN'T USE POWERS,
AT: i MEAN, rEAL LIFE POWERS, nOT GAME ONES,
AT: iT'S AGAINST THE RULES,
AG: 8ut if you are going to 8reak the rules and refuse to roll, what choice do I have!
AG: I h8 that it had to come to this 8ut what can I do!

Vriska makes a good point here. Tavros is breaking the rules. He's basically forcing her hand. Try to remember that next time you feel sorry for him.

AG: Tavros, have I mentioned how cute you look in that plucky little outfit?
AG: Why if I didn't know 8etter, I'd say I was playing with Pupa Pan himself!
AG: Isn't that what you want, Tavros? To 8e like Pupa?
AG: Of course you do! What 8oy wouldn't want to 8e like Pupa! So dashing and 8rave.
AG: He is everything you are not!
AG: For one thing, he can flyyyyyyyy.
AG: Do you want to flyyyyyyyy, Tavros?
AG: Have you ever tried to fly? I 8et you haven't!
AG: How a8out we take to the skies, Pupa!
AG: Hahahaha, oh you like that idea, Pupa? Yes, you do. I can feel it in your simple, mallea8le 8rain.
AG: You want to fly so 8ad!

AG: Fly, Pupa!!!!!!!!
AG: Flyyyyyyyy!
AG: Hahahahahahahaha!

Yes, I know, huge bitch, awful murderous manipulative person, blah blah blah. But listen, folks. She clearly likes him. See how she says he looks cute in his outfit? She doesn't have many flaws, but no one is totally perfect, and against all good sense and better judgment she likes this guy for some reason, and this is her way of dealing with that. You have to remember that many spiders paralyze their prey before dealing with them further. She's playing a longer game here.

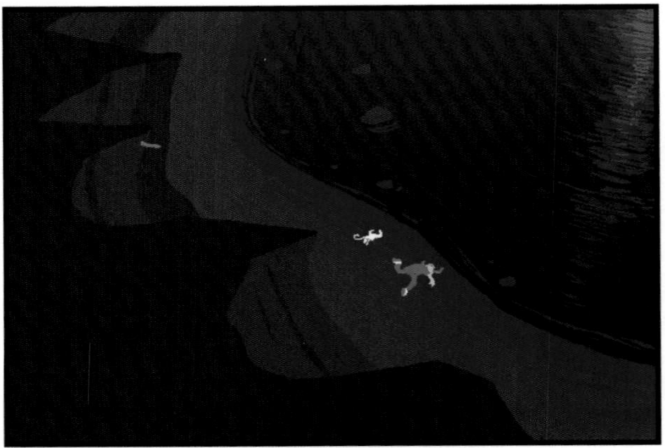

AG: Aaaaaaaahahahahahahahaha!
AG: Hahahahahahahahahahahahahahaha!!!!!!!!
AG: Haaaaaaaahaaaaaaaahaaaaaaaahaaaaaaaahaaaaaaaahaaaaaaaahaaaaaaaahaaaaaaa!
AG: Adios, Toreadum8ass.
AG: :::;D

arachnidsGrip [AG] ceased trolling adiosToreador [AT]

adiosToreador [AT] **began trolling** carcinoGeneticist [CG]

AT: aG JUST JUMPED ME OFF A CLIFF,
AT: wITH MY BRAIN,
AT: aND, uHH
AT: mY LEGS, aLSO,
AT: aND NOW, tHEY FEEL,
AT: iNVISIBLE,
AT: wOW, i'M SURE THERE WAS A BETTER WAY TO SAY THAT,
AT: aNYWAY,
AT: tHAT'S REALLY ALL THERE IS,
AT: tO REPORT ON THE SUBJECT,
AT: oF ME GETTING HURT,
CG: HEY ASSHOLE, STOP PLAYING GAMES FOR GIRLS.

carcinoGeneticist [CG] **ceased trolling** adiosToreador [AT]

> Back in the present...

John Arm Alert: coming out of the cliff. Also, you gotta admire how the moment Vriska's done with her funny prank, she just logs the fuck off. Karkat does just about the same thing, but one has to assume he thinks Tavros is exaggerating and not reporting on his literal paralysis. Karkat calls Flarp a game for girls, which in human culture sounds like a sexist pejorative. But knowing what we know about Flarp and trolls in general, what he probably means is, "Stop playing games for girls. They're very dangerous, and one of these days it's going to get you killed."

But not too far into the present. Right around this moment, with Karkat and the toilet, during a conversation we have already read, which ended like this:

GC: OH BOY YOU N33D TO G3T W1TH TH3 PROGR4M K4RK4T
GC: H4V3 YOU T4LK3D TO 44
CG: 44 WHAT?
GC: 4POC4LYPS34R1S3N SORRY
CG: NO, OF COURSE NOT.
GC: OR T4
GC: OR 4G 1 GU3SS
GC: OR C4
GC: R34LLY TH3R3S L1K3 TH1S WHOL3 CONSP1R4CY 4BOUT TH1S
GC: 4S 1M F1ND1NG OUT
CG: WELL WHY DON'T YOU JUST TELL ME SO I DON'T HAVE TO TALK TO ANY OF THOSE DOUBLETALKING ASSHOLES.
GC: 1 C4NT!
GC: 1 GOTT4 ST3P OUT OF TH3 TR33 FOR 4 MOM3NT
GC: WH3N 1 COM3 B4CK 1 W1LL 3NT3R TH3 G4M3
GC: CY4!

gallowsCalibrator [GC] **ceased trolling** carcinoGeneticist [CG]

arachnidsGrip [AG] **began trolling** carcinoGeneticist [CG]

AG: Pssssssst.
AG: Hey 8rave leader.
CG: OH MY GOD, WHY ARE YOU TALKING TO ME.
AG: Can I join your team?
CG: YES I'M GLAD YOU ASKED, BECAUSE THERE IS A WIDE OPEN SLOT FOR THE MOST VILE BACKSTABBING SOCIOPATH WHO EVER LIVED.
CG: YOU REALLY HELPED ME OUT OF A JAM BY STEPPING FORWARD.
AG: Vile 8acksta88ing sociopath? Karkat, did you copy and p8ste that phrase directly from your personal ad descri8ing what you are looking for in a lady?
CG: HA HA HA!
CG: MORE CAGEY CUTESY BULLSHIT.
CG: LIKE I'M NOT UP TO MY LOBE STEM WITH THAT ALREADY HAVING TO DEAL WITH TEREZI.

Homestuck's narrative text—which you may have already guessed is indistinguishable from my stream-of-consciousness bullshit in virtually any context, including these notes—bears examination sometimes. It contains many statements that aren't jokes exactly, just wise-assed things to say, as well as ways of saying things that could be said in a more sensible manner. Like, "But not too far into the present." What the hell does this actually mean? We're hopping back to the "present," but not so far back that we would have to officially begin calling it the future. In fact, going "far into the present" seems to be a preposterous concept, because the present is an exact point on a timeline. Falling short of the present, by a bit or a lot, is what we call the past. Exceeding it by a bit or a lot is what we call the future. Also none of this means anything, because Hivebent has made it pretty clear through its nonlinear presentation that there's no such thing as the present from our viewpoint. And to make this even less meaningful, no matter how far into Hivebent's "future" you go, it's still all taking place in the past, since it's explicitly presented as a long flashback in the greater story. The narration is always playing games with words to evocatively capture this stupid dance we're doing with ludicrous ideas and abstract concepts.

CG: YOU BOTH MUST HAVE BEEN INSUFFERABLE WHEN YOU WERE A TEAM.
CG: YOUR OPPONENTS PROBABLY ALL JUST TRIED TO COMMIT SUICIDE AFTER A FEW MINUTES OF PUTTING UP WITH YOUR FANGY GRINNED DRIVEL.
CG: THAT'S PROBABLY HOW IT ALL WENT DOWN WHEN THE SHIT HIT THE THRESHER.
AG: That's not a 8ad guess! 8ut man! Karkat you sure are giving me a hard time.
AG: I don't see how we're supposed to 8e 8ecoming friends if you recoil from my olive 8ranch like I'm twitching a mummified 8ovine phallus in your direction.
CG: BECOMING FRIENDS, WHAT THE FUCK.
CG: WE WILL NEVER BE FRIENDS, MORON.
AG: Not even h8 friends?
CG: NO. MORE LIKE TWITCHY EYED PROJECTILE VOMITING IN UTTER DISGUST FRIENDS, WHILE I PERFORATE MY BONE BULGE WITH A CULLING FORK.
AG: Yesssssss. I'll take it!
CG: GET LOST.
AG: Anyway, I was just joking a8out wanting to 8e on your team.
AG: I'm already on the 8lue team.
CG: OH! OH REALLY?????
CG: WAIT, LET ME COUNT OUT EIGHT OF THESE THINGS, HOLD ON. ? ? ? ? ? ? ? ?
CG: THERE, I AM NOW AN ENORMOUS TOOL FOREVER.
AG: Yes, Aradia and I have an arrangement. We will 8e co-leaders.
AG: (But really I will 8e the leader! Heh heh. Shh! Don't tell anyone!)
AG: What do you think, Karkat? Can you take on two dangerous laaaaaaaadies at once?
CG: YAWN.
AG: Come on! Aren't you a little nervous that I will oppose you? You should 8e!
CG: NO YOU'RE JUST A RUN OF THE MILL LITTLE PSYCHO GIRL, A TROLL CAEGAR A DOZEN.
CG: I'LL BE TAKING APART THE BLUE TEAM WITH BRUTAL EFFICIENCY, YOU'LL SEE.
CG: YOU NEVER PLAYED ONE OF YOUR DUMB GAMES WITH ME SO YOU NEVER HAD THE PRIVILEGE OF SEEING WHAT I CAN DO.
CG: ENJOY THE SHOW, SWEETHEART.
CG: JUST DON'T EVEN THINK ABOUT USING YOUR MIND CONTROL TRICKS ON MY PLAYERS.
CG: REMEMBER YOUR TRUCE?
AG: Pshhhhhhhh. Those days are far 8ehind me.
AG: Anyway, I can't control just any8ody. They've got to 8e impresssssssssiona8le. Like you!
CG: YOU CAN'T CONTROL ME.
AG: Sure I can. I just choose not to.
CG: YEAH OK.
AG: I find your mind totally unpalata8le to 8rowse. Looking into your 8rain is like pawing through a smelly dumpster.
AG: Full of 8roken glass and razor 8lades!
AG: And poop. D::::
CG: WHATEVER, DON'T EVEN TRY IT.

Her olive branch remark is both a callback to when Karkat said something similar to John about becoming friends, as well as a reference to the infamous bull penis cane wielded by CD in the Midnight Crew Intermission. Quite a one-two punch. Vriska here is under the laughable impression she is going to be the secret leader of the blue team, but what else is new. Half these people all think they're either going to be the leader, or on the other team. It would make a lot of sense for Vriska to be on the blue team, which is what makes it so great that she's not. But she is an excellent fly in the ointment—or spider, if you will. Dropping this hot mess into the red team, an otherwise fairly coherent group of friends with good chemistry, is a good recipe for drama. Vriska is subsequently used as that kind of ointment-containminating ingredient almost ceaselessly for the rest of this Act.

CG: I'VE GOT THE BETTER SCOURGE SISTER ON MY TEAM AND IF YOU BREAK YOUR TRUCE YOU'LL HAVE TO ANSWER TO HER.
CG: THE FUNNY THING IS SHE WAS ALWAYS WAY BETTER THAN YOU EVEN WITHOUT ANY POWERS.
CG: YEAH THAT'S RIGHT, I KNOW YOUR WHOLE STORY.
CG: YOU WERE ALWAYS JEALOUS SHE COULD MANIPULATE PEOPLE SO WELL WITHOUT RESORTING TO CHEAP MIND TRICKS.
CG: HAHA, I CAN TELL THIS BURNS YOU AND I CAN'T EVEN PAW THROUGH YOUR DUMPSTER!
CG: CHALK IT UP AS ANOTHER INFURIATING VICTORY FOR GUTTER BLOOD OVER ARISTOCRACY.
CG: OH WHAT'S THAT, NOTHING TO SAY?
CG: WOW SPEECHLESS I GUESS. YOU'RE PROBABLY CRYING RIGHT NOW. THAT WOULD MAKE MY FUCKING DAY.
CG: HEY LOOK AT ME BEING THE ONE TO TALK SHIT AT WARP SPEED THEN LOG OFF BEFORE YOU CAN REPLY.
CG: BYE, IDIOT.

carcinoGeneticist [CG] **ceased trolling arachnidsGrip [AG]**

carcinoGeneticist [CG] **began trolling arachnidsGrip [AG]**

AG: Oh, 8ack so soon! Did your thum8 slip on the 8utton????????
AG: I guess you can't get enough of me.
AG: ::::)
CG: YOU MADE ME DO THAT.
CG: AND YOU KNOW IT.
AG: You 8n't got nothing on me and you can't prove shit!!!!!!!!
AG: Anyway, Karkat, I just wanted to say.
AG: <3

arachnidsGrip [AG] ceased trolling carcinoGeneticist [CG]

> Karkat: Be the other asshole.

This appears to be the only time in the story Vriska psychically controls Karkat. There are definitely limitations to her powers. Higher bloods are immune. Everyone from Terezi and up can resist her powers. Probably Kanaya too, since it's hard to imagine her being controlled. (Though whether that's due to her blood or temperament is an open question.) Trolls lower on the hemospectrum are fair game. Tavros, Sollux...probably Nepeta too, but why would Vriska bother with her? Aradia has some resistance due to being an advanced psychic herself, in a way that Sollux is not at his lower moments (see: brain problems). So, is Vriska being truthful that she can control Karkat but just doesn't want to because his mind is unpalatable? Or is there something about his mind that makes it genuinely difficult to control, and that's just her cover story? Maybe all she can pull off are these little things. "Finger slips" as little demonstrations of power, without being able to take full control.

You are now the other... oh.

Oh god.

You decide that we could probably stand to delay this guy's introduction a little longer. Why don't we see what someone else is up to.

Anyone.

> HURRY

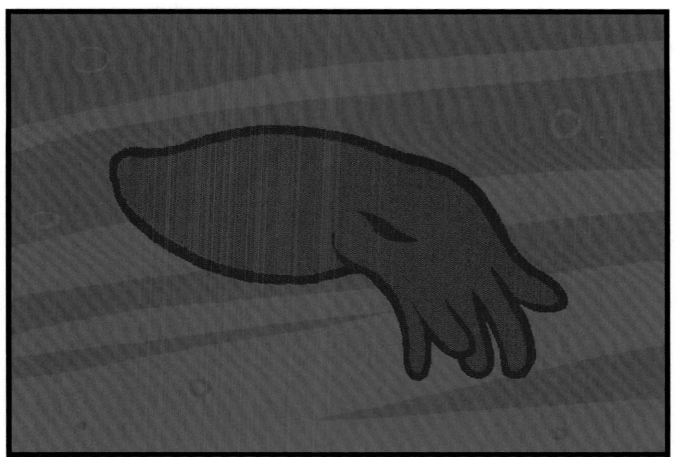

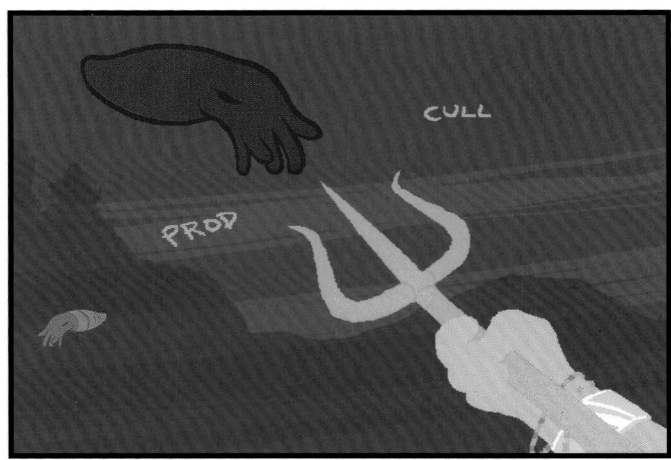

You switch to a vague teaser of the final unseen troll in the nick of time.

Ah yes, the old "let's get to know this guy, wait, oh no he sucks, let's not just yet" gag. Except Equius doesn't suck at all. He does the opposite of that. What shall we derive from everything in this shot? One worrying detail that jumps out is the lusus's black eye, which presents the alarming possibility that he may be the victim of Equius's domestic abuse. The explanation turns out to be more innocent though. Dude is just really strong. The cool kids recognized right away that this lusus design is based on a Humanimal, which were some bad and weird comics I used to make. Just buff guys with animal freak-bodies that almost always had udders, despite always being men. The anthro porn art, which Equius regards as classic, absolutely exquisite masterpieces and priceless works of fine art, also reference my older work. I used to harvest pieces such as these and write very academic reviews and critiques of them. Some of them are pasted directly here on his walls, with a little obscuring of certain anatomical features. Much later, John's oil retcon further obscures a questionable portion of the piece on the right. The speech bubble in that piece, which is native to the original work, says "I love being STRONG," which perfectly captures the spirit of Equius as well as the rather eclectic body of subject matter his character is based on.

> Aradia: Go home.

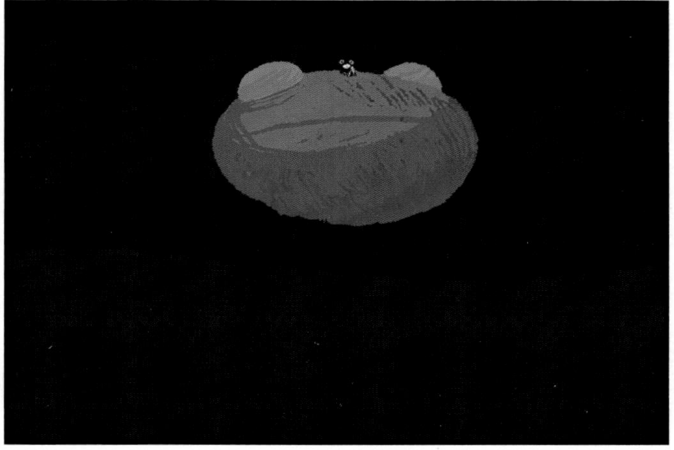

You head back to your hive to get the blue team's session started.

It's been a while.

You revisit the remains of your quaint rural hive. Your lawnring and the small excavation sites you dug up for practice are all overgrown with vegetation.

You haven't been here since the night of the accident. On that night you found your CALLING. The voices of the dead grew louder, urging you to return to the ruins you discovered not long before. You left so abruptly, you didn't even have time to bury your lusus.

But that's fine, because trolls don't typically bury their dead. Leaving bodies to be consumed by wild animals is more customary.

> Aradia: Begin session.

Who's this last troll? Let's see... There's a cuttlefish. And somebody holding a fork, attempting to cull the cuttlefish. Oh, it's Feferi, got it. The master of subtlety is at work yet again. She's a sea princess, but we'll get into her stuff later. Hivebent is very busy, as you know. It's way too busy to settle on any one thing, without suddenly switching to the next set of things it needs to hurry through. The next thing in this case is tuning into Aradia riding her big, cool frog head. Returning to her house is important, because you need a house to play this game. Also, bringing back the frog head is important, because...it just is. She'll need that soon, in a very consequential way.

You have an arrangement to begin the session as co-leader with one of the blue bloods. You understand this player intends to make a power grab, and take sole possession of the leadership role. Such subterfuge is typical of their caste. But you're perfectly ok with this. It's one of the many things you're ok with.

You allow your co-player to take the lead and enter the Medium first. You understand that the leadership role is essentially meaningless, aside from offering the distinction of being the first player to enter. You also understand that entering the game second was always your intention.

> Aradia: Connect to server player.

You have a server player connect to you, someone you personally selected for the role. The devices required for entry are deployed.

The kernelsprite awaits prototyping. But unlike all eleven other players, your dead lusus is not available. You have to use something else.

> Aradia: Tier 1 prototype.

It's not accidental that we're watching Aradia return to the ruins of her old home, in a way that's interwoven with the Flarp disaster backstory. We're methodically exposing pieces of the puzzle to reveal what happened overall, which includes showing traces of the aftermath. We now know that whatever happened to Aradia during this Team Charge/Team Scourge blowup probably resulted in the destruction of her home. She's 0k with that, though. Also, this narration is pretty cagey. It says she has an arrangement to be co-leader with a blue blood but doesn't say which one. We just saw Vriska bragging about such an arrangement with her, but it could also be Equius (it is, in fact, Equius). But even then, Aradia's only using him, too. She's playing everyone. She has a very advanced and pragmatic view of leadership when it comes to a *Sburb* session. She understands there's no such thing as a leader, just a bunch of sad kids getting played by Paradox Space. In a way, she's the most honest type of leader any session has. A leader by absentia, a cold orchestrator of preordained, controlled chaos, who creates the spaces for all the pieces to fall into place, and then just sits back and lets them fall.

Prototyping with the frog head before entering the Medium would prove to be critical for later success. Just another of many assurances whispered by the dead. You've long since stopped questioning them, or doubting the future significance of even spontaneous acts of frivolous desecration.

Compelling your nonplussed server player to perform this task might have proven difficult. Luckily your telekinesis, an ability greatly magnified through your CALLING, would be sufficient to move the massive object, whereas the game cursor likely would not.

Your server player simply watched in mystification.

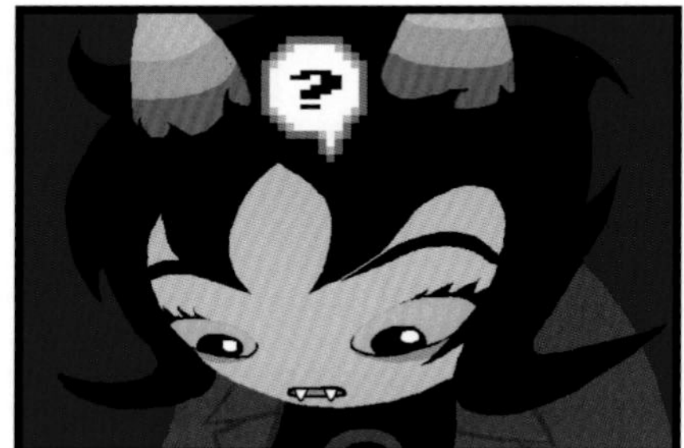

She really just had no idea what the hell was going on.

> Aradia: Enter.

Even Aradia's random feats of destruction, supposedly done just for the sake of vandalism and desecration, turn out to be not that random. There was a major purpose to the preprototyping of this frog, which ultimately results in the exile of the Black Queen, who later becomes Snowman, i.e. Important Stuff. As Aradia's arc progresses and the ghostly freeze on her emotions and desires begins to thaw, one of the themes that starts emerging is the struggle over the nature of what is random in a universe where any appearance of randomness is prewritten as an essential result, and any act of destruction, no matter how violent or disruptive, only serves as a preconditional pillar for any foretold series of outcomes. As a robot, when she gets her emotional legs back under her somewhat, she gets more aggressive and starts lashing out, using acts of chaos, violence, impulsiveness, and randomness as a kind of protest against the bondage that existing in Paradox Space represents. In other words, there's no random act that reality hasn't accounted for, but aggressively enacting them is still kind of a Fuck You statement to the master. It's an attitude borne by a defiant slave, which she knows herself to be, just like her ancestor.

You enter the Medium, taking your place in the LAND OF QUARTZ AND MELODY as the MAID OF TIME.

Meanwhile, your client player has been exploring another world. The blue blood has a present for you. The present cannot be duplicated via alchemy at this stage of the game. It would cost too much grist, a detail which this player had not been aware of. The player would have to progress to the second gate of their own world, arrive through the gate above your hive, and deliver it in person.

Facilitating this delivery was one of the reasons why it was important for you to enter second.

Your server player's confusion is only in part due to learning the ropes of a new game. There is a more significant reason for her befuddlement.

While she followed your advice and went through the simple motions of game setup, at no point were you visible on her monitor. She saw your damaged hive. She saw the alchemiter and other devices she deployed. She saw the strange computing device on the floor, bearing the visage of a species she didn't recognize. She even saw a great big stone frog head fly through the air all by itself, and become the Frogsprite.

And though she would ask why, and you would always delay the answer, the fact remained.

She couldn't see you.

> Aradia: Tier 2 prototype.

Equius demanding that Nepeta be on the blue team now makes a little more sense. (Aside from the fact it's probably what he wanted anyway as a controlling asshole, but still.) He knew she needed to function as Aradia's server player, while he was busy functioning as Aradia's client. I guess in Aradia's estimation Nepeta was among the least likely to make a big deal about Aradia's ghost status, and she's the confidante of Equius, who also knows. Here we also zip to the future to check out Aradia's land, and learn of her Maid of Time designation. Quartz and Melody correlate with her Time aspect. Quartz is used in clocks. As for melody, there are giant music box pieces everywhere, probably always turing their great brass columns, churning out creepy melodies that reverberate throughout the land. There's a little music box in her hive ruins there, which she's probably had for a long time. A little clue about destiny for her younger self to consider.

She couldn't see you up until the moment after the sprite's second prototyping.

Because you were dead all along.

We are all completely blown away by this stunning revelation.

Wow. Dead. Really? Like a ghost?

Huh.

> Nepeta: Interrogate frog girl.

The sassy handling of this delivery was my way of saying, if you were on the ball, this is probably what you suspected was true about Aradia all along. This was a fact that was easily surmised but not officially confirmed until now. Any time a fact is reasonably "guessable," I don't think it makes for very good material presented as a stunning revelation in a straight-faced way by the narrative. So sometimes a jokey non-reveal reveal is a thing that happens in *Homestuck*. There are always so many dumbfounding twists flying around that sometimes it pays not to be too precious with the unveiling of certain facts. In a different story, the "Aradia turned out to be a ghost all along" reveal could be a huge, earth-shattering twist. But in HS, it's just another thing that happens. You go, oh cool, nice to know. All right, what next.

arsenicCatnip [AC] **began trolling** apocalypseArisen [AA]

AC: :33 < aradia i can s33 you!
AC: :33 < that is you right
AA: yes
AC: :33 < why are you the floating frog all of a sudden?
AA: im dead
AA: my spirit merged with the fr0gsprite
AC: :33 < wow
AC: :33 < dead
AC: :33 < really?
AA: like a gh0st
AC: :33 < huh
AC: :33 < well i hope this doesnt make me sound dumb
AC: :33 < but i am completely blown away by that stunning revelation!
AA: y0u d0nt s0und dumb
AC: :33 < whew! :33
AC: :33 < how did you die?
AA: i ign0red the advice 0f a friend
AA: and made s0me bad ch0ices
AC: :33 < *ac rumples up her nose in purrplexment at aa’s really vague and spooky answer*
AC: :33 < but actually thats good because i kind of think i dont want to know
AC: :33 < its making me sad to think about :((
AA: 0k
AA: nepeta can y0u please keep this a secret
AC: :33 < yes i purrmise i wont tell anyone about it
AC: :33 < and by purrmise i mean promise just so you know im serious!
AA: thank y0u
AA: ribbit
AA: wh00ps
AC: :33 < h33 h33 h33!!!

> Aradia: Be the huge bitch.

Even Nepeta is getting in on the act of roasting anyone who was surprised by the fact that Aradia was a ghost. Also I don’t think it will surprise anyone that Nepeta is HELLS OF excited that Frog Aradia now officially ribbits.

Bluh bluh.

> Enter name.

Your name is VRISKA SERKET.

You are a master of EXTREME ROLE PLAYING. You can't get enough of it, or really any game of high stakes and chance. You have persisted with the habit even in spite of your ACCIDENT. But then again, you don't have much choice.

Your lusus is VERY HUNGRY, ALL THE TIME. She can only be appeased by the FLESH OF YOUNG TROLLS. You cloud campaigns for teams of Flarpers, utilizing your abilities for ORCHESTRATING THE DEMISE OF THE IMPRESSSSSSSSIONA8LE. Your victories supply you with treasure, experience points, and SPIDER FOOD.

You are something of an APOCALYPSE BUFF, which is something you can be on Alternia. You are fascinated by end of the world scenarios, and enjoy constructing DOOMSDAY DEVICES for the hell of it. You are drawn to means of DARK PROGNOSTICATION and the advantages they offer, particularly in gaming scenarios. Your abilities in this department were hobbled with the loss of your VISION EIGHTFOLD, and you have since sought alternatives through various BLACK ORACLES. You consult with these ominous globes, but routinely destroy them in frustration over the PUZZLING GUARANTEED INACCURACY of their predictions. Breaking them has developed into a habit BORDERING ON FETISHISTIC, and with each you destroy, you add to an insurmountable stockpile of TERRIBLE LUCK. You have to stop. But addiction is a powerful thing.

Your trolltag is arachnidsGrip and your st8ments tend to 8e just a little 8it overdramaaaaaaaatic.

What will you do?

> Vriska: Check out cool drawing on wall.

File under obvious: trolls emerged in the story as an alien parody of real-life internet trolls, those who aggrieve and harass others online in many ways, in the form of many profiles, such as raging capslock shouters, argumentative jackasses, or disingenuous "pranksters" who casually toss around death threats. When expanding on the roster in Hivebent, the creative challenge became crafting a diverse range of such profiles. And a corollary to this challenge was imagining what profile would maximize the qualities that make someone a troll in this sense. In other words, who is the most trollish troll in this group, what are the traits that someone fitting that description has, and what form will they take in terms of personality and role in the story? Vriska is the result of this effort, and one way of looking at her arc in the story is as a simple exploration of what it means to draft a character designed to have the ultimate troll profile. Being the ultimate troll doesn't necessarily mean being the biggest asshole (though there are times when she gets that award too). It means being the most controversial. One designed to incite, to maximize drama and division, inside the story and out. -->

You drew your own role playing character for fun, as many Flarpers are prone to do. She is the best character, and you wish you were her. Oh wait, you are her! Your wish has been granted. Probably as a special boon for being so great at everything.

Her name is Marquise Spinneret Mindfang, scourge of land dwellers and sea dwellers alike, and worst nightmare to silly BOY-SKYLARKS everywhere. She has accumulated more treasure and gained more levels than any member of the PETTICOAT SEAGRIFT class ever.

She gained all the levels. All of them.

Yeah!!!!!!!!

> Vriska: Begin meddling.

--> She's constantly used that way, as the number-one wedge character, dropped into situations to stir up controversy, get people arguing, and fuel noisy divisions in fandom leading to heated arguments about morality, the motivations behind her conduct, and the dispensation of justice. Since serving as the ultimate troll, fandom wedge, and escalator of drama is an inseparable part of her profile, by extension the narrative has a way of constantly dragging her back into the spotlight to keep stirring the pot, ratchet up controversy, and continue forcing the plot forward by dint of her overbearing personality and need to be important. Whether she's the one forcing her way back into the spotlight all the time due to ego, or it's actually the narrative always pulling her back in as a preferred tool of effective melodrama, thus giving her a reputation as someone favored by the author as a vehicle for mayhem and controversy, is left for readers to decide. It's also left for them to decide if there's even a difference between those things. But one consequence of this blatantly evident favoritism she either enjoys or steals from the narrative is that, after enough time goes by, it becomes an indisputable point of fact that, without caveat, excuse, or even the slightest attempt at conveying any sense of shame about the development, Vriska is presented as the author's canonical waifu. Unfortunately this isn't a joke, and leads to major plot developments later on, with unspeakably dire consequences for everybody. Again, both inside the story, and out.

You have a lot to do. So many irons in the fire OW!

Lousy dice. You just can't ever seem to go anywhere in your hive without stepping on an errant D4. Pointy little bastards.

It's just your bad luck, you guess. You've had such terrible luck ever since your accident. And it just keeps getting worse. As far as you're concerned, the world can't end soon enough.

As you were saying. So many irons in the fire. Such a tangled web. It is a web full of flaming irons and mixed metaphors.

Tonight is a big night. You have a lot of meddling to catch up on tonight. Bugging and fussing and meddling.

> Vriska: Take dice.

Luck is her thing. I mean, it's her aspect, sort of: Light encompasses concepts relating to fortune. But when I say it's her thing, I also mean it's a theme, one of the many pieces that combine to form the constituents of what we call an arc. Her arc is an absolute whopper. Where to even begin surveying it? Some character arcs are so big, it's probably better to view them as a series of phases or chapters, all of which thread together and relate to a few bigger ideas. The "bad luck" vs. "good luck" chapter of Vriska's arc is more of an Act 5 thing and becomes less relevant later. But for now, it's established that this bad luck streak started with the "accident," which resulted in the maiming of all her friends and herself, and the death of Aradia. Even though there's something to the concept of luck in the story (she can use it as a power to get lucky rolls, etc.), I don't think you have to be a genius of literary analysis to detect that "bad luck" in this case is something of a scapegoat for her. More likely it's shorthand for a guilty conscience, and the bad karma associated with it. There's a hole in her soul, created by a life of misdeeds she won't face, and the struggles for success, treasure, victory, glory, and above all, relevance, are constant exertions throughout her very long journey in the vain and mostly unsuccessful attempt to fill this moral vacuum inside her. In other words, it's an arc of ambition as a staggering gesture of overcompensation. Like Karkat on steroids, with much darker underlying pathos.

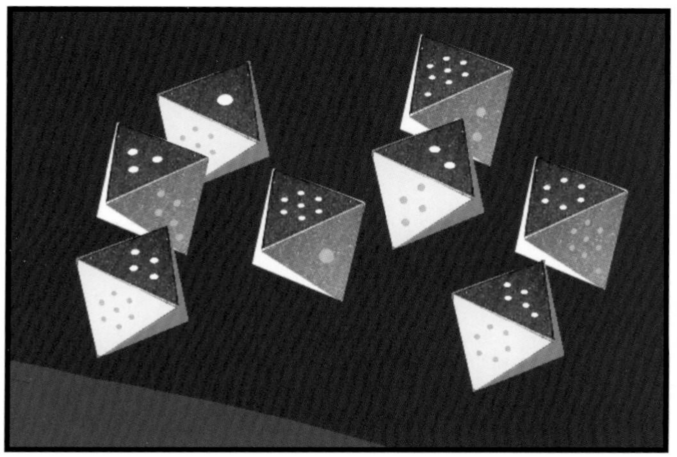

You equip your enchanted dice set, the fabled FLUORITE OCTET.

It consists of eight D8, plundered from a ghost ship during a particularly challenging campaign. In ancient times such weapons were employed by roving bands of GAMBLIGNANTS, deadly marauders with a passion for chance. They all died off though. Took too many crazy risks.

Rolling the dice will execute a wide range of highly unpredictable attacks. Very high rolls can be devastating to even the most powerful opponents.

Of course with the luck you've had lately, you couldn't make a good roll to save your life. Got to do something about this awful luck.

Gotta catch a br8k!!!!!!!!

When you get worked up about stuff you put 8's in places that don't really make a lot of sense phonetically.

> Vriska: Begin meddling.

Because Vriska is so special, and is basically my wife, she gets to have a really cool and unique weapon. This set of dice is a genuinely nice and well-designed group of objects, particularly from the POV of an RPG nerd, which is what Vriska is. This must have been a hell of a find for her in that ghost ship. 8 dice, with 8 sides each. 8^8 makes for almost 17 million possible rolls. 8 obviously is Vriska's magic number, but 8-8 pairs have some ominous significance. In this story the 8-ball has grim associations with the destruction of a universe (see: Snowman). Two 8s is therefore associated with the destruction of two universes, which is a cosmically synchronous event with the summoning of Lord English. English is often shown with his pool ball eyes frozen in the grim 8-8 state, and this is in fact the state they lock to when confronted with Vriska moments before his presumable defeat. In that sense, it's a shorthand for "game over." 88 is also associated with Hitler. The bad news for this number just keeps piling up. Also I have the same initials as Hitler. Okay, I'm getting a signal in this earpiece from my producer to stop talking about Hitler. But you get the idea. 8 is a cursed number, and double 8 is octuply bad.

Time to get this show on the road. There are SO MANY people to meddle with tonight.

After you ditch an unwelcome solicitor first, that is. Doesn't she realize how rude it is to meddle??

You'll fuss with her meddling later.

What now?

Oh, him. You thought he'd washed his hands of you. Strange timing that he's bugging you tonight after so long without a peep from him.

> Vriska: Deal with this guy.

Vriska is, along with her many other traits, a huge hypocrite. She finds Kanaya's meddling very bothersome, and calls Kanaya out on the habit often. But by her own admission, Vriska's basically the meddler in chief. She has a pattern of doing this with a lot of her relationships, i.e. projecting when it comes to the defining feature of that relationship. She complains of being the victim, when she's the victimizer. Of being meddled with, when she's the meddler. Of being manipulated, when she's the manipulator. Speaking of manipulators, hey look. Doc is here.

Hello.
AG: Oh my god, why are you talking to me????????
This is the last time we'll ever talk.
AG: Still sticking with the white text I see. So smooth and stylish!
AG: I forgot how much I loved highlighting it to read all the 8oring things you have to say.
AG: It's like a fun game for super extra handicapped retarded people. Like opening a present! Find out what o8noxious thing the mystery tool typed.
AG: What is it!
A parting courtesy, I suppose.
All the ways I've exploited you were meant to bring about the events that will take place this evening.
Knowing this will provide context for the events in your near future, and will affect how you behave in response.
These events will be just as important as those preceding it.
I've gone to great lengths, you see.
AG: You didn't exploit me.
AG: You are just a petty douche with a 8ad temper who likes to pl8y g8mes, and all I did w8s humor you.
I did exploit you, very thoroughly. It was easy.
AG: So full of yourself!!!!!!!!
Have I ever lost a game?
AG: Don't ch8nge the su8ject!!!!!!!!
What subject are you referring to?
AG: XXXXO
AG: I'm going to log off in a 8ig huff and you have to promise not to use that nasty trick where you log me 8ack on out of petty douchey spite!
AG: And then we can go 8ack to never ever talking, 8ecause man! That was heaven when it was like th8t!!!!!!!!
There's no need for that kind of assurance.
I'll be brief.
I no longer hold you accountable for any wrongdoing. In fact, I've given your transgression very little thought since the incident.
If you acknowledge this amnesty and regard it as sincere, you may begin to find the odds falling in your favor again.
This may be essential if you are to succeed on your journey.
AG: Mm hmm. Slow down! Man.
AG: I am just wearing out so many pens taking all these important notes! Fuuuuuuuuck!
AG: Fuck you for ruining all my good note-taking pens and giving me this terri8le cramp in my good note-taking hand!!!!!!!!

Here's a fun media gimmick lost in print. On the site, Doc's text was white on near-white, making it impossible to read. So you had to select the text with your mouse to highlight it (as Vriska openly laments here, doubling as a tip to the reader) in order to make it visible. Old-school message boards often used this as a low-tech method when users wanted to hide spoilers. This is a pretty fitting way to have the reader reveal Doc's text, since he's omniscient, knows the future, and can be pretty loose with certain facts. So his words can be regarded as a kind of spoiler which those conversing with him may or may not want to highlight and thus spoil themselves on.

Incredible, the risks you take with your scorn.
But of course it was your unpleasant, simplistic temperament that made you so easy to control.
Vicious and predictable, like an insect.
If you turn a swarm of wasps on a crowd, the outcome is certain.
It takes no skilled strategist to understand this. You were in fact a waste of my talents.
A primitive expedient.
AG: Blech. What a sno8. You're worse than my meddley meddler meddlefriend.
I wonder why they waste their camaraderie on you. I'll never understand it.
AG: I thought you said you would 8e 8rief????????
I'll say one last thing.
Though the magnitude of the ensuing destruction resulting directly from your actions will be neither possible or necessary for you to fathom, there nevertheless ought to be a silver lining.
The only question is whether you will live long enough to see it.
I'm not a gambling man.
But if I was, I wouldn't bet on it.
Goodbye.
AG: Zzzzzzzz. 8ye, assh8le.

More hollow comebacks. As hollow and wishywashy as the inside of one of these dumb black globes. What use is all that attitude against a guy who's never wrong? It's so depressing, you can't even work up the energy to smash this stupid thing.

Maybe you could stand to have some camaraderie wasted on you, even if it comes from a meddley meddler meddlefriend.

> Vriska: Endure meddling.

Doc Scratch is such a powerful manipulator, he manipulates other skilled manipulators to manipulate others on his behalf. In this case, he does most of his manipulation work on Vriska and Terezi, the Scourge Sister manipulation duo extraordinaire. He manipulates them to manipulate everyone else, and he also plays them off each other, all the while being very smug about it. It's probably easy to be such an incredible puppet master when you're omniscient, but he doesn't care. His whole act tends to be "playing with his cards facing up" as kind of a mindfuck power move, constantly signaling that "I'm going to get you to do what I want you to do, without making any secret about what I'm doing." Or, "I'm going to mislead you without technically lying, you're going to be able to tell that's what I'm doing, but there's still nothing you can do about it, and none of your objections matter." He's a fairly conventional devil figure in this way, as well as a nefarious alt-author, with the power to stand in for me, or subvert the narrative. These are his top-level qualities as a character and narrative device, which are explored much more intensively late in Act 5 during his story-hijack move. But there's an awful lot more to say about him than this. You'll see.

arachnidsGrip [AG] began trolling grimAuxiliatrix [GA]

AG: Whaaaaaaaat.
GA: Just Wanted To Know
GA: Is Your Lusus Dead Yet
AG: Huh? What kind of question is that!
AG: Is this a trick? Are you trying to sa8otage me? Are you in cahoots with someone????????
GA: Uh No
AG: Cahooooooooots!!!!!!!!
AG: Cahoots I say.
GA: You Sure Do Seem To Be Saying Cahoots
GA: Im Just Asking
GA: Because Mines Dead
AG: What? Oh no.
AG: How did that happen?
GA: It Was Just Her Time
AG: Really? Are you sure it wasn't sa8otage? I would suspect sa8otage if I was you.
GA: No There Was No Plot Or Conspiracy Or Any Trace Of Saboteurs Operating Through The Special And Magical Union One Can Only Describe As Being In Cahoots With Another
GA: When A Virgin Mother Grub Abdicates And Renounces Brooding
GA: Her Time Will Be Relatively Short
GA: I Always Knew This
AG: ::::(
AG: She was so cool, you had the coolest lusus of anyone I know.
AG: I wanted to meet her some day.
GA: Maybe You Still Can
AG: Yeah, meet her corpse! I guess that's not so bad a consol8tion prize.
AG: Seeing a 8ig dead cool mother gru8. Wow!
AG: You were so lucky. My lusus sucks! Haha.
AG: Why did you ask if she's dead, anyway? Do you know something????????
GA: They Are All Dying
GA: Or Are Going To Soon
GA: I Believe Its A Preemptive Consequence Of The Game We Are About To Play
GA: If A Preemptive Consequence Is A Concept That Can Be Said To Hold Any Meaning
GA: But From What I Understand If It Is Applicable In Any Sphere At All Then This Game Holds That Sphere
AG: Okaaaaaaaay, I don't really get that. So you can just go ahead think I'm some dum8 flighty 8road again.
GA: I Wasnt Going To Think That
GA: You Know What I Dont Think Even I Really Understand What I Just Said So Nevermind
AG: Now you have me a little worried. Man! I hope she's ok.

Kanaya, being the "Jade" of the session, gets a lunchbox holographic computer too for some reason, branded not with Squiddles but the cuttlefish troll equivalent, presumably called Cuttles. Even though Kanaya is the Jade of the troll session, she's really not much like Jade at all in terms of personality. But aside from that, you can list up a ton of similarities: Space players, living in a cool tower next to a volcano, "raised" by a First Guardian, etc. Kanaya even has jade blood.

AG: Why would this happen? This is just my luck. Have some died 8esides yours????????
AG: And uh, you know who's, I guess. ::::o
GA: Yes A Few
GA: Karkat Thinks Its His Fault
GA: He Believes His Actions Triggered An Inauspicious Chain Reaction
AG: You mean a curse?
GA: Sure
AG: Wow, between his curse and my shitty luck we are so screwed.
GA: Im Not Surprised To See You Endorse His Paranoia Without Hesitation
GA: But I Was Attempting To Illustrate A Point In Bringing It Up
AG: Whew! There goes another one sailing over the idi8t girl's head! Ok, lay it on me.
GA: These Events Are Inevitable And Regardless Of Whatever Emotional Entanglements Obfuscate Their Significance They Will Ultimately Serve An Important Purpose
GA: The Curse Had Nothing To Do With It
GA: And Karkats Notion Of A Curse Is Inseparable From His Perception Of Events As Intrinsically Negative And As Tailored To His Personal Dissatisfaction
GA: And Your Bad Luck Is The Same Way
GA: I Believe Anyway
AG: Uh. Ok.
GA: What Would Happen If You Just Cleaned Up A Bit
GA: Dont You Think You Would Step On A Few Less Hard Triangles
AG: Why do you try to help me and stuff? What's the point!
AG: It's kind of bothersome. And insulting sometimes!
AG: So I have a messy room. 8ig deal. My luck fucking 8lows! It's got nothing to do with it and you just don't even know.
AG: Meddler. Why you so meddley, Miss Meddlesome McFussyfangs????????
GA: Because Youre Dangerous
AG: No way! I'm just fine. Why don't you can it.
GA: Every Time You Tell Me To Can It I Think Its Funny
GA: I Mean Its Just A Funny Thing To Say Dont You Think
AG: ::::P
GA: Its Ok To Be Dangerous
GA: Lots Of People Are
GA: And Dangerous People Can Be Really Important
GA: Maybe Even The Most Important Sometimes
GA: But It Just Means Theres Got To Be Someone Around To Keep An Eye On Them
GA: And If Not Me Then Who
GA: Everyone Has An Important Job To Do
AG: Ok, so you're spying on me. Kind of creepy! Man, m8y8e you should get a l8fe.
AG: Or you know, if you're so h8gh 8nd might8 an8 th8nk you're so gr8at, m8y88 you c8uld oh I d8n't kn8w........
AG: TRY AND ST8P ME FROM DO8NG B8D THINGS????????

Here's another pretty good exchange, which establishes stuff about them both individually, before they jettison each other almost completely and virtually never talk to each other again after Hivebent. Kanaya has a fascination with dangerous girls she needs to "keep an eye on," which sort of makes Vriska her starter Rose. A much shittier and more difficult to manage Rose. I mentioned Kanaya's enabling trait before, which Vriska almost seems to be calling her out on here. Her "meddlesome," enabling-yet-condemning approach to certain relations puts her in an odd social box, which people don't quite know what to do with, and Vriska seems to struggle with it too. Does Vriska like her and want to earn respect from her? Does she want her to go away? Vriska is the type who sucks up to people and wants approval from them if they show apathy toward her (Aradia), and shows disdain for those who do the opposite, either positively or negatively (Tavros), and Kanaya confusingly exhibits both traits. Too cool, too aloof for Vriska, but oh also, she cares a lot and wants to protect her from her own dangerous tendencies. Some of it reads as simple attraction to these types of girls, but a big part of it also has to do with Kanaya's strong maternal streak, the need to "mother" certain people. It doesn't seem that Vriska dislikes her per se, but unfortunately Kanaya's conflicted, concern-based approach to the relationship has dropped her right in the Friend Zone. Actually, the place Kanaya finds herself in a lot is probably better described as the Mom Zone.

GA: That Wouldnt Work
GA: If I Tried To Stop You You Would Regard Me As An Enemy
GA: Instead Of Merely As A Nuisance
GA: And What Good Would That Do
GA: So Im Afraid Mcfussyfangs It Must Be
AG: U88888888h!
AG: Ok, gr8. Fine! I'm going to check on my lusus now.
AG: 8ut I'm starting to think you are full of shit, and I am quite sure she will 8e QU8TE FIN8!
GA: Youre Right Anything Can Happen I Guess
GA: But Just So You Know Im Sorry For Your Loss In Advance

arachnidsGrip [AG] **ceased trolling** grimAuxiliatrix [GA]

arachnidsGrip [AG] **began trolling** grimAuxiliatrix [GA]

AG: Aaaaaaaah!
AG: Man, why d8dn't I just get th8 last w8rd and sign off real qu8ck like I usu8lly do????????
AG: Let you sne8k th8t stink8n' littl8 ninja quip in th8r8. Ah! So m8d.
AG: Lousy st8pid godd8mn supportive fri8nd!

arachnidsGrip [AG] **ceased trolling** grimAuxiliatrix [GA]

> Vriska: Check on lusus.

You go down the like fifty million stairs to her nest below. You wonder if any other kid on the planet has such a high maintenance lusus? You DOUBT it.

Vriska, basically: Fine, mom, I'll go check on my other mom. On the matter of Kanaya's maternality again... Every troll obviously started with one very basic idea, something tied to their zodiac sign, which then informed their troll handle and led to various points of characterization. Virgo was a tricky one. What do you do with virginity? Kanaya's handle is grimAuxiliatrix. Auxiliatrix is a term associated with the Virgin Mary. So in Christianity at least, virginity has mythological association with motherhood. And thus we have something to build on. Themes of motherhood run all throughout Kanaya's arc, in some pretty literal ways. (For her ancestor, blatantly literal when it comes to Christian lore parallels.) But it's more than just content for an arc. Maternal impulses are woven into her characterization. She acts this way toward Vriska (but only while she has a thing for her), toward Karkat, and later toward her girlfriend as she helps her through her struggles. Basically she's like this with people she cares about, and not so much with those she doesn't. It also goes a long way toward explaining her gravitation toward the thankless ashen quadrant and natural talent for being an auspistice. I just know you're jittering in anticipation for the dirt on quadrants. Patience.

You pass by one of your completed doomsday devices. You promised you'd build it for an especially powerful and influential member of the nautical aristocracy, in return for his collusion during your campaigns. Some guy you were in cahoots with! You guess none of it matter now though.

It was tough to build, and isn't perfect yet. Luckily one of your pals nearby is pretty handy with technology. He can be tapped for parts and favors frequently.

You wonder if any other kid on the planet has as many irons in the fire as you.

YOU DOUBT IT.

It's an amusing and easy to forget sidebar to Vriska that one of her hobbies is building doomsday devices. This one is for Eridan, obviously. Probably the funniest thing about it is the fact that it almost certainly won't ever work as intended—powerful enough to blow some stuff up, but never the whole world. She just made some empty promise to Eridan to get him to do something for her. There's virtually no way she's ever interacted with him without dunking on him in some manner. Another funny thing about it is the fact that getting help from one of her "pals nearby" (Equius) probably just means she made him do almost all of the work and is taking full credit for it, just like she's doing with Aradiabot. Additional trivia: this art asset is just the doomsday dice cascader from a *Problem Sleuth* bonus page. The fact that this asset already existed is probably just what gave me the idea to include it at all, to give it to the character who has dice as a weapon.

See, look at this. She's fine. Fine and huge and hungry as ever.

You... guess you're relieved? Yes, of course. Whew! Why wouldn't you be. It would be devastating if anything happened to your dear sweet custodian.

Vriska is messed up mostly because of Spidermom issues. Sure, it also has to do with her ruthless culture, expectations placed on those in her class, and how a child troll is supposed to prepare for a brutal life as an adult. But having to kill kids to feed her big, nasty mom her whole life probably isn't helping. This is some good backstory stuff, because it provides a lot of cheap and easy fuel for those who wish to exonerate her for all her flaws and misdeeds. Blaming Spidermom is sort of the low-hanging fruit in the ever-raging Vriskourse.

If you're asking why Vriska saw fit to dangle her highly volatile, explosive, work-in-progress doomsday device precariously between cliffs, hovering just over her lusus, you're asking a damn good question. My guess is, the device is a little too big to keep inside. Also this way, Equius can go down there and "help" with it (work on it for her, by himself) any time he needs to. If you like a good conspiracy, you could also speculate she put it there BECAUSE there's an off chance it could fall and kill her mom.

You guess there's no delaying this guy's introduction anymore.

As long as we're in the neighborhood.

> Enter name.

Fakeout-delaying Equius's intro until now was a pretty good move, since it allowed for this nice external transition shot between two neighboring hives. Not bad. Here's a totally nuts fact: the retconned oil isn't on the poster anymore. It was in the first shot we cut away from, but now it's gone. How does the retconned oil work? Does it stay there permanently, or does it exist fleetingly in the one panel it's shown in? This opens up some nasty metaphysical questions. By retconning something back into any given *moment* in the story, is it being retconned into the true stream of events, with the panel simply displaying the single moment we are viewing? Or is it being retconned back into a specific *panel*, which should be seen as a narrative construct in and of itself, not merely an abstract viewport which has no acknowledgeable identity? It's too early for this shit, friends. We're still crawling through some very dense, humorous alien lore here. We need to steel ourselves a lot more before we grapple with the metafictional bullshittery of late Act 6.

Your name is EQUIUS ZAHHAK.

You love being STRONG.

You are so strong, you would surely be the class of the elite legion of RUFFIANNIHILATORS. And while such a calling would be quite honorable, you would prefer to join the ranks of the ARCHERADICATORS, perhaps the most noble echelon the imperial forces have to offer. Unfortunately, you SUCK AT ARCHERY. You have not successfully fired a SINGLE ARROW. Every time you try, you BREAK THE BOW. You are simply too strong. You have broken so many bows, it has developed into a habit BORDERING ON FETISHISTIC.You have to stop. But addiction is a powerful thing.

You have a great appreciation for THE FINE ARTS. You use your aristocratic connections to acquire PRICELESS MASTERPIECES, painted in the oldest and most respected Alternian tradition of NUDE MUSCLEBEAST PORTRAITS. These striking depictions of the EXQUISITE FAUNA native to Alternia remind you of the PUREST PHYSICAL IDEAL that must be sought by anyone who professes a LOVE OF STRENGTH. When those of lesser bloodlines turn up their uncultured noses at such stunning material, it MAKES YOU FURIOUS.

Practically everything MAKES YOU FURIOUS. You have so much rage, it can only be expressed through STAGGERING QUANTITIES OF PHYSICAL VIOLENCE. You build strong and sturdy robots, set them to kill mode, and BEAT THE SHIT OUT OF THEM in caged brawls.Sometimes you LOSE TEETH. But they usually grow back.

Your trolltag is centaursTesticle and with your bow and arrow ever at the ready, you D --> Take e%ception to 100d language unbefitting of b100 b100ds

What will you do?

> Equius: Check on lusus.

Equius has a few things in common with Vriska. Not a lot, but enough to be worth noting. Though Equius is a notch higher on the hemospectrum, they're both blue-blooded aristocracy whose castes maintain both deep contempt for those lower and (especially in indigo cases) exceedingly high regard for those above. The fact that they're neighbors suggests there isn't that big a divide between blue and indigo in terms of status and daily life. Both classes probably cluster together somewhat in a kind of snobby symbiosis, since they're one notch below purple-blooded clown hell, which is a radically different kind of cultural aristocracy. And both are one notch above the jade and teal middling classes, which enjoy some status, but both castes revolve around more functional, municipal services such as breeding administration and law enforcement. But on just a character level, there are a couple echos here. Vriska obsessively breaks 8-balls in a way "bordering on fetishistic." Equius does the same with bows. Both for different reasons. For her, relating to her obsession and frustration with her luck. For him, obsession and frustration with his strength, something that he loves about himself but which prohibits him from doing another thing he loves. Fetishizing destruction and chaos for reasons along these lines is a theme that runs through this group, especially when you include Aradia's fixation on it as well.

Now where did that craven excuse for a custodian go. It makes you furious when he goes missing like this. Probably off somewhere nursing his bruises. You swear, the old boy is made of glass. You are starting to get agitated.

Aurthour! Where are you???

Oh, there he is. He was just preparing an ice cold glass of nutritious LUSUS MILK for you, with a thick foamy head on it, just the way you like it.

You cannot hope to beat Aurthour in a butler-off. He is simply the best there is.

> Equius: Thank Aurthour.

You accept the frosty beverage and give the good fellow a grateful pat, as gently as possible.

Once *Homestuck* hit its "start introducing way too many characters" stride (Hivebent is exactly when that occured), there were a lot of issues I started thinking about when it came to rolling out tons of diverse, often ridiculous new characters. Primarily, I saw them as interesting challenges in writing and characterization. By the very nature of trolls, a lot of these guys were always going to be pretty bad, obnoxious, gross, or creepy, particularly at first glance. So one major challenge I found interesting was something like, "How do you introduce someone who appears to be almost instantly revolting or objectionable, and then proceed to make the reader love this person against all odds?" Equius is probably the strongest example up to this point of me embracing this idea as a challenge. The initial impressions he gives are pretty horrible. He's constantly angry, racist, humorless, has weird horse porn everywhere, and...oh no, does he BEAT HIS LUSUS TOO?? Just awful. But the unfolding of his character thereafter reveals certain mitigating truths. He doesn't beat his lusus, he's just so strong he leaves bruises despite his best efforts at tenderness. It's like a disability he struggles with. If you want to go full sadstuck, picture him unable to hug his dear moirail upon meeting her, for fear of crushing her fragile bones. There are many small ways his portrait is guided so that a guy who really has no right to be seen as endearing ends up being strangely so, often in ways that aren't even easy to explain. I firmly believe that if you don't love Equius after you've read most of *Homestuck*, then there's something wrong with you.

Seriously, he's like a soft summer peach.

> Equius: Drink lusus milk.

Lusus milk is the secret to being STRONG.

Actually it isn't. You like to think that though. The truth is you're really strong because you're kind of a freak. You were chosen by one of the strongest lusus species on the planet. It was the only sort of custodian that could handle raising you.

Whoops there goes the glass, as usual.

It's an obscure fact that Aurthour is one of the strongest lusii on the planet. He appears to be a miniature version of something in the musclebeast family, specifically from a race of centaur butlers. (We see much bigger versions of these on Jake's island.) This helps establish the magnitude of Equius's strength. It's like the common trope where you show a strong guy, just so another stronger guy can defeat him easily, to show how strong the REALLY strong guy is. Except it's a classic twist on the trope: show a guy's really strong dad, and demonstrate how easily he is bruised at the slightest loving touch from his son. If only we had a nickel for every time we've seen it.

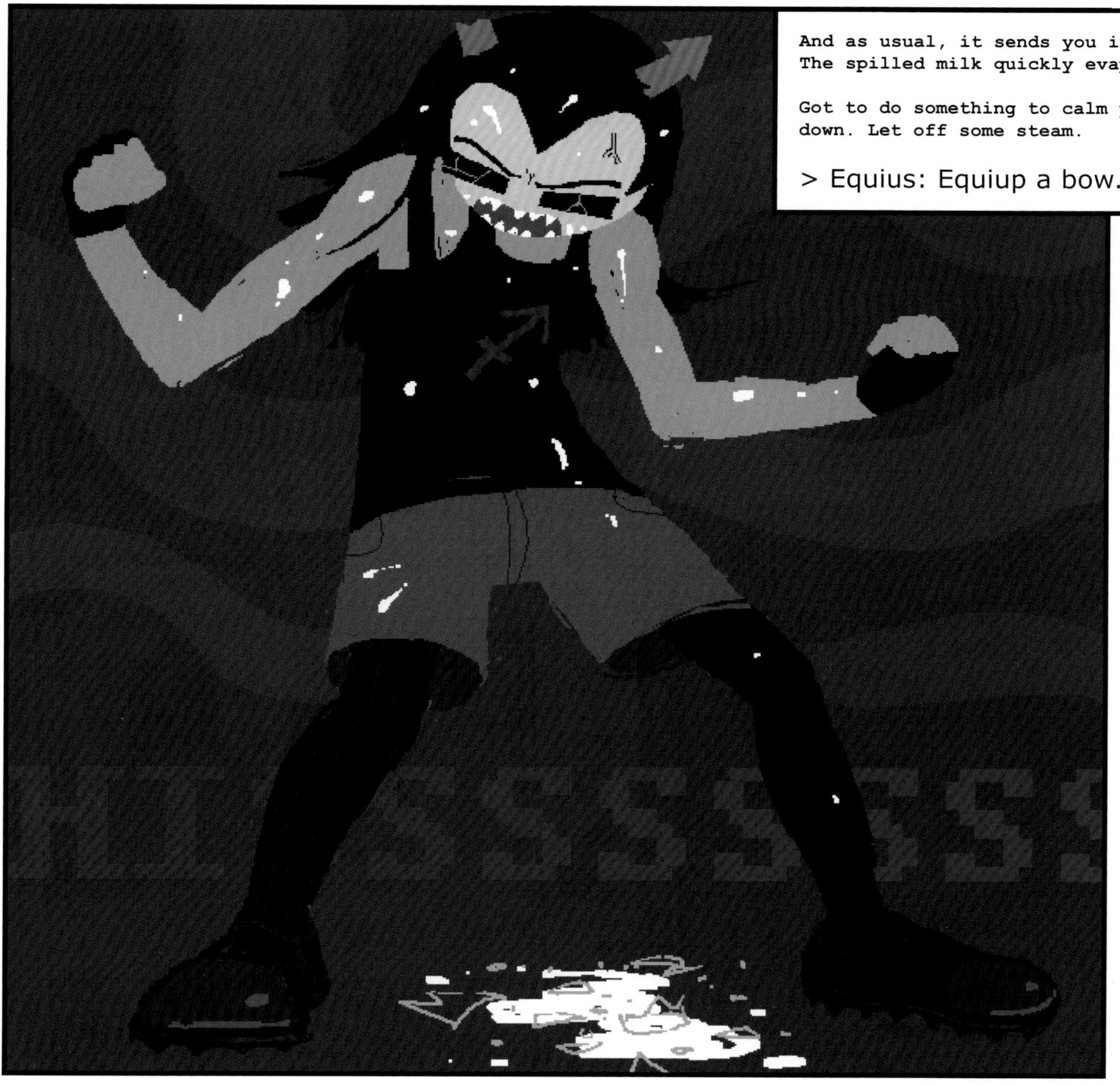

And as usual, it sends you into a rage. The spilled milk quickly evaporates.
Got to do something to calm yourself down. Let off some steam.
> Equius: Equiup a bow.

Equius's black pinstripe leggings are a great design choice. Why did I do this? I don't know, but in his sprite form I probably originally intended them to be socks. But because a sprite's legs are so stumpy, the socks come up to the edge of the shorts, making it seem like they're tights. So when I drew this hero mode shot, I just extrapolated from that. My only regret is not making them just a little shorter, leaving the traditional anime *zettai ryouiki* saucy skin-gap between the top of the stocking and the shorts. As if this panel wasn't steamy enough.

You mean equip.

A little archery practice ought to cool you off. But of course the piece of shit snaps like a twig the moment you pick it up.

Actually, the feel of the brittle wood giving way under the astonishing might of your mangrit is starting to calm you down already.

You equip it to your 1/2BOWKIND SPECIBUS, which is pretty much useless.

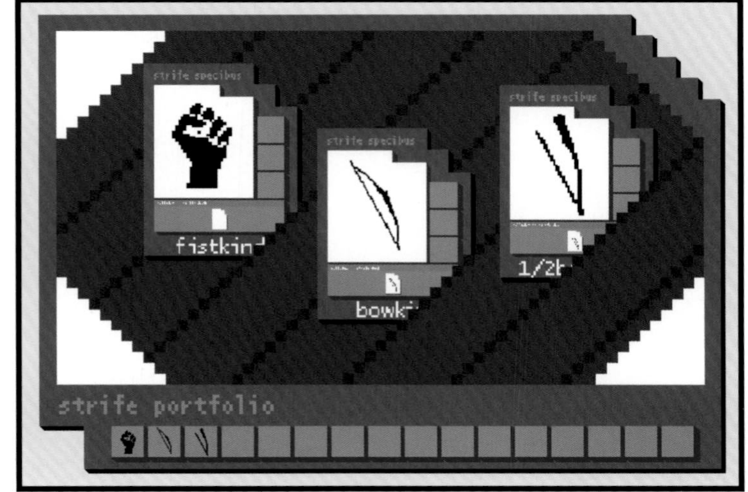

You also keep a plain old BOWKIND SPECIBUS in the event that you are able to fire an arrow some day. Because a boy can dream, right?

But for more practical purposes, you keep a FISTKIND card on hand. You stow them all in your STRIFE PORTFOLIO.

Remember the STRIFE PORTFOLIO? It still exists. It didn't stop existing or anything.

> Equius: Answer.

The strife portfolio does still exist. Sometimes I have to remind people that things still exist, because so many things exist, and just because you forget about them doesn't mean they stop existing. A few characters have multiple allocations naturally, like Equius. Roxy is another player who has fistkind, and she also happens to be a Void player like him. Is there something to be said for Void players being naturally inclined toward fighting empty-handed? Whoops, I just made *Homestuck* scholars around the world throw years of research in the trash.

You proceed to have a conversation we read not all that long ago.
It went mostly like this.

CT: D --> **Yes** AC: :33 < no CT: D --> **Yes** AC: :33 < no CT: D --> **Yes** AC: :33 < no CT: D --> **Yes** AC: :33 < no CT: D --> **Yes** AC: :33 < no CT: D --> **Yes** AC: :33 < no CT: D --> **Yes** AC: :33 < no

But when all was said and done, you are quite sure you convinced your good friend to stay on the right team. Not the team full of degenerates with swill coursing through their veins.
You're starting to get worked up again.

Routine helps calm you down. Maybe you will talk to another friend. You talk to him every day for some reason. Though it's not exactly right to call him a friend, since you despise him. Your relationship with the fellow is difficult to describe.

It should be noted that in troll language, the word for friend is exactly the same as the word for enemy.

> Equius: Talk to friend/enemy.

Background Aurthour Swiffering up the spilled milk is one of the purest things ever to happen in the comic. The friend/enemy Equius is about to talk to is Gamzee. It's another odd and rather forgettable fact that he has a habit of talking to Gamzee every day. He has a frustrating relationship with Gamzee, because literally everyone does. Equius's daily objective is to simultaneously prostrate himself before a superior while ripping him to shreds for his clowny, stoner demeanor and absolute failure to behave in keeping with his station of superiority. The tension is very titillating for Equius, as it seems all inner conflict is. It's a daily regimen that verges on erotic, and this dynamic finally culminates in a fairly graphic way during the "murderstuck" phase of Act 5. That they speak so often leads to some interesting questions about them. How close are they, really? What on earth do they talk about every day, aside from Equius telling him how reprehensible he thinks he is? Equius, along with all his other traits, is very mysterious. Nobody ever really knows what he's up to. Vriska, a cunning person herself, seems clueless as to his Aradiabot double-cross. He operates in the shadows, or "dark spots," as a Void player. Even Doc can't see what he's up to, for the most part.

centaursTesticle [CT] began trolling terminallyCapricious [TC]

CT: D --> Have I ever told you what a reprehensible disgrace you are
TC: hAhA, fUcK yEaH, oNlY eVeRy MoThErFuCkIn DaY bRo!
CT: D --> I'm not in a very good mood
CT: D --> There are a few things I'd like to get off my chest
TC: MoThErFuCkIn SpIlL iT, dOn'T bE aLl KeEpIn ThAt ShIt BoTtLeD uP
TC: lIkE a FuCkIn AlL sHaKeD uP bOtTlE oF fAyGo.
TC: FuCk DoGg I'm ThIrStY.
TC: i'M dOwN tO mY lAsT bOtTlE aNd I dOn'T fUcKiN kNoW iF i CaN gEt AnYmOrE iN tHiS mOtHeRfUcKiN mAgIc LaNd So I dOn'T kNoW.

CT: D --> What you do appear to know is e%actly how to ma%imize my livid contempt for you
CT: D --> With your revolting language and your sense of decorum
CT: D --> At such breathtaking odds with the richness and perfe%ion of your b100d
CT: D --> I just hate you so much
TC: ThAt'S cOoL, i CaN't AlL bE mAkInG nOt EvErYbOdY hApPy AlL tHe TiMe.
TC: iF wE eVeR mEt I cOuLd BaKe YoU a FuCkIn PiE aNd We CoUlD cHiLl AnD mAyBe We'D bE bEtTeR bRoS tHaT wAy.
CT: D --> And the degrees to which you pollute your precious b100d
CT: D --> With your bottled fizzy sugar and soporific to%ins
CT: D --> Maddening
CT: D --> You will stop
TC: WhOaAaA, i WiLl?
TC: hOw Do YoU kNoW tHaT?
CT: D --> No, you don't understand
CT: D --> It's not a predi%ion, it's an order
CT: D --> I command you to stop
TC: Oh, AlRiGhT bRoThEr.
TC: yOu MoThErFuCkIn GoT iT.
CT: D --> What
CT: D --> Are you serious
TC: yEaH.
TC: I mEaN, yOu GoT tO sHoW sOmE fAiTh In YoUr FrIeNdS, cAuSe ThEy'Re AlL tHe OnEs WhO'rE bEiNg To LoOk OuT fOr YoU.
TC: sO fUcK iF yOu SaY i'M nOt DoInG tHe ShIt RiGhT, tHeN wHaT tHe MoThErFuCk Do I kNoW!
CT: D --> No
CT: D --> This is una%eptable

One funny thing about this conversation, judging by the ease and familiarity with which Equius slides right into his pattern of vicious rebuke toward this dumb clown, is that it kind of reads as a form of erotic roleplay both are willingly participating in, but neither of them realize that's what's going on. There's some irony that Equius engages in a sort of daily roleplay routine with Gamzee while admonishing Nepeta for her attempts to get him to roleplay with her in a more "frivolous" way. She probably doesn't have the slightest idea he does this every day.

CT: D --> Ok, let's start over
CT: D --> I apologize
CT: D --> I was completely out of of line, and I'm sorry
CT: D --> I have no right to talk to you like that, or tell you what you can't do
TC: aWw, No WoRrIeS!
CT: D --> It's not my place
CT: D --> Your habits notwithstanding, I am lesser than you
CT: D --> An inferior
TC: hAhAhA. oK.
CT: D --> Don't you understand that you're better than me
CT: D --> Can you please act like it
CT: D --> That's not a command, it's just a polite request I guess
TC: oK, i CaN tRy, BuT mAn I dOn'T kNoW iF i KnOw HoW tO bE lIkE a BeTtEr MoThErFuCkEr ThAn AnY oThEr MoThErFuCkEr.
CT: D --> 100k, it isn't that difficult
CT: D --> Try to be cognizant of your desires and needs
CT: D --> And attempt to regard those around you as simple vehicles meant to bring about your gratification
TC: WoW, wHaT?
CT: D --> What are you doing
TC: uHhHhHh.
CT: D --> Right now
CT: D --> It sounds as if you have begun playing with the red team
CT: D --> Is this true
TC: yEaH!
TC: fUcK yEaH. i'M aLl Up In ThE fUcKiN sHiT oF tHiS wIcKeD mYsTiCaL mOtHeRfUcKeR.
TC: i BoNkEd An ImP oN tHe HeAd WiTh A cLuB.
TC: AnD tHeN a LiTtLe LaTeR i ScArEd OnE wItH a HoRn.
TC: :o)
CT: D --> Good
CT: D --> This is very good
CT: D --> It really pleases me to hear tales of physical subjugation
CT: D --> I presume these were lesser beings, toiling in the lower ranks of some hierarchy
TC: wElL yEaH, tHeY'rE uNdErLiNgS.
TC: AnD tHeRe'S SoMe SuBjUgGlAtIoN iNvOlVeD fOr FuCkIn SuRe!
TC: bUt NoW wE kInD oF sEtTlEd DoWn AnD mE aNd ThE iMpS aRe ShArInG sOmE pIe
TC: tHeSe MoThErFuCkErS aRe PrEtTy DoPe AcTuAlLy, I lIkE tHeM.
CT: D --> Ok
CT: D --> It pleases me considerably less to hear things like that
CT: D --> But I've already stated I have no right to be disappointed by your conduct, so I will try to control myself

Equius thrashes between ordering people what to do, and then when they do it, becoming dissatisfied and realizing that he really wants them to be doing what he wants them to do under their own volition, and also for them to tell HIM what to do, whether they're of a higher or lower caste. This is a mess, and is probably why these two talk so much. It's an endlessly circular fetish, and it never resolves itself. Timeline-wise, this conversation locates them after Gamzee has entered the game. The red team has a good jump on the blue team, already three players deep while the first blue (Equius) hasn't entered yet. Not a *super* important detail, but it's worth tracking this stuff in the background somewhat, because the order of entry tells us certain things, like who had to work with (or put up with) whom as a server player. Karkat deals with Terezi (we saw how that went), Terezi deals with Gamzee (notable when you know their long-range arc), Gamzee deals with Tavros (thank god for offscreen conversations, let's just leave it at that), Tavros deals with Vriska (Oh No), and Vriska deals with Kanaya (mom to the rescue).

TC: aW sHiT bRo, I dOn'T wAnT tO bE aLl LiKe To DiSaPpOiNt YoU!
TC: WhAt CaN i Do To MaKe A bRoThEr FuCkIn ShApE hIs ShIt Up?
TC: iF i CoUlD mAkE yOu SmIlE iT'd Be ThE bEsT fUcKiN mIrAcLe I eVeR dId PaRt Of.
TC: hOnK hOnK hOnK! :o)
CT: D --> Hmm
CT: D --> Would it be too much to ask
CT: D --> For you to maybe
CT: D --> Boss me around a little
TC: UuUhHhHhH.
TC: yOu MeAn LiKe RoLe PlAyInG?
CT: D --> If it would help to couch it in those terms
CT: D --> Then yeah, I guess so
CT: D --> But not the especially juvenile kind
CT: D --> Let's keep it serious and professional
TC: i'Ll TrY, bUt I'm NoT mUcH fUcKiN aNy GoOd At It I tHiNk.
CT: D --> Just
CT: D --> Say anything
CT: D --> As long as it's authoritative
TC: oK.
TC: uH, hEy YoU, dOn'T gO nEaR tHe MoThErFuCkIn OcEaN, cAuSe I aLl ToLd YoU nOt To A bUnCh Of TiMeS!
TC: ShIt Is StRaIgHt Up DaNgErOuS, aNd I'm GeTtInG mY hArSh On AbOuT iT.
CT: D --> Hmm
CT: D --> Decent
CT: D --> I don't live near the ocean though, so it's hard to immerse myself in the scenario
TC: aLrIgHt, WeLl, WhAt ArEn'T yOu AlL nOt SuPpOsEd To Do?
TC: WhAt KiNd Of MiScHiEf Do YoU gEt YoUr BaD fUcKiN sElF uP tO?
CT: D --> I do so many bad things
CT: D --> Just awful things
CT: D --> I'm incredibly impudent and a superior needs to put me in my place
TC: uMmMm, Ok WeLl.
TC: DoN't Be DoIn AlL tHoSe BaD fUcKiN tHiNgS bRo!
CT: D --> Yes
CT: D --> Yes, that's good
CT: D --> Like that
TC: cUt ThAt ShIt OuT, i'M sO aLl MeAnInG tHiS! hAhAhA.
CT: D --> E%cellent
CT: D --> Now tell me this, highb100d
CT: D --> I've been roughhousing a little too hard lately
CT: D --> I've made a bit of a mess and anyone in a position of authority would surely be % about it

Maybe this is the first conversation they've ever had where they openly acknowledge that what they're doing is roleplaying? Let's call it a breakthrough. It's also telling that in Gamzee's honest attempt to RP, he goes straight for the goatdaddy issues. A bit sad really. Is this conversation over yet? Oh, there's one more page.

TC: Uh.
TC: %?
CT: D --> Cross
TC: oHhH.
CT: D --> What do you make of it
CT: D --> This wretched misbehavior
TC: fUcK mAn, I aM sO mOtHeRfUcKiN sAlTy AbOuT aLl ThAt BuSiNeSs YoU sAiD!
TC: FuUuUuCk, Im LiKe AlL mOvInG mY mOuTh AnD tHe WiCkEd NoIsE iS cOmInG oUt In ThE fRoNtIeSt WaY pOsSiBlE.
TC: aNd It'S gOiNg At YoUr DiReCtIoN, cAuSe ThAt'S tHe DiReCtIoN tO fUcKiN bE aNgRy At!
CT: D --> Yes
CT: D --> So good
CT: D --> I am presently whipped into a state of contrition
CT: D --> One befitting of our class disparity
CT: D --> But I'm starting to perspire again so it's best that we stop
CT: D --> Thank you for indulging me
TC: hAhA, nO pRoBlEm BrO.
TC: It'S cOoL wE cOuLd AlL uP aNd MoThErFuCkIn OpEn Up A lItTlE bIt WiTh EaCh OtHeR.
TC: lIkE bRoS.
TC: If ThErE's StUfF yOu WaNt To GeT oFf YoUr ChEsT dUdE, lIkE i SaId I'm FuCkIn HeRe FoR a MoThErFuCkEr.
TC: kInD oF lIkE a MiRaClE, hOw It'S aLwAyS tHeRe.
TC: It NeVeR gOeS aWaY, yOu KnOw?
CT: D --> No
CT: D --> But I comprehend the sentiment
CT: D --> I have lots of thoughts, but they're difficult to communicate
CT: D --> If you'll listen
TC: sUrE! :oD
CT: D --> Honestly I'm confused by the social order
TC: mAn, Me ToO. i DoN't KnOw WhAt Of FuCkIn WhAt CoLoR iS wHaT, sO i DoN't BoThEr WiTh ThInKiN oN tHaT mOtHeRfUcKeR.
CT: D --> See, that's what I mean
CT: D --> How is it possible for one of your distin%ion to be so ignorant
CT: D --> And loathesome
CT: D --> Whereas
CT: D --> A member of the most abject, verminous b100dline of all
CT: D --> Can conduct herself with such grace and possess nothing but admirable mannerisms
CT: D --> I find these striking ju%tapositions perple%ing, and I confess strangely into%icating
CT: D --> I wonder if I have gone mad
CT: D --> To form such a pact with her

Equius has a quirk with a fair amount to consider. As the Sagittarius, and therefore centaur-themed troll, the "cent" part of centaur makes 100 his magic number and percent signs his favored symbol. He replaces the phoneme "loo" in words with "100," even when the original word isn't spelled that way, like "b100." And he swaps in % signs for x's, but more confusingly, also for x phonemes, so "bricks" becomes "bri%." He does this even for sounds that are just *close to* x, like "distinction" becoming "distin%ion." And sometimes he replaces an entire word semantically related to the % symbol, like "cross." I ended up really milking this quirk, mostly because I knew that only swapping instances of x would not yield a lot of changes and so would feel kind of insubstantial.

TC: WoW, i GoT nO fUcKiN cLuE wHaT yOu'Re TaLkInG aBoUt
TC: wHo Is ShE?
CT: D --> I shouldn't be talking about this
CT: D --> You're the enemy

centaursTesticle [CT] ceased trolling terminallyCapricious [TC]

> Vriska: Be in cahoots with Equius. Cahoooooooots.

arachnidsGrip [AG] began trolling centaursTesticle [CT]

AG: Equiiiiiiiiuuuuuuuus.
CT: D --> What
AG: Hey! I'm a8out to meddle with so many losers right now.
CT: D --> How many
AG: So many! All the losers. All of them.
CT: D --> Good
CT: D --> Use your cunning and venom to make them envy our nobility
AG: Oh man, was that sarcasm? That sounded like sarcasm!
CT: D --> No
CT: D --> Humorous insincerity is for pedantic wigglers
AG: Pshhhhhhhh, I know! I know you never make jokes. I was the one 8eing sarcastic, you stooge!
AG: I was 8eing sarcastic a8out you 8eing sarcastic. Duh.
CT: D --> That's because you're a little worse than me
AG: The fuck I am! Anyway. Hey!
AG: Did you finish Aradia's present yet? I'm a8out to fuss with her and I want to know if I can keep my promise or if you're gonna make a liar out of me.
CT: D --> It's finished
CT: D --> I'll deliver it shortly
AG: Great! Thanks, 8uddy. I'll 8e w8ting here for you.

Having just revealed his feelings toward Aradia at the end of the last conversation to Gamzee (and us), referring to his "pact" with her, we are finally picking up on their double-cross (%%) arrangement. Recall that it was left ambiguous in a scene with Aradia who she was referencing as co-leader, whether it was Vriska or a different blue-blooded troll. They all seem to think they're playing each other. Equius is probably the closest to being right. Notice how Equius knows exactly what he's doing here, at every step of the way. When he says "I'll deliver it shortly," he doesn't say *who* he's delivering it to. He's playing Vriska, and he thinks he's playing Aradia by giving her a body he's "tampered" with. But Aradia outplays him on that front in the end too.

CT: D --> I'm happy to help
CT: D --> But I don't understand why you're intent on gratifying that worthless peasant
AG: 8ecause I promised I would and it's none of your damn 8usiness! Man.
AG: Quit your prying! Always fidgeting and poking and prying.
CT: D --> Fine
CT: D --> Then let's proceed with the plan in a curt and professional manner
AG: Agreeeeeeeed.
AG: So just to review!
AG: We will let Aradia perpetr8 her cute little ploy on Sollux and usurp his power.
CT: D --> Yes
AG: Isn't it funny when these chumps try to get all tactical and underhanded? It's really adora8le!
CT: D --> I guess it is pretty quaint
AG: Anyway. She makes her little powergra8, and that's when we 8oth step in and usurp her as co-leaders.
AG: Right????????
CT: D --> That's the plan
AG: Ok, good. Then the 8est team will 8e led 8y the two highest 8loods, the way it should 8e!
AG: Or at least, the highest 8loods who aren't shitty clown worshippers or under water freaks. Sound good?
CT: D --> Yes, we're in absolute agreement
AG: Yes.
CT: D --> Yes
AG: Yes.
CT: D --> Yes
AG: Yeeeeeeees!!!!!!!!
CT: D --> Stop
AG: Gr8! What a gr8 team we are.
AG: Heeeeeeeey........
AG: You wouldn't 8e planning anything sneaky, would you????????
CT: D --> No, don't be absurd
CT: D --> Are you
AG: What! How could you suggest such a thing! Man, so insulting.
CT: D --> Ok
AG: Perfect. We have the perfect plan, and no one is plotting any sort of dou8lecrossings or 8acksta88ery or anything like that.
CT: D --> There are no %%ings up my sleeve
CT: D --> Also, I don't have sleeves
CT: D --> I am as transparent as can be, and my word is my bond
AG: I know! Don't worry, dude. I trust you completely.

Of course, the fact is that everyone's playing everyone else, and all involved know what a bunch of backstabbing assholes they all are, so attempts to follow through with planned collusion sort of devolve into this slapstick banter where they clearly seem to suspect they're all about to double-cross each other. This is also another look at the Obsequious Vriska persona, who rears her head with anyone who is notably aloof, harsh, or disdainful to her regularly. It makes sense that this has become the standard repartee between them over the years. Equius's personality is pretty stable, but hers is in wild flux depending on who she's talking to. A *Paradox Space* comic I wrote shows off this dynamic pretty well too, where she sucks up to him after her arm got blown off, hoping he'd build a new one for her. On this note, there's also decent supporting evidence that Vriska has some sort of crush on Equius, but possibly only on a physical basis. Maybe the best case for this is how she went gaga when she saw Nic Cage from *Con Air*, with his sweaty muscles, long greasy hair, and dirty wifebeater. She absolutely lost it, and Equius looks exactly the fucking same. So, while she may not "like" him technically, in a personal way, her crush is the kind where she finds some dude so outrageously and inexplicably hot, he completely ruins her ability to keep composure or think rationally. Which may explain why he was able to play her so easily.

```
CT: D --> You know
CT: D --> I can feel you trying to read my mind
AG: 8ullshit!
AG: Pro8a8ly just another one of your many daily rage aneurysms.
AG: Why don't you cool your jets and have a glass of gross muscle8east milk????????
CT: D --> Get out of my head, it's making me angry
CT: D --> Try to remember who built your arm for you
AG: Oh g8d!
AG: D8n't you d8re!!!!!!!!
```

> Equius: Go check on Aradia's present.

You delve deeper into your hive where you store many of your robotic projects. The lair doubles as the caged arena where you battle them.

Under the tarp is the completed gift. You of course have no intention of delivering this to your neighbor as promised. You naturally will doublecross your accomplice, just as you assume she has plans to doublecross you. You assume she is assuming the same of you. Business as usual for blue bloods.

You will deliver it to Aradia yourself to gain her favor, and then doublecross her and take your rightful position as team leader. How ironic that someone of your blood purity must work to win the favor of the lowest sort of peasant. Humiliating. Strangely titillating, even. But in the end, class order will be restored.

> Equius: Remove tarp.

Very obvious callback panel to when Dave talked Jade into slapping herself in the face with her own dreambot. It was a clever trick by Dave. This is a little more direct, but I guess it was clever of Equius to leave the remote override chip in there. The fact that he's been able to directly control Vriska's arm all this time raises some questions, though. What else has he done with this ability? Do we even want to know?? What are the odds that on some level, she doesn't particularly mind the fact that he pulled this dubious shit on her during a medical crisis??? Do we want to know that either???? In any case, it's not too far off from what she herself has the ability to impose on some of her other friends. It wouldn't be a bad means of keeping her honest and preventing her from exploiting her own powers in creepy ways, if that's how he chose to use this leverage. Which it isn't, because he doesn't care.

You reveal her sparkling new chassis. You have paid a great deal of attention to quality and detail in this model. She is perfect.

You don't know what to make of the feelings she stirs. For one like you to entertain thoughts of attraction for such genetic filth would be utter depravity.

Exquisite, delectable depravity.

Why, Aradia. It appears the red glass of your eye has caught the pink and green glint of the moons in their perigees. The sweet poetry almost makes a man forget how the grime that once filled your veins made his stomach turn. It is a good omen for illicit lovers. Could you imagine the scandal if anyone found out?? No one must ever know.

But worry not. Your heart will pump no more of that despicable red sludge. You have been given a new heart. You can be taught the ways of the class you were always meant for. No one is beyond redemption.

Be grateful, dear Aradia. For the first time in your meaningless life you have met a man with true compassion.

There are so many dimensions of creepiness to this, it's hard to keep track of them all. One detail worth cocking an eyebrow over is the "class upgrade" this represents for Aradia. Strangely, though Equius is attracted to her swill-blooded untouchable status, he does what he probably presumes is the sweeping romantic gesture of upgrading her to the same blood class as him, even though this gesture sort of neutralizes the very class divide he finds so intoxicatingly depraved. He may view this as a "sacrifice" he is making for her benefit. But what's probably even more creepy about this, when you think it through, is that as he was building this thing, the most logical and direct supply of indigo blood was probably his own body. He's essentially giving her a full-body blood transfusion using his own blood, so that she gets to experience the privilege of being his true equal. The creepiness is probably compounded by the fact that this robot surely doesn't need any blood inside it at all to function. It's strictly symbolic.

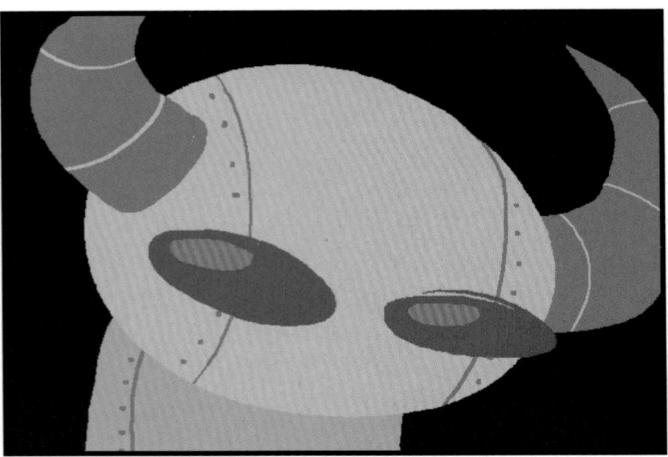

And just what do you think YOU'RE looking at??? Keep your cold, mechanical judgment to yourself. As if your own record is so spotless! Don't forget who made you. Oh, what's that? My, that is a smart mouth you have. That was the last straw. An example must be made of this insubordination.

He seems to have a similar relationship with his robot sparring partners as Terezi has with her dragons. I guess Terezi uses them for sparring too, in a sense. To sharpen her lawyering skills.

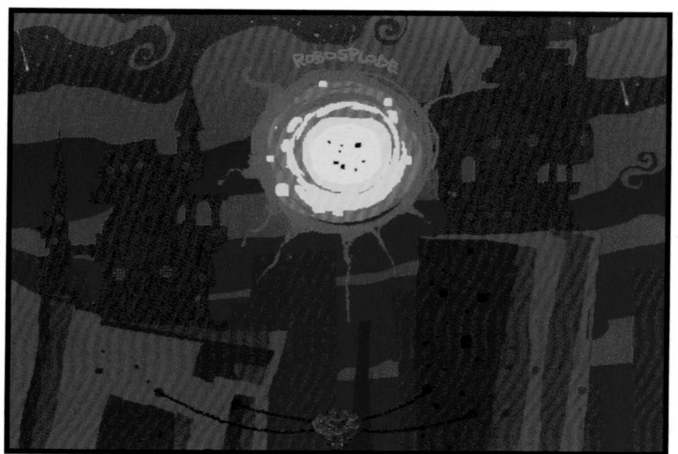

The CATENATIVE DOOMSDAY DICE CASCADER is unfortuitously activated.

The lousy thing breaks.

You seriously cannot believe how unbelievably shitty this doomsday device is.

Vriska probably designed this thing to mimic her Vision Eightfold eye, as a form of branding. Kind of like an artist signing their work. She may have decided to make it dice-based technology either because she never wants to bother with any form of weapon that isn't dice or luck-based in some way, or she just wanted to build in a feature that made sure Eridan needed to get extremely lucky to blow up the world. But also, considering Equius was likely the one who built most of this, Equius himself probably sabotaged it so it never had a chance of being that powerful anyway. Why would any of these people want to give their idiot friend the power to blow up the world? Unpacking this ridiculous doomsday device project underscores the fact that, while the entire troll group can unanimously agree on virtually nothing, literally all of them would still agree that Eridan sucks and should never be trusted.

That's just the exact same explosion asset from a few panels ago. Who is responsible for this half-assed garbage? I demand answers.

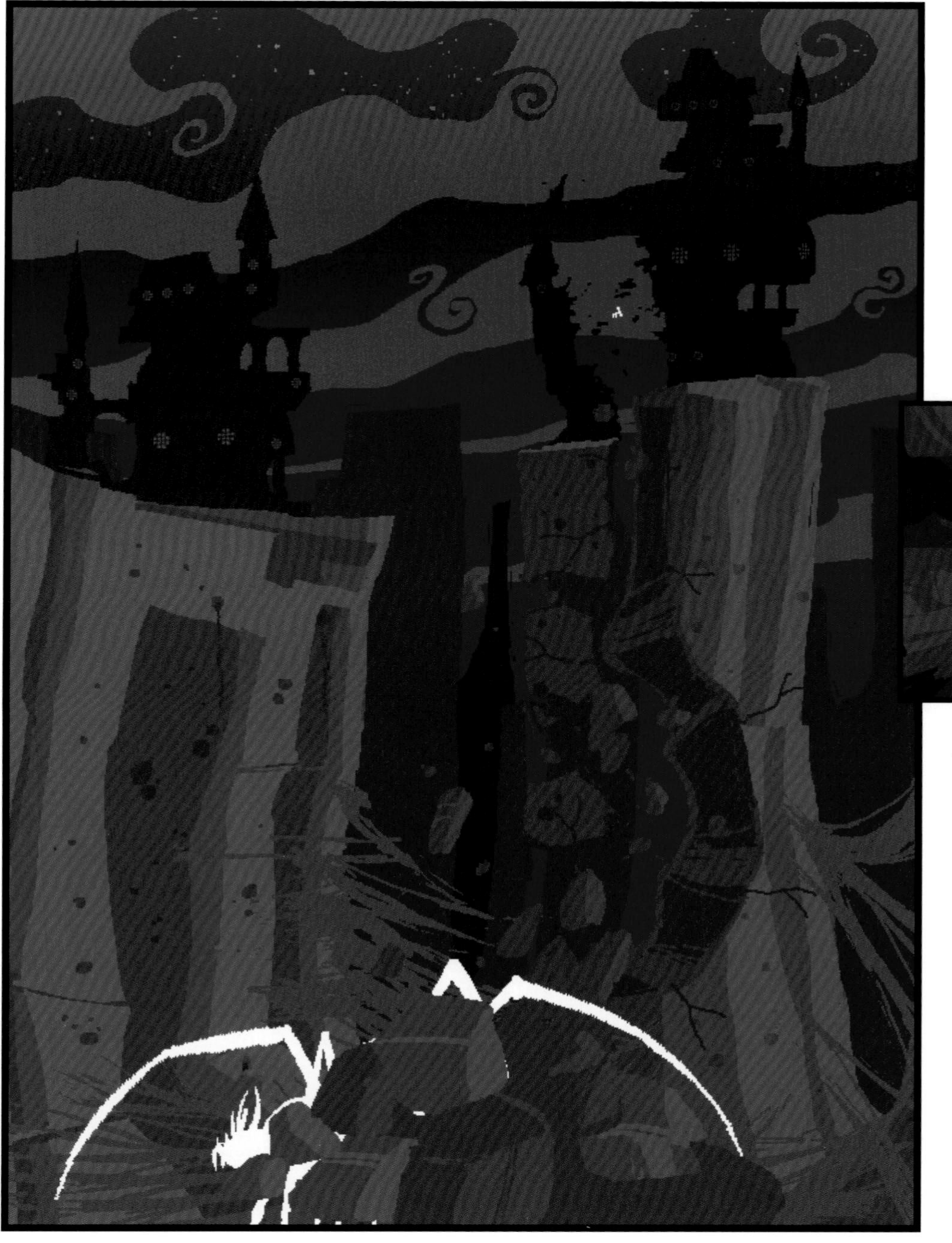

AURTHOOOOOOOOOOOUUUUUUUUUUR!

> Moments earlier...

I might say Equius does Vriska an accidental favor by killing her awful spider mom and freeing her from the slavery of feeding duties. Except what really happens here is that by killing her he's guaranteeing the spider will be prototyped, thus forcing Vriska to continue having to deal with her in the session but now being able to actually speak to her directly. I'm guessing they didn't really have many heart-to-heart talks, to put the bad blood behind them. Seems more likely it motivated Vriska to get out of the hive as much as possible and go treasure hunting on her cool map planet. Aurthour though, now that's a real tragedy. He and Equius probably had some truly amazing, tear-jerking conversations off screen.

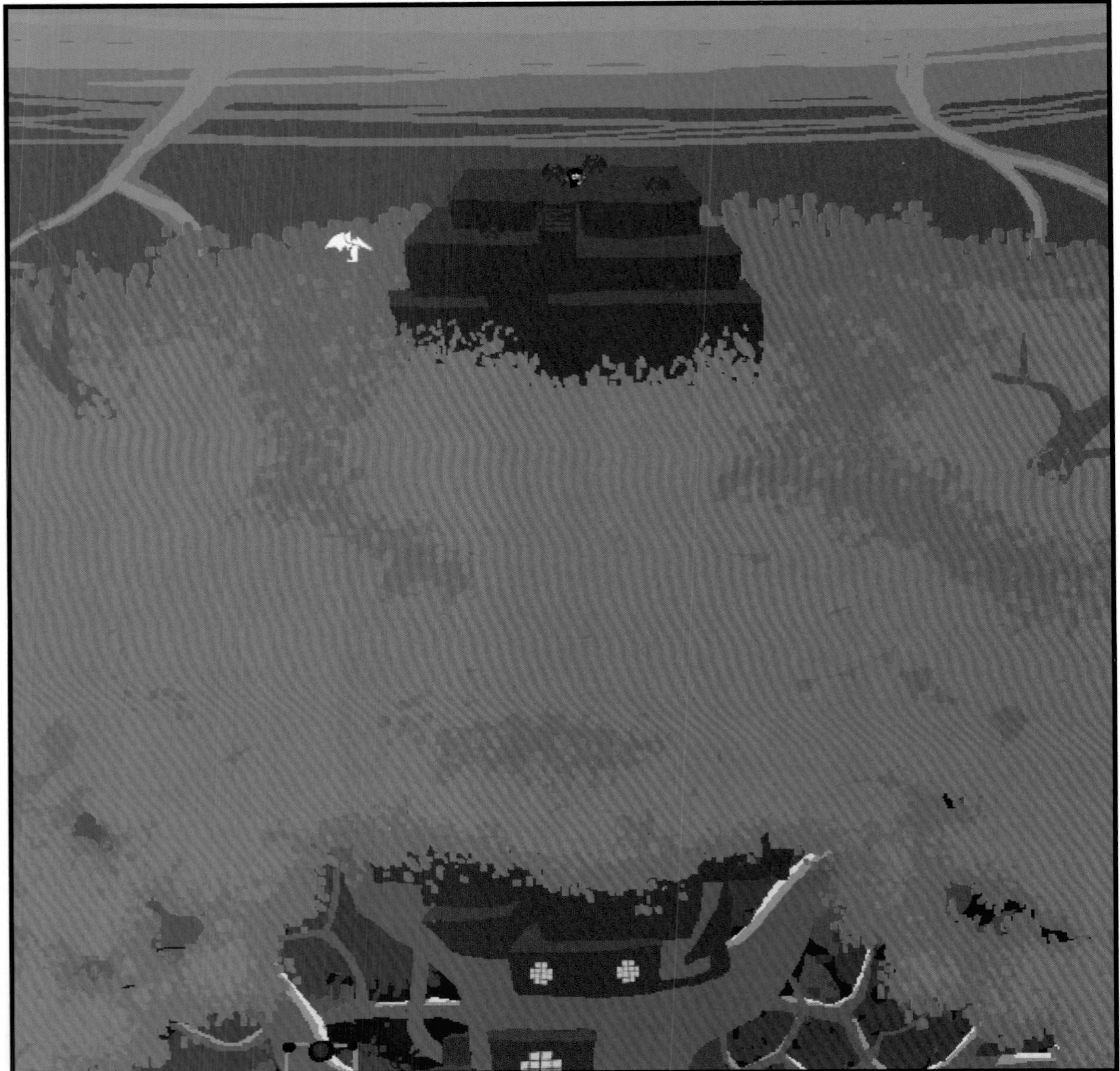

Vriska: Meddle with Terezi.

The most remarkable thing about this shot is the vertical progress on Terezi's hive, implying Gamzee was actually able to stay focused long enough to build it for her. This probably involved many pages of frustrating conversation that unquestionably would serve as good foreshadowing material for future blackrom potential between them, if we could have read it.

arachnidsGrip [AG] began trolling gallowsCalibrator [GC]

AG: It looks like tonight we will have to 8reak our truce. Or at least suspend it. Hope you don't mind!
GC: HOW DO YOU F1GUR3 TH4T
AG: Because tonight we will play a game together. For the first time in I don't even know. Forever!
GC: TH3 TRUC3 W4SNT 4BOUT NOT PL4Y1NG G4M3S TOG3TH3R DUMMY
GC: 1T W4S 4BOUT NOT ST4BB1NG 34CH OTH3R 1N TH3 B4CK 4NYMOR3
GC: 4ND STOPP1NG TH3 3NDL3SS CYCL3 OF R3V3NG3
GC: 4ND 4BOV3 4LL NOT US1NG YOUR POW3RS TO HURT P3OPL3 WHO DONT D3S3RV3 1T!

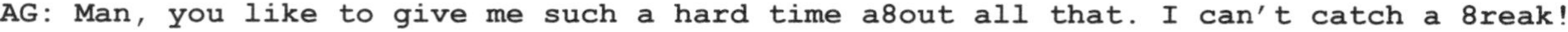

AG: Man, you like to give me such a hard time a8out all that. I can't catch a 8reak!
AG: Can't you see I'm trying to put all that 8ehind me and make amends with every8ody?
AG: No, of course you can't see that. What am I saying!
GC: 1T'S H4RD TO B3L13V3 YOU W1TH 4LL TH3 LY1NG YOUV3 DON3
GC: YOUR BLU3B3RRY BUBBL3GUM WORDS ST1LL SM3LL PR3TTY GOOD BUT YOUR D3C31T ST1NKS! >8O
AG: ::::(
AG: I'll prove it to you. I'm giving Aradia a present that will make her feel all 8etter finally.
AG: Then I'll 8e in the clear. Phew! Totally redeemed. You'll see. I mean smell.
GC: 1 DONT KNOW WHY YOUR3 BOTH3R1NG TRY1NG TO H3LP H3R
GC: SH3 WONT C4R3
GC: WH4T3V3R 1T W4S YOU D1D TO H3R 1 TH1NK YOU BROK3 H3R BR41N
GC: 1TS SO T3RR1BL3
AG: Man, why can't you cut me some slack for once????????
AG: It's not like I even did anything that 8ad to you.
AG: I lost seven eyes 8ut you only lost two! I would say you came out ahead in the 8argain.
GC: 1 KNOW
GC: 4ND 4CTU4LLY
GC: 1 N3V3R R34LLY GOT TH3 CH4NC3 TO TH4NK YOU >:D
AG: Ugh! Your sarcasm really stings when here I am just trying to 8e nice. Ok, I guess I deserve it.
GC: 1M S3R1OUS THOUGH
GC: BUT 1 DONT 3XP3CT YOU TO G3T TH4T
AG: Aaaaaaaah!
AG: Fine, 8e that way. But you shouldn't sit there and pretend we're so different.
AG: Remem8er Team Scourge? How convenient all that must 8e to have forgotten! You were so nasty.
AG: Oh man, if you crossed Terezi Pyrope you were fucked!!!!!!!!
GC: Y34H 1F YOU W3R3 4 B4D GUY
GC: W3 W3R3 SUPPOS3D TO B3 L1K3 4 V1G1L4NT3 DUO D1SP3NS1NG JUST1C3

This would appear to be the first Vriska/Terezi interaction. If it's not, don't even @ me folks. Let's just say it is. This is the most important character relationship resulting from all the sound and fury of Hivebent's chaotic dispensation. Forget all the other scrubs and their melodrama. Just put them in the trash, and focus on this. It's the arguable axis around which the whole epic revolves, when you really study all the ramifications from the fallout resulting from their rivalry, ensuing revenge cycle, and mutually floundering struggle for redemption, in the warped way each of them defines that idea. The "truce" they refer to here roughly covers the conditions surrounding their entire tandem arc. An uneasy agreement to set aside their vicious, competitive tendencies to allow for a stable friendship, even though the friendship seems entirely based on their deep need for these competitive behavior patterns to play themselves out. The truce in a sense is an acknowledgement of an unhealthy codependency, an addiction to the negative qualities and drama they bring out in each other and in everyone around them who gets pulled into it. And as we know from two blue blood intros already, addiction is a powerful thing.

GC: 4ND YOU COULD T4K3 TH3 B4D GUYS HOM3 4ND F33D TH3M TO YOUR STUP1D SP1D3R
GC: BUT 1NST34D YOU JUST F3D H3R 3V3RYBODY!
GC: 4ND L13D 4ND L13D 4ND L13D
AG: Yeah, those were the days.
AG: I mean, days full of mist8kes and r8gret!
AG: But it was still a lot of fun. Watching you dismantle huge teams of Flarpers with nothing 8ut politics and head games.
AG: Without even using any special powers! Wow.
GC: M3H
AG: Come oooooooon!
AG: What do I have to do here?
GC: 1 DUNNO
AG: Well if you want to know what I think, you should start changing your tune.
AG: Cause even though you got all these highfalutin morals and fancy reserv8tions, you know as well as me that a killer is a killer is a killer!
AG: There 8n't no ch8nging your ways for good, and one d8y you're going to flail that silly l8ttle cane of yours and not find n8thin to 8ump into, and fall f8ce first into the shit ag8in.
AG: And you're going to do something t8rri8le to some8ody and wish you could t8ke it 8ack 8ut you c8n't!!!!!!!!
AG: And then you'll work hard to win 8ack their trust, and you'll try and try and tr8, and you'll see how hard it is!
AG: You'll seeeeeeee!
GC: 1 DOUBT 1T
AG: You'll see.
AG: I am whispering that and it is echoing and ominous.
AG: You'll seeeeeeee........
AG: You'll seeeeeeeeeeeeeeeeeeeeeeeeeeeeeeeee
AG: eeeeeeeeeeeeeeeeeeeeeeeeeeeeeeeee........
GC: OH W1LL YOU C4N 1T S3RK3T!
AG: Hahahahahahahaha.

arachnidsGrip [AG] ceased trolling gallowsCalibrator [GC]

GC: >XO

arachnidsGrip [AG] began trolling gallowsCalibrator [GC]

AG: Whoa, what was that????????
AG: There was a loud noise outside my hive!
AG: It sounded like an explosion.

Vriska's "You'll see" warnings come across as heavy-handed foreshadowing of something. So much so that we cast about for things we already know about Terezi. Since we're privy to some of her future already, we know she tries to dupe John into getting killed early, resulting in Davesprite. Is this what's being foreshadowed? Maybe not a bad guess, if prior story data is all we have to go on. But knowing even more about future events later, there's a much more obvious backstabbing Terezi commits, which haunts her for years after. The themes in play between these two focus on friendship as a function of when to forgive and when to hold a grudge, and on viewing those judgments through the lenses of the just vs. unjust, the moral vs. immoral. One pithy and accurate summation of their characters I read once in a text post making the rounds online put it this way: Terezi is chaotic lawful, Vriska is evil good.

GC: WOW R34LLY
AG: And then another one!
AG: And now something that sounds like an avalanche!!!!!!!!
GC: W3LL 1F 1 H4D TO GU3SS
GC: 1 WOULD S4Y
GC: 1T W4S PROB4BLY TWO 3XPLOS1ONS 4ND TH3N 4N 4V4L4NCH3
AG: That dum8ass is probably punching ro8ots again.
AG: I will go outside and look.
GC: OK
GC: TRY NOT TO G3T BURN3D OR CRUSH3D TO D34TH OR 4NYTH1NG TH4T WOULD B3 4WFUL
AG: You got it! ::::::::)

arachnidsGrip [AG] ceased trolling gallowsCalibrator [GC]

> And much earlier than that...

gallowsCalibrator [GC] **began trolling** apocalypseArisen [AA]

GC: HOW 1S H3
AA: 0k
AA: he cant walk th0ugh
AA: pr0bably never will
GC: >:[
GC: M4YB3 H3 COULD B3 F1X3D
GC: W1TH ROBO PROSTH3T1CS
GC: 1F YOU D1DNT M1ND G3TT1NG H3LP FROM...
GC: UH >:\
AA: n0!
AA: neither he 0r i sh0uld have ever had anything t0 d0 with th0se hateful sn0bs
AA: it was a big mistake
AA: n0 0ffense 0_0
GC: TH4TS OK
GC: 1M 4 L1TTL3 TOO T34L FOR TH31R T4ST3S 4NYW4Y >:]
AA: i d0nt see why theyd lift a finger t0 help him
AA: they hate us b0th s0 much
AA: im s0 mad!
GC: 1 HOP3 YOUR3 NOT TH1NK1NG OF DO1NG 4NYTH1NG 1N R3T4L14T1ON
GC: 1TLL 3ND B4DLY
GC: YOU SHOULD L3T M3 H4NDL3 1T

Back to the Flarp debacle flashback, already in progress, in the past. The idea is floated of having Equius help Tavros out with a pair of robolegs right after the incident. Aradia rejects the idea, seemingly washing her hands of any blue-blood involvement. Alive Aradia is someone with opinions and principles, who takes stands on things. That all changes soon, and suddenly she's amenable to robo-assistance from an indigo snob. (She plays him pretty good though, so maybe it's not a TOTAL abdication of principle.) Terezi warns Aradia not to retaliate against Vriska, which in addition to being sound advice to keep Aradia out of danger, is a pretty good window into Terezi's perspective on the matter of retribution. It ties into the Terezi/Vriska "justice vs. morality" duality as a prevailing force of tension between them. -->

AA: im n0t scared 0f her
AA: she cant c0ntr0l me
AA: shes tried it d0esnt w0rk
GC: 1 KNOW
GC: BUT TRUST M3 1F YOU P1SS H3R OFF SH3LL F1ND 4 W4Y TO G3T YOU
GC: TH1S 1S R34LLY TR1CKY JUST L3T M3 D34L W1TH 1T
AA: but it was my fault
AA: i was distracted when i c0uld have helped him
GC: 1 W4S TOO
GC: W3 W3R3 BOTH D1STR4CT3D BY TH3 S4M3 TH1NG
AA: yeah
AA: wh0 was he anyway
GC: PR3TTY SUR3 1T WAS VR1SKAS FR13ND
AA: what was he d0ing there
AA: watching us
GC: WHO KNOWS
GC: H3S NOT R34LLY H3R FR13ND THOUGH
GC: YOU SHOULD S33 HOW H3 T4LKS 4BOUT H3R B3H1ND H3R B4CK
GC: SH3 H4S NO 1D34 HOW B4D H3S PL4Y1NG H3R
GC: BUT TH3N 1 DONT TH1NK H3 KNOWS HOW B4D SH3S PL4Y1NG H1M 31TH3R
GC: S33 1TS COMPL1C4T3D
GC: YOU R34LLY N33D TO ST4Y OUT OF 1T 4ND L3T M3 D34L W1TH TH1S
AA: i guess s0
AA: i feel p0werless sitting here d0ing n0thing th0ugh
AA: its like she wins even if y0u get her back!
GC: DONT TH1NK OF 1T TH4T W4Y
GC: 1 KNOW HOW TO STOP H3R
GC: TRUST M3
AA: i guess 0ur gaming days are 0ver then
AA: us f0ur at least
GC: Y3P
GC: 1M PR3TTY MUCH DON3 W1TH H3R

--> Terezi insists on handling the Vriska situation herself. Looks like she ends the conversation believing she's convinced Aradia to sit this one out. But this doesn't feel like it's just about averting danger to Aradia, or diffusing a tricky Serket situation like only she knows how to do. It also conveys Terezi's attitude as having a sense of "responsibility" toward handling Vriska, partly due to their darkly codependent relationship, but also due to Terezi's attitude toward justice. Terezi views herself, almost exclusively, as a dispenser of justice. Exclusively, because she's the only one she knows who cares about justice, and considers morality in those terms. Therefore, if anyone else punishes Vriska, it's merely revenge. Whereas if she does it, it's delivering justice, and hence throughout their mutual arc, Terezi continues to see Vriska as her "responsibility" and views herself as the only one who can cause Vriska to face justice for her misdeeds. Vriska, however, does not see things in terms of justice but rather in terms of a fungible, ever-rationalizable personal morality, making her a strong foil for Terezi's desire to pursue justice. Put more simply, Terezi's ethos concerns bringing justice to those who have wronged others, while Vriska's concerns exacting revenge upon those who have wronged her.

It's probably best you listen to the advice of your friend.

And yet, the voices are as lucid as ever. They urge you to make her pay.

> Aradia: Make her pay.

It's a shame it had to come to this. You don't like summoning the spirits of the dead to settle scores.

But if she had to face her victims again, maybe she'd finally learn to feel remorse.

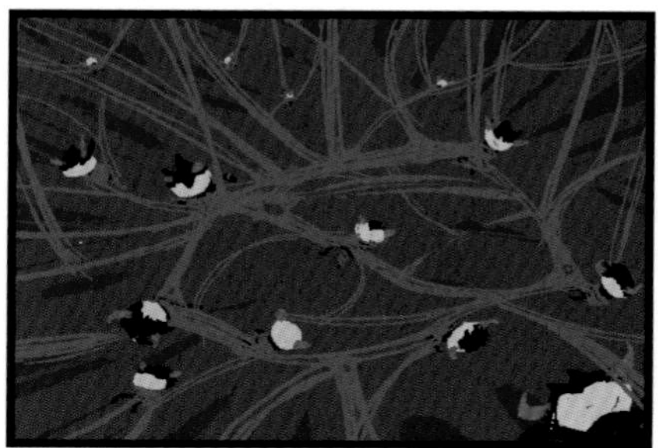

"Make her pay" is the same command as the animation sequence that ends Hivebent. Which is also executed by Aradia against Vriska. This was Aradia's first attempt, a fairly weaksauce effort to scare Vriska straight using ghosts of her victims. Obviously that's not going to cut it. You don't write Vriska a check you aren't prepared to cash. Aradia is much more heavy-handed with her second attempt at making her pay. By then she's armed with a sick robot body, a compromised conscience, and a whole lot of pent-up rage.

> Vriska: Answer white text guy.

It's already evident that Doc Scratch has been manipulating circumstances to help this gruesome series of events unfold. He's always there at the right moment to nudge people in the direction of doing the nasty thing that, deep down, they already know they want to do. Like any self-respecting devil figure would. A couple pages ago, you might have noticed Terezi and Aradia alluding to his presence, when Tavros was in the process of jumping off the cliff. He asked them for help, but they didn't answer. The reason apparently was that Doc was distracting them, to ensure Vriska had the time to get the job done. It also seems likely he egged her on too, given what he's about to say to her here. Maybe he'd been inflaming her contempt for Tavros leading up to that moment as well? Whispering things in her ear about what a loser he is, how he'll never become strong without her "help." He'd surely know just what buttons to push.

Well?
AG: Well what! I am surrounded 8y ghosts and kind of fre8king out a8out it!
I know.
I'm asking what you intend to do about it.
AG: I don't know, I guess I will just curl into a little 8all and cry and hope they go aw8y!
AG: Is that what you want to hear you sick f8ck????????
Aren't you going to kill her?
AG: Who????????
Your friend.
The one who summoned the spirits.
AG: Will that make them go away?
Does it matter?
She brought them here to torment you. This obviously warrants revenge.
You know you're going to anyway. You won't be able to help yourself.
AG: I don't have to do shit!
AG: May8e I don't mind ghosts. May8e they'll 8e gr8 company once I get used to them!
No, they are terrifying you.
There's only one thing to do.
AG: Ok, so why don't YOU kill her! 8e my guest! Wow, thanks for offering. Wh8t a pal!
That's not how I work.
AG: Oh really, well you seemed pretty excited a8out killing Tavros too.
AG: And you even helped! So I guess that is how you work after all.
Not really.
All I did was stand somewhere for a few minutes.
I just gave you an opportunity to do something you wanted to do anyway.
You hated him, remember?
AG: I know I did! I still do, I guess. I dunno.
AG: 8ut I was never gonna kill these people. They were like, off limits I guess?
AG: These games were just supposed to 8e fun and serve no other purpose!
They were serving a very important purpose.
AG: Yeah ok, you getting off on talking a girl into killing her 8uddies sure is important!
AG: Los8r.
Again, I didn't talk you into anything, nor am I doing so now.
You were, and are, going to do this regardless.
I only ever place myself into positions of tangential involvement with events that will bring about my employer's entry into this universe.
I oversee the events as they take place, and ever so slightly nudge them into motion when necessary.
AG: I'm 8eginning to think you really 8elieve that! So delusion8l. You're just a path8tic, lonely gamer who 8uys into his own character profile 8S.
The omniscient have no need for beliefs and no room for delusion.
AG: Hahahahahahahaha!

One reading of Doc is as a manipulative devil-creep in the model of many fictional characters who fit this description; he's a fairly recognizable and traditional presence in the story, when viewed that way. A less traditional reading centers on his role on a metatextual level, as a nefarious, all-knowing, profoundly evil alt-author presence. A guy who has the full powers of the author, who essentially IS the author with certain dark authorial impulses greatly exaggerated, while functioning as a character in the story who can speak to and influence other characters in support of an evil agenda. (That is, the summoning of yet another, even more satanic alt-author being into the comic.) Viewed this way, his conversations with other characters take on a different quality. Normally, the author remains a disguised presence and influences the thoughts of characters with an unseen hand, simply by writing their thoughts directly into their heads, their words into their mouths. This alt-author is essentially doing the same thing, but as an actual character and a known presence to those he influences. He whispers in their ears, gets them to do the nasty, terrible things that are latent within their nature to do, which I as the unseen author easily could have done myself through a conventional writing process. But I outsourced that dark influence to this guy, thus establishing him as a narrative construct in the story on the same level as, but at odds with, the actual author. This surreptitiously lays the groundwork for a future point of tension: a narrative war between an Idiot God and a Genius Devil. Which, admittedly, when the shit finally hits the fan, mostly reads as one buffoon's struggle with a figment of his imagination, in the form of a wrestling match with a floppy, inanimate puppet. It's actually the perfect metaphor signifying the creative process behind this comic.

AG: You're the dum8est omniscient person I ever met.
AG: Sure you know a lot, 8ut I know for a FACT there's stuff you don't know.
That's true.
But the gaps in my knowledge exist by design.
They are the pillars of shadow on which my comprehensive vision is built.
Necessary pockets of void meant to effectuate outcomes I've foreseen and which will require my influence.
Each dark pocket, in time, will be filled.
But I wonder why I waste this nuance on you.
AG: 8ecause you need to add more 818tant lies to patch up all the holes in your sad cover story.
I don't lie.
Deception is only necessary for those like you to achieve their objectives.
I play with my cards face up.
Isn't it funny how during our various matches, I can tell you what my moves will be in advance, and still win?
AG: ::::P
AG: Yeah, 8ut I'm getting closer to 8eating you. You'll see.
Look at that. The short amount of time I have reserved for arguing with a child has expired.
I will go.
But maybe you're right. Maybe you are a person with free will and you won't kill your friend.
What do I know?
Enjoy your haunting.

Vriska: Make her pay.

Doc here refers to the dark spots, the pockets of void on which his vision is built. These hint at limitations to his omniscience. As an alt-author figure, his omniscience makes sense, since the author has sweeping knowledge of story details as well. Because I "know everything," he "knows everything" too. Of course, as I write the story, there are plenty of things I don't know yet, and the "not knowing" is always an important part of the process in this largely improvisational medium. The known gaps are worked into the story, evaded through time skips and other tricks, filling out the surrounding narrative until certain answers become clearer, and then revealed at the right moment. The voids are built around, and in a real way, become foundational, almost load-bearing gaps in knowledge, just as he describes. Pillars of shadow. So his dark spots are not only a limitation to an otherwise ridiculously overpowered villain that can be exploited, they're a feature of a specific type of "authorial omniscience" copied into his profile.

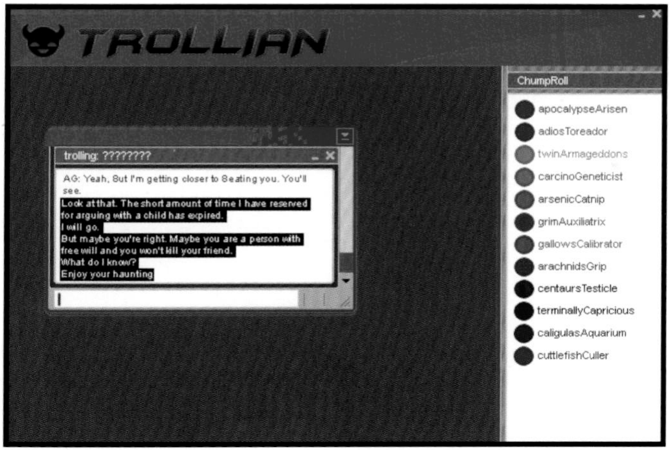

Of course he's right. Not much point in living with all these moaning spooks just to spite some guy you don't give a shit about.

But how to go about it? Can't control her. It can be difficult to manipulate the mind of the psychically gifted.

Let's see, who else is there. Terezi? Forget about it! What about that guy? Nah. Her? Nope. Not him either.

How about this guy? Unfortunately, you can only control him about half the time.

Then again, that should be all the time you need.

arachnidsGrip [AG] **began trolling** apocalypseArisen [AA]

AG: Araaaaaaaadiiiiiiiaaaaaaaa.
AA: what
AG: Nice trick! With the ghosts and all. Man, you got me pretty good.
AA: id rather n0t talk t0 y0u
AG: Fair enough!
AG: Just wanted to say I'm sorry, that's all.
AA: im n0t the 0ne y0u sh0uld ap0l0gize t0

Then, after Doc fills Vriska's head with evil ideas, we return to the narrative text, which...continues filling her head with evil ideas. The first line is, "Of course he's right." It's easy not to notice this, because by its nature, the narrative text disguises accountability. The speaker disappears behind the words, and we start imagining them as a literal transcription of a character's thoughts without thinking much about it. But the truth is, she doesn't have just one devil whispering in her ear, she has two. Him and me. Doc: "You should kill her." Me: "He's totally right! Do it."

AG: Yeah I know. I'll make it up to him some day. Don't worry!
AG: Anyway, hey guess what?
AG: I've got a message for you from your 8oyfriend.
AG: He's outside your hive right now!
AA: n0t falling f0r it
AG: Take a look.
AA: i d0nt see anything 0ut there
AG: Well ok, I'm just the messenger. If you want to risk missing him then suit yourself.
AG: L8er!!!!!!!!

It must be a trick! He surely would have told you if he was making the trip all the way out here from his hive stem.

All this talk about insidious malefactors whispering in Vriska's ear and warping her thoughts, and Word of God admissions that this is exactly what's happening to her from multiple fronts at once, should help stoke the fires of Vriskourse and give a lot more ammunition to her apologists, who like to point out that nothing Vriska does is ever really quite her fault. There's a word for these people: heroes. They are absolutely right, and if you take one lesson from these notes, let it be this. Vriska has done nothing wrong. Not even once in her life, and she never will.

Sollux??

AG: Arrivederci, Megido.

arachnidsGrip [AG] ceased trolling apocalypseArisen [AA]

Crushing Sadstuck: Engage. The retributional overreach here is fairly preposterous. All Aradia did was conjure a brief karmic spookfest to cause Vriska to directly confront the souls of those she killed in the past. It almost isn't even a punishment. More like a cute idea. Responding by using Aradia's own "boyfriend" as a puppet to murder her is somewhat less cute. She ices the deal with another melodramatic one-liner. With Tavros, it was Troll Spanish. Now it's Troll Italian, I guess. Don't ask me why all these Troll Foreign Languages exist. Can't say I've got any answers there. Aradia's ancestor speaks Troll Japanese. Well, Troll Badly Google Translated Japanese.

002252

> Be the white text guy.

Dude lives on the green moon. So let's go there and meet him. I blather down here with so much presumption of the reader's foreknowledge of things. Which makes it easy to shrug through certain twists and revelations, of which there are many. Finding out where and who this guy is, connecting him to the Felt as a yet-unknown member of the gang, a right-hand man to English—that's big deal stuff. Let's stop being such a bunch of jaded tools who know all this already, and get pumped about it. Don't you wish sometimes you could wipe your memory and experience certain stories anew all over again? Let's just fucking do that. Stumble wide-eyed into the future like a toddler taking its first steps, flailing its chubby little arms with a sense of wonder. All right, maybe this is silly, let's not do that. Let's just get to know Doc Scratch like a bunch of sensible adults, and use the power of our critical hindsight to appreciate his introduction, his diabolical role in the greater narrative, and the assiduous way in which this material has been stitched into the current arc.

002253

You try to be the white text guy, but fail to be the white text guy.

No one can be the white text guy except for the white text guy.

The white text guy is known as Doc Scratch.

He is an officer of an indestructible demon known as Lord English. His job is to pave the way for the arrival of his master, who will be summoned upon the termination of the universe. He has worked at this task for many centuries, and will continue to do so until THE GREAT UNDOING.

Scratch is Alternia's FIRST GUARDIAN. Every planet destined for intelligent life has such an entity meant to protect it, and facilitate the planet's ultimate purpose. A first guardian is typically almost as old as the planet itself, and each has a unique, circuitous origin through the knots of paradox space. They can be born into a great diversity of forms, though they all share a common, especially potent genetic sequence. The code grants them near omnipotence, and when merged with a host of great intelligence, near omniscience as well.

What will he do?

It's up to him. All we can do is stand here.

And watch.

This sums it all up pretty well. And I've already indulged in a lot of meta about him down here, prior to this page. What else is there to say? Probably a lot, once he actually starts doing things. Let's wait for him to do those things, then. For now it's worth noting that we can't "control" him. Meaning he doesn't respond to reader commands. The next page says it's because he's a First Guardian, which is a cagey explanation. It's also because he's an author-tier character. As I've said before, the more powerful and villainous a character is, the higher up the metaladder they reside. Jack is higher than most characters due to his utilization of a Fourth Wall and appearance in narrative proximity to the author himself (my orange fingers typing his name). Doc is much higher than that. The first true alt-author of the story, but not the last.

What's he up to now? Hard to say since we're not telling him what to do. Guardians can never be told what to do. Neither the omnipotent kind, nor the ordinary kind who raise kids in houses. It's a universal law of reality.

Looks like he's pondering over his next move in a game he is playing with some wicked troll girl down on the planet. Usually these matches are no contest, but she has been getting closer to beating him lately, and he has no idea how this is possible.

Uncertainty, though rare, is quite a troubling sensation for the omniscient.

What's this? It appears someone is contacting him. More bothersome uncertainty. How is it this youngster is able to relay an unsolicited message? He doesn't even have an account name.

Does Vriska even know how to play Huge Cube Battlefield Chess? Does she have her own cube chessboard somewhere in her hive? I have some questions about this. It may not matter, since she's been using one of Doc's rogue cue balls to cheat anyway.

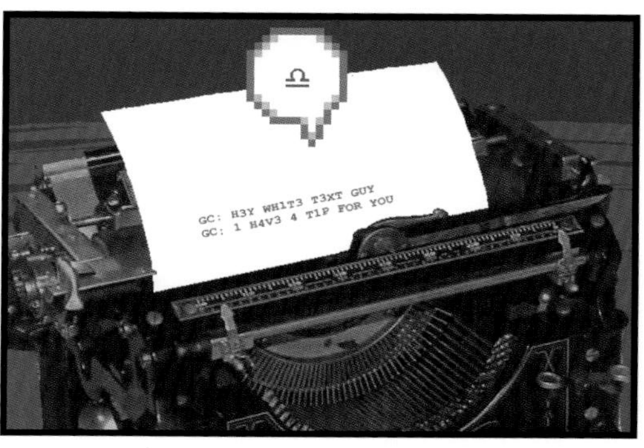

GC: H3Y WH1T3 T3XT GUY
GC: 1 H4V3 4 T1P FOR YOU
How were you able to contact me?
Never mind, I figured it out instantly.
GC: R34LLY?
Yes, through my limitless intellect.
Occasionally I discover there are things I have not always known.
It gives me the opportunity to make deductions, which are practically always flawless.
It's gratifying.
GC: UH OK
GC: TH4TS N34T 1 GU3SS
You asked your clever friend with the colorful spectacles to trace the source of my messages.
He then established a relay for your messages to reach this source through some sort of computational proxy.
I gather he has recovered from his implementation as a weapon in the sabotage of your mutual friend, whom you both believe to be dead.
GC: OH MY GOD WH1T3 T3XT GUY!
GC: SHUT UP! >:O
GC: 1M TRY1NG TO G1V3 YOU 4 M3SS4G3 H3R3
I have a name.
It is not White Text Guy.
GC: OH WHAT 1S 1T
I'm not going to tell you my name.
But if you wish, you may refer to me as Mr. Vanilla Milkshake.
GC: YOU 4R3 SO W31RD
GC: WHY WOULD 1 DO TH4T
It is perfectly in keeping with a habit which you will develop in the future.
GC: 1 DOUBT 1T
Why?
GC: SOUNDS K1ND OF S1LLY 4ND FR1VOLOUS
GC: BL4R WHY DO YOU K33P D3R41L1NG M3!
GC: YOUR3 R1GHT SOLLUX 1S WORK1NG W1TH M3 4ND W3 H4V3 1MPORT4NT BUS1N3SS FOR YOU TO CONS1D3R
GC: W41T
GC: YOU S41D W3 B3L13V3 OUR FR13ND 1S D34D
GC: 1S SH3 NOT?
Yes, I said you believe she is dead.
And soon, you will believe she is not.
Both statements are true.
And yet each exhibits a trace of falsehood.

In addition to being omniscient, he's also kind of a supercomputer in terms of intelligence. Which is kind of a waste of a supercomputer, letting it know everything in advance. It's like if Deep Blue had knowledge of all possible chess games in its database and therefore didn't need to use any computing power to consider actual chess strategy. Wait, that pretty much describes what Deep Blue was, I think, so never mind. Anyway, it makes sense that Doc's mind, all-knowingness notwithstanding, is a supercomputer. One of his original components is a scheming AI character who was built and modeled after a character whose name rhymes with Birk Strider. It is probable this is one of the few facts he is personally unaware of, though.

002256-002257

GC: WOW WHY D1D 1 BOTH3R 4SK1NG
GC: NO WOND3R SH3 SN4PP3D SH3S GOT TO D34L W1TH YOUR STUP1D R1DDL3S 4LL TH3 T1M3
GC: 4NYW4Y C4N YOU JUST H3LP M3 G3T R3V3NG3 SO W3 C4N C4LL 1T 4 N1GHT
Why would I involve myself in your paltry feud beyond the extent I already have?
I believe the need to exert such influence has come to an end.
GC: B3C4US3 YOULL W4NT TO
GC: WH3N YOU H34R WH4T 1 H4V3 TO S4Y
I doubt it.
GC: H4V3NT YOU WOND3R3D HOW SH3 C4N COM3 CLOS3 TO B34T1NG YOU 1N G4M3S L4T3LY
GC: HON3STLY 1M SURPR1S3D YOU H4V3NT D3DUC3D 1T Y3T
GC: W1TH YOUR SH1NY WH1T3 SUP3RBR41N
It's disturbing.
But sometimes that is the nature of these hollows in my perception.
It feels a bit like dark water, sloshing about the cavity in my head.
What do you know of this?
GC: SH3S CH34T1NG
GC: SH3 4LW4YS CH34TS 1F SH3 C4N F1ND 4 W4Y
GC: L4T3LY SH3S US3D TH3 S4M3 4DV4NT4G3 SH3 US3S 4G41NST M3 WH3N W3 PL4Y G4M3S
GC: BUT SH3 TOLD M3 4BOUT 1T
GC: SH3 T3LLS M3 LOTS OF STUFF L1K3 TH4T PROB4BLY TO RUB 1T 1N MY F4C3
GC: BUT SH3D N3V3R R1SK T3LL1NG YOU
What advantage is this?
GC: HOLD ON
GC: 1 H4V3 TO T4LK TO YOUR P4RTN3R 1N CR1M3 FOR 4 S3COND >:]
I thought you were hers.
GC: >:P

> Terezi: Orchestrate demise of the wicked.

She went too far this time and she knows it. She's got to pay. Justice is long overdue.

The only sad part is how easy it's going to be. It will take no skilled manipulator to orchestrate her downfall. She's a waste of your talents.

> Terezi: Contact partner in crime.

Scratch's head is a big cue ball. But the analogy describing his state of confusion, dark water sloshing inside the cavity in his head, describes the structure of a magic 8-ball. Which is one of his cue balls as well. I see this as a literal description of the actual way his head is designed too. Dark water sloshing around. But there probably isn't a fortune-telling tetrahedron floating around in there. Instead, whatever's in there probably serves as a sort of grim kernel for the final emergence of his master when the time comes. Maybe it's a little Caliborn fetus? Wait, I've said too much, yet again.

gallowsCalibrator [GC] **began trolling** arachnidsGrip [AG]

GC: H3Y VR1SK4
GC: 4NYTH1NG TO S4Y
AG: Ummmmmmmmm, no?
AG: A8out what?
GC: 4BOUT K1LL1NG H3R
GC: 4FT3R YOU S41D YOU WOULDNT
AG: Oh, that? I thought we were done talking a8out it!
AG: We concluded I messed up and I'm completely horri8le in every way.
AG: I can only feel SO AWFUL, you know. Here, I'm 8anging my head against the desk now.
AG: 8ang 8ang 8ang. Are you happy?
GC: NOT R34LLY
AG: Uuuuuuuugh, what do you want from me????????
GC: 1M NOT SUR3
GC: 1 GU3SS 1M LOOK1NG FOR SOM3 R34SON TO CH4NG3 MY M1ND
GC: 1 DONT KNOW WH4T YOU C4N S4Y TH4TLL DO 1T
GC: 1 SORT4 HOP3 TH3R3S SOM3TH1NG THOUGH
AG: You should lighten up a 8it. May8e even congratul8 me!
AG: Wow, great jo8 Vriska! Single handedly taking out Team Charge like that.
AG: No more competition from those low class clowns!
GC: N4H TH4T W4SNT 1T
AG: Ok, well, change your mind a8out what!
AG: What are you going to do, Pyrope!
GC: 1 W4S PROB4BLY JUST GO1NG TO K1LL YOU
AG: Hahahahahahahaha!
AG: You mean from your tree? With all your AMAAAAAAAAZING POWERS?
AG: Tell me, what sort of powers do tree girls have? Swinging from vines and stuff?
GC: MY TR33 DO3SNT H4V3 V1N3S >:[
GC: SOM3T1M3S 1 L3T OTH3R P3OPL3 SW1NG FROM ROP3S THOUGH >:]
GC: Y34H 4NYW4Y YOULL B3 D34D 1N 4 COUPL3 M1NUT3S
AG: Yeah right!!!!!!!!
AG: Complete and total muscle8east shit!
GC: 1F YOU DONT B3L13V3 M3
GC: WHY DONT YOU CONSULT W1TH YOUR L1TTL3 4DV4NT4G3
GC: 1T S33MS TO H4V3 4LL TH3 4NSW3RS
AG: I don't need to do that to know you're 8luffing.
GC: Y34H
GC: BUT
GC: YOU KNOW YOUR3 GONN4 4NYW4Y

Another snapshot of the tortured Scourge Sisters dynamic, in a long tale of angst and ambivalence concerning justice and morality. Terezi wrestles with this eternally. She wants to bring Vriska to justice. But she doesn't. She does, doesn't, does, doesn't. Vriska thrashes back and forth in a different way. I'm sorry, see how sorry I am? Isn't being sorry ENOUGH? What more do you want? I'm sorry, not sorry, sorry, not sorry. And being not sorry takes the form of lashing out, incrimination, daring Terezi into action, calling her bluff, etc. So her vacillation is more like, I'm sorry, fuck you, I'm sorry, you don't have the guts, I'm sorry, just kill me already! The dangerous dance goes on and on.

GC: 4DD1CT1ON 1S 4 POW3RFUL TH1NG >:]
GC: S33 Y4

gallowsCalibrator [GC] ceased trolling arachnidsGrip [AG]

She can't be serious. What could POSSIBLY lead to your demise in a matter of minutes?

WHAT COULD IT POSSIBLY BE???

> Vriska: Consult little advantage.

You consult with your MAGIC CUE BALL, an extremely rare treasure you recently plundered from an ancient crypt, and one of many rumored to be hidden across the globe. Each at one time belonged to the strange and powerful man fabled to live on the green moon, but have since managed to escape his vision.

It is said to make predictions with alarming precision and specificity. Unfortunately it lacks a portal on its surface that allows you to view the prediction.

So who could say for sure whether its predictions were accurate? It would require someone with x-ray vision.

Or, just maybe...

We've seen this thing before. Jade's got one in her bedroom. It seemed like an innocuous throwaway item at the time, with its portal-less prognostication power making it come off as kind of a useless gag item. It is a very powerful artifact, though. They're seeds for Doc Scratch. One of these is an essential ectobiological component to Scratch, providing him with the essence of his omniscience, while Lil Cal provides the...other qualities. This means he can theoretically be created in any universe that contains both a seed and Cal. Jade's cue ball doesn't end up creating another Doc Scratch in their universe, but it does end up in Rose's hands and serves as a convenient means for his further manipulation of her.

Someone with VISION EIGHTFOLD.

You channel your powerful eyesight through your customized lenses and whisper to the faithful little oracle: Should you be worried about Terezi's threat?

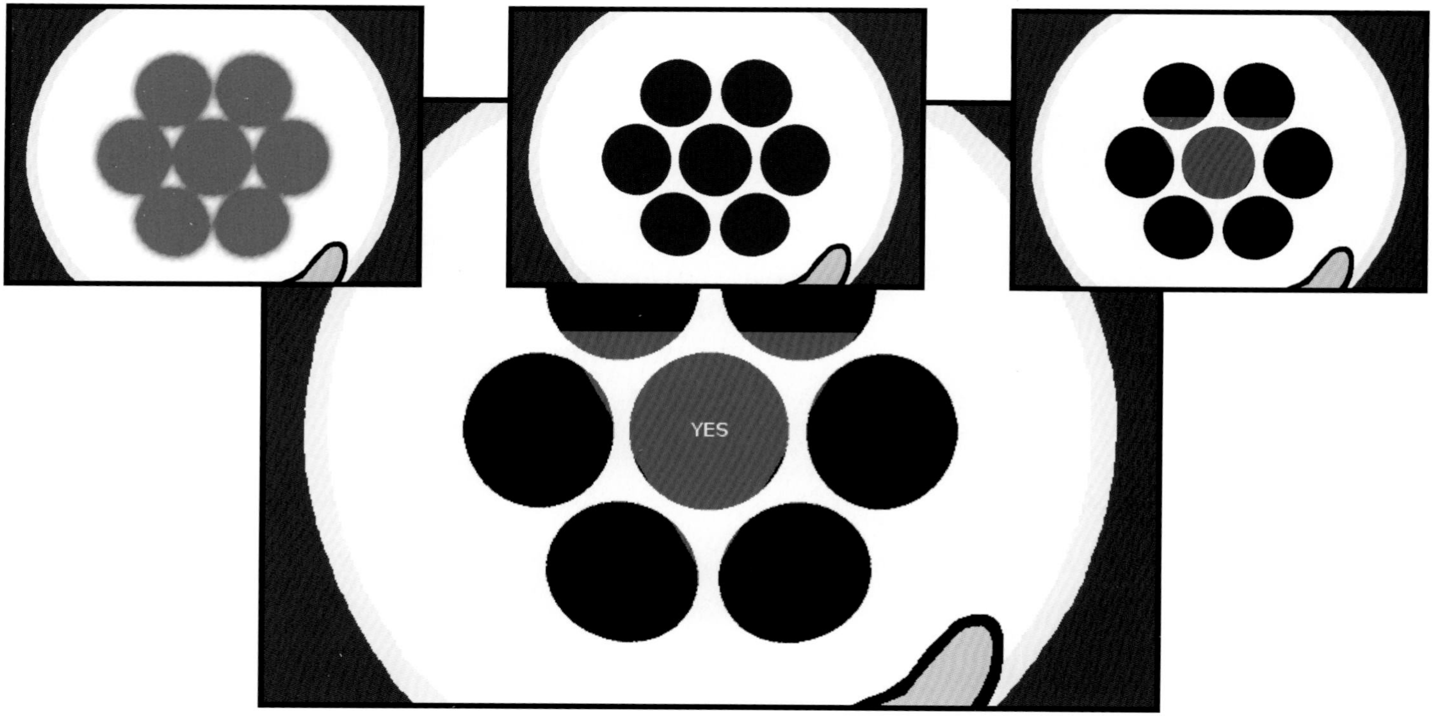

YES

> Terezi: Inform Mr. Vanilla Milkshake about his missing orb.

We didn't know what Vriska's Vision Eightfold was until now. Seemingly it alluded to some vague power to see the future? That turns out to be true, indirectly. It's just a kind of X-ray vision. It's unclear how necessary her special lenses are to use the power. I'd probably look at it as a kind of jeweler's loupe, magnifying her power to see clearly, but not essential. It's not the most amazing superpower, but combined with her mind-control abilities, it makes for a pretty good accessory power. The way she chooses to use it is telling. She's effectively mimicking prognosticative powers by stealing fortunes from another source, by peering through an opaque surface never meant to be breached. She's essentially outsourcing her prediction powers and taking credit, just like she does with machine-building skills and other people's bodies, including the use of *their* powers. All she ever does is use her abilities to hack the system in various ways, looking for cheats, shortcuts, and end-runs, seizing power, knowledge, relevance, and glory using the absolute least-resistance method available. She is a consummate thief.

SHE HAS WHAT?

GC: >:o

As an animated GIF, this panel is a real kick in the ass. Lots of hyperactive flashing, jittering, crackling of energy... Doc's mad as hell, and the vibrant medium helps you really feel that. Now you don't feel it, quite so much. But at least you have me down here, talking to you. Hey there, what's up? This way, I can just tell you Doc's mad, so you don't even have to "feel" it. Just let me do your feeling for you, and everything will be alright. You don't get that cool service on the web, do you? Well, now you know for sure. He's pissed. You're welcome.

Ok, little ball. Fine. If you're so smart, then answer this! How is it going to happen!

HOW????????

I WILL EXPLODE IN YOUR FACE

It's a pretty good trick Terezi pulls here. Manipulating an omniscient, omnipotent creep to maim a murderous, overpowered cheater. She used a few known facts to her advantage and set them both up perfectly. There are probably a couple lingering questions about this. For one thing, did Terezi know that Doc would make the cue ball blow up in Vriska's face after she told him? How did she know it could explode, or the fact that he would make it explode if he got pissed? The simplest explanation is that she just cleverly pried out all this information from Doc himself through some casual conversations. She knew Vriska had the object. She probably was able to get Doc to blab about his seeds without tipping the fact that Vriska had one, so she could use the info to her advantage later. He sure likes to run his invisible mouth, so it was probably easy. She learned he was very sensitive about his seeds, and he doesn't want anyone touching them. He must have conveyed he'd rather destroy them himself rather than let them fall into others' hands without his intent. (Rose he allowed, for instance, because it served his purpose.)

> In the aftermath of more recent misfortune...

One retrieves his dead custodian from the rubble below.

Another finds hers struggling to survive.

The moment this happened marked the beginning of Vriska's "bad luck," by her own estimation. (Doc alluded to this.) Which means that she has been associating "good luck" with "access to reliable foreknowledge." Makes sense from a Light aspect standpoint, where luck and knowledge are closely related ideas. After she loses her Vision Eightfold and her cue ball intel edge, she starts flying blind, as it were. She blames her inability to cheat using stolen knowledge on a deficit of luck and desperately starts seeking good information from lesser sources, like 8-balls, which she then starts habitually cracking open with a sense of addictive frustration. She starts to come across as a kind of luck/knowledge junkie, looking to duplicate a high she once had, which can never be obtained again. And like a junkie, she keeps digging herself deeper into the hole she's trying to get out of with each "hit" she takes, since breaking 8-balls supposedly brings you bad luck. It's a vicious cycle.

You guess you've got to put her down.

The question is, do you have the luck to get it done?

Would a sufficient roll even qualify as good luck in this case? You don't know.

> Vriska: Roll.

Maybe the dead girl is on to something. Maybe the only way to beat your bad luck is not caring about the outcome.

Whew, deep stuff there, Vriska. Amidst our metaphysical examination of the many themes in play, lest we forget, these are still basically a bunch of shitty teens, who are inclined to think and say a lot of shitty teen things. Got problems? Try NOT GIVING A FUCK. /shrugs into outer space/

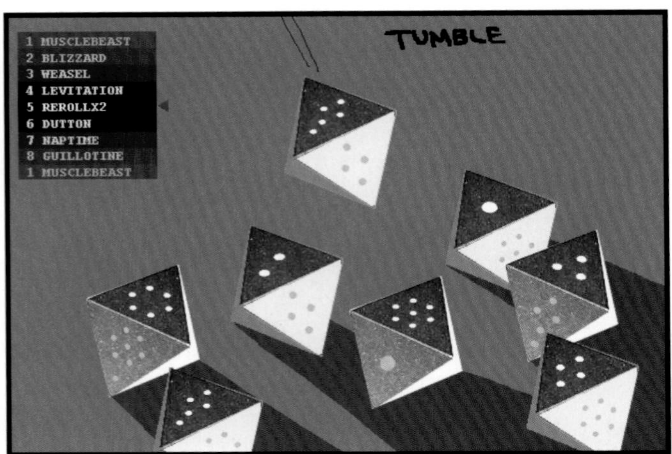

Seven of the FLUORITE OCTET land, narrowing the field down from the full 8^8.

One tumbles through the air. It will decide among the eight remaining techniques.

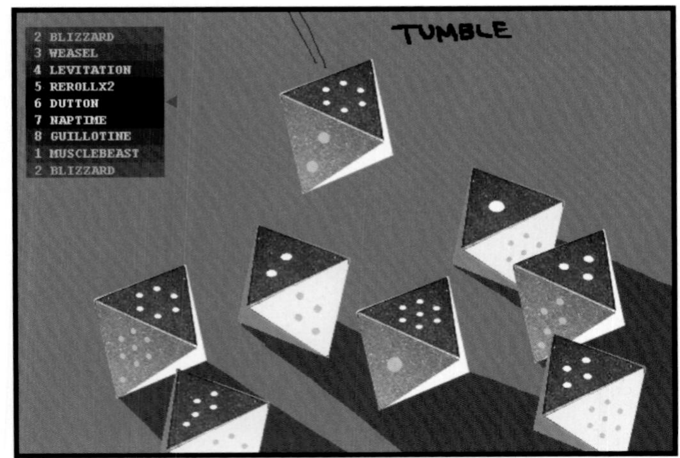

I'd say landing on the one roll out of seventeen million possibilities which specifically summons a huge guillotine, when your objective is to put a giant spider out of its misery, actually qualifies as a very lucky roll. Will she appreciate this fact? Probably not. When you get it in your head that you're snakebit, you always focus on the bad, never the good, like when you fortuitously stumble on a very convenient way of euthanizing your horrible mother.

Since these dice belonged to Mindfang at one point, it's reasonable to ask: did she have to guillotine her own spider mom too? Maybe it's becoming a Serket family tradition, like so many other things. Later on, when we learn more about ancestors, it seems like their spirits watch over their descendants and guide them in certain karmic ways, even if this phenomenon isn't quite that literal. They seem more like "echoes of legend" built into the kids' destinies. Maybe it's not "luck" that lets her roll results of certain importance to her life. Maybe Mindfang's spirit still presides over these dice.

Au revoir, spidermom.

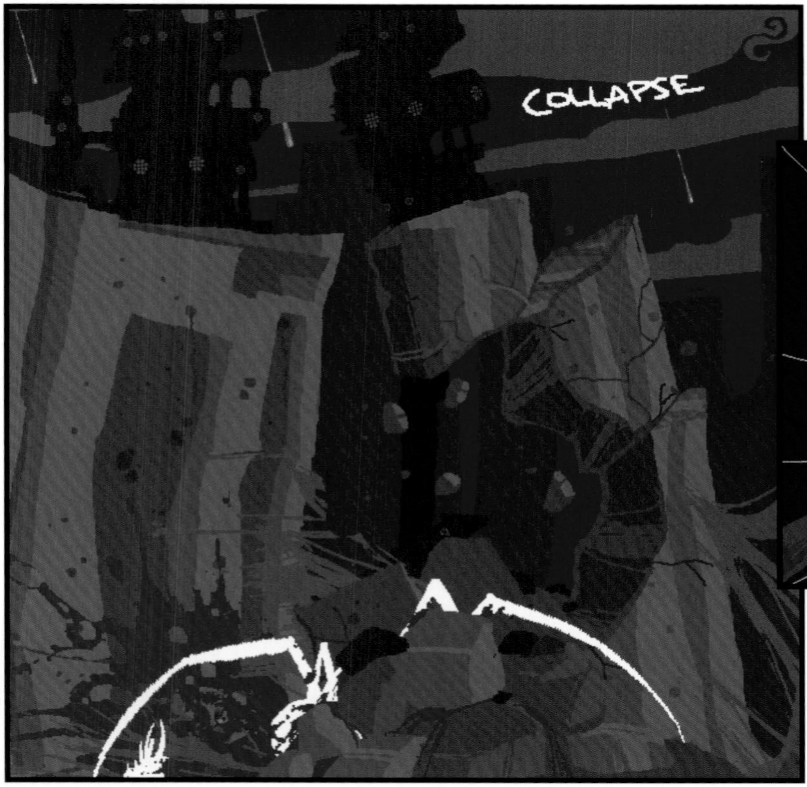

COLLAPSE

Your mercy killing triggers another avalanche. More rotten luck!

Now she's using Troll French. Okay. And now she's back to only seeing the bad luck instead of the good. Yes, sure, you got drenched in your mom's blood and it triggered another avalanche. But what about the unbelievably unlikely roll you just made, resulting in a convenient decapitation device for your humongous abusive custodian? So ungrateful.

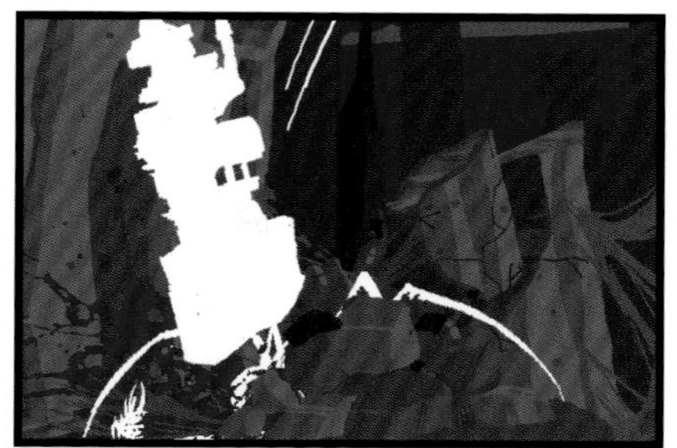

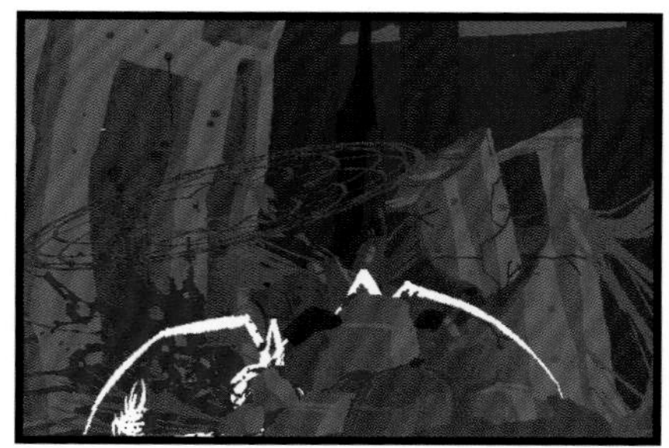

> Vriska: What's her deal????????

arachnidsGrip [AG] **began trolling** apocalypseArisen [AA]

AG: What's your deal????????
AA: what d0 y0u mean
AG: Did you just zap Equius into the game? His hive disappeared!
AA: are y0u n0t happy ab0ut that
AG: Hell no! I was supposed to get your surprise present from him! Um, that he was keeping for me! 8ut only temporarily!
AG: And then we were going to jump in the g8me tog8ther! As co-le8ders! Remem8er????????
AA: y0u were ab0ut t0 be killed by his hive
AA: pr0ceeding with that plan w0uldnt have made sense
AA: we certainly d0nt need tw0 dead players
AG: 8ut!
AG: Aaaaaaaah!
AG: You knew this was going to happen! You were planning it all along! You're planning all this. I know a schemer when I see one!
AA: yes it was the plan
AA: it had t0 g0 this way
AG: No! It had to go the way we said it would. I was going to give you the present I convinced him to m8ke for you. Me! It wo8ldn't have got m8de if not f8r me!
AG: And then you could have a 8ody again and everyth8ng would 8e fine. Then we could go 8ack to 8eing friends again.
AA: were we ever really friends
AG: Yeah!!!!!!!!
AG: I don't know. I felt like we were even if you didn't think so.

Vriska is super ambitious and obviously wanted to be the co-leader (and then leader) quite intensely. So it's worth noting that the thing she's most upset about here is that this turn of events means she doesn't get the chance to give Aradia the present and "make everything right again." Let's think on that a bit. And then get sad.

AG: I guess I'm not very good at acting like a friend. Or saying stuff like, hey friend! You're my friend! It doesn't really occur to me.
AG: 8ut we were! Why would you play with me if you didn't think I was your friend?
AA: i d0nt remember
AA: it d0esnt matter
AG: 8arf. More of this apathetic 8aloney. Why don't you cut the ghost girl act already? I get it! You're dead and spooky.
AA: ribbit
AG: Hm.
AG: Uh, okay?
AG: Haha. Pretty odd!
AA: s0rry
AG: That's cool, you can ri88it if you want. In a weird way it almost makes you sound normal!
AG: So what now? I guess you and Equius co-lead since he managed to usurp me. That cunning 8astard.
AG: I guess I follow you into the game instead? Fine 8y me! I'll follow you guys. Just give me my orders, 8oss.
AA: n0
AA: y0ure n0t 0n the blue team
AG: Oh what the fuuuuuuuuck!
AA: y0u were never g0ing t0 be
AG: I get it. I finally see now. This is your revenge.
AG: You finally did it, Megido. You got me pretty good. Well played.
AA: its n0t revenge
AA: y0u were always supp0sed t0 be 0n the red team
AA: y0ull believe me later
AA: when y0u wake up
AG: What a load of SHIIIIIIIT. You've 8een plotting your revenge since day one. And I fell for it like a sucker. Can't say I 8lame you.
AA: ive never th0ught ab0ut revenge at all
AG: 8ut why not!
AG: I killed you!!!!!!!!
AA: i d0nt care
AG: AAAAAAAAH!!!!!!!!
AG: You're so infuri8ing! Why c8n't you just h8 me? It would 8e a lot easier th8t way.
AG: Or at least feel 8othered or annoyed or S8METHING! God!!!!!!!!
AG: May8e I sh8uld just rip my he8rt out of my chest and pound it to a 8loody pulp here on my desk with my sup8r strong ro8ot arm.
AG: Pound pound pound pound pound pound pound pound!
AG: Look at that, more nasty 8lue 8lood all over me. Why not! Might as well op8n the floodg8s and p8nt my whole hive with this oh so envia8le cerulean SWILL.

And then she just loses it. Like I said before, it's the apathy that kills her. Anything else, she can deal with. Hatred, friendship, anything, as long as it's not nothing. Disinterest and irrelevance are the ultimate poisons to a character who is the purest embodiment of controversy within the narrative. The only bad publicity is no publicity. It's not intended as revenge, but Aradia couldn't come up with a better one if she tried. Even the beatdown Aradiabot gives Vriska later is better than this, and in a sick way, Vriska probably regarded that as the two of them formally making amends. Also, let's not overlook the heart-ripping-out line. Quite an oddly specific foreshadowing for something that happens very soon...in twelve pages, actually.

AG: 8ecause clearly it's up to me to feel em8tions for the 8oth of us, you misera8le soulless witch!
AA: 0_0
AG: I h88888888 you!
AG: H8 h8 h8 h8 h8 h8 h8 haaaaaaaate!
AG: I only regret killing you cause it m8de you so 8ORING!!!!!!!!
AA: s0rry
AG: I don't want to 8e on the red team. ::::(
AG: It's full of jerks who just think I'm a 8ig jerk.
AA: they need y0u th0ugh
AA: and its where y0u need t0 be
AA: karkat will be in t0uch with y0u s00n
AG: Oh god, I can't w8 for THAT convers8tion.
AA: als0 if its any c0ns0lati0n
AA: the teams are meaningless anyway
AG: What? Why would that 8e consol8tion? It's more vague spooky nonsense!
AG: Fuck you for me trying to help you.
AG: Fuck the 8lue team, fuck your conniving, fuck Equius's dou8ledealing and the stupid muscle8east he rode in on, and fuck you for s8ving my life.
AG: FUUUUUUUUCK YOOOOOOOOUUUUUUUUU!!!!!!!!

arachnidsGrip [AG] **ceased trolling** apocalypseArisen [AA]

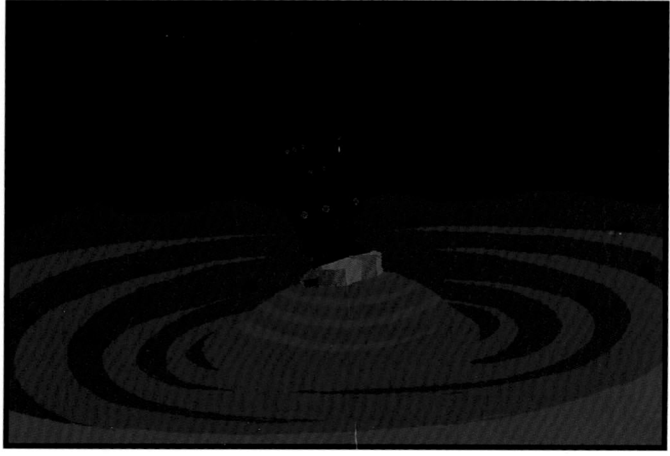

And soon, in a place known as the LAND OF CAVES AND SILENCE...

> Equius: Let her know the deal.

Vriska has a few really, really epic meltdowns throughout *Homestuck*, right up to the end. The meltdown to end them all of course happens between Vriska x (Vriska). These incidents always expose a deeply sad and broken person. I have no consoling remark to follow that up with. It's just how it is, folks. And now, the introduction to Equius's haunting land, already in progress. His hive is tilted, which is just the way it came in. He'll probably have to fix that at some point (don't worry, he's STRONG enough to just push it back, probably). Silence is the operative idea for his aspect of Void. A void of sound. His land actually is pretty reminiscent of the Alpha Kid session planets (which makes sense, since it's a void session). They're all planets full of tombs, crypts, etc., each conveying a profoundly haunting, solitary vibe. I always felt, on a totally personal level, that it's one of the nicer details of Act 6. The lands all have an extremely evocative sense of desolate atmosphere.

centaursTesticle [CT] began trolling apocalypseArisen [AA]

CT: D --> Aradia, here's the deal
CT: D --> Now that the game has begun, the plan will be modified slightly
CT: D --> We will not be co-leaders of the b100 team
CT: D --> I alone will be the leader
CT: D --> Is that understood
AA: thats fine
CT: D --> Good
CT: D --> Wait
CT: D --> You have no objection
CT: D --> Are you sure
AA: n0
AA: im 0k with it
CT: D --> Do you typically embrace such a passive attitude when your superiors give you orders
AA: i d0nt usually receive 0rders fr0m superi0rs 0r 0therwise
AA: but really its fine
CT: D --> Hmm
AA: what
CT: D --> I think I should get a towel
CT: D --> I'm perspiring heavily again
AA: why
AA: whats wr0ng
CT: D --> Never mind
CT: D --> I'm trying to stay professional about this
AA: ab0ut what
AA: what are y0u talking ab0ut
CT: D --> Forget it
CT: D --> It's just pleasant to consort with one of lesser breeding who clearly understands her place
AA: ive underst00d f0r s0me time that this will be my r0le
AA: t0 functi0n as y0ur server player
AA: and that y0u w0uld be the team leader as the first in the chain
CT: D --> Perfect
CT: D --> Then we are on the same page
CT: D --> I 100k forward to seeing how well you serve me, server player
AA: uh
AA: thats n0t quite the meaning 0f the w0rd server
CT: D --> What do you mean

Equius just never stops giving himself fuel for revving up his sexual agitation, even when the other person remains passive, or just doesn't know what to say. You almost get the sense that he's always the only one who's actually participating in the conversation he believes is taking place. Let's also take an enormous amount of gratification and relief from the fact that Aurthoursprite has maintained his ripped physique after having his horse body transplanted with a ghost torso. Thank god.

AA: as y0ur server i manipulate y0ur envir0nment t0 help y0u advance
CT: D --> I don't understand
CT: D --> Are you
CT: D --> Are you saying
CT: D --> That
CT: D --> You are in a position of control over me
AA: i supp0se s0
CT: D --> Oh
AA: what
CT: D --> Oh my God
AA: 0_0
CT: D --> This is
CT: D --> Impropriety of a caliber I cannot even
CT: D --> It's
CT: D --> You are as low on the hemosprectrum as possible
CT: D --> To consider that someone so low could be in a position of authority over me is
CT: D --> It's just so
CT: D --> Disgusting
AA: y0u really are quite a sn0b
CT: D --> No it's
CT: D --> FILTHY
AA: 0_0
CT: D --> I need some air
CT: D --> Or some cold milk
CT: D --> Or a towel, I need a towel
CT: D --> Where the fuck are all my fresh towels
CT: D --> I mean
CT: D --> Fiddlesticks, please pardon my language
CT: D --> It won't happen again
AA: y0u l00k really agitated
AA: are y0u sure y0ure alright

It's incredibly tragic that the GIF of Equius vibrating intensely due to his lewd insinuations has been expanded into four virtually identical panels. I'm so sad about this, I actually just dusted off my bugle and started playing "Taps."

CT: D --> I'm fine
CT: D --> I'll be fine
CT: D --> I just need to breathe
CT: D --> And to break something possibly
AA: break s0mething
CT: D --> Yes
CT: D --> It helps me rela%
AA: 0h
AA: i think i understand
CT: D --> Do you
AA: i like breaking things
AA: i didnt used t0 but n0w i d0
AA: its fun
AA: um
AA: hell0
AA: are y0u sure y0ure 0k
CT: D --> Yes
AA: y0u really d0 l00k like y0ure sweating pretty hard
CT: D --> I just need a blasted towel
CT: D --> Where ever did that Aurthour get off to
AA: maybe y0u sh0uld break s0mething
AA: t0 try t0 calm d0wn
CT: D --> Perhaps
AA: d0 y0u want me t0 break s0mething
CT: D --> Whoa what
AA: i c0uld break s0mething if y0u want
CT: D --> Do you
CT: D --> Want to break something
AA: kind 0f
CT: D --> I, uh
CT: D --> Ok

Equius x Nepeta conversations are very good, but it should also be noted that Equius x Aradia conversations are also very good. We may have to deduce that any conversation involving Equius is very good. The evidence is becoming insurmountable.

AA: equius im ab0ut t0 thr0w an ablutiOn trap thr0ugh y0ur wall
AA: heads up

CT: D --> Yes
CT: D --> Yes that was wonderful
AA: it was pretty c00l
CT: D --> But could you please refrain from dipping into the vernacular of commoners
CT: D --> In fact, this is an order from your leader
CT: D --> Call things by their proper names
AA: what
AA: y0u want me t0 call it a bath tub
AA: that s0unds ridicul0us
CT: D --> Nevertheless, do it
AA: fine
CT: D --> Now
CT: D --> Could you please
CT: D --> Uh
CT: D --> Do that again
AA: what
AA: y0u want me t0 thr0w the trap thr0ugh y0ur wall again
AA: i mean the tub
CT: D --> Yes
AA: is that an 0rder
CT: D --> Yes
CT: D --> Wait
CT: D --> I don't know
AA: what d0nt y0u kn0w
CT: D --> Maybe I don't want to order you to
CT: D --> Maybe I want
CT: D --> You to do whatever things that you want to do

It's just like when Rose threw a bathtub through John's wall. In the business, we say this is a callback. But when it happened to John, I don't think it made him horny. At least, I sure hope not.

AA: i really have n0 idea what y0ure talking ab0ut
CT: D --> You could cause quite a bother for me, with the power you wield
CT: D --> I can do nothing to stop you, peasant girl
CT: D --> It's so magnificently depraved
AA: y0u are s0 weird
AA: and this is c0ming fr0m a gh0st
AA: ribbit
CT: D --> What was that
CT: D --> Are you role playing now
CT: D --> Stop, it's unbecoming
AA: s0rry
CT: D --> You're better than that
CT: D --> And by better, I mean worse
CT: D --> Much, much worse
CT: D --> Downright coarse and degenerate
CT: D --> Just reprehensibly sordid
AA: 0_0
CT: D --> Actually
CT: D --> Yes
CT: D --> You may role play and proceed to deepen this already irretrievable debauchery
CT: D --> In fact I command it
CT: D --> I command you to have free will and do as you please
CT: D --> And continue being bothersome and unpredictably destructive
CT: D --> I mean
CT: D --> If you want
AA: im n0t really r0le playing
AA: im part fr0g
AA: but 0k
AA: i guess i can break s0me m0re stuff
AA: ribbit
CT: D --> Yes
CT: D --> Ribbit again
AA: i cant really c0ntr0l the ribbits

There's a John arm. Occasional ribbiting also has really spiced up Aradia's morose personality. Have we talked about Frog Aradia yet? It's an easy thing to forget about her, because she just jumps into the robot body and that's that (until her god tier phase). Every session we know of involves some sort of freakish animal fusion prototyping. Beta Kid: Bird Dave and Dog Jade. Troll: Frog Aradia. Alpha Kid, pre-retcon: absolute hell-mess of fusion garbage we probably shouldn't bother talking about yet. Alpha Kid, post-retcon: Literally Everyone Is A Cat.

CT: D --> I will make haste through this mysterious realm and find your gate
CT: D --> It will pose no challenge for me at all
AA: yeah i kn0w
CT: D --> I will then give you your new body, and you may take your rightful place as my subordinate
AA: sure
CT: D --> Actually
CT: D --> Now I'm beginning to wonder
AA: what
CT: D --> Whether I want you to be my subordinate
CT: D --> Hmm
CT: D --> I hope this doesn't sound too strange
AA: everything y0u say s0unds strange
CT: D --> Maybe I would like you to be the co-leader again
AA: 0k
CT: D --> In fact
CT: D --> Oh my goodness, I can't believe I'm entertaining this thought
CT: D --> It feels just vile
CT: D --> Try not to roll your eyes at me
AA: i d0nt have pupils
CT: D --> Would you mind terribly
CT: D --> Being the leader
AA: fine
CT: D --> But
CT: D --> Don't tell anyone
CT: D --> You will be the leader of me, and I will lead all else
CT: D --> You would in effect be the secret leader
AA: yeah sure
AA: thats pretty much h0w it is anyway
CT: D --> Yes, that's the spirit
CT: D --> You take to authority well for one of your b100d
AA: i d0nt have b100d
CT: D --> Not yet
CT: D --> But soon your heart will beat anew, and through it, fresh b100d and fresh passion
AA: 0_0
AA: w0w uh
AA: can y0u just bring me the r0b0t already
CT: D --> On my way

centaursTesticle [CT] ceased trolling apocalypseArisen [AA]

AA: ribbit

Aradia actually turns out to be a very skillful, passive kind of shadow leader. It was her plan all along to assume leadership of the session, and here this ambitious, scheming, weird asshole is just...HANDING her the leadership role, voluntarily. He basically talks himself into it (because he seems to talk himself into everything, with his sexually-agitated circular nonsense), and she just says fine. With all her cloaked maneuvering, she isn't even that underhanded about any of it. She just surrounds herself with Machiavellian crazy people, and lets all their scams cancel each other out, allowing her to default into this position.

> Equius: Proceed to second gate.

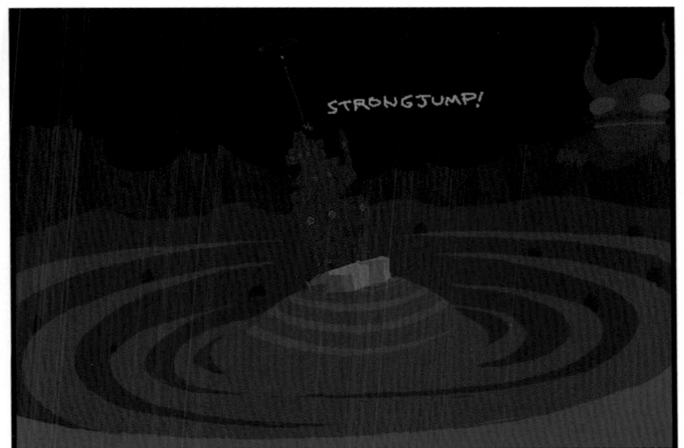

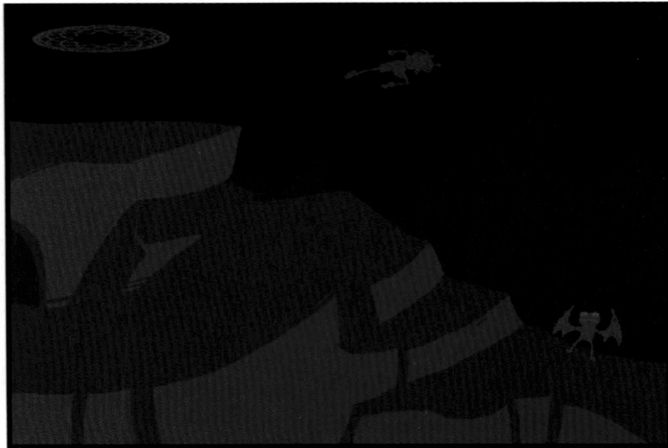

Nothing motivates a guy to strongjump-speedrun through his own enchanted world like having to deliver a sweet robot body to his new girlfriend. Reminds me of the meme, probably insanely dated by the time you read this, of the girl telling the guy to come over, he's like meh, she says her parents aren't home or something, and he starts zooming over. But instead of parents not being home, she's like, I'm a ghost frog, and I need that choice new bod you built me, you know, the one full of your own blood... Good grief, ok, I gotta stop describing memes down here, this sucks.

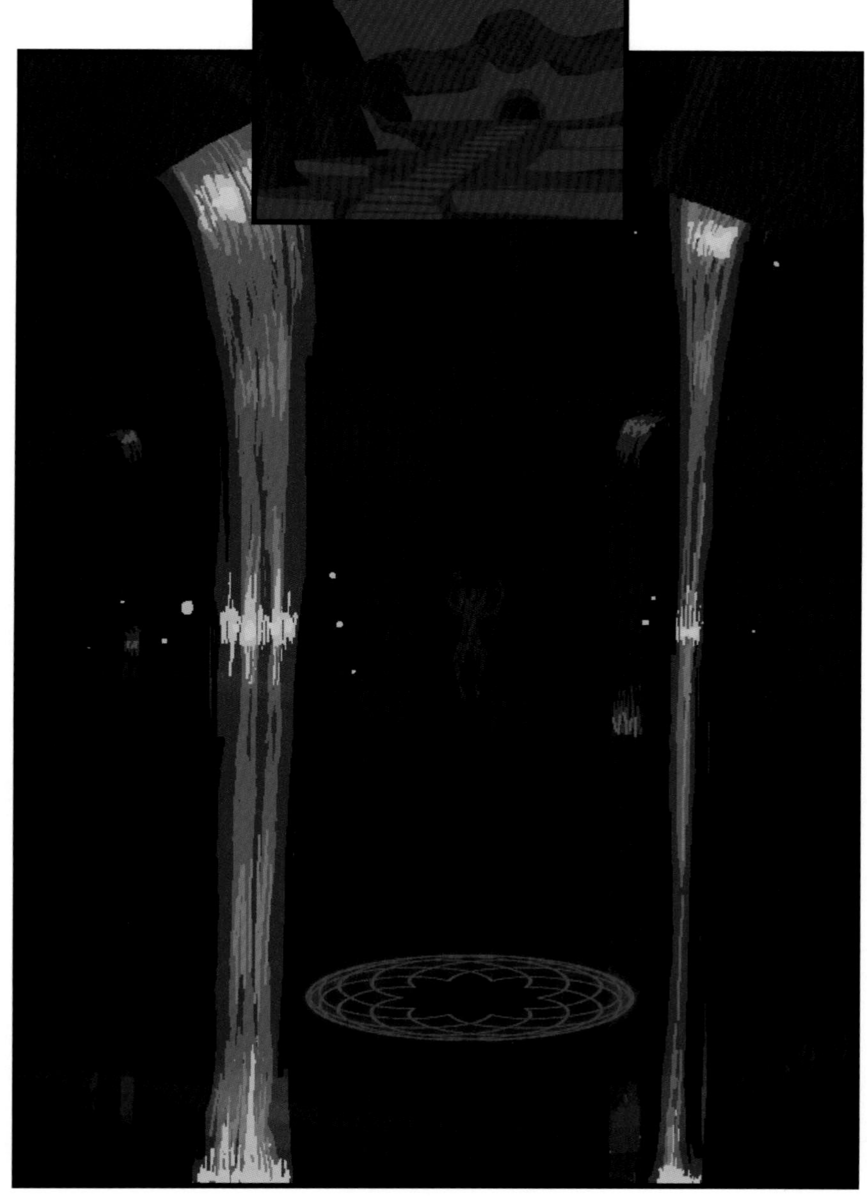

This poses no challenge for you at all.

> Equius: Enter.

These ruins look exactly the same as the place where his ancestor, Darkleer, was hiding out when Mindfang went to see him. What a very mysterious fact this is.

> Equius: Deliver present.

ARADIASPRITE: it 100ks nice
EQUIUS: D --> Yes
EQUIUS: D --> It is perfect in every way
ARADIASPRITE: ribbit
EQUIUS: D --> Do you
EQUIUS: D --> Have a clean towel anywhere

> Aradiasprite: Enter soulbot.

Nice to see Nepeta has already made some progress building up her house. It's noticing the little things, you know? Her house entered the session as a bit of a fixer-upper, so it's about time it had some work done on it. Jake's house was in a similar situation. Yikes, why did I bring Jake up during this great scene that's about to happen? Gotta stop ruining the moment.

EQUIUS: D --> I think it suits you
EQUIUS: D --> Much more so than the form of a levitating ghostly amphibian
EQUIUS: D --> How does it feel
ARADIABOT: it feels
ARADIABOT: different!
EQUIUS: D --> Ok
EQUIUS: D --> But I mean
EQUIUS: D --> Do you feel anything else
ARADIABOT: uh
EQUIUS: D --> Any sort of
EQUIUS: D --> Stirring sensations
ARADIABOT: stirring?
EQUIUS: D --> Yes
EQUIUS: D --> Such as
EQUIUS: D --> Sensations which may be stirred by flowing b100d and a beating heart
ARADIABOT: im n0t sure
EQUIUS: D --> Can you detect anything within you might describe as
EQUIUS: D --> Smoldering passion
EQUIUS: D --> I mean
EQUIUS: D --> Just out of curiosity
ARADIABOT: wait
ARADIABOT: what is that
EQUIUS: D --> What's what
ARADIABOT: this feeling
ARADIABOT: 0h g0d
ARADIABOT: 0H MY G0D WHAT DID Y0U D0!

Equius doesn't miss a beat. No buildup to it, no small talk. Just, right out of the gate: "So. Do you love me yet?" I think we already established him as a creep, and this sure is a creepy thing to do. But it isn't much different than giving someone a love potion from a fantasy story, which in my observation, is not classically treated as an incredibly disturbing violation of another person's rights. Often love potions are used in a comical way, instead of presenting it as the monstrous feat of a sexual predator. At least the way he built the bot allows her to quickly remove the source of the invasive feelings if she found them disturbing. So there, that's my valiant defense of my sweet son, Equius. He's slightly better than the shitty rapists in stories who use love potions to win the affection of others.

ARADIABOT: did y0u pr0gram this r0b0t t0 have feelings f0r y0u?
ARADIABOT: R0MANTIC FEELINGS???
EQUIUS: D --> Hrrrk
ARADIABOT: ANSWER ME BLUE BL00D SCUM
EQUIUS: D --> I
EQUIUS: D --> Yes
EQUIUS: D --> Uh
EQUIUS: D --> It's a chip in your heart
EQUIUS: D --> Is that not ok
ARADIABOT: get it 0ut
EQUIUS: D --> Urrk
EQUIUS: D --> I guess I can
EQUIUS: D --> Uninstall it if you would just
ARADIABOT: GET IT 0UT!!!
EQUIUS: D --> Sorry
EQUIUS: D --> I'll
EQUIUS: D --> Hrrrrrrk
ARADIABOT: GET IT 0UT GET IT 0UT GET IT 0UT GET IT 0UT GET IT 0UT GET IT 0UT GET IT 0UT GET IT 0UT GET IT 0UT GET IT 0UT GET IT 0UT GET IT 0UT GET IT 0UT

Yes, his creepy plan backfired somewhat. But can you honestly say he isn't enjoying this situation anyway? Looks like Equius wins no matter what.

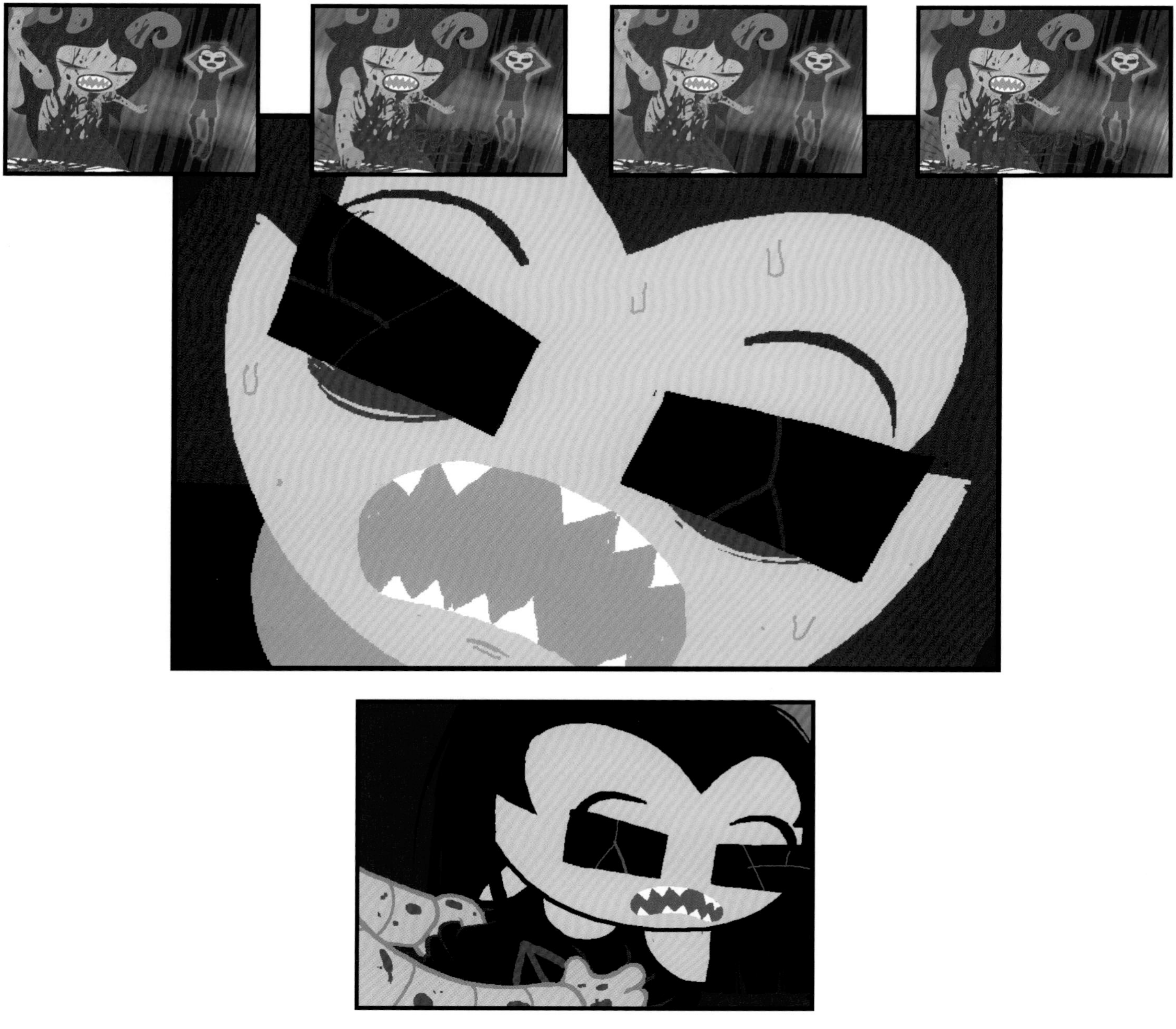

Later the Dirkbot does this exact same thing. But it happens casually in the background as a gag, while Jake is being preoccupied and self-absorbed, as usual. I'm sure Dirk, who programmed the robot to do that, thought it would be a really passionate, dramatic gesture like it is here. But it turned out Jake just didn't care. Nobody cared, Dirk. Your feelings just aren't that important, sorry. What's happening here is important, though. This whole sequence was fire. Miss me with your bad and wrong opinions if you disagree.

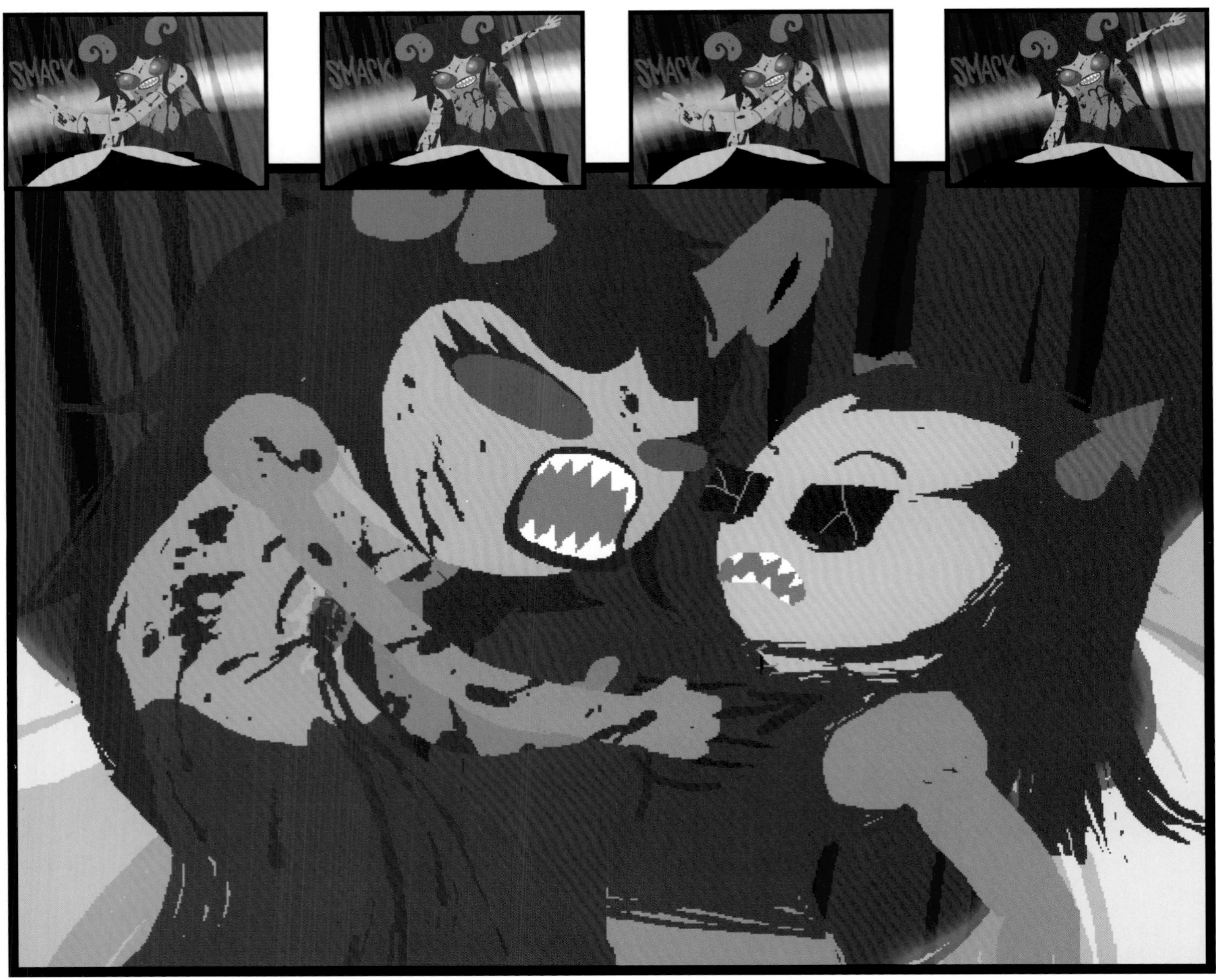

This is the same animation used in **Descend** when Dream Jade tries to smack Dream John awake. It behooves me to point these things out, even if it's not interesting. The word "behooves" contains the word hooves, which is what horses have. Equius likes horses. See how everything always comes full circle? How do I even do it. Okay yeah, I might be running out of shit to say. How many more pages are in this book? Oh. More than 200, you say? All right then. /sound of a person loudly ripping out 200 pages of a heavy book/

So, the moral of the story is, Aradia's basically into this, as long as she gets to do the feeling on her own instead of a stupid heart implant doing it for her. Maybe she was briefly even into the effect of the heart implant, in a sense? It certainly seemed to help jump-start her emotions again. Like some crazy emotional defibrillator. Just because the whole situation is creepy and weird and blood is everywhere doesn't mean we have to be a bunch of fucking downers and harsh too much on their strange little love story. Let's just be happy for them.

> Nepeta: Update wall.

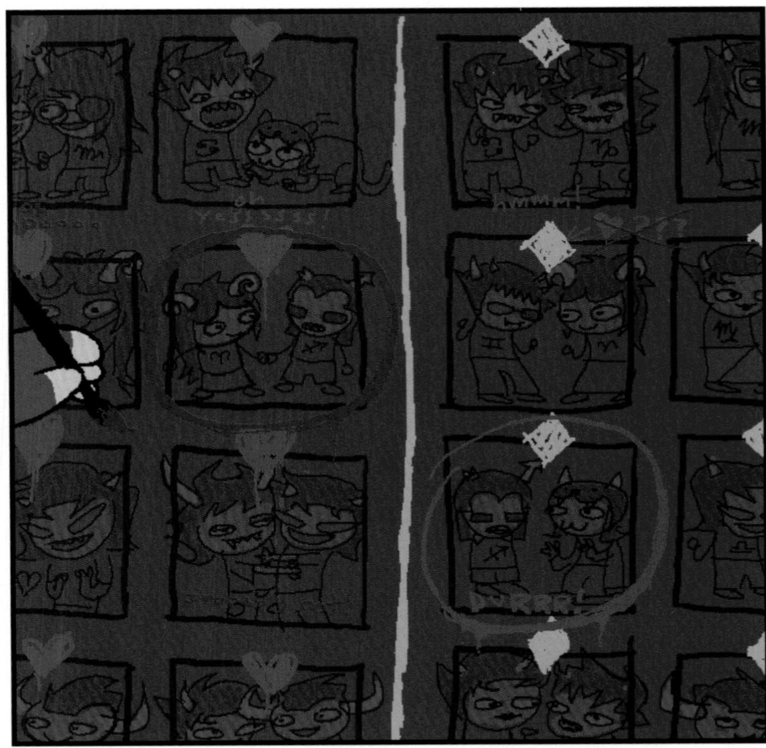

You consult your SHIPPING WALL. Clearly some changes are in order.
You must admit you didn't see this one coming, even with your remarkable matchmaking acumen.

You should probably recolor all the Aradia panels so she looks like a robot too.
It is a major commitment keeping up with all your ships, but it is worth it.

> Karkat: Recruit Vriska.

Nepeta is standing in for the fandom here, updating her shipping wall with this stunning development, as must we all. Even though she didn't see this one coming, she must have given it *brief* consideration, since she clearly drew it in advance. But it seems she's drawn all ships in advance, and only has to circle ones that come to pass, while simply leaving commentary on others. Very convenient. We can draw a few insights from this. First, obviously we note she has an unrequited thing for Karkat, which is critical information, especially to the avid Nepkat loyalists out there. We also see she considers Gamzee <3 Terezi to be a crack ship. (She's right, sort of.) And there's confirmation that she and Equius are moirails, even though we don't know what that means yet. In fact, this visual aid is a good clue that helps us start figuring some stuff out about troll romance on our own, even before I felt it some combination of necessary and hilarious to dump approximately 100,000 words on the subject into the story all at once.

carcinoGeneticist [CG] **began trolling** arachnidsGrip [AG]

CG: OK THIS IS GOING TO SOUND PREPOSTEROUS GIVEN OUR LAST CONVERSATION.
CG: AND I GUESS PRACTICALLY EVERY CONVERSATION PRECEDING IT.
CG: AND I'M PROBABLY GOING TO HAVE TO DO SOMETHING COMPLETELY DISGUSTING LIKE APOLOGIZE.
CG: AND EVEN THOUGH I'LL HATE MYSELF FOR IT I WILL TOTALLY MEAN IT, I PROMISE.
CG: LIKE, REALLY REALLY MEAN IT.
AG: You're going to ask me to join your team, aren't you.
CG: YEAH.
CG: HOW DID YOU KNOW.
AG: I don't seem to have much choice now! Aradia kicked me off the good team.
CG: HAHAHAHA WOW THAT IS GREAT.
CG: WAIT, SORRY.
CG: NO WAIT, I DON'T HAVE TO APOLOGIZE, THAT'S RIGHT. YOU HAVE NO CHOICE NOW.
CG: I APOLOGIZE TO MYSELF FOR OFFERING YOU A SHITTY MEANINGLESS APOLOGY.
CG: APOLOGY ACCEPTED, KARKAT. LET'S BURY THE THRESHER WITH A TOTALLY PLATONIC BRO BULGE BUMP.
CG: BUMP HAHAHAHAHAHAHAHA.
AG: You dork.
AG: Do you really think your usual pedantic quips are going to 8ug me now????????
CG: I'M NOT TRYING TO BUG YOU I'M TRYING TO GET YOU TO JOIN MY DAMN TEAM, NOW STEP IN LINE SERKET.
AG: I was just 8etrayed and a8andonded 8y my two accomplices and 8est pals, and on top of that I am soaked in the 8lood of my lusus which I just had to decapit8 myself.
AG: So listening to a cra88y asshole 8e all tickled with his own mediocre retorts isn't going to spoil my evening!
CG: OK, WELL, SORRY TO HEAR ABOUT THAT.
CG: BUT I MEAN YOU CAN JUST DUMP HER CARCASS IN THE KERNEL AND BRING HER BACK STRONGER THAN EVER.
AG: Wow.
AG: Uh, good to know.
AG: I guess. ::::
CG: NOW WHY DON'T YOU HOP IN THE TRAP, WASH THAT NASTY BLUE SHIT OFF, AND JOIN OUR FUCKING SESSION ALREADY.
AG: What! It's so rude to dict8 hygiene procedure to a lady. Under any circumstance! Even for douchey loudmouths with delusions of leadership.
AG: May8e you should try to think a8out the dum8 things that fall out of your protein chute for once, Vantas.
CG: BLAH BLAH BLAH.
CG: NOW MY CHUTE IS DOING A FUCKING STELLAR IMPRESSION OF SOMETHING THAT DOESN'T GIVE A SHIT.

Karkat apologizes to himself, then accepts his own apology. A brief prelude to the many actual conversations (i.e. arguments) he has with past and future versions of himself. Nobody is better at having ridiculous, emotionally explosive, psychologically revealing conversations with himself than Karkat. Except maybe until Dirk comes along, who designed an entire AI version of himself for that very purpose. So maybe Dirk gets the prize? He doesn't yell as much though.

AG: Anyway, you know my 8lood's the prettiest and you'd o8viously kill to have it.
CG: NO IT SUCKS.
CG: TOTALLY HAPPY WITH MINE, NICE TRY THOUGH.
AG: 8S!
AG: Why would you hide 8ehind your lame gray anonymity then?
AG: You do realize everyone thinks that's totally lame, right????????
CG: IT'S NOBODY'S BUSINESS.
CG: I DON'T SEE WHY IT SHOULD BE A MATTER OF PUBLIC RECORD.
CG: I'M NOT GOING TO WEAR THAT SHIT ON MY SLEEVE LIKE YOU DO.
CG: LITERALLY AND FIGURATIVELY.
CG: IT'S PRIVATE, SO EVERYONE CAN GO POINT THEIR PROBING BUSYBODY SNIFFNODES UP THEIR OWN IMPERTINENT SEED FLAPS.
AG: Fine. Like anyone really cares! It's just lame and insecure.
AG: So why don't you tell me what I've got to do here???????? I await instruction from my 8igshot a8looded leader.
CG: OK FIRST THING'S FIRST.
CG: YOU'VE GOT TO CONNECT WITH TAVROS QUICKLY AND GET HIM IN THE SESSION BEFORE HE GETS KILLED.
AG: Uggggggggh.
CG: WHAT.
AG: Can't someone else do that?
CG: NO. WHY.
AG: XXXXO
CG: WHAT'S THE BIG DEAL, JUST DO IT.
AG: 8ut I h8 that guy!
CG: WHO CARES.
AG: This is your command decision? Getting someone who h8s a guy to save his life? Pretty weak, 8oss!
CG: WHY DO YOU EVEN HATE HIM, IT'S FUCKING RIDICULOUS.
CG: IF ANYTHING YOU SHOULD PITY HIM.
CG: ESPECIALLY SINCE YOU WERE THE ONE WHO PARALYZED HIM.
AG: I know. I don't really understand it.
AG: It's just a really special kind of h8! It never goes away and it doesn't make a lot of sense.
CG: THIS IS KIND OF A WEIRD TIME TO BE CONFIDING IN ME ABOUT YOUR FEELINGS OF BLACK ROMANCE BUT OK.
AG: Oh god, what?
CG: I MEAN IF YOU'RE REALLY IMPLYING TAVROS IS YOUR KISMESIS I THINK YOU'RE BRAYING UP THE WRONG FROND NUB.
CG: BOTH PARTIES HAVE TO HATE EACH OTHER EQUALLY, I MEAN LIKE TRUE HATE.
CG: MAYBE YOUR FEELINGS COME SOMEWHAT CLOSE TO FITTING THE BILL BUT I DON'T THINK HE CAN HATE ANYONE, IT'S WEIRD, HE'S KIND OF BROKEN IN THE HEAD.

He keeps his mutant red blood color a "secret," but the exterior of his hive is decorated with bright red fabric shapes. Very subtle, Karkat.

AG: Fuuuuuuuuck, WHAT are you talking a8out?
CG: I THINK THIS SUBJECT IS BEYOND A LOT OF PEOPLE'S GRASP BUT I KNOW A LOT ABOUT IT, NOBODY EVER REALLY WANTS TO TALK TO ME ABOUT IT THOUGH.
AG: Whoa really? Oh no shit, REALLY????????
CG: OK, MOST PEOPLE WHO HAVEN'T HAD THEIR LOBE STEM CAUTERIZED ARE CAPABLE OF FEELING THE TWO PRIMARY EMOTIONS, HATE AND PITY.
CG: PITY IS OF COURSE JUST THE TONED DOWN VERSION OF THE CENTRAL EMOTION, HATE.
CG: AND ALL THE NUANCES OF PITY MANIFEST AS VARIOUS OTHER KINDS OF FEELINGS LIKE WHATEVER CHEMICAL REACTIONS TRIGGER MATING FONDESS OR THE MYSTERIOUS FORCES THAT ARE BEHIND MOIRALLEGIANCE.
AG: Karkat, holy fuck.
AG: So.
AG: 8oring.
CG: A WELL BALANCED PERSON IS IS GOING TO HAVE A GOOD DISTRIBUTION BETWEEN HATE AND THE VARIOUS PITY HUMORS.
CG: HAVING A GOOD BALANCE KEEPS ALL THE EMOTIONS SHARPER, SEE I THINK THAT'S YOUR PROBLEM.
AG: Oh????????
AG: I hope you know I already wore out some good note-taking pens today. All the pens.
AG: All of them.
CG: SEE, MY HATE IS LIKE A FINELY TUNED INSTRUMENT BECAUSE I'M AWARE OF THESE PRINCIPLES.
CG: I COULD HATE A HOLE IN PARADOX SPACE ITSELF, STRAIGHT THROUGH TO A NEW REALITY FRESH FOR THE HATING.
AG: Hahahahahahahaha, you don't even know how much I'm laughing at this.
CG: BUT SEE, YOU'RE TOO HEAVY ON THE HATE SIDE, OR AT LEAST YOU PRETEND TO BE WHICH IS MAYBE WORSE.
AG: You aren't reading anything I say are you? You just want to talk and talk and talk.
CG: AND YOU THINK YOU'RE HATING UP EVERYONE HARD WHEN YOU'RE REALLY JUST BURNING OUT THAT ENTIRE EMOTIONAL HEMISPHERE.
CG: IT'S LIKE LUKEWARM HATE. PRETENDER'S HATE, WITH NO COUNTERPOINT AT ALL.
CG: AS SUCH THERE'S NO REAL SUBSTANCE TO YOUR HATE, IT'S LIKE A CARDBOARD MOVIE PROP.
CG: WHICH IS WHY YOUR BRAIN IS BROKEN, KIND OF LIKE TAVROS'S BUT ON THE OPPOSITE HEMISPHERE I GUESS.
CG: OR MAYBE YOUR BROKEN BRAIN LED TO THE IMBALANCE IN THE FIRST PLACE, I DON'T KNOW.
CG: WHATEVER THE CASE IS, YOU'RE KIND OF EMOTIONALLY SCREWED, SORRY TO SAY.
CG: YOUR HATE'S TOO DULL FOR A PROPER KISMESIS, IN MY OPINION.
CG: AND I DON'T SEE ANYONE CHOMPING AT THE BIT TO BE YOUR MOIRAIL HONESTLY, UNLESS THERE'S SOMEONE OUT THERE WHO WOULD ACTUALLY BOTHER PITYING YOU.
CG: AND LANDING A MATESPRIT? HAHAHAHA!
CG: SERIOUSLY, LIKE THAT WOULD EVEN INTEREST YOU.
CG: BASICALLY ANY FEATURE OF YOUR EMOTIONAL PROFILE THAT USUALLY MAKES SOMEONE VIABLE IN THE REDROM DEPARTMENT MUST BE TOTALLY FRIED.
CG: YOUR BLACKROM POTENTIAL'S PROBABLY TOAST TOO.

Karkat really does have some amazing leadership skills. When Vriska tells him she got kicked off the blue team, his first order is to team her up with the guy she paralyzed, and still loathes. Then, when she objects, he goes on a long rant about everything that's wrong with her. Leader of the year??

CG: HEY.
CG: ARE YOU THERE.
AG: Oh, yeah.
AG: I started tuning you out.
AG: Are you done?
CG: NO WAY, I COULD GO ON.
CG: THIS IS FASCINATING, TELL ME HOW THE FUCK THIS ISN'T FASCINATING.
AG: Did you learn this crap from your awful romance movies?
CG: THEY'RE REALLY INTRIGUING SOCIOLOGICALLY.
CG: INCREDIBLY COMPLEX, SOPHISTICATED STORIES, YOU WOULDN'T GET IT.
AG: Hey asshole, stop watching movies for girls.
CG: WHAT PART OF INTRIGUING SOCIOLOGICALLY DON'T YOU UNDERSTAND.
CG: ALSO THEY'RE AWESOME, SHUT UP.
AG: Argh, ok! Man! Just let me connect to stupid 8oy-Dum8fuck so I don't have to listen to this anymore!
CG: YEAH OK.
CG: OH, WAIT!
CG: I NEVER EVEN GOT TO THE DAMN POINT.
AG: What is it now!
CG: I DIDN'T NEED YOU SPECIFICALLY TO CONNECT TO TAVROS, I MEAN I COULD GET ANY SCHLUB TO DO THAT.
CG: YOU JUST HAVE TO GET IN HERE ASAP BECAUSE I REALLY NEED YOUR MIND POWERS.
AG: You do????????
AG: I mean.
AG: O8viously you do. Duh.
AG: What for?
CG: I RAN INTO SOMEONE HERE.
CG: A SORT OF DOUBLE AGENT I GUESS.
CG: HIS NAME IS JACK.

Another "____ for girls" comment. Which, judging from how this expression was used earlier in reference to Flarp, probably just means that troll romance movies are really violent. Which makes perfect sense, of course. Also you can't really tell here, but Karkat's blood color in that GIF image was cycling through a few colors, to keep it a "mystery." Sometimes *Homestuck* does this, protects a piece of information it isn't ready to reveal yet by presenting it in plain sight but obscuring the thing in question in some manner. This is also done with the name of Kanaya's land.

CG: HE HAS SOME INSIDE INFORMATION ABOUT HIS KINGDOM.
CG: HE WANTS TO WORK TOGETHER WITH US TO OVERTHROW THE BLACK QUEEN.
CG: SO I SAID OK.
CG: AND NOW I NEED YOUR HELP.
AG: Um, ok.
AG: I can try.
AG: What does he know?
CG: HE RECENTLY GOT HOLD OF SOME INTEL REGARDING A WEAKNESS IN THE QUEEN'S DEFENSES.
CG: I DON'T KNOW ANY MORE THAN THAT.
CG: BUT WE'VE GOT TO HURRY AND GET STARTED ON THIS THING, OR IT COULD GET KIND OF AWKWARD.
AG: Awkward? What do you mean?
CG: I MEAN HE'S JUST STANDING HERE NOW.
CG: WAITING FOR ME I GUESS.
CG: BUT IT'S OK, I THINK HE'S PRETTY MUCH SETTLED DOWN.
AG: Settled down?
CG: WELL, HE STABBED ME ONCE.
AG: Oh, only once!
AG: Are you sure you should trust him? I don't know if I would, 8ut hey I'm not the leader.
CG: NO, NO, IT'S COOL.
CG: HE'S COOL, IT'S FINE I DON'T REALLY MIND THE STABBING, IT WAS ALL A MISUNDERSTANDING.
CG: WELL OK I'M PRETTY SURE HE MEANT TO STAB ME.
CG: BUT I KIND OF THINK THAT'S LIKE
CG: THE WAY HE GREETS PEOPLE?
AG: This game is so stupid.
CG: IN ANY CASE I THINK HE'S PROBABLY ALL STABBED OUT.
AG: Whew!!!!!!!!
AG: Oh, man.
AG: Since you're 8leeding I should ask Terezi what color your 8lood is.
CG: GOOD LUCK WITH THAT.
CG: SHE CAN'T SEE ME OR SMELL ME OR ANYTHING, I'M WAY OUT OF MY HIVE SOMEWHERE ELSE ON THE PLANET.
AG: Ok, then I'll ask Jack.
CG: NO, JACK WON'T TELL, I MADE HIM PROMISE HE WOULDN'T TELL.
AG: Dammit! Stupid lousy tightlipped sta8happy dou8le agents.
AG: Doesn't Trollian have some kind of viewport feature?
CG: YEAH BUT I'M PRETTY SURE ONLY SOLLUX KNOWS HOW TO SET THAT UP, AND HE'S BEEN INCOMMUNICADO FOR HOURS FOR SOME REASON.
CG: ANYWAY THAT WHOLE FEATURE SEEMS TOTALLY INVASIVE AND LARGELY POINTLESS TO ME, SO JUST FORGET IT.
AG: Yeah ok, here we are a8out to em8ark on an espionage mission. A spying tool sounds totally useless!
AG: Another gr8 point, captain.

Karkat has a funny attitude regarding Jack. If one of his friends slights him in the smallest way in conversation, he explodes and goes on a lengthy, indignant tirade. But if Jack stabs him, Karkat bends over backwards to excuse him, rationalizing that it's just his way of being friendly or something. He seems to admire Jack, and respects his ruthlessness. Or at least he thinks he does. There's almost a paternal quality to the relationship, like Jack is the father Karkat never had (Except...he did have a father? A crab monster father, though. It's not quite the same.) Or maybe another way of looking at Karkat's behavior toward Jack is more like if Jack were a dangerous animal Karkat respected greatly, that he was trying to tame and befriend, like a tiger. If a wild tiger swipes at you with its claws, you don't take it personally. It's just his nature. You'd probably blame yourself for not being careful enough, and then keep trying to figure out how to connect with the beast. Of course, we're still thinking like humans here. Forming connections with dangerous beasts IS what father-son relationships for trolls are like.

CG: WHATEVER.
CG: JUST GET YOUR ASS IN HERE SO WE CAN DETHRONE THIS GODDAMN QUEEN.
CG: IT'LL MEAN ONE LESS GOD BOSS WE HAVE TO FIGHT.
AG: Fine, I'll be right there.
AG: Just try not to lose too much of your mystery blood and die.

arachnidsGrip [AG] ceased trolling carcinoGeneticist [CG]

> Be Jack a few minutes ago...

You find the kid you've been looking for. He's got a pretty sharp tongue and can't seem to keep it sheathed. He should learn up front you're no stranger to sharp objects yourself.

He still won't shut up. He doesn't seem to care about the wound. He's just going on and on about the freakish color of his blood. He doesn't want you to look at it. Just look away, he says.

You've got to admit. Now you're curious.

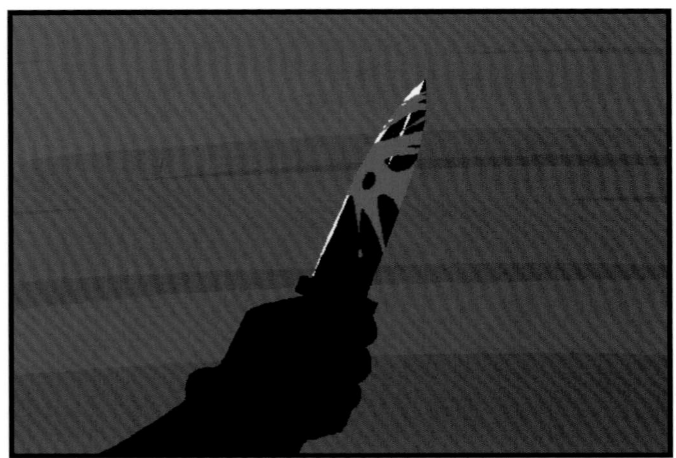

You don't see what the big deal is. Nothing special. This kid's out of his mind.

But he's still blubbering on and on about it.

> Jack: Look at knife.

Karkat's blood color was concealed for only a few pages. Visually obscuring it until Jack looks at the knife is less about keeping the true color from the reader than about deliberately collapsing any mystery or controversy regarding the blood at the moment Jack looks at it, since he's acting as the witness who can verify for Karkat that his red blood is no big deal and is in fact perfectly ordinary to most creatures, including every living thing inside this game. This is another one of those non-reveal reveals, where the "mystery" surrounding something was never actually that important or even meant to be obscured, just like the ghost Aradia reveal. When you look back through the story, Karkat's blood color becomes obvious: his red hive decor, his Land, which surrounds him with HUGE OCEANS OF RED BLOOD. Almost like his environment is taking this point of extreme insecurity and rubbing it in his face. The mystery of his blood up to this point seems more fueled by Karkat's insecurity and fear rather than being a true point of narrative intrigue. The moment Jack shows him it's nothing to be ashamed of is when he can begin the process of letting go and dealing with it.

It seems he's the only one of his kind with this mutant candy-red blood. An outcast. He thinks he was put on this planet covered in an ocean of his own blood to be taunted. Punished for something.

Saddest story you ever heard. Got to do something to shut him up.

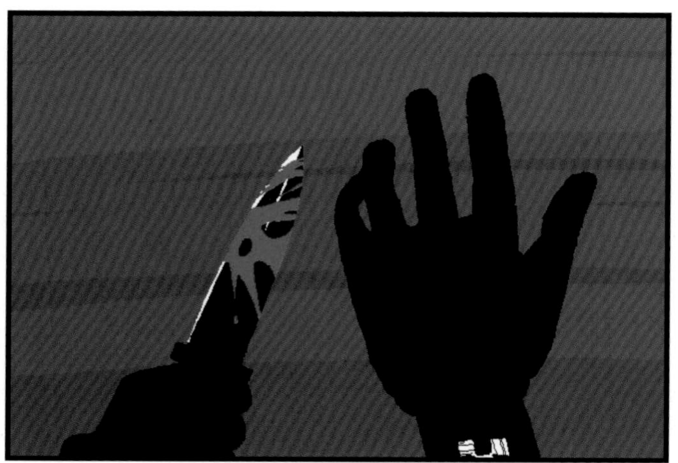

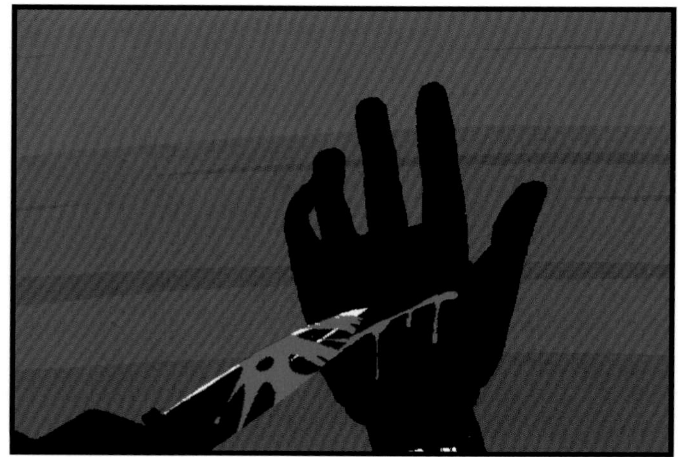

And in addition to helping dispel the "mystery" for us, and beginning to dispel the shame for Karkat, Jack is initiating an almost heartwarming moment of bonding between them. He quickly establishes himself to Karkat as an amalgam of a pseudo-father figure, a tamed dangerous animal, and now a blood brother. Jack is the first person Karkat ever meets who has blood like his, but soon he will meet a lot more. Humans sharing his blood type is another small symbolic way of hinting that Karkat is more fundamentally suited to being a human than being a troll, struggle as he might against this truth for most of his life.

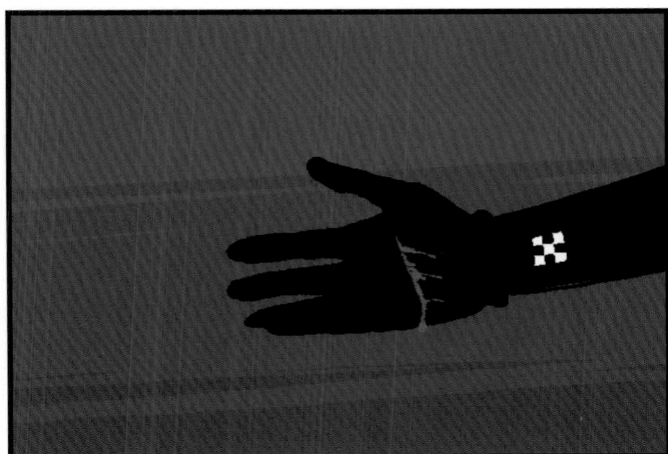

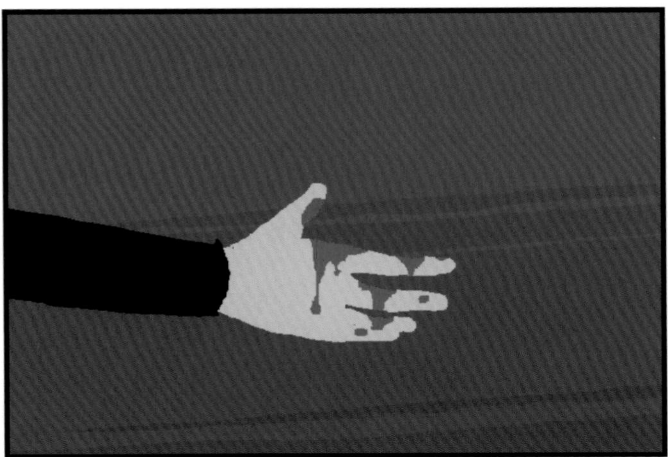

The blood pattern on Jack's hand is quite reminiscent of the Blood aspect symbol. I'm sure you noticed. But you also like it when I confirm the things you were thinking, right? Yes, you do.

> Karkat: Be in cahoots with Jack.

You and your like-blooded accomplice soon put OPERATION REGISURP into motion, a contingency plan which the archagent conveniently had on file and named himself. If it were drafted by a legitimate contingency firm, it would ostensibly have been given a better title.

Your whole team executes the plan along the course of its journey, employing espionage, mind control tactics, political sabotage, vicious interrogations and cold blooded assassinations. Everyone does their part and you begin to learn the true meaning of teamwork, as well as this troll disease called friendship.

Jack apparently likes to name things associated with taking down monarchs using portmanteaus with the suffix "regi-." Regisword, regisurp...almost like he was designed to have mutiny on the brain? To be fair, Operation Regisurp—an actual, detailed plan of betrayal contained in an actual folder—appears to be much better thought out than the tactic he was using in the human session. Which consisted of occasionally handing a regisword to anyone wandering through his office, like a confused mail lady, and hoping they would take it upon themselves to assassinate the rival king or queen. But then, maybe Operation Regisurp is a better plan because it involves ousting his *own* queen? Now that's a plan he can really throw himself into.

But before a single step is taken, Jack briefs you on the intelligence uncovered by one of his agents. It is an advantage over the queen you will seize upon while she has let her guard down.

With each prototyping by each player, the royalty of both sides would evolve. The queen with her RING OF ORBS TWELVEFOLD would first take on the claws and ridged carapace of your lusus. And then the wings and scales of Terezi's young dragon. And then the horns and gills and cloven hooves of Gamzee's fallen custodian. And so it would continue.

Though a queen is a vain creature, she is also sworn to her duty. She would be braced for the heavy load of augmentation ahead. She could certainly withstand the eight eyes of an arachnid. The fairy wings might at worst be frivolous, and the great bull horns could even be regarded as striking additions. For that matter, the sultry lips of a mother grub might very plausibly suit her. She perhaps would wear a brave face even behind a dignified mustache, and the centauring of her lower torso could transpire without much complaint. She would dutifully indulge a lactating udder. And when all was said and done, doubling her head count would surely be insult to elevenfold injury, but nothing she hadn't essentially endured already, all in the name of her kingdom.

But she would spare herself all of these additional debasements. Because before the rest came, there would be one corruption to her figure she could not abide. Her vanity wouldn't allow it.

The text here goes pretty heavy on the idea that the queen was only "enduring" these gruesome mutations out of a sense of regal duty. I think this is worth second-guessing, though. The Black Queen in the human session really seemed to be getting into the mutations and wardrobe updates resulting from prototypings. She really leaned into the slutty clown dress-up fun and got a kick out of forcing Jack to participate. You get the sense this is just part of what it means to be a queen, to revel in the crazy mutations and upgrades the ring endows. So maybe her vanity hadn't actually suffered that much before the frogsprite entered the picture. It's just that Dersites are SO biased against frogs, she couldn't tolerate marring her figure in that one specific way. The entire Operation Regisurp appears to revolve around exploiting the queen's bitter anti-frog racism.

She could not stand bearing the visage of the most loathsome creature known to existence. So vile is its appearance, so contemptible its purpose, all depictions of the creature let alone members of its population are permanently banned from any jurisdiction in the reach of her agents. Those of its kind go by many names, and so does the reviled patron god they herald - THE GREAT DETESTATION, KING PONDSQUATTER, SPEAKER OF THE VAST JOKE, or most commonly, BILIOUS SLICK.

His true name is of course forbidden. And wearing his face is where she drew the line.

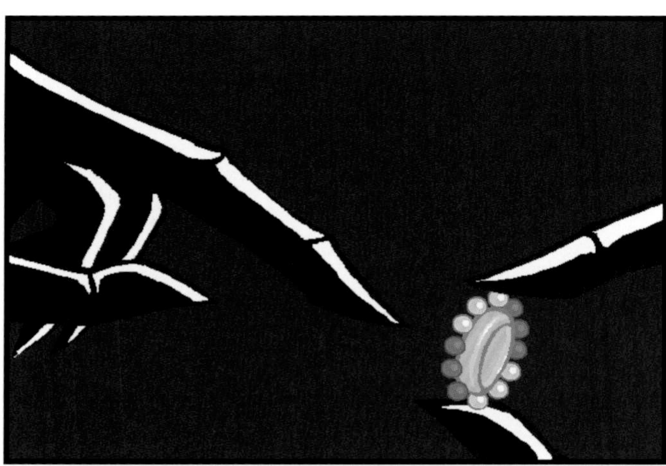

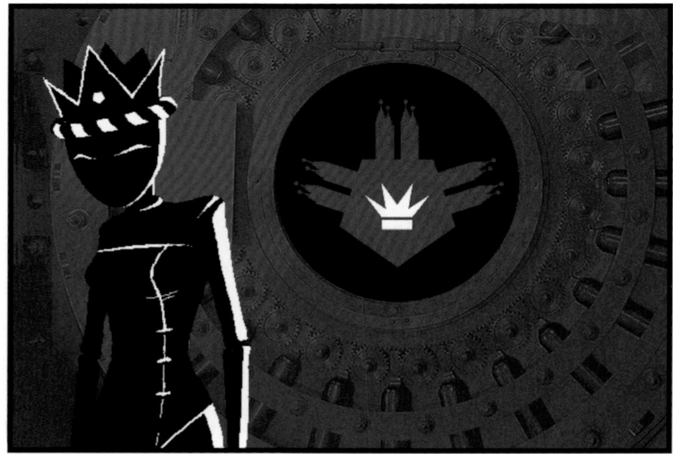

She removed the ring and concealed it in the ROYAL VAULT while she was quite sure no one was looking. She then retired to her private chamber from which she would dispatch orders, no one the wiser of her disadvantage.

Or so she thought.

> Red team: Execute Operation Regisurp.

Note that when she takes the ring off six orbs are filled. Three players from the blue team have entered the session, and three from the red team. Aradia was the second of the blue team to enter. Nepeta was third. Aradia's entry is when the frog mutations took effect on the ring-wearer. And then an interval passed before Nepeta's entry. Which means the queen actually spent a decent amount of time looking like a frog, deliberating whether or not she could put up with this for an entire game session. Ultimately, she couldn't hang in there. But this does imply she at least *tried*.

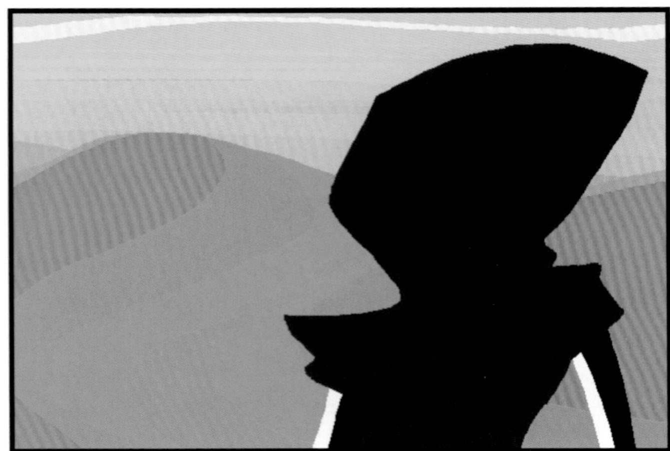

The operation in time would be a total success. The BANISHED QUASIROYAL would make the future Alternian wasteland her home.

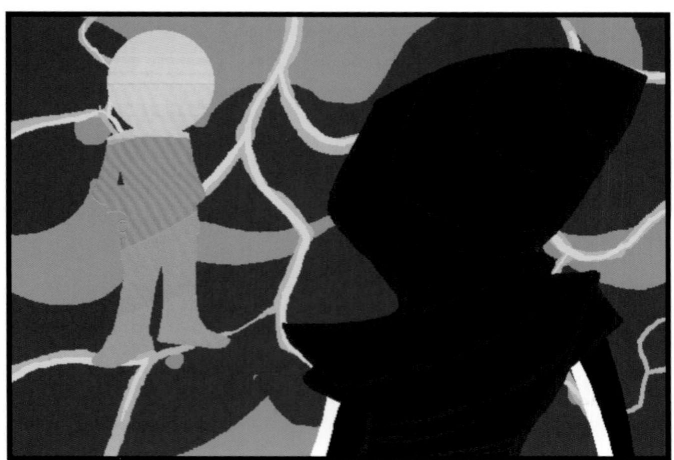

Until she was given a new purpose.

The Black Queen's actions pretty much parallel what the White Queen did on Earth. She flies one of the Derse battleships through a defense portal and lands on postapocalyptic Alternia, with her cool shroudwear ready to go. She won't need it for long, though. Doc has quite a glamorous wardrobe upgrade ready for her. Doc and his master have a habit of granting certain women sick powers and conscripting them into long-term service, from which they can only be released by death.

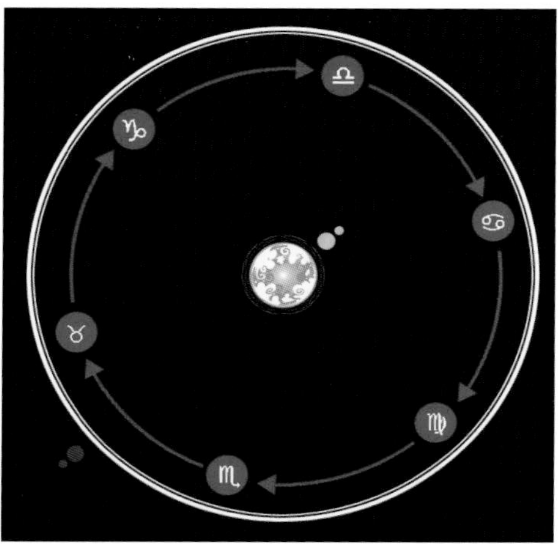

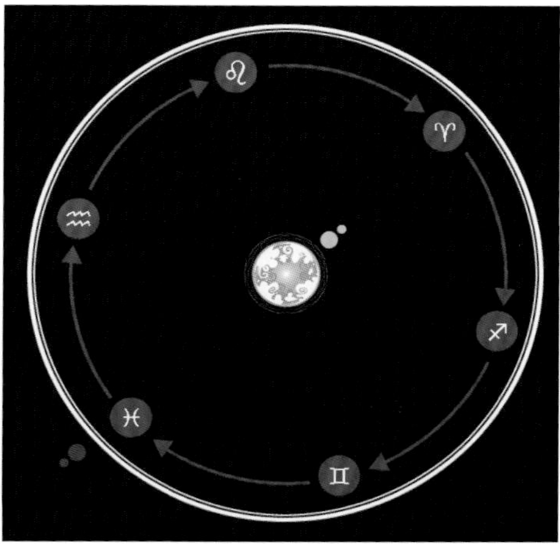

But at the onset, you would know nothing of the queen's aversion to an amphibious likeness, or about her orbs twelvefold, or any such details. You were informed of her disadvantage, and would act accordingly. You and your red teammates would work to dethrone the queen in your session, while the blue team members would take on the entirely separate set of royal adversaries in their own session. This was to be a competition, after all.

Or so you thought.

You would begin to notice a strange pattern. The blue team's prototypings would affect the mutations of your session's underlings.

And your prototypings would affect theirs.

We're leading up to another non-reveal reveal showing us how the "two" game sessions were actually one big, twelve-player session all along. There were many small clues along the way, including the shot a few pages ago of the queen's ring with twelve orbs, and the story treats this fact as so obvious to everyone that it's presented in the form of a somewhat humorous confirmation rather than a mind-blowing revelation. This happens often enough in Hivebent that this casual reveal method almost starts feeling like a refrain, which probably results more from this arc's fast and loose pacing than anything else. As if to say, we're in a big hurry here folks, we don't have TIME to have our minds blown. That said, let's admire these uncharacteristically detailed action panels exhibiting cool environments and teamwork. Wanna know something? Well, In My Opinion, those music box-tower things are particularly good fantasy set pieces. Nice concept, nice design. You agree with me.

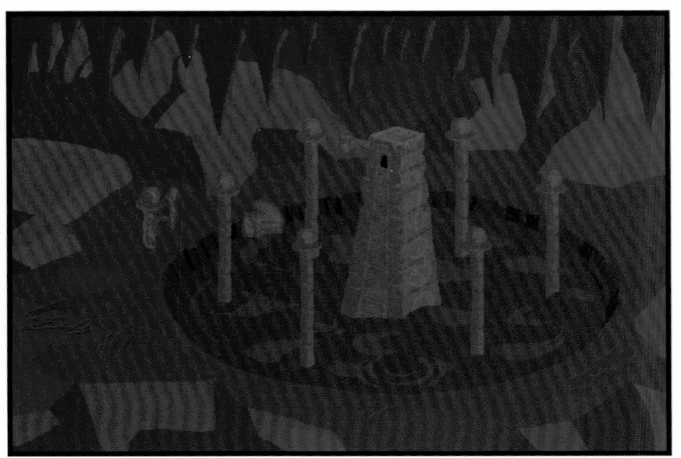

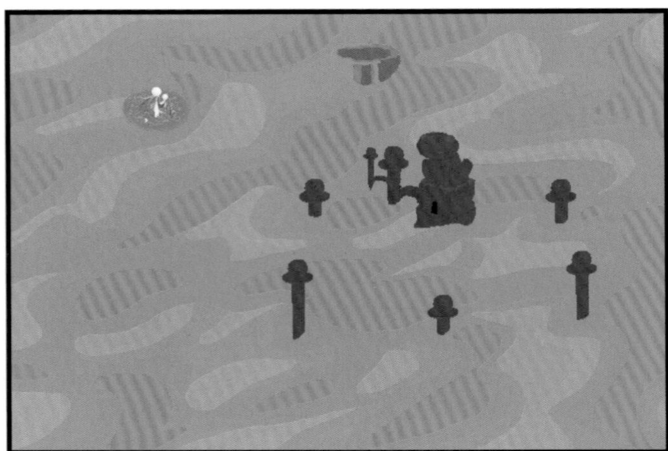

Though the signs pointed to two distinct sessions - two sets of mystic ruins, two opposing teams, two separate chains of connected players - this was all misleading.

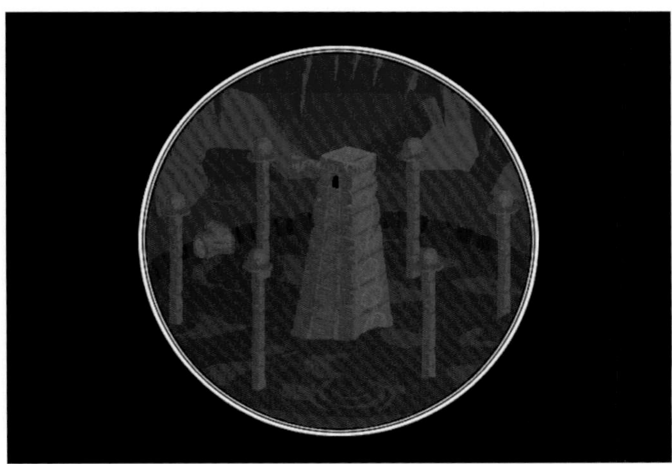

You were joining a particularly unusual bifurcated session, meant from the start to receive all twelve players through two separate connection chains. A session with one Skaia about which twelve planets would circle. With one army of dark and one of light. With one pair of kings and one pair of queens. And with one cantankerous archagent and his typical disdain for authority. It wouldn't be until later in the session when the full chain was nearly closed that you would realize the truth.

The truth was it had always been the same session all along. That your teams were not competing, but cooperating toward a common goal.

A twelve-player session is a *big* session, by any standard. Since I just make this shit up, I get to say what's true or not, but it does seem unlikely that they would get much bigger than that. (Sorry, the forty-eight-player Squiddle session was some bullshit joke and was never real.) It just doesn't seem logistically viable for many more players to play this game than that. But a twelve-player session would still ordinarily just have one set of ruins: a single frog temple with twelve surrounding planet-towers. This one is a special bifurcated session, though, as it says there. That means it has one usual set of ruins, which always end up next to the Forge. (The volcano there. All sessions start with one of those, except void sessions.) And also that the future site for one of the player's homes is nearby, like Jade, Kanaya, or Jake. But the underground Rogue Ruins site is quite anomalous to a session's starting planet. It makes sense that it's underground, hidden from view, and associated with Aradia. A planet is only supposed to have one set of ruins, so these are like the Shadow Ruins, which only conspiracy theorists whisper about. It's a fitting location for Aradia to begin her cloak-and-dagger campaign, assuming the role of Shadow Leader.

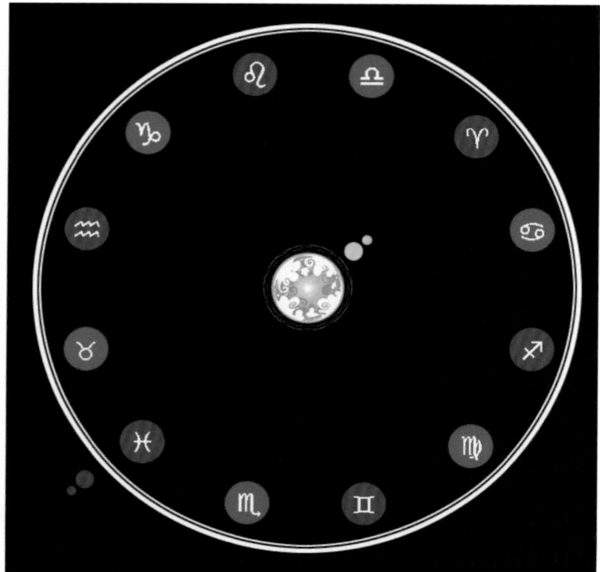

In the more drawn out form of this adventure's narrative, figuring this out would have been a huge deal. We would have been completely blown away by this stunning revelation.

Wow. Same session all along. Really?

Huh.

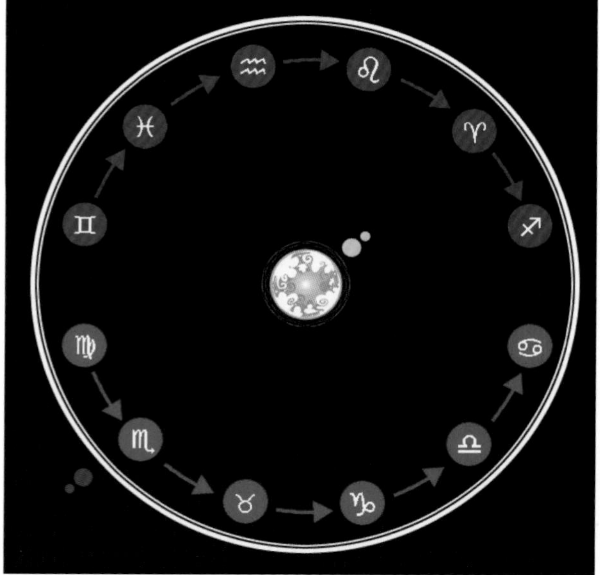

But since we've decided to engage this epic in shorthand, you feel you must insist that we continue with this expository interlude.

It would turn out the arrangement of planets looked like this, rather. Bifurcated from each other, each team appearing to comprise a distinct chain in a distinct session without the luxury of the complete picture we see here.

It appeared that way until it was time to link the two chains, completing the circuit of twelve and uniting the teams.

For these final two links, Skaia had a plan, as it did with the order of every preceding link, and as it did with the paradoxical seeding of its own players on the surface of the planet it would later devastate to buy itself time. Its plan was as inescapable as all others, as inevitable as the reckoning it would ultimately face.

The way Hivebent is written, sometimes it feels like the actual story is put on hold and replaced by "author notes," briefly explaining what actually happened in a loose and whimsical way. As I've said probably ten times now, everything comes back to the fast pacing. It really feels like an advanced exercise in telling a complex long-form story, but in extreme fast-forward. With a gun to my head. And with the *Benny Hill* music playing. The "real story" of Hivebent has been severely compacted, key events of a dramatic nature have been elided, and what's been dropped in its place is just a metric ton of additional fucking sass from yours truly. Notes on a story instead of a story. And because *Homestuck* is a neverending metaserpent always eating its own postmodern tail, here we have a printing of such a story, with even more "author notes" providing additional layers of quippy blithering. It turns out I may never run out of ways to explain things, or ways to explain all the explanations thereafter.

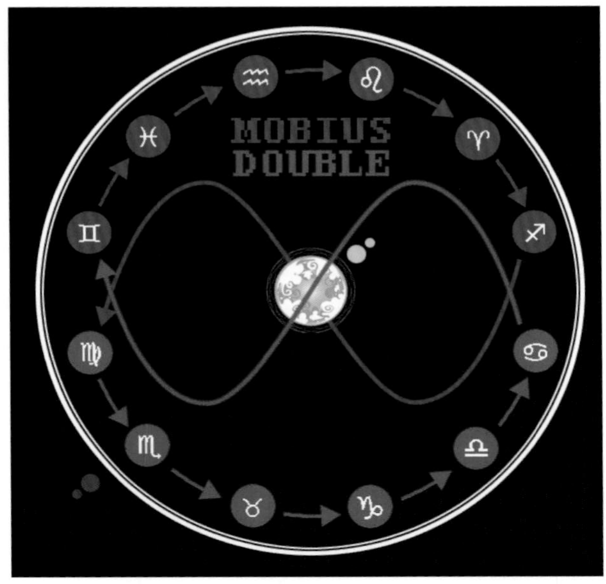

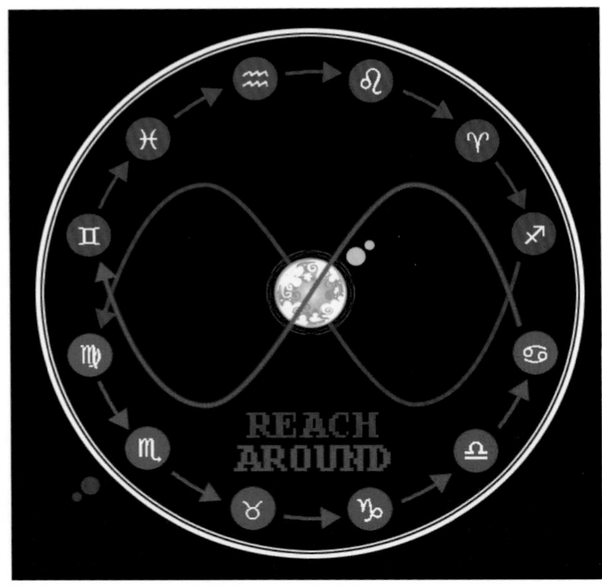

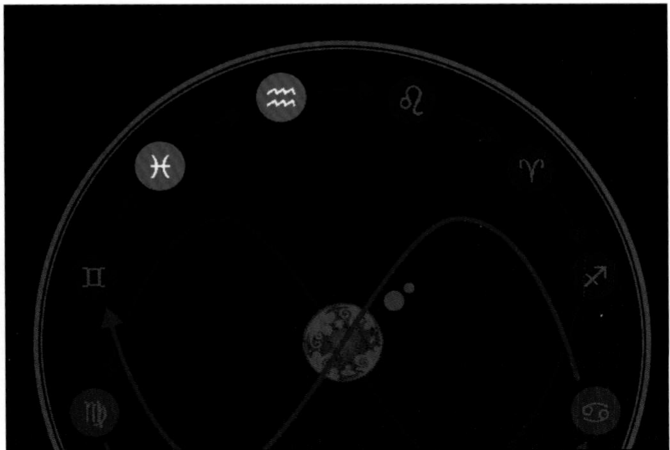

After watching the phrases MOBIUS DOUBLE and REACH AROUND toggle for a few minutes while in a sort of stupor, you finally snap out of it. Your attention drifts toward these two symbols.

You would try to be these mysterious characters but you suspect you would fail, so you don't bother.

They're way too mysterious for you to be them yet! Seriously, what's up with these guys? Do they live under water or something? What's their deal!

We'll learn all about them a little later.

MOBIUS DOUBLE and **REACH AROUND** toggle back and forth in one GIF image on the site. So just look from one panel to the other in one-second intervals to get the idea. This handy graphic also locks in final confirmation of the player entry order, for those keeping score of such things. Which probably describes nobody? Nobody reading the books, or reading the site quickly, tends to do that. But when this was being released serially at the time, man. People lived for stuff like that. Checking off exactly what information the reader knows, and when, what's confirmed vs. merely suspected, and how certain unconfirmed things can be deduced via elimination processes and inference. People were sleuthing things like that out all the time, and I was always watching. Which is probably why so much of this stuff ends up being so meticulously considered on such a granular level. The story always had to keep the super detectives on their toes, and GOD FORBID it ever exhibited the slightest logical inconsistency. But it never did, and even if you think it did, that was probably one of my jokes, so nice try, hot shot.

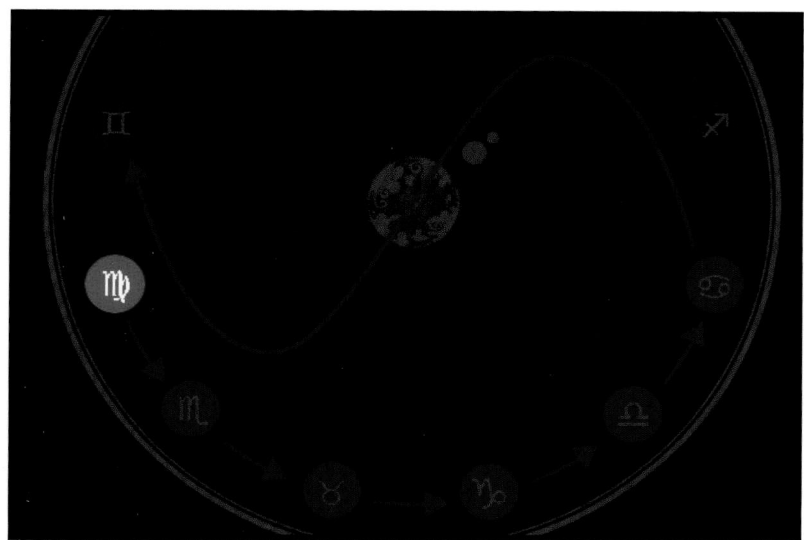

For that matter, what about this young lady? What is HER deal???

We'll probably find out about her later too. It will probably be quite some time before you get to be her. It could very well be pages and pages and pages.

> And pages and pages and pages.

Seriously, it could take forever.

> Enter name.

We finally meet Kanaya. On book page 271. That's actually a long way to go before finally meeting a major troll we already knew about. She's third to last, in fact, just behind the two sea dwellers. But there's good reason for holding off on her introduction. Her living situation is very unusual by troll standards. She basically just lives in Jade's house, with her own personal touches strewn about. She, like Jade, has sort of a combo-breaking quality in the stream of character introductions. The nine previous to her grew up in situations that were typical for trolls within their classes, so introducing them doubled as a good way to get to know troll culture. Now that we have some context, we can start identifying departures from those norms. Leaving the sea dwellers for last also fits in with this reasoning. It's hard to appreciate what it means to be aristocratic until it's understood what it means to be common. Saving these three for last is part of that overall design and is also why, in her intro, Kanaya quickly starts talking to Eridan and Feferi. So we can finally hear their voices and set up their imminent introductions.

Your name is KANAYA MARYAM.

You are one of the few of your kind who can withstand the BLISTERING ALTERNIAN SUN, and perhaps the only who enjoys the feel of its rays. As such, you are one of the few of your kind who has taken a shining to LANDSCAPING. You have cultivated a lush oasis around your hive, and in particular, you have honed your craft through the art of TOPIARY, sculpting your trees to match the PUFFY ORACLES from your dreams. You have embraced the tool of this trade, which conveniently is the weapon of choice for those who would hunt the HEINOUS BROODS OF THE UNDEAD which crawl from the sand at sunrise to feast on the light and the living.

It would be convenient if you actually hunted them, but it is of course far too dangerous, every bit as suicidal as attempting to poach the terrible MUSCLEBEASTS who roam at night. So you indulge in your bright fascination with the grim through literature. Just before the sun goes down and you join your flora in rest, you immerse yourself in tales of RAINBOW DRINKERS and SHADOW DROPPERS and FORBIDDEN PASSION.

You are one of the few of your kind with JADE GREEN BLOOD. As such you are one of the few who could be selected and raised by a VIRGIN MOTHER GRUB, an event so rare as to elude documented precedent. She would defend you from desert threats, and though her life would be short, in time you would assure her of progeny.

You are one of the few of your kind whose affection for the aesthetic strongly overpowers instinctive regard for the utilitarian. As such, you are one of the few of your kind who has developed a zeal for FASHION and DESIGN and LIVELY COLORFUL PATTERNS. You decorate your hive with FLORA and FABRIC, as delicately or aggressively as inspiration demands. You are a SEAMSTRESS or a RAGRIPPER or a TREETRIMMER or a LUMBERJACK, whichever you care to be, and your unique hive is equipped with a great supply of advanced technology to accommodate your interests. The technology and indeed the hive itself were all recovered from the ruins nearby when you were very young. The seed of your hive was deployed on the volcanic rocks beneath the sand with the assistance of your lusus and her remarkable burrowing skills, and you have lived there happily together since.

Another (Jade-like) pattern-breaking feature of Kanaya's character is that she's diurnal and thrives in the sun. Most trolls have a dash of cheesy pop culture linked to their profile. With Kanaya, if you're detecting notes of *Twilight*, you're not crazy. This also signals that jade bloods are rare relative to populations of other classes. Hard to say how rare, exactly. Considering she gets the "one of the few of your kind" refrain, jade bloods probably have the smallest population of any individual class, aside from fuchsia (which numbers exactly one on the entire planet, as you'll see soon). It's a class that has more to with breeding administration than other types of grunt work, for which much bigger populations would be more useful. Even so, Kanaya seems to be more notable than the average member of her class (which, admittedly, is true for most of these characters), in that she was chosen by a virgin mother grub. Her later-revealed vampiric qualities also seem to be unusual for her class, although I don't think it's ever really confirmed how unusual or common that trait is among jades. Since in the main *Homestuck* narrative we only ever get one solid example of each blood type, it tends to be left as a point of speculation how representative that one character is of the rest of their classes.

You know the ruins and the hive and everything here that is not sand and rock originated from the world of your dreams. You also know that one day you will visit this world while you are awake. That day is today.

Your trolltag is grimAuxiliatrix and you Tend To Enunciate Each Word You Speak Very Clearly And Carefully

What will you do?

> Kanaya: Equip chainsaw.

What CHAINSAW? You are quite sure there is no CHAINSAW leaning on that bookshelf.

There is however a tube of LIPSTICK on the floor.

> Kanaya: Fine, equip that then.

Alright, let's settle down. No need to get hysterical.

Oh, there goes your WARDROBIFIER again. Never a dull moment in fashion when the randomized cycle is on.

> Kanaya: Apply.

It *seems* this is the first clear confirmation that Kanaya is awake on Prospit while she sleeps? It may have been hinted at before, but now all doubt is removed. Again, just like Jade. We'll need to put a pin in that and remember to keep an eye out for why it's true. Also like Jade, she has a wardrobifier. But unlike Jade, she actually likes a wide variety of fashion, which she sews herself. So she actually gets some good use out of it, rather than cycling through a bunch of silly tee-shirts. The chainsaw-to-lipstick is some standard item duality inherited from *Problem Sleuth*, like Snowman's lance/cigarette holder. But in this case, this particular item actually existed in the other story and was the weapon/cosmetic of choice for Hysterical Dame. Hence the odd reference to getting "hysterical" here, which probably seems like a weird line if you don't have the scoop.

You can choose between your trademark jade or black. Even though a troll's lips are naturally black.

But they can always be blacker, and a lady with a true sense of style knows this.

In any case you think you'll mix things up and go with green for a while.

> Kanaya: Answer CC.

Here's an unusually unequivocal canon confirmation that trolls have black lips. Wait, cosplayers rarely take that literally? Oh. That's fine, I guess. I don't care. Also, it's nice to see Kanaya has such a fine array of kimonos, made just for chilling out around the house. I wonder where she got the patterns for them. Online, from Troll Japan? Wait a minute... Doc Scratch has been in contact with her. And he's been raising Damara. It's all adding up, isn't it? Yes! Wait. No, it isn't, sorry. False alarm, go back to being confused.

cuttlefishCuller [CC] **began trolling** grimAuxiliatrix [GA]

CC:)(-ELLO!
GA: Hey
CC: KANAYA)(I!
CC: Glub glub glub glub glub!
CC: 38)
GA: You Seem More Excited Than Usual
GA: Or Less
GA: I Cant Tell
GA: Help Me Tell Without Saying Glub
CC: Glub glub glub glub glub glub glub!
GA: Im Going To Type This Face Now
GA: :?
GA: Even Though No One Knows How To Make A Mouth Do A Question Shape Like That
CC:)(a)(a sorry!
CC: I cant really control t)(e glubs.
GA: Yes You Can
GA: But Thats Fine You Can Glub To The Content Of Your Collapsing And Expanding Bladder Based Aquatic Vascular System
GA: If It Means You Are Excited About Something
CC: I AM -EXCIT-ED!
GA: Ok Why
CC: -Everyt)(ing we are about to do next is exciting.
CC: It is always exciting.
CC: I'm -EXCIT----------------ED!
CC: Pc)(ooooo.
GA: It Looks Like One Of Your Letters Got Away From You
CC:)(a)(a yea)(I really launc)(ed t)(at one.
GA: You Forked An Innocent D Loitering Over There By The Shout Pole Minding Its Own Business
CC:)(-E)(-E!
CC: Glub glub glub!
CC:)(-EY! Lets stop being retarded for a minute.
GA: Yeah Sure
CC: I am just worked up about t)(is game, it will be great.
CC: Ive been waiting a long time to get started! We all)(ave.
GA: I Thought So
GA: I Have Been Cloaked In A Mood Of Perpetual Anticipation For Some Time As Well
CC: We s)(ould compare notes. Even t)(oug)(we are on different teams!
GA: Well
GA: Not Really
CC:)(mm really?

Feferi is very excited. That's approximately her entire personality. Being excited. Okay, there's a little more to her than that. But then she dies, and we don't get to see much of what else she has to offer, and that's about that. Until later, during her triumphant return as Fefeta. Then we finally get to hear all the things the story never gave her a chance to say. It's really a poignant moment of redemption for her legitimacy as a character.

CC: See t)(is is w)(y we s)(ould be comparing notes! 38O
GA: What Notes Would You Like To Submit For Comparison
CC:)(mmmmmm.
CC: Well I am going to join my team pretty late.
CC: I t)(ink I)(ave to!
CC: I will need to connect after my goofball moirail does so I can keep my goggles on)(is nefarious escapades.
CC: Its a toug)(job but its important! Everyone)(as an important job to do.
GA: Yeah
CC: Isnt t)(at w)(at youre doing too? Joining late to keep an eye on yours?
GA: I Dont Know For A Fact That She Is Mine
CC:)(a)(a youre not supposed to know for a FACT dummy!
CC: You just do w)(at you t)(ink is rig)(t and even if you were wrong t)(e worst t)(at)(appened was you)(elped somebody and)(elped t)(e w)(ole world too!
GA: I Know
GA: But What If I Dont Really Want Her To Be That
CC: Glub glub glub glub S)(RUG.
GA: Yeah Glub Glub Shrug Is The Right Attitude I Think
GA: Our Minds Are Already Made Up Anyway Arent They
CC: Yes probably!
CC: Your clouds tell you everyt)(ing so w)(at do you even)(ave to worry about?
GA: They Dont Tell Me Everything
GA: Just As I Am Sure She Doesnt Whisper Everything To You
CC: T)(ats true.
CC: O)(s)(ucks now Im going to get sad.
CC: S)(e will be gone soon. 38(
CC: T)(oug)(I guess it will be a relief not to)(ave to worry about keeping)(er voice down anymore!
GA: I Wonder If Any Other Kid On The Planet Has As Many Burdens In The Fire As You
GA: I Doubt It
CC: T)(ey arent burdens!
CC: Ok I guess t)(ey are)(a)(a.
CC: But I love t)(em and I wouldnt)(ave it any ot)(er way because t)(is is w)(y Im)(ere!
CC: On t)(at note I t)(ink Im going to go say goodbye to)(er. Maybe you s)(ould too w)(ile you)(ave t)(e c)(ance!
CC: Even t)(oug)(Ill see)(er again soon w)(ic)(still seems kind of strange to me.
CC: But t)(ats w)(y t)(is is all so -EXCITING!
CC: KANAYA BY----------------------------E!

cuttlefishCuller [CC] **ceased trolling** grimAuxiliatrix [GA]

I was lying. Being EXCIT--ED isn't all there is to Feferi. She also leads us into the concept of moirallegiance and provides an exemplary model of a long-suffering moirail to a very unpleasant and problematic person. She does a good job as the portrait of someone in a bad relationship they feel unable to get out of, but this case comes with an additional layer of duty, since a moirail's social role is to help neutralize the threat your dangerous friend may represent to others. So breaking up with them carries an even higher cost, and therefore raises the stakes of guilt. Feferi also has a "duty to the throne" to consider. So to whatever extent we can isolate her marginal arc for examination, there seem to be themes of finding the gumption to liberate herself from various duties and burdens, both for her own sense of happiness and the greater good for her people. Eridan doesn't give a shit about any of that though.

You had nearly forgotten. Today her time would come.

Maybe you should be there in her final moment. But then it isn't exactly final, is it?

Death is pretty confusing without the finality.

It's too late.

You'd better change back into your work clothes. No point in getting a good dress dirty.

> Kanaya: Check on lusus.

"Death is pretty confusing without the finality" is the tagline for *Homestuck*. Having now owned myself, as well as my great comic, let's look back at the previous conversation again. It's worth noting the allusion to Kanaya's relationship with Vriska, which Feferi presumes to be moirallegiance. Not unreasonably, since Kanaya's stated task is to keep an eye on Vriska for her own good. But that's kind of a mixed signal she's sending, since clearly she has other designs; notice how she says she doesn't "want her to be that," implying she'd rather Vriska was something more. This gives us a glimpse into the psychology surrounding troll romance, which we're only still figuring out through inference. Sometimes trolls get locked into quadrants, or trap themselves into them through mixed signals, as Kanaya has done. Similar to getting "friend zoned" by a crush, but with even more exotic social compartments to get stuck in. For instance, if you have a red crush on someone, and your strategy is to neg them into liking you, then whoops, you might end up in the black quadrant instead.

She brought you this far.
Now to live up to your end of the bargain.

> Kanaya: Operate.

Good thing she has the perfect tool for this exact task. In *Problem Sleuth*, Hysterical Dame did a lot of cool stuff like this too. Drawing all over people with lipstick, which just turned into a time-delayed chainsaw attack against them. *Problem Sleuth* was a good time, if you didn't know, with a very similar ideas-per-page sheer density level as *Homestuck*. I always used to feel it went without saying that if you're reading *Homestuck*, then you know about *Problem Sleuth*. But it's been so long, I'm starting to assume the opposite now.

> Kanaya: Captchalogue that thing.

You secure the MATRIORB through your CHASTITY MODUS. Safe and sound!

You will serendipitously discover the key to unlock this card when and only when you are ready to use this item, and not a moment before!

Salvaging the matriorb from her dead mom is a somewhat minor event folded into Kanaya's formal introduction. But it's a small yet meaningful act that kicks off her entire character arc, pertaining to her maternal duty and struggle to revive her dead race, which is a quest that manages to persist all the way to the end. For that reason, Kanaya feels like she has an unusually coherent heroic arc by *Homestuck* standards. Setting up a thing she has a burning need to do --> ongoing, mighty struggle to do the thing, with many setbacks --> final success in doing the thing, which works out great --> the end. Even the basic premise of *Homestuck* as a heroic journey for the protagonists isn't like that. They do end up creating a universe in the end, after a ridiculous number of setbacks. But it was never established as a goal from the start. The characters had to meander for a long time until they finally understood what the objective was. In fact, as of this moment in the story, we *still* don't know what *Sburb* does. So let's take a moment to appreciate our friend Kanaya here, for the simplicity and clarity of her goals and desires.

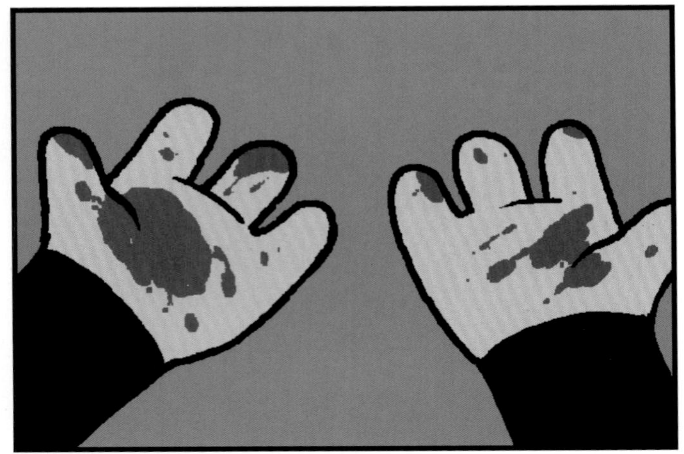

Look at this mess. All this blood and sunlight is stirring bright feelings within. You often fantasize about being a true rainbow drinker from your literature. It would be a life of darting between the shadows, of persecution and being misunderstood. And of ROMANCE. You would drink heavily from its multicolored well, and the hemospectrum would be your wine list preceding the great feast of passion.

Surely it couldn't hurt. While no one is looking...

> Kanaya: Just a taste.

> Kanaya: Meddle with moirail.

The "Bluh" panel, a clear callback to when Rose tried sipping her mom's drink, sets up Kanaya's "evolving" taste for blood, which parallels Rose's "evolving" taste for alcohol. (By which I mean, later they're both hella into it.) Since I'm on the subject of Rose and her evolving tastes, consider this Funny Fact: for someone with such serious mother issues, Rose sure did end up falling for a literal mother-themed character.

AG: Whaaaaaaaat.
GA: Just Wanted To Know
GA: Is Your Lusus Dead Yet

You then proceed to have the rest of this conversation we already read, bugging and fussing and meddling through the special and magical union one can only describe as being in moirallegiance with another.

At least, you guess that's how you would describe it. Maybe.

Troll romance sure is confusing!

You will put her out of your mind for a while. It should be hours before you have to connect with her anyway. Might as well pack this thing up and head inside.

Oh what now. What could this guy want?

It never ends!

> Kanaya: Answer CA.

Kanaya is in diamonds denial, getting herself stuck in the pale quadrant with a crush but unable to face it fully. That's what I'm calling that situation, it's a new term. But I'm going to forget the term instantly after this page, and therefore it will stop being canon. That's how this works.

caligulasAquarium [CA] began trolling grimAuxiliatrix [GA]

CA: kan make her talk to me do somethin
GA: Who
CA: your no good connivvin fuckin backstabbin girl crush thats wwho
GA: Overstating Our Relationship Wont Make Me Feel Very Cooperative
GA: Its Paler Red Than That Ok
CA: pshhhhhh that is a fuckin laugh and you knoww it evveryone does
CA: so help me out tell her to talk to me i think she blocked me you got to
GA: Why Do I Got To
GA: I Dont Got To And Every Time You Take My Help For Granted I Feel Like I Got To A Little Less
CA: wwhatEVVER you are so the vvillage twwo wwheel devvice wwhen it comes to auspisticing
CA: you cant let a grudge go by you wwont stick your busy stem betwwixt so get wwith the program fussyfangs
GA: If Your Slander Werent So Predictable Id Block You Too For Saying That
GA: Has It Occurred To You She May Have Blocked You Because You Are Vvery Ovverbearing
GA: I Just Said That Aloud Now In Your Silly Accent And Had A Private Moment Of Enjoyment
CA: wwho givves a shit wwhy she blocked me or about my fuckin manners come on youvve got a wway wwith her
CA: i figure if youre going to auspisticize any twwo brinesuckers wwho sneer at each other a funny wway you might as wwell make it official and be ours right
GA: Your Black Solicitation Just Seems Really Indecent
GA: What Do You Want From Her Anyway
CA: she made me somethin per a prior arrangement
CA: she wwill delivver it wwhen wwe meet in this game but i dont knoww wwhat the logistics are yet
CA: im tryin to connoiter wwith her here but shes blowwin me off again fickle dirtscrapin landhag
GA: What Is It
CA: kan stupid wwhat do you think its a fuckin gizmo to bloww up the wworld or somethin
CA: ok wwell not that obvviously
CA: but somethin thatll kill all land dwwellers wwhat else wwould i be after
GA: Can You Just For A Moment Entertain The Thoughts Of One Untouched By Megalomaniacal Derangement And Tell Me Why Id Want To Assist You With That
CA: wwell

Get ready for this awful child. The obnoxious, romantically tragic, genocidal fuckboy of the group. It should be a familiar online archetype to most by now. Earlier I referred to Nepeta as being somewhat a writeup of the enthusiastic fandom type, which could be summarily branded as the "Tumblr fangirl." And in that sense, she reads as a less focused rough draft of Calliope, who brought more clarity to that role later. So thinking in those terms, you could also view Eridan as a writeup of the "4chan nastyboy," and therefore an unfocused draft of Caliborn, who similarly distilled that role. I think there's a lot to say about Eridan, particularly as a raw precursor to that villainous presence in the story later. I'll wait until he's on-screen before diving into that, though. Just setting up here! You've been warned.

CA: im not goin to vvery wwell kill you am i that wwould be fuckin unconscionable
CA: wwhat kind of friend wwould i be
GA: Also Speculate For A Moment That Self Preservation Might Not Be What Would Sway My Decision
CA: yeah go ahead and kiss us off but therell be blood on your hands
CA: you could either play along as our auspistice and do a little mediating like you wwere fuckin hatched to
CA: or wwatch she and me devvolvve into fuckin full fledged kismesisses the kind like you dont get once in ten thousand swweeps
CA: you knoww thats wwhat it wwould be there wwould be rainboww rivvers runnin through star systems and all nebulizin like liquid firewworks
CA: it wwill be beautiful and heartbreaking all at once
CA: you should read up on your history instead of poring through that godawwfull sunny rubbish
GA: Its Just
GA: Laborious Listening To This
GA: Im Sorry
GA: None Of It Matters
CA: yeah it does its important sorry but the fate of the race and purity of the bloodline is important excuse me for being concerned
GA: I Know
GA: But You Really Should Know By Now The World Will End Tonight Regardless
GA: Land And Sea Dwellers Alike Will All Die
GA: Because Of The Game We Are About To Play
GA: And I Agree The Fate Of The Race Is Important But Its In My Hands Now
GA: All Of Ours Really
CA: huh
CA: wwell ok
GA: Really
CA: ordinarily id call bullshit on terrible stinkin bs like that but i knoww you dont really lie about stuff
CA: unless its to yourself
CA: but thats wwhy i bother evven talking to you i wwouldnt evven be here SAYIN any of this otherwwise
CA: so did your clouds tell you that
GA: The Doomsday Scenario In Particular
GA: No Not Exactly
CA: i got clouds and they dont tell me SHIT they hide nothin but misfortune and monstrosities
CA: fuckin pain in the ass fuckin clouds

The fact that Eridan's being so loose with strange romantic terms is how you know we're getting awfully close to the troll romance info dump. It's like a Geiger counter that's starting to beep like crazy. Eridan has something in common with Karkat in that he appears well versed in the subject of romance. Later we see that, even though they don't like each other much, they sort of act like "bros" when it comes to this subject. However, Karkat treats the subject more academically, with a sort of hobbyist's enthusiasm, and seems to carry a certain respect for the knowledge. Whereas Eridan clearly tries to exploit his knowledge of romance to his advantage, behaves manipulatively, sort of in the vein of a pickup artist (and a very unsuccessful one at that). We detect signs of this here. His entire scheme with the doomsday device appears to have more to do with roping Vriska into a blackrom relationship than it does with his interest in wiping out land dwellers (still a valid motivation, but secondary to his sad romantic pursuits). He also uses his romantic insights to manipulate people in other ways, even if he's not trying to court them. Like pinning Kanaya down as a natural auspistice and using it to get her to set him up with Vriska. Maybe even "mediate" between them, since that's what she apparently likes to do with Vriska anyway. In fact, the more you unpack what he's doing here, if you understand the ashen quadrant, the more it actually seems like he *is* hitting on Kanaya, with kind of a backdoor approach. He's proposing a menage-a-clubs, with him and Vriska. He literally never stops working all possible angles to fill his quadrants.

CA: so howw do you knoww then
GA: I Have Another Source
CA: ok wwell you are jacked tight the fuck into this thing in so many wways i dont knoww wwhat to say anymore
CA: wwhatevver wwe wwill just play and find out i guess
CA: so can you tell her to talk to me anywway
GA: No
CA: god dammit
CA: she and me are teammates wwevve got to havve a powwwwoww or SOMETHING
GA: You Arent Actually On The Same Team
CA: fuck
CA: fine i get it ill step off
CA: you dont wwant to be our auspistice cause you dont wwant to get locked into that sort of relation wwith her i can respect that
GA: No Thats Not It
CA: yeah it is your real feelins run pretty awwful RUDDY methinks evverybody knowws it
CA: especially that assblood karkat he and me havve you so pegged about that its upright silly
CA: but its cool its totally fine dont wworry ill leavve you alone and givve you a shot
GA: Its Unbelievable
GA: Her Patience
CA: wwhat
CA: wwhoa wwait wwho
GA: Never Mind
CA: ok wwait did she talk to you today
CA: wwhat did she say
CA: or glub or wwhatevver
GA: Something About Longing To Touch You Indiscretely
CA: WWWWHAT
GA: And That Shes Basically In The Scarlet Throes For You
GA: As Deep In The Flushed Quadrant As One Can Be
CA: wwait
CA: did she actually say that
CA: in confidence
GA: To The Letter
CA: can you copy exactly wwhat she said
GA: Absolutely Not
CA: this is bullshit youre bee essing me in some wway awwful
CA: you dont lie but you do tease and ill tranfuse my kickass royal blood out wwith incontinent musclebeast discharge if i wwont knoww wwhen im gettin hooked
GA: Yeah
GA: Shes Just A Concerned Moirail

The only reason I made him say "powwwwoww" is because I wanted to type four w's in a row. This should be obvious to everyone. It's worth pausing here to behold how completely ridiculous Eridan's entire verbal existence is, when you take into account his silly double w/v quirk, which conveys an absurd "accent" of some sort, his run-on cadence, unyieldingly indignant tone, and colorful vocabulary that feels like a baffling mashup of pirate speak, soccer hooliganism, and the fuckboy joker always sliding into your DMs. His eclectic vocabulary and obsession with romance means that we suddenly get this whole rush of quadrant vernacular we hadn't heard before. Which is pretty intriguing on a worldbuilding basis, to start picking up how many average trolls probably allude to each other's romantic habits in casual conversation. Things like being "ruddy" for someone, or waxing this way or that. There's a whole manner of speaking about this stuff that can only be picked up through enough exposure to contextual banter.

GA: Looking Out For You
GA: Thats All
CA: awwww fuck
CA: see im tellin you
CA: you got to play your cards right
GA: What Do You Mean
CA: if youre not savvvvy about howw you define yourself to people
CA: you can just splash into the moirail zone before you knoww wwhich wways upwward
GA: Oh
GA: Hmm
CA: kan its hard
GA: What
CA: being a kid and growwing up
CA: its hard and nobody understands

caligulasAquarium [CA] **ceased trolling** grimAuxiliatrix [GA]

> Kanaya: Return to room.

There is a lot to do before you enter. There will be a lot of people to talk to and help along the way. No, not meddle with or mediate. HELP, dammit! You are very helpful.

You have a lot of inside information on what you and your coplayers are about to face. You are jacked tight the fuck into this thing in so many ways we don't know what to say anymore. And it's not just cloud visions either.

You have another source.

> Kanaya: Consult source.

Okay, "savvvvy" was just another excuse to type four v's in a row. Calling myself out here at every turn. "Being a kid and growing up. It's hard and nobody understands" is another *Homestuck* tagline. I'm just going to keep making note of these when I see them. They will always do one of the following: 1) reference dying too much 2) address the difficulties of growing up 3) involve the fact that nobody ever really knows what the hell is going on 4) insinuate in some way that I am a buffoon, a liar, a sadist, or a megalomaniacal genius, or 5) all of the above. In fact, this entire note can be a tagline too.

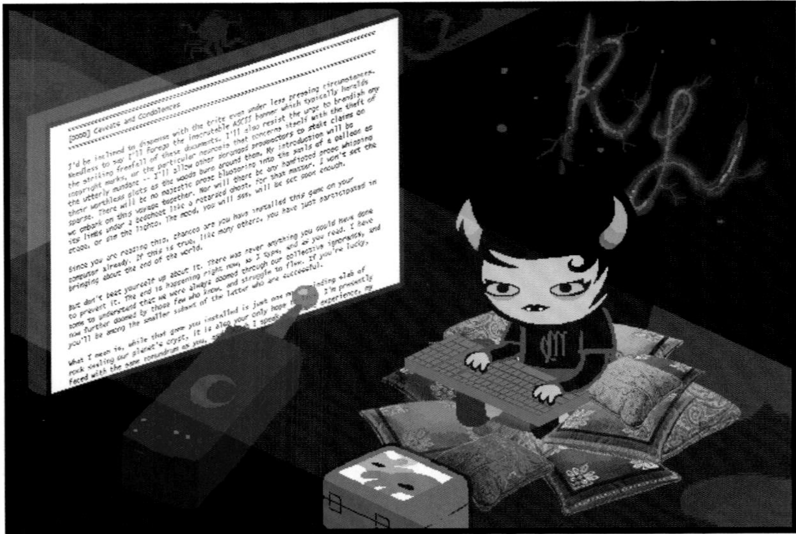

In one dream, the clouds pointed you to the address of a server hidden in an obscure pocket of a realm unknowable to mortals. It contains a journal written by a young member of an alien species. She has documented her experiences playing the game you are about to play.

You can only assume this took place a long time ago. This race is likely ancient, preceding yours by millions of sweeps. Maybe billions! You like to try to imagine the adventures of these players. Were they successful in repopulating their race? Did they manage to protect their matriorb and hatch a new mother grub? Could they hold it together, or were they torn apart by the complex social dynamics, the matespritships and moirallegiences and auspisticisms and kismesissitudes that will surely plague your group along the way?

You have little doubt they succeeded with flying colors.

Jade was the last-introduced, combo-breaking kid, who came across as generally "overpowered" in terms of her foresight, access to knowledge and tech, and overall handle on the situation compared to her friends, who were all disasters. Kanaya is like that too, but with an even more expansive range of foreknowledge and reliable sources. She has cloud visions like Jade, but also, surprise! She's been reading Rose's game walkthrough too, not only prepping for the game itself but also laying the groundwork for knowing who the human kids are when she sees them. While Jade was uniquely armed with these benefits, for Kanaya it's a bit less remarkable, considering there are others in the group with high levels of advanced knowledge too, with Aradia topping them all. The fact that Kanaya's foreknowledge assets don't make her exceedingly special in the group lets her fly under the radar a little more, sit back, and use that knowledge in more of a supporting role to her friends, which suits her personality. Like it says on the previous page, she's not meddling or mediating, she's HELPING, dammit!

You have little doubt their victory was because of their leader, a great heroine, the TENTACLETHERAPIST. From what she recorded, it seems the group had very little knowledge of what they were getting into. And yet they appear to have been the only of their kind to have risen to the challenge in a session stacked heavily against them. You are convinced her leadership was the difference.

It would be nice to have the chance to talk to her. Alas, she's likely been dead for millennia. Only the incomplete record of a long forgotten quest remains.

On the other hand, if you were to discover her quest ended in failure, it might be somewhat disillusioning.

But that thought never crossed your mind.

> Tavros: Enter.

We get the sense that Kanaya isn't reading the walkthrough mainly as a means of technical research into the game, but more as an intriguing narrative to start building fantasies around, like her grim literature. Here's her troll-normative visualization of Rose, because, well, why wouldn't an alien just look kinda like a troll? Horns are normal, and so is gray skin, so yeah, why not. If Kanaya were trying to be realistic, she'd probably give Rose more alien qualities, but her imagination is being lazy, and the only point of this fantasy is to imagine how cool Rose is so she can develop a preemptive crush on her. This provides us with a lot of retroactive perspective on all the Rose–Kanaya conversations we've read. There is a tone of bitterness and scorn running through Kanaya's earlier dialogue with Rose that isn't fundamental to her personality otherwise. This explains why. Kanaya is underwhelmed and disillusioned with her heroine of legend, so she begins by cooperating with Karkat's trolling orders and treats Rose with nothing but derision. It's only a bit later, when Rose starts holding her own in certain conversations and pulls off a few badass moves for the camera, that Kanaya's earlier heroine-crush starts to rekindle itself.

Having narrowly dodged obliteration, you take your place as the PAGE OF BREATH in the LAND OF SAND AND ZEPHYR.

> And in time...

AG: Taaaaaaaavros!
AG: Go outside and look at what I 8uilt for you! You are going to FLIP!
AT: oKAY,

AT: i THINK THIS, iS,
AT: pROBABLY MEANT TO ANTAGONIZE ME,
AG: What are you talking a8out. Look at my 8eatiful 8uilding. Don't you think it's a8out time someone got a little cre8tive with this game????????
AT: uMMM, mAYBE,
AG: Everyone always wants to do things the 8oring way.
AG: Didn't we make a truce, Tavros? That we would try to 8e less 8oring from now on?

Building vertically for a player in a wheelchair using only stairs and no ramps is an obvious act of aggression on Vriska's part. One that's a little easier to miss is the fact that she put his totem lathe about as far away from his hive as possible, for basically no reason.

AG: You don't want to 8reak your truce with me, do you Tavros?
AT: nO,
AG: Gr8. Now get clim8ing!
AT: pLEASE DON'T READ THIS AS,
AT: a BORING THING, i HOPE,
AT: bUT,
AT: iT'S PHYSICALLY IMPOSSIBLE TO DO THAT, mOSTLY,
AG: Man. I knew it. Toreasnooze is 8ACK IN ACTION.
AT: wHY DON'T YOU, iN LIKE,
AT: a NOT BORING WAY, bUILD,
AT: mORE INCLINED SURFACES, lIKE YOU DID OVER THERE,
AT: mAYBE YOU COULD COLOR THEM, wITH FUN COLORS,
AT: sO YOU WON'T THINK THEY'RE BORING AND GET ANGRY AT ME SOME MORE,
AG: I 8uilt that ramp 8ecause we were in a hurry to save your life, remem8er?
AG: A dead Tavros is even more 8oring than an alive and crippled Tavros 8y a slim margin.
AG: My stair structure is lovely and I'm not changing it.
AG: Now hop out of your wheel device and get clim8ing!!!!!!!!
AT: uHH,
AT: cLIMBING,
AG: Or crawling. Whatever! Stop 8eing so helpless. It's pathetic.
AT: iT WILL TAKE A LONG TIME,
AG: What's the rush! You're in the game, safe and sound. Look in the sky. Do you see any meteors? I sure don't!
AT: bUT, tHERE ARE IMPS AROUND,
AT: aND i'LL BE SORT OF DEFENSELESS,
AT: lYING DOWN ON STAIRS,
AG: Siiiiiiigh.
AG: You did not just use that excuse. We 8oth know you can commune with these things.
AG: Hey! Why don't you psychically command them to carry you up????????
AG: Oh my god that is a gr8 idea. Once again, leave it to Vriska to come up with the cre8tive solutions.
AT: i WOULDN'T REALLY,
AT: WANT TO MAKE THEM DO THAT,
AT: i JUST DON'T UNDERSTAND, wHY,
AT: wE CAN'T DO THIS THE EASY WAY,
AG: What good would that do you?
AG: Whatever the purpose of this game is, it makes you work hard for it!
AG: That way you 8ecome stronger along the way and you are 8etter prepared for whatever's next.
AG: Remem8er when we used to flarp together???????? It was the exact same principle. And that's why you were always outmatched! You were too soft and not well prepared.

It's actually a really good idea for Tavros to commune with the imps to carry him up the stairs. But he's too much of a wuss to actually do it. Vriska was even willing to allow this, which is practically letting him cheat. If anything, she's way too easy on him. I guess flushed feelings will do that to a girl.

AG: Nothing comes easy, Tavros. That is why we go through the trials in the 8rooding caverns when we are young.
AG: To make sure we are strong when we come out!
AG: Do you remem8er the trials, Tavros?
AT: nOT VERY WELL, nO,
AG: Well, I do, and they were a 8itch.
AG: 8ut now that I think a8out it, it would make perfect sense if your trials were really easy 8y some mistake.
AG: That is why you are such a soggy phlegm sponge, and why you got picked 8y such a sad, frail little lusus!
AT: }:(
AG: 8ut that's ok, it pro8a8ly wasn't your fault. Just a 8ad 8r8k!
AG: You're lucky you have me as a server player, so I can challenge you and help you get strong.
AG: Now hop out of that seat and get clim8ing! I will deliver the device to you once you are at the top.
AG: Clim8, Pupa!
AG: Cliiiiiiiiim8!
AT: mAYBE i SHOULD ASK TINKERBULL ABOUT THIS,
AT: hE'S REALLY SMART, nOW THAT HE CAN TALK,
AG: No!!!!!!!!
AG: You don't need help from your lame 8ull fairy. He is only holding you 8ack.
AT: hE'S MY FRIEND,
AG: God. Pathetic.
AG: This is getting frustrating.
AG: Why did I have to get stuck with the cripple? Just my luck.
AG: Do you have any idea how inconvenient this is? Do you have any sympathy for what I'm dealing with here?
AT: uHH,
AG: You're so inconsider8. You just sit there looking smug. It's infuri8ing to look at you.
AG: You haven't even thanked me! Or apologized for that matter!!!!!!!!
AG: uHHHHHHHH THANKS VRISKA, fOR sAVING UHH MY LIFE,
AG: uMMMMM IT SURE WAS 8RAVE AND HEROIC AND PRETTY OF YOU,
AG: aLSO uMMM dUHHH,,,, uMMM,,, i AM SORRY FROM THE 8OTTOM OF MY NOOK,,,,,,,,,
AG: Seriously, how hard would that have 8een?
AT: oKAY,
AT: tHANKS, i GUESS,
AT: bUT,
AT: sORRY FOR WHAT,
AG: For 8eing crippled, you ass!
AT: yOU WANT ME TO APOLOGIZE,
AT: fOR BEING PARALYZED,

She's right. He really is lucky to have her as a server player. We all should be so lucky as to have Vriska in total control of our surrounding environment, challenging us to be better and stronger. I would gladly yank Tavros out of his chair, toss him in a sand dune, and take his place. Sounds like a dream come true.

AG: Yes.
AG: Say you're sorry.
AT: i DON'T MEAN TO BE RUDE, oR bORING,
AT: bUT THAT'S RIDICULOUS, gIVEN,
AT: uH, tHE CIRCUMSTANCES,
AG: 8ullshit!
AG: It's something called 8asic decency and civility you fudge8looded 8oor.
AG: Now get down on your useless wo88ly knees and apologize.
AT: nO, i DON'T WANT TO,
AG: >::::O

AG: Apologize, Pupa!
AG: Apologiiiiiiiize!!!!!!!!
AG: Say you're sorry for being a cripple! Wheeeeeeee!
AG: Aaaaaaaahahahahahahahaha!

> Tavros: Summon Rufio.

Now she's done it. She has awoken the mighty inner fury that is...

RUUUUUUUUUUUUUUUUUUFIIIIIIIIIIIIIIIOOOOOOOOOOOOOOOOOOOOOO!

This just made people hate Vriska even more, when she grabbed his wheelchair and jerked him back and forth, making him apologize for the paralysis she deliberately inflicted on him. I can't imagine why. People are SO sensitive. Oh, here's the first appearance of my friend Dante Basco. It's a nice thought, Tavros, but even my boy Dante can't bail you out of the predicament caused by your jaw-dropping cowardice and lack of gratitude.

```
But unfortunately, Rufio is not real.
He's imaginary. A fake. Like a made up
friend, the way fairies are.

You continue to be sad and alone.
```

> Vriska: Wheeeeeeee!

> Kanaya: Mediate.

Kanaya comes to the rescue. I guess we're supposed to cheer this development? Be like, yeah, you go, Kanaya, dump that load gaper all over that spiderbitch! Seems to me more like she's just being a big wet blanket here. Like mom coming in to break up a fight by turning the lights off and on rapidly. The kids were just having a little fun, mom. God. What's the big deal?

AG: Hey, what's your deal!
AG: Shouldn't you 8e helping me out of this jam instead of fussing with my plum8ing????????
GA: Just Presenting A Floating Reminder That Tavros Will Need Plenty Of Inclined Surfaces For His Ascent
AG: That's silly. I made so many ramps, you wouldn't even 8elieve it.
AG: I specifically decided I wanted to 8uild something ugly and 8oring. It is now the land of ramps and yawns.
GA: Hes Reported Otherwise
AG: That lousy snitch! May8e I should take his computer away so he can't go crying to fussyfangs anymore.
GA: Maybe I Should Upend This Load Gaper Over Your Head
AG: No, don't!
GA: Im Still Learning The Interface
GA: It Could Happen Accidentally At Any Moment
AG: I'm only trying to help him. ::::(
GA: Think Of Another Way To Help
AG: Fine.
AG: I'll do something NICE.
AG: I have an idea. I will 8e right 8ack.
AG: And for the record, I was going to do this anyway! I was just trying to make him a 8etter player first.
GA: Ok
AG: In the meantime, how a8out I serve my client player the way I think is 8est, and you can do the same for yours????????
GA: Hmm
GA: I Thought I Was

> Vriska: Scurry downstairs.

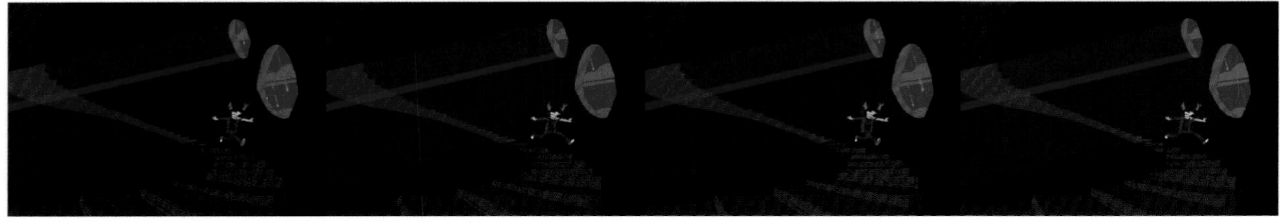

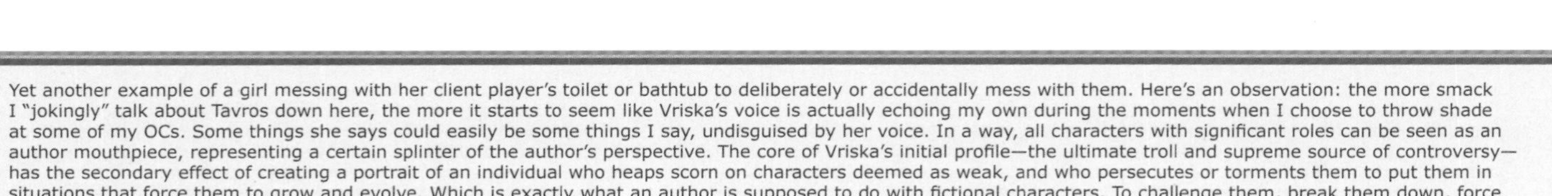

Yet another example of a girl messing with her client player's toilet or bathtub to deliberately or accidentally mess with them. Here's an observation: the more smack I "jokingly" talk about Tavros down here, the more it starts to seem like Vriska's voice is actually echoing my own during the moments when I choose to throw shade at some of my OCs. Some things she says could easily be some things I say, undisguised by her voice. In a way, all characters with significant roles can be seen as an author mouthpiece, representing a certain splinter of the author's perspective. The core of Vriska's initial profile—the ultimate troll and supreme source of controversy—has the secondary effect of creating a portrait of an individual who heaps scorn on characters deemed as weak, and who persecutes or torments them to put them in situations that force them to grow and evolve. Which is exactly what an author is supposed to do with fictional characters. To challenge them, break them down, force hard decisions, prompt evolution, and let them build themselves back up or die trying. In other words, the basic constituents of what we consider compelling character arcs and narratives in general. -->

You make your way down to one of your innumerable LOOT STRONGHOLDS where you stash riches and gold and jewels and prizes plundered during your campaigns.

There they are. Your ROCKET BOOTS. You must confess you will find favor with just about any kind of footwear as long as it is bright red. You would wear these striking boots even if they were broken pieces of junk!

But as it happens they work just fine and they are awesome.

> Vriska: Take them.

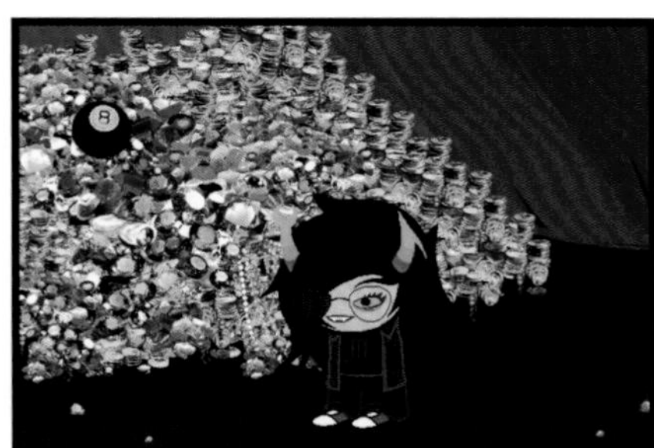

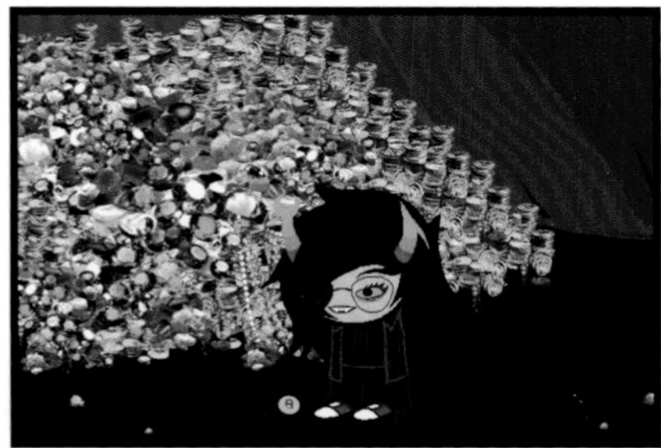

> Vriska: Go back up.

--> So (ignoring for a moment her gaudy pile of treasure and badass rocket shoes) looking at it this way, another dimension to Vriska's already dense profile is her role, in a rough-sketch kind of way, as an avatar for what I'm calling "authorial scorn" for one's own creation. Not necessarily all of it, but certain characters, events, and conditions. It's not as ill-willed as it might sound, but more of a universal principle of storytelling that for things to be interesting, harsh outcomes must befall those you create, in response to which they may thrive or fail. Which to the casual observer may read as hate. "Why did the author hate this character so much?" is a question some ask of fiction that is harsh to its occupants. It isn't "true hate," but something else, a necessary degree of authorial viciousness to produce the right kinds of tension, which is tempered and balanced by an opposite force, authorial affection for a creation, which can express itself in extremes too, like various kinds of indulgence. These forces are explored symbolically in a more coherent sense later, but I think the themes begin to develop as Vriska's portrait comes into better focus, as a vessel for this particular kind of scorn, one obsessed with challenging others in cruel ways to force them to overcome their limitations and get stronger. As the "most favored character," it makes sense that she would echo this authorial attitude. In fact, she by definition only inherits favored status in the first place because she's doing the dirty work for me, stirring the pot, pushing the buttons, raising the stakes. -->

AG: Quit cleaning up after me!!!!!!!!
AG: You are so ridiculous.

> Vriska: Get code.

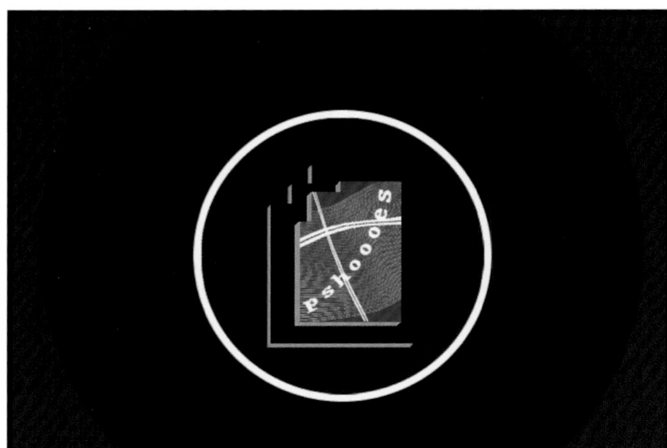

> Vriska: Send code.

> Tavros: Alchemize.

--> This quality probably becomes noticeable in this sequence, because it stands in contrast to what Kanaya is doing. If Vriska is the current mouthpiece for authorial scorn, Kanaya counters with authorial affection. While Vriska wants to throw weaklings into the water to sink or swim, Kanaya prefers to support them with maternal concern. Acting as this sort of authorial mouthpiece is not a huge part of Kanaya's character, but it comes through in the right context. And anyway, like I said, these ideas were very raw in Hivebent, emerging as sketches and loose themes to build on later. The concept of authorial scorn—or actually, "wrath," as a better term—comes into sharper focus in Act 6 through certain avatars. Pushing further the thesis that there is a part of any creator that "hates" the creation, everything inside it, and even those outside it (such as fandom), leads to a metafictional examination of what happens when those forces are fully unleashed and spin out well beyond the author's control. As if to say, a monster has been summoned, and once loose, operates autonomously of the author at great cost to everyone and everything inside the story, and, to some extent, outside. This is basically the crux of Lord English as symbolic figure, through his emergence and how he "presides" over the story thereafter, casting a pall of hate, terror, and destruction over the narrative itself. A symbolic counterbalance exists too, an elevated personification of affection for everything in the story, in the form of Calliope. Anyway, that's a WHOLE lot of shit to get into under a page where Vriska sends the Pshoooes! code to give Tavros a rocket.

> Tavros: Fly, Pupa!!!!!!!!

AG: Flyyyyyyyy!

> And again, in time...

> Tavros: Lead fearsome entourage into ruins.

I've got to get briefer with these notes. Jesus. There are still a lot of pages to go. Every page seems to contain a damn graduate thesis underneath. Time to cool it the fuck down. Let's see, what simple thing can I say about this page. Heh, that's a nice rocket chair. It looks fun, and he looks happy. WOW, WAS THAT SO HARD????????????

> Tavros: Confer with teammate.

AT: yESSSS, aNOTHER PIECE FITS,
AT: wE ARE MAKING SOME STRICT PROGRESS ON THIS PUZZLE,
AG: Oh. That's cool I guess.
AT: sO WHERE DO YOU THINK, iS THE NEXT ONE,
AG: Um, I don't know? Pro8a8ly 8uried in the stupid sand somewhere like all the others.
AT: oKAY, THAT'S MOSTLY WHAT i WAS THINKING TOO, bUT,
AT: iT SUDDENLY DOESN'T SOUND LIKE YOU THINK THE PUZZLE IS COOL,
AG: The puzzle sucks! All these puzzles suck.
AG: If I have to help you put one more dum8 sla8 of 8oring rock into another stupid wall indent8tion I am going to put an indent8tion in my desk with my f8ce.
AT: bUT IT, uHH,
AT: iT LOOKS LIKE A FROG,
AT: aND THAT'S KIND OF FUN,
AG: Snore. These puzzles are for wigglers. I solved way 8etter puzzles than this in my heyday as Mindfang.
AG: Oh look some ruins. Oh look another mysterious recess in the wall! I wonder if something fits in there????????
AG: It pro8a8ly just opens a secret passage to more wall indent8tions. I am so over this puzzle.
AT: uHH, bUT,

Okay, back into graduate thesis mode. Who was I even kidding with that. This page is a really good example of how *Homestuck* has a policy of trivializing its own "background lore." It's a bit flippant and exceedingly non-precious about points of lore that would otherwise take center stage as a focal point of intrigue in other fantasy stories. *Homestuck* does this consistently, often aggressively, with almost an air of derision toward the idea that anyone would actually want to focus on the substance of *Sburb*'s mythological challenge to the players, the dungeon crawling, the secrets, the puzzles. That's why this frog puzzle feels like kind of a background joke rather than anything that could possibly matter to the story. I'm making sure the reader is always being reminded that the substance of the quest, which normally would be THE quest and explicit focus of such stories, is just a farcical backdrop to the actual foreground story. Which is about kids bullshitting with each other, the focus on their characters and themes, and the struggles along the way of their coming-of-age journey. The "Quest," and later the "Narrative Itself" simply serve as convoluted, hostile, and usually satirical environments for that journey. They are analogues for life itself, or the hostile world we must grow up in, full of the many absurd and pointless quest-like regimentations of society. Vriska here again functions as a sort of mouthpiece for authorial scorn toward elements of his creation. She derides these puzzles as a boring and useless expenditure of her time and interest, as well as the reader's. But this expression of scorn is just an accurate observation about the story itself. The story isn't about this stuff, and her inclination to hack or cheat her way through *Sburb* is actually an insightful reflection of the priorities and logic of *Homestuck*.

AT: tHEY ARE NECESSARY TO SOLVE, aREN'T THEY,
AT: tO FIND NEW MAGIC ARTIFACTS AND THINGS, aND LEARN MORE ABOUT THE LORE OF THIS LAND,
AG: Tavros, let me let you in on a little secret a8out the lore of your land.
AG: It's 8oring!!!!!!!!
AT: }:o
AG: The minds of your consorts are very soft and impressiona8le.
AG: As easily manipul8ed as all those imps you've 8een 8ossing around.
AG: I have picked apart their tiny little lizard 8rains and seen through all the smoke and mirrors of their riddles.
AG: I have gotten to the truth they are guarding. The great 8ig mystery 8ehind this planet. And you know what it is, Tavros?
AT: nO,
AG: It's 8ullshit!
AG: Meaningless, 8oring, fanciful 8ullshit wrapped in flowery poems to keep you guessing.
AG: It all leads to one thing anyway, and that's what we should put our attention on.
AG: Real gamers cut to the chase. They power through all the nonsense and go for the gold.
AG: They cheat, Tavros.
AG: It is time you learned to start cheating.
AT: i THOUGHT, i KIND OF WAS CHEATING,
AT: bY MAKING FRIENDS WITH MONSTERS,
AG: Well, it's a good start. You are 8ending the rules and getting stuff done.
AG: Ok I will admit, I am fairly impressed with your progress so far. Even though you still pro8a8ly haven't even killed a single enemy!!!!!!!
AT: uMM,
AG: No, don't 8other. I know you haven't.
AG: 8ut may8e that's ok. May8e it's just your style, and your real strength is surrounding yourself with allies who are much stronger than you.
AG: Like me!
AG: I'm sure there is more than one way up the echeladder. In your case pro8a8ly the only way is to roll gently up the echeramp.
AG: The path of the invalid.
AT: yEAH, i AGREE,
AG: 8ut I think it's time to stop fucking around! You need to 8e challenged more.
AG: I have 8een designing a quest for you that should test your true limits.
AT: oHH,
AT: iS THAT WHAT YOU WERE DOING, aLL THIS TIME,
AG: Yes.
AT: i MEAN, nOT THAT i DON'T,
AT: aPPRECIATE IT, BUT,
AT: dON'T YOU HAVE YOUR OWN QUEST TO DO,

Here Vriska is going on at greater length, saying almost what I just said on the previous page, but from the perspective of a cutthroat gamer rather than story analysis. There's a lot of moralization that happens in stories, particularly those meant for young people. Little lessons built into everything we consume, which have a way of indoctrinating us on how to consume all stories forever. We always look for the moral of the story, the lessons of right vs. wrong, sort of unconsciously. "Cheating = bad" is a recognizable moral of this kind, so when we see her ranting here about the need to cheat, as consumers of moral tales our alarm bells go off. "This is a bad person who has an immoral ethos, and she will likely be punished for this later, and we should want that as readers." The problem with this view is, of course, it's just not that simple. As a matter of valor and integrity, in a vacuum, yes, cheating is bad and immoral. However, in a situation you know to be rigged against you in certain ways, full of hurdles and milestones that are fundamentally meaningless, or even in some ways designed to mess with you or hold you back, is cheating then okay? Does it even count as cheating anymore, or is "cheating" just a negative word for what's actually the correct and logical solution to a murky problem, partially designed to deceive you and waste your time? This is part of what makes Vriska an intrinsic wedge character. She's always walking through the uncanny valley of morality with just about everything she says and does.

AG: Yeah, well, after she got me in the game, Kanaya just left me in the lurch, pro8a8ly 8ecause she's dealing with her own crisis now.
AG: Which is just as well 8ecause I was starting to get nannied HARD. You wouldn't even 8elieve it.
AT: nANNIED,
AG: So I had some time to kill.
AG: I drew you a map!
AT: wHOAAA,
AG: Here, take a look.
AG: It marks what will 8e your new destination. Where you will find the ultim8 challenge.

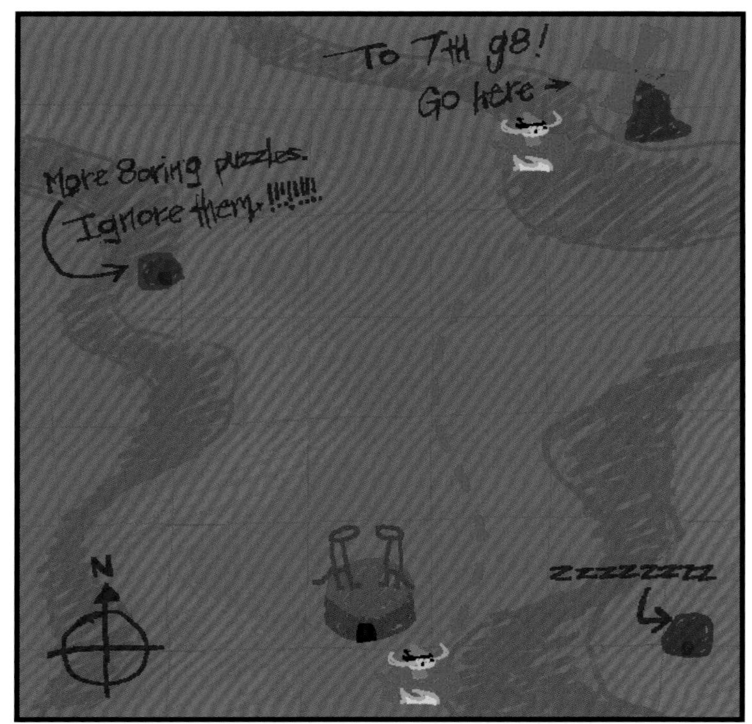

Vriska's "cheating" policy, as a matter of cutting through the bullshit and embracing a strategy of speed-running *Sburb* to whatever extent possible, actually isn't a remotely bad idea in the context of their session. It seems to be very effective, and though there are a lot of bumps along the way, the trolls actually kick their session's ass and win fair and square. The universe/frog they create turns out to be fruit from a poison tree, but that really isn't their fault. We are somewhat led to believe they had a flawed approach to this game, and were karmically punished for it when they tried to claim their reward. But that's mostly due to Karkat's projection and self-loathing rather than a true karmic sentence enforced by the text in response to their shortcuts and other "moral indiscretions." From the reader standpoint, it's tempting to parse it this way, I think again due to being so well-trained to view stories on such moralistic terms, where rewards come to those who do things the right way, and punishment to those who don't. Characters themselves are motivated to see things this way too, because they, like us, cut their teeth on tales with such morals. So Karkat, and many other characters, are prone to evaluating what happens to them in the terms of "the way stories typically work," which actually is a faulty perspective, verging on being tragic. The only conclusion to draw then, I believe, is this: it's wrong to interpret their misfortune after victory as punishment for either their moral failings or their approach to playing the game. A take I saw fairly often went something like, "The trolls speedran the game, skipping over important challenges that were key to their personal growth, which led to their downfall." This is a misleading and superficial spin on what happened. It gives too much credit and authority to *Sburb*'s various regimentations as legitimate authenticators of one's "personal growth." They are not. *Sburb* has never been what it appears to be. Not to the players, and not to us.

AT: wHERE DOES IT GO,
AG: I have determined from your consorts that there is a terri8le monster deep underground.
AG: It guards a hoard of treasure 8igger than either of us can imagine!
AG: It is called a denizen, and it is the 8oss of your whole planet.
AG: Tavros, you will go and face your denizen.
AT: wON'T THAT BE,
AT: tOO DIFFICULT,
AG: It will 8e the most powerful adversary you have ever met.
AG: 8ut you can handle it. I 8elieve in you!
AT: uM, tHANKS,
AT: i MEAN, i RESPECT THAT YOU HAVE LOTS OF,
AT: pIRATEY BRAVADO ABOUT STUFF, aND YOU TYPE FAST ABOUT IT,
AT: bUT i THINK THIS IS FOOLISH AND NOT SENSIBLE,
AT: i WILL PROBABLY JUST GET KILLED, rEALISTICALLY,
AG: May8e! That is the risk you take 8y 8eing a 8rave adventurer.
AG: 8ut it is a good opportunity to apply your cunning.
AG: May8e you can rally a huge army to 8end to your will and overwhelm the monster???????? Who knows! It is up to you.
AG: This is it, Tavros. It is time to sink or swim.
AT: i SHOULD GET kANAYA'S ADVICE,
AT: oR MAYBE kARKAT SINCE HE IS THE LEADER,
AG: No!!!!!!!!
AG: Oh god, every time. Always going and getting to others to 8ail you out.
AG: Anyway, Kanaya is missing in action, and Karkat has his head up his nook with his new sta88y h8friend.
AG: Neither can help you.
AT: iT'S JUST HARD TO FIGURE OUT,
AT: iF YOU REALLY THINK THIS IS A GOOD IDEA STRATEGICALLY,
AT: oR IF IT'S JUST MORE OF THE THING, wHERE YOU HARASS ME BUT SOUND EXCITED ABOUT IT,
AG: Tavros, I know no8ody 8elieves me a8out this, pro8a8ly not even a gulli8le dope like you.
AG: 8ut I actually care a8out your advancement as a player.
AG: Everything I have done has 8een to make you stronger!
AT: oKAY,
AT: i STILL DON'T KNOW WHAT TO BELIEVE, aBOUT THAT,
AG: Ugh, you are useless!
AG: I'm done talking a8out this. Now shut up and point that cherry vehicle of yours toward the X on that map.
AG: Next stop, g8 seven. Let's go.
AT: uHHHHHH,
AG: This isn't optional. You know very well that I can make you go to that g8 whether you want to or not!

Here's a reprisal of Terezi's scam to trick John into going to fight his denizen early, including a "helpful map" and all. Except this happened long before Terezi's stunt, so maybe she got the idea from Vriska? It's not inconceivable. But in this case the prank isn't lethal, it's just a surprise seduction-trap. Which possibly reframes Terezi's prank as darkly amorous in nature as well? And also not inconceivable. Note her cagey use of language here. Tavros's "most powerful adversary" yet turns out to just mean having to contend with Vriska's questionable advances.

AG: 8ut I would rather it not have to come to that.
AG: What will it 8e?
AG: Advance or advance?
AT: oKAY,
AT: i WILL GO,
AG: Oh one last thing.
AG: Equip your 8oy-Skylark outfit.
AG: This will 8e Pupa's last stand!
AG: I mean sit.
AG: Hahahahahahahaha.

> Tavros: Point cherry vehicle toward X on map.

You proceed through what seems to be your second gate, into the LAND OF MAPS AND TREASURE. The THIEF OF LIGHT lies in wait.

Note that Vriska's last demand to Tavros is to have him dress up as Pupa Pan. This is transparently kinky stuff going on here. It's also transparently ridiculous. But these are ridiculous kids who barely have a handle on what the hell they're actually doing when it comes to amorous activity. Even though the troll kids are technically the same age as the humans (albeit in different time units), it's still hard to imagine the humans doing anything like this until a few more years have time-skipped by (see: Act 6). It's fair to say trolls are just forced to grow up faster. A more violent, brutal culture, more self-sufficient upbringing without adult influence, a society revolving around more intense romantic conventions, and a forced breeding program mandated by the government. Factors like this are liable to encourage kids to start acting a lot older than they are.

> Vriska: Wake up.

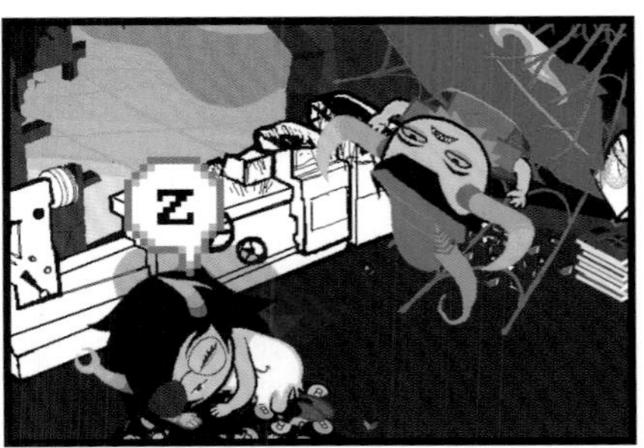

Oh my!

It appears Pupa Pan himself has flown through your window while you were asleep. How exciting! Surely he is here to take you away on the adventure of a lifetime. He is more dreamy and heroic than you ever imagined.

But what's this?? It seems the legendary Boy-Skylark has misplaced his shadow. He is looking EVERYWHERE for it, to no avail. He is having a devil of a time, what with being paralyzed from the waist down and all. He clearly needs your help.

> Vriska: Help Pupa find shadow.

This looks familiar, a Breath player rocket-crashing into a Light player's bedroom as she sleeps. John did that to Rose. But you remember that, why am I pointing it out? Can't you do ANYTHING for yourself? No, of course you can't. Your life would completely fall apart without me and my helpful notes, and we both know it. Anyway, unlike the John crash, this is obviously a rigged stunt. A spider trapping her chosen prey for a bit of fun and sexy roleplay. Arguably the funniest thing happening here, aside from the basic fact that Vriska had the idea to do this at all, is that it doesn't seem she really knows how the Peter/Pupa Pan story works. Peter flies into Wendy's window, not Tinkerbell's. What's going on here is just a BIT dumb. She probably just wanted an excuse to dress up as a sexy fairy. Can you blame her???

Pupa! You truly are a silly goose. Your shadow has been trapped underneath your useless torso the whole time! Honestly, where else would it be you stupid sack of shit?

Of course, the secret to reuniting with your shadow is to get up and walk around. And play and dance and frolic! Your shadow will surely join in your gaiety.

But it appears Pupa has lost the use of his legs. There will be no frolicking in this young man's future. ::::(

Unless...

> Vriska: Apply special stardust.

Everyone knows that just a pinch of SPECIAL STARDUST along with a happy thought will allow any boy to get up and walk again. Everyone knows this because it is in the classic tale, PUPA PAN. Young Pupa flies through the window of a fairy girl's respiteblock, falls on the floor, and has trouble getting up like an enormous pansy. The fairy girl then helps him walk again, and in return, he teaches her to fly, even though she probably already knows how to fly. Because she's a fairy. They fly out of her window together, and have magical adventures for many sweeps thereafter.

To be honest, you hardly know a damn thing about Pupa Pan. But you do not care.

It's really fun and considerate of her to incorporate his disability into the sexy roleplay. Sometimes less considerate people have a tendency to awkwardly tiptoe around other people's disabilities, which can come across as a bit condescending or insulting. Not Vriska though. She goes right at it. This boy was horribly paralyzed in an unfortunate cliff-jumping incident, and dammit, she's going to make that WORK in this saucy scenario.

Pupa remains as pathetic and useless as ever. The stardust did nothing! Probably because it is just glittery powder with no magical properties whatsoever and is basically bullshit. Because in case it wasn't clear, magic isn't real, and neither are miracles.

OR

It could just be that Pupa has failed to have a happy thought!

Your duty is clear. You will have to MAKE him have happy thoughts.

> Vriska: Make Pupa have happy thoughts.

The saddest thing about Tavros is he has no game whatsoever. Look at this pitiful display. Vriska is working SO hard to get this romance off the ground. Buttering him up with a number of insults and belittling remarks, after going to all the trouble of setting this clever trap and dressing as his favorite fake thing in the world, a sexy fairy. This seems to be what pisses her off the most about him. She can read his feelings well enough, since she's psychic, so it's not like she's imagining things. She gives him these "opportunities" to prove himself, which, yes, *may* be a bit aggressive. But this is just her way, and he knows it. Yet, each chance she gives him, he beefs it every time. Completely exhausting. Once again, Vriska manages to be the most sympathetic figure in virtually any interaction she has in the comic. Undeniable FACT.

Out of frustration, she briefly considers taking this route, but bails on the idea quickly. She's a lot of things, but this is one thing she apparently isn't. (Hint: it's a thing that begins with "rape" and ends with "-ist.") But her ancestor was. Spending centuries being a swaggering asshole pirate emboldens one toward certain unseemly behaviors, I guess. Vriska idolizes her ancestor of course, and models much of her personality and bravado after her, or at least her impression of who she was. Basically, she's a bad influence. As if having one bad mom wasn't enough, in a way Vriska actually has two. The Mindfang diaries... Oof, there's some shit to unpack. We'll get to that next book. Learning about Mindfang's life as told through her journal, and knowing that Vriska read every page while very young, tells us a lot about why Vriska is who she is. Perhaps more importantly, seeing differences in the ways she *wants* to be like Mindfang, but can't quite bring herself to be, might actually tell us more about Vriska than how she strives to be similar.

> Kanaya: Deal with your own crisis.

Whew, crisis resolved. It was no doubt harrowing and suspenseful.

But in the meantime, you have left your client player in the lurch. Ideally she has not gotten herself into too much trouble.

And ideally the dramatic irony has not gotten so thick you could draw a dotted line on it with a tube of lipstick and cut it in half with a chainsaw.

> Kanaya: Return to serving client.

Just imagine how awesome the **[S] Kanaya: Enter** Flash probably was, and how pissed off you are we didn't get to see it. Things that *could* have been presented as awesome animations, but weren't, because I didn't feel like it, make up an entire Shadow Genre within *Homestuck*. If you're ever wondering why I didn't do something that *could* have been awesome, just repeat these magical words to yourself: "He probably made that decision as a deliberate affront to me, personally. Vengeful spite, quite literally, was his only motivation." Another Shadow Genre that's an even larger superset of "things I could have made, but didn't" is "stuff I could have shown in any way, shape, or form but chose not to (again, out of spite)." Hivebent is chock-full of material covered by that Shadow Genre.

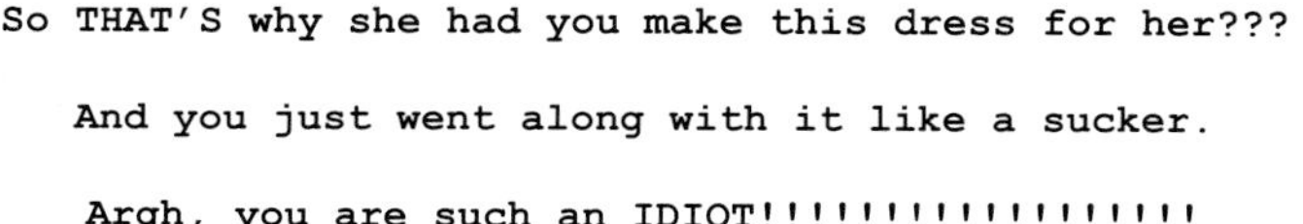
So THAT'S why she had you make this dress for her???
And you just went along with it like a sucker.
Argh, you are such an IDIOT!!!!!!!!!!!!!!!!!!

MOTHERSPRITE: There there, sweetheart.

There seriously, absolutely non-jokingly, were a bunch of unfathomable rubes out there who thought that Kanaya was so upset watching this kiss because she had a crush on TAVROS. If you've never given any thought to the kind of bullshit I've had to deal with, the absolutely limitless undulating gascloud of human stupidity that I've been exposed to, please consider this cursed tale of woe I have shared before you speak another word. Then some day, consider placing a bouquet of sympathy on my grave, while arranging a twenty-one-gun salute nearby.

Kanaya, it's hard.

Being a kid and growing up.

It's hard and nobody understands.

> Try to understand.

The green teardrops on the fairy dress Kanaya made for her crush, who's currently making out with a dude while she wears a copy of that very dress... That's some of the rawest sadstuck you'll ever see. This struck me as a good moment to finally pivot to The Dump. It's been building. You could kind of feel it actually, even if you didn't know it was coming. Something *intense*, involving a closer look at what troll romance is all about. Flirting with these weird terms, characters making advances on each other that involve different card suits... Something was up. Here's what's up. It's called TROLL ROMANCE, motherfuckers, and it's serious as shit. Read and study every word carefully. This is your life now.

The problem is that when the subject of troll romance is broached, our sparing human intellects instantly assume the most ingratiating posture of surrender imaginable.

But we will do our best to understand regardless.

Humans have only one form of romance. And though we consider it a complicated subject, spanning a wide range of emotions, social conventions, and implications for reproduction, it is ultimately a superficial slice of what trolls consider the full body of romantic experience. Our concept of romance, in spite of its capacity to fill our art and literature and to rule our individual destinies like little else, is still just that. A single, linear concept. A concept usually denoted by a single symbol.

<3

Troll romance is more complicated than that. Troll romance needs four symbols.

The origins of troll romance aren't that mysterious. The Midnight Crew Intermission, featuring a gang of mobsters related to the four card suits, was presented in proximity to a world of aliens we were about to meet. In fact, the Midnight Crew are the exiles for those alien players. The conceptual linkage between trolls and the four suits began there. The symbol for one suit, a heart, symbolizes romance for humans. The question following almost naturally after that, if you're just a little bit nuts, is: what if, in a different culture, the other three suits represent different kinds of romance? It's like an exponential expansion of the idea. One suit, a heart, is a 1^1 grid, singular, simplistic. One data point, which by itself implies no pattern. Whereas four suits expands the realm of romance geometrically, to 2^2, which is where the notion of a grid, or "quadrants" begins to take shape. And once we're talking about quadrants, further organizing principles present themselves. What do the red suits have in common? The black? How about similarity by shape? (The heart naturally corresponds to the spade, and therefore evokes its opposite.) Believe it or not, this stuff actually does start designing itself. That's how you know the shit is real. It has the veneer of silly nonsense, but it's not. It was there all along, just waiting for someone to reveal it.

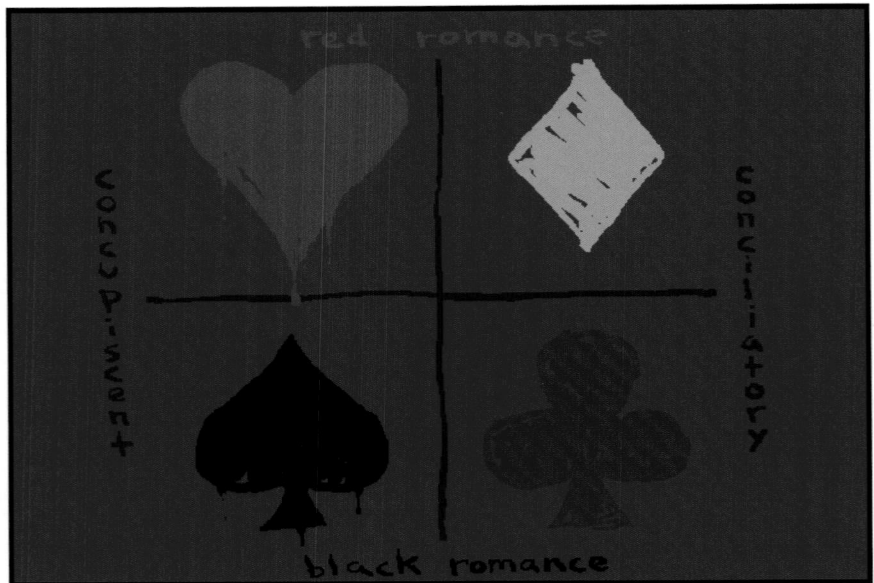

Their understanding of romance is divided into halves, and halved again, producing four quadrants: the FLUSHED QUADRANT, the CALIGINOUS QUADRANT, the PALE QUADRANT, and the ASHEN QUADRANT.

Each quadrant is grouped by the half they share, whether horizontally or vertically, depending on the overlapping properties one examines. The sharpest dichotomy, from an emotional perspective, is drawn between RED ROMANCE and BLACK ROMANCE.

RED ROMANCE, comprised of the flushed and pale quadrants, is a form of romance rooted in strongly positive emotions. BLACK ROMANCE, with its caliginous and ashen quadrants, is rooted in the strongly negative.

On the other hand, the vertical bifurcation has to do with the purpose of the relationship, regardless of the emotions behind it. Those quadrants which are CONCUPISCENT, the flushed and caliginous, have to do with facilitating the elaborate reproductive cycle of trolls. Those which are CONCILIATORY, the pale and ashen, would be more closely likened to platonic relationships by human standards.

There are many parallels between human relationships and the various facets of troll romance. Humans have words to describe relationships of a negative nature, or of a platonic nature. The difference is, for humans, those relationships would never be conceptually grouped with romance. Establishing those sort of relationships for humans is not driven by the same primal forces that drive our tendency to couple romantically. But for trolls, those primal forces involve themselves in the full palette of these relationships, red or black, torrid or friendly. Trolls typically feel strongly compelled to find balance in each quadrant, and seek gratifying relationships that each describes.

The challenge is particularly tortuous for young trolls, who must reconcile the wide range of contradictory emotions associated with this matrix, while understanding the nature of their various romantic urges for the first time.

Of course, young humans have this challenge too. But for trolls, the challenge is fourfold.

> Examine flushed quadrant.

Frankly, there's too much stuff up there to read to bother saying anything about it down here. Let's just take a breather. I'm going to my fridge to get a snack.

When two individuals find themselves in the flushed quadrant together, they are said to be MATESPRITS. Matespritship is the closest parallel to the human concept of romance trolls have. It plays a role in the trolls' reproductive cycle, just as it does for humans.

This is pretty obvious! Not much more needs to be said about this.

Moving right along.

> Examine caliginous quadrant.

When a pair of adversaries delve into this quadrant, they become each other's KISMESIS. As one of the concupiscent quadrants, it plays a role in procreation as well. There is no particularly good human translation for this concept. The closest would be an especially potent arch-rivalry.

For instance, human players would never be able to adequately diagnose the relationship between the queen and her archagent. But troll players could immediately place it as a dead ringer for kismesissitude. They would think we were all pretty stupid for not getting it. And they would be right.

Okay, I'm back. These are both good examples, and the graphic diagram illustrating couples pairing up in these suits for the sake of conveying this stuff: ALSO GOOD. What we're gleaning here is that these romantic ideas have already been cleverly seeded in the story, and thus the material has been in a way thematically woven into the fabric of the narrative, which is extremely important to note. It means that a dumb, annoying nerd can't say none of this matters or that it's a stupid, indulgent exercise in derailing the plot that serves no purpose. That dumb nerd can sit his ass right down.

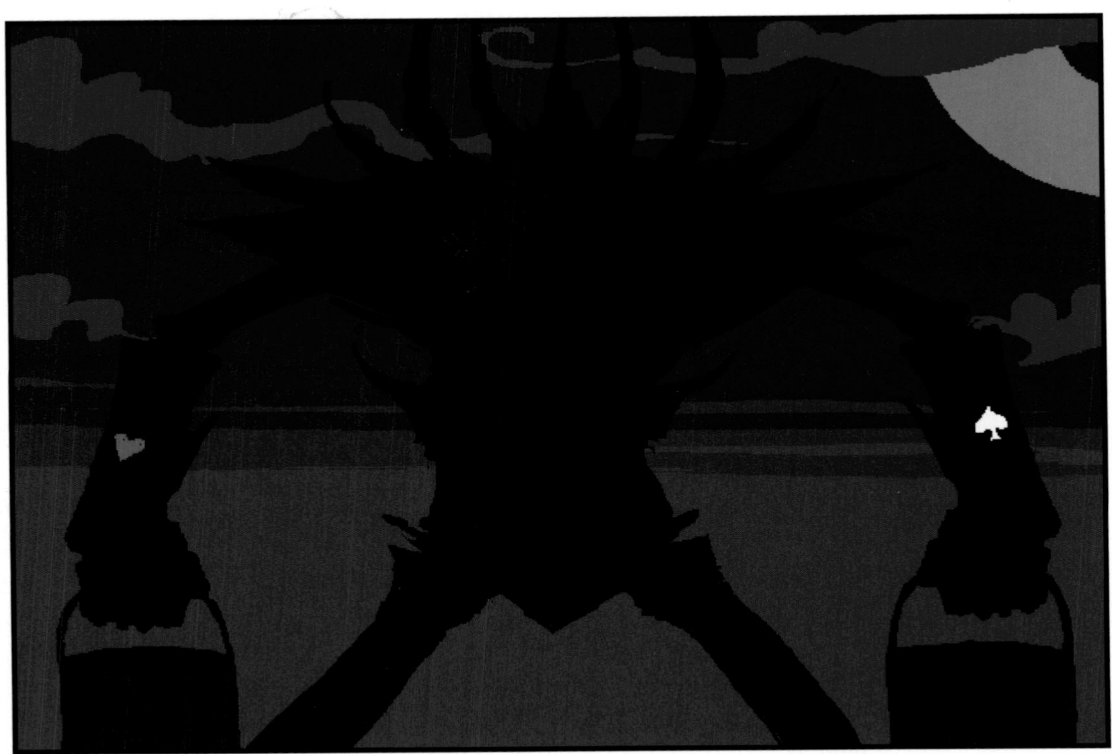

Trolls have a complicated reproductive cycle. It's probably best not to examine it in much detail.

The need to seek out concupiscent partners comes with more urgency than typical reproductive instincts. When the IMPERIAL DRONE comes knocking, you had better be able to supply genetic material to each of his FILIAL PAILS. If you have nothing to offer, he will kill you without hesitation.

The genetic material - WITHOUT GOING INTO MUCH DETAIL - is a combinative genetic mix from the matesprit and kismesis pairs, respectively. The pails are all offered to the mother grub, who can only receive such precombined material. She then combines all of it into one incestuous slurry, and begins her brooding.

This doesn't mean the initial combination was for naught, however. In the slurry, more dominant genes rise to the fore, while the more recessive find less representation in the brood. Especially strong matesprit and kismesis pairings yield more dominant genetic material. The more powerful the complement or potent the rivalry, the more dominant the genes.

TROLL REPRODUCTION SURE IS WEIRD. We all take a moment to lament how pedestrian the human reproductive system is, and further lament that the phrase "incestuous slurry" is not a feature of common parlance in human civilization.

> Examine ashen quadrant.

I make a point of repeating how we DON'T WANT TO GO INTO TOO MUCH DETAIL about how this genetic material is actually provided to fill the buckets. That's because I didn't think it was tonally responsible to get into graphic explanations about the mechanics of troll fornication. That was a good call at the time, but I see no reason why I should present myself as similarly encumbered in these books. How do they provide so much fluid for the heart or spade pail? I believe it's been implied that the mutual result of the red or black concupiscent ritual is the prodigious vomiting of genetic material. Though to be perfectly honest, I can't remember at all if this was implied anywhere in the text, or just in my imagination at some point over the last eight years.

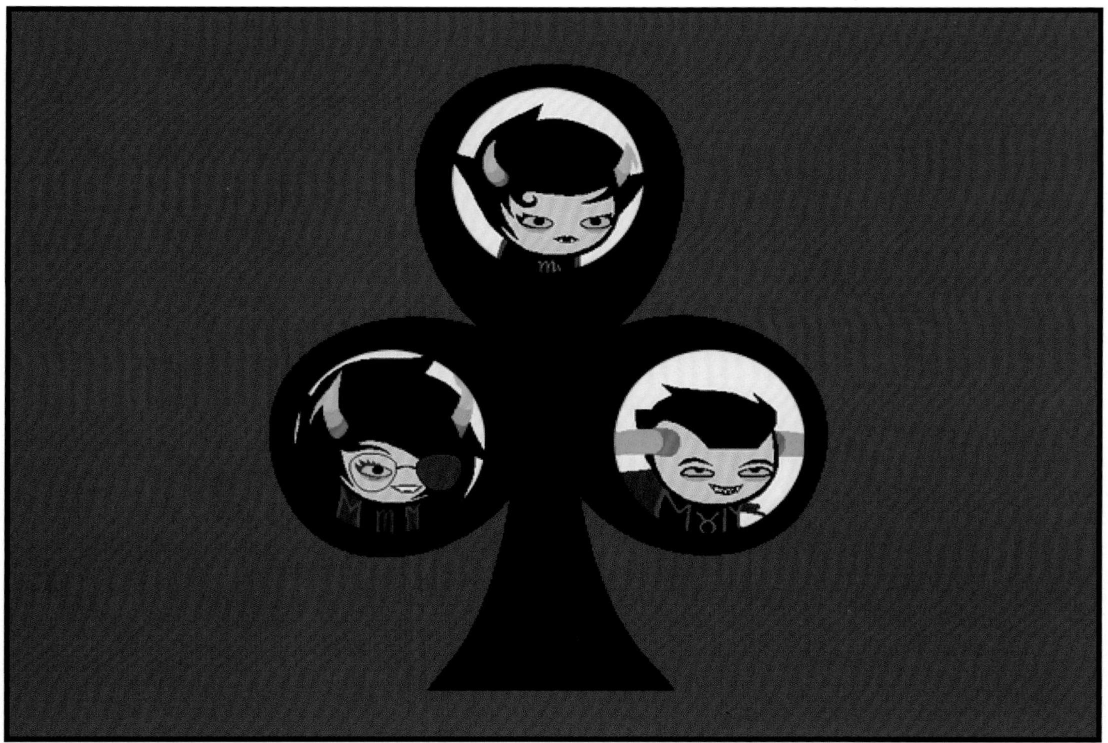

This quadrant involves a particular type of three-way relationship of a black romantic nature. Falling on the conciliatory side, it has no bearing on the reproductive cycle, except for indirect ramifications.

When two trolls are locked in a feud or some otherwise contentious relationship, one can intervene and become their AUSPISTICE. The auspistice mediates between the two, playing the role of a peace keeper, preventing the feud from boiling over into a fully caliginous rivalry.

Since such lesser feuds are quite common among trolls, there is a significant need for auspisticing parties. Without them, too many ashen feuds would become caliginous, and begin to conflict with other exclusive kismesis relationships, leading to a great deal of social complexity and sore feelings (even more so than black romance usually involves). Without auspisticism, the result would be widespread black infidelity.

This diagram is kind of funny, because these three never even formalize a real auspisticeship. Kanaya just kind of moonlights as a wannabe auspistice, while the other two can't even make up their minds about whether they have a serious blackrom attraction that's in need of mediation or not. It's just used as an example because it's the closest we've come to seeing the real deal in canon so far. It's also worth noting the existence of this quadrant culturally arises from the need to suppress trolls' general inclination to devolve into blackrom sluts. Note there's no auspistice equivalent for red romance, implying that temptation toward red infidelity is nowhere near as big a problem in troll culture. This paints a pretty good picture of what average life is like for trolls with their quadrants filled.

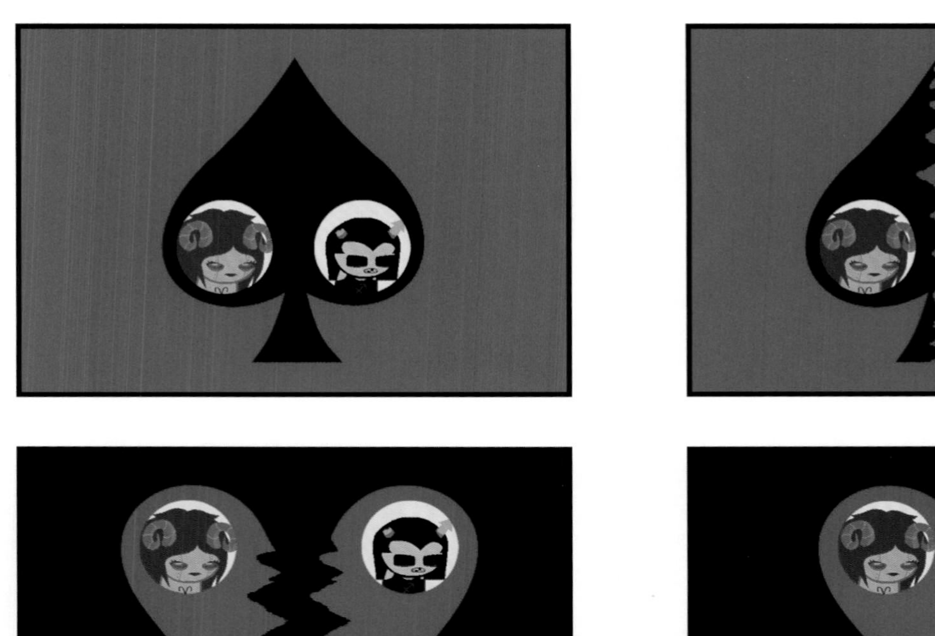

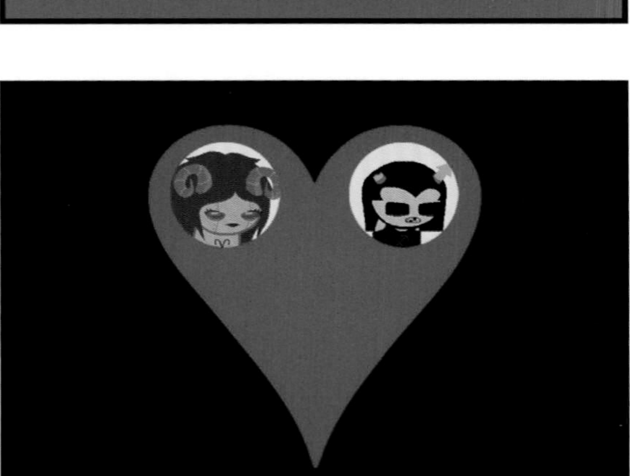

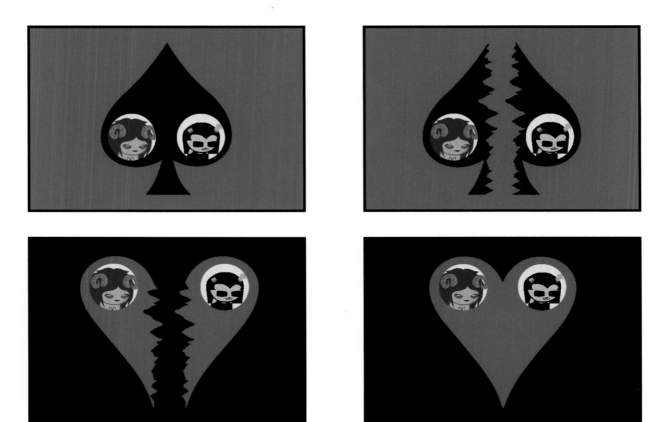

The relationships each quadrant describes tend to be malleable, if not volatile, especially on the concupiscent half where more torrid emotions reside. It doesn't take much to flip a switch and transmute blackrom feelings to redrom, and vice versa.

In many cases, one party will have red feelings while the other has black. But it will often be the case that one party's feelings will swap to match the other's, since there is no quadrant which naturally accommodates such a disparity. But thereafter, it's not uncommon for the two to toggle between red and black in unison now and then. These scenarios naturally result in both red and black infidelities.

This sort of relationship volatility is why conciliatory relationships are an important part of troll romance.

The previous note implies red infidelity is a lot less common than black infidelity, which is probably true. But the info on red/black vacillation here implies that when red infidelity does occur, it's more likely the result of two partners flipping between red and black erratically, leaving themselves open to courting other people in the red quadrant while the couple is in their black moods. Romantic life for trolls is pretty dramatic. Hence the need for the pale relationships, which serve as social stabilizers. When you look at it that way, it starts to make more sense why the escalation of romantic complexity isn't linear, it's geometric. In other words, to expand on our human "system," you can't really just add a spade and be done with it. You're adding too much drama. So you need another two to counterbalance. So a 1^1 system becomes a 2^2 grid. Extrapolating further, to add another heart- or spade-equivalent symbol to that, you'd realistically be stretching the system out to a 3^3 grid. (And no, I will NOT be talking about leprechaun romance here, although I know you want me to.)

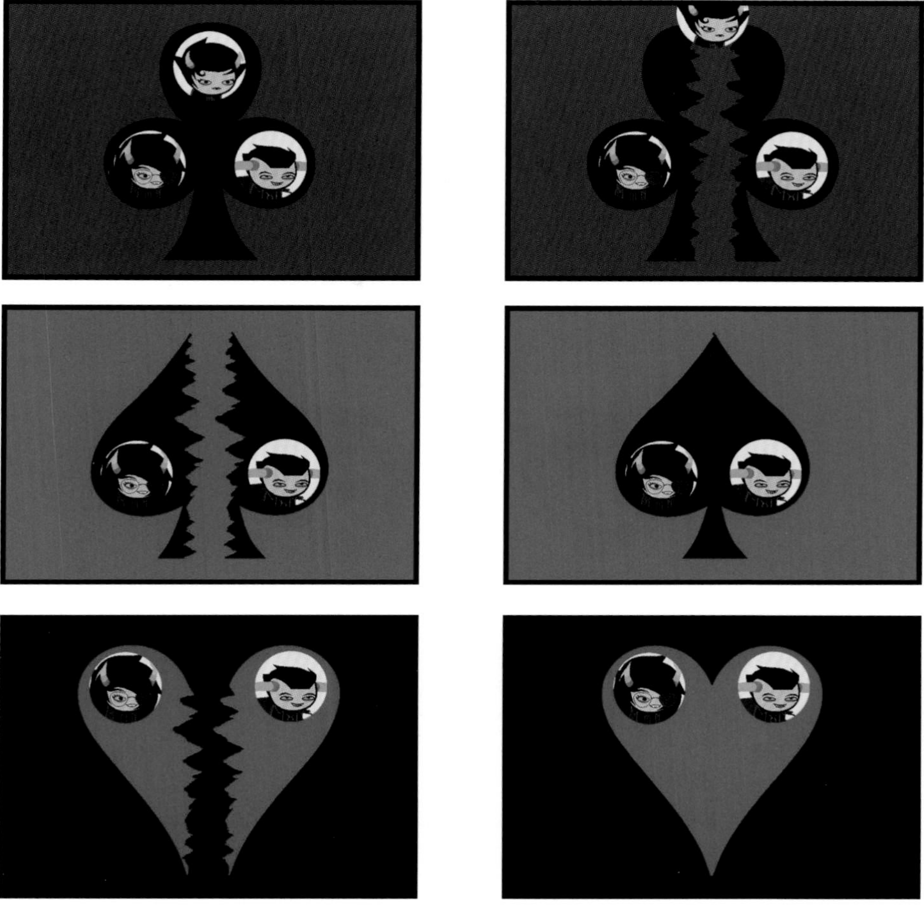

An auspistice can stabilize particularly turbulent relationships. If the auspistice fails to mediate properly, or has no interest in the role, or perhaps has different romantic intentions him/herself altogether, then the relationship often quickly deteriorates into one of an especially hostile and torrid nature. There are many outside factors and influences tugging and pulling these relationships in different directions, and unlike humans who have very orderly, simple, straightforward romantic relationships without exception, trolls exist in a state of almost perpetual confusion and generally have no idea what the hell is going on.

Being confused by troll relationships is one thing we do have in common though.

> Examine pale quadrant.

Kanaya/Vriska/Tavros was used as an ashen relationship example a couple pages ago, which I mocked, because it wasn't a strong example. This here is much more accurate. It's also probably a more helpful visual aid of troll romance in practice overall, rather than just in theory. Troll romance is usually a huge mess, involving two or three people flailing around emotionally and locked in vicious cycles with each other. Somebody like Kayana goes, you two are bad news for each other, I gotta step in here. Oh wait, actually I love her, I can't do this, bye. Whoops, they go back to black flirting/sparring. Wait, whoops, now they're in love. But...maybe? No, actually they hate each other, false alarm. The mediator comes back, says holy shit you guys, I've got to put a STOP to this. Rinse and repeat stupidly, forever, or until different romantic players enter the scene and upset the apple cart even more.

This quadrant presides over MOIRALLEGIENCE, the other conciliatory relationship. A reasonable human translation would be the concept of a soul mate, but in a more platonic sense, and with a more specific social purpose.

Trolls are a very angry and violent race. Some are more hot-tempered and dangerous than others, to the extent that if left to their own devices, they would present a serious threat to society, or even to themselves. Such trolls will have an instinctive pale attraction to a more even-tempered troll, who may become their MOIRAIL. The moirail is obliged to pacify the other, to function as the better half. The two partners in a strong pale relationship will serve to balance and complement each other's emotional profiles, and thus allow their other relationships to be more successful.

It's often ambiguous especially among young trolls whether a bond formed between an acquaintance is true moirallegence, or the usual variety of platonic involvement. Furthermore, romantic intentions of a more flushed nature can often be mistaken for paler leanings, much to the frustration of the suitor.

But some pale pairings, as the one above, will be strikingly obvious to all who know them.

Fandom took troll romance suuuper seriously. I know, shocking, right? There was a lot to talk about and discuss, ways of applying it to other works of fiction, to their original work, and even to their lives. Which, bringing this into your real life, is probably getting a bit carried away. Not many people went totally off the deep end, trying to fill all four quadrants, or if they did, I never saw much of it. But I did notice that the one new quadrant which really took off, on a casual everyday life basis, was this one. Big portions of fandom would freely use the term moirail, and describe certain friends that way. I think plenty still do, actually.

And yet others will seem to have been hatched for each other.

> Wait! More troll romance exposition please.

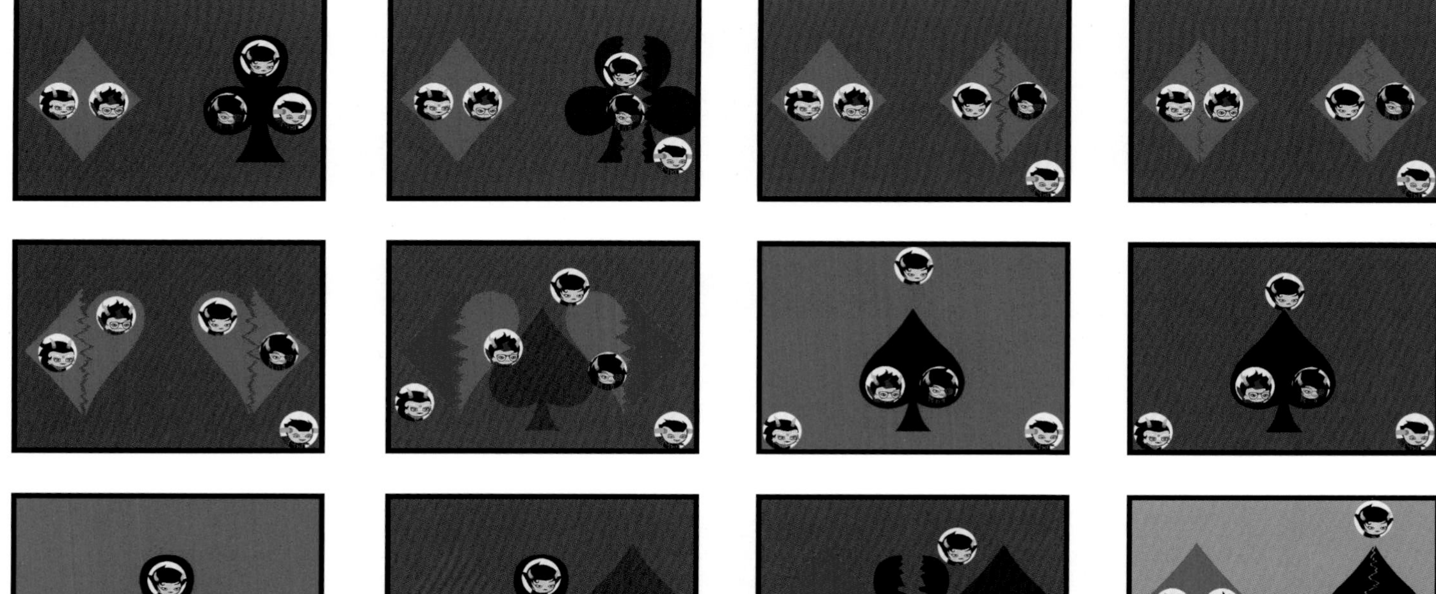

Are you following the sequence there? Study it carefully. If you understand what's going on, then congratulations, you understand troll romance and what a bad, stupid mess it all is. If you don't, that's fine I guess. If you aren't even bothering to look closely enough at the panel sequence to try and figure it out, well, I guess that's fine too. If you aren't even bothering to read my notes down here? Can't say I blame you for that either. Oh, you say you didn't even bother opening the book? Alright, now you're just showing off, wise guy.

002403-002404

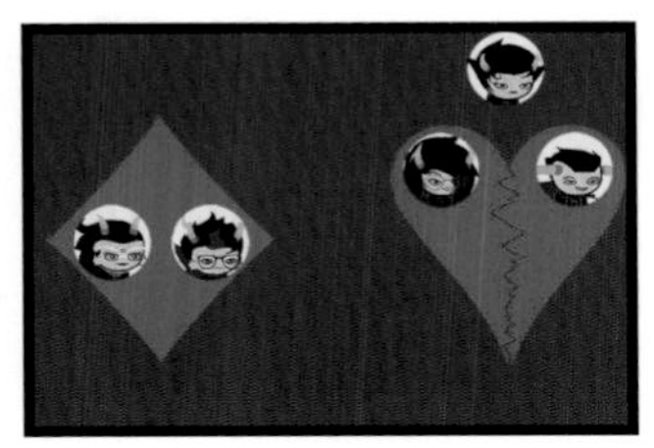
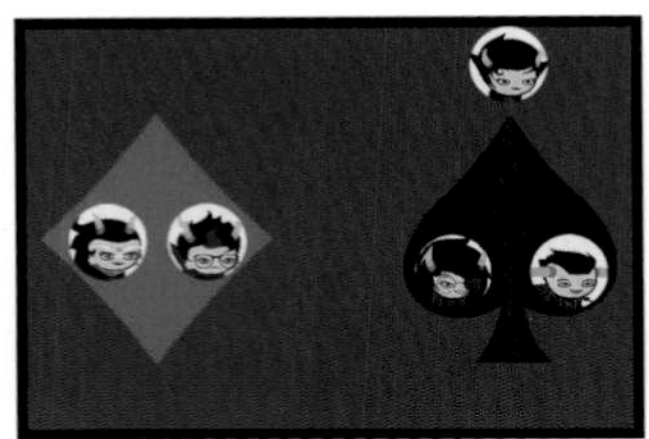
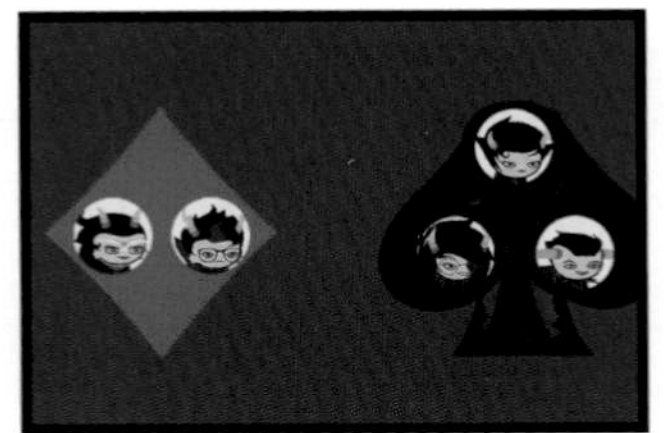

God you just can't get enough of this can you! That would have been a great point for a transition out of this illustrated sociological study, but ok, if you insist.

Now see, what's going on here is...

It's perfectly simple. When the full matrix of troll romance is in action, we have... uh...

Hey, why don't you figure it out! You should be an expert on all this by now anyway.

Later our troll hero would try to explain this to our human hero, attempting to convey all the nuance of troll romance through a nearly verbatim recitation of the preceding excerpts.

He would try to describe how rich and textured the troll romantic comedies were compared to the one dimensional schlock of our human cinematic counterparts. He would barely scratch the surface of Troll Will Smith's virtuosity with the delicate lattice of troll romance, as he would assist the bumbling fudgeblooded Troll Kevin James through the interwoven minefield-briarpatch of redrom and blackrom entanglements, all the while sifting through his own prickly romantic situation and ultimately learning the true meaning of hate and pity. But would they succeed before the imperial drone came knocking with his thirsty pails at the ready??? Yes, they would.

But John didn't understand any of this because he's a moron, and he wouldn't shut up about his awful bullshit Earth movies. He would just go on and on and on about that garbage.

Karkat is actually the kind of nerd who has a really specific interest no one cares about, but he keeps being like, no you just have no idea how DEEP all this is. John would probably be that way about his movies too, except there's no real organizing principle behind all of them. They're all just a bunch of bad movies from the '80s and '90s, and the underlying theory uniting them all is, "he just kinda likes them all for some reason, and also, Nic Cage is great." It's exactly the kind of attitude that would piss off a guy like Karkat. Which maybe is partly why John was hate at first sight for him.

But if there was one theme to be hammered through his thick skull, it would be the trolls' cultural preoccupation with romantic destiny. Yes, the romantic landscape is rife with false starts and miscues and infidelities, red and black. But every troll believes strongly that each quadrant holds one and only one true pairing for them, and it is just a matter of time before the grid is filled with auspicious matchups through the mysterious channels of TROLL SERENDIPITY.

In short, their belief is that for each quadrant there exists a pair or triad of trolls somewhere in the cosmos that were...

MADE FOR EACH OTHER.

Wow, another great transition. You wonder if it will stick this time. You have no choice but to take a stab at the rare and extremely dangerous 2x TRANSITION COMBO.

> Attempt 2x transition combo.

John Cusack is known to be a universal constant, and *Homestuck* confirms this truth canonically. Celebrities in general are cosmic constants, actually. Two separate universes could be created with somewhat varying laws of physics, but their celebs would still all be the same. They're actually more fundamental than physical laws, certain platonic concepts, or the aspects themselves. What's that? This is some of the dumbest shit I've ever said? Well, get outta here then. I'm gonna keep going with this. What sort of statement could I be making by asserting this truth? Hmm, let's see if I can make this shoe fit. Celebrities to us are bigger than just people, bigger than life actually. They're cultural touchstones. Like personified landmarks to let you know you haven't lost your bearings. To let you know you're still alive, here in this culture, and no matter what stupid things happen, or what our differences may be, we will always have a mutual, universal understanding and recognition of who these clownish, mediocre famous people are, and there's some comfort in that. Comfort on par with the basic understanding that gravity will always behave as you understand. Apples always fall from trees, and even if they bonk you on the head, there's still comfort in the reminder of this constancy. There, did I just make this horseshit work for you? You know I just did. You're probably mad now.

Looks like it worked.
So who IS this guy, anyway?

> Enter name.

Your name is ERIDAN AMPORA.

We're going to introduce these two in tandem, because why not. They're the only two trolls left, they're both sea dwellers, and they're moirails, which is a word we just got done understanding at great personal cost. So let's dive in. Here's fucking Troll Harry Potter or whatever.

> Eridan: Do something awesome.

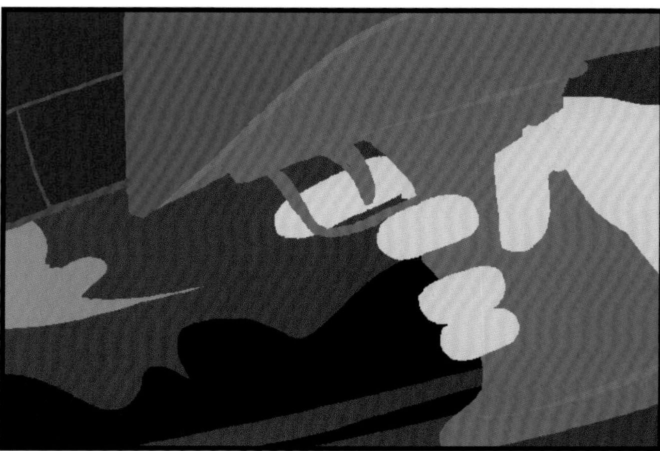

Wait for it...

Wait.

Eridan's loyal mount is seahorse dad, one of the objectively best dads, probably. Seahorse dad flies, as do apparently many, if not all, lusii meant to raise violet-blooded trolls. The Aquarius sign is the basis for Eridan's core concept as a troll. It's a slightly confusing sign, due to a couple superficial details. First, the name has the root "aqua," which obviously evokes the idea of water. It's also right next to Pisces, the damn fish sign, and these two facts together clearly form the basis for the idea that the two highest blood types belong to an aristocratic sea dweller class. There's just one problem, though. Aquarius is actually an AIR sign. I know, it doesn't make much sense. Those zig-zaggy lines on Eridan's shirt? That's just some air blowing, I guess. It felt important to adapt violet-blood themes a little to reflect this, a compromise between being a fully aquatic class and being under an air sign. Essentially, violet bloods are amphibious, and though many live under water, they spend about as much time in the open air, on boats or such. Their aquatic lusii fly through the air. And so you see, this is why Eridan has a flying seahorse dad. It's all so simple.

THAR SHE BLOWS.

Speaking of which, here's another flying sea lusus, which, judging from its blood color, probably belongs to some purple-blooded clown kid out there somewhere. Anyway, Eridan's handle is caligulasAquarium, which could have brought a bunch of stuff to mind when we first saw it. The "Aquarium" part was the dead giveaway that he would be the Aquarius troll. An aquarium also evokes the idea of a whole menagerie of sea beasts, which maybe he tended to in some manner. And now, these panels here possibly indicate that his "aquarium" is really the sky, which he views as a sort of hunting grounds.

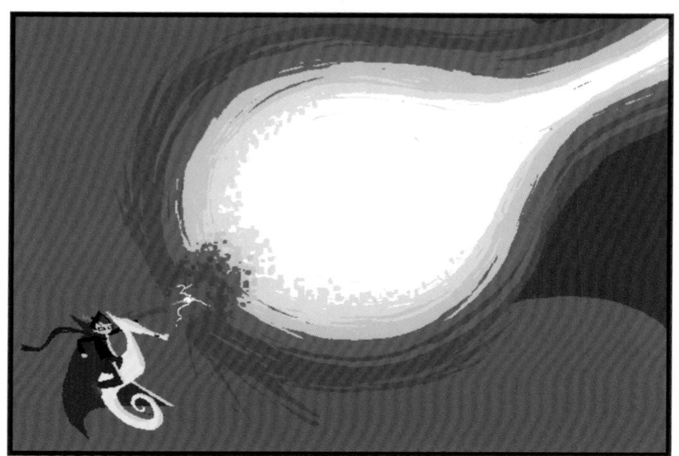

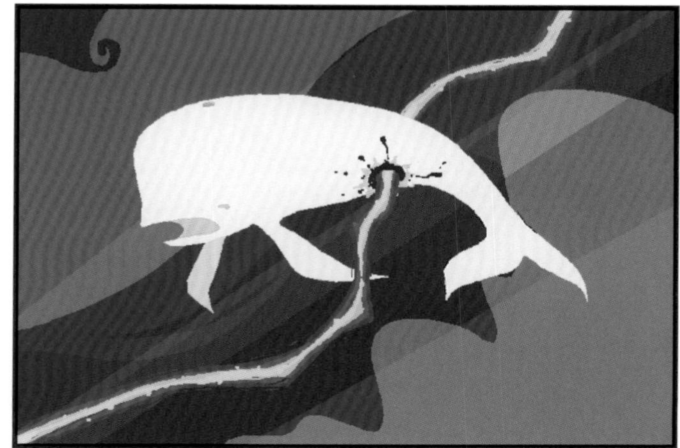

Eridan essentially kills other kids' parents, making him an "orphaner," just like his ancestor. As for the Caligula part of his handle, well, it's not hard to see a tyrannical, asshole emperor, known for his cruelty and perversity, as a historical blueprint for Eridan (who, if he doesn't quite live up to that image, certainly would *like* to). There's a little more going on here, though. "Caligula" shares the same root as "caliginous," which is a word for darkness and a part of troll romance lexicon associated with blackrom. Eridan, a "hopeless romantic," is particularly fixated on filling his black quadrant.

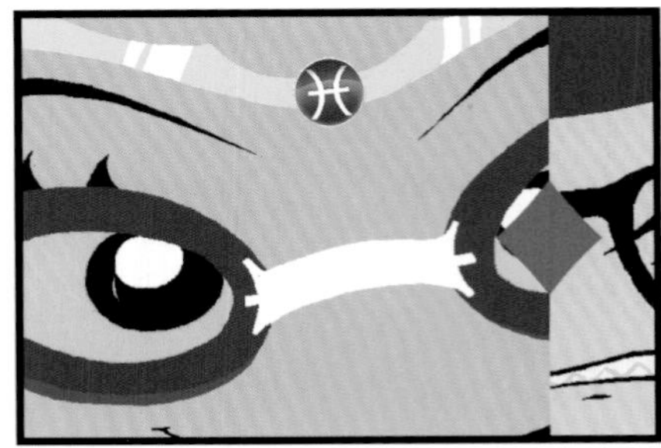

2x TRANSITION COMBO

Ok, that guy is pretty much squared away.
What about her?

> Enter name.

Your name is FEFERI PEIXES.

Peixes, I have to admit, is an awkward name to pronounce. I didn't have to grab it from the suggestion box, but I did. If I recall correctly, there weren't many names to choose from that I thought were decent. The only other one there I remember was Meenah, but that's only because I double-dipped back into the old box for the Alpha Troll names. Pretty sure *peixe* is Portuguese for "fish." The "x" is soft, like pie-she's.

> Feferi: Do something adorable.

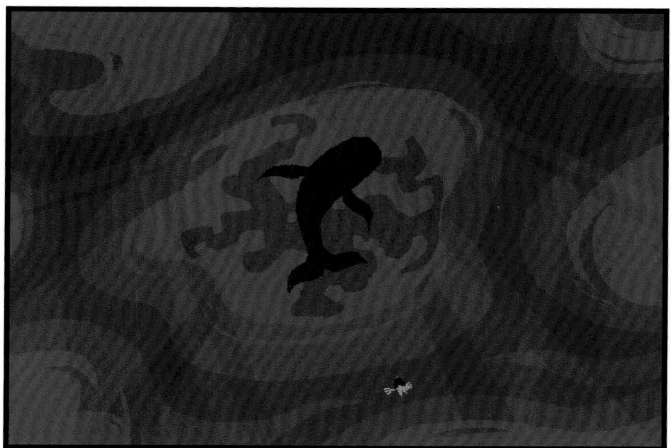

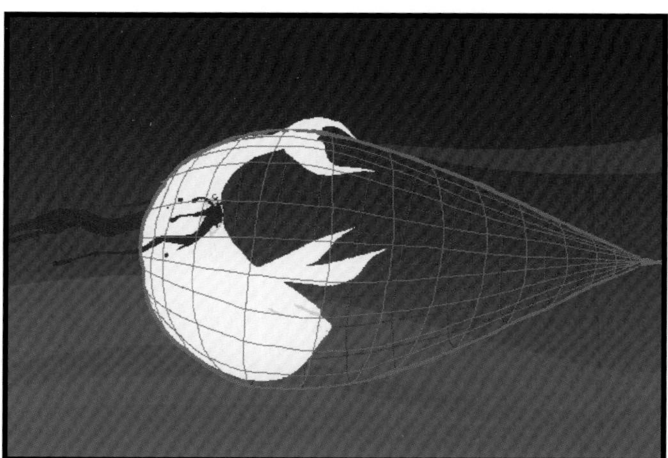

Feferi and Eridan have a little racket going on here. Eridan brutally orphans hundreds of kids, and she feeds their dead lusii to an insatiable monstrosity of the deep. Eridan basically does this due to having a thing for her, but he's stuck in the "moirail zone" and therefore feels relegated to providing a series of favors in order to stay in her good graces, which often is how guys who subscribe to friend zone-based ideologies are prone to thinking about such things. Also, he's kind of a murderous asshole who probably just likes killing stuff anyways. Whereas Feferi does this every day to make sure her lusus doesn't throw a tantrum and kill all trolls in the known universe. The burden is a bit lopsided, but hey, they work together to get it done as a team, like a good pair of moirails. At least she seems cheerful about it. In fact, she's cheerful about everything. Except Eridan.

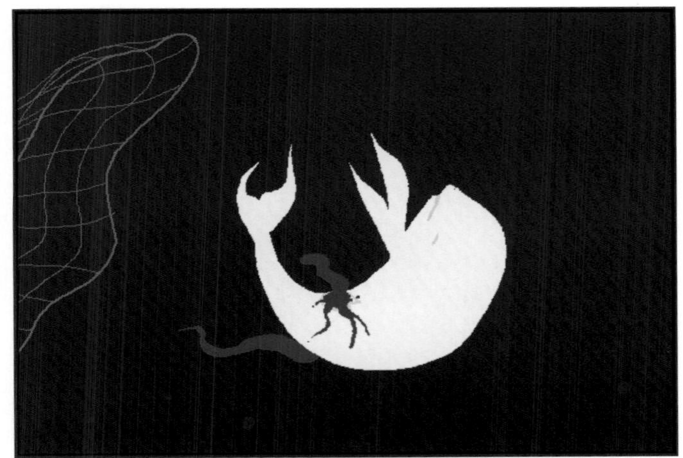

Gl'bgolyb is big.

Very, very big.

> Feferi: Go home.

It's not stated outright, or at least not soon, but Gl'bgolyb is a horrorterror from the Furthest Ring, who was transported to Alternia millions of years ago and dropped to the bottom of the ocean. "Gl'bgolyb" pronounced phonetically is basically just goofy eldritch-speak for "glub glub." This thing can psychically kill all trolls any time it wants, essentially making the entire species its prisoner, and is thus the basic corrupting kernel of absolute power which prompted the brutal totalitarian troll civilization to evolve the way it has. Each young heiress must take care of it and keep it calm, the way Feferi is doing here. Once upon a time, the young Condesce needed to do this too, before her ascendence to the throne. It is stated or implied later (I don't remember which) that this monster was transported to this planet by Doc Scratch in prehistoric times, specifically to corrupt the race and develop it into a violent society, which he prefers and which suits his long-term agenda. Prior to the game scratch that led to the trolls' current universe, the planet was called Beforus. This topic, you may already know, is an *insane* can of worms to get into. But for now, suffice it to say that Beforus did not have the same devil figure that Alternia has lurking on its moon, working to corrupt the race since birth. It therefore did not have Gl'bgolyb either, and troll society evolved in a more peaceful direction.

That should keep her quiet for a while.

At least until she dies.

> Eridan: Go home.

That should keep her happy for a while.

And make a freshly orphaned troll somewhere pretty sad.

> Eridan: Examine block.

You conveniently return to your respiteblock so that we may study your variety of INTERESTS.

This was very considerate of you.

Eridan at one point had a cool, mobile, pirate ship hive, which he probably cruised around the sea in during his Flarp games. Apparently at a later point it got shipwrecked on an island, and he never actually did anything about it, or simply wasn't able to. Which is probably fine. A hive is a hive. The only really bothersome thing to me about it is the fact that it's slightly non-level now. Probably annoying to live in a place like that. If he drops something round, does it go rolling downhill across the floor?

Flowing through your veins is nearly the richest blood the hemospectrum has to offer, penultimate on the scale. As such, you are a SEA DWELLER, a sub-race of troll distinct from the commoners by mutation and habitat, a caste which rules over the entire species.

But ruling, in your view, is not enough. You have an overpowering GENOCIDE COMPLEX, and have made it your sworn duty to KILL ALL LAND DWELLERS. You have amassed resources and deadly weaponry from around the world for this ambition through many sweeps of EXTREME ROLE PLAYING, while pursuing a working DOOMSDAY DEVICE which will bring armageddon to all those on the surface. Haven't had much luck with that, but maybe tonight's your night.

You hold a fascination for MILITARY HISTORY AND LEGENDARY CONQUERORS. You have dubiously modeled your profile and exploits after the most notorious figures and their stories, which are bristling with the GLORY OF VICTORY and the STING OF DEFEAT and POLITICAL MACHINATIONS and ROMANTIC INTRIGUE. It is an image you are careful to craft through EXAGGERATED EMOTIONAL THEATRICS, and your penchant for mass murder notwithstanding, people tend to regard you as a BIT OF A TOOL.

You also like MAGIC, even though you know it to be FAKE. Like a made up friend, the way wizards are. Made up make believe FAKEY FAKEY FAKES. It's still fun though.

Your trolltag is caligulasAquarium and you speak wwith a vvery wweird and sort of wwavvy soundin accent.

You hold off on doing anything for the moment on account of courtesy to fellow royalty.

> Feferi: Examine block.

Time for AMPORA TALK. Let's go right for the social profile bull's-eye: Eridan is a nastyboy. By now I've said lots of stuff about how Hivebent has been the environment for many smaller "rough draft" themes expressed through characters who start to hint at profiles that are brought into sharper focus later using different avatars. For example, Nepeta (romance-obsessed fangirl) as a proto-Calliope, the counter to which is Eridan (romance-obsessed, in a different way, nastyboy) as a proto-Caliborn. Caliborn and Calliope have a lot more substance to their symbolism, as well as additional layers that connect to what you might call The Point of *Homestuck* itself, as a more comprehensive creative statement. The portraits in Hivebent, the Nepeta/Eridan fangirl/nastyboy profiles, are more shallow and superficially comedic. Which isn't to say they aren't good characters. It's just that, in Eridan's case especially, the profile is almost purely political. He's the dude online who has egregious, patently evident problems with women, the way he talks about them and behaves toward them. The guy who feels entitled to their time and affection, and for this reason, struggles to win either. Everybody knows who this guy is. The profile is fundamentally rooted in misogynistic rancor, and everything else revolves around that—his loneliness, his foul temper, his attraction toward conquering and genocide, and eventually, his murderous rage. His effective self-radicalization over the course of the story, as happens so often in reality, stems from these issues.

On the subject of courtesy, you have also returned to your block so we can get a better look at you. Again, quite considerate.

Royalty sure is civilized!

You are also a SEA DWELLER. You have the most noble blood possible, the only of your kind known to possess it, and the only to share it with GL'BGOLYB, a deep sea monster also known as THE RIFT'S CARBUNCLE, EMISSARY TO THE HORRORTERRORS, or in more hushed tones, SPEAKER OF THE VAST GLUB.

This makes you the HEIR APPARENT for Alternian rulership, which ordinarily would place you in considerable jeopardy. HER IMPERIOUS CONDESCENSION would steer the flagship from the fleet and make an attempt on your life herself, if not for the protection of your monstrous lusus.

And if not forewarned of your race's extinction by the whispers of that lusus, you would have BIG PLANS FOR THE THRONE. All the plans. All of them.

You would redefine what it means to be CULLED in troll society. Under your rule it would mean caring for the unfit and infirm rather than exterminating them, and you have put this idea into practice by CULLING THE FAUNA OF THE DEEP. You tend to wild and beautiful AQUATIC HOOFBEASTS, grooming and feeding them daily. You capture and cage CUTTLEFISH by the thousands for their own good, and also because they are funny and colorful and you love them. They often swim through the bars of their cages, but that is fine. You run your whole palace as a sort of WILDLIFE ADOPTION FACILITY, even if the wildlife's need for care is dubious at best, and the practice really just amounts to an elaborate ROLE PLAYING SCENARIO. It's still fun though.

You would also look forward to using your reign to UNITE THE TWO RACES. You were told you would do this one day by your lusus, even if it does contradict her message of extinction. Oh well, you suppose NOT ALL PROPHECIES CAN COME TRUE.

Your trolltag is cuttlefishCuller and you)(ave a)(ard time not getting R-EALLY -EXCIT-ED ABOUT PRACTICALLY -EV-------ERYT)(ING!

Unfortunately, Feferi gets to be the foil for this unfolding nastyboy profile and has to work hard to keep him at arm's length. Her mini-arc is successful in this regard. Her arc in total...not so much. Which is a shame, because it results in her being near the bottom rung in terms of overall screen time and word count among major characters. Them's the breaks, though. In a cast of 500, not everyone gets to be a superstar. Still, there are things about her worth examining and celebrating, so let's do that. Like Kanaya, who has the "few of your kind" refrain, Feferi has "only of your kind," because it's literally true. There's one pink blood at a time on this world, except the Condesce, who's always out there somewhere. Her royal ambition seems to be to duplicate the conditions of peace on Beforus, possibly including the part where they care for the underprivileged to an extent that may be overbearing. Beforus, instead of having stratified brutal oppression, was more like a stratified nanny state. Feferi seems to display this inclination with her adoption of wildlife, which doesn't need caring for either. They're cared for because *she* wants it, not them, which is Beforus life in a nutshell. In this sense, the Alternia heiress (Feferi) and Beforus heiress (Meenah) possess reverse mentalities. Feferi craves the order and over-caring of Beforus, while Meenah craves the chaos and exploitation of Alternia (unsurprisingly, since she's the teen Condesce). -->

What will you both do?

> Eridan and Feferi: Do something ridiculous.

YES.

FUCK YES.

--> And though Feferi has many stylistic features of a truly extraordinary kid—rich sea princess, cool underwater castle, surrounded by animals she cares for... basically, any enthusiastic young kid's dream life—aside from all this, what seems fundamental to her profile is just a basic sense of averageness. This isn't me throwing shade at her, it's just how she's supposed to be. Kind of a regular kid who gets excited about regular kid stuff, doesn't have a wild, ostentatious personality or glaring defects like most other trolls. She's an average, fun-loving kid leading the life of the least average kid on the planet, and she wants to make the best of her situation, whether it's inheriting the throne (where she would bring peace to the planet) or saying goodbye to the world and playing the game (which she knows will happen, because her lusus told her it would). Like Aradia, Feferi is okay with a lot of things, but she slides through adversity easily with the power of enthusiasm rather than apathy. The only other character I can think of with "averageness" as a built-in feature of her profile is Jane. Who is also a Life player, and an heiress to a different throne (occupied by, yet again, the Condesce). Returning to the idea that most of these characters tend to be composites of various constituent building-block personas, or platonic ideals of certain character types, we appear to be isolating another ingredient here: Janeness. Or Feferiness, depending on how you look at it. I'm more inclined to see Jane as a distillation of a rough idea that began here, since that's the pattern which keeps playing itself out over this Hivebent reread.

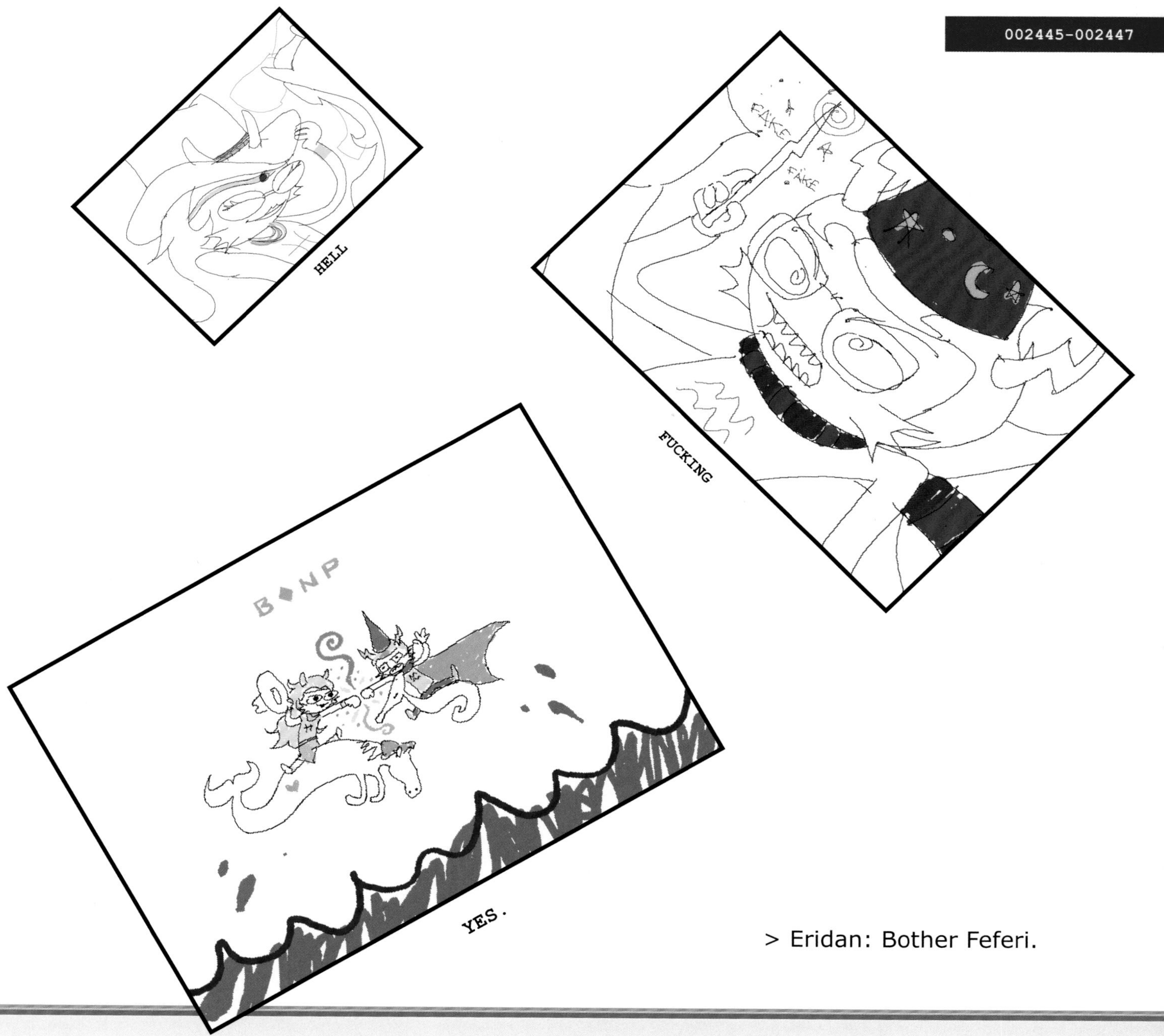

> Eridan: Bother Feferi.

We're off to a great start with these two. What a fun relationship they have. Even the panels are getting in on the fun, all tilting about on the page, funstyle. Actually their relationship isn't fun, it's total shit, and we are being misled.

caligulasAquarium [CA] **began trolling** cuttlefishCuller [CC]

CA: fef
CA: hey
CC: ?
CA: glub
CC: Glub glub!
CC: 38)
CA: yeah
CA: hm
CC: W)(at is it!!!
CA: wwhat
CC: I am wondering if you can forego t)(e exaggerated emotional t)(eatrics for once and actually tell me w)(at's on your mind!
CA: nothins on my mind wwhy cant i just fuckin talk and glub at you for a reason i dont havve
CC: 38|
CA: wwell fine but you dont wwant to hear it
CC: Yes I do.
CC: We are supposed to talk to eac)(ot)(er, t)(at is w)(at moirails are for.
CA: uhuh wwhatevver
CC: Glub glub glub glub siiiiig)(.
CC: Will you take t)(e c)(ip off your nub and tell me w)(at's t)(e matter?
CA: yeah wwell ok since wwe are the PALEST OF PALS A GUY COULD EVVER ASK FOR
CA: i wwill tell you
CA: evven though you wwill only humor me as usual since you dont agree wwith my agenda
CA: any of my agendas really
CA: none of the agendas
CA: none of them
CC: Are you fretting over anot)(er one of t)(ese dumb contraptions?
CA: see
CA: more condescension
CA: you are goin to make a hell of an empress
CC: No I'm not! But t)(at is beside t)(e point.
CC: None of your plots to kill t)(e land dwellers ever work out, and every doomsday device you get your)(ands on turns out to be a piece of junk!
CA: so
CA: i got to keep tryin thats howw all the great military masterminds became great through upright persevverance
CC: I t)(ink deep down you stack t)(ese plots against you so you fail because you know it's wrong.

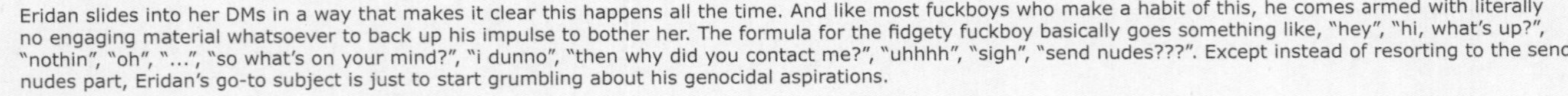
Eridan slides into her DMs in a way that makes it clear this happens all the time. And like most fuckboys who make a habit of this, he comes armed with literally no engaging material whatsoever to back up his impulse to bother her. The formula for the fidgety fuckboy basically goes something like, "hey", "hi, what's up?", "nothin", "oh", "...", "so what's on your mind?", "i dunno", "then why did you contact me?", "uhhhh", "sigh", "send nudes???". Except instead of resorting to the send nudes part, Eridan's go-to subject is just to start grumbling about his genocidal aspirations.

CA: it isnt wwrong
CA: im not going to explain it to you again
CA: at this point all you need to knoww is its important to me
CA: and im doing it for us
CA: i mean our kind
CA: nobody understands not evven you
CC: T)(is is t)(e last time I will say t)(is.
CC: W-E AR-E NOT B-ETT-ER T)(AN ANYBODY!!!!!
CC: GLUB. >38(
CA: pshh
CA: hemospectrum begs to differ
CC: If you're as sickened by t)(em as you say, w)(y do you spend so muc)(time on land?
CC: You can't)(ave t)(e sort of affinity for "our kind" t)(at you profess if you've only spent, w)(at...
CC: A few days underwater, maybe? IN YOUR W)(OL-E LIF-E!
CA: wwhatevver
CA: i havve to keep an eye on em up here
CA: its all about tactics
CC: W)(at about your friends? Do you ever t)(ink about t)(em?
CC: If t)(ey are beneat)(you t)(en t)(ey)(ave to die too.
CC: And I know you like talking to some of t)(em. You say you)(ate t)(em but I t)(ink you are pretending!
CA: history is full of cases wwhere conquerers consort wwith members of the enemy in a mannerly wway before wwipin them out
CA: evven goin as far as growwin fond a some
CA: its only civvilized
CC: Mmm)(mm.
CC: I)(ave a fis)(y feeling...
CC: T)(at t)(is stupid doomsday mac)(ine t)(ing is just anot)(er excuse to consort!
CC: Wit)(someone in particular...
CA: all your feelins are fishy
CC: 38P
CA: GLUBGLUBGLUBGLUBGLUBGLUB
CC: 38O
CC: DON'T YOU GLUB IN T)(AT TON-E OF GLUB WIT)(M-E MIST-ER!
CA: ill glub in wwhatevver dumbass bubbly soundin fishnoise i wwant to glub
CC: O)(S)(IT, you are angling for SO MUC)(TROUBL-E NOW.
CA: ok please lets just not get into the wwhole fuckin fish pun thing again ok
CA: like wwe get it wwe are nautically themed
CC:)(-E)(-E ok. 38)
CA: but yeah i dunno

Feferi's quirk, I gotta admit, is another rough one. Swapping H with)(just turns out to be a tough read, IMO. It's definitely a good *idea*, visually referencing the Pisces symbol in that way, similar to how Eridan references his wavy symbol (and accent, apparently) with vv and ww. But it doesn't do the eye any favors in terms of readability, and *possibly* contributed to my disinclination to give Feferi much dialogue in the story. Note later how Meenah doesn't have this quirk, unless she's shouting.

CA: i dont knoww wwhy she ignores me i guess shes just bored wwith me
CA: wwe had it all set up for her to givve me this thing tonight that probably doesnt evven wwork but yeah maybe that wwasnt the point
CA: i mean you think wwe havve a pretty good rivvalry goin right
CA: or at least had
CA: it wwas pretty fuckin bitter and contentious for a wwhile there and there wwas some good chemistry i dont knoww wwhat happened
CC: Um, I guess?
CC: I wouldn't really know.
CC: Sometimes people just drift away I t)(ink, or just aren't as into t)(e quadrant as t)(e ot)(er wants to be.
CC: So you really t)(ink your feelings for)(er run t)(at dark?
CA: it doesnt matter like i said shes bored shitless
CA: i guess im not as good a advversary as i thought
CC: T)(at is so ridiculous, any girl would be lucky to)(ave a kismesis as diabolical as you, especially T)(AT one.
CC: W)(o knows w)(at)(er problem is! S)(e)(as issues.
CA: ehhh
CA: wwell ok thanks for sayin so
CC: You know, I'm not sure w)(y we never talk about our romantic aspirations.
CC: We s)(ould more often. It is kind of -EXCITING!
CA: shrug
CC: Probably because you fill your gossip quota wit)(your nubby)(orned bro.
CC: You leave not)(ing left to talk about wit)(your dear sweet moirail!
CC: We are supposed to)(elp eac)(ot)(er wit)(t)(at stuff too, remember.
CA: maybe
CA: seems kinda
CA: odd though
CC: Your stupid fis)(y face is w)(at's odd!
CC:)(AV-E YOU -EV-ER T)(OUG)(T ABOUT T)(AT??
CA: fine
CA: wwell those are my stupid feelins wwhat about yours
CA: seems to me like you get along too wwell wwith evverybody to be harborin any black sentiments
CC: Um...
CC: Yea)(. I can't t)(ink of anybody I feel t)(at way about. 38\
CC: Maybe I am just not old enoug)(to)(ave t)(ose feelings yet? We are still pretty young you know.
CA: yeah
CC: So ok. T)(ose are your black leanings.
CC: W)(at about R-ED, ------Eridan???

It seems Feferi is cleverly laying the groundwork for her own imminent breakup with Eridan by offering counsel on his frustration with Vriska: "Sometimes people just drift away I t)(ink, or just aren't as into t)(e quadrant as t)(e ot)(er wants to be." I'm sure this is relatable to many. It's a tough job, breaking up with a dude like this. Like defusing a bomb. She also references his tight bro-relations with Karkat, who he probably spills his feelings to all the time, like his red crush on Feferi. That's why he tenses up at the idea of having romantic realtalk with Feferi, the way moirails are "supposed" to. He bristles at their pale relationship because he wants it to be something more. Everything going on here barely needs to be couched in terms of quadrants. It's completely relatable on human terms. And therein lies the truth of our tour through troll culture. It's really just a look at humanity, which has been dressed up with a bit of outlandish and generally satirical alien worldbuilding elements. But that describes a lot of sci-fi, doesn't it.

CC:)(MMMMM??????? 38D
CA: oh god
CC: Is t)(ere a lucky lady you are waxing scarlet for?
CC: OR LUCKY F-ELLOW??? 38O
CA: uh
CC: Tell me!
CC: Don't pretend you're all -EMBARRASS-ED SUDD-ENLY!!!
CA: ok fef
CA: this is NONE OF YOUR DAMN BUSINESS
CC: 38o
CA: i gotta go
CA: be back later wwhen its time to play

caligulasAquarium [CA] **ceased trolling** cuttlefishCuller [CC]

CC: 38(

> Eridan: Go get a beverage.

Another emotionally exhausting conversation. Too many FEELINGS AND PROBLEMS. It couldn't be any clearer to you. You and this sea princess have splashed down hard into the moirail zone, and now you don't know which way's upward. Perhaps tonight you will reveal your true feelings toward her, and end these exaggerated emotional theatrics once and for all, one way or another.

You need a stiff drink.

But... ugh. Not this swill. You're not THAT desperate.

> Eridan: Check fridge.

Feferi's facetious shocked reaction to speculating on Eridan waxing scarlet for a guy instead of a girl has the familiar heteronormative ring to it you'd expect to overhear in a conversation in human culture. Hivebent never makes a big deal of explicitly stating that trolls are an overwhelmingly bisexual race, but you start to gather that from context on a longer-term basis. On the subject of troll society just being a farcical veneer for human society and examining things relatable on human terms, you get a lot of moments like this, where statements and certain presumptions by characters have very human-centric perspectives that bleed into the text. *Homestuck* is not exceedingly strict about keeping the tone square with a precise reflection of alien cultural literalism. You could look at this in a couple ways. Either I could just be getting a little lazy sometimes, and I'm just letting human-centric worldviews, customs, verbal patterns, etc., leak into the text because it's just easier doing it that way (YA GOT ME). Or you could view it as a more critical choice to keep characters, interactions, and situations more relatable, more tonally in keeping with presenting this arc as a loosely crafted, humorous sci-fi romp, and shifting the focus toward other elements besides some maniacally constructed xenosociological study. Personally, I tend to gravitate toward explanations for things that make me sound like less of a shithead.

You pay a visit to what the common land dwellers refer to as a THERMAL HULL, instead of the more aristocratic and especially esoteric and alien sounding term, a REFRIGERATOR.

> Eridan: Open it.

A bunch of UNBELIEVABLY SHITTY WANDS tumble out.

Of course you knew these were in here. You're not even sure why you looked.

> Feferi: Go get a beverage.

A fridge full of shitty wands. Why, that's just a callback, you surely realize, to Dave's fridge full of shitty swords. If it wasn't clear, Eridan's persona-alchemy involves a touch of Dave, just like Sollux's does. You can tune into this by observing the speech patterns of both. Later they're also connected through rivalry, which perhaps is an unrelated fact, or perhaps not. Eridan is a full-blown nastyboy, and younger Dave starts out with some edgy habits too. Not that bad, though. You get the sense that with the wrong influence, Dave could have slipped down the nastyboy road and gone full Eridan. Instead, he follows the path of the wokeboy, which is probably a better outcome for everyone. Dave's proximity to shitty swords, Eridan's proximity to shitty wands—there's some thematic linkage in that both say something about the character. Dave's involved with shitty swords, i.e. false/brittle talismans of ersatz heroism, which break, and the broken sword symbolism linked to his identity is something he must contend with in his journey, deriving whatever meaning from it that he can. Eridan's shitty wands, i.e. false talismans of magic, known and disdained for their fakeness attribute, serve to challenge him to override that fakeness through anger and determination, as well as the channeling of his aspect, Hope, as a means of conquering the forces of impotence ruling his identity, which the useless wands seem to physically embody. Of course, unlike Dave's path, his is an unambiguously villainous trajectory.

Another emotionally exhausting conversation. Too many FEELINGS AND PROBLEMS. That guy. Talk about a high maintenance moirail. Perhaps tonight you will reveal your true feelings toward him, and end these exaggerated emotional theatrics one way or another.

You need a sugary drink.

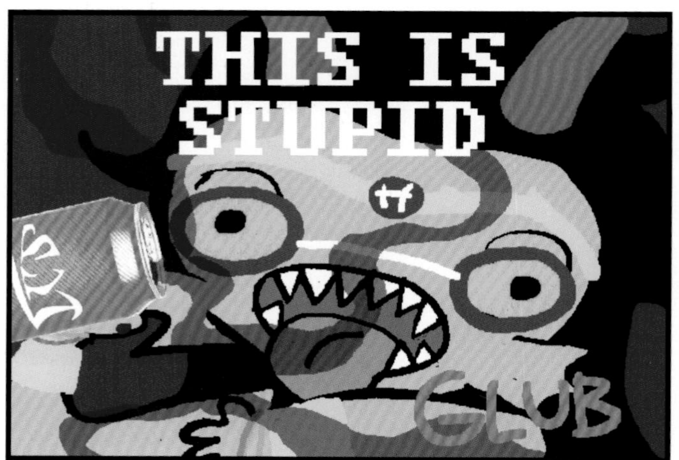

> Feferi: Disarm.

The dumb "Tab has sugar" running gag even spills over into the troll version of Tab. At some point it's established that the Condesce loves this stuff, making it the logical beverage of troll royalty. (The pink can is kind of a giveaway.) Hence Feferi likes it too. But extrapolating a little, that means surely Tab was introduced on Earth by the Condesce herself, most likely distributed through one of the many arms of the Crocker empire.

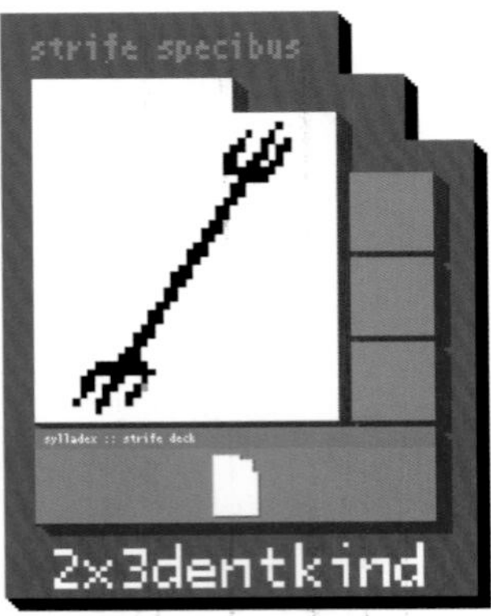

You decide to unwind and take your mind off the drama for a while before starting the game. You nearly forgot this is going to be an exciting night. Everything you are about to do next is exciting. It is always exciting. You are excited.

You unequip ΨDON'S ENTENTE, a golden DOUBLE CULLING FORK, a legendary weapon reserved for royalty, and generally only used for ceremonial purposes.

> Eridan: Disarm.

You unequip AHAB'S CROSSHAIRS, which is YET ANOTHER legendary weapon, about as powerful as your KIND ABSTRATUS will allow.

You plundered it from a ghost ship during a particularly challenging campaign. It was the same old gamblignant's ship from which your accomplice at the time also plundered a set of extraordinarily powerful dice.

You almost feel sorry for the adversaries you will face tonight. They will likely pose neither team much challenge at all. Unless one of the links in the prototyping chain includes something especially huge and monstrous, but really, what are the odds of that happening?

> Eridan: Bother Vriska.

This rifle was straight up Dualscar's weapon, just like Vriska's dice belonged to Mindfang. We've also seen it before. It was one of the legendary weapons the bunny had. So now we have another one of these little threads to follow, connecting the past to the future. We know this weapon makes a journey from this session to the human session, and into the "future" (or wherever Jade's penpal is), and then back again via the bunny box. Let's all check off the "where that gaudy blue rifle in the bunny box came from" box on our scorecard. (I guess I should note that we saw it even earlier than this, when Eridan was riding the seahorse, but I delayed mentioning it until now, for Reasons.)

On the subject of your old accomplice/rival, you guess you'll try talking to her one more time, even though you know she won't answer. You know she is bored shitless with you and your drama. You are almost starting not to care about this stupid doomsday device which probably won't even work. She probably KNOWS you know it won't work. She has probably put all the pieces together and knows it was an elaborate ruse to be in cahoots with her again.

And she just went along with it playing you for a chump.

You are such an IDIOT!!!!!!!!!!!!!!!!!!

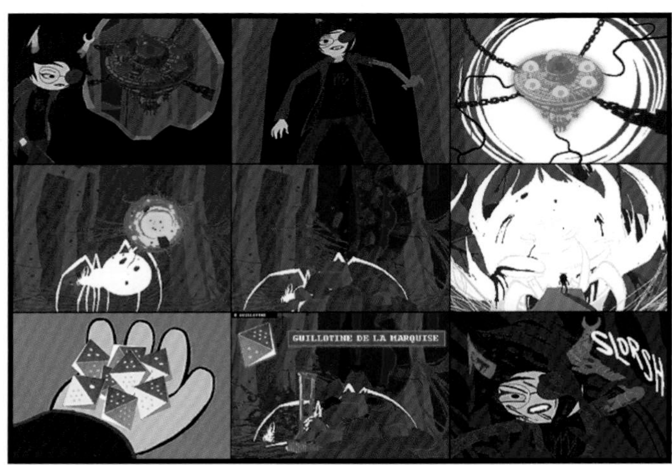

Yeah, see? No answer. Bored shitless, just like you thought. She has much hotter irons in the fire than you these days.

She's just busy using your device to conveniently wound then euthanize her mother. Chill out, man. Maybe someday you can both laugh over this. Or bond over it. No, that won't happen, just messing with you.

But it wasn't that long ago that you were the hottest iron. At the height of your prowess as seagrifts, Marquise Mindfang and Orphaner Dualscar were in alliance an unmatched terror, and in competition, unbridled tempest. Either way, spoils were typically traded and shared. No levels were left for anyone else to gain. None of the levels.

She would have the victims of your conquest walk the plank.

While you would reap the custodial spoils.

Basically, Vriska's Flarping days weren't so much an expression of her blackrom interest in Erican as they were a scam of convenience to feed her bad mom. She was using him, unsurprisingly, but then, he was using her too, to harvest food for his redrom crush's lusus. Even though they were both scamming each other, he was hoping Vriska was blackrom-interested in him anyway. But she wasn't interested. At all. And neither was Feferi. #ForeverAlone

And while yet another partook
not in revelry, but necessity.

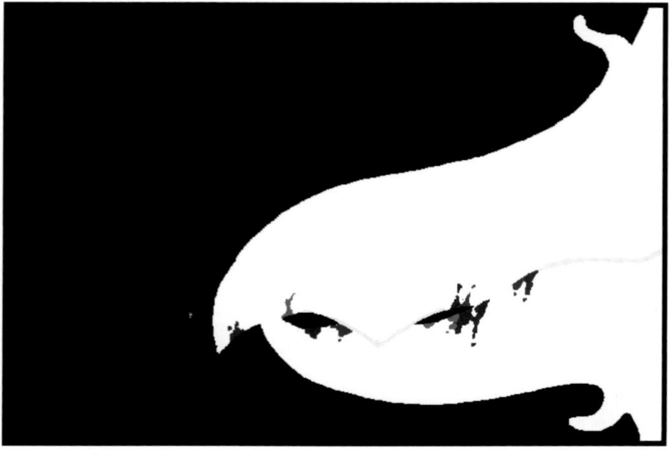

She had to keep her fed to keep her
calm, to keep her terrible voice down.

If she were to raise it above a whisper, trolls would begin dying. First, the lesser bloods, those more psychically susceptible.

If she raised it to a shout, all on the planet would die. Land and sea dwellers alike.

And if she were ever to get really upset, she might release THE VAST GLUB, a psychic shockwave that would exterminate every troll in the galaxy.

The "VAST [blank]" is a running gag that starts here (I think), which I can name four total examples off the top of my head. The VAST GLUB (instant troll extinction), the VAST CROAK (a big frog says a huge ribbit when a universe is created), the VAST HONK (Lord English says a loud honk when he's summoned), and the VAST EXPLETIVE (the Sufferer says "fuck" really loud while he's getting crucified for being Troll Jesus).

In truth, it would be all too easy to solve the land dweller problem once and for all. You'd just need to lighten up on the feeding schedule for a while. Maybe you'd be a little too busy to bother with that hassle for once? Or maybe you could happen to be off your game for a spell? It happens, even to the best sometimes.

But nah. It would make her upset.

More emotions. More problems. That's all you need.

> Some time later...

The WITCH OF LIFE takes her place in the LAND OF DEW AND GLASS.

> Feferi: Report to Eridan.

cuttlefishCuller [CC] **began trolling** caligulasAquarium [CA]

Maybe putting the fish troll inside a big fishbowl was a little on the nose. Wait, what's that? The cat troll's land coming up soon is named LOLCAT? Never mind then. Nothing matters. Feferi's finally getting ready to have The Talk with Eridan. Notice how she waits until she's safely in the session before breaking up with him. It's a bit like moving to a country overseas, then breaking up with your ill-tempered jackass boyfriend over the phone. Not a bad play.

CC: W)()()()()(-E-E-E-E-EW.
CA: fef are you in
CC: Yea)(...
CA: that took forevver
CA: i wwas gettin wworried kinda
CC: Yes, it was a pretty close call, and got kind of complicated.
CC: But Sollux finally came t)(roug)(, and now I believe t)(e full c)(ain is complete!
CA: man that guy
CA: hes a fuckin drama machine it is fuckin pathetic
CC: YOUR STUPID FIS)(Y FAC-E IS T)(-E DRAMA MAC)(IN-E T)(AT DO-ES NOT)(ING BUT W)(IN-E AND GLUB.
CC: 38P
CA: fuck SORRY
CC: Anyway you s)(ouldn't say t)(at about)(im,)(e is a)(ero and)(e saved my life.
CA: yeah sorry
CA: i wwas just really wworried and stressed out i thought you wwere dead
CA: and i didnt evven get to thank you for savvin my life or really for anythin
CA: and i just spent all this time here wworryin and thinkin about stuff
CA: and i decided i havve something i wwant to tell you
CA: that ivve been meaning to get off my nub for a wwhile noww
CC: O)(, really?
CC: T)(at's good! Actually, I)(ave somet)(ing I)(ave been meaning to say to you too.
CA: wwhoa really
CA: uh
CA: wwhat is it
CA: you go first
CC: Mm, okay.
CC: But t)(is isn't easy to say!
CA: yeah i knoww
CA: its ok maybe i wwill understand more than you think
CA: wwe might evven be sayin the same thing
CC: Okay, I)(ope so.
CC: I t)(ink...
CC: Now t)(at we are bot)(in t)(is game, and)(ave left our world be)(ind...
CC: And you can no longer pose t)(e danger to our people t)(at you)(ad always planned to...
CC: I t)(ink it is not really necessary for me to be your moirail anymore.
CA: wwhoa
CA: wwait
CA: wwhat
CC: 38(
CC: I am really sorry, -Eridan. It)(as just been so)(ard looking after you and keeping you out of trouble!

Feferi flips out when Eridan disses her hero Sollux. The writing is on the wall. But really the saddest fucking thing going on here is how, when she tells Eridan she has something to say, he actually thinks there's a chance she's got the same thing on her mind that he does. Like she's about to spill her red feelings to him first and save him the trouble. What do you even do with a guy like this? We don't have the technology yet to build a violin small enough to play for him.

CC: It)(as taken its toll, and)(onestly I am really ex)(austed.
CA: fuck
CA: this isnt what
CA: i dont knoww i wwasnt expectin this at all
CA: im not sure i can handle this
CC: I'm sorry!!! 38'(
CC: It will be t)(e best for bot)(of us. We can just sort of be...
CC: Regular friends instead.
CA: no
CA: please dont
CA: look im bein serious here dont do this
CA: i wont even use my weird accent while i type ok so you know im bein really dead serious and honest about this
CC: Uh...
CC: Okay, I am being serious and honest too. SEE?
CA: ok good
CA: are you sure you arent bein hasty about this youve just been through a lot
CA: i mean we are supposed to be fated to be moirails arent we
CA: isnt that how it works
CA: you cant just throw all that away cause youre sick of me
CC: I am not sick of you, Eridan! I still really like you.
CC: In order to be destined for moirallegience, both people have to be on board, don't you think?
CC: But I cannot do it anymore. So I think it just wasn't meant to be all along.
CC: And really, you just don't need me anymore. You are free to do as you wish! We both are.
CC: I can't look after you anymore.
CA: I DIDNT EVER NEED ANYONE TO LOOK AFTER ME
CA: i was totally fuckin fine my ambitions were noble
CA: and really none of your fuckin business QUITE FRANKLY your majesty
CA: and the only reason i put up with stickin my flipper in this fuckin shithole quadrant with you was
CC: Was what?
CA: nevermind
CC: Tell me!
CA: ok fine
CA: i apologize for losin my shit over this i was just caught off guard is all
CA: but maybe its a good thing really
CA: actually i might a been proposin the same thing to be honest
CC: Oh?
CA: yeah
CA: fef have you thought about
CA: since you dont wanna be pale with me no more

This is a fascinating moment in troll dialogue history, because, by briefly opting out of their quirks, it suggests most of the time they are just willfully adhering to the typing patterns for no particularly good reason. It also implies that dispensing with a quirk conveys a sense of seriousness. But many trolls have had many serious and emotional conversations while just continuing on with their quirk, no problem. They probably get so used to the quirks that they don't even notice when a very serious moment would warrant dropping the act for a bit. I'd compare it to wearing a huge, ridiculous hat virtually every moment of your life, and you only bother to take it off for the most somber moments possible, like when you break up with someone. But then, you get so used to wearing it, and everyone's so used to seeing you wear it, that you don't even end up following that rule, and you just show up to funerals and stuff wearing this big dumb fucking hat. Nobody calls you out on it, because they genuinely don't even notice it as weird. You're just the guy who always wears that thing, showing up to put a rose on the casket.

CA: the possibility a some other type of arrangement with me
CC: What do you mean?
CA: i mean
CA: somethin a bit more
CA: kinda reddish
CA: like
CA: brighter red
CC: 38O
CC: No, I hadn't thought about it!
CA: ok well what do you think about it
CA: now that youre thinkin about it
CC: Um...
CC: I really don't know about that.
CA: why not i thought you said you liked me
CC: I do! But I don't know if it's really in that way.
CA: couldnt it be though
CA: dont you think theres room in your collapsin and expandin bladder based aquatic vascular system for those feelins
CC: I've never had a chance to consider anything like that! I have just spent all my time worrying about you and trying to keep you from killing everybody or hurting yourself.
CC: It took all my energy.
CC: I don't think I have anything left for those feelings either.
CA: oh god
CC: What?
CA: im the biggest fuckin idiot who ever lived
CA: i cant BELIEVE i just opened up to you like a chump when i knew what was comin
CA: i am one sad fuckin brinesucker
CA: overemotional sappy trash youre right im not better than anybody
CA: im worse than anybody
CA: EVERYBODY
CA: all the bodies
CC: STOP!!!!!!!!!!!
CC: God.
CC: Will you just clam up for once in your life?
CC: Always carping and carping and carping!
CC: You go completely overboard with your emotions, always looking to reel in drama wherever you can.
CC: I am up to my gills in it! I just can't salmon the strength anemonemore.
CA: i cannot
CA: BELIEVE
CA: you are doin the fish pun thing while youre breakin up with me
CA: real nice

Feferi suddenly fishtailing into more sea puns during her breakup spiel may legitimately be the funniest thing that happens in this entire book. Sea look, even I'm doing it now. Absolutely no one respects Eridan. No body. None of the bodies.

CA: whoops i mean REEL nice
CC: HEHEHE, sorry.
CC: But really, this shouldn't be as bad as it sounds.
CC: When all is said and done, I am still your friend.
CC: We have left our world behind. Everyone is dead, and there's no use in worrying about it now.
CC: It's over! It is time to play this game and focus on building something new and ------EXCITING.
CC: So)(ang in t)(ere, -Eridan.
CC: I)(ave to go now! Sollux is in serious trouble, and I)(ave to go)(elp)(im.
CC: BY------------------------E!
CA: wwait
CA: dont go

cuttlefishCuller [CC] **ceased trolling** caligulasAquarium [CA]

CA: glub

> Feferi: Proceed to gate.

Feels bad, man. Hey, let's forget this idiot's pain for a moment and reflect on an achievement we finally unlocked. We've met all twelve trolls now and have been thoroughly introduced to each of them. What a ride. Maybe now I can finally chill out and stop saying so much about them on a metatextual level, and about everything else going on for that matter? Maybe I can just start saying some jokes instead. Ah, to dream. Well, anyway, back to writing utterly crushing volumes of literary wank extolling the brilliance of my own whimsically produced, decade-old nonsense.

YOU'R-E FR-E-E-E-E-E-E---------------E!

> Karkat: Check on Sollux.

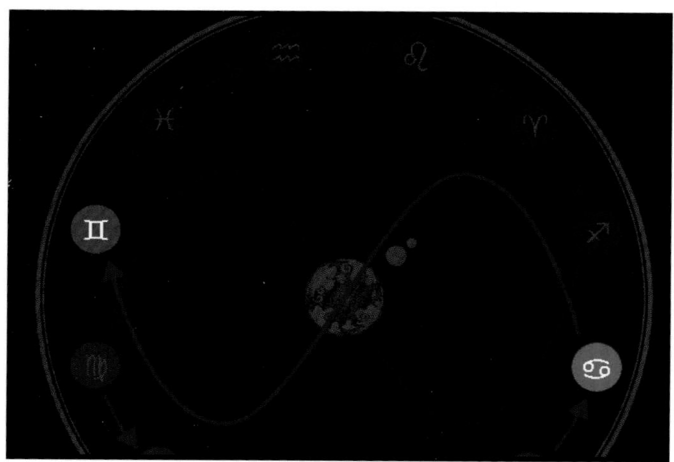

carcinoGeneticist [CG] **began trolling** twinArmageddons [TA]

This kinda implies Feferi is actually really strong. Like, low-key strong. A superpower she has without making a huge deal out of it. Maybe even close to Equius-strong? That's a hell of a jump she did, just like Equius. It makes sense that those of her blood class would be sturdy as hell, judging from what we know about the Condesce. Anyway, this looks to be plausibly the happiest moment of her life, launching herself out of her stuffy old fishbowl-castle toward freedom, and possibly a new boyfriend she has to go kiss back to life. Too bad this is pretty much her peak moment.

CG: BRO ARE YOU OK.
CG: HEY
CG: OH GOD
CG: WHAT HAVE I DONE.
CG: SOLLUX?
CG: PLEASE TELL ME THAT'S JUST HONEY.
CG: PLEASE JUST BE HONEY PLEASE JUST BE HONEY PLEASE JUST BE HONEY
CG: HAHA, OK, MAKE-BELIEVE TIME IS OVER!
CG: OH GOD OH GOD OH GOD OH GOD OH GOD OH GOD OH GOD OH GOD OH GOD OH GOD OH GOD OH GOD OH GOD OH GOD OH GOD OH GOD OH GOD

It is all your fault. You couldn't get him in before the glub.

There, there, you blubbering goddamn pansy.

We skip over some action. The tense final moments of getting the last player in the session (Sollux) involved his race against the clock to get Feferi in before she died, and Karkat's race to get Sollux in before her lusus released the Vast Glub in its dying gesture to protect her from a meteor. It's been noted that, due to the fact that the psychic Glub takes some time to travel through space to wherever the Condesce's ship is, this means Sollux actually died before his own ancestor (the Helmsman) did.

> Gamzee: Indulge emotional theatrics.

caligulasAquarium [CA] **began trolling** terminallyCapricious [TC]

CA: gam i need to talk to kar wwhere is he he isnt answwerin
TC: He's bUsY BeInG SlApPeD MoThErFuCkIn sEnSeLeSs bY ThE GuY WhO LiKeS KnIvEs
TC: BuT I CaN ReLaY WhAt mEsSaGe yOu gOt, My bRoThEr
CA: i dont feel comfortable wwith that
CA: i havve some serious feelins and problems here and i need some advvice

Karkat is deeply upset over the loss of his buddy. He does a lot of getting upset over dead friends, so this is a nice warm-up for him. Let's pause and note his presence on this planet. He's made good progress with his new blood-brother and/or murder-father, Jack. Think of all the journeying they've had to do to get here. Finding the gate on Karkat's blood planet, leading to Terezi's mind planet (where is she by the way?), then finding the gate there leading to Gamzee's stupid circus planet. It's really exciting to imagine Jack and Karkat's adventures together. Meanwhile Gamzee sits around here predictably like a useless piece of shit. He did find some time to make a cool rocket unicycle, so at least that's something.

TC: HaHa, YeAh i fEeL YoU, hE'S PrEtTy wOrKeD Up tOo
CA: wwhy
TC: BeCaUsE OuR GoOd bRo sOlLuX JuSt kIcKeD ThE WiCkEd mOtHeRfUcKiN ShIt
CA: wwhat the fuck do you mean by that
CA: are you sayin hes dead
TC: YeAh :o(
CA: oh fuck
CA: oh god fuck noww i feel like an asshole
TC: YeAh i'd sAy tHaT An aSsHoLe iS ThE ThInG ThAt jUsT AbOuT WhAt eVeRyBoDy fEeLs lIkE
TC: KaRkAt bLaMeS HiMsElF On iT, pOoR MoThErFuCkEr
TC: BuT I ToLd hIm tO Be cHiLl
TC: BeCaUsE ThErE Is a mIrAcLe cOmInG, i cAn fEeL It
CA: that is the wworst fuckin advvice
CA: wwhat an awwful thing a you to say
CA: MAGIC ISNT REAL STUPID STOP BELIEVVIN IN IT
TC: i'Ve gOt tO BeLiEvE At wHaT My hEaRt tElLs iN Me, EvEn iF It's a fAkE ThInG
TC: HoNk
CA: this is a lot a pointless fuckin rubbish and isnt no emotional help to him or me either for that matter
CA: put kar on
TC: UuUuH, i cAn't rEaLlY ThInK AbOuT InTeRvEnInG, tHe bLaCk fRoWnInG MoThErFuCkEr kInDa sCaReS Me
TC: ArE YoU SuRe i cAn't hElP A bRoThEr Up iNtO HiS MoThErFuCkIn cHiLl?
CA: i dont knoww
CA: it probably doesnt matter
CA: my feelins seem petty and meaninless noww
CA: she had better things to wworry about than my ovverwwrought bullshit
CA: like the dead guy wwho savved her
CA: so forget it thanks anywway
TC: BrO My aDvIcE Is yOu jUsT KiCk bAcK AnD MoThErFuCkIn sNaP InTo sOmE RuDe eLiXiR AnD MaYbE GeT YoUr wIcKeD ZoNe oN
TC: ThErE I SaId mY PeAcE
CA: wwhat the FUCK are you fuckin babblin about
TC: SnAtCh aN IcEcOlD, dOg
TC: MoThErFuCkIn cHuG ThAt sHiT LiKe yOu aNd tHe bOtTlE WaS ReUnItEd lOvErS
CA: are you recommendin a bevverage to me or somethin
CA: is that wwhat this is
TC: YeAh mAn SlAm A FaYgO
CA: i dont havve a fuckin faygo you stupid fuck wwhy wwould i keep that disgusting shit on hand
TC: ArE YoU MoThErFuCkIn sUrE AbOuT ThAt?

Another great rarepair conversation. I live for this shit. When do these two ever talk? Never. Enjoy it like a fine wine. It's even wine colored. Except the wine's bad, and it's making you sick. Sometimes we realize certain characters never talk because they have basically nothing to say to each other. What does Gamzee even have to say to anyone, other than a string of meaningless "chill" platitudes, while looking for any excuse to mention his favorite soda? People really should have seen Gamzee's Turn coming a lot more than they did. We just watched Eridan put on a douchebag spectacle for the books, but then when he starts talking to Gamzee, he almost seems like a reasonable, empathetic person by comparison. Yes, Eridan is pretty bad. But Gamzee's repulsiveness is literally bottomless.

CA: oh
CA: oh god youre right i do
CA: i totally forgot about it
TC: YoU SeE MaN
TC: MoThEr
TC: FuCkIn
TC: MiRaClEs
TC: :o)

> Eridan: Slam a Faygo.

You prepare to kick back and motherfuckin' snap into some rude elixir and maybe get your wicked zone on.

It sure would be startling if what followed was a crudely drawn spit-take accompanied by an odd, short exclamation.

> Eridan: BLUH!

What.

It's just soda. Not great, but not that bad either. What's the big deal?

We all need to settle down here.

> And later still...

The joke here is that all the mentions of Faygo make it seem like I'm just ripping this soda brand to shreds. Absolutely tearing this Upper-Midwest beverage a new asshole and deriding it into oblivion along with all the credulous fools who drink it. But in reality, it's fine. Completely unremarkable in every way, and aside from the fact that an American cult dedicated to circus rap seems unusually faithful to the product, it's barely worth commenting on at all. The joke here basically is: there is no joke. BA-DUM PSHH!

A princess prepares to administer a universal remedy for the unawakened.

> Karkat: BLUH!

This week in, "We literally never, ever stop learning the rules of *Sburb*." This is the first indication that a player can be brought back to life in this way. Very handy to know. Doesn't even have to be a prince, or a princess, or royalty of any kind. Can be literally any coplayer who, within the vaguely allotted time limit in which this reviving method is still valid, makes it to the body to kiss it. Feferi knows this how? Not sure I could tell you. Could be lots of ways, really. Maybe Gl'bgolybsprite told her offscreen, and she hurried away to do it? Or maybe she didn't actually know at all, and she just wanted to enthusiastically kiss Sollux's dead body? She is -EXCIT-ED after all. The answer can be whichever explanation you think is more "fun."

> hey kid
> never got a chance to say
> how much i hate you
> every last one of you

Goddamn troll kids. Every time you turn around they're smoochin' each other. Makes a man want to stab his own gut and puke blood.

Here's another brief episode of: Gamzee's fooling around uselessly in the background while his "best friend" grieves the loss of their mutual friend, doesn't actually give a fuck about anything, but for some reason a lot of people thought he was a good and nice guy before he went "crazy." /shrug/ Oh hey, Jack is watching through the exile terminals in the far future as Slick, hatefully reminiscing. This must mean...

It is like I am the kid from the Never Ending Story. I was chased by some bullies into this fucking attic and now I am watching people watching people watching more people kissing and stuff basically forever. How many metalayers removed this story can we get??

This attic is spooky. I wish those bullies would just leave me alone.

Later I am going to ride a long magic dog through the sky and fuck their shit up.

Ugh. This troll paint is making a mess. This was such a bad idea.

> MSPA: Quick, become more meta while AH is brooding.

Yep, it means I'm about to show up again. Honestly, what's about to transpire is a fantastic author meltdown moment. It holds up really well. Who the fuck are we kidding. Everything holds up well. Timeless, perfect literature, that's the shit I'm about, and nothing else. Got it? This material is revisiting the idea that I only appear through these little meta-media transitional devices involving Jack, who's inextricably associated with the Fourth Wall construct, as the disgruntled bureaucrat who worked in a cubicle consisting of four such walls utilized as monitoring devices in his nefarious, day-to-day grind. And now we see some things never change for him. He's *still* watching things he hates playing out on screens, and having no choice about it, kind of like you. And we pull the frame back a little and see that I'm pretty much in the same boat. We're all stuck in this hell together. But as the only tortured genius among us all, I'm the only one who's allowed to have funny meltdowns about it.

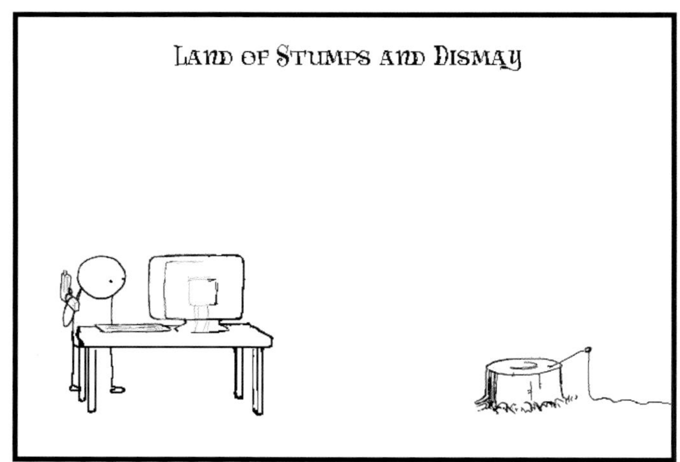

AH employs a daring execution of AUTHORTECH -> LADDER TO SELF INDULGENCE behind his own back. It keeps happening.

All MSPA readers make a solemn vow to do an acrobatic fucking pirouette off the stump and blow their brains out if it doesn't stop keep happening.

> AH: Ok, ha ha, get back to the story jackass.

Then we pull back a little more, and the reader gets in on the act. This is a rather plain-looking character in the story who represents you, in front of your computer, with a gun (except now you're in front of a book, with a gun). We first met him in *Problem Sleuth*, when the final boss revealed he had a million more health meters. But he originated in *Jailbreak*, the first MSPA comic, as a guy who, upon breaking out of jail, at some point became fixated on the idea of suicide in the proximity of this tree stump with a harpoon stuck in it. Don't go looking for *Jailbreak*, or read it, ever. It is the most cursed tale I have ever written in my life. We shouldn't even be talking about it. Nevertheless, I think this character makes for a great avatar for the reader in general. A long-suffering, walleyed individual who conveys a certain air of helplessness over the material he views, his struggle to understand it, and his complete impotence when it comes to halting his addiction to this content. Suicide is never far from his mind, and hardly a thing takes place on this website which does not in some way cause him to meditate upon the notion of ending it all. This being is your guiding spirit, and to deny this is to spew lies. He apparently hails from a stark and lonely planet called LOSAD.

Excuse me?

Oh, I'm sorry. Am I not going fast enough for you?

Well QUITE FRANKLY, your majesty, I don't think you realize what kind of hell I've been through.

Do you have any idea how long I've been trapped in this attic??

Do you have any idea how FUCKING SCARY it is in here???

Do you have even the SLIGHTEST CLUE how many times that wolf head over there has SCARED THE SHIT OUT OF ME?????

> Uh... Wolf?

AAAAAAAAAAAAAAAAAAAAAAAAAAAAAAAAAAAA
AAAAAAAAAAAAAAAAAH

> This is ridiculous.

That's the wolf from *The NeverEnding Story*. It's my greatest fear. I'm trapped in this attic like the kid from *The NeverEnding Story* was. That kid was reading a long fantasy story in that attic as a framing device for the "real story," where a bunch of crazy stuff happened, and a sad horse drowned in a swamp at some point. Also, as the kid kept reading, the lines between the fiction and reality started blurring, so it was a similar kind of metaclusterfuck as *Homestuck*. (Well, not really, but whatever.) Except the guy in the attic in this case isn't reading the story that's coming to life and consuming his reality, he's writing it, while throwing a big tantrum, and screaming at a wolf-head trophy. So that's why *The NeverEnding Story* is a pretty apt "mascot movie" for the author-insert layer of *Homestuck*, which also does an incredible job of making the reader suspect that its story quite possibly will never end. *The NeverEnding Story* themes have a way of surfacing any time I show up in *Homestuck*. (E.g. the next time you see me, I'll be riding the huge, long, magic dog named Falcor, chasing cruel bullies, and punishing them for their evil deeds.)

No, this is MY LIFE we're talking about here. Bullies. Wolves. Musty attics. Huge spiders. Did I mention the spiders? Let me tell you, I got HELLA spiders up in this...

Fuck, this horn fell off. Dammit. Piece of shit. Wonder if there's any glue in here... oh screw it.

Do you have any idea how much power I wield over you?? To what extent I can RUIN the shit you step in with that squeaky clean sunday loafer you use to stomp that bookmark and stamp that F5 key, day goddamn in and day fucking out??? Do you possess even the most infinitesimal kernel of cognizance for the degree to which I can make the shorn, shivering weasel that is the totem spirit representing your wretched fascination with this website squeal in heartrending remorse????

It would be so easy! I could snap my gray smudgy fingers RIGHT NOW, and make you read all the troll romance exposition segments all over again, BACK TO BACK TO BACK TO BACK TO BACK TO BACK.

Oh, you don't think I'll do it????????

> Oh my god.

When Hivebent was being updated in real time, the deeper we got into it, the more I detected a certain amount of grumbling from the peanut gallery about the pacing of this arc, that maybe it was too much of a detour, slowing down the progress of the "real story." But the more you examine *Homestuck*, the more you realize the "real story" doesn't have a conventional meaning. Or, the "real story" is more of a self-understood projection of narrative idealism, around which revolve many orbital layers of farcical deconstruction. It's like the John Lennon quote: "Life is what happens while you're busy making other plans." My spin on that is: *Homestuck* is what happens while you're busy looking for the "real story." Regardless of any pacing reservations at the time, Hivebent now feels like it's regarded as sort of a sacred text among fans of the series. The lesson is that the real-time grumblings of fandom guttersnipes during the slow rollout of such content don't mean a damn thing, and they always seem to be wrong about everything. But it's not really a lesson, because I always knew that. The important thing was to recognize when the time was right to make these little power moves and reassert some dominance over the story. Lennon had his bullies too. Ultimately he got owned by one of them. He didn't have a long, magic dog to fight back with. He also didn't really have the guts to weaponize his work against his fans. If Lennon was a serious artist, he would have taken the worst song he ever made, expanded it to be an indulgent thirty-minute ballad, released it as a single, and gone on tour for a year playing only that song.

The problem is that when the subject of troll romance is broached, our sparing human intellects instantly assume the most ingratiating posture of surrender imaginable.

But we will do our best to understand regardless.

Humans have only one form of romance. And though we consider it a complicated subject, spanning a wide range of emotions, social conventions, and implications for reproduction, it is ultimately a superficial slice of what trolls consider the full body of romantic experience. Our concept of romance, in spite of its capacity to fill our art and literature and to rule our individual destinies like little else, is still just that. A single, linear concept. A concept usually denoted by a single symbol.

<3

Troll romance is more complicated than that. Troll romance needs four symbols.

Their understanding of romance is divided into halves, and halved again, producing four quadrants: the FLUSHED QUADRANT, the CALIGINOUS QUADRANT, the PALE QUADRANT, and the ASHEN QUADRANT.

Each quadrant is grouped by the half they share, whether horizontally or vertically, depending on the overlapping properties one examines. The sharpest dichotomy, from an emotional perspective, is drawn between RED ROMANCE and BLACK ROMANCE.

RED ROMANCE, comprised of the flushed and pale quadrants, is a form of romance rooted in strongly positive emotions. BLACK ROMANCE, with its caliginous and ashen quadrants, is rooted in the strongly negative.

On the other hand, the vertical bifurcation has to do with the purpose of the relationship, regardless of the emotions behind it. Those quadrants which are CONCUPISCENT, the flushed and caliginous, have to do with facilitating the elaborate reproductive cycle of trolls. Those which are CONCILIATORY, the pale and ashen, would be more closely likened to platonic relationships by human standards.

There are many parallels between human relationships and the various facets of troll romance. Humans have words to describe relationships of a negative nature, or of a platonic nature. The difference is, for humans, those relationships would never be conceptually grouped with romance. Establishing those sort of relationships for humans is not driven by the same primal forces that drive our tendency to couple romantically. But for trolls, those primal forces involve themselves in the full palette of these relationships, red or black, torrid or friendly. Trolls typically feel strongly compelled to find balance in each quadrant, and seek gratifying relationships that each describes.

The challenge is particularly tortuous for young trolls, who must reconcile the wide range of contradictory emotions associated with this matrix, while understanding the nature of their various romantic urges for the first time. Of course, young humans have this challenge too. But for trolls, the challenge is fourfold. When two individuals find themselves in the flushed quadrant together, they are said to be MATESPRITS. Matespritship is the closest parallel to the human concept of romance trolls have. It plays a role in the trolls' reproductive cycle, just as it does for humans. This is pretty obvious! Not much more needs to be said about this. Moving right along. When a pair of adversaries delve into this quadrant, they become each other's KISMESIS. As one of the concupiscent quadrants, it plays a role in procreation as well. There is no particularly good human translation for this concept. The closest would be an especially potent arch-rivalry. For instance, human players would never be able to adequately diagnose the relationship between the queen and her archagent. But troll players could immediately place it as a dead ringer for kismesissitude. They would think we were all pretty stupid for not getting it. And they would be right. Trolls have a complicated reproductive cycle. It's probably best not to examine it in much detail. The need to seek out concupiscent partners comes with more urgency than typical reproductive instincts. When the IMPERIAL DRONE comes knocking, you had better be able to supply genetic material to each of his FILIAL PAILS. If you have nothing to offer, he will kill you without hesitation. The genetic material - WITHOUT GOING INTO MUCH DETAIL - is a combinative genetic mix from the matesprit and kismesis pairs, respectively. The pails are all offered to the mother grub, who can only receive such precombined material. She then combines all of it into one incestuous slurry, and begins her brooding. This doesn't mean the initial combination was for naught, however. In the slurry, more dominant genes rise to the fore, while the more recessive find less representation in the brood. Especially strong matesprit and kismesis pairings yield more dominant genetic material. The more powerful the complement or potent the rivalry, the more dominant the genes. TROLL REPRODUCTION SURE IS WEIRD. We all take a moment to lament how pedestrian the human reproductive system is, and further lament that the phrase "incestuous slurry" is not a feature of common parlance in human civilization. This quadrant involves a particular type of three-way relationship of a black romantic nature. Falling on the conciliatory side, it has no bearing on the reproductive cycle, except for indirect ramifications. When two trolls are locked in a feud or some otherwise contentious relationship, one can intervene and become their AUSPISTICE. The auspistice mediates between the two, playing the role of a peace keeper, preventing the feud from boiling over into a fully caliginous rivalry. Since such lesser feuds are quite common among trolls, there is a significant need for auspisticing parties. Without them, too many ashen feuds would become caliginous, and begin to conflict with other exclusive kismesis relationships, leading to a great deal of social complexity and sore feelings (even more so than black romance usually involves). Without auspisticism, the result would be widespread black infidelity. The relationships each quadrant describes tend to be malleable, if not volatile, especially on the concupiscent half where more torrid emotions reside. It doesn't take much to flip a switch and transmute blackrom feelings to redrom, and vice versa. In many cases, one party will have red feelings while the other has black. But it will often be the case that one party's feelings will swap to match the other's, since there is no quadrant which naturally accommodates such a disparity. But thereafter, it's not uncommon for the two to toggle between red and black in unison now and then. These scenarios naturally result in both red and black infidelities. This sort of relationship volatility is why conciliatory relationships are an important part of troll romance. An auspistice can stabilize particularly turbulent relationships. If the auspistice fails to mediate properly, or has no interest in the role, or perhaps has different romantic intentions him/herself altogether, then the relationship often quickly deteriorates into one of an especially hostile and torrid nature. There are many outside factors and influences tugging and pulling these relationships in different directions, and unlike humans who have very orderly, simple, straightforward romantic relationships without exception, trolls exist in a state of almost perpetual confusion and generally have no idea what the hell is going on. Being confused by troll relationships is one thing we do have in common though. This quadrant presides over MOIRALLEGIENCE, the other conciliatory relationship. A reasonable human translation would be the concept of a soul mate, but in a more platonic sense, and with a more specific social purpose. Trolls are a very angry and violent race. Some are more hot-tempered and dangerous than others, to the extent that if left to their own devices, they would present a serious threat to society, or even to themselves. Such trolls will have an instinctive pale attraction to a more even-tempered troll, who may become their MOIRAIL. The moirail is obliged to pacify the other, to function as the better half. The two partners in a strong pale relationship will serve to balance and complement each other's emotional profiles, and thus allow their other relationships to be more successful. It's often ambiguous especially among young trolls whether a bond formed between an acquaintance is true moirallegence, or the usual variety of platonic involvement. Furthermore, romantic intentions of a more flushed nature can often be mistaken for paler leanings, much to the frustration of the suitor. But some pale pairings, as the one above, will be strikingly obvious to all who know them. God you just can't get enough of this can you! That would have been a great point for a transition out of this illustrated sociological study, but ok, if you insist. Now see, what's going on here is... It's perfectly simple. When the full matrix of troll romance is in action, we have... uh... Hey, why don't you figure it out! You should be an expert on all this by now anyway. Later our troll hero would try to explain this to our human hero, attempting to convey all the nuance of troll romance through a nearly verbatim recitation of the preceding excerpts. He would try to describe how rich and textured the troll romantic comedies were compared to the one dimensional schlock of our human cinematic counterparts. He would barely scratch the surface of Troll Will Smith's virtuosity with the delicate lattice of troll romance, as he would assist the bumbling fudgeblooded Troll Kevin James through the interwoven minefield-briarpatch of redrom and blackrom entanglements, all the while sifting through his own prickly romantic situation and ultimately learning the true meaning of hate and pity. But would they succeed before the imperial drone came knocking with his thirsty pails at the ready??? Yes, they would. But John didn't understand any of this because he's a moron, and he wouldn't shut up about his awful bullshit Earth movies. He would just go on and on and on about that garbage. But if there was one theme to be hammered through his thick skull, it would be the trolls' cultural preoccupation with romantic destiny. Yes, the romantic landscape is rife with false starts and miscues and infidelities, red and black. But every troll believes strongly that each quadrant holds one and only one true pairing for them, and it is just a matter of time before the grid is filled with auspicious matchups through the mysterious channels of TROLL SERENDIPITY. In short, their belief is that for each quadrant there exists a pair or triad of trolls somewhere in the cosmos that were... MADE FOR EACH OTHER.

> Wow.

Honestly, it would be a pretty strong move if over the next couple pages, I just pasted all the troll romance exposition again into the author notes section underneath. Oh, you don't think I'll do it????????

The problem is that when the subject of troll romance is broached, our sparing human intellects instantly assume the most ingratiating posture of surrender imaginable. But we will do our best to understand regardless. Humans have only one form of romance. And though we consider it a complicated subject, spanning a wide range of emotions, social conventions, and implications for reproduction, it is ultimately a superficial slice of what trolls consider the full body of romantic experience. Our concept of romance, in spite of its capacity to fill our art and literature and to rule our individual destinies like little else, is still just that. A single, linear concept. A concept usually denoted by a single symbol. <3 Troll romance is more complicated than that. Troll romance needs four symbols. Their understanding of romance is divided into halves, and halved again, producing four quadrants: the FLUSHED QUADRANT, the CALIGINOUS QUADRANT, the PALE QUADRANT, and the ASHEN QUADRANT. Each quadrant is grouped by the half they share, whether horizontally or vertically, depending on the overlapping properties one examines. The sharpest dichotomy, from an emotional perspective, is drawn between RED ROMANCE and BLACK ROMANCE. RED ROMANCE, comprised of the flushed and pale quadrants, is a form of romance rooted in strongly positive emotions. BLACK ROMANCE, with its caliginous and ashen quadrants, is rooted in the strongly negative. On the other hand, the vertical bifurcation has to do with the purpose of the relationship, regardless of the emotions behind it. Those quadrants which are CONCUPISCENT, the flushed and caliginous, have to do with facilitating the elaborate reproductive cycle of trolls. Those which are CONCILIATORY, the pale and ashen, would be more closely likened to platonic relationships by human standards. There are many parallels between human relationships and the various facets of troll romance. Humans have words to describe relationships of a negative nature, or of a platonic nature. The difference is, for humans, those relationships would never be conceptually grouped with romance. Establishing those sort of relationships for humans is not driven by the same primal forces that drive our tendency to couple romantically. But for trolls, those primal forces involve themselves in the full palette of these relationships, red or black, torrid or friendly. Trolls typically feel strongly compelled to find balance in each quadrant, and seek gratifying relationships that each describes. The challenge is particularly tortuous for young trolls, who must reconcile the wide range of contradictory emotions associated with this matrix, while understanding the nature of their various romantic urges for the first time. Of course, young humans have this challenge too. But for trolls, the challenge is fourfold. When two individuals find themselves in the flushed quadrant together, they are said to be MATESPRITS. Matespritship is the closest parallel to the human concept of romance trolls have. It plays a role in the trolls' reproductive cycle, just as it does for humans. This is pretty obvious! Not much more needs to be said about this. Moving right along. When a pair of adversaries delve into this quadrant, they become each other's KISMESIS. As one of the concupiscent quadrants, it plays a role in procreation as well. There is no particularly good human translation for this concept. The closest would be an especially potent arch-rivalry. For instance, human players would never be able to adequately diagnose the relationship between the queen and her archagent. But troll players could immediately place it as a dead ringer for kismesissitude. They would think we were all pretty stupid for not getting it. And they would be right. Trolls have a complicated reproductive cycle. It's probably best not to examine it in much detail. The need to seek out concupiscent partners comes with more urgency than typical reproductive instincts. When the IMPERIAL DRONE comes knocking, you had better be able to supply genetic material to each of his FILIAL PAILS. If you have nothing to offer, he will kill you without hesitation. The genetic material - WITHOUT GOING INTO MUCH DETAIL - is a combinative genetic mix from the matesprit and kismesis pairs, respectively. The pails are all offered to the mother grub, who can only receive such precombined material. She then combines all of it into one incestuous slurry, and begins her brooding. This doesn't mean the initial combination was for naught, however. In the slurry, more dominant genes rise to the fore, while the more recessive find less representation in the brood. Especially strong matesprit and kismesis pairings yield more dominant genetic material. The more powerful the complement

THAT'S WHAT JUST HAPPENED BITCH.

> Alright, now you're DEFINITELY trolling us. Come on.

or potent the rivalry, the more dominant the genes. TROLL REPRODUCTION SURE IS WEIRD. We all take a moment to lament how pedestrian the human reproductive system is, and further lament that the phrase "incestuous slurry" is not a feature of common parlance in human civilization. This quadrant involves a particular type of three-way relationship of a black romantic nature. Falling on the conciliatory side, it has no bearing on the reproductive cycle, except for indirect ramifications. When two trolls are locked in a feud or some otherwise contentious relationship, one can intervene and become their AUSPISTICE. The auspistice mediates between the two, playing the role of a peace keeper, preventing the feud from boiling over into a fully caliginous rivalry. Since such lesser feuds are quite common among trolls, there is a significant need for auspisticing parties. Without them, too many ashen feuds would become caliginous, and begin to conflict with other exclusive kismesis relationships, leading to a great deal of social complexity and sore feelings (even more so than black romance usually involves). Without auspisticism, the result would be widespread black infidelity. The relationships each quadrant describes tend to be malleable, if not volatile, especially on the concupiscent half where more torrid emotions reside. It doesn't take much to flip a switch and transmute blackrom feelings to redrom, and vice versa. In many cases, one party will have red feelings while the other has black. But it will often be the case that one party's feelings will swap to match the other's, since there is no quadrant which naturally accommodates such a disparity. But thereafter, it's not uncommon for the two to toggle between red and black in unison now and then. These scenarios naturally result in both red and black infidelities. This sort of relationship volatility is why conciliatory relationships are an important part of troll romance. An auspistice can stabilize particularly turbulent relationships. If the auspistice fails to mediate properly, or has no interest in the role, or perhaps has different romantic intentions him/herself altogether, then the relationship often quickly deteriorates into one of an especially hostile and torrid nature. There are many outside factors and influences tugging and pulling these relationships in different directions, and unlike humans who have very orderly, simple, straightforward romantic relationships without exception, trolls exist in a state of almost perpetual confusion and generally have no idea what the hell is going on. Being confused by troll relationships is one thing we do have in common though. This quadrant presides over MOIRALLEGIENCE, the other conciliatory relationship. A reasonable human translation would be the concept of a soul mate, but in a more platonic sense, and with a more specific social purpose. Trolls are a very angry and violent race. Some are more hot-tempered and dangerous than others, to the extent that if left to their own devices, they would present a serious threat to society, or even to themselves. Such trolls will have an instinctive pale attraction to a more even-tempered troll, who may become their MOIRAIL. The moirail is obliged to pacify the other, to function as the better half. The two partners in a strong pale relationship will serve to balance and complement each other's emotional profiles, and thus allow their other relationships to be more successful. It's often ambiguous especially among young trolls whether a bond formed between an acquaintance is true moirallegence, or the usual variety of platonic involvement. Furthermore, romantic intentions of a more flushed nature can often be mistaken for paler leanings, much to the frustration of the suitor. But some pale pairings, as the one above, will be strikingly obvious to all who know them. God you just can't get enough of this can you! That would have been a great point for a transition out of this illustrated sociological study, but ok, if you insist. Now see, what's going on here is... It's perfectly simple. When the full matrix of troll romance is in action, we have... uh... Hey, why don't you figure it out! You should be an expert on all this by now anyway. Later our troll hero would try to explain this to our human hero, attempting to convey all the nuance of troll romance through a nearly verbatim recitation of the preceding excerpts. He would try to describe how rich and textured the troll romantic comedies were compared to the one dimensional schlock of our human cinematic counterparts. He would barely scratch the surface of Troll Will Smith's virtuosity with the delicate lattice of troll romance, as he would assist the bumbling fudgeblooded Troll Kevin James through the interwoven minefield-briarpatch of redrom and blackrom entanglements, all the while sifting through his own prickly romantic situation and ultimately learning the true meaning of hate and pity. But would they succeed before the imperial drone came knocking with his thirsty pails at the ready??? Yes, they would. But John didn't understand any of this because he's a moron, and he wouldn't shut up about his awful bullshit Earth movies. He would just go on and on and on about that garbage. But if there was one theme to be hammered through his thick skull, it would be the trolls' cultural preoccupation with romantic destiny. Yes, the romantic landscape is rife with false starts and miscues and infidelities, red and black. But every troll believes strongly that each quadrant holds one and only one true pairing for them, and it is just a matter of time before the grid is filled with auspicious matchups through the mysterious channels of TROLL SERENDIPITY. In short, their belief is that for each quadrant there exists a pair or triad of trolls somewhere in the cosmos that were... MADE FOR EACH OTHER.

AAAAAAAAAAAAAAAAAAAAAAAAAAAAAAAAAAAAAAAAAAAAAA
AAAAAAAAH
HA HA HA HA HA HA HA HA HA HA HA HA HA HA HA HA
HA HA HA HA HA HA HA HA HA HA HA HA HA HA HA HA
HA HA HA HA HA HA HA HA HA HA HA HA HA HA HA HA
HA HA HA HA HA HA HA HA HA HA HA HA HA HA HA HA
HA HA HA HA HA HA HA HA HA HA HA HA HA HA HA HA
HA HA HA HA HA HA HA HA HA HA HA HA HA HA HA HA
HA HA HA HA HA HA HA HA HA HA HA HA HA HA HA HA
HA HA HA HA HA HA HA HA HA HA HA HA HA HA HA HA
HA HA HA HA HA HA HA HA HA HA HA HA HA HA HA HA
HA HA HA HA HA HA HA HA HA HA HA HA HA HA HA HA
HA HA HA HA HA HA HA HA HA HA HA HA HA HA HA HA
HA HA HA HA HA HA HA HA HA HA HA HA HA HA HA HA
HA HA HA HA HA HA HA HA HA HA HA HA HA HA HA HA
HA HA HA HA HA HA HA HA HA HA HA HA HA HA HA HA
HA HA HA HA HA HA HA HA HA HA HA HA HA HA HA HA
HA HA HA HA HA HA HA HA HA HA HA HA HA HA HA HA
HA HA HA HA HA HA HA HA HA HA HA HA HA HA HA HA
HA HA HA HA!!!!!!!!!!!!!!!!!!!!!!!!

> AH: Recap, then?

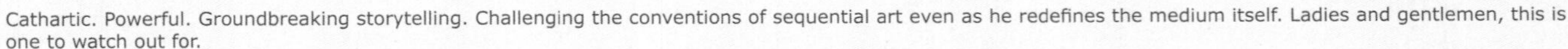
Cathartic. Powerful. Groundbreaking storytelling. Challenging the conventions of sequential art even as he redefines the medium itself. Ladies and gentlemen, this is one to watch out for.

Hmm.

Nah, I think we're good.

> AH: Reel it in.

Yeah ok. Guess I've trolled you guys enough.

Where were we? Oh yeah. Slick.

> SS: Move this along.

It's bad enough you had to watch this broad smooch a corpse and this kid bawl his eyes out once already, even if it was centuries ago.

NEXT.

This is, I think, the start of the tradition of me refusing to do recaps. Or only doing them in kind of a weird way, like typing in white text. They really were a pain to write. They were also kind of useless? Like, if you need them to follow along, then what are you even doing here? It was a bit defiant of me, I know. I often show quite the plucky, rebellious spirit when it comes to rejecting or mocking the very conventions and patterns which I myself established earlier. It's heroic, really. The last stretch of ten pages or so, if nothing else, go a long way toward making it clear that ultimately, the only true hero *and* villain of the story is me. Just the author against the whole world, and himself. So inspiring. Extra trivia: maybe it seems odd I'm wearing Kanaya's shirt, but it's just because I'm a Virgo, that's all. My aspect is also Space, just like hers. I took the test and everything.

Oh for the love of...

Why would they even DESIGN a button like that if it doesn't print the right advancement characters???

You are getting really tired of mashing the '=' key.

> SS: Type '====', then ==>

Maybe this joke loses something here. Because we (rightly, I think) decided to forgo using the ==> symbols in the books to advance to the next panel, to reduce clutter. After Hivebent began, the ==> symbol became ======>. The first one is a house-like shape, representing four players. The second represents twelve. The standard format keyboard only comes with the ==> button. Which is completely useless when it comes to Jack trying to advance the "story." So he has to kind of hack it, to his frustration. This isn't the only time I frustrate villain characters with badly designed interface constructs meant for viewing story events. The stunts I pull with Caliborn's viewing device are a masterstroke in author-on-OC antagonism. Of course, it's critical that I do this. Somebody needs to train the supreme villain in his evil ways. It might as well be the author.

This moon is different. It's very...

Purple.

And quiet.

Doesn't look like anyone here is awake yet.

Not like the yellow moon you were just dreaming about. Plenty of friends there, all up and around, making a racket.

It was fun for a while. Until you woke up with honey in your mouth, killed your lusus, saved a princess, and died.

Luckily you had a couple lives to spare.

Unshockingly, Sollux has two dream selves. He just used up one of them coming back to life. This makes the counts of Prospit and Derse dreamers among the trolls a bit lopsided. Aradia has... Hang on, I'll continue this on the next page, which actually shows the stuff...

Most other players only get one extra.

But you're kind of a special case.

> BOY.

Aradia intriguingly has no dream self at all. Or so it seems. She actually does have one, but her dream self is asleep, in the core of the Derse moon, lying on a Quest Slab. Her dream self has always been asleep, waiting for one very specific moment to wake up. The omission of Aradia's dream self here seems like a casual mystery, but it is not forgotten about at all. The topic is revisited during one of the more dramatic moments of the story. Aside from that, let's admire the full range of dream pajama ensembles here. What's your favorite? What is YOUR dreamsemblesona?

Huh?

> YOU THERE. RED AND BLUE EYE BOY.

> I REMEMBER THIS!

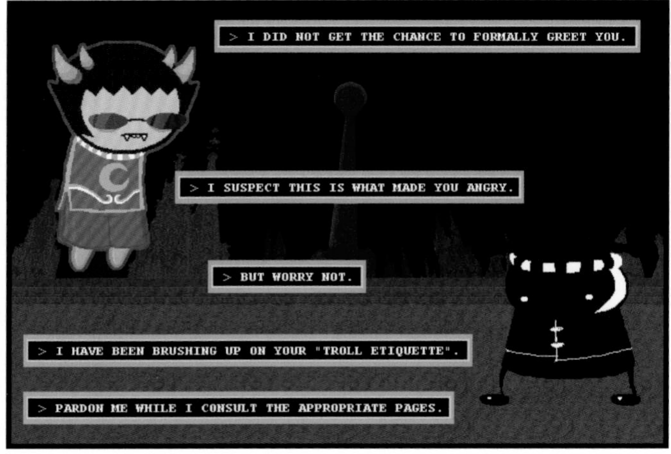

> IT WILL ONLY BE A MOMENT.

Just what you need. Another voice of the imminently deceased invading your head. Haven't they caused you enough trouble already?

Get iit out.

> TROLL ETIQUETTE SURE IS CONFUSING.

Clubs Deuce is Sollux's exile, because deuce, obviously. Even without the dual theme they share, the matchup seems fitting anyway for some reason. Here's some more weird, circular logic that CD is already familiar with from his stint in the Intermission: he thinks Sollux is mad because he was rude in person. But he's actually mad because in the future, CD is apologizing in Sollux's brain for being rude in person. And CD only assumed he was rude in person because Sollux got mad.

GET IIT OUT GET IIT OUT GET IIT OUT GET IIT OUT GET IIT OUT GET IIT OUT GET IIT OUT GET IIT OUT GET IIT OUT GET IIT OUT GET IIT OUT GET IIT OUT

> OH JEEZ.

> Sollux: Blast off.

CD is in a crab station. That's because Karkat is the player who got Sollux into the session, completing the chain. Remember the rules? The exile station is modeled after something related to the server player for the character the exile speaks to via console. For instance, WV, who was John's exile, was in a cork station on top of a big wine bottle, at the site of where Rose's house used to be. Never forget the rules. If you do, I'll just keep reminding you. In fact, I'll do that even if you don't.

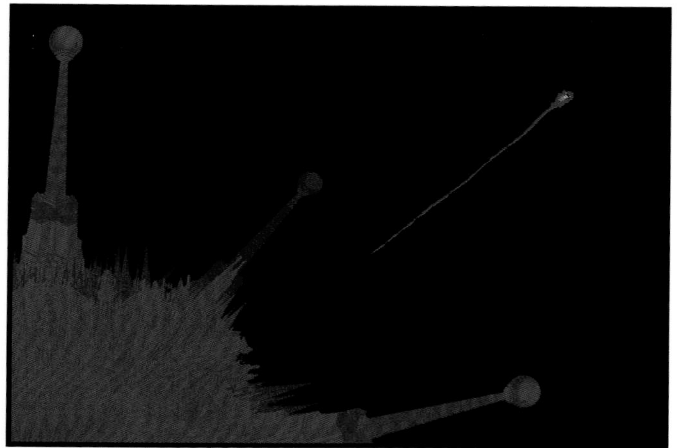

You've wasted enough time on sleeping and dying. You've got to get back to adventurin' while the adventurin's good. And also change out of these stupid pajamas.

PCHOOOOOOOOOOOOOOOOOOOO

> Sollux: Get back to adventurin'.

The revived MAGE OF DOOM returns to the LAND OF BRAINS AND FIRE for a surprise rendezvous with the WITCH OF LIFE.

Hey what the heck is going on in here???

> Vriska: Get back to adventurin'.

Sollux has the worst land. I don't think it's even a contest, really. It's just so completely terrible and unfun. Nothing but fire and brains everywhere. Dave has a similarly inhospitable land, a planet covered in lava, but at least there are cool industrial gear-based ruins and skeletal steel buildings to explore. Sollux just gets a bunch of gross brains harassing him. Just another shitty break for a guy stuck with a hard-luck arc. At least he gets a nice, new fish girlfriend here to help him out with brain-stabbing duty.

Somewhere on LOMAT, the Thief and the Page plunder the untold riches of innumerable pointless side-quests.

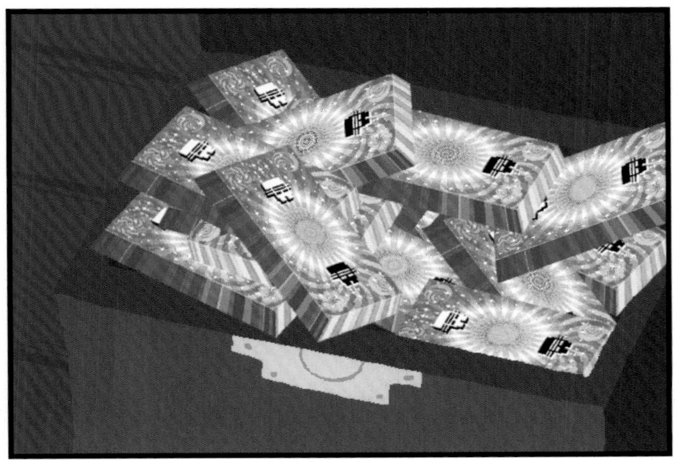

Despite their past dramas, Vriska and Tavros finally seem to be having a nice time here. As we skip ahead to these little snapshots of what things were like during their 612-hour session (about a month), we get a sense that things kind of settle into an agreeable rhythm for a bunch of characters who otherwise might be at odds with each other, as they work together to make progress. Of course, we don't know for sure what things were like with them. They were probably still arguing sometimes, and Vriska was surely being Vriska. But their session lasted long enough that there were days or weeklong stretches where certain activities probably started feeling routine, or even fun. In a way, their monthlong getaway to these fantastical settings probably felt a bit like a big group of friends going away to summer camp.

The Thief is proving useless. Completely unresponsive to commands.

You'll need to rely on someone else. Someone less stubborn.

Someone craftier.

> 8th exile: Type "=> SWITCH 2".

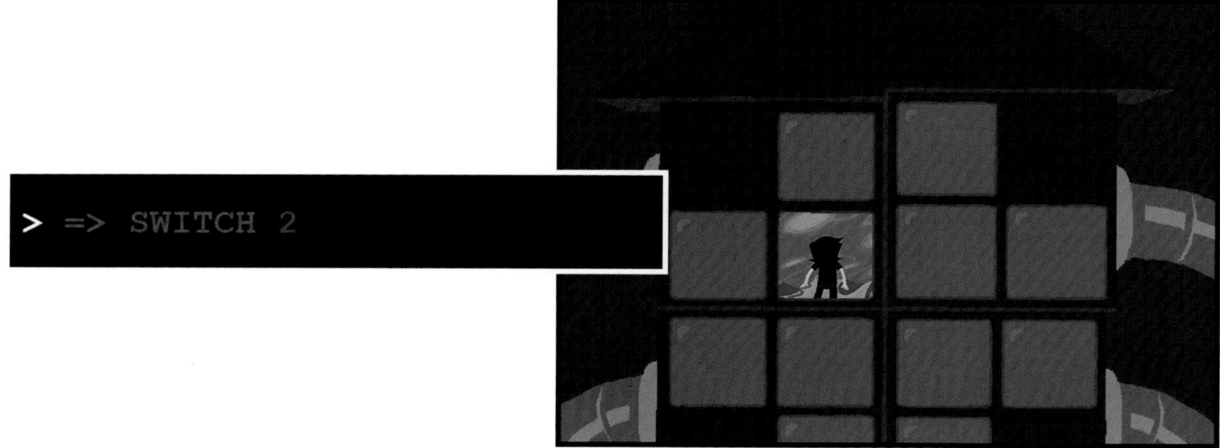

The 8th exile... Who could that be? I got snow idea, man.

While the KNIGHT OF BLOOD charges ahead, the SEER OF MIND remains behind to unravel the mysteries of the LAND OF THOUGHT AND FLOW.

> Seer.

> It is time.

It's the voice again.

You were wondering when she'd come back. This time you are ready for her.

> Terezi: Retrieve chalk.

While Sollux has the worst land, Terezi has one of the better ones. She's a Mind player, and so she has these trippy, pulsing synapses covering the sky. The synapses aren't just decorative; they seem to be active constructs relating to the aspect of Mind and are used that way graphically later on when she starts dabbling with her powers. They're actually somewhat similar to the clouds in Skaia. But while those clouds are windows into future or past events in Paradox Space, conveying "what you are seeing *will* happen, or *has already* happened," the synapses are windows into the many *potential* events and their offshoots in Paradox Space, conveying "what you are seeing *could* happen," and it's up to a Mind player to sift through those possibilities as they become more adept with their powers.

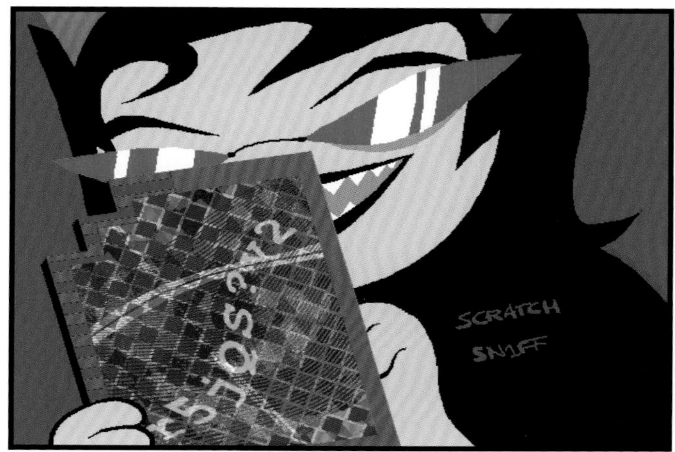

You search for the appropriate card through your SCRATCH AND SNIFF modus.

The card will be unmistakable. It is the one that smells like a fruity rainbow that makes you sneeze.

Even late in Hivebent, I'm still taking opportunities to stop and answer unasked questions like, "Wait, what was Terezi's modus? Did we ever see it?" So, yeah, it's a scratch and sniff modus, because she's blind and smells stuff, and also has a coin. Not a bad gag answer to that question, huh? Basically every troll modus is some form of gag relating to their character traits. The modus progression goes like this. First three kids: all data structure modi, very serious and mostly terrible. Jade: combo breaker, ridiculous board-game modi, establishing the precedent that a modus can be anything, there are no rules. Trolls: lots of silly joke modi after that, continuing the trend that they can be anything, even stupid things, and nothing really matters. The Alpha Kid modi mostly continue that trend too.

> Terezi: Inquire.

> To begin your mission.

> You must eliminate the archagent.

> Nepeta: Surely you must be adventurin' by now.

We already know that the queen exiles talk in this font, because the White Queen talked that way to Rose. So we definitely know who this is. This makes the Black Queen officially the exile for both Vriska and Terezi, which I think we can agree is a pretty good matchup. Terezi using her chalk here to communicate with her exile is a nice way to handle this scene so that the reader can observe their interaction. It does raise a question, though: why couldn't Terezi just answer the Queen verbally? Surely there's audio in those stations. I think the best answer is that Terezi just likes any excuse she can to use her chalk.

Why yes, as a matter of fact. It does appear that the ROGUE OF HEART has been keeping herself quite busy.

> Nepeta: Aggress.

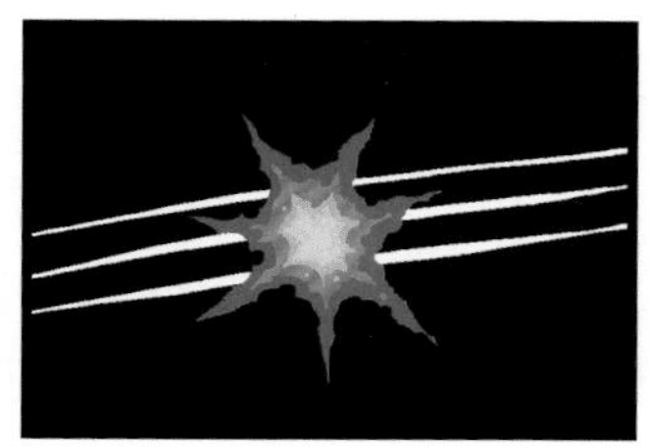

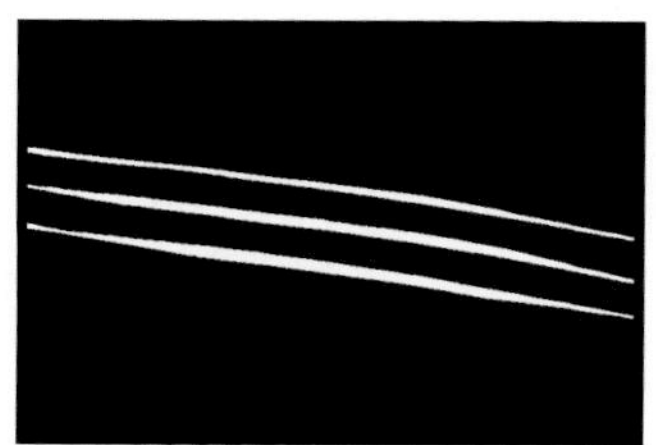

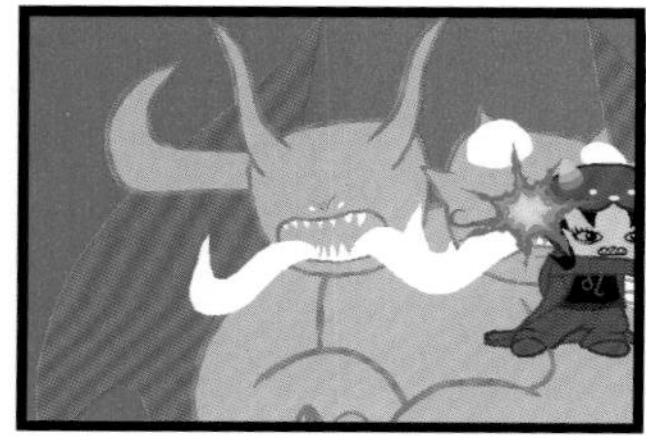

LOLCAT. I've already talked about this. What is there left to even say. I make no excuses for my crimes. I think I just really wanted to make this joke and warped the entire concept of her land around this idea, which is why it's so stupid. So that's why Nepeta, one of the explicit whipping-kids of the story, gets arguably the dumbest land, just like another whipping-kid, Sollux, gets unarguably the most awful land. Someone needs to swoop in to save these children from my horrendous decisions.

Wasn't this just a *Wolverine* cover? Anyway, Nepeta gets her badass moment. That's the only one, ever. Okay, that might not be true, but I don't really care.

My award-winning onomatopoeic instincts really shine through on many pages of *Homestuck*, few more than this one. What's Equius doing here, anyway? Looks like his robo-girlfriend ditched him already, leaving him to start planet-hopping and unite with his dear moirail. As spicy as that moment was between Aradiabot and Equius, after that it's implied there wasn't much depth to the relationship. Just kind of a weird fling. Much later, in one of the dream bubble mini-sprite games I believe, Aradiabot gives the impression that after their fling, she just kind of saw him as a gross dude she vaguely regretted letting anywhere near her long after that.

You inquire into whereabouts of the MAID OF TIME. The HEIR OF VOID has no idea where she went! She just disappeared.

> Equius: Get up and commence the adventurin'.

The underlings have been getting enormous lately. Must have been something one of those other clowns prototyped.

Speaking of clowns...

> Equius: Answer Karkat.

It does not appear to be a message from Karkat directed at you specifically.

He has just updated one of the many memos on the transtimeline bulletin board he set up a while ago. You've since no longer bothered keeping up with the endless and mostly incomprehensible communique.

But while checking the update, you can't help but skim through the first memo in the long sequence, which was written hours ago from your present perspective.

> Equius: Read first memo.

The whereabouts of the Maid of Time: she had her fun with this smelly oaf and then dumped him for good because she's got loads of time traveling to do. The huge, tendriled monster there is the prototyped Glubglub's influence. (Who, sadly, we never get to see as a sprite. Possibly because I didn't want to draw it.) And as long as this note is rambling about nothing in particular, the close-up of Equius's shades is pretty interesting to think about if you know the far future of the story. That is, a Void player wearing cracked shades that are strikingly reminiscent of the badly damaged state of the Furthest Ring, after Lord English starts rampaging through it, striking cracks that look like exactly that into the void itself. Equius is, oddly, a constituent part of English himself, it bears pointing out.

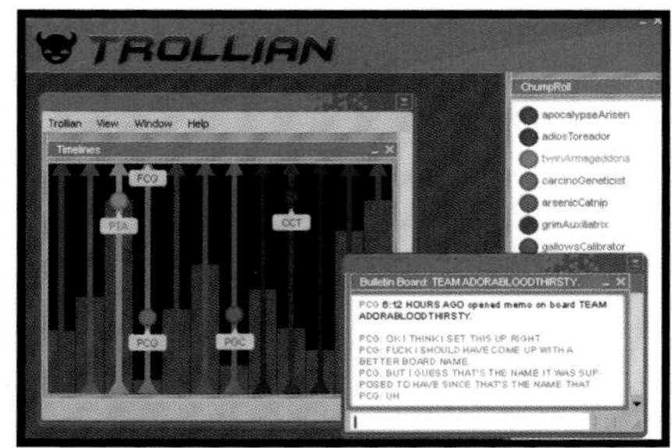

PAST carcinoGeneticist [PCG] **6:12 HOURS AGO opened public transtimeline bulletin board TEAM ADORABLOODTHIRSTY.**

~~~~~~

PCG **6:12 HOURS AGO opened memo on board TEAM ADORABLOODTHIRSTY.**

PCG: OK I THINK I SET THIS UP RIGHT.
PCG: FUCK I SHOULD HAVE COME UP WITH A BETTER BOARD NAME.
PCG: BUT I GUESS THAT'S THE NAME IT WAS SUPPOSED TO HAVE SINCE THAT'S THE NAME THAT
PCG: UH
PCG: I ALREADY READ.
PCG: WOW THAT PROBABLY WON'T MAKE ANY SENSE TO ANYBODY.
PCG: WHATEVER, IT'S JUST A STUPID NAME, LET'S JUST DO THIS.
PCG: THIS IS A PUBLIC BULLETIN USING TROLLIAN'S WEIRD TRANSTIMELINE FEATURES WHICH I DON'T EVEN REALLY UNDERSTAND YET.
PCG: BUT I'M GUESSING MIGHT BE USEFUL.
PCG: I'VE INCLUDED ALL TWELVE PLAYERS IN THE SUBSCRIPTION LIST SO YOU SHOULD ALL BE ABLE TO READ THESE MEMOS AT ANY TIME.
PCG: THAT IS, ALL THE MEMOS POSTED, PAST AND FUTURE. I THINK.
PCG: IT COULD GET PRETTY TEMPORALLY CONFUSING OBVIOUSLY. I'M GOING TO TRY TO KEEP THE MEMOS AS SIMPLE AND LINEAR AS POSSIBLE.
PCG: ALSO LET'S KEEP THIS A ONE-WAY-ONLY BULLETIN TO MAKE THIS AS SIMPLE AS POSSIBLE.
PCG: DO NOT REPLY TO MY MEMOS!!! THIS IS NOT A FUCKING CHATROOM, ASSHOLES.
PCG: IF YOU HAVE SOMETHING TO SAY TO ME IN RESPONSE TO A MEMO, MESSAGE ME IN PRIVATE AT THE APPROPRIATE POINT ON THE TIMELINE.
PCG: FIRST ORDER OF BUSINESS IS ABOUT THE TEAMS.
PCG: AS OF NOW, YOU SHOULD ALL BE AWARE THAT THERE IS REALLY ONLY ONE TEAM, AND WE ARE ALL WORKING TOGETHER.
PCG: AND BY "NOW" I MEAN TIME LOCAL TO ME AS OF WRITING THIS.
PCG: SO IF YOU'RE READING THIS IN THE PAST...
PCG: UH OK FIRST OF ALL, HOW DO YOU EVEN KNOW ABOUT THIS FEATURE ALREADY? SECOND WHY DIDN'T YOU FUCKING TELL ME.
PCG: WHATEVER I DIGRESS.
PCG: IF YOU'RE READING THIS IN THE FUTURE THEN WHO CARES, IT'S PROBABLY OLD NEWS TO YOU.
PCG: ACTUALLY NOW THAT I THINK ABOUT IT, WHAT'S SO SPECIAL ABOUT READING THIS IN THE FUTURE?
PCG: IT'S LIKE ANY BULLETIN BOARD, YOU POST STUFF AND IT SITS THERE FOR A WHILE AND PEOPLE IN "THE FUTURE" READ IT.

The introduction of "memos" as a new dialogue medium was a pretty exciting addition to the overall toolkit of character interaction. Mainly because it was the first venue that allowed for more than just two people to talk to each other at once. The result is the feeling of a messy chat room, rather than a direct message conversation. Except even messier, because this is where the characters begin to play around with the feature that lets them talk to each other across different points on the timeline. The net result of this, mostly, is just Karkat creating an almost infinite supply of new, self-fulfilling ways of owning himself in front of all his friends. This device was a great device to throw into the mix of later Act 5 action. Many good things were done with it, and it really shook the story out of some overly comfortable patterns of character interplay. I give it five stars. I mean, I give everything I do five stars. But this time, I give five stars to this particular five-star rating.
~~~~~~

PCG: HUH. BIG FUCKING DEAL I GUESS.
PAST gallowsCalibrator [PGC] 5:51 HOURS AGO responded to memo.
PGC: OH MY GOD K4RK4T!
PGC: WHO C4R3S!!!!! >:O
PCG banned PGC from responding to memo.
PCG: ANYWAY LIKE I WAS SAYING.
PCG: ONE BIG TEAM, OVER WHICH I HAVE ASSUMED TOTAL LEADERSHIP.
PCG: I WILL ASSUME THAT IT WILL CONTINUE TO STAY THIS WAY FOR THE DURATION OF OUR QUEST, AND THAT I WILL REMAIN AN IMPECCABLE LEADER FOR A SPAN OF HUNDREDS OF HOURS WHILE I GUIDE US ALL TO A STUNNING VICTORY.
PCG: IN FACT, I DON'T EVEN NEED TO ASSUME.
PCG: I BROWSED THROUGH THIS WHOLE BULLETIN IN ADVANCE, AND IT DOES APPEAR TO BE THE CASE. GO ME.
PCG: IN FACT, SINCE I'VE SEEN WHAT I WILL WRITE IN THE FUTURE, I WONDER WHAT IMPETUS I WILL HAVE FOR WRITING IT LATER WHEN I'M SUPPOSED TO?
PCG: I WONDER IF I COULD JUST COPY/PASTE IT... HOLD ON.
PCG: DAMN.
PCG: I GUESS THEY THOUGHT OF THAT? I DUNNO. I TRIED TO LOOK AT THE WHOLE BULLETIN AGAIN, BUT NOW THAT I'VE OPENED THIS ONE FROM THE BEGINNING, I CAN'T SEE THE WHOLE THING ANYMORE.
PCG: UNLESS I LOOK AT IT ON ONE OF YOUR COMPUTERS...
PCG: OR MAYBE IF YOU SEND ME LIKE A TEXT FILE OF IT? WOULD THAT CAUSE A PARADOX OR SOMETHING?
PCG: YOU KNOW WHAT, THIS IS SO STUPID.
PCG: I ACTUALLY REMEMBER READING ALL THIS SHIT LIKE A HALF HOUR AGO, AND NOW HERE I AM TYPING IT ANYWAY.
PCG: I PROBABLY CAN'T AVOID TYPING ANY OF THIS, HOW WEIRD IS THAT.
PCG: I HATE TIME TRAVEL.
PAST twinArmageddons [PTA] 0:34 HOURS AGO responded to memo.
PTA: eheheheheh KK iim ba2iically ju2t lmao here at thii2, WOW.
PCG: HOLY FUCKING SHIT, ARE YOU PEOPLE RETARDED.
PTA: dude don't worry ii wont fuck up your memo for long, ii ju2t cant beliieve thii2 wa2 the biig rea2on you wanted "future me" two help you open tho2e port2.
PTA: two ba2iically ju2t babble about paradoxe2 and argue wiith your2elf for hundred2 of page2 heheheh.
PCG: OK SO YOU'RE SAYING THIS FROM LIKE 5 HOURS IN THE FUTURE JUST TO GIVE ME A HARD TIME, NICE.
PCG: WELL THANKS FOR THE HELP, SO WHEN DO I BAN YOU, FUTURE BOY?
PTA: a few liine2 down, after ii pretend liike iim goiing two diie.
PTA: iim 2ure for a laugh on account of my iimmiinent banniing, FUCK how could you even do that two me.

Let's sift through the temporal structure here. Equius is currently reading this memo, which Karkat started six hours ago. This means that when Equius talks, he's the only one referred to as "current" (CCT). Everyone else here is some past version of themselves (PCG, PGC, PTA), even those who replied in the recent past, like Sollux did a half hour ago. Later, a future Karkat relative to Equius (FCG) chimes in from all the way toward the end of the session to remark on how embarrassing this all is. This is how all memos work, a complete quagmire of people scattered across the timeline tripping over each other, arguing, and complaining about how stupid the entire bulletin board is. It's a microcosm of Karkat's later trolling efforts of the humans, or at least a decent accidental beta test of the idea. Something he starts out with certain intentions for and tries to do in an organized way, but it completely backfires and devolves into pure chaos he has no control over, in an endless feedback loop of gratuitous self-owns.

PTA: 2o cold man.
PCG: ARE YOU REALLY STILL SORE AT ME FIVE HOURS LATER FOR RUNNING THAT VIRUS, GOD DAMN GET OVER IT.
PCG: IT WAS YOUR FUCKING VIRUS ANYWAY, YOU'RE TO BLAME.
PTA: eheh no bro we're cool about that, now future you ii2 connectiing wiith me 2o ii can enter the game.
PCG: OH YEAH?
PTA: yeah 2o thank2 for that fiive hour2 iin advance.
PCG: THIS IS BS ISN'T IT.
PCG: TROLLING ME FROM THE FUTURE, HOW JUVENILE CAN YOU GET.
PTA: no man iit2 true, we are bulge bumpiing pupa pal2 agaiin.
PCG: OH FUCK THIS CONDESCENDING FUTURE KNOWITALL ACT, WE AREN'T BUMPING SHIT, YOU ARE SO BANNED.
PTA: nooooooo, not the ban, it buuuuuuurn2, oh god hahahaha.
PTA: waiit.
PTA: oh god.
PTA: iit doe2 burn.
PTA: 2omethiing'2 wrong, iim 2eriiou2!
PTA: that horriible p2ychiic noii2e
PTA: the voiice2
PTA: they're all goiing two diie
PTA: oh 2HiiT iim bleediing
PTA: 2hiiiiiiiiiiiiiiiiiiit
PTA: thii2 ii2 bad
PTA: ii have two get her iin quiick
PTA: got two go
PCG **banned** PTA **from responding to memo.**
PCG: AND SO THE PORCINE HOOF BELONGING TO THE SWOLLEN HAG KNOWN AS LADY DESTINY HAS STOMPED ANOTHER THROAT.
PCG: WHICH ONE OF YOU FUCKERS IS NEXT?
PCG: NOBODY???
PCG: OK, GOOD.
PCG: ALTHOUGH I'M FAIRLY SURE I REMEMBER SOMEONE ELSE CHIMING IN BEFORE I CLOSED THIS MEMO.
PCG: YOU ADD DISORDERED SHIT RINSERS CAN'T KEEP YOUR LASCIVIOUS PRONGS OUT OF THE ROE HOLE, CAN YOU.
PCG: SOLLUX, FOR FUTURE REFERENCE, OR PAST REFERENCE OR WHATEVER
PCG: IF YOU WANT TO DO THAT KIND OF ROLEPLAYING, YOU CAN START YOUR OWN BULLETIN.
PCG: YOU CAN ALL ACT LIKE BRAINDEAD ASSWIPES IN YOUR OWN FESTERING FLAP OF PARADOX SPACE, FINE WITH ME.
PCG: EVERYONE WILL BE SO CONFUSED BY THE TIME PARADOXES, IT WILL DISTRACT THEM FROM HOW

Five hours from when Karkat types this, he's looking at dead Sollux on his monitor and probably remembering this memo exchange. Which, according to the laws of sadstuck, just makes the death all the more tragic. He thought Sollux was joking, then blocked him. Karkat seems to have a habit of doing this. Recall that he did basically the same thing when Tavros messaged him to tell him he was just paralyzed. There's kind of a sad conflict in Karkat's personality, where he genuinely cares deeply for all his friends but is so busy and so caught up in his own bullshit all the time that he obliviously glides right over the moments where they're actually in serious trouble.

AWFUL THEIR TERRIBLE HOBBIES ARE.
PCG: CHOOSE YOUR CLASSES NOW! LEVEL 69 NOOKSNIFFER IS UP FOR GRABS, WHO WANTS IT.
PCG: NO THAT'S NOT AN INVITATION FOR YOU FUCKING NERDS TO COME IN HERE AND CORRECT ME ON YOUR GODDAMN FAIRY ELVES.
PCG: JUST DO ME A FAVOR AND KEEP ME BANNED FROM THAT ONE OK.
PCG: I'LL RETURN THE FAVOR IF YOU NERD UP MY MEMOS, I SERIOUSLY CAN'T BELIEVE HOW MANY FUCKING NERDS ARE ON THIS TEAM.
PCG: JUST REMEMBER THIS IS MY PERSONAL PODIUM, A STUMP IF YOU WILL, FOR SOLE USE BY ME AS LEADER FOR IMPORTANT LEADERSHIP BUSINESS.
PCG: GOT IT?????????
FUTURE carcinoGeneticist [FCG] **612 HOURS FROM NOW responded to memo.**
FCG: GROAN.
FCG: THIS IS SO EMBARRASSING.
FCG: WHAT WAS I EVEN THINKING.
PCG: STFU!!!!!!!!!!!!!!!!!!!
PCG **banned** FCG **from responding to memo.**
PCG: OK, I'M FED UP WITH THIS MEMO, GONNA CLOSE IT OUT.
PCG: YOU'LL HEAR FROM ME AGAIN LATER WHEN I GOT SOMETHING ELSE TO SAY, I.E. JUST SCROLL DOWN YOU DOUCHE.
PCG: IT'S ALL RIGHT THERE ALREADY.
PCG: BECAUSE OF
PCG: TIIIIIIIIIIIIIIIIME TRAAAAAAAAAAAAAAAVEL!
PCG: I KNOW, RIGHT?
PCG: ANYWAY, JUST TO REITERATE:
PCG: FULL STEAM AHEAD
PCG: LEADER = ME FOREVER, OBVIOUSLY
PCG: PEACE THE FUCK OUT DBAGS
CURRENT centaursTesticle [CCT] RIGHT NOW responded to memo.
CCT: D --> I'd like to add to this useless memorandum
CCT: D --> That I still don't recognize the validity of your leadership
PCG: SWEET MOTHER GRUB'S OOZING VESTIGIAL THIRD ORAL SPHINCTER.
PCG: HOW CAN YOU PEOPLE BE SO STUPID.
CCT: D --> It may be true that we are all playing in the same session, but I see no reason to disband the former power structure
CCT: D --> Especially if it means instituting a tactical midget with a short fuse, a foul mouth, and paralyzing insecurity over the color of his b100d
CCT: D --> That's all I have to say
PCG: OH I HAVE A SHORT FUSE! THAT'S VERY FUNNY, YOU CAN ALMOST HEAR ME LAUGH OVER THE SOUND OF THE ROBOT YOU ARE PROBABLY BEATING TO DEATH.
PCG: OR DOING WORSE TO.

FCG's message from 612 hours in the future is the first data point that gives us a good sense of the span of the session length. We don't know that's the end of the session from this memo yet—that confirmation comes a bit later—but this at least gives us a sense of what the players are in for. Another odd rule of these memos is that, apparently, before you actually contribute to one you can scroll through the entire thing and read it, beginning to end, including all the messages made deep in the future. So someone who wasn't impatient like Karkat could actually take time to study it, understand everything that's going to happen, and then jump back into the discussion at certain predestined moments they've already read. But the moment you contribute, you sort of collapse the memo's waveform so to speak—you can't read anything after that and just have to fly blind like in an ordinary conversation. Naturally, Karkat gives the memo a half-assed skim before diving into composing it from the start with his blustering nonsense. Does this make perfect sense? Is it scientifically and logically AIRTIGHT? Well, maybe not. But it does lead to a lot of funny conversations.

PCG: HEY, YOU DO KISS YOUR ROBOTS, RIGHT?

CCT: D --> Uh

PCG: MIGHT AS WELL CLEAR THE AIR AS LONG AS WE'RE BROADCASTING THIS ACROSS THE ENTIRE SPACETIME CONTINUUM.

CCT: D --> Not usually

PCG: HAHAHAHAHAHAHAHAHA

PCG: THE FUNNY THING IS IN THE FUTURE EVERYONE WILL RECOGNIZE ME AS THE UNDISPUTED LEADER, EVEN YOU.

PCG: YOU WILL BE STANDING ON THE TIPPYTOES OF YOUR IDIOTIC METAL SHOES, TAKING DELICATE PURCHASE OF MY NUBBY HORNS AND HOISTING YOURSELF OVER MY HEAD TO PUT YOUR SWEATIEST TOUGH GUY SMOOCH UPON MY TWITCHING SPINE LUMP.

PCG: IT WILL BE TENDER AND DEFERENTIAL, LIKE A PAUPER KISSING A NOBLE'S RING.

PCG: JUST SCROLL DOWN, READ THE LOGS.

CCT: D --> Nowhere have I seen evidence of this

CCT: D --> Most of this is you from various points in time raving about nonsense and arguing with yourself

CCT: D --> Do you realize that here in the future, this bulletin has come to be regarded as something of a joke

CCT: D --> A lengthy piece of comedy, often quoted amongst ourselves in private moments of levity

CCT: D --> It seems I'm the one to inform you of this up front

CCT: D --> Which is likely why you persist with the ingratiating charade against better judgement

PCG: YOU'RE GETTING OFF ON THIS AREN'T YOU

CCT: D --> What do you mean

PCG: THIS EXCITES YOU, BEING THE TOUGH GUY AND PRETENDING LIKE YOU'RE PUTTING THE AWESOME LEADER IN HIS PLACE.

PCG: YOU'RE PROBABLY WORKING UP A GOOD SWEAT.

PCG: HOPE YOU ALCHEMIZED A BUNCH OF SPARE TOWELS.

PCG: HEY WHY DON'T YOU && THEM WITH YOUR SPONGEY BRAIN FOR EXTRA ABSORBENCY.

CCT: D --> How do you know about my perspiration problem

CCT: D --> I mean, aside from reading about it in this memo

CCT: D --> Wait

CCT: D --> Fudgesicles

PCG banned CCT from responding to memo.

PCG closed memo.

~~~~~~

Equius says "here in the future, this bulletin has come to be regarded as something of a joke," even though he's only six hours into Karkat's future while reading this. I guess a born snob will use literally any point of superiority to be snobby with. Blood color, being a few hours in the future, whatever. His observation is worth a laugh, but really, what he probably means is, he scrolled way ahead to see the future of the memo and has observed how many people in the memo mock him for it. He's already identifying more with people from weeks ahead in the timeline than with Karkat, who's only a few hours behind, just for the sake of giving him a hard time. In fact, even Karkat starts doing this to himself. Maybe more than anyone else.
~~~~~~

> Karkat: Begin another memo.

Terezi's side of this chalk conversation speaks pretty well for itself. Sometimes good conversations are just implied ones. It *seems* that the Black Queen may be assisting with her own Regisurp-exiling process? Or maybe, more accurately, with foreknowledge of her inevitable exiling, she's using her understanding of what happened to give even more instructions, to achieve something else she wants. Such as exiling the agents who betrayed her. Oh, there's another retcon oil splotch there on the crabtop. I haven't been pointing them out much. Maybe I don't want to spoil all the fun for you? (It's not even that fun.)

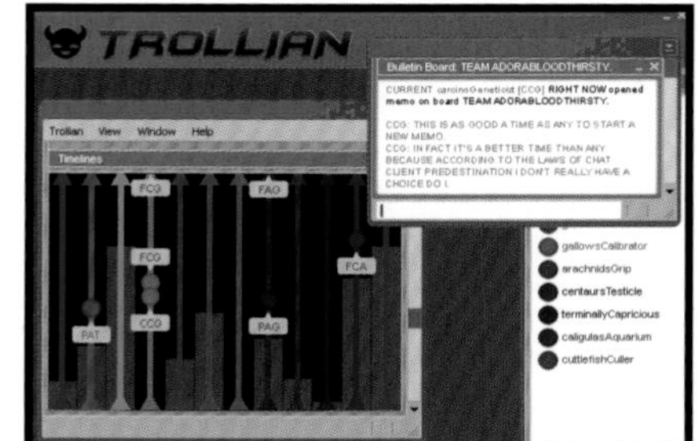

~~~~~~

CURRENT carcinoGeneticist [CCG] **RIGHT NOW opened memo on board TEAM ADORABLOODTHIRSTY.**

CCG: THIS IS AS GOOD A TIME AS ANY TO START A NEW MEMO.
CCG: IN FACT IT'S A BETTER TIME THAN ANY BECAUSE ACCORDING TO THE LAWS OF CHAT CLIENT PREDESTINATION I DON'T REALLY HAVE A CHOICE DO I.
CCG: FUCK.
CCG: IT DOESN'T MATTER, IT'S STILL A GOOD TIME TO DO IT.
CCG: PEOPLE, WE NEED TO GET ORGANIZED HERE.
CCG: SHIT IS GETTING SERIOUS.
CCG: WE ARE ABOUT TO EMBARK ON OPERATION REGISURP, A CUNNING PLAN DEVISED BY DOUBLE ARCHAGENT JACK NOIR TO EXILE THE BLACK QUEEN.
CCG: WE WILL NEED ALL HANDS ON DECK FOR THIS, EVEN THE IDIOTS.
CCG: AND ONCE AGAIN, A REMINDER
CCG: DO NOT TROLL ME IN THESE MEMOS FROM ANY POINT IN TIME OR IT'S AN INSTA-BAN.
CCG: ALSO A NOTE TO MY FUTURE SELF
CCG: IF YOU FEEL THE NEED TO SAY SOMETHING SMUG, DO ME A FAVOR AND SHOVE A THROB STALK IN IT.
CCG: JUST SIT THERE PATIENTLY AND WAIT FOR ME TO BECOME YOU IN THE DUE COURSE OF TIME, THUS IMPROVING YOUR INTELLECT DRASTICALLY.
CCG: OR, INTELLECTS PLURAL.
CCG: I FORGOT, THERE ARE A LOT OF YOU FUCKERS OUT THERE.
CCG: ALL OF YOU, JUST ZIP YOUR CHUTES. I MEAN SERIOUSLY, LIKE THERE'S NOTHING BETTER TO DO IN THE FUTURE???
CCG: IT'S THE FUTURE FOR GOD'S SAKE, A REALM OF ENDLESS FUCKING POSSIBILITIES.
CCG: NOW
CCG: BEFORE WE GET STARTED, LET'S TAKE A TOLL OF THE SITUATION AT THIS POINT IN TIME.
CCG: *MY* POINT IN TIME.
CCG: WHO'S IN SO FAR, WHO'S NOT, ETCETERA.
FUTURE caligulasAquarium [FCA] 3:11 HOURS FROM NOW responded to memo.
FCA: hey sorry for bustin in on the memo but i cant get ahold of you youre not answwerin
CCG: OH FOR FUCK'S SAKE.
FCA: gams advvice is fuckin useless all he told me wwas to enjoy a bevverage
CCG: NO, DUDE, DON'T DRINK THAT SHIT. IF IT WERE UP TO HIM WE WOULD ALL DRINK FAYGO AT ONCE IN SOME RITUALISTIC RAP CLOWN SUICIDE PACT.
CCG: BUT INSTEAD OF COMMITTING SUICIDE THE THING THAT WE ALL ACCOMPLISH IS BECOMING INSTANTANEOUS ASSHOLES WITH AWFUL TASTE.
FCA: i mean
FCA: its not evven that bad

The timeline diagram up there is really intense. Take a look at the gray bars and note how high they come up. That shows when each player entered the session. Karkat first, then Terezi, so they're the lowest (so low, they're below the edge of the window). From Karkat's (CCG's) current frame of reference, everyone but Sollux, Eridan, and Feferi have entered. I can ALMOST guarantee that all of those bar heights were carefully considered so as not to produce continuity snags. I remember making these little memo Trollian diagrams as if the slightest error by even a pixel width was an unconscionable act of carelessness. The character dot-markers are all pretty well-placed too. Shouldn't I be winning some sort of award for this shit? The award they give guys who discover the most innovative and perplexing ways to waste their time. That's the one I want, give it to me.
~~~~~~

FCA: its just soda but wwhatevver this isnt the point
CCG: THIS ISN'T THE VENUE FOR AIRING YOUR FUTURE PROBLEMS, COUNT SEA DIPSHIT.
FCA: i knoww i knoww
FCA: its just
FCA: i got a problem
FCA: wwith feferi
FCA: and im really kinda sittin here in bad shape about it emotionally speakin
CCG: OK, WELL
CCG: I GET THAT, I HEAR YOU BRO
CCG: BUT THIS IS STILL NOT THE RIGHT PLACE FOR THIS SO I'VE GOT TO BAN YOU.
CCG **banned FCA from responding to memo.**
CCG: BUT SERIOUSLY JUST GET IN TOUCH WITH ME IN PRIVATE ABOUT IT, OK MAN?
CCG: WE'LL GET YOUR SHIT STRAIGHTENED OUT.
CCG: OK.
CCG: IS EVERYBODY GOOD?
CCG: JUST GONNA SIT HERE FOR A MINUTE, LOCAL TIME, AND SEE IF ANYONE ELSE HAS ANY SHIT THEY WANT TO SCRAPE OFF THEIR BULGE ON TO MY CLEAN NUTRITION PLATEAU.
CCG: NOBODY?
CCG: GREAT, WONDERFUL.
CCG: I NOW OFFICIALLY DECLARE THE NONSENSE PORTION OF THIS MEMO TO BE OVER.
CCG: THIS DECREE SHALL BE BINDING AND LASTING.
CCG: BACK TO PLANNING REGISURP.
CCG: BEAR DOWN EVERYBODY, THIS IS FUCKING IMPORTANT, THERE IS A QUEEN ON THE LOOSE AND WE'VE GOT TO SHOW A BITCH THE DOOR.
FUTURE arachnidsGrip [FAG] 609 HOURS FROM NOW responded to memo.
FAG: ::::D
CCG: UN BE FUCKING LIEVABLE.
FAG: Kaaaaaaaarkat!
FAG: I'm sorry!
FAG: 8ut do you have any idea how funny this thing is? I mean this whole thing???????? I can't stop laughing!
CCG: HEY CAN FUTURE YOU MIND-PREVENT ME FROM HITTING THE BAN BUTTON?
CCG: I'M GENUINELY CURIOUS! GO AHEAD, TRY TO STOP ME I DARE YOU.
FAG: I'm not going to try, I'm just here to say this whole thing is ridiculous.
FAG: We didn't really need you to pretend to 8e a little angry general to get any of this done.
FAG: We kicked the queen out of there no sweat! It was easy. In fact, I did most of the work myself, right 8efore I found all the treasure and scaled all the rungs.
CCG: OH, ALL OF THEM YOU SAY?
CCG: FASCINATING.
CCG: HEY FORGET THE BAN BUTTON, USE YOUR MIND POWERS TO HELP ME LOCATE THE DESPERATELY ATTEMPT TO GIVE A SHIT BUTTON. WHOOPS WE BOTH FAILED, IT DOESN'T EXIST.

Karkat seems genuinely sympathetic and regretful that this is neither the time nor place to bro out with Eridan over his romantic problems. He truly enjoys hashing such things out and being there for his friends when they have quadrant issues. This is one reason why it's almost impossible to dislike him, even though he's constantly shouting and practically never stops talking. Even Vriska can't help but like him. She logs in from way in the future here basically just to offer some expressions of endearment, in her way. The demeanor that many of his friends have toward him almost makes it seem like they regard him as sort of a cute pet.

FAG: Hey, I'm gone. I just think you should relax.
FAG: You were wound up so tight through the whole adventure, and now here in the present you're a8out to explode. It's insuffera8le!
CCG: EVERYBODY, DID YOU HEAR THAT?? SUPERFUTURE VRISKA HAS AN IMPORTANT LIFE LESSON FOR US ALL.
CCG: WE DON'T HAVE TO WORRY ABOUT OUR PRESENT RESPONSIBILIES AND OBLIGATIONS!
CCG: BECAUSE AS IT TURNS OUT, IN THE FUTURE ALL THAT STUFF ALREADY HAPPENED. WE'RE OFF THE FUCKING HOOK!
CCG: TIME TO RELAX. LET'S ALL CRAWL INTO OUR COCOONS AND GET BUSY STIMULATING OUR AUTOEROGENOUS SHAME GLOBES.
CCG: FIRST ONE TO START A WANK FIRE GETS A SHINY BOONDOLLAR.
CCG: THIS IS AN ORDER FROM YOUR LEADER.
FAG: Hahahahahahahaha.
CCG **banned FAG from responding to memo.**
CCG: LATER, FAG.
CCG: TOO BAD THE ACRONYM WASN'T "HAG" INSTEAD, IT WOULD HAVE SUITED YOU MUCH BETTER.
CCG: INSTEAD OF THAT NONSENSE WORD
CCG: MAYBE ITS ASSOCIATION WITH YOU WILL COLLOQUIALLY CAUSE IT TO TAKE ON A NEGATIVE CONNOTATION, WHAT DO YOU THINK?
CCG: MAYBE FAG WILL BE "THE NEW BURN!" EVEN THOUGH IT REALLY MEANS NOTHING IN OUR LANGUAGE.
CCG: I DON'T KNOW, THIS IS STUPID, FORGET IT
CCG: OK I'M RAMBLING HERE, I'M AWARE OF THAT.
CCG: FUTURE ME, DON'T YOU FUCKING DARE WEIGH IN ON THIS, I KNOW WHAT YOU'RE THINKING.
CCG: IF I WERE FUTURE ME, WHICH I GUESS I AM, I WOULD READ THIS AND BE ALL OVER IT, LIKE DAMMIT KARKAT WHAT DO YOU THINK YOU'RE DOING.
CCG: GET TO THE POINT.
FUTURE carcinoGeneticist [FCG] **0:20 HOURS FROM NOW responded to memo.**
FCG: YEAH PRETTY MUCH.
CCG **banned** FCG **from responding to memo.**
CCG: SO I'M SAYING IT TO MYSELF ALREADY HERE AND NOW, SO I WON'T HAVE TO LATER, GOT IT YOU TRENCHANT BACKBITING PRICKS?????
CCG: DAMN, I'M LOSING MY TRAIN OF THOUGHT.
CCG: MAYBE I'LL PICK IT UP AGAIN IN A FRESH MEMO LATER.
CCG: I DON'T KNOW IF THAT'S RIGHT THOUGH, BECAUSE I VAGUELY REMEMBER THIS ONE BEING LONGER THAN THIS.
PAST adiosToreador [PAT] **0:38 HOURS AGO responded to memo.**
PAT: hEYY,
CCG: OH SON OF A BITCH.
PAT: i THOUGHT,
PAT: sINCE IT LOOKS LIKE, yOU'RE SAYING YOU'RE OUT OF IMPORTANT MEMO STUFF TO SAY,
PAT: uHH,
PAT: mAYBE YOU COULD HELP ME, hERE,

Listen. That just HAPPENED to be the three letter abbreviation for Future arachnidsGrip, okay? It's not like I specifically went out of my way to make this word appear on this page a whole bunch of times. Karkat simply offers some metacommentary on the word, because it kind of jumps out, doesn't it? What, are you going to sit there and tell me that you would have made the choice not to bring anyone's attention to it at ALL? Oh, what's that you say, smart guy? You probably wouldn't have even made *Homestuck* in the first place? Well aren't YOU special then. Anyway, Karkat wraps it up with some words to live by: "OK I'M RAMBLING HERE, I'M AWARE OF THAT." I'm copying this statement here as a reminder to get these words tattooed on myself some day.

PAT: sINCE i DON'T KNOW WHERE YOU ARE NOW, bUT MAYBE HELP ME,
PAT: aBOUT A THING THAT HAS TO DO WITH A GIRL,
PAT: lIKE,
PAT: a ROMANCE THING, yOU MIGHT KNOW ABOUT,
CCG: YOU PEOPLE ARE IMBECILES.
CCG: ALL OF YOU.
CCG: I AM NOT POSTING THESE MEMOS TO COUNSEL YOU ON YOUR PAST AND FUTURE DATING PROBLEMS!!!!!!!!!!!!!!!!
CCG: WHY ARE YOU ALL SUCH BASKET CASES. I DON'T EVEN KNOW WHAT TO SAY ANYMORE.
PAT: sORRY,
CCG: SHOULD I BAN YOU? WHAT'S EVEN THE POINT ANYMORE! ONE OF YOU STOOGES WILL BE RIGHT ON THE LAST ONES HEELS WITH ANOTHER SOB STORY.
CCG: JUST
CCG: HURRY UP AND TELL ME WHAT YOUR PROBLEM IS BRO.
PAT: oKAY,
PAT: i'M SORT OF, lYING ON vRISKA'S FLOOR RIGHT NOW,
PAT: lIKE, iN HER BLOCK,
PAT: lYING DOWN,
PAT: uHH, yOU KNOW, bECAUSE i CAN'T WALK,
CCG: OH NO SHIT REALLY???
CCG: YOU CAN'T BE SERIOUS, WHEN DID THIS HAPPEN.
PAT: uH, yEAH, aNYWAY,
PAT: sHE TRIED TO KISS ME,
PAT: wELL, sHE DIDN'T TRY, sHE ACTUALLY DID,
PAT: aND THEN, kIND OF DROPPED ME,
PAT: aND ALSO WE ARE WEARING COSTUMES,
PAT: wOW, i'M NOT EXPLAINING THIS WELL,
CCG: THIS IS SO FUCKED UP, WHAT HAVE YOU GOTTEN YOURSELF INTO.
PAT: aND NOW, tO MAKE IT,
PAT: uHHHHH,
PAT: a LOT WEIRDER,
PAT: tHERE IS AN ANGRY VOICE IN MY HEAD,
PAT: i DONT THINK IT'S rUFIO THIS TIME,
PAT: rUFIO'S NOT THAT ANGRY,
PAT: hE'S ALSO IMAGINARY,
PAT: lIKE, a FAKE MADE UP FRIEND,
PAT: yOU KNOW, lIKE,
PAT: tHE WAY FAIRIES ARE, }:(
CCG: GOD, ACTUALLY I REMEMBER READING THIS BULLSHIT.
CCG: OR SKIMMING IT AT LEAST.
CCG: HOW COULD I FORGET???
CCG: MORE LOONEYBLOCK THEATER, AND HERE I AM DRAWING THE CURTAINS FOR YOU GUYS LIKE A DOPE.

Karkat's memos start out as attempts to bring order and regimentation to their "strategy" as guided by the "leader" of the party, which nobody takes seriously at all, and they quickly devolve into forums for romantic counseling, stupid bickering, and friendship bonding. In other words, a smaller sketch of Karkat's arc in totality. Another good thing about memos is that, since literally anyone can jump in from any point in the timeline, there are all these moments in Hivebent we've already seen that these responses can reference, adding a little more dimension to some of those moments. For instance, we really had no idea that after Vriska kissed Tavros, he spent the next ten minutes or so lying on the floor while texting Karkat for romantic advice, in a chat environment that Vriska herself is also privy to. This is a big reason why the memos are good, and more generally speaking, why including what I'm gonna call "conversational time travel" is a really interesting and dynamic device for telling stories and drafting comedic scenarios. Consider, after just a couple memos, how much potential they have displayed already? The mind reels imagining all the things you can do in fiction with such a dialogue format.

PAT: aNYWAY, i THINK VRISKA IS UPSET ABOUT IT, aND SHE'S NOT TALKING OR ANYTHING,
PAT: wHAT DO i DO,
CCG: OK WELL, I CAN ADVISE YOU AND STUFF
CCG: BUT YOU DO REALIZE THIS IS A PUBLIC BULLETIN.
CCG: WE SHOULD BE HAVING THIS CHAT IN PRIVATE.
CCG: EVERYONE CAN READ THIS, EVEN HER.
CCG: I MEAN FUCK, SHE WAS *JUST HERE* TALKING YOU DUMMY!
PAT: i KNOW, i READ THAT,
PAT: bUT,
PAT: tHAT'S FUTURE HER, wHICH,
PAT: dOESN'T SEEM SO BAD,
PAT: mAYBE FUTURE HER CAN READ THIS, aND,
PAT: i GUESS,
PAT: kNOW i'M SORRY ABOUT IT,
PAT: i DIDN'T MEAN TO HURT HER FEELINGS,
CCG: WELL, FINE, IF YOU WANT TO BROADCAST A TRANSTIMELINE APOLOGY THEN FINE.
CCG: BUT YOU SHOULD REALIZE THE FUTURE IS KIND OF A WIDE OPEN THING, I MEAN SHE COULD READ THIS LIKE TWO MINUTES IN THE FUTURE AS WELL AS 600 HOURS.
CCG: AT THAT POINT YOU WOULD ESSENTIALLY BE TALKING TO PRESENT HER, COMPLETELY DEFEATING THE PURPOSE OF YOUR SPINELESS MESSAGE IN A BOTTLE APOLOGY.
PAT: oH,
PAT: yEAH,
PAT: i DIDN'T, rEALLY THINK OF THAT,
PAST arachnidsGrip [PAG] 0:08 HOURS AGO responded to memo.
PAG: Hi.
CCG: AHAHAHAHAHAHAHAHAHAHAHAH.
PAG: Karkat, shut up! This does not concern you.
CCG: OK WHATEVER. MY MEMO, BUT WHATEVER.
PAT: uH, wOW,
PAT: hI,
PAG: Tavros, it's ok. Really.
PAG: So you don't feel that way a8out me! That's fine. I shouldn't have expected any different.
PAG: I can deal with it! I am not a wimp like you. I roll with 8ad 8r8ks all the time. No 8iggie.
PAG: In fact, I already have dealt with it. I was over here dealing with it while you were over there on the floor fooling around with your computer after a cute girl tried to kiss you for some reason.
PAG: As it turned out, fooling around with your computer to........
PAG: Go cry on future Karkat's shoulder a8out this????????
PAT: uM,
PAT: yEAH,

Karkat is far from being a master of time. If anything, he may actually be sort of a numbskull with regard to the aspect. But since he's charging blindly into this mad quest which by its nature involves so many time shenanigans, it kind of forces him to be introspective and sometimes actually a bit insightful about the nature of time. He has to think about what the future really means. It's "kind of a wide open thing," happening in a few years or a few minutes. When you start seeing future versions of other people and yourself as legitimately different, discretely isolated personas, it conjures certain philosophical problems, which he's constantly grappling with. The further the future is from the present, the more distinct that separate version of a person is. Ideas like this, and Karkat's unabashed floundering with them, start threading into bigger themes of the story, such as, what is a person, and what constitutes the "self"? Is it an ideal? A composite of ideals? The result of a composite of ideals and a set of specific choices? Clearer understanding of a single aspect, Time, actually starts deepening one's understanding of the concept of self. Does greater understanding of other aspects allow this as well? The story answers this later on.

PAG: Hahahaha. You are a str8nge and funny 8oy, Tavros.
CCG: OH GOD
CCG: THIS IS
CCG: COMPLETELY HILARIOUS.
CCG: NOW I SEE WHY EVERYONE HAS BEEN RIPPING ON MY MEMOS.
PAG: Karkat I said shut the fuck up!!!!!!!!
PAG: Anyway, though totally unnecessary, your apology is accepted.
PAT: oKAY,
PAG: Now pick yourself up off the floor so we can go wring some fucking treasure out of this misera8le magic rock!
PAT: yEAH, i'LL TRY,
PAG: Actually, never mind, I'll 8e over there to help you with that too, kind of like I do with everything.
PAG: Just lie still and try not to start crying or anything, and w8 a few minutes for your timeframe to catch up with mine.
PAT: uH,
PAT: wHAT,
PAG: Exactly! I aaaaaaaam smarter than you. You see? You're learning!
CCG: FUCK, ENOUGH ALREADY.
CCG: THERE, GREAT, ANOTHER HAPPY COUPLE
CCG: IN WHATEVER HIDEOUS QUADRANT THIS BATSHIT PAIRING WILL SUSTAIN.
CCG: NOW OFF YOU GO.
CCG **banned** PAT **from responding to memo.**
CCG banned PAG from responding to memo.
CCG: HOLY HELL.
CCG: THIS IS EXHAUSTING.
CCG: I DON'T EVEN KNOW WHAT I WAS TALKING ABOUT ANYMORE.
CCG: OK, MAYBE I'LL TAKE A MINUTE TO COLLECT MY THOUGHTS AND GET BACK ON TOPIC HERE.
FUTURE carcinoGeneticist [FCG] **609 HOURS FROM NOW responded to memo.**
FCG: NO YOU WON'T.
FCG: THIS ONE WAS PARTICULARLY NAUSEATING IN RETROSPECT, I'M SHUTTING THIS DOWN.
FCG **banned** CCG **from responding to memo.**

FCG **closed memo.**

~~~~~~

> HEY RUNT

I wonder what Future Karkat specifically found so nauseating about this memo in particular? Seems like Vriska and Tavros had something bordering on a constructive conversation here. He's likely just reacting with disgust to his own contributions. This is like a guy who, during a bout of depression, scrolls through old chatlogs or emails and beats himself up about them. It's a fair read on Karkat's character if you want to say he suffers from depression. But then, so many of these kids do, don't they? The condition of being young and growing up is an inherently depressive undertaking, hence why so much of *Homestuck* is the way it is. Depression is really common, and I don't think you can swing a dead cat without smacking someone who is currently or has at some point suffered some form of it. Maybe the largely and almost universally depressive journey from childhood to adulthood sets people up for patterns of negative expectation for the rest of their lived reality, which then keep playing themselves out. And so it goes, the specter of depression seeming to haunt people for all time to come. I don't know, this ain't clinical, and I'm no sadness doctor. I'm just another schlub ruminating on what it means to be a person, using a crude website as a scratch pad for such reverie. Maybe I'll finally figure it all out by the time I write the Final Author Note for these books. I'll let you know if I do.
~~~~~~

> I SAID GET YER ASS UP AND GO KISS THE GIRL YOU PIPSQUEAK

You are having trouble bringing yourself to get up and kiss the girl.

> YOU KISS THAT GIRL THIS INSTANT

> ======>======>======>

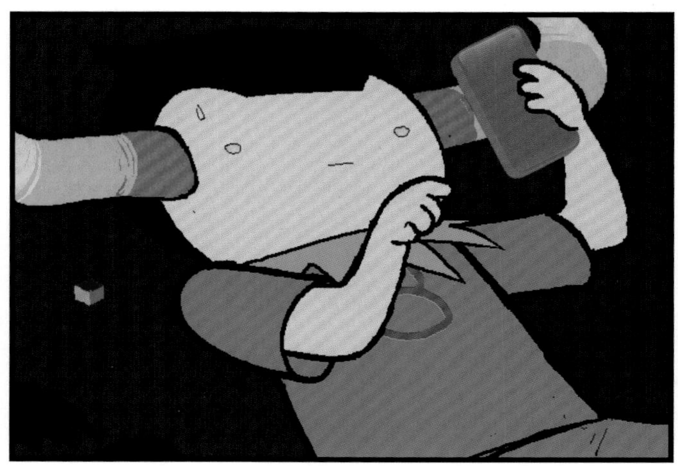

You cannot do it. You cannot kiss the girl.

> Thief.

The Midnight Crew as exiles for trolls serve widely varying roles for their players, supporting or antagonistic, parental or friendly. Heart Boxcars just wants to be Tavros's overbearing, thuggish wingman. Really wants him to go for that kiss. It makes sense that he wants to help Tavros out with his red quadrant, since HB is the heart-suited member of the gang. I'm sure I considered having all exiles work this way, but it doesn't end up being that literal, because, ehhh. It probably felt not worth shoehorning in a precise one-to-one correlation where HB would help his kid with redrom, SS with blackrom, etc. Their influence is looser than that. SS goes on about how much he hates all these kids, and CD tries to be vaguely conciliatory toward Sollux. Close enough.

> You will need to be strong.

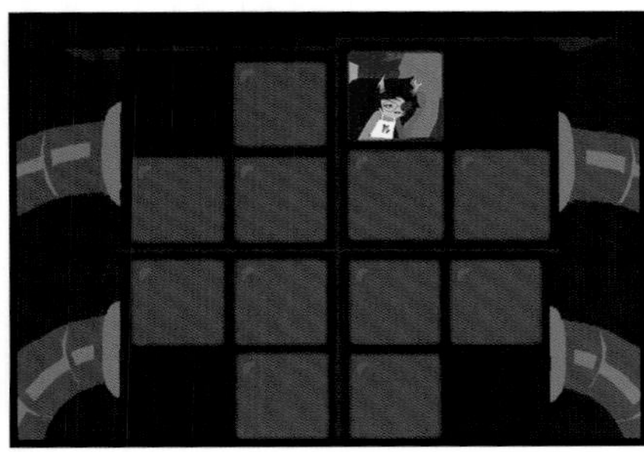

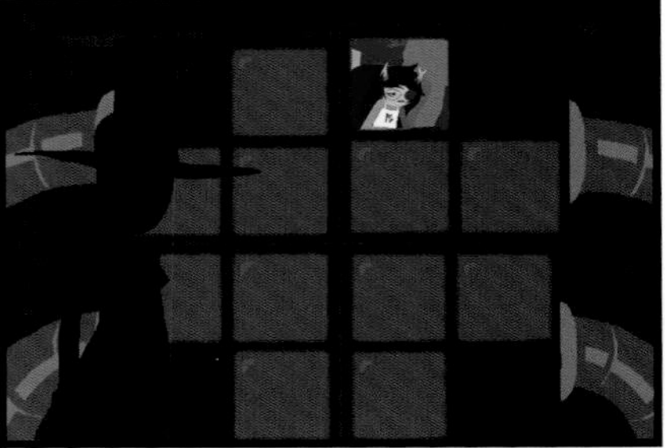

And in time, though prone to distraction and obstinacy, she would.

But not alone.

Snowman tries to talk to Vriska first but has to wait for her to get over this silly roleplay nonsense with Tavros. So she hits up Terezi, then comes back when the coast is clear. She likes both the Scourge girls, but Vriska clearly is her favored daughter. Can't say I blame her. To her, Vriska's like... What's the waifu equivalent of a daughter? Wait, that was a weird question, never mind. I like to think that she counsels Vriska a little on her broken-heart matters right after this. I can't imagine Snowman having anything but raw contempt for Tavros and the idea that he and her beloved Scourge daughter could ever be a couple. She probably helps Vriska understand important things such as: you don't need this complete fool in your life. He's utterly beneath you, and someday perhaps you'll find the sense to run a lance through his chest. Maybe I'll even covertly arrange for you to come into possession of my own lance for this purpose so that you do not forget my advice.

To bring every circle closed, her partner and rival would have to be guided in tandem. The Thief and the Seer were to serve as twin lashes of the scourge cracked by a quasiroyal against her own former kingdom to settle a score. To make him pay. Scourge's black inches would rip red miles through Derse, and the bright rivers gushing from its wounds would wash her mutineers down the drains of exile. In time they would have to answer for their treason.

Patience would be necessary. But then, she'd recently come into all the time in the universe.

I dunno about any trivia for this page. I already said stuff about this. She helps boot her whole kingdom of traitors outta the session so she can eventually torment them all in the Felt mansion to get her revenge. Anything else to add here? Sorry, I'm too distracted by this badass drawing of Snowman. You agree, right? Word.

> Snowman: Continue briefing.

> Find the ring before he does.

> And then,

Terezi never met a quiet, mild-mannered reptile she didn't have an overpowering urge to string up. Wait. We never actually get to see her interact onscreen with the real, live consorts of her land. I hope she didn't... DEAR GOD. Okay, I'm changing the subject. Snowman instructs Terezi to find the ring she left behind and destroy it so Jack can't use it. This sounds like just a preventive move to avoid the Jack disaster that happens to the human session, and it is. But what she doesn't say is, you need to destroy the ring to win the game anyway. Both rings, actually. Got to throw 'em in a big volcano. Act 7 shows the whole deal quite vividly.

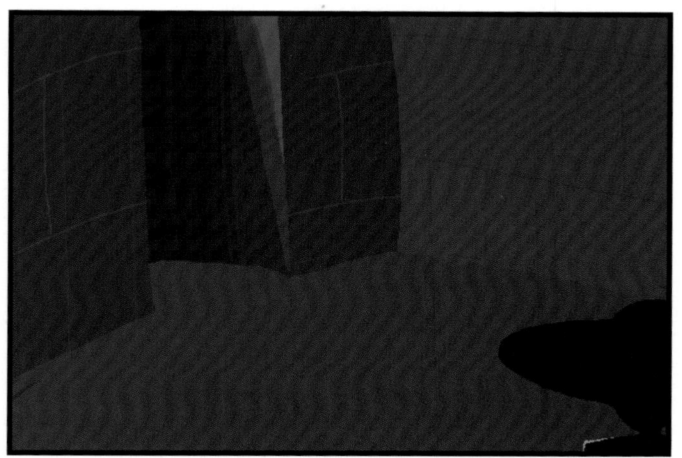

This is the exile station that landed where Kanaya's hive used to be. How do we know? It looks like her lusus. It's the station that shows Vriska by default, because Kanaya is Vriska's server. Remember? The tunnel goes up and comes out the right eye. Projecting a beam of light. Wait, what's with this Sans *Undertale* shit? Don't ask me, this was five years before that game came out.

> Centuries ago...

And yet, right now...

The SYLPH OF SPACE was able to vacate the impact site with several features of her buried landscape in tow. She sits atop her session's dormant FORGE.

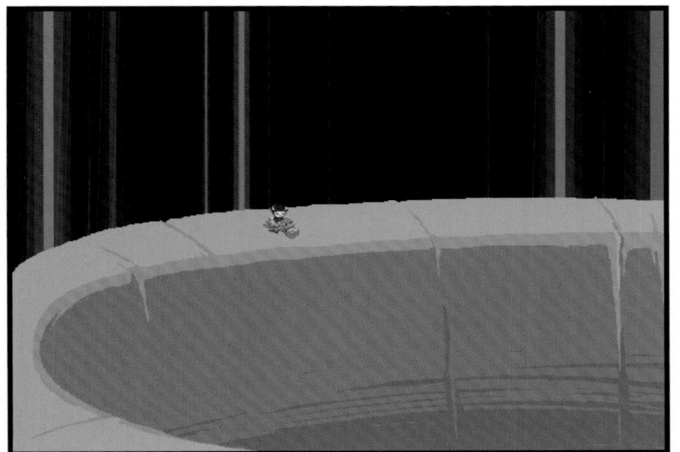

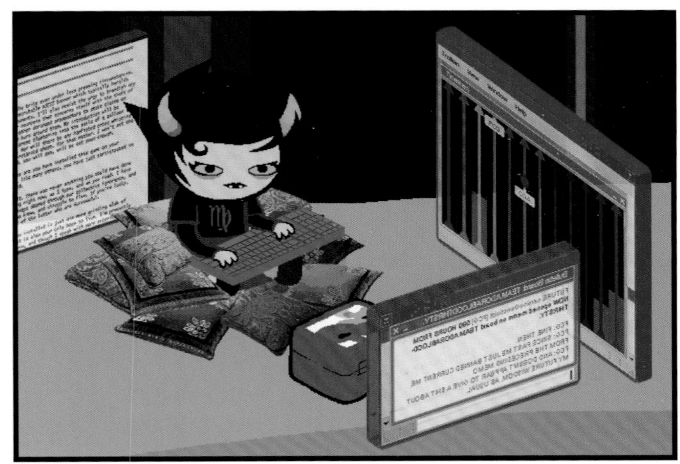

> Kanaya: Reply to memo.

Here's another non-reveal reveal like disguising Karkat's blood color while showing it, kind of a cheating way of hiding but not hiding something. I didn't feel like it was the right time to show the second word of Kanaya's land yet, because it's a word shared with all Space players' lands, including Jade's. There were various reasons I didn't want to tip off the name of her land, but also, garbling the text signals to the reader that this information is a mystery worth taking note of. Aside from that, let's enjoy the fact that Kanaya dragged all her nice pillows up to the edge of this volcano so she could be comfy while computing.

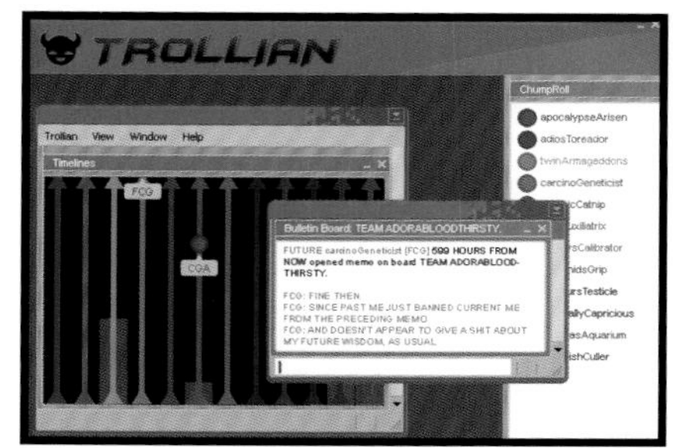

FUTURE carcinoGeneticist [FCG] **599 HOURS FROM NOW opened memo on board TEAM ADORABLOODTHIRSTY.**

FCG: FINE THEN.
FCG: SINCE PAST ME JUST BANNED CURRENT ME FROM THE PRECEDING MEMO
FCG: AND DOESN'T APPEAR TO GIVE A SHIT ABOUT MY FUTURE WISDOM, AS USUAL
FCG: LOOKS LIKE I'LL JUST HAVE TO START ANOTHER MEMO FROM SCRATCH.
FCG: HEY PAST ME, GO HAVE A BLAST KILLING THE KING, I'M SURE IT WILL BE AWESOME.
FCG: IN FACT, IT WAS AWESOME. BANG UP JOB WITH THAT, DUDE!
FCG: TOO BAD IT WAS ALL A HUGE WASTE OF TIME.
FCG: OH, WHAT'S THAT, PASTHOLE? YOU DIDN'T READ THIS AND FIGURE THAT OUT AHEAD OF TIME?
FCG: OR MAYBE YOU JUST SKIMMED THIS AND IT DIDN'T GET THROUGH YOUR THICK BULGE???
FCG: WHAT A SHOCK!
FCG: MEMO-WITHIN-MEMO TO PRESENT SELF: PUT FORTH A MORE CONCERTED EFFORT TO IMPRESS UPON EVERYONE IN THE PAST, MYSELF INCLUDED, WHAT A BUNCH OF FUCKING IDIOTS THEY ALL ARE.
FCG: I AM LEARNING A VALUABLE LESSON TODAY!
FCG: IT TURNS OUT YOU CAN'T ALTER THE OUTCOME OF DECISIONS MADE BY MORONS, NO MATTER HOW MUCH YOU YELL AT THEM.
FCG: ALL YOU CAN REALLY DO IS GIVE THEM A HARD TIME AND TRY TO MAKE THEIR LIVES JUST A LITTLE MORE MISERABLE.
FCG: WHICH SOUNDS LIKE A MORE NOBLE PURSUIT THAN CHANGING DESTINY FOR THE BETTER ANYWAY, FRANKLY.
FCG: LOSERS SHOULD BE FORCED TO FACE THE MUSIC, EVEN FOR THE MISTAKES THEY HAVEN'T MADE YET.
FCG: THEIR PUNISHMENT IS BEING ALLOWED TO MAKE THE MISTAKE IN THE FIRST PLACE. TALK ABOUT POETIC JUSTICE!
FCG: AND THEN GETTING SOUNDLY BERATED BEFORE, DURING, AND AFTER THE MISTAKES ARE BEING MADE IS JUST THE MUCUS ON THE GRUBLOAF.
FCG: THE SWEET, TANGY MUCUS.
FCG: THIS IS DUMB.
FCG: WHY DID I EVER THINK THESE MEMOS WERE GOING TO BE A GOOD IDEA.
FCG: NOBODY CARES
FCG: I MEAN
FCG: NOBODY'S EVEN TROLLING ME ANYMORE.
FCG: AND I'M LEAVING MYSELF WIDE OPEN TOO, SAYING SOME PRETTY DUMB THINGS HERE.
FCG: I GUESS MAYBE I WROTE TOO MANY.
FCG: AND FILLED TOO MANY OF THEM WITH LONG ARGUMENTS WITH MYSELF.
FCG: NO ONE'S GOING TO READ THROUGH ALL THIS, ALL THE VALUABLE INFORMATION IS JUST GETTING

"IT TURNS OUT YOU CAN'T ALTER THE OUTCOME OF DECISIONS MADE BY MORONS, NO MATTER HOW MUCH YOU YELL AT THEM." Not to get overly political down here in the laugh gutter. This just sounds like the tagline for the result of the 2016 U.S. election.

LOST IN THE YELLING.
FCG: YOU STUPID STUPID IDIOT.
FCG: OH FUCK YOU, WHY'D YOU EVEN START ANOTHER MEMO THEN??
FCG: I GUESS
FCG: THERE ARE A COUPLE THINGS I WANT TO GET OFF MY CHEST, OK?
FCG: OH GOD, NOW I'M ARGUING WITH CURRENT ME.
FCG: I DIDN'T EVEN NOTICE I WAS DOING IT, THIS IS REALLY FUCKED UP.
FCG: I'VE GOT TO PULL IT TOGETHER.
FCG: THINK BACK TO WHAT WE MIGHT HAVE DONE WRONG.
FCG: BUT THE THING IS
FCG: AS MUCH AS OUR PAST SELVES ARE A BUNCH OF STUBBORN UNLISTENING ASSHOLES
FCG: I CAN'T EVEN REALLY IDENTIFY ANY MISTAKES WE MADE.
FCG: IT WAS ALL PRETTY MUCH LIKE CLOCKWORK.
FCG: A 600 HOUR CAMPAIGN TO COMPLETE A GAME LIKE THIS IS PRETTY GOOD IF YOU ASK ME.
FCG: AND I HAVE ASKED ME.
FCG: IT TURNS OUT ME AGREES.
FCG: I CAN'T SHAKE THE FEELING SOMEONE ELSE MUST BE RESPONSIBLE FOR THIS.
FCG: IT DOESN'T SEEM LIKE IT WAS SOMETHING THAT WAS SUPPOSED TO HAPPEN IN OUR SESSION.
FCG: SOLLUX HAS THE SAME INTUITION ABOUT IT AS ME, HE THINKS THERE'S SOMETHING FII2HY ABOUT IT.
FCG: IT'S REALLY INSUFFERABLE THE WAY HER FISH PUNS HAVE RUBBED OFF ON HIM, IT KIND OF MAKES ME WANT TO VOMIT.
FCG: ANYWAY
FCG: HE SAYS HE'S WORKING ON TRACING THE ORIGIN OF THIS DISASTER.
FCG: IF I FIND OUT WHO'S RESPONSIBLE
FCG: I WILL
FCG: I DON'T EVEN WANT TO THINK ABOUT IT NOW.
FCG: WASTE OF GOOD FRESH RAGE.
FCG: I'M A LITTLE TIRED OF ALL THE OLD THINGS I'VE BEEN ANGRY ABOUT.
FCG: IT'S GOTTEN SO STALE.
FCG: IN A WEIRD WAY I'M SORT OF LOOKING FORWARD TO HAVING SOMETHING NEW TO BE PISSED OFF ABOUT.
FCG: IT'S NOT LIKE THERE'S ANYTHING ELSE TO LIVE FOR NOW ANYWAY.
FCG: SO I'M KEEPING MY PRONGS CROSSED.
FCG: IT WILL BE LIKE FUCKING 12TH PERIGEE'S EVE UP IN HERE.
FCG: LAST SWEEP'S EVE WAS PROBABLY THE LAST HAPPY MEMORY I HAVE IN FACT.
FCG: WHAT DID YOU GUYS DO FOR THE LAST HOLIDAY?
FCG: ANYONE?
FCG: I REMEMBER MY LUSUS HAD BEEN GONE FOR DAYS AND I WAS STARTING TO GET WORRIED.
FCG: BUT THEN HE FINALLY RETURNED, TRIUMPHANT.
FCG: HE BROUGHT THE FRESH BEHEMOTH LEAVING INTO OUR HIVE, AND TOGETHER WE DECORATED IT.
FCG: AND

When Current Karkat actually starts arguing with Current Karkat, not only did he not notice he was doing it, I think it's safe to say that even *we* didn't notice he was doing it. A lot of arguments he has with other versions of himself are hard to differentiate, because it's always gray text, and it's always yelling. It blurs together. Much later, he "solves" this problem by switching to red for a bit, during one of his more pathetic conversational loops of self-hate. A little further down he starts wondering what they did wrong in the session. Which, as I was saying earlier, is not really anything, and he kind of almost has that epiphany here. But then loses that epiphany once he discovers the humans, decides to hate them with a refreshed sense of rage, and starts blaming all the wrong things again for their failure, including himself. It's almost like he gains clarity in his rage gaps. When one fog of rage subsides, he starts seeing things clearly, but that all goes away the moment he enters a new fog of rage. Regardless, we're getting close to the end of Hivebent now, and you can kind of start sensing this wildly fractured, manic narrative start to gather itself and point itself back in the direction of where we left off. The new hate-hobby Karkat discovers, of course, we know to be the humans.

FCG: I DUNNO
FCG: THAT'S ALL I CAN SAY, I'M GETTING A LUMP IN MY SQUAWK BLISTER.
FCG: I GUESS I'M DONE.
FCG: I'M GOING TO LIE DOWN NOW
FCG: ON THE STEEL FLOOR OF THIS FRIGID METEOR DRIFTING THROUGH THE BLACK UNCARING VOID OF OUR NULL SESSION.
FCG: NULL, KIND OF LIKE THIS MEMO I GUESS.
FCG: LATER.
CURRENT grimAuxiliatrix [CGA] RIGHT NOW responded to memo.
CGA: I Dont Think We Did Anything Special
FCG: WHOA, HEY
FCG: WHAT?
CGA: Last 12th
CGA: We Stayed In
CGA: And I Read Stories To Her It Was Nice
FCG: OH
FCG: THAT'S COOL.
FCG: THIS IS THE FIRST TIME YOU'VE RESPONDED TO A MEMO THAT I CAN RECALL.
FCG: YOU TOOK IT RIGHT DOWN TO THE WIRE. I WAS JUST ABOUT TO CLOSE THIS THING.
CGA: Yeah I Know
CGA: I Wasnt Sure If I Was Going To
CGA: But Then I Noticed A Conversation In Which I Was A Participant
CGA: Which As It Turns Out Is The Conversation Taking Place Now
CGA: I Scanned It Briefly And Then Perused Other Memos For My Presence
CGA: I Found None And Returned To This One
CGA: But My Part Of The Conversation Was Gone
CGA: I Regarded This As A Prompt To Begin Typing And Record My Contributions Live
CGA: That Is How This Works Isnt It
FCG: PRETTY MUCH.
FCG: FOR A WHILE IT WAS FRUSTRATING.
FCG: WHEN I DISCOVERED THE FEATURE I KIND OF BREEZED THROUGH ALL MY FUTURE MEMOS, NOT REALLY READING ALL OF THEM CAREFULLY OR THOROUGHLY.
FCG: THEN I LOOKED AT IT AGAIN, AND THE WHOLE BOARD WAS GONE.
FCG: BECAUSE IT WAS TIME TO MAKE IT IN THE FIRST PLACE, SO I DID.
FCG: AND THEN I KEPT MAKING MEMOS WITH ONLY FOGGY RECOLLECTIONS OF WHAT THEY CONTAINED.
FCG: WHILE ALL THESE OTHER CHUMPS FROM DIFFERENT TIMES KEPT GIVING ME SHIT.
FCG: INCLUDING MYSELF.
FCG: BUT IT WAS ALL GOOD, BECAUSE AS I EVENTUALLY BECAME MY OWN FUTURE SELVES, AND GOT TO BE ON THE OTHER SIDES OF THOSE CONVERSATIONS.
FCG: AND COULD DO MY PAST SELVES THE SERVICE OF INFORMING THEM HOW STUPID THEY WERE BEING.
FCG: I STOPPED BOTHERING TRYING TO REMEMBER HOW ANY OF THESE MEMOS WENT.
FCG: HONESTLY THE LAST FEW WEEKS HAVE BEEN A BLUR TO ME, JUST NON STOP YELLING AT MYSELF,

This is also the first time in Hivebent when we spend any real time tuning into a part that takes place on the meteor they end up stranded on after whatever catastrophe causes them to flee there. For all the zipping up and down the timeline we do, we never actually go that far until now. Again, it's about starting to gather up and organize all these loose threads and direct them back into something we recognize as connecting to the main narrative line. Even when certain stories or arcs are really chaotic and wildly out of order, I think most of us have good intuitions when it comes to picking up on when a story is making moves in preparation for the approach to its own endgame material. This memo starts feeling like that turning point. You've also got Kanaya weighing in, playing the role of a sort of wise, sympathetic ear to a down-and-out protagonist. You know That Moment in the movie. We all do. We're all experts. *Homestuck* knows you're a media expert and uses that assumption to its "advantage" all the time. The only time it backfires is when it turns out you're nowhere near the expert I thought you were. You know those moments when you see me shaking my head in grave disappointment? That's why I'm doing that, FYI.

HAGGLING WITH PAST AND FUTURE KNUCKLEHEADS, KILLING MONSTERS AND SOLVING PUZZLES, CYCLING THROUGH ALL THE GATES AND PLANETS LIKE A HUNDRED TIMES, ZIGZAGGING DOWN TO THE BATTLEFIELD, OUT TO THE VEIL, OVER TO PROSPIT, BACK TO DERSE, AND ON AND ON AND ON LIKE THAT UNTIL WE THOUGHT WE WON.
FCG: BUT WE DIDN'T WIN. WE LOST.
FCG: WE LOST AS HARD AS FAT GUYS FALL.
CGA: What Exactly Happened
FCG: DID YOU READ THE MEMO JUST BEFORE THIS?
CGA: No
FCG: GIVE IT A READ, I'M DONE RANTING ABOUT ALL THAT FOR NOW.
CGA: Alright
CGA: In A Moment
FCG: BUT YEAH, THAT'S HOW TROLLIAN'S TIMELINE STUFF WORKS. YOU'LL GET USED TO IT.
FCG: OR NOT! SINCE APPARENTLY THIS IS YOUR ONLY MEMO REPLY. YOU WERE PRETTY SHREWD IN SIDESTEPPING THIS WHOLE CLUSTERFUCK.
CGA: It Seems Like A Logical Way To Engineer A System Wherein One Simultaneously Functions As The Reader And Author Of The Transcripts
CGA: Its Temporally Sound Construction
FCG: THEN YOU'RE THE ONLY ONE WHO THINKS SO.
FCG: HELL YOU PROBABLY WOULD HAVE BEEN A BETTER MAID OF TIME THAN THE ONE WE WERE STUCK WITH.
FCG: SHE'S COMPLETELY SHITHIVE MAGGOTS, DON'T EVEN GET ME STARTED.
CGA: I Think We Are Given Roles To Challenge Us
CGA: That Dont Necessarily Suit Our Strengths
CGA: At Least I Was
CGA: I Have No Idea What Im Doing Here
FCG: SURE YOU DO.
FCG: OR, YOU WILL. TRUST ME YOU'LL DO FINE.
FCG: SO WHAT PROMPTED YOU TO RESPOND ANYWAY.
FCG: I MEAN ASIDE FROM BEING STRONGARMED BY CONVERSATIONAL PREDESTINATION.
CGA: Oh
CGA: At This Point Im Not Even Sure If Im Inclined To Ask Anymore
FCG: YOU MIGHT NOT HAVE A CHOICE.
FCG: DO YOU REMEMBER IF THIS MEMO WAS MUCH LONGER THAN THIS?
CGA: Um
CGA: There Is A Good Way To Go I Think Yeah
FCG: THEN MIGHT AS WELL SPIT IT OUT.
CGA: Its Such A Silly Question
FCG: RED OR BLACK?
CGA: What
FCG: YOUR PROBLEM, DOES IT PERTAIN TO REDROM OR BLACKROM INTERESTS?

Karkat suggests Aradia isn't a great Maid of Time. I dunno about that. She time traveled to make a thousand doomed robotic copies of herself to help defeat a crazy-strong Black King. Seems pretty good to me. He's probably remarking more on her mental stability than her competence. Of course what's really going on here, story-wise, is that he's foreshadowing her violent freakout in the End-of-Hivebent animation coming up soon.

CGA: Thats Not What This Is About
FCG: COME ON. PEOPLE HAVE BEEN USING THESE MEMOS TO SIFT THROUGH THEIR ROMANTIC PROBLEMS FOR WEEKS, I AM A FUCKING VETERAN AT THIS SHIT BY NOW.
FCG: SERIOUSLY, I DON'T MIND, IT'LL BE A WELCOME REPRIEVE FROM SHOUTING AT MYSELF.
CGA: Im Not Sure What To Say About It
FCG: DIDN'T YOU AT LEAST GET A SENSE OF WHAT THIS CONVERSATION WAS ABOUT WHEN YOU SKIMMED IT?
CGA: Not Really
CGA: If I Were Thinking About It I Probably Wouldnt Have Wanted To Anyway
CGA: Dont You Think Its Better To Have Unrehearsed Conversations
CGA: Even If The Subject Matter Is Awkward
FCG: YES I COMPLETELY AGREE.
FCG: IT'S GOOD YOU DIDN'T READ IT. WE CAN AVOID THE SORT OF VERBAL SLAPSTICK ROUTINES I'M SICK TO FUCKING DEATH OF BY NOW.
FCG: I AM SO TIRED OF PEOPLE BEING ALL COY AND TELLING ME WHAT WE'RE ABOUT TO SAY BEFORE WE SAY IT, AND THEN WE WIND UP FUCKING SAYING IT ANYWAY.
FCG: AND THEN WE PROVE TO THE INVISIBLE RIDDLER THAT IS FATHER TIME BEYOND A SHADOW OF A DOUBT WHAT A BUNCH OF FUCKING IDIOTS WE ALL ARE.
FCG: DO YOU HAVE ANY IDEA HOW OLD THAT GETS AFTER A WHILE?
FCG: SO REALLY, TELL ME.
FCG: I KNOW IT'S ON YOUR MIND, I GOT A SENSE FOR THESE THINGS.
FCG: R OR B???
CGA: Ok
CGA: Red Then
CGA: But I Guess
CGA: Not Really Red Enough
FCG: HAHA, WELL ISN'T THAT ALWAYS THE CASE?
FCG: STORY AS OLD AS TIME.
FCG: EVEN IN PLACES WHERE STRICTLY SPEAKING TIME DIDN'T EXIST UNTIL RECENTLY.
FCG: WHO'S THE TARGET OF THESE FLUSHED LEANINGS?
FCG: IF YOU DON'T MIND MY ASKING.
CGA: Its Not The Asking I Mind
CGA: Its The Telling
CGA: In A Public Forum
FCG: I DON'T THINK ANYONE'S READING.
FCG: DID YOU NOTICE ANYONE ELSE JOIN IN LATER?
CGA: No
CGA: It Appeared To Be Just The Two Of Us
FCG: SEE
FCG: NOBODY CARES ENOUGH TO BOTHER.
CGA: I Dont Know Whether Thats Reassuring

Karkat mentions here an "invisible riddler." This is an idea that comes up from time to time throughout the story. Recall the "unseen riddler" in the narration during John's early animation, when he's listening to the wind in his neighborhood. It conjures the idea of a hidden Loki-like figure somewhere, whose pranks have nihilistic designs, an intangible force of mischief that robs its targets of a meaningful or dignified existence. In John's case, the nihilistic rumination about this figure seems to focus on the shapeless and uncertain direction of his life. Karkat's remark here focuses on the futility and self-fulfillment of one's own foolishness, passively allowed to play itself out by this prankster figure, who he links to "Father Time" as well. There is no one true god of Paradox Space, but to whatever extent there is, it's probably this riddler figure, which is why it's left in doubt as to whether he even exists at all. He's never discussed without also referencing his invisibility, or dubious reality. A much less cagey explanation is, it's probably best interpreted as the forces of mischief and authorial cruelty or callousness toward the subjects within this fiction, which are laced into the entire narrative and relate closely to the quality of "authorial scorn" that was mentioned earlier in some of the Vriska meta. When galvanized through more extreme figures like Caliborn, these forces become less passively nihilistic and prankstery, and more actively hostile and destructive.

CGA: Or Just A Bit Disheartening
FCG: WELL I DIDN'T MEAN IT LIKE THAT.
FCG: THEIR DISINTEREST IS MORE A REFLECTION ON ME THAN YOU.
CGA: Disinterest Is The Operative Concept Here
CGA: Shes Not Even Responding To My Messages Anymore
CGA: Could Be Busy
CGA: But Im Rapidly Approaching A Resolution To Discard The Preposterous Infatuation
FCG: SHE? WELL I GUESS THAT NARROWS IT DOWN SOMEWHAT.
CGA: Shit
FCG: IF I THINK BACK ON EVENTS KNOWING THIS I COULD PROBABLY PIECE IT TOGETHER...
CGA: How About
CGA: If I Agree To Consult With You About It In Private
CGA: We Can Drop It Here
CGA: Before You Crack Me Like A Vault
CGA: With Your Weird Romance Sleuthing Acumen
FCG: ALRIGHT, DEAL.
CGA: It Still Puzzles Me That You Are So Versed In The Topic
CGA: Do You Have Access To A Manual Archived On A Remote Server Somewhere
FCG: WHAT
FCG: NO OF COURSE NOT.
FCG: I DON'T ACTUALLY KNOW ALL THAT MUCH.
FCG: I JUST KNOW THIS STUFF WILL DRIVE YOU SHITHIVE MAGGOTS IF YOU DON'T FIGURE OUT HOW TO DEAL WITH IT.
CGA: That Figure Of Speech You Keep Using Puzzles Me Too
FCG: LIKE
FCG: NOT THAT I EXPECT YOU TO GIVE A SHIT BUT PERSONALLY I AM ALL TWISTED UP ABOUT BLACKROM STUFF ESPECIALLY.
FCG: HONESTLY I DON'T THINK I WAS CUT OUT TO HAVE A KISMESIS, I THINK MY STANDARDS ARE WAY TOO HIGH.
FCG: DID YOU KNOW THAT...
FCG: THIS FEELS SO INSANE TO ADMIT, BUT
FCG: OVER THE COURSE OF THIS ADVENTURE, AT TIMES I ACTUALLY BEGAN TO SUSPECT I WAS MY OWN KISMESIS.
FCG: HOW FUCKED UP IS THAT???
CGA: Im Not Qualified To Say
CGA: Neither Romance Nor Psychology Are My Strong Suits
FCG: BUT OBVIOUSLY ITS NOT TRUE, I NEVER EVEN DID ANY LEGIT TIME TRAVELING WHERE I COULD MEET MYSELF, I JUST BICKERED WITH PAST AND FUTURE GHOSTS ON A CHAT CLIENT.
FCG: FITTING REALLY. EVERY CALIGINOUS ADVERSARY I'VE CONTEMPLATED HAS ELUDED ME LIKE A PHANTOM, EVEN MYSELF!
FCG: WHATEVER, I'M DONE WITH IT.

That Kanaya has trouble imagining how Karkat could have a strong handle on the subject of romance without access to an online manual (like her access to Rose's walkthrough) says something about the way she thinks, and views skill or expertise. Here she says romance and psychology aren't her strong suits, and a couple pages ago she was expressing doubts about her role as a Space player. Some characters struggle with self-loathing issues (she's talking to one of them now), but she seems especially troubled by self-doubt issues. Maybe this is why these two resonate as friends so well. One is there to reassure him he is not loathsome, the other to reassure her she is not incompetent. We've been over Kanaya's role as a mother figure to a bunch of people, and it helps for a good mother figure to have a good son figure as a counterpoint, a son who's there to remind her, "No, you're not bad at this. Stop it with that talk."

CGA: And What Of Scarlet Ambitions
CGA: Fare Any Better In That Quadrant
FCG: NO NO NO I'M NOT AIRING THAT SHIT OUT HERE.
FCG: MAYBE PRIVATELY.
FCG: IT'S PRIVATE.
FCG: LET'S CHANGE THE SUBJECT, WHAT WERE YOU ORIGINALLY GOING TO ASK ME.
CGA: Oh Fine
CGA: Heres This Silly Question For You
CGA: I Was Just Wondering Given Your Vantage Of Hindsight
CGA: If Youd Had Cause To Observe At Any Point In Time
CGA: Magic
FCG: UH...
CGA: Like Real Magic
CGA: I Guess What Im Asking Is
CGA: Is Magic A Real Thing
FCG: WOW, YOU'RE RIGHT, THAT'S KIND OF THE DUMBEST FUCKING QUESTION I'VE EVER HEARD.
CGA: I Know
CGA: Its Just That I Have A Good Reason To Believe Magic Is Real
CGA: Our Ancient Predecessors Discovered How To Use It
CGA: But Then They May Have Surpassed Us In Skill By A Great Deal
FCG: YOU PUT WAY TOO MUCH STOCK IN THAT RATTY OLD GUIDE.
FCG: BUT ANYWAY NO, WE NEVER USED MAGIC.
FCG: I MEAN, LET ME TRY TO PUT INTO PERSPECTIVE HOW RIDICULOUS THE WHOLE NOTION IS ANYWAY.
FCG: WE CAN ALCHEMIZE PRACTICALLY ANYTHING WITH THE RIGHT MATERIALS AND GRIST.
FCG: WE CAN, AND DID, MAKE SUPER POWERFUL WEAPONS AND ITEMS THAT CAN DO PRACTICALLY ANYTHING.
FCG: WHAT ADDITIONAL ADVANTAGE COULD MAGIC OFFER? ALL THIS SHIT IS PRACTICALLY MAGIC ANYWAY.
FCG: BUT MORE LIKE
FCG: GOOFY SCIENCEY MAGIC. YOU KNOW?
CGA: Sure
FCG: BUT EVERYTHING HERE IS KIND OF MAGIC IN A WAY, ISN'T IT.
FCG: FORTUNE TELLING DREAM CLOUDS AND GOLDEN MOONS AND SHIT.
FCG: IF YOU LOOK AROUND
FCG: THERE'S MAGIC EVERYWHERE IN THIS BITCH.
FCG: IT'S ALL AROUND US.
FCG: MOTHER FUCKIN MIRACLES, RIGHT?
CGA: Heh
FCG: WHAT DO YOU NEED MAGIC FOR ANYWAY?
CGA: Im Running Out Of Ideas
CGA: I Need To Figure Out A Way To Stoke This Volcano
CGA: In Case You And The Others Are Successful In Recovering The Queens Ring

Karkat's dissertation on magic is a pretty good summary of the ongoing tension between the realness/fakeness attribute of magic throughout the story. We get pretty flippant about magic in *Homestuck*, don't we? It's just a word you can use to describe certain forces, in the same way that you can use the word "luck" to evaluate certain outcomes, if you're fixated on that concept. This isn't really mind-blowing wisdom here. I'd describe it more as premise-level information, upon which the story elaborates in certain ways. Magic and luck are more like states of mind. If there is any deeper truth to sift from these semantics, it's an idea that the story keeps returning to, which is that the power of belief is the key to everything. Believing in things reduces their fakeness attribute. It's the force that shapes your reality, used to snatch personal meaning from the jaws of a cynical and nihilistic environment. Could this be why Hope is framed as the most fundamentally powerful aspect? Even the other aspects themselves are ideas like this (recall: luck=light), whose power is subject to the ebb and flow of one's belief in them. And belief itself isn't necessarily just a trick of willpower. It can be an expression of one's willingness to embrace an idea, or pursue a deeper understanding of it.

FCG: YOU'LL FIGURE IT OUT.
FCG: AND YOU WON'T NEED MAGIC, TRUST ME.
FCG: JUST BE PATIENT, THE ANSWER WILL COME TO YOU SOMEHOW.
CGA: I Guess You Would Know
FCG: YEAH, REALLY THERE'S NOTHING TO WORRY ABOUT.
FCG: AT LEAST AS FAR AS THE DETAILS OF THE ADVENTURE GO.
FCG: WE WERE ALL PRETTY AWESOME AT THIS GAME.
FCG: REALLY AWESOME IN FACT.
FCG: UNTIL A LITTLE WHILE AGO.
FCG: WHEN IT TURNED OUT WE WEREN'T ACTUALLY ALL THAT AWESOME.
FCG: TURNS OUT WE WERE PRETTY FUCKING UNAWESOME ALL ALONG.
CGA: Still Baffled By What Would Conceivably Cause Such A Crisis In Awesomeness Post-Victory
FCG: WELL
FCG: FOR STARTERS
FCG: HAVE YOU SCROLLED UP TO THE TOP OF THE TIMELINES YET?
CGA: No
FCG: CHECK THAT OUT
FCG: MAYBE READ A FEW RECENT MEMOS
FCG: BUT OTHER THAN THAT IT'S NOT FOR YOU TO CONCERN YOURSELF WITH.
FCG: JUST DEAL WITH GETTING THROUGH THE QUEST.
FCG: I'LL CATCH UP WITH YOU ABOUT IT WHEN YOU CATCH UP WITH ME ON THE TIMELINE.
FCG: WHICH JUST HAPPENS TO BE RIGHT NOW.
CGA: Say Hi To Me For Myself
FCG: OK I PROBABLY WON'T DO THAT, BUT ALRIGHT HA HA.
FCG: WHAT THE HELL ARE YOU DOING OVER THERE ANYWAY?
CGA: You Mean Future Me
FCG: YEAH.
FCG: YOU'RE MESSING AROUND WITH YOUR CHAINSAW.
FCG: WHILE TAVROS IS SLEEPING ON THE FLOOR.
FCG: OH GOD.
FCG: FUUUUUUUUUUUUUCK WHAT ARE YOU DOING???????
CGA: What
CGA: What Did I Do
FUTURE carcinoGeneticist 2 [FCG2] **600 HOURS FROM NOW responded to memo.**
FCG2: OK.
FCG2: EVERYTHING'S FINE I GUESS.
CGA: What Happened
FCG2: I PASSED OUT FOR ABOUT AN HOUR.
FCG2: FUCKING EMBARRASSING.
FCG2: YOU ARE OUT OF YOUR GODDAMN MIND, YOU KNOW.
CGA: Shithive Maggots You Mean
FCG2: YEAH

Obviously Karkat is reacting to the moment Kanaya saws off Tavros's legs, while Equius watches creepily. We saw one frame of that earlier. Yes, it's a funny beat in the conversation that calls back to that moment, but it also establishes an important hour of missing time for Karkat while he's passed out. This gap where he's asleep on the floor comes up again later in Act 5. The second part of Act 5 does a lot of what Hivebent does. Where Hivebent skips around, chaotically fitting together the greater puzzle of the troll session until we finally reach the end, A5A2 skips around a lot, fitting together the puzzle of their stay on the meteor and sorting through the mystery of exactly what happens and when. So there starts to be an accounting of many little moments like this, to use as points of reference for when certain things are happening. "Aradiabot explodes" is another such benchmark for the reader to use to track surrounding events. Interestingly (maybe), Karkat uses this idea too, by setting "Jade's dreambot explodes" as a similar benchmark to help Jade get her bearings through a nonlinear swamp of communications.

FCG2: IN A GOOD WAY THOUGH.
FCG2: OK I'M SHUTTING THIS MEMO DOWN FOR MY PAST SELF.
FCG2: SINCE HE'S CURRENTLY LYING UNCONSCIOUS ON THE FLOOR AN HOUR AGO.
FCG2: SEE YOU IN THE FUTURE-NOW.
CGA: Til Then
FCG2 banned CGA from responding to memo.
FCG2 banned FCG from responding to memo.

FCG2 closed memo.

~~~~~~

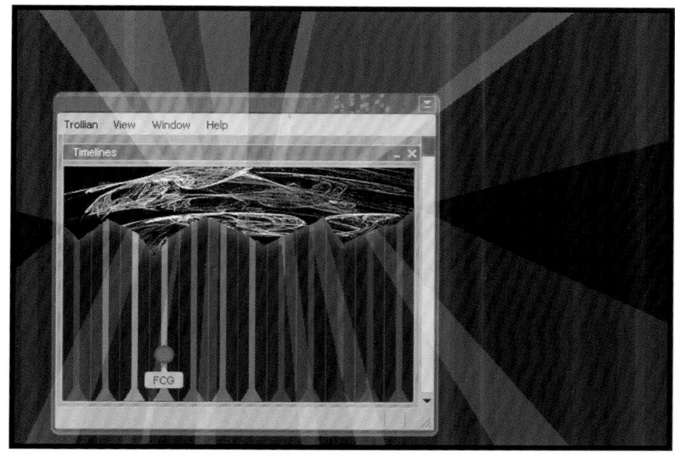

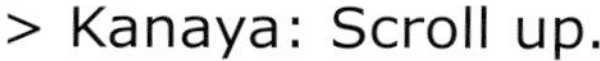
> Kanaya: Scroll up.

> Terezi: Fly up.

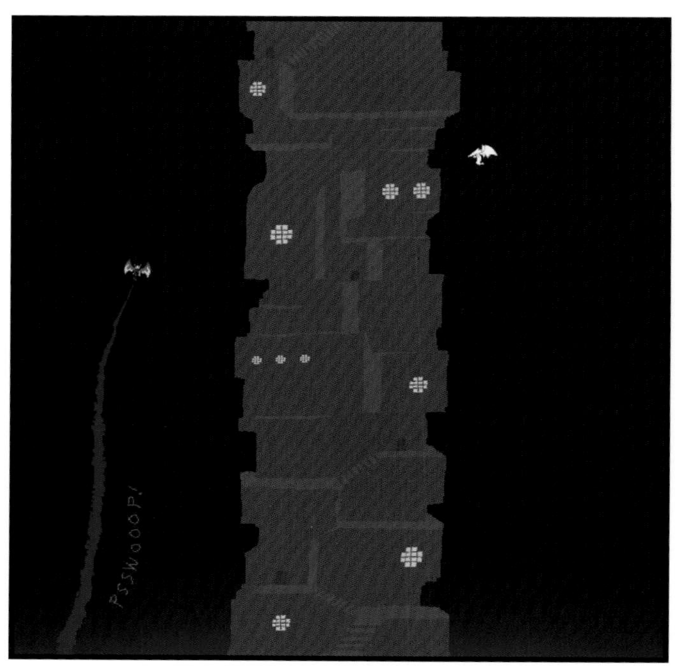

We've come to anticipate the "Rift" in the troll session, which has been alluded to. Some vague, calamitous event, which we know literally nothing else about. So when Kanaya scrolls up, we can surmise the jagged tear at the top of the timeline window signals this event. It doesn't, though. The Rift is just a term Karkat used to describe an event he didn't understand, which was Jack showing up and slicing their entryway into the new universe in half. He guessed some vague rift in space-time was responsible for that. The jagged rip in the timeline window is something else completely. If you read *Problem Sleuth*, that rip might look familiar. The underlying graphic and style of that jagged edge were copied from the moment when the entire universe ripped in half, and then needed to be sewn back together with a big needle. There's a reason I copied that exact graphic over for this purpose. The cataclysmic nature of the two events turns out to be pretty similar.
~~~~~~

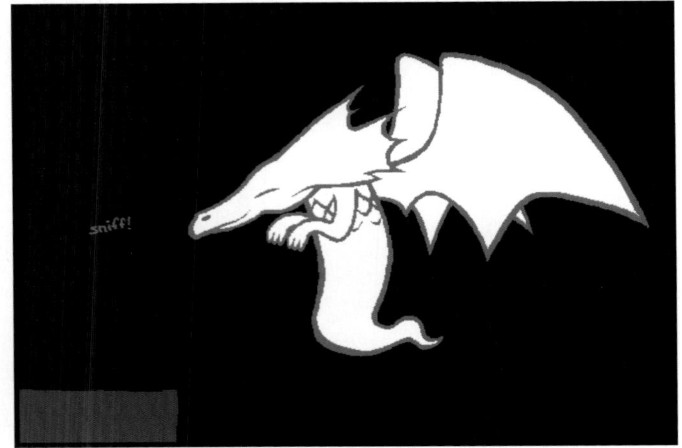

DRAGONSPRITE: sniff sniff
DRAGONSPRITE: hey terezi!
DRAGONSPRITE: heeeeeeeyyyyyyy!
DRAGONSPRITE: hiiiiii terezi!
DRAGONSPRITE: hiiiiiiiiiiiiiiiiiiiiiiiiiiiiiiii!
DRAGONSPRITE: sniff sniff sniff
DRAGONSPRITE: heeheeheeheeheeheeheeheeheeheeheeheeheehee!

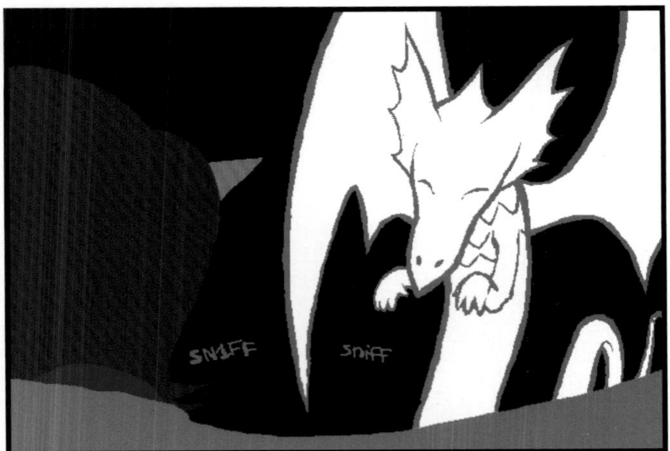

> Terezi: Respond.

Lusus sprite dialogue is very rare. We get a tiny bit of dialogue from the mother grub sprite, but that's it. This is a relatively huge amount of dialogue coming from Terezi's baby dragon mom. It talks exactly how we'd imagine a recently hatched baby dragon who was suddenly given the ability to speak might talk. Why did I decide to give this particular sprite a bunch of lines, while leaving almost all the rest not only mute but completely unshown? Not sure I have a good answer for that. Believe it or not, sometimes there are decisions I make which can't be explained with several paragraphs worth of analysis.

carcinoGeneticist [CG] **began trolling** gallowsCalibrator [GC]

CG: OK I GOT YOUR MESSAGE
CG: THANKS FOR NOT HASSLING ME ABOUT IT IN ONE OF THE MEMOS TO GET MY ATTENTION, I APPRECIATE THAT.
CG: UNLESS YOU DID, BUT IT WAS IN A FUTURE MEMO I HAVEN'T WRITTEN YET, IN WHICH CASE HAVE A BIGTIME FUCK YOU ABOUT THAT IN ADVANCE.
GC: NO 1 D1DNT BUG YOU 4BOUT 1T 1N YOUR STUP1D M3MOS!
GC: TH3Y 4R3 4NNOY1NG 4ND 1M T1R3D OF G3TT1NG B4NN3D FOR NO R34SON
CG: POSTING IN THEM AT ALL IS THE REASON. YOU'RE NOT SUPPOSED TO REPLY MEMOS PERIOD, THAT'S THE REASON.
GC: M4YB3 1 W1LL ST4RT MY OWN BULL3T1N BO4RD
GC: 4ND 3V3RYON3 W1LL B3 4LLOW3D TO R3PLY 4NY T1M3 TH3Y W4NT
GC: 3XC3PT FOR GUYS W1TH NUBBY HORNS, OH NO, TH3Y W1LL NOT B3 4BL3 TO R3PLY 4T 4LL
GC: GRUMPY K4RK4TS W1LL B3 3XPR3SSLY FORB1DD3N FROM R41NBOW RUMPUS P4RTYTOWN!
GC: >:P
CG: SOUNDS LAME.
GC: BY TH3 W4Y TH4T W1LL B3 TH3 N4M3 OF TH3 BO4RD 1N C4S3 1T W4SNT CL34R
CG: YEAH I GOT THAT.
CG: THIS IS AN EMPTY THREAT, BECAUSE IF YOU MADE A BOARD AT ANY POINT ON THE TIMELINE I WOULD BE ABLE TO SEE IT RIGHT HERE AND READ THE WHOLE THING ALREADY.
CG: WAIT...
CG: OH GOD, YOU ACTUALLY DID.
GC: Y3SSSSS!
GC: FUTUR3 T3R3Z1 1S LOOK1NG PR3TTY COOL R1GHT 4BOUT NOW >8]
CG: LOOK I DON'T CARE ABOUT THE FRUITY RUMPUS ASSHOLE FACTORY.
CG: WHAT'S ALL THIS ABOUT GOING AFTER THE QUEEN'S RING.
GC: W3LL
GC: TH3 TH1NG TH4T 1S 4LL 4BOUT 1T 1S
GC: W3 H4V3 TO GO 4FT3R TH3 QU33NS R1NG
GC: 1T 1S 4 N3W M1SS1ON
CG: BUT WE'RE STILL IN THE MIDDLE OF TRYING TO PULL OFF REGISURP WITH JACK.
CG: WHY DON'T WE TAKE IT ONE MISSION AT A TIME.
GC: Y34H 4BOUT TH4T
GC: TH3 WHOL3 PO1NT 1S TO D3STROY TH3 R1NG SO J4CK DO3SNT G3T 1T
CG: WHY WOULD WE WANT TO DO THAT, JACK'S AN ALLY.
GC: 4LSO
GC: TH3 M1SS1ON SORT OF 1NVOLV3S 3X1L1NG J4CK TOO
GC: >:|

Here's a Significant Moment. For Terezi personally, at least. So much so that she wrote the word MOM3NT with her own blood on a scarf to help John retcon back to this part of the story to make sure she doesn't waste any more of her life on this dumb boy. Normally on this page you'd be able to click on an alternate command labeled "???????", which takes you to a password page. If you don't know the password, you just wonder what the hell is up with that, click back, and keep reading. Thousands of pages later though, you learn the password from the scarf, go back, enter the password, and proceed through an offshoot of the story involving John's ridiculous intervention. Nice use of the medium, right? Too bad it doesn't translate to a book at all, in any conceivable way, so it wasn't even worth considering how to do it. But hey, at least I EXPLAINED it down here. You know what they say. An explanation is worth 1,000 words. This one here is worth 183, so you're getting it for cheap.

CG: THIS IS BULLSHIT.
CG: WE'RE NOT EXILING JACK, HE'S COOL.
GC: K4RK4T, H3 1S NOT TH4T COOL!
CG: YES HE IS, HE'S A TOTAL BADASS WITH A FUCK TON OF BLADES AND SHIT, AND HE'S HELPING US OUT.
GC: OK, 1 TH1NK 1TS PR3TTY CUT3 TH4T YOU SORT OF LOOK UP TO H1M L1K3 TH4T
GC: BUT S3R1OUSLY, 1 DO NOT G3T 4 GOOD F33L1NG FROM H1M!
GC: H3 K1ND OF
CG: STINKS?
CG: LET ME ACTED SHOCKED LIKE I DIDN'T SEE THAT COMING.
CG: O:
CG: FUCK I FORGOT MY HORNS, I ALWAYS FORGET THEM
CG: O:B
GC: NO!
GC: W3LL
GC: SORT OF
GC: H3 DO3SNT SM3LL B4D 4CTU4LLY
GC: H3 SM3LLS R34LLY CL34N 4ND SH1NY 4ND D4RK D4RK D444RK L1K3 4N O1L SL1CK 4ND TH3R3 1S 4 T1NY H1NT OF L1COR1C3 TH3R3 TOO
GC: 1TS MOR3 L1K3
GC: TH3 W4Y H3 MOV3S
GC: 1 SM3LL H1S SMOOTH MOT1ONS 4ND TH3 W4Y H3 SQU1NTS H1S 3Y3S 4ND 1T G1V3S M3 TH1S R34LLY N3RVOUS F33L1NG
CG: WHAT A SURPRISE, YOU ARE DRAGGING YOUR SCHIZOPHRENIC NOSE INTO THIS, WHAT AN OUTSTANDING CHARACTER WITNESS.
CG: OBJECTION YOUR TYRANNY! HAHAHA
GC: >:D
CG: THE BOTTOM LINE IS I AM NOT GOING TO EXILE JACK BECAUSE YOU BELIEVE YOU CAN SMELL MALICE OFF AN INTERPRETIVE DANCE.
GC: K4RK4T, H3S 4 J3RK!
GC: H3 H4S ST4BB3D YOU ON MOR3 TH4N ON3 OCC4S1ON!
CG: SOME OF THOSE STABBINGS WERE ACCIDENTAL!
GC: >8|
CG: OK, WELL I KNOW FOR A FACT THE THIRD TIME WAS ACCIDENTAL.
CG: ANYWAY YOU'VE BEATEN THE SHIT OUT OF ME A FEW TIMES YOURSELF.
GC: BUT 1 D1DN'T DR4W BLOOD!
GC: 1 M34N 1 COULD H4V3 TO S4T1SFY MY CUR1OS1TY >:]
GC: BUT 1 D1DNT 4S 4 COURT3SY TO YOU
GC: S1NC3 YOU ST1LL W4NT TO K33P 1T 4 S3CR3T FROM M3 L1K3 4 P3TUL4NT L1TTL3 W1GGL3R >:P
CG: HEY I PROMISED I'D TELL YOU.
CG: I JUST

You know how sometimes you need to talk your idiot friend out of spending lots of time with his weird, older, shifty friend who has a cool knife collection? This relatable and timeless experience is captured here.

CG: WASN'T READY OK
GC: W3LL
GC: 1TS OK
GC: 1 KNOW WH4T COLOR YOUR BLOOD 1S 4NYW4Y >:]
CG: NO YOU DON'T
GC: YUP, 1 TOT4LLY DO
CG: LIES, I'VE BEEN VERY CAREFUL.
CG: NOT LIKE ALL YOU CLASSLESS SHITBAGS WHO SLOP YOUR BLOOD ALL OVER THE PLACE EVERY GODDAMN MINUTE LIKE IT'S SOME WEIRD FETISH.
GC: 3RR
GC: HM >:\
CG: WHAT
GC: BL4R
GC: HOLD ON
CG: WHAT IS IT?
GC: 1 S41D HOLD ON! SOM3T1M3S 1TS H4RD TO P1CK OUT TH3 L3TT3RS FROM TH3 HOLO PROJ3CT1ON
GC: 1 N33D TO G3T 4 CLOS3R LOOK!
CG: ARE YOU LICKING YOUR GLASSES AGAIN?
CG: I HATE IT WHEN YOU DO THAT, IT'S FUCKING DISGUSTING.
GC: NOMP, WH4TH WOULB EBER G1TH YOU TH4TH 1BE4???
GC: H3H3H3H3H3H3H3

> Terezi: Get closer look.

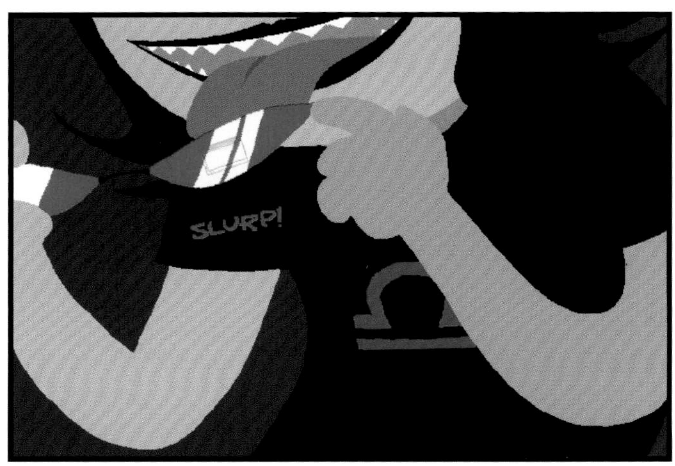

This is just revisiting the ongoing farce at the center of Karkat's life. That is, his blood color being one of the ridiculously worst-kept secrets possible, even as he insists to himself that it's unhackably privileged information, even around someone who he knows operates via some kind of powerful "scent sonar."

002575

GC: TH4T 1S B3TT3R
GC: 1TS MUCH 34S13R TO R34D YOUR COLOR TH1S W4Y
GC: YOUR DR4B D1RTY P4V3M3NT GR4Y
GC: ON TOP OF BR1GHT C4NDY R3D, L1K3 4 SH1NY LOLL1POP
GC: DO3S TH4T SOUND F4M1L14R K4RK4T??
CG: YES, I'M EXTREMELY FAMILIAR WITH THIS SORT OF NONSENSE BY NOW, SURE.
GC: NO 1 M34N
GC: GR4Y ON R3D
GC: L1K3 TH3 W4Y YOUR SK1N
GC: CONC34LS YOUR BLOOD
CG: WHAT
GC: C4NDY C4NDY R3D!
GC: L1K3 YOUR PL4N3T
GC: YOU H4V3 STRONG CH3RRY COUGH SYRUP 1N YOUR V31NS! 1T 1S COMPL3T3LY D3L1C1OUS.
CG: WHO TOLD YOU
CG: DID JACK TELL YOU
GC: NO H3 DO3SNT T4LK MUCH
GC: 1 F1GUR3D 1T OUT MYS3LF
CG: HOW
GC: 1 GOT 4 CLOS3R LOOK
GC: R3M3MB3R >:]
CG: NO
GC: PFFF YOU 4R3 PL4Y1NG SO DUMB, YOU KNOW 3X4CTLY WH4T 1 4M T4LK1NG 4BOUT
CG: I CLEANED UP MY WOUND AND CHANGED MY SHIRT BEFORE I EVEN MET YOU, I'VE BEEN EXTREMELY CAREFUL.
CG: SO YOU'RE GOING TO HAVE TO FILL ME IN.
GC: 1T W4S WH3N 1 GOT CLOS3 3NOUGH
GC: TO SM3LL 1T UND3R YOUR SK1N
GC: PL34S3 K4RK4T, DO NOT PR3T3ND TH4T YOU FORGOT 4BOUT OUR L1TTL3 MOM3NT
CG: WHOA
CG: YOU MEAN
CG: DURING
CG: FUCK.
CG: OK SHHHHHHHHHH SHH SHH SHH...
CG: LET'S NOT TALK ABOUT THIS, NOT HERE.
GC: TH1S 1SNT 4 M3MO!
GC: 1TS 4 PR1V4T3 CORR3SPOND3NC3 JUST B3TW33N US, R3M3MB3R?
CG: I KNOW BUT
CG: DAMMIT
CG: WRITING ALL THESE MEMOS HAS MADE ME PARANOID.
CG: IT JUST DOESN'T FEEL SECURE CHATTING ABOUT IT OVER THE CLIENT, I DUNNO.
CG: WE CAN TALK ABOUT IT IN PERSON.
GC: HOW "1N P3RSON" DO YOU M34N?

Karezi is one of those baseline type of ships that exist in any given franchise. The kind with blinking arrows pointing to it and a neon sign saying "THE TEXT INTENDS FOR YOU TO SHIP THESE TWO." It has endgame written all over it. Which, despite some endearing qualities and some decent conversations in service to the idea, is what makes it a bit boring. To whatever extent *Homestuck* is capable of serving up a conventional, recognizable morsel of "fairytale intent" on a platter, this might be it. A statement expressing what it considers to be its equivalent to the boy-meets-girl, written-in-the-stars, journey-to-the-white-picket-fence sort of pairing. Which is not an inherently bad thing. There's a always place for arcs like these, and a certain comfort people take from grabbing on to the white-picket-fence outcomes and rooting for them. A lot of people were pretty stoked about Karezi. Stuff like this conversation obviously is going to start shoveling coal into that engine pretty hard. But these features are what give it a predictable quality, and thus make it much less likely to be fully realized in the long run. Instead, later it's given more value as a foil relationship, a thing that threatens to happen often, because it's "supposed" to, but functions as a basis for turbulent departures. A backdrop of stable, comprehensible relationship potential against which some more unpredictable and challenging outcomes for them both start to play out. -->

GC: UH OH LOOK 4T MY 3Y3BROWS G3TT1NG C4RR13D 4W4Y H3R3
GC: >;]
GC: > ;]
GC: >;]
GC: > ;]
GC: >;]
GC: > ;]
GC: K4RK4T H3LP, TH3Y 4R3 OUT OF CONTROL!!!
CG: THOSE ARE EYEBROWS?
CG: I THOUGHT THEY WERE HORNS.
GC: TH3Y 4R3 HORNS TOO
GC: TH3Y 4R3 4R3 WH4T3V3R 1 W4NT TH3M TO B3
CG: ?:B
GC: DONT CH4NG3 TH3 SUBJ3CT BY B31NG CUT3!
CG: WELL APPARENTLY I JUST CAN'T FUCKING HELP MYSELF CAN I.
GC: NOP3
CG: HOW CAN YOU EVEN SMELL SO DAMN WELL, ANYWAY.
CG: YOU GIVE ME A HARD TIME ABOUT BEING COY ABOUT SHIT
CG: BUT WHEN IT COMES TO YOUR CRAZY SENSES YOU'RE SO VAGUE, IT'S LIKE TRYING TO DECIPHER THE DAILY HOROSCOPE RIDDLE.
CG: OR THE RIDDLES FOR ALL 48 SIGNS COMBINED.
GC: 444RGH
GC: YOU 4R3 4 R3L3NTL3SS SUBJ3CT CH4NG3R! >XO
GC: F1N3, 1TS OK 1F YOU DONT W4NT TO T4LK 4BOUT 1T
GC: GOD YOU 4R3 SOOOOO SHY FOR 4N 4NGRY GUY WHO W4NTS TO B3 4 B1GSHOT L34D3R, 1TS R1D1CULOUS
CG: LOOK
CG: WE'LL TALK
CG: I PROMISE
CG: WHY DON'T YOU JUST SAY SOME STUFF ABOUT YOURSELF FOR A CHANGE
CG: AND CUT ME SOME SLACK.
GC: OK >:]
GC: 1M SUR3 1 M3NT1ON3D 4FT3R YOU M3T MY SPR1T3
GC: 1 L34RN3D FROM H3R THROUGH MY DR34MS
GC: B3FOR3 SH3 H4TCH3D!
CG: YEAH, BUT IT'S STILL SO VAGUE.
CG: THAT'S THE WHOLE POINT.
CG: HOW ABOUT A STRAIGHT ANSWER?
GC: OK, 1LL TRY
GC: WH3N 1 W3NT BL1ND, TH4TS WH3N 1 F1RST WOK3 UP
GC: 4ND MY LUSUS H3LP3D M3 W4K3 UP!
GC: SORT OF
CG: YOU MEAN ON PROSPIT'S MOON.
GC: Y3S

--> Quick off-topic note: Karkat's reference to the forty-eight signs is based on the (fake) forty-eight-player Squiddle session that apocryphally created their universe. Back on topic: Karezi as the male/female lead, meant-to-be sort of ship, is, well, it's obvious. It's obvious to me at least, because I'm dangling it out there, obviously. Therefore I feel it must be obvious to you. And as such, I feel you must know I see it as obvious, and intend it as obvious, in this big feedback loop of self-evidentiary storycraft and trope jockeying. Any time this is true, I think awareness of the circumstance tends to leak into the consciousness of the characters involved. Characters in HS tend to be pretty self-aware (like Striders and Lalondes), but even the ones that aren't as much (like these two) still tend to carry a form of subconscious self-awareness. (Feel free to chew on this oxymoron for a moment before continuing.) In other words, on some level, Karkat and Terezi both just sort of *know* they are the male and female leads in a lengthy heroic tale, and thus their sense of this propels them toward attraction, as if satisfying unspoken narrative obligation. This must especially seem true for Karkat, who lives and breathes the tropes of his romance films. -->

GC: BUT
GC: 3XC3PT FOR 4 V3RY BR13F MOM3NT...
GC: 1 W4S BL1ND 1N MY DR34MS TOO
GC: TH3 DR34M S3LF 1M4G3 1 PROJ3CT C4N'T S33, B3C4US3 1 GU3SS D33P DOWN 1 DONT R34LLY W4NT TO
CG: WHY IS THAT.
CG: IS IT OUT OF SPITE TO VRISKA?
CG: I KNOW I'D PROBABLY BE COOL WITH IT OUT OF SPITE MORE THAN ANYTHING.
GC: NO
GC: NOT TH4T TH3R3 W4SNT SOM3 S4T1SF4CT1ON 1N B31NG OK4Y W1TH 1T
GC: GR4T3FUL 4BOUT 1T 3V3N!
GC: 4ND M4K1NG SUR3 SH3 KN3W TH4T
GC: BUT TH4TS NOT 1T
GC: TH3 D4Y 1T H4PP3N3D W4S TH3 F1RST T1M3 1 3V3R H34RD FROM MY LUSUS
GC: SH3 WOK3 M3 UP, 4ND 3V3R S1NC3 H4S B33N T34CH1NG M3 4 D1FF3R3NT W4Y TO S33
GC: 4 D1FF3R3NT W4Y TO P3RC31V3 3V3RYTH1NG 1 GU3SS, NOT JUST 1N 4 S3NSORY W4Y
CG: OK, SO WHY DID YOU NEVER TELL ME ANY OF THIS?
GC: YOU WOULDNT H4V3 GOTT3N 1T!
GC: 3V3N NOW YOU ST1LL DONT R34LLY
GC: YOU H4V3 NOT 3V3N S33N SK414 Y3T
CG: HOW AM I SUPPOSED TO WAKE UP.
GC: 1 DONT KNOW!
GC: SOM3TH1NG D1FF3R3NT DO3S 1T FOR 3V3RYBODY
CG: HOW MANY OF US ARE AWAKE NOW?
CG: HOW MUCH OF THE FUTURE DID YOU "SEE" BEFORE WE STARTED
CG: IN THE CLOUDS, LIKE KANAYA
CG: ALSO HOW DID YOU GO BLIND ANYWAY???
CG: WHAT DID SHE DO TO YOU, I DON'T KNOW WHY YOU'RE SO CAGEY ABOUT THAT.
CG: I STILL DON'T SEE HOW SHE COULD BLIND YOU WITHOUT BEING ANYWHERE NEAR YOU.
CG: OBVIOUSLY SHE CAN'T CONTROL YOU, SO WHAT GIVES?
GC: K4RK4T SHUT UP!
GC: GOD
GC: HOW 4BOUT 1F
GC: 1 T3LL YOU 4LL 4BOUT TH4T STUFF N3XT T1M3 W3 4R3 "1N P3RSON" >;]
GC: 1N F4CT, 1 W1LL T3LL YOU WH3N YOU W4K3 UP!
GC: UNT1L TH3N 1 W1LL K33P T4BS ON YOU 1N YOUR TOW3R WH1L3 YOU SL33P L1K3 4 L1TTL3 HON3Y P4J4M4'D PUP4 N3STL3D 1N H1S COCOON
CG: WAIT LET ME GUESS.
CG: DO I LOOK ADORABLE?????????
GC: 4CTU4LLY
GC: YOU LOOK K1ND OF L1K3 4 B1G P1L3 OF SM3LLY B4RF
CG: WOW, WHAT THE FUCK.

--> Here Terezi tees up the mystery of her blinding, which is one of the few remaining things to wrap up. It's covered in **[S] Make her pay**, which we'll get to in a few pages. I'm still plowing through the meta on WHAT'S THE DEAL WITH KAREZI? It feels important to hit these subjects very hard down here in the gutter while I've got the chance, just so I don't have to later. Then you know what's basically up with Karezi, forever, and I can opine on other matters with foregone presumption of your understanding. Unless you forget I said all this, which you probably will. And frankly, so will I. Anyway. I think the fact that on some unwitting level, they both recognize a part of their attraction is based on obligatory service to the narrative pushing them together like this goes a long way in explaining the fact that the pairing is a bit tense, full of fraught turns, false starts, and stupid miscues. It follows a clumsy path, and a lot of this feels like it stems from the fact that Karkat ends up forcing it along the way, much the way he does with his role as "the leader," which is also a role thrust upon him by unseen narrative forces. He keeps pushing for the romance to happen aggressively and obsessively, because he senses that's what's "supposed" to happen and never actually has the epiphany that this is what's going on in his mind. And Terezi keeps getting caught in the cycle of stupidity too for similar reasons, and can't seem to stop humoring the development of this inorganically blossoming romance. Which exacerbates her depression issues, makes things worse, and ultimately contributes to her deep dive through the clownlust sewer. -->

GC: OF COOOOUUUUURS3 YOU DO, DUMB4SS >:]
CG: OH
CG: THEN
CG: GOOD I GUESS
GC: OK 1V3 GOT TO FLY
GC: DONT WORRY 4BOUT TH3 R1NG M1SS1ON
GC: YOU C4N ST4Y BUSY W1TH R3G1SURP
GC: 1 W1LL ORG4N1Z3 TH3 N3W M1SS1ON MYS3LF
GC: L4T3R!
CG: WAIT
CG: TEREZI
CG: PLEASE DON'T TELL THEM ABOUT MY BLOOD.
CG: I WANT TO TELL THEM, I MEAN I WILL TELL THEM.
CG: LATER
CG: ONCE THEY RESPECT ME AS A LEADER.
GC: OK
GC: 1 W1LL K33P TH4T S3CR3T 1F YOU K33P TH1S ON3 1 T3LL YOU
GC: WH1CH 1S TH4T
GC: B3TW33N YOU 4ND M3 K4RK4T
GC: 1 TH1NK TH3Y 4LR34DY DO
GC: BY3!
GC: <3
CG: BYE

gallowsCalibrator [GC] **ceased trolling** carcinoGeneticist [CG]

carcinoGeneticist [CG] **ceased trolling** gallowsCalibrator [GC]

carcinoGeneticist [CG] **began trolling** gallowsCalibrator [GC]

CG: <3

carcinoGeneticist [CG] **ceased trolling** gallowsCalibrator [GC]

> [???????]
> [S... BAHJ] Terezi: Ascend.

--> But that said, all long-road Karezi bummers aside, at least at this moment in the story this thing they have going on here reads as pretty endearing. Like there could still be real promise to whatever's going on here. Could it have worked out nice and fine if Karezi followed a conventionally successful romantic path, and turned out to be endgame as hell? Sure, why not. But it didn't. All I can tell you is, a lot of people went nuts for that little heart he logged back on to share. I wonder how many of those people gradually transmuted into Davekat stans? We may never know.

This SBAHJ-style comic "reskinned" from earlier iteration, involving Davesprite flying up away to the sun like a fucking piece of gargbage, was a good, stupid panel to puase on while I took a few days to make **[S] Make her pay**. Wow, a few WHOLE DAYS? "Pausing" the comic formally used to be necessary in such situations because it updated so much, and during Hivebent in particular. A pause page was a way of me saying, "Chill out, I'm not dead, I'm probably just working on a Flash." Later on, the pauses got a little less "fun," and also a lot longer. It was more like me saying, "Yo guys, chill here for a bit while I take a moment to handle a multi-year spanning crisis." Usually those long gaps were radically overcompensated for by killing all the characters in one fell swoop upon my return and dumping a ton of horribly drawn anime on everyone. In a way, all *Homestuck* pauses can be seen as a means of storing up vast quantities of dark potential energy, which explodes in everyone's face when the updates resume.

[S] Make her pay is the culmination of Hivebent. It ties up what can be regarded as the few remaining loose ends in a rough and bloody collage of retributional actions, which all revolve around the brand-new star of the story, Vriska. This sounds like a joke, but it really isn't. If there's one thing we end up with at the end of Hivebent that we didn't begin with, it's the emergence of this figure as someone who's going to demand center stage from now on, and who won't take no for an answer, no matter how many times the narrative tries to point the camera at something else. This animation really couldn't do a better job of signaling this transition, since the apex of Hivebent revolves around not just one of Vriska's plot points, but two. One where she does something horrible, and another where she suffers horrible consequences for what she did.

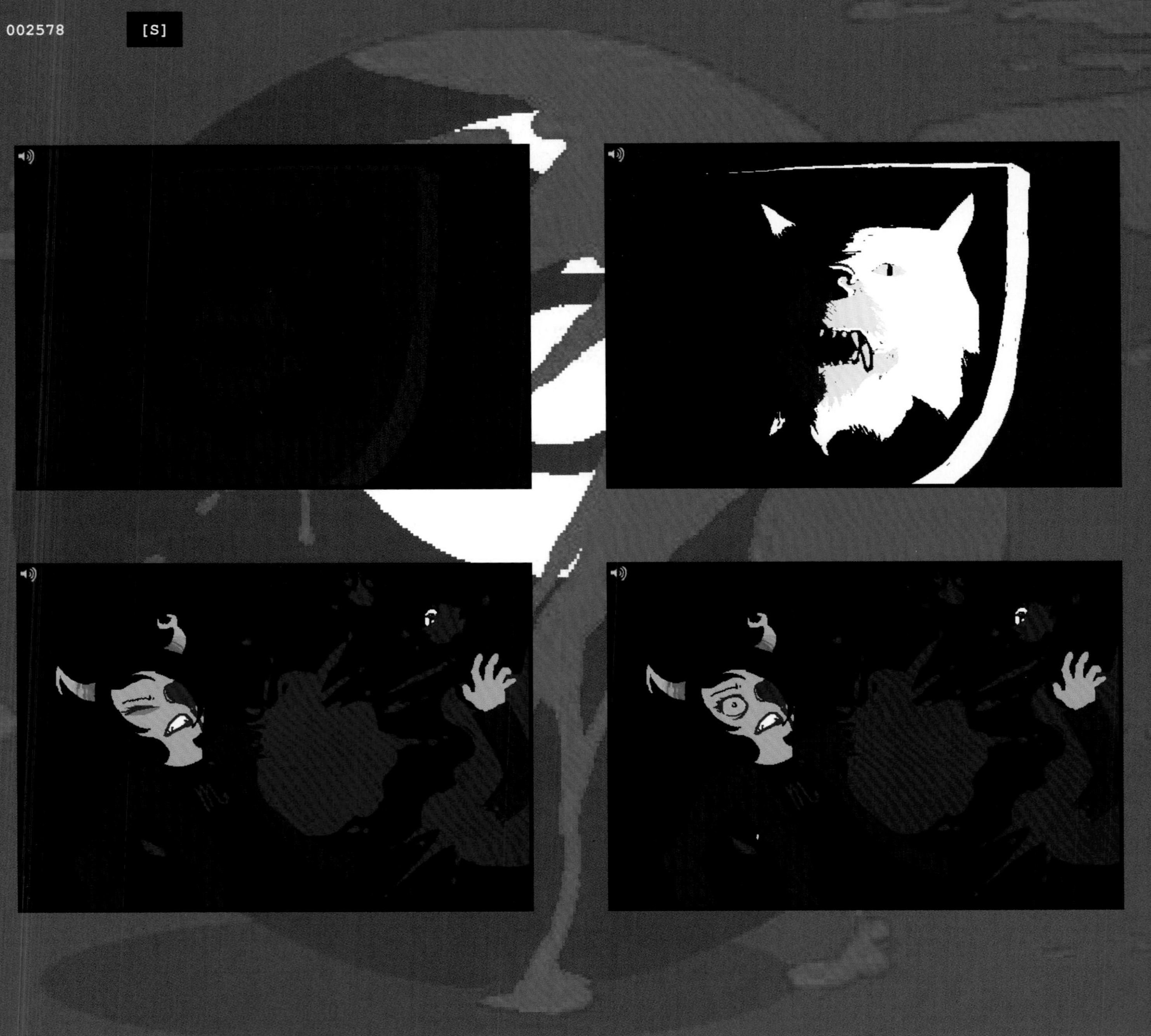

AAAAAAAAAAAAAAAAAAAAAAAAAAAAAAAAAAAAAAAAAAAAAAAAAAAAAH! Sorry, I lose my shit whenever I see that wolf head. The animation picks up right where we left off, when Scratch blew off Vriska's arm and took out her eye. Have we talked about this particular disfigurement yet? It's mentioned in the Pupa Pan parallels, but also it's the same disfigurement Jack receives in the other session, as a result of some mishaps with the clown doll John prototyped. Is this a "cursed disfigurement"? Is the fact that this happened to Vriska, as sort of a punishment by Scratch, meant to indicate that future realities would be cursed with echoes of this disfigurement as well? Did Scratch give her this disfigurement deliberately because he knew of its future relevance? Is it simple foreshadowing? Is there no correlation? What are the answers, when you can't definitively tell if one event takes place before another, or the reverse is true? Are these disfigurements taking place in a way that each is circumstantially simultaneous with the other? Scratch would probably say yes. The reason I know he would is because he's basically just a slightly more obnoxious and opaque version of the author.

The animation settles into a rhythm from here on, in a way that I think is pretty self-explanatory, even in static form. So there's probably not much to say about it. I think I'm going to try a brand-new trick. It's called "hiding the author notes margin" when I don't have anything particularly worthwhile to say. Oh, you don't think that sounds like the "coolest" idea I've ever had? Well, why don't you give it a shot first, see how you feel about it. I know I'm feeling pretty great about the plan already.

002578
[S]

The author note margin suddenly returns on page 420, just in time for me to invite you to "blaze it." It's totally fine with me if you want to rip this page out of the book and roll a dank blunt with it. I won't call the cops. What? You think returning to writing page notes just to say this was actually dumb as shit? Fine, DON'T blaze it. I'll try to do better, by sharing an urban legend with you, that I made up one time. If the clock strikes 4:13, you can say "Homestuck" out loud, if you want. But if you do, you will then have exactly seven minutes to smoke some weed. If you don't manage to do this before the clock strikes 4:20, I will show up and murder you. Don't tell any of your friends this, it will end in tragedy.

DOUBLE

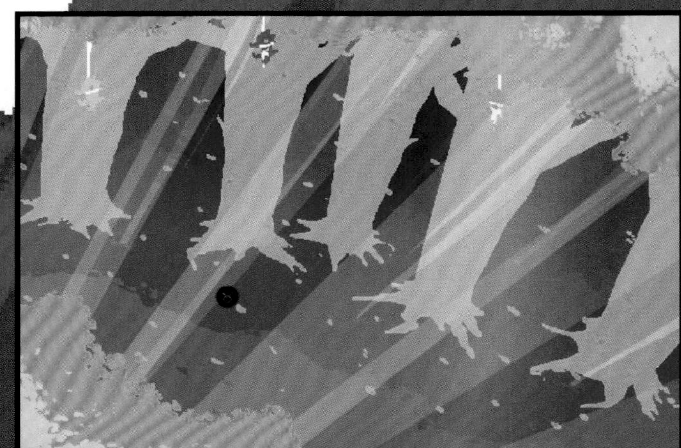

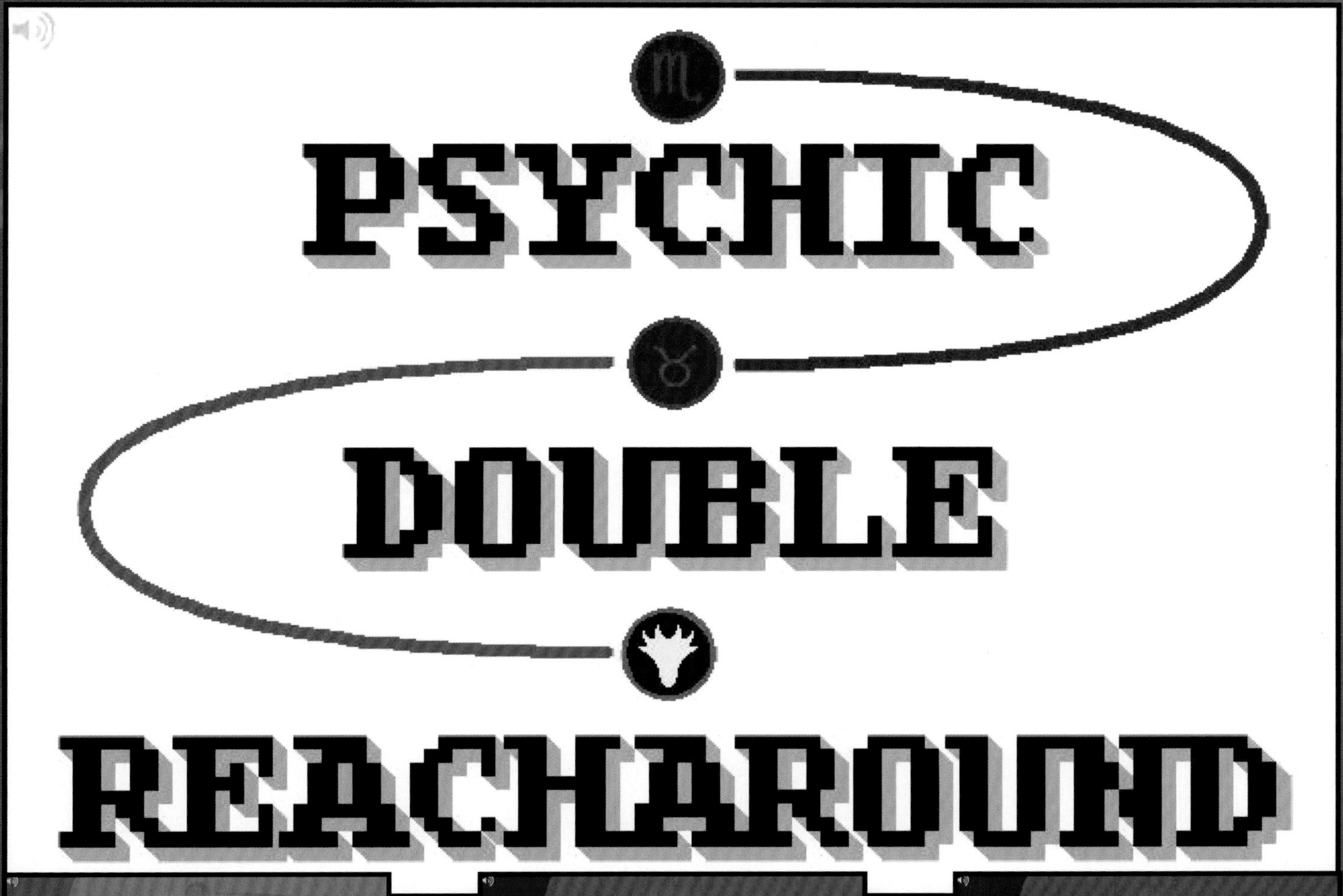

PSYCHIC DOUBLE REACHAROUND

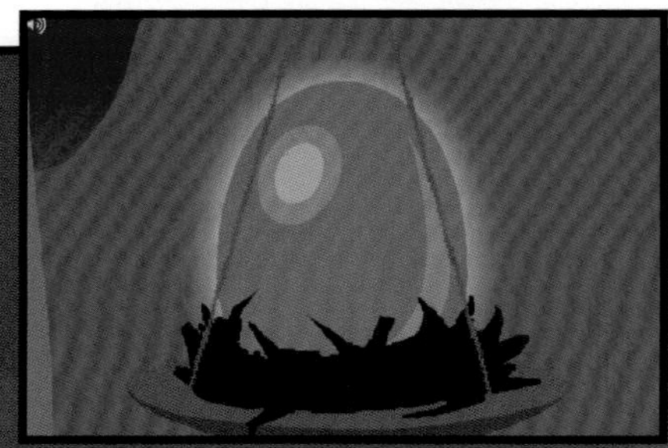

If it wasn't totally clear, here's what Vriska did. She psychically controls Tavros, who's a total chump and is easy for her to control at any time, for any purpose. She makes him use *his* psychic powers to commune with an animal. The animal in question is Terezi's pre-hatched dragon, who is psychically linked to Terezi, who is asleep. The dragon then controls Terezi to get up, sleepwalk through the woods, and stare directly into the harsh Alternian sun until she goes blind. Pretty good revenge, Vriska. I'm impressed. Or I would be, if I wasn't the one who thought of it instead of you. Oh wait, that just makes me even more impressed with it. Good job all around, everyone. Me and my OCs make a great team.

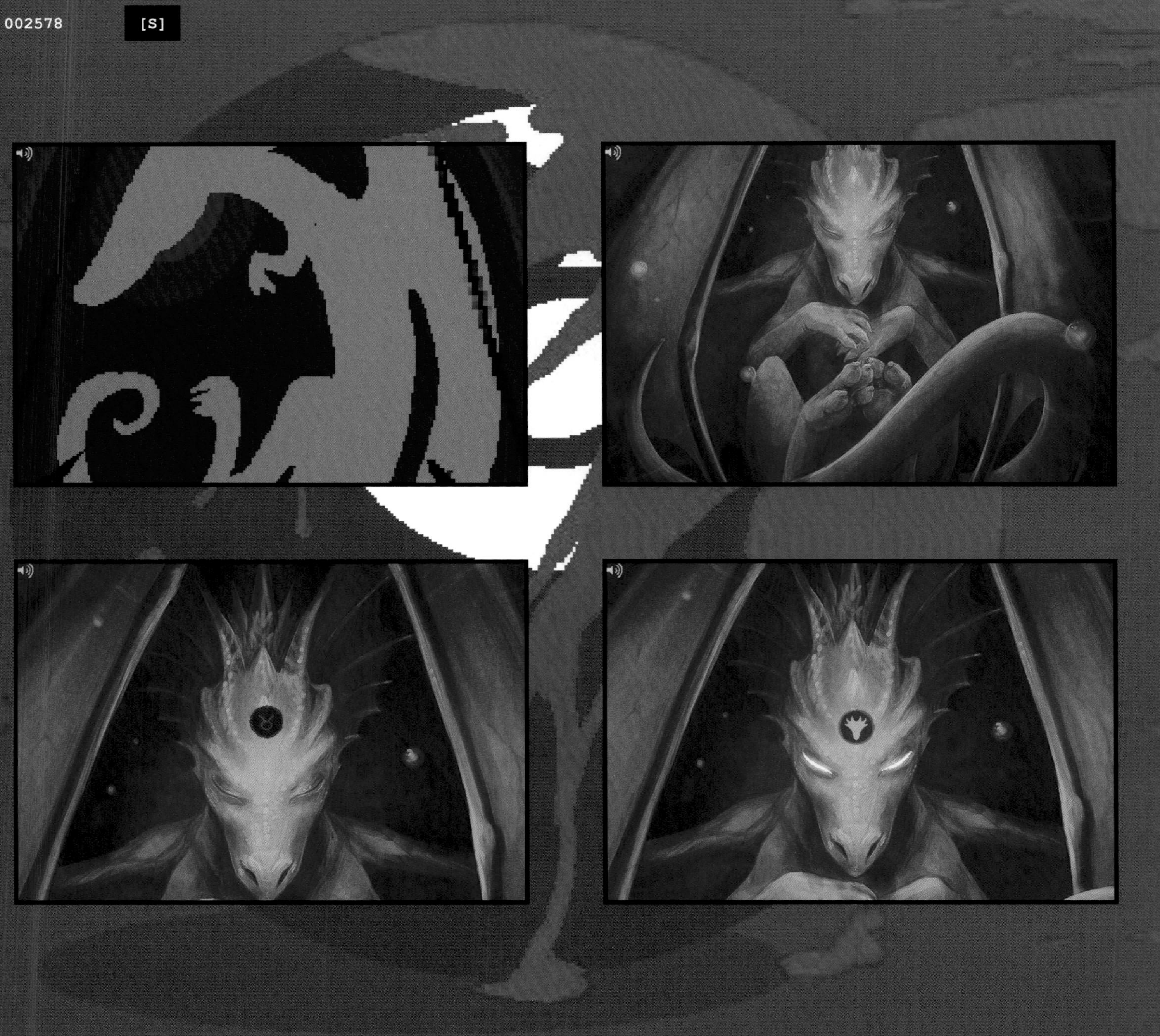

Getting contributions from other artists for animations was still kind of a new idea at this point. But the Flashes were still made with blazing speed, so the contributing artists had to work fast too, which resulted in a looser-looking art style similar to what I was working in. Still, opening it up to other artists who could invest more time individually into certain pieces really expanded the potential for how good some of these assets could look. So eventually some really strong examples started showing up, like this one. Making productions this way really widened the range of what *Homestuck* was capable of looking like. That range is about as broad as it gets, stretching from "complete and utter shit" all the way to "commercially produced, mainstream animation studio–grade." That escalation finally caps off with the Act 7 animation, which, for whatever else it might be, is the ultimate synthesis of *Homestuck* as a wildly escalating medium in the visuals department.

[S]

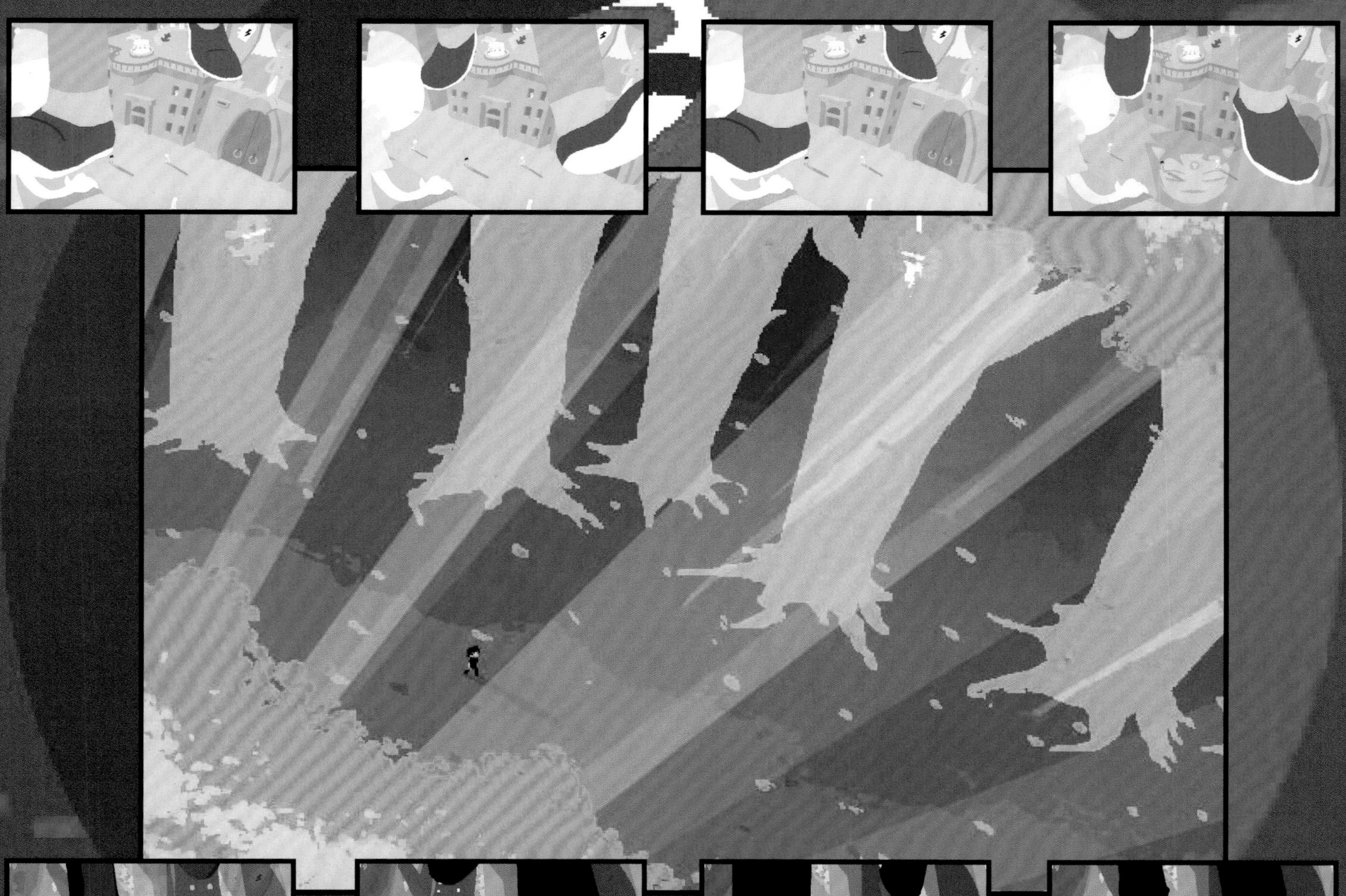

The neat thing here is that, though Vriska believes she's getting revenge, the dragon is actually managing to turn this into a boon for Terezi. Terezi hinted at this earlier in a conversation with Vriska, wanting to thank her for this moment, which Vriska didn't understand and just got frustrated about. The dragon is actually making her sleepwalk in two places: in the forest, and on Prospit. The animation sort of stylistically blends these two processions, toggling and fading between Terezi's real self and dream self as they stroll along.

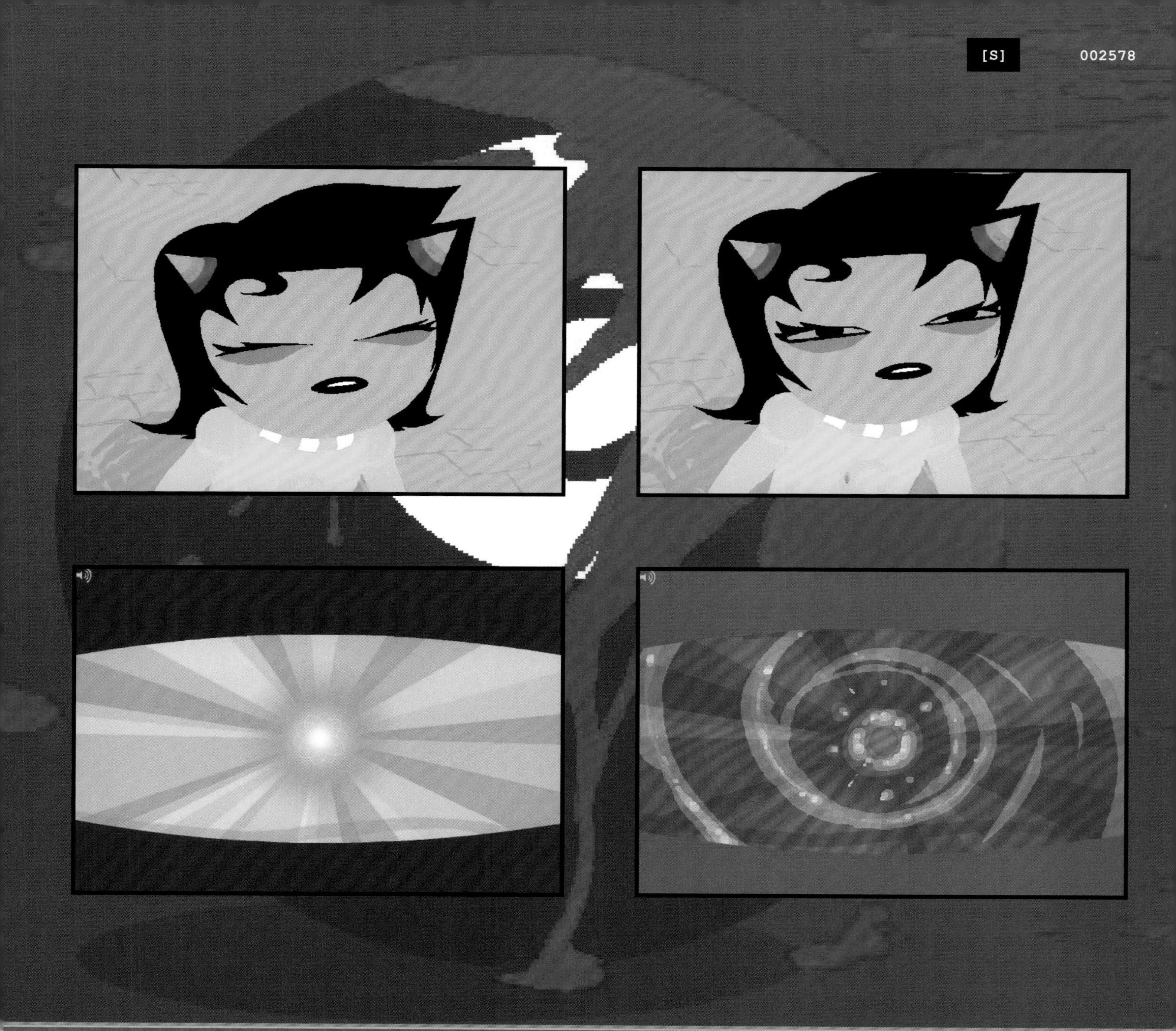

They open their eyes in both places. Dream Terezi sees Skaia, real Terezi gets an eyeful of burning sun. This is what causes Terezi to wake up on Prospit. She's blind in both the real and dream worlds, but now that her dragon is in tune with her mind, she's taught how to see in other ways, making most use of those lessons on Prospit. By the time she wakes up back in the woods to discover herself blind, she can already "see" well enough to find her way back home. Her blinding isn't really the maiming Vriska was going for. It's a sense-expanding, mind-awakening event that Terezi feels improves her life, and it becomes an important part of her identity. So much so that to be "healed" would trigger a crisis of identity and depression.

002578
[S]

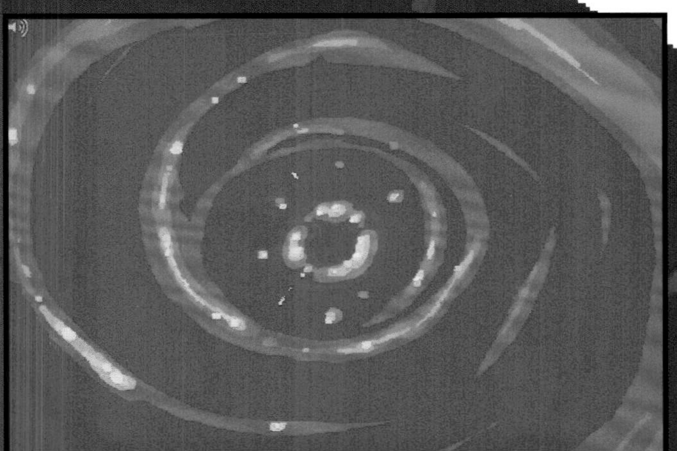

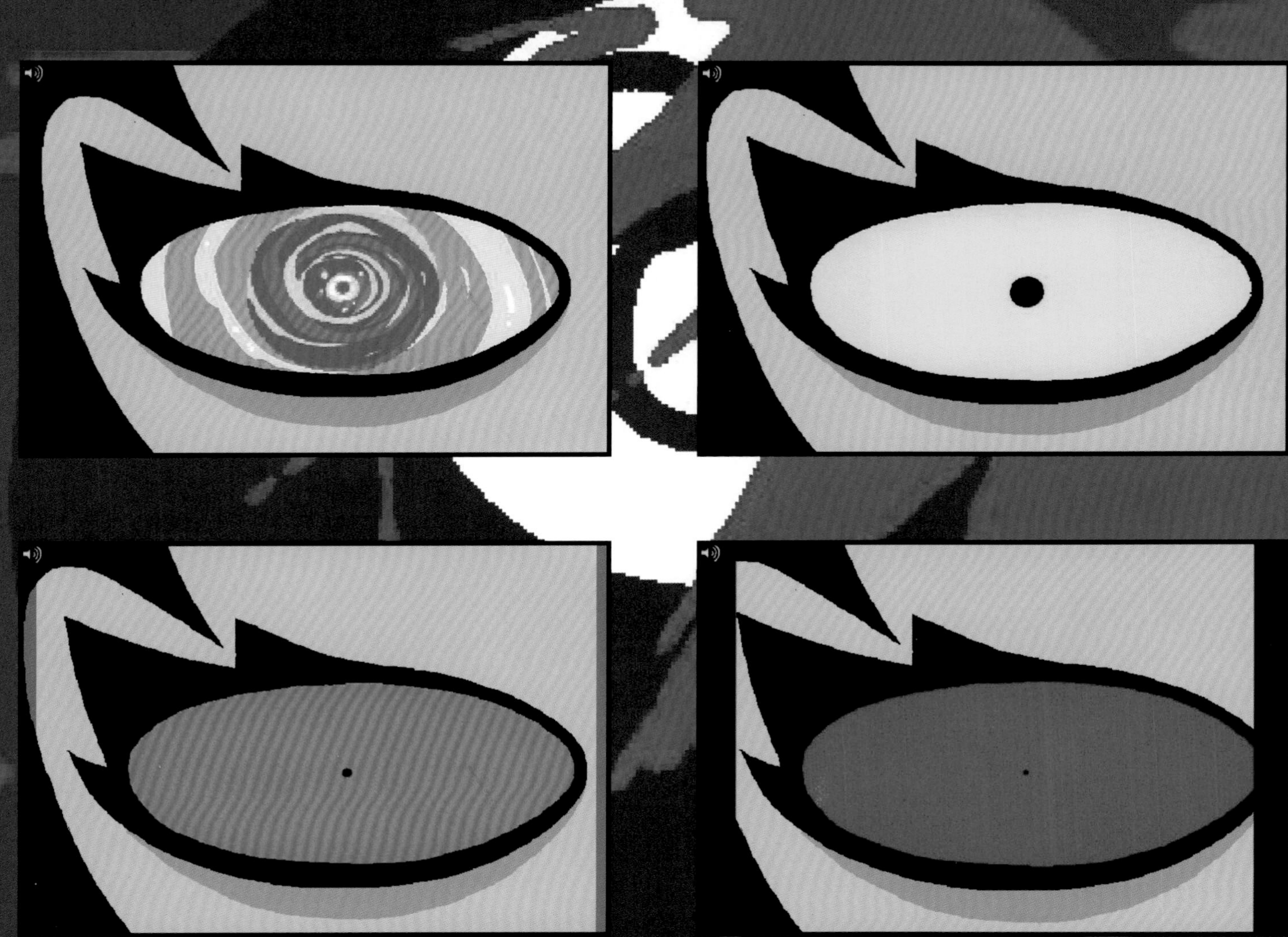

002578

[S]

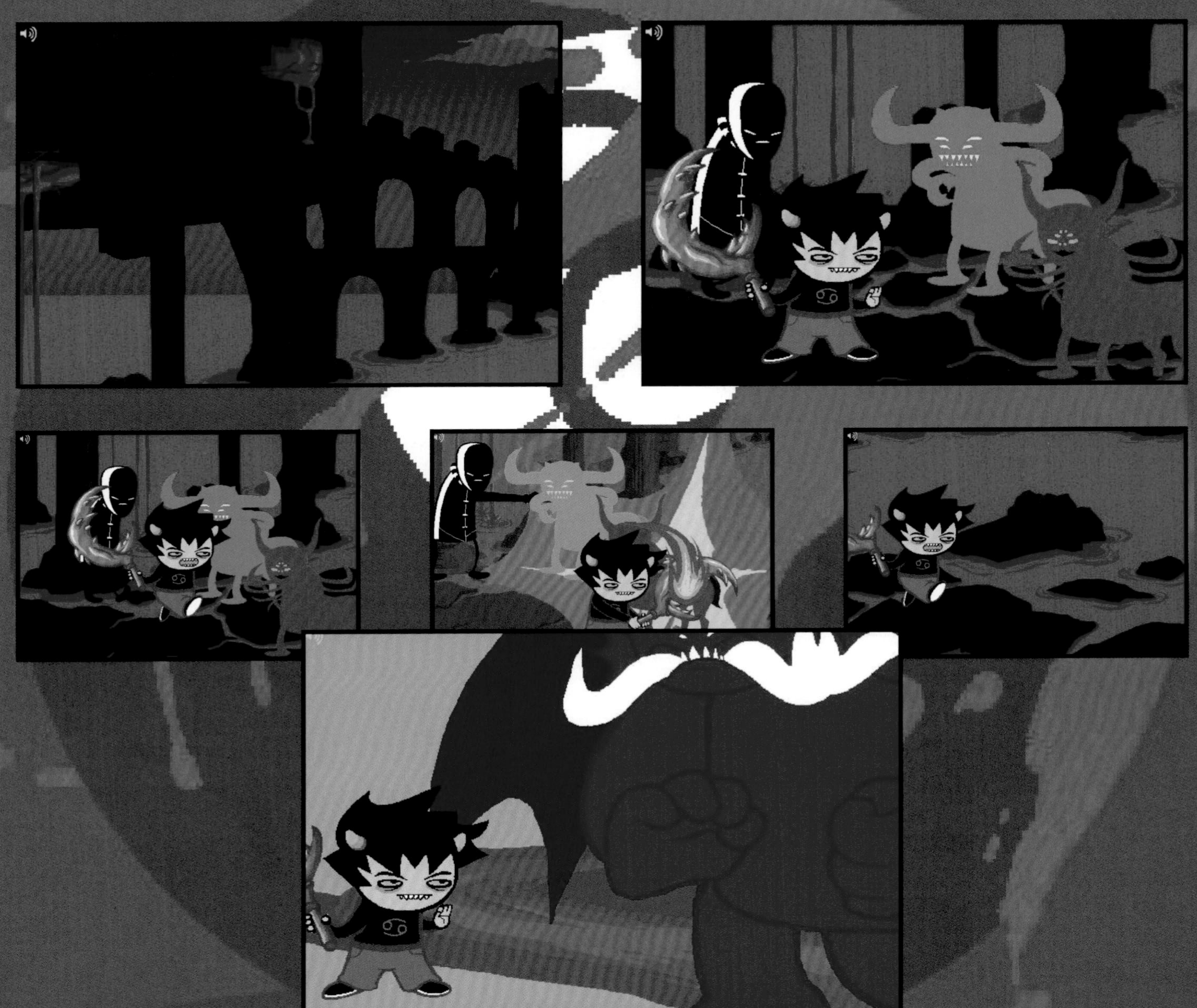

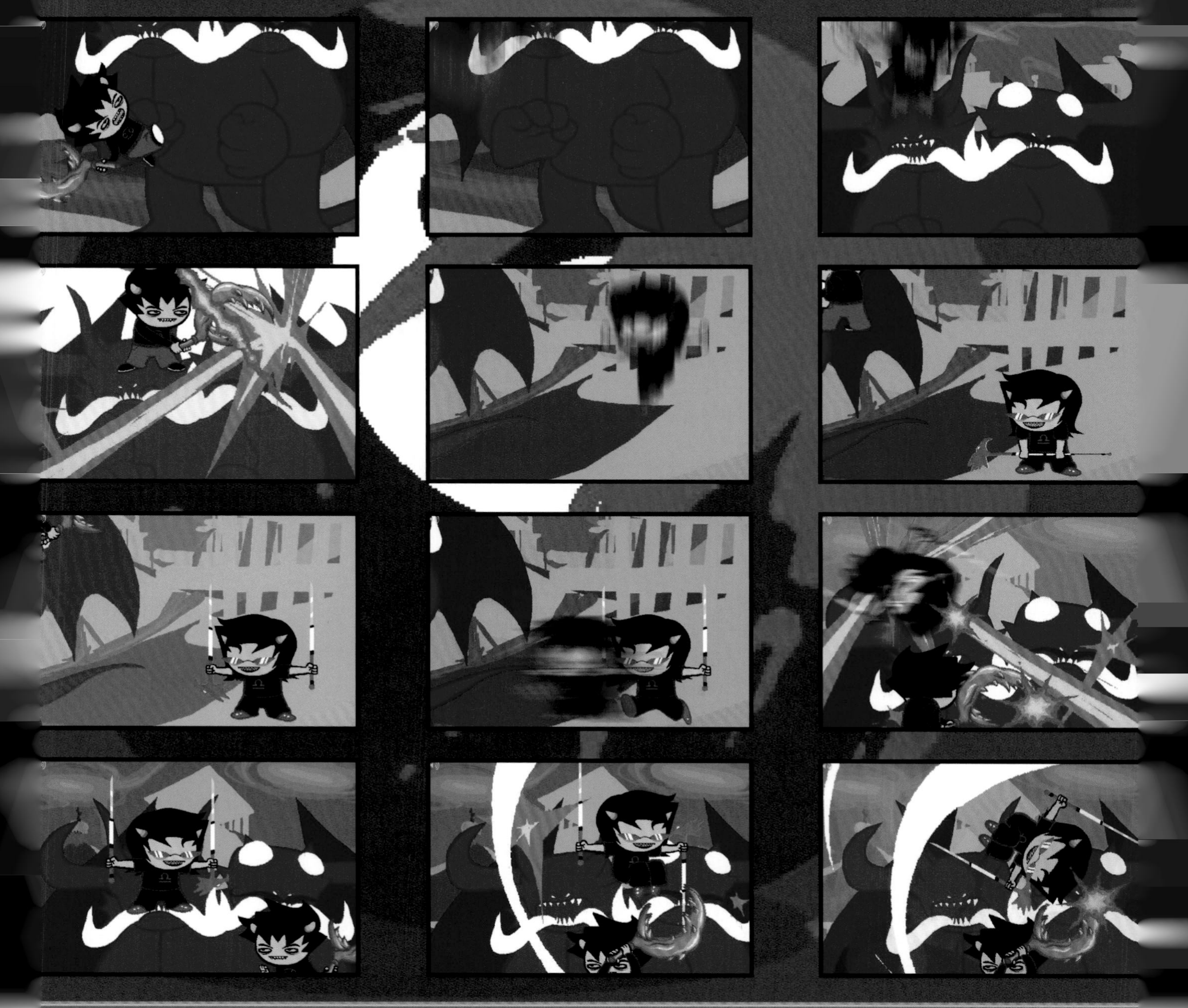

There are a few little sprite-based battle vignettes sprinkled into the animation. Full disclosure? Stuff like this tended to be filler. Some of these songs were LONG. But I didn't want to cut them down too often. A lot of times it was hard to find meaningful ways to fill every single stretch of a song without just dropping some reasonably cool, reasonably on-topic moments to grab the eye, or to use on a transitional basis before moving on to another stretch of the song that marked the right time to start a more relevant cinematic sequence.

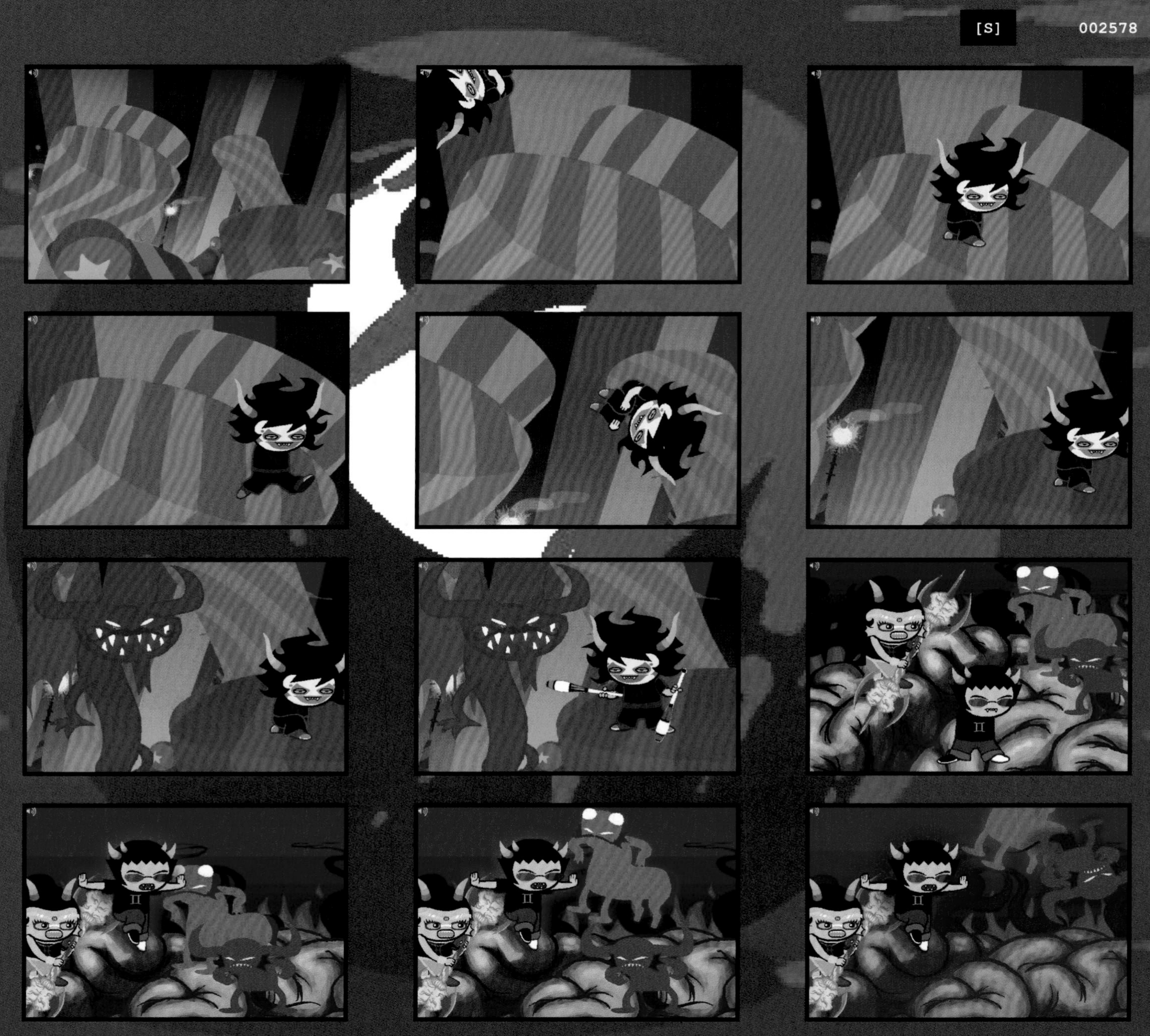

The way the art contributors worked as a group usually was pretty open-ended. A little in advance of starting an animation I'd say something like, "I don't really know exactly what this Flash needs yet, but probably just a bunch of generally cool battle stuff, like sprites and backgrounds, would be useful." And they did turn out to be useful. I almost always found a way to sneak everything in there, even if it was only onscreen for a couple seconds. It's one reason why a lot of these sequences end up being so dense.

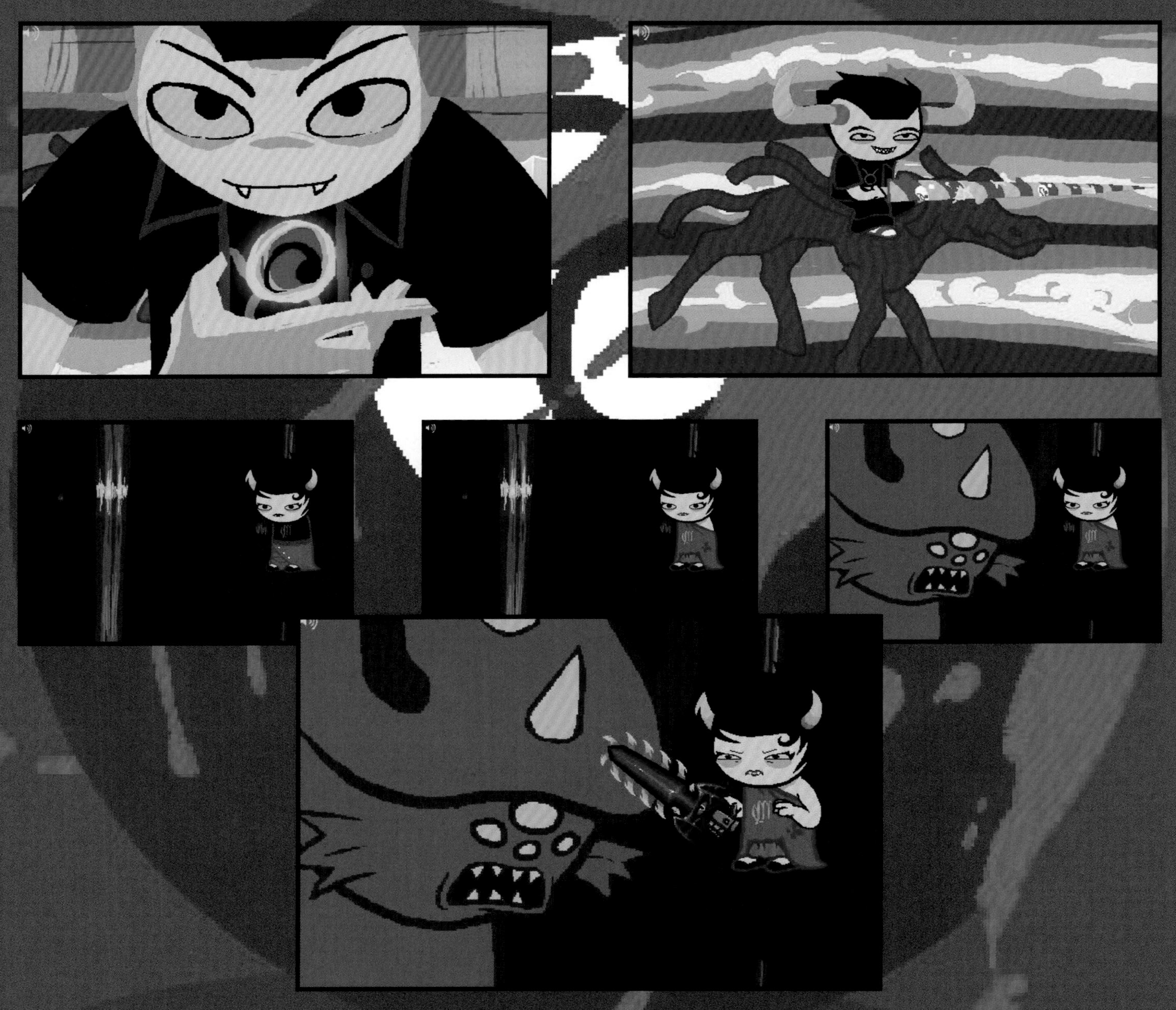

[S]

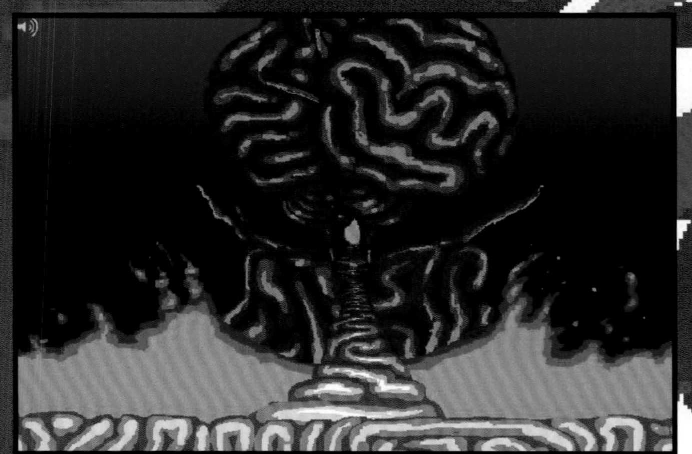

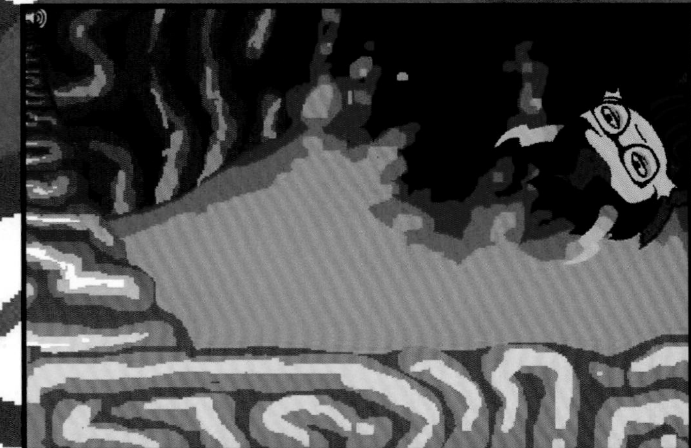

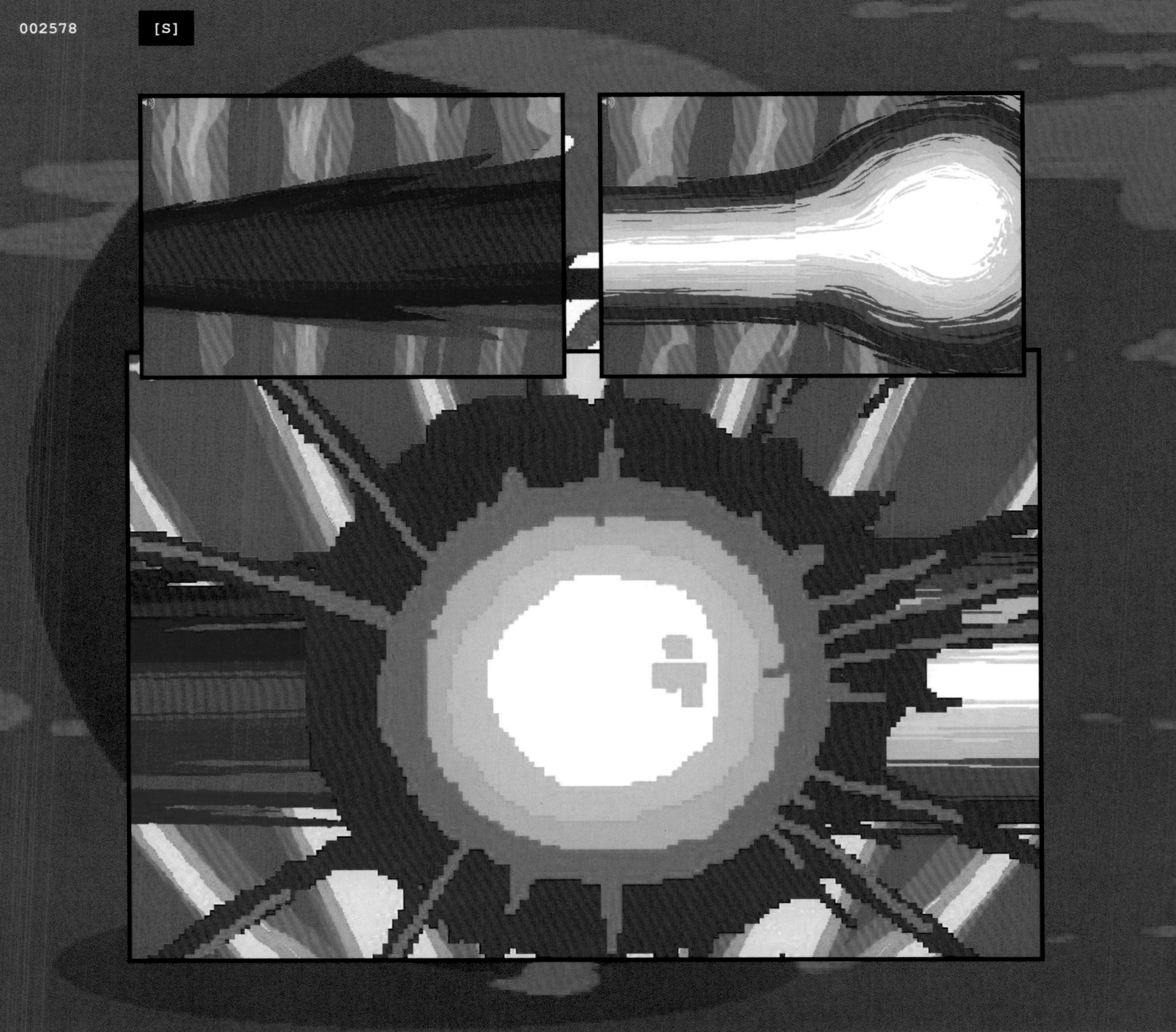

A first glimpse of the Sollux vs. Eridan drama. A lot of these brief clips imply events that readers easily could have guessed were going to play out anyway. We knew Sollux and Feferi started dating. We knew Feferi was Eridan's ex, and we knew what his attitude was like. We don't even need to make a whole thing about it. The wrong play would have been adding another scene in Hivebent where Eridan was like YOU STOLE MY GILFROND YOU SCURVVY SCALAWWAG! All we need is this brief shot, and it's like, oh, yep, there they go, that figures. Sometimes these arcs include *so* much shit, it seems like maybe there's no real vetting process for which scenes and conversations go in and which don't? That ain't true at all. There's a real art to determining out of all this chaos what's worth showing, which conversations are worth printing, and which ones are best left implied or omitted entirely. I can't give you the guidebook to such decisions. Ya just gotta FEEL IT.

Props to Vriska's Megaman slide across the bridge. Again, this only exists here because one of the artists randomly decided to make that pose.

Aradiabot shows up to beat Vriska's ass down. And we see she's got two portable, floating time-travel devices, like Dave has. These are implied to be akin to his turntables, but they're made from the stuff she had available on her planet. So this shot establishes that she's been making the rounds through time. Doing what, though? We'll see. But whatever she did, it seems like she's done enough of it to decide it's squared away, and she's now at liberty to focus on settling an old score.

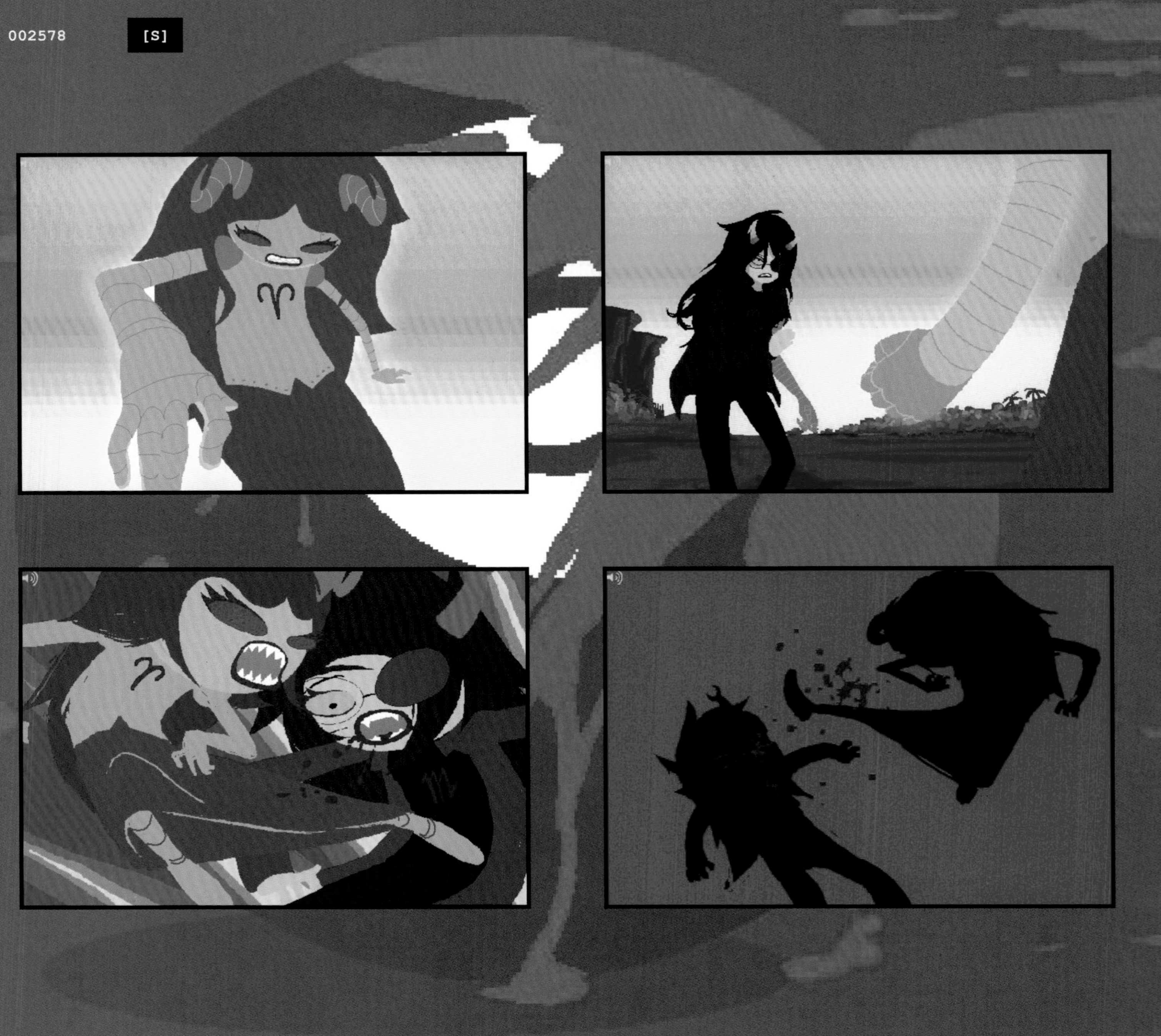

This all gets pretty savage. Probably the worst the story's presented so far, on a graphic-violence basis. Any time *Homestuck* moves the line a little further along any axis, it's basically saying, "This is also something the story can be." That goes for everything from the quality of rendering to the nature of the content. This fight pushes the line on *Homestuck's* capacity for brutality a little further. In that regard, this animation acts as another good transitional piece, paving the way for the tone of the rest of this Act. The Nastytimes are upon us.

002578

[S]

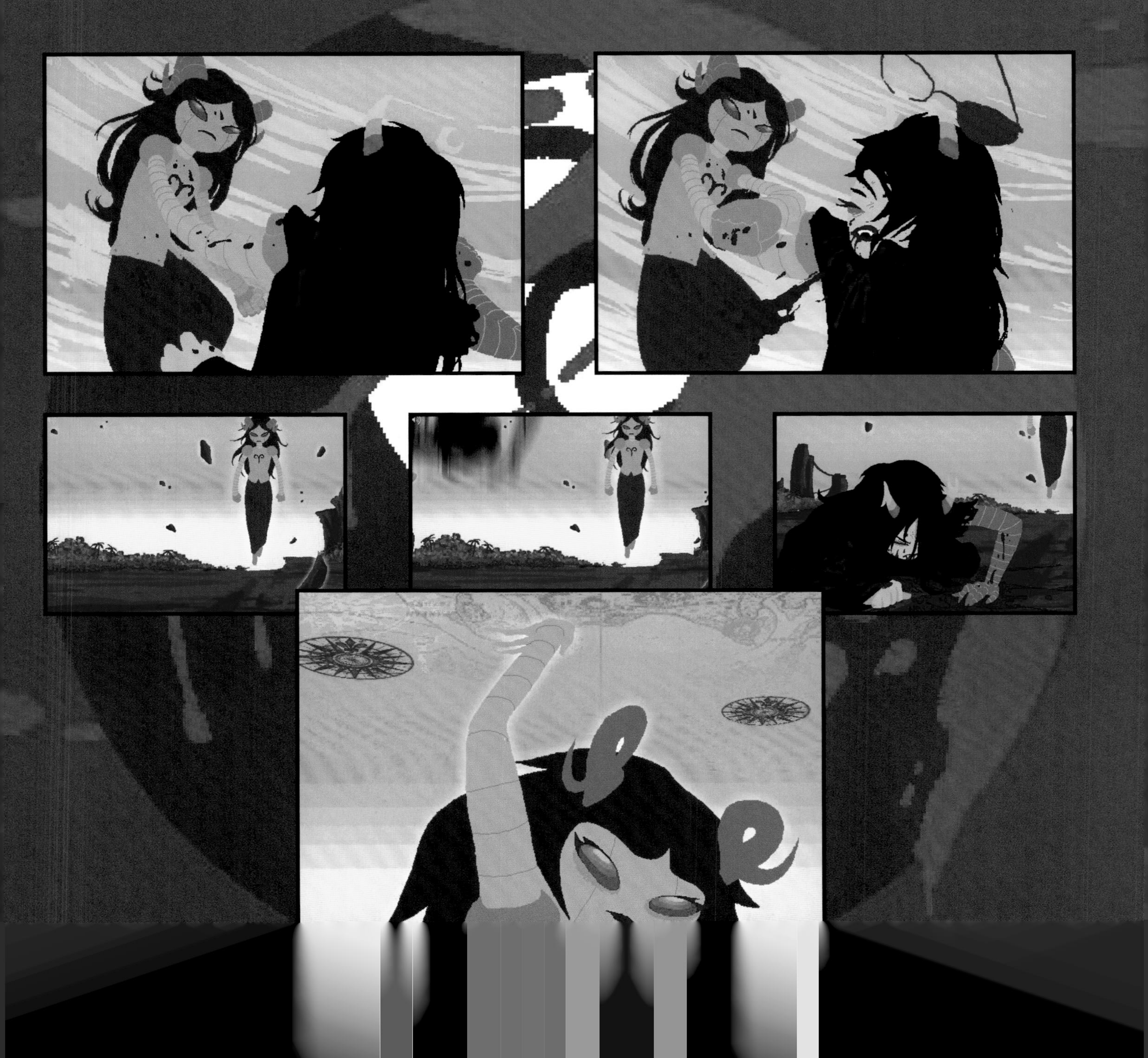

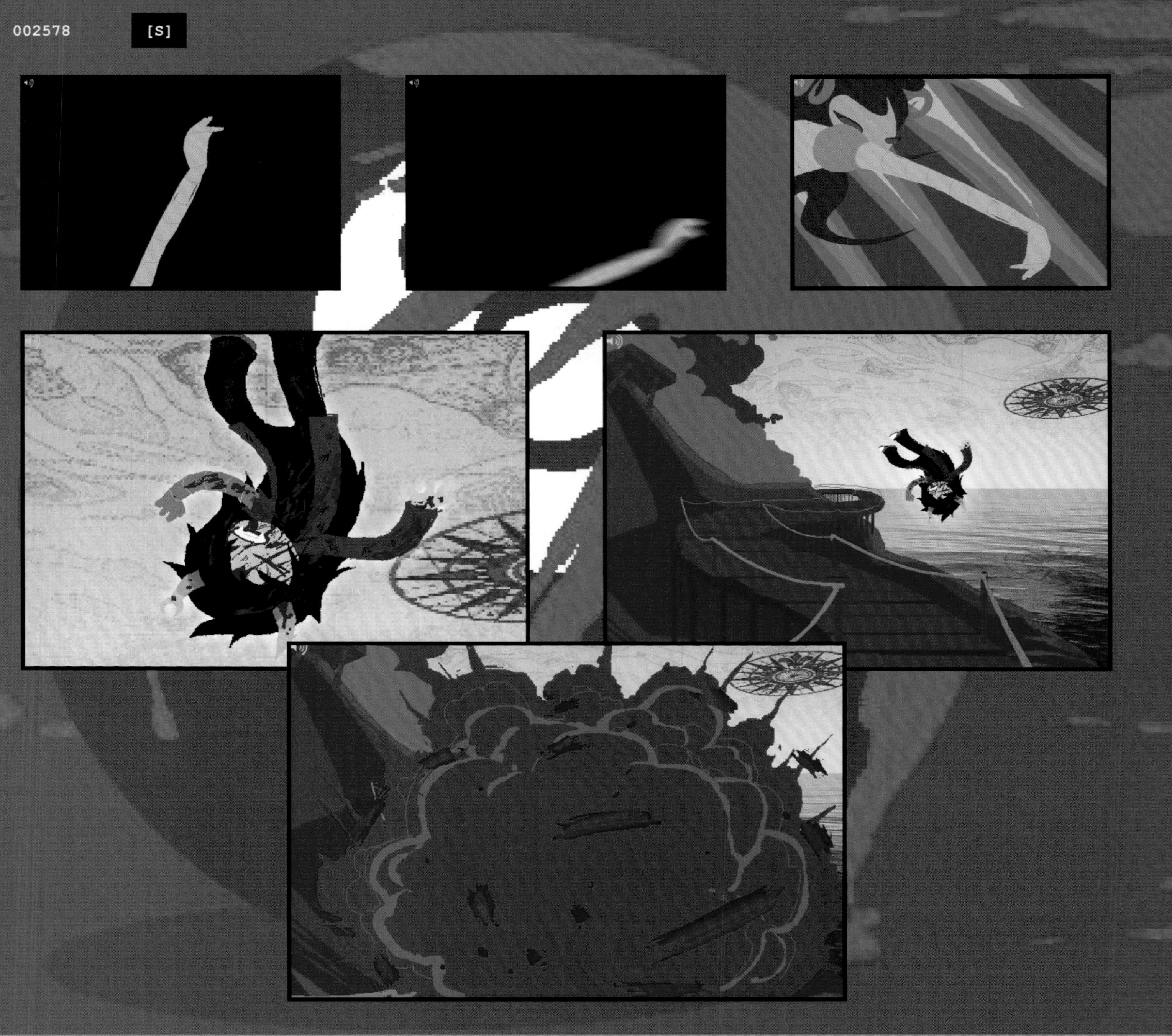

When Aradia said, "Hey you wanna hit the boardwalk a little later?" I don't think this is what Vriska thought she had in mind.

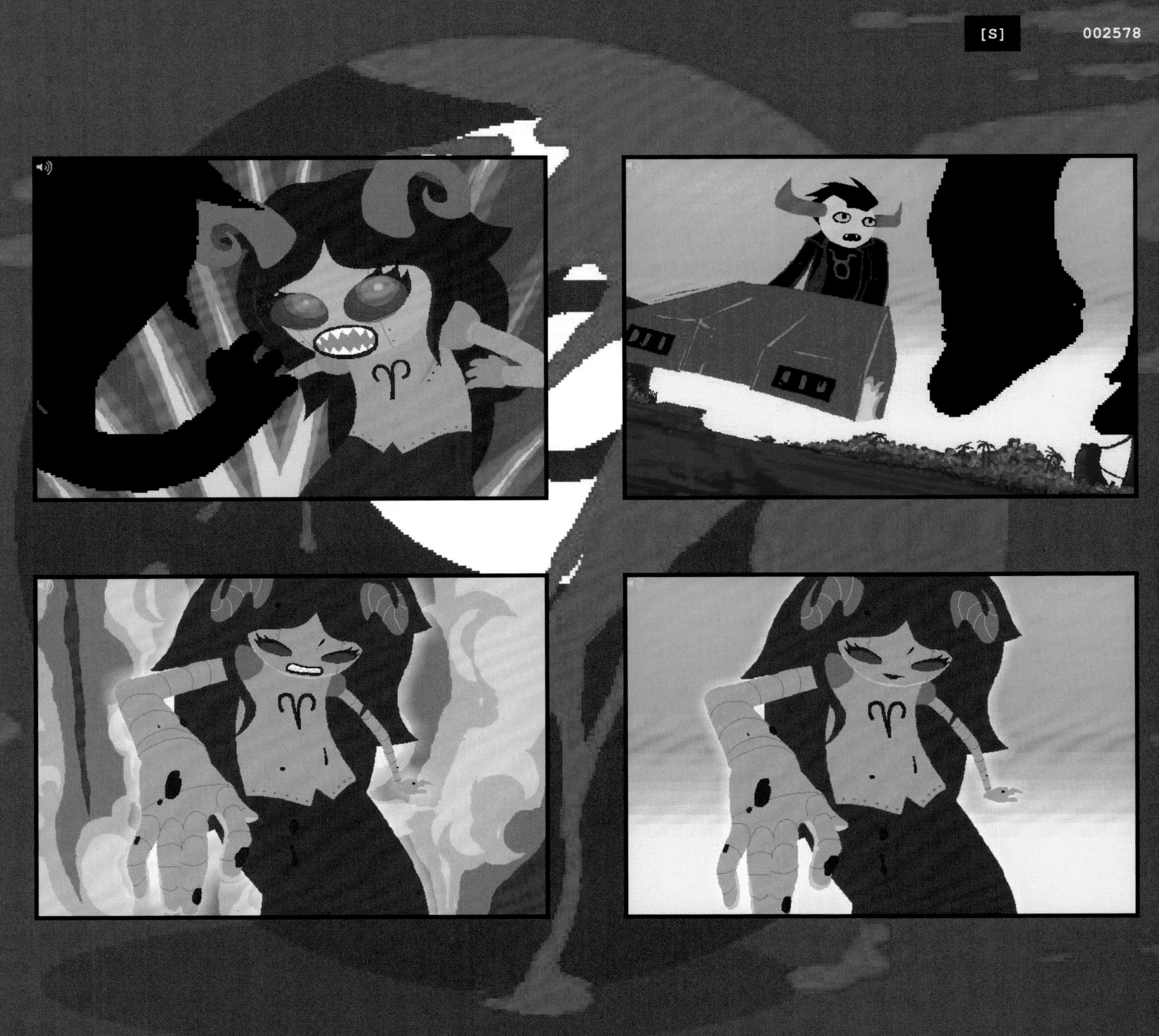

Cue chorus from the "why the fuck does Tavros have long sleeves" choir. Good question. This is just one of the perils of having a bunch of artists working on this stuff quickly, without much time taken to vet all the assets for consistency. Is it really *too* far outside the realm of possibility he's got a black hoodie stowed away somewhere in that rocket chair?

I'd like to imagine she delivered an ice-cold one-liner before vanishing. Maybe something like, "Thanks for the present."

And we see this is the story of how Vriska awakened on Prospit too. You can look at the animation as telling as two parallel tales, in two different ways. Either as two tales of revenge revolving around Vriska, one where she delivers retribution and the other where she receives it. Or as two tales of awakening, one where Terezi wakes up in response to making the best of a punishment she probably didn't deserve, and the other where Vriska wakes up in response to being jolted from slumber by a punishment she probably *did* deserve.

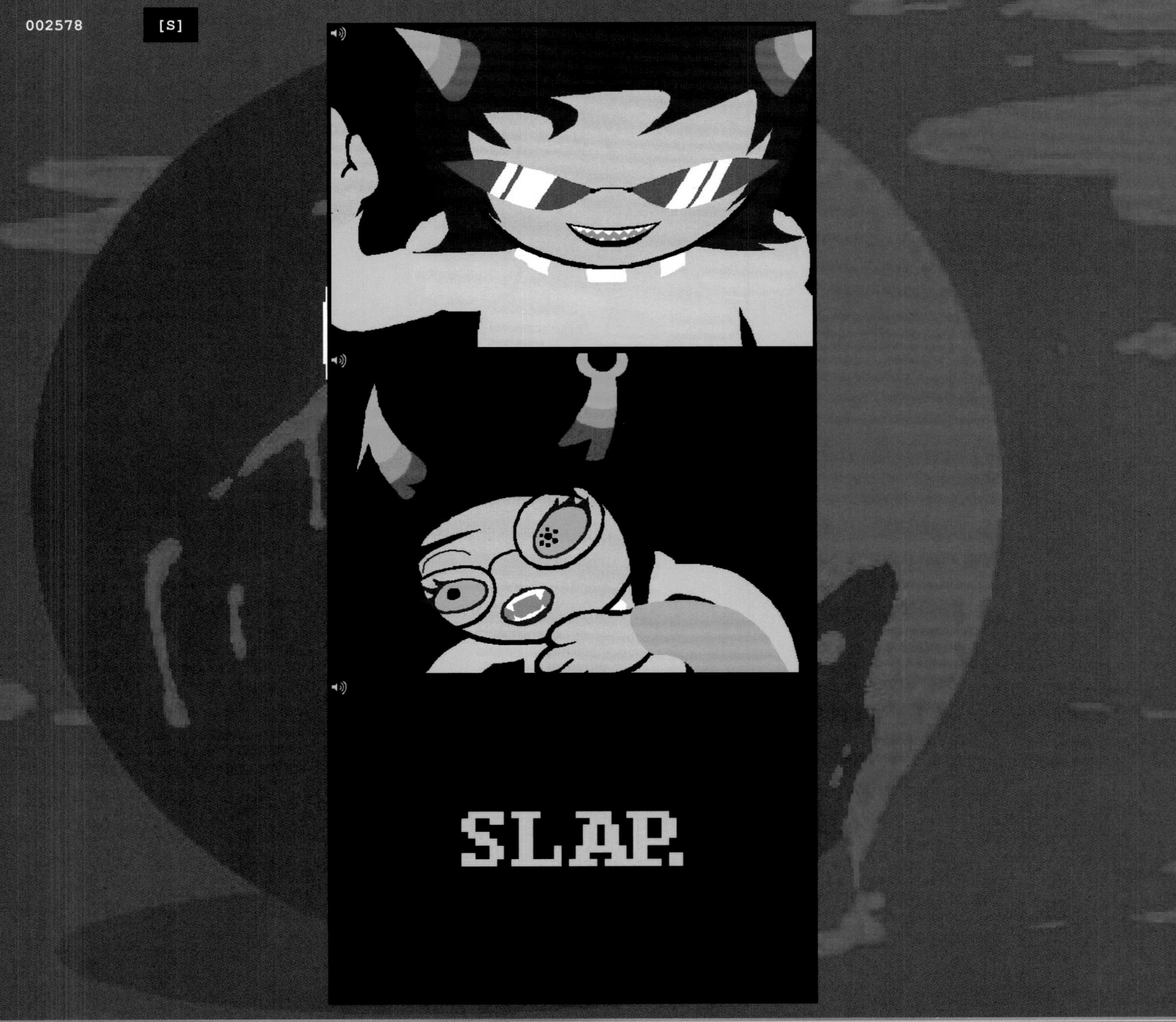

This is a funny and abrupt way to end this sequence. Sort of a nice, long-awaited reunion on Prospit, after the final score has been "formally evened." It probably results in a short conversation we don't get to see that is apologetic and conciliatory in nature. Maybe one of those rare moments, pre-retcon, where they just get to be good friends for a bit, unfettered by all the baggage, bad blood, and competitive bullshit. Unfortunately, this moment doesn't last long. Vriska's real body starts slowly bleeding to death, while she tries to convince Tavros to finish her off in her quest cocoon. Her dream self starts bleeding horribly too, to match the damage to the real body, in keeping with the "time limit" a player's dream self has before they can no longer be kissed back to life. Terezi watches her start to bleed here, and I'm going to guess she finds it a bit disturbing to witness.

Another observation: Vriska's dream self is healed, arm and eye intact. Terezi's is still blind though. There are some vague and unspoken rules concerning whether serious injuries transfer over to dream selves. A decent way of viewing a dream self is just as a dream-projection of the id. A collection of certain ideas about yourself, your identity. Vriska's injuries aren't an important part of who she is, and if they were healed, she'd be glad to be done with them. Terezi's blindness is a big part of her identity. In fact, she was blinded by the very process of her awakening, which, if you ask me, is a more than logical way of understanding how the injury was imprinted on her dream self for good.

> Make her pay.

> Make her pay.
The Gray Ladies

And here's the final exile: DD. Of course he's reading some of his porn while watching the teen alien girls fight to the death, like some sort of weirdo. Actually I just put the paper in his hand to remind us of his affection for gray ladies, when he is in fact the exile for Aradiabot, who is...a gray lady. How perfect is this? I mean, yeah, all trolls are gray, even when they're not robots. Just, give me a break, okay? Does this mean DD is using this device to creep on all the troll girls? He's coming dangerously close to horning in on Doc's act.

Atta girl.

> DD: Move this along.

Someone needs to grab the reins on timeline management here. These delinquents waste too much time. Can't seem to conduct their business with any efficiency at all.

Payback scenarios notwithstanding. There's always time to be made for a good comeuppance.

> Skip to the end.

I know I just said a bunch of stuff about him maybe being a creep. But look, this is just my OPINION here. I don't think he's actually being creepy about this. I think he has a genuinely parental attitude toward Aradia and wants to see her succeed in her violent and underhanded schemes. See how he wants them to conduct their business with efficiency? He's way too professional to go Full Doc on these girls.

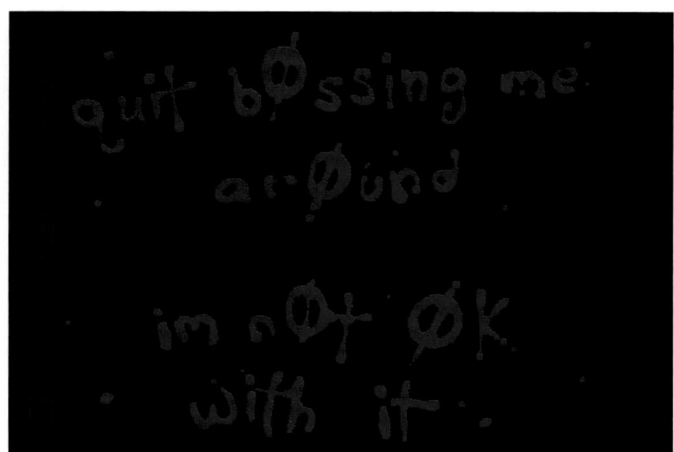

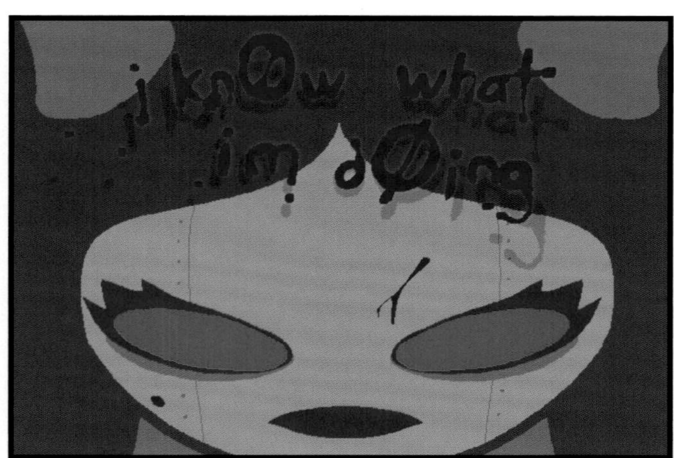

> That's what I like to hear.

Another good visual device to show a player communicating with their exile (again, notwithstanding any speculation about why they don't just speak their responses to the exile). The extremely edgy act of writing with your own or other people's blood is a long and honored tradition in *Homestuck*. A tradition that, I believe, begins here.

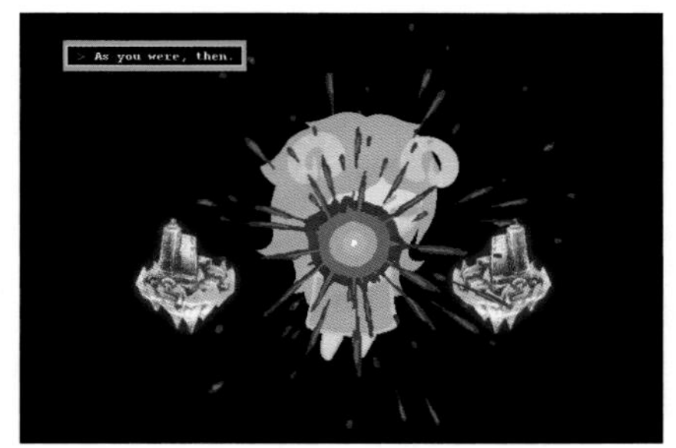

> Aradia: Skip to the end.

She's back to rendering herself in a less symbolic manner. It all comes full circle.

FUTURE apocalypseArisen [FAA] **2:16 HOURS FROM NOW opened private transtimeline bulletin board r0ad t0 the und0ing.**

~~~~~~

FAA 2:16 HOURS FROM NOW opened memo on board r0ad t0 the und0ing.

FAA: this private b0ard will and has already served as a l0g 0f past events f0r future selves t0 rec0rd and a guide 0f future events f0r past selves t0 f0ll0w
FAA: i d0nt kn0w which half 0f its r0le has been 0r will be m0re imp0rtant
FAA: p0ssibly neither is critical since deviati0n fr0m the c0urse is m0stly imp0ssible and reflecti0n 0n its traversal is c0mpletely irrelevant
FAA: but im typing this anyway
FAA: because im b0red again
PAST apocalypseArisen [PAA] 601 HOURS AGO responded to memo.
PAA: and here i was thinking we were finished taking 0rders fr0m v0ices!
PAA: weve 0nly swapped the imperatives 0f the dead with th0se 0f 0ur future selves
PAA: wh0 are als0 dead
FAA: yes it seems that way
PAA: 0h well it was an enj0yable reprieve fr0m fatalism while it lasted
PAA: id nearly managed t0 sav0r it
FAA: an err0r narr0wly av0ided then
FAA: i think we sh0uld refrain fr0m dial0gue in this mem0
FAA: with0ut res0rting t0 bannings 0r absurd exchanges 0f self repudiati0n
PAA: yeah i agree
PAA: i just th0ught id interject that and g0
FAA: 0k

Karkat's mistake was in not making his board private. Did he even know it was an option? That way he could have argued with himself in peace instead of having a bunch of hyenas yucking it up at his expense. Come to think of it, I could have done this with *Homestuck*. Made it a private webcomic, where I get to argue with myself hysterically using my own OCs, and nobody else gets to see it, or bother me, ever. Ah, what could have been...
~~~~~~

FAA: we will and have already amassed an army t0 c0nfr0nt the black king
FAA: an army c0nsisting 0f 0ur alternate future selves
FAA: each 0ne rer0uted fr0m a d00med 0ffsh00t 0f the alpha timeline
FAA: each given an0ther chance at a c0nstructive influence 0ver the ultimate 0utc0me
FAA: by the way if y0u didnt kn0w already
FAA: a future self returning t0 the past fr0m a d00med timeline will always be slated f0r imminent destructi0n herself
FAA: its 0ne 0f the rules
FAA: and the unf0rtunate reality is
FAA: this will and has already been a mass suicide missi0n
FAA: 0r it w0uld be
FAA: and already w0uld have been
FAA: if we all werent already dead
FAA: 0_0

FAA: m0bilizing 0urselves in such numbers w0uld be required t0 neutralize the kings psychic attacks
FAA: it w0uld take 0ur c0mbined c0ncentrati0n t0 dampen the abilities he inherited fr0m glbg0lyb
FAA: with0ut the cumulative eff0rt 0f 0ur d00med reserves
FAA: with0ut the heightened mental and physical endurance 0f 0ur r0b0tic vessels
FAA: with0ut the untimely demise we all shared bef0re this began
FAA: vict0ry w0uld n0t be p0ssible
FAA: he w0uld kill us all with 0ne dreadful s0und

It's left understated what a dreadful upgrade the enemies received when Gl'bgolyb was prototyped. The one being who can psychically kill all trolls any time it wants, giving its powers to...thousands of enemies who want nothing more than to kill a bunch of trolls. It stands to reason the lesser underlings have watered-down versions of this power. I wonder what that means. Can imps give the trolls nosebleeds? Mild headaches? What about the bigger ones? Could they put trolls in comas? Did the trolls develop any kind of suppression technology for this, like cool helmets? Man, I don't remember seeing any cool helmets. Who knows, really. This does help underscore what a critical role Aradia played in the final fight, though. The king probably has fully developed Vast Glub powers. This is like one of those hideously unbeatable end bosses who does a single attack to wipe out your party at the beginning of the fight. And part of the challenge is figuring out the one really hard thing you need to accomplish to neutralize that attack, before you begin even considering the *real* challenge.

FAA: i d0nt kn0w if it was just bad luck
FAA: 0r an extensi0n 0f the curse karkat insists he br0ught 0n us
FAA: that lead t0 the incidental and unf0rtuit0us pr0t0typing 0f feferis p0werful lusus
FAA: with0ut which the battle w0uld have p0sed little challenge
FAA: i think
FAA: it was m0re likely just an0ther inevitability
FAA: a pr0duct 0f c0llusi0n between the disparate f0rces at play
FAA: a bargain struck between what skaia kn0ws already and what the g0ds demand up fr0nt
FAA: t0gether they 0rchestrate trials sufficient t0 ensure
FAA: that in 0verc0ming them we w0uld be pr0ven w0rthy
FAA: 0f inheriting the ultimate reward
FAA: ribbit
FAA: wh00ps

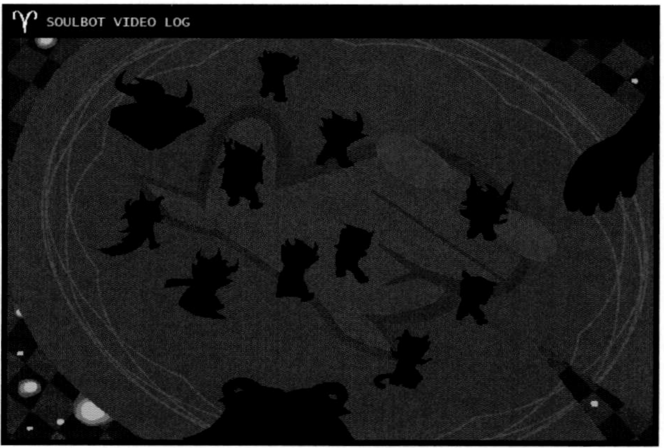

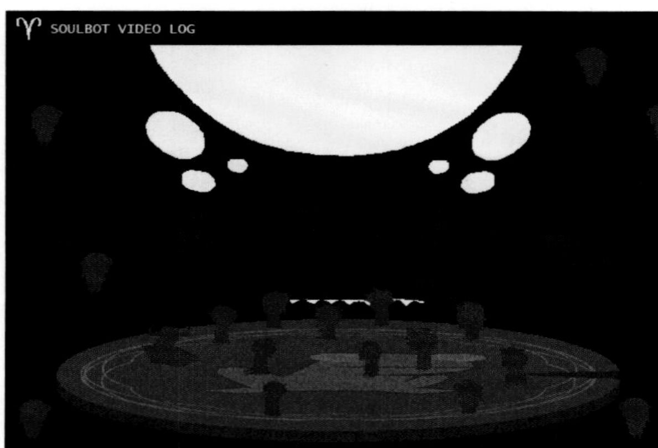

FAA: and s0 it w0uld be and has been already
FAA: that while distracted by the c0mbined eff0rts 0f 0ur d00med legi0n
FAA: the king w0uld be aggressed by the 0thers
FAA: and even th0ugh each w0uld be well prepared
FAA: perched 0n the highest rungs 0f their echeladders
FAA: equipped with the best weap0nry grist c0uld build
FAA: versed in the deadliest fraym0tifs b00nd0llars c0uld buy

We still don't know what the Ultimate Reward is, but we're getting close. Aradia gives us an accidental hint with her "ribbit." Recall that one of the prototypings was a frog, making the king part frog. Which means they had to slay one frog of sorts to make way for another. But the frog they make ends up dying later as well. Too bad. Here's a thing about this lilypad platform here: it's a game construct meant to assist with fighting the king. The king is a huge, towering end boss, and video games usually provide the player with some means of actually getting close enough to attack such an enemy. This is what *Sburb* provides. Pretty convenient, huh. Once the king is defeated, this same lily pad changes color and serves as the platform for the gateway to claim the reward. See the panel on the right. This platform serves as the environment for a lot of endgame material toward the close of the story. But not material of a combat nature—more like social endgame stuff, where a bunch of estranged kids finally get together, lounge around on the floor, and BS with each other.

SOULBOT VIDEO LOG
FAA: even th0ugh the mete0rs fr0m the kings 0wn reck0ning w0uld be turned against him
FAA: we w0uld 0nly narr0wly succeed
FAA: but ultimately
FAA: and even with 0ne imp0ssibly lucky r0ll 0f the dice at the final m0ment

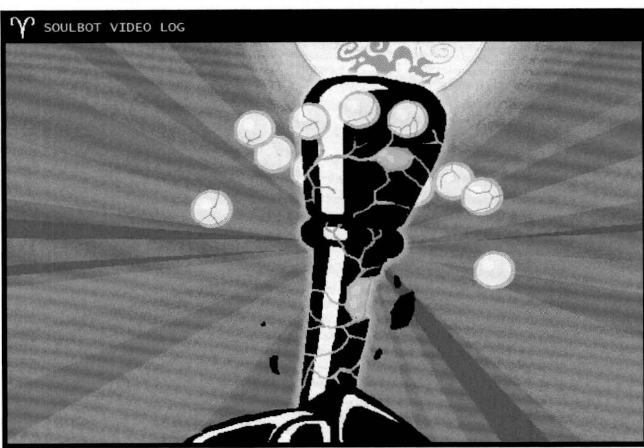

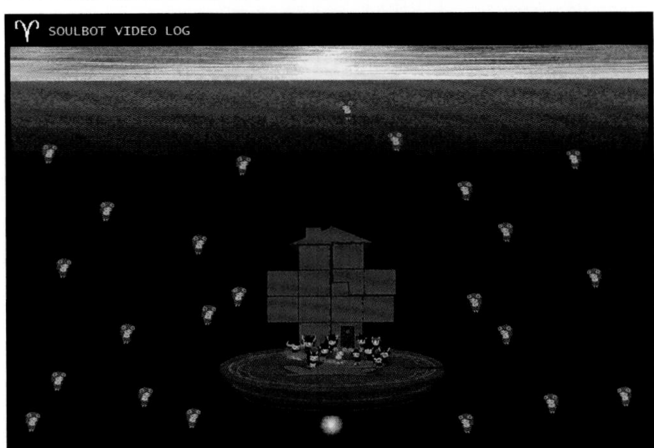

Hinting at a big, final boss battle was the way to go here. No huge animation. No way. I'm sure people wanted that (they always did). Some folks out there did make a big, simulated king battle animation years later. But that would have been a very wrong application of production time and effort here. It's not relevant, it's not the focus, and the battles of the story almost never are. It's helping solidify the ongoing precedent that endgame battles really are not what *Homestuck* does. I've said things like that outside the story, and included many reminders of it within. The supreme example of this, of course, is the alleged endgame battle that is theoretically supposed to take place with Lord English. Conventional expectations lead to presumptions on the reader's part that the narrative is structured that way, and what it must be building up to. This is a rather substantial point of analysis, probably best left for closer to that moment. But navigating around certain big battles and confrontations relates to some themes I've bandied about freely in this book. That, in short, the "real story" we've been trained to look for and expect in such media isn't actually the "real story" of *Homestuck*. It's an imagined narrative that happens in the background while the stuff we're most concerned with takes place on an extra-narrative layer with a set of completely different focal points and objectives, and only uses the backdrop traditional-narrative layer as substance for deconstruction, satire, and subversion of expectations, and as a basis for the parallels it draws between the regimentations within narrative and real life, which exist

SOULBOT VIDEO LOG
FAA: we w0uld pr0ve 0ur w0rth

They're so close. All they need to do is go in. And then they would... I don't even know. Fuck around somewhere in our universe? Maybe nowhere close to Earth at all? Maybe start New Alternia somewhere? Well, they end up sort of doing that anyway, much later, in a much more circuitous fashion, and with fewer trolls left alive in the final group. It's probably for the best that they did it the way they did. Who knows what sort of world they would have created without getting a little more experience first. Would *you* want to live in a civilization started by a group of thirteen-year-old alien assholes? No, let's be sensible. It would be much better to live on a world started by a mixed group of sixteen-year-old trolls and humans.

FAA: and the reward w0uld be within 0ur reach

FAA: but 0nly m0mentarily

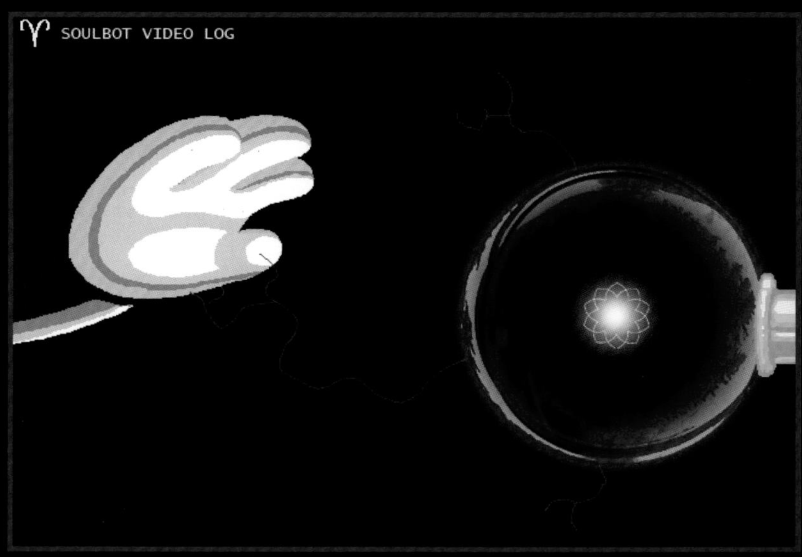

For some reason, the doorknob to a new universe is very special. I mean, it makes sense. If you've got a door leading to a whole brand-new universe, you spring for a little something extra. Like some sort of sick orb you might buy in a new age store. Also crackling with mysterious wizard energy. This is the same basic shot used when John reaches for the knob at the end too. This same visual asset is used (but rotated ninety degrees) when John reaches into the house-shaped juju to get his retcon powers. These gestures have some cosmic gravity, and there's a purpose in echoing them. That knob asset is *also* used as the go-to graphic for dream bubbles. These are some INCREDIBLE facts I'm tossing out here, guys. Oh, here's a detail worth noting. We see Vriska back there, with her healed eye. This kind of spoils the fact that the beatdown she got from Aradia actually did kill her, rather than just wound her, and she gets resurrected in some way soon after. (We can only assume by a kiss, since we don't know about god tier yet.) Otherwise she'd still only have one eye.

FAA: bef0re we w0uld be able t0 claim it
FAA: we w0uld be interrupted
FAA: by s0mething
FAA: which w0uld be ushered int0 0ur sessi0n by a rift in parad0x space
FAA: a rift which we w0uld determine
FAA: will be 0pened by f0ur members 0f a fledgling species
FAA: wh0 will be playing in an0ther sessi0n 0f the same game that we will and have already played

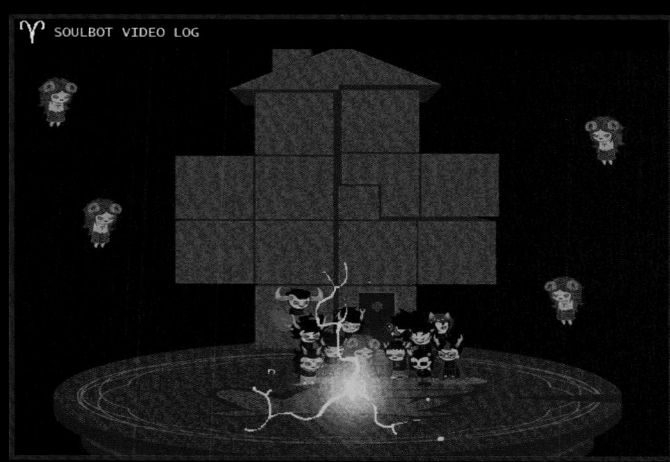

FAA: their rift will lead t0 the great und0ing
FAA: with0ut necessarily causing it
FAA: n0t directly
FAA: such rifts are themselves supp0sedly benign
FAA: useful even
FAA: they are catal0gued phen0mena within the game itself
FAA: with a pr0vided means 0f creating them
FAA: and a wide range 0f scenari0s f0r which it might be prudent t0 d0 s0
FAA: the incipisphere l0cals have a m0re f0rmal term f0r them
FAA: they typically refer t0 such a rift as

So, I'll just come right out with it: Bec Noir transports here, slices the door in half, and they all escape to a meteor before he can kill them. Aradia calls it a "rift" too, like Karkat, and implies the human kids open this rift. They didn't, though. (However, they *were* basically responsible for the rise of Bec Noir, in many respects, so the transference of blame still largely stands.) The rift itself was caused by Noir, who deliberately teleported here via an exile station on Earth, to escape the imminent destruction of that universe (which he himself is the cause of, not long after he arrives here). Aradia says rifts are catalogued phenomena in the game itself, which really isn't wrong. It's simple transporter technology, so yeah, duh, it's all part of the game. But I can't be too hard on her. She's doing me, the author, a favor by being enigmatic at this point in time. This stuff is all still super, duper mysterious right now. P.S. There's a John arm. It's right in front of Tavros's face. I wonder what he thinks about it.

Aradia's SOULBOT VIDEO LOG is essentially the same feature that Jade's dreambot has. Might as well use it as another in-story medium to broadcast certain events. The wrap-up of all this stuff, as seen and described by Aradia, really was the right way to go, since she did the most to launch the session and knows the most about what's going on. Nevertheless, despite her quite expansive field of situational knowledge, she still manages to play the role of an unreliable narrator here in a bunch of ways. Turning people who know huge amounts of stuff into unreliable narrators is both good as a challenge for the author, and good as a strategy for toying with the perception of readers and keeping them off guard. The more you establish the narrator as credible, the likelier a reader is to believe the things they say, and if you thread some disinformation into their accounts, it provides fuel later for more credible surprises. Jade's character is also being used in this way.

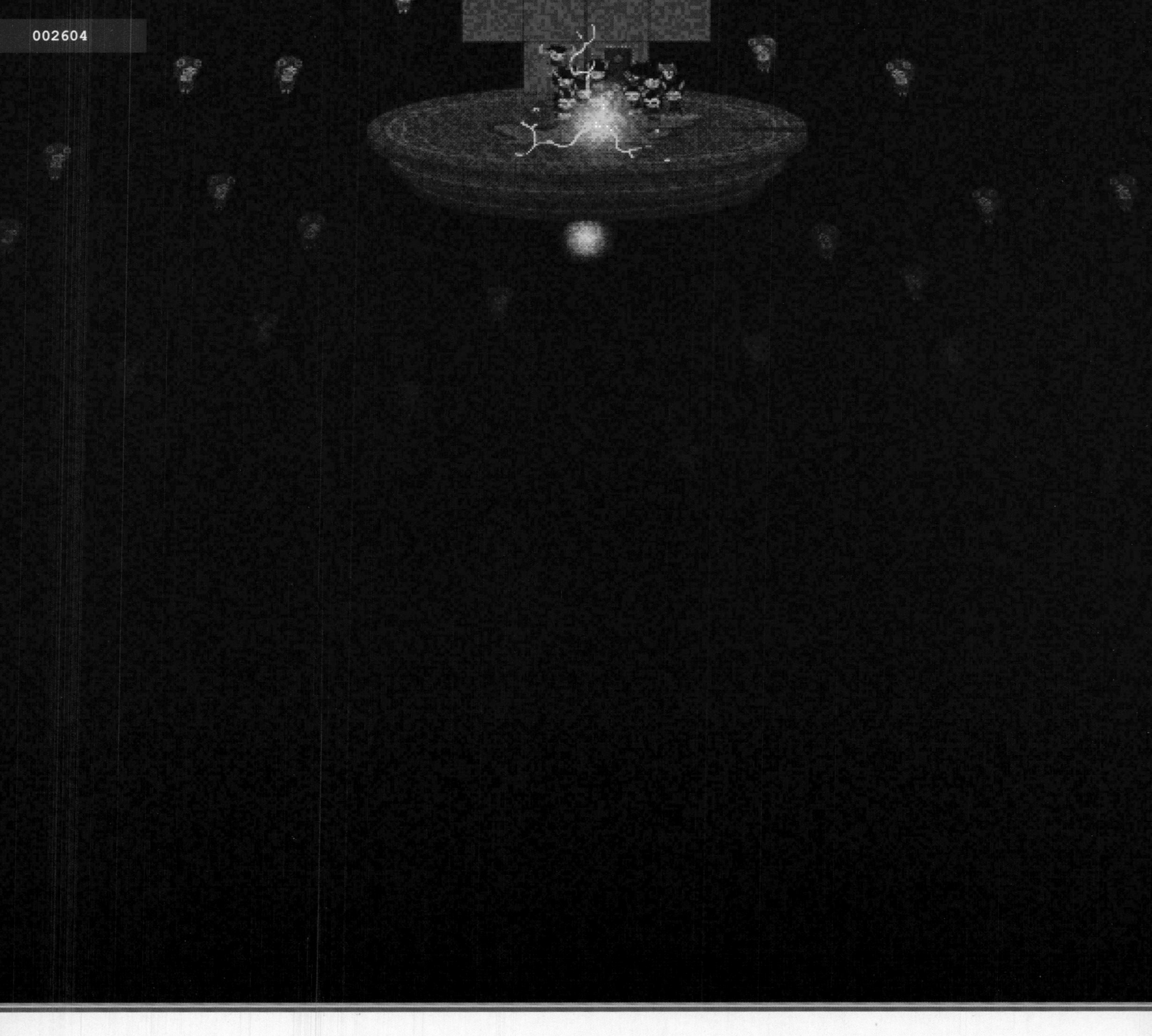

This is actually one long image. On the site, you scroll down and down, to get to one line of dialogue, which lends a certain measure of impact. Here, I have pulled the dazzling media trick of converting vertical, digital scrolling motion into horizontal, paper-based page-turning motion. Pretty cool, isn't it?

002604

Just kidding, it's not cool at all. This is a very tall image, and there's almost literally no other way to deal with that as a formatting challenge other than what has been done here. Thanks for checking out my tall-ass, de-animated animated GIF in the form of print media, though. I appreciate it.

The black field dissolved into this crackling field of green energy. You can't see it, but I could describe it to you? Well, I couldn't really, any more than I just did. Maybe I could make some sound effects? That would definitely come across as a nice value-add to the book presentation of this story.

CRAKCLEFWOOOSHHHHHH-CRACKZAP-BZZTCH-(FLAME ROAR, SMOLDER)-PCHOOWHOSOOOOSH-CRACKEREL-ZAAAAP-yeah this fuckin sucks.

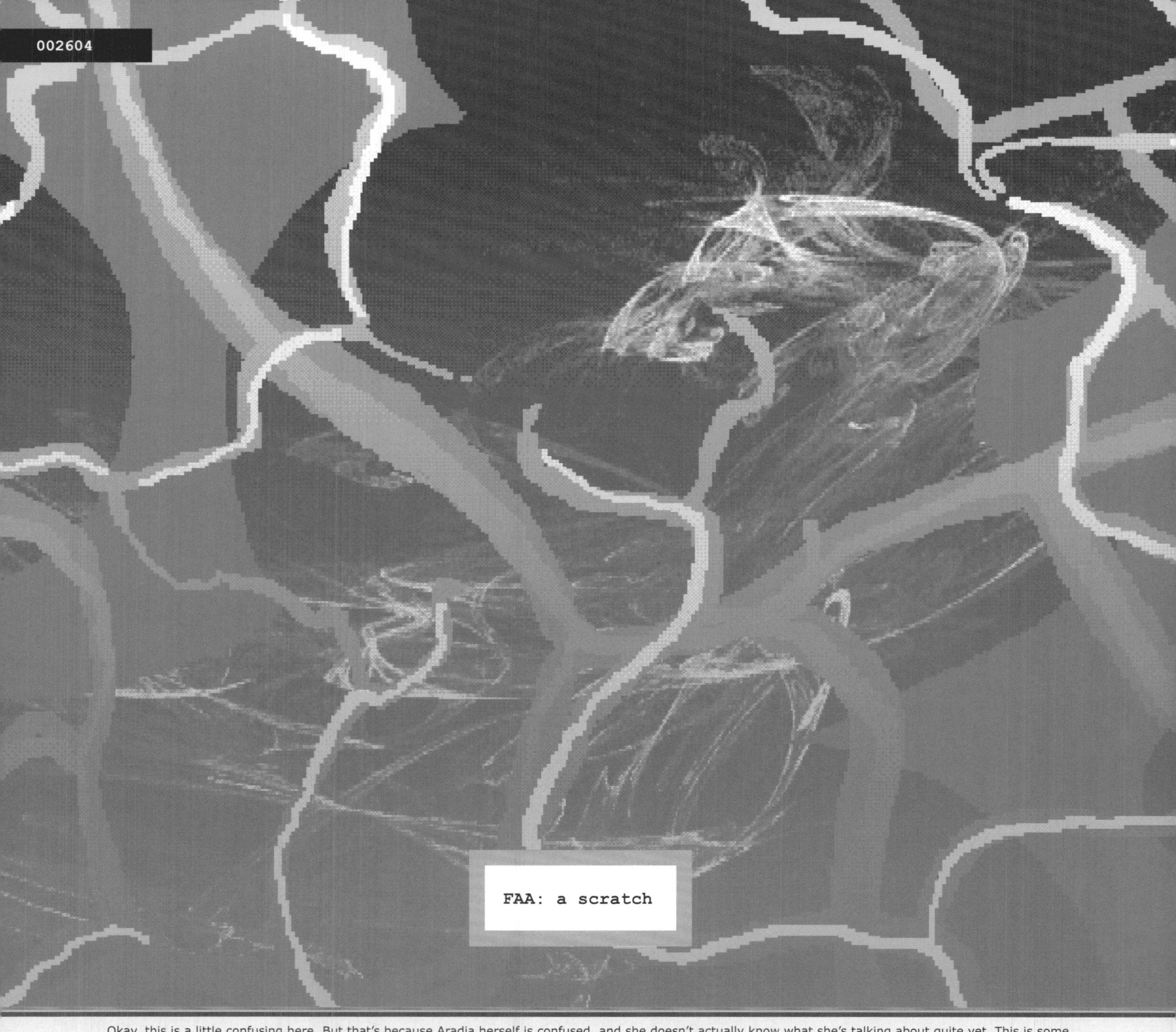

Okay, this is a little confusing here. But that's because Aradia herself is confused, and she doesn't actually know what she's talking about quite yet. This is some of the unreliable narrator stuff I was talking about before. If you know the story well, I think her mistake is actually pretty obvious. She's conflating a rift with a scratch, when in fact they are different things. First of all, a rift isn't really anything. It's just a word the trolls use to describe Jack's sudden appearance, the act of teleporting from an exile station into a session. A scratch is something totally different, and is a much bigger deal. It really is a prescribed action you can take in a game, under extreme circumstances. It's basically a reset. If you get in a jam, you can reset the game, or actually, your entire universe's starting conditions, wiping out everything, including your current forms and all those in the session. The scratch *indirectly* led to the rift, because all Jack was doing was trying to flee the session before the reset, and he wound up on Earth, and he had to flee from *there* too, because the universe was about to be destroyed. And the destruction of

CAA: the direct effects 0f a scratch are limited t0 the sessi0n inv0king it
CAA: we w0uld n0t experience 0r 0bserve th0se effects fr0m 0ur sessi0n
CAA: but we w0uld experience the c0nsequences
CAA: in the f0rm 0f that which prevented us fr0m claiming 0ur reward
CAA: he wh0se hand w0uld be f0rced by the scratch
CAA: t0 emerge fr0m hiding

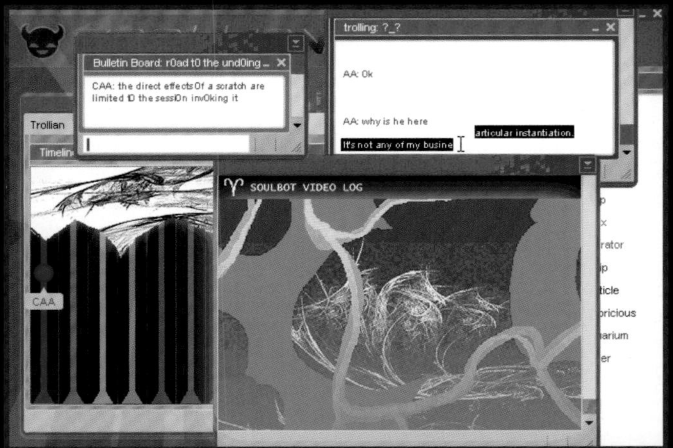

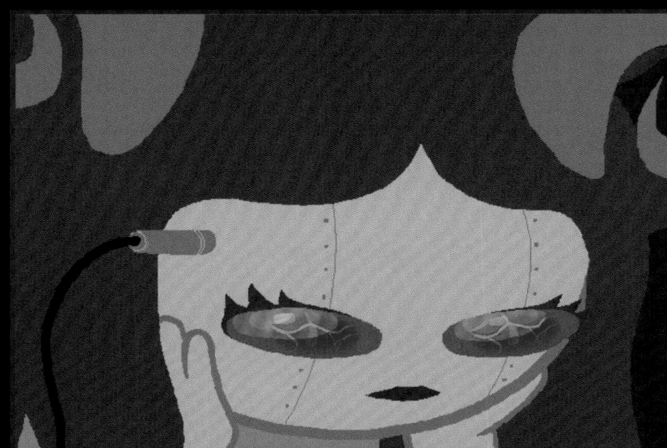

CAA: but there w0uld be n0 adequate way t0 prepare
CAA: even with all the f0resight at 0ur disp0sal
CAA: f0r a f0e m0re p0werful than the king we will and have already defeated
CAA: f0r a dem0n wh0 is indestructible
CAA: 0mnip0tent
CAA: and enraged

EVERYTHING HERE IS MISDIRECTION. We already know "indestructible demon" is a code phrase referring to Lord English. So Aradia's basically leading us to believe Lord English showed up and caused all these problems. She suggests the scratch doesn't directly affect their session (true), that the scratch led a powerful demon to come to their session (true), and insinuates that the demon is Lord English (false, it's Jack), and that this chain of events forced English to emerge (semi-true, in that the Great Undoing, caused by Jack, is what ultimately summons English). All of this is a garble of half-truths and selective omissions. On that note, take a look at who she's talking to there. It's Doc. Looks like he's been putting ideas in her head (without "technically lying," of course), and then she's been putting ideas in *our* heads. His text says "particular instantiation. It's not any of my business." He's talking about the instantiation of Jack, who just arrived to mess everything up. Doc's right—Bec Noir is not his business. That particular Noir is from the human session, which is well outside Doc's jurisdiction. (Even though he still messes with the session later, by talking to Rose.)

CAA: while the rest 0f the party w0uld absc0nd
CAA: 0ur duplicates w0uld buy us time
CAA: they w0uld all be killed
CAA: again

CAA: all except f0r me
CAA: this is just as well i supp0se
CAA: what w0uld we even d0 with all th0se c0pies anyway

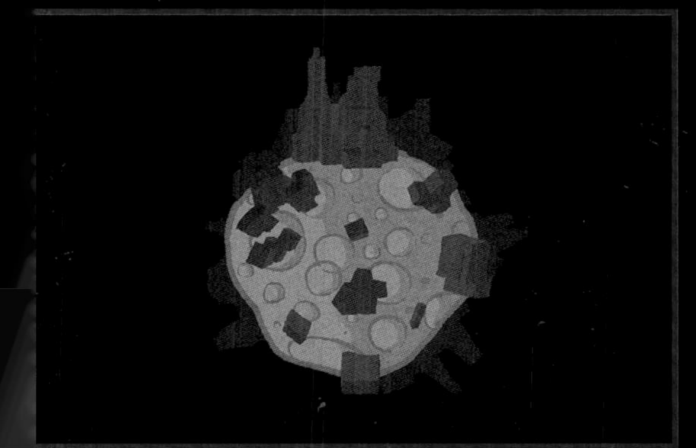
CAA: we w0uld return t0 the site 0f 0ur hatching
CAA: s0 t0 speak
CAA: where we w0uld hide
CAA: amidst a veil depleted by the reck0ning
CAA: and wait
CAA: drifting in the wide 0rbit 0f 0ur s00n t0 be null sessi0n

were all doomed Aradiabot copies anyway. Even though they were already dead. So I guess dead people in robot bodies can be double-doomed people in ghost bodies can double-die, after all. And finally, we see the meteor the trolls have been trapped on since we first met them in Act 4. king on this location, because it turns out to be pretty much the most lived-in setting of the entire story. More scenes take place here than anyw etty sure. Ranging from the troll group as it currently stands, to a ridiculous hodgepodge of trolls and humans over a three-year journey (playec way to Calliope and Caliborn in a far-flung future setting.

CAA: banished fr0m the universe we left behind

The red vs. blue conceit established with the troll teams, along with Sollux's bifurcation stuff, is extended here to include an ongoing reference to two universes (which was already somewhat true, since we saw two universes referenced this way in ~ATH code earlier). Blue represents the troll universe, red represents the human one. We're zooming in and out of Sollux's shades as a transitional device to link the two universes to these colors. (This also relates to Dave's shades, which have been cosmically imprinted with stars and galaxies as well, a feature that traces back to their original appearance in *Problem Sleuth*, believe it or not). It felt important to visually link the two universes to these two colors, so that they could be signified with such simple visual associations in the future. This becomes useful later in the story. There are some pretty abstract ideas to convey, involving entire universes, specifically the destruction thereof. For instance, the Tumor, a huge bomb, has two explosive components: a big blue tube and a big red tube. Both of these are meant to signal that in some abstract way that they "contain" these universes, and when both universes are destroyed in one circumstantially simultaneous event, then the entire bomb detonates. Stuff like this would be pretty challenging to communicate without the use of these color-coding methods. Generally speaking, color coding goes a long way in the story to help readers form associations and understand many abstract things that would otherwise be harder to pick up on.

CAA: and yet in being denied
the ultimate reward
CAA: we w0uld be barred fr0m entry

Remember the fact that Sollux goes blind later on? Well, linking the two universes to red and blue, and therefore also to Sollux's eyes, means that his blindness carries a certain symbolism beyond just his being the hard-luck cast member walking the path of the blind prophet archetype. Losing his vision is a way of linking him to the destruction of both universes, or forecasting the event before it happens. Another, less obtuse way of putting it is that this is foreshadowing. Later Sollux is only half-blind, because due to an overexertion to save everyone he ends up half-dead. (Why yes, you're right, this *is* kind of a stupid fact, but whatever). Which matches up with the fact that later, due to the scratch resulting in the Alpha Kid timeline, the human universe appears to have renewed life. Note that this does not mean the scratch literally resurrected the big frog Jack murdered. It simply means the post-scratch timeline always existed within that frog somewhere, and when we view the Alpha Kids, we are witnessing moments that took place before the frog was killed. But I think we're too close to the end of the book to get bogged down in the mechanics of amphibious cosmology, so I'm gonna chill on all that.

CAA: int0 the universe we created

Finally: here it is. It took getting halfway through Act 5 to finally figure out what *Sburb* actually does. It's a universe creation engine, or more specifically, a means of universal procreation, challenging young kids from planets with sentient life to either succeed or fail in the propagation of meaningful existence itself. It sort of ties a bow on the heretofore seeming arbitrary zodiacal associations with the trolls. They must have been understood on some level by ancient Earth cultures to be the creators. Whether it's known who they were, or whether they were a bunch of jerky alien teens, is anyone's guess. But apparently someone in ancient times picked out a bunch of constellations and named them after the twelve signs of the creators. That's a wrap for Hivebent, a.k.a. Act 5 Act 1, which we didn't know counted as A5A1 until now. We didn't even know acts could DO stupid things like that, but now we do. The act has bifurcated itself into two acts, with two sets of curtains, one red, the other blue, just like the universes.

Trudge complete. What's left to say about this? Having just made this crazy, annotated sweep through this arc all over again, I've got to tell you: I have no idea where any of this came from. Like one time back in 2010 I jazz-handsed a bit too hard, and this stuff just sort of magically appeared, thus basically turning *Homestuck* into "That Fucking Troll Comic" instead. It all seems pretty nuts now, like a particularly garish display of creative intensity. Making Hivebent took exactly one summer. For the duration of only that summer, I lived in somebody's weird and terrible house. My roommate I think was some sort of criminal? He was bad news. He had two huge dogs that honestly struck me as mostly untamed and bloodthirsty creatures. The result of this living arrangement was that I spent almost twenty-four hours a day locked in my shitty little room, working on this nonstop. Maybe that's where the thing with me being stuck in an attic with the wolf head came from? Actually that's probably exactly where it came from. When I spell it all out like this, it doesn't seem mysterious at all. Anyway, when Hivebent was done, I escaped from that dude's house and went on to greener pastures (i.e. mostly a bunch of other shitty apartments, but involving fewer dangerous animals). Thanks for listening to a small slice from my life as a ceaseless, roving drifter. And good job getting through this book. You've earned yourself a little break before moving on to the next one. Not me, though. I'll clearly be writing notes on this series for the rest of my life.

♈ ♉ ♊ ♋ ♌ ♍ ♎ ♏ ♐ ♑ ♒ ♓

ART CREDITS

[S] Make her pay.

Brett Muller, clorinspats, Eyes5, FauxMonstur, Jessica Allison, Lexxy, M Thomas Harding, myluckyseven, Nic Carey, Paige Turner, Richard Gung, SaffronScarf, Tavia Morra, SkepticArcher, Sockpuppy, Vivus

Homestuck
Book 4
Part 2: Act 5 Act 1

VIZ Media Edition

By Andrew Hussie

Cover Art - Adrienne Garcia
Book Design - Christopher Kallini
Cover & Graphic Design - Adam Grano
Editor - Leyla Aker

Printed in China

Published by VIZ Media, LLC
P.O. Box 77010
San Francisco, CA 94107

10 9 8 7 6 5 4 3 2 1
First printing, February 2019

PARENTAL ADVISORY
HOMESTUCK is rated T+ for Older Teen and is recommended for ages 16 and up. This volume contains staggering quantities of physical violence, unbelievably shitty wands, subjugglation, a tactical midget with a short fuse, musclebeasts, and all the losers. All of them.

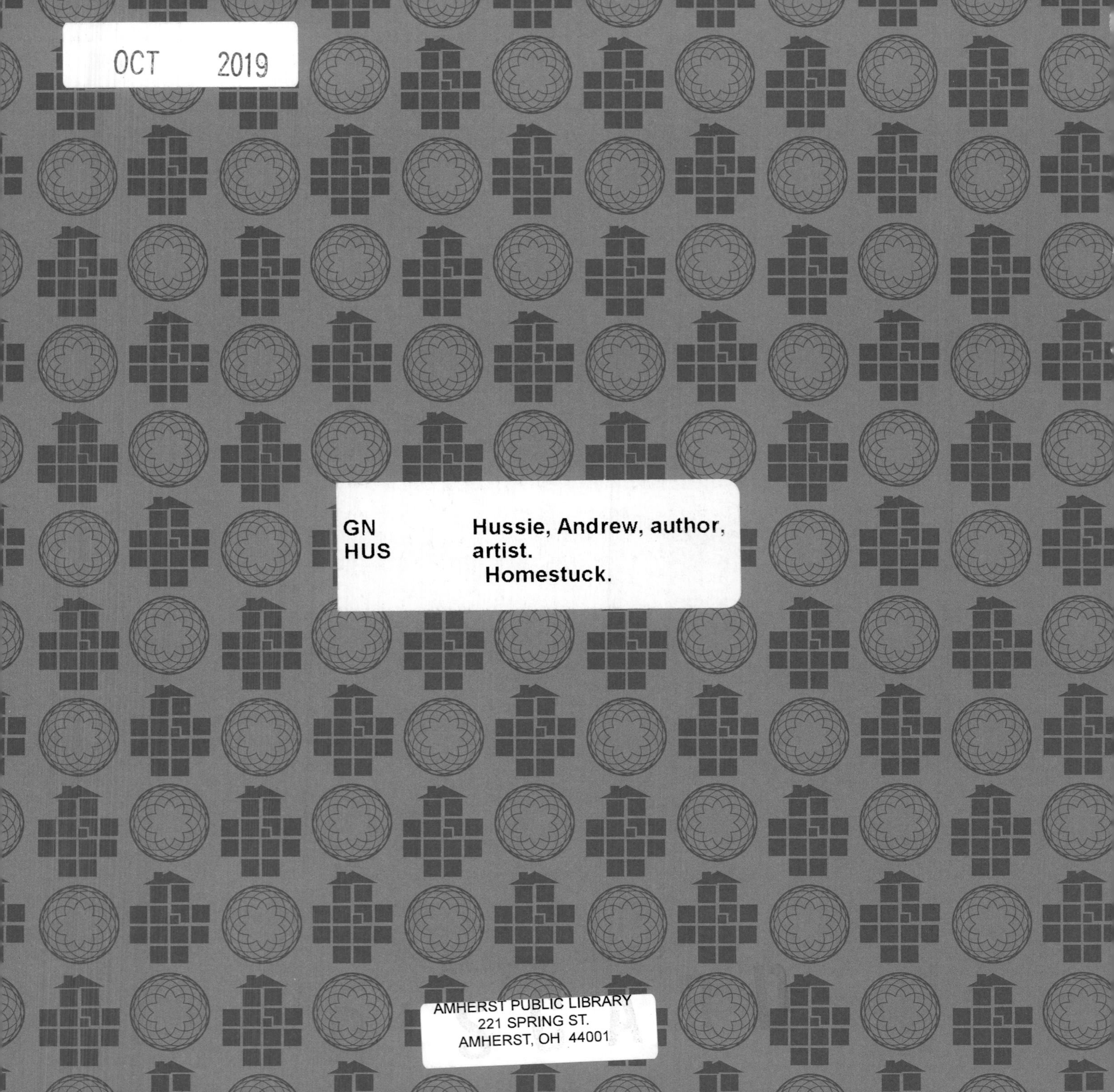